THE CONSTITUTIONALIZATION OF INTERNATIONAL LAW

The Constitutionalization of International Law

by

JAN KLABBERS

Professor of International Organizations Law,
University of Helsinki

ANNE PETERS

Professor of Public International Law
and Constitutional Law, University of Basel

and

GEIR ULFSTEIN

Professor of International Law, University of Oslo

OXFORD
UNIVERSITY PRESS

OXFORD
UNIVERSITY PRESS

Great Clarendon Street, Oxford OX2 6DP
United Kingdom

Oxford University Press is a department of the University of Oxford.
It furthers the University's objective of excellence in research, scholarship,
and education by publishing worldwide. Oxford is a registered trade mark of
Oxford University Press in the UK and in certain other countries

First published 2009
First published in paperback 2011
Reprinted 2012

British Library Cataloguing in Publication Data
Data available

Library of Congress Cataloging in Publication Data
Data available

ISBN 978-0-19-969354-2

Printed and bound by CPI Group (UK) Ltd, Croydon, CR0 4YY

Preface

This book has been a long time coming. It started when, some five years ago, the present authors met at a conference in Turku/Åbo, Finland, and agreed to 'do something together'. It became readily apparent that none of us were interested in organizing a conference or series of seminars. It also became clear that none of us would be terribly keen on editing other people's work. And so we decided we should write a book together.

The next question then was what the book should be about. Well, that was easy: we were all three of us intrigued by the constitutionalization of international law. We also settled, fairly soon, on our general approach. We were not so much interested in being merely descriptive, but instead were keen on trying to decide what shape constitutionalization could possibly take. And then the process started: we started to draft reading lists and send them around. We started to share literature tips more generally. We had a few meetings on the phone, and we met a number of times, over the years, in various places. We had a first session together in Berne, where some of the earlier drafts were first presented to a larger (but still comfortably small) audience. We met in Helsinki for a few days, just the three of us. We met in the Swiss resort of Kandersteg, where some of the drafts—more advanced by now—were presented to a high-profile audience. We met in Heidelberg, in the margins of a larger conference, and we met in Paris, again just the three of us. And sometimes it seemed like we were chatting on email, with handfuls of messages flying back and forth within a few hours.

There is a nice symbolism at work here. As the opening chapter will suggest, the very idea of the constitutionalization of international law must be understood against the background of globalization, and the above makes abundantly clear that the production of this very book owes much to globalization. It would have been difficult, perhaps impossible, to produce a book in this particular manner even as recently as 15 or 20 years ago: the availability of affordable air travel and quick means of communication helped us immensely. Not to mention, of course, the possibility that without globalization we would not have had a topic to begin with.

The one thing that we would have expected is that, on some deeper level, our political differences might come back to haunt us: how is it possible for three people to write a book on such a highly charged and politicized topic despite them having differences of opinion? In the end, this proved to be not much of a problem, and the most plausible explanation for this would be that over the years some mutual learning took place. Through discussions of the general approach and extensive comments to each others' chapters, our opinions have converged at least to the extent that it proved possible to write together. This does not mean that we agree on every analysis and all conclusions of the book. And we were not willing to harmonize our individual writing style. As a result, we felt the need to be clear as to who wrote which chapters. Jan Klabbers wrote chapters 1 and 3; chapters 2 and 4 were written by Geir Ulfstein; and chapters 5, 6, and 7 by Anne Peters. Although the book was conceived and written as a joint undertaking, each of the authors bears responsibility only for her or his chapters.

In the process, we owe a debt of gratitude to many people. Our spouses and families, of course, have had to put up with this strenuous collective effort, sometimes literally: both Geir Ulfstein's wife and Jan Klabbers' son have been kept awake while we were discussing things in the adjacent room, and Anne Peters' daughter was supervised in her homework by mobile phone. Geir Ulfstein would like to extend his gratitude to Professor Hélène Ruiz Fabri for providing excellent and hospitable research conditions, assisted on the practical side by Sophie Guy, during his sabbatical in Paris. Then there are the many people who have listened to the various chapters of the book in draft form, and have provided detailed and pointed comments, especially Andreas Føllesdal on chapter 2, Simone Peter on chapters 5 and 6, and Oliver Diggelmann and Steven Wheatley on chapter 6. Claudia Jeker from the Basel law faculty not only co-organized meetings and workshops, but also produced a perfect manuscript and compiled the bibliography out of numerous files flowing in from three sides. At Oxford University Press, we are indebted to Merel Alstein and John Louth for their unflinching support, and to the anonymous reviewers whose feedback on our proposal proved very helpful. Substantial financial support was granted by the Swiss National Funds and by the Freie Akademische Gesellschaft Basel. Workshops were financed as part of the Swiss National Centre of Research 'World Trade Law: From Fragmentation to Coherence'. We owe a lot to the generosity of the director of that NCCR, Thomas Cottier, for hosting and sponsoring our work, even in its not so trade-law-related aspects. But most of all, perhaps, we are indebted to the many, many authors who have gone here before us, working—through different disciplines—in the rich tradition of the constitutionalization of international law.

Jan Klabbers, Anne Peters, Geir Ulfstein
Helsinki, Basel, Paris
March 2009

Table of Contents

Table of Cases

List of Abbreviations

ACHR	Inter-American Commission on Human Rights
AI	Amnesty International
AJIL	American Journal of International Law
AP I	Protocol Additional to the Geneva Conventions of 12 August 1949, and relating to the Protection of Victims of International Armed Conflicts (Protocol 1)
ATCM	Antarctic Treaty Consultative Meeting
ATS	Antarctic Treaty System
BGE	Entscheidungen des Schweizerischen Bundesgerichts (Decisions of the Swiss Supreme Court)
BINGO	business interest organization
BIS	Bank for International Settlements
BIT	Bilateral Investment Treaty
BVerfG	Bundesverfassungsgericht (German Federal Constitutional Court)
BVerfGE	Sammlung der Entscheidungen des Bundesverfassungsgerichts (Collection of the Decisions of the German Federal Constitutional Court)
BYIL	British Year book of International Law
CAT	Convention against Torture/Committee Against Torture
CEDAW	Convention on the Elimination of All Forms of Discrimination against Women
CEPAA	Council on Economic Priorities and Accreditation Agency
CESCR	Committee on Economic, Social and Cultural Rights
CFI	Court of First Instance
CITES	Convention on International Trade in Endangered Species of Wild Fauna and Flora
CLCS	Commission on the Limits of the Continental Shelf
CoE	Council of Europe
COP	Conference of the Parties
CRC	Convention on the Rights of the Child
CSCE	Conference on Security and Co-operation in Europe
CSD	Commission on Sustainable Development
CUP	Cambridge University Press
DSU	Dispute Settlement Understanding
EC	European Community
ECHR	European Convention of Human Rights and Fundamental Freedoms/European Court of Human Rights
ECJ	European Court of Justice
ECOSOC	United Nations Economic and Social Council
ECOSOCC	Economic, Social and Cultural Council of the African Union

ECR	European Court Reports
ECT	Treaty establishing the European Community
EEC	European Economic Community
EJIL	European Journal of International Law
EP	European Parliament
ESC	European Social Charter
ETI	Ethical Trade Initiative
ETS	European Treaty Series
EU	European Union
FAO	Food and Agriculture Organization of the United Nations
FIFA	Fédération Internationale de Football Association
FSC	Forest Stewardship Council
G7 (or G8)	Group of 7 (or 8)
GA	United Nations General Assembly
GATT	General Agreement on Tariffs and Trade
GEF	Global Environment Facility
GGI	Global governance institutions
GRI	Global Reporting Initiative
GSP	Generalized System of Preferences
HAP	Humanitarian Accountability Project
HRC	Human Rights Council
IASB	International Accounting Standards Board
IBRD	International Bank for Reconstruction and Development
ICAO	International Civil Aviation Organization
ICC	International Criminal Court/International Chamber of Commerce
ICCPR	International Covenant on Civil and Political Rights
ICESCR	International Covenant on Economic, Social and Cultural Rights
ICISS	International Commission on Intervention and State Sovereignty
ICJ	International Court of Justice
ICLQ	International & Comparative Law Quarterly
ICon	International Journal of Constitutional Law
ICRC	International Committee of the Red Cross
ICSID	International Centre for the Settlement of Investment Disputes
ICTR	International Criminal Tribunal for Rwanda
ICTY	International Criminal Tribunal for the former Yugoslavia
IDA	International Development Association
IFRS	International Financial Reporting Standards
IHL	International Humanitarian Law
ILA	International Law Association
ILC	International Law Commission
ILM	International Legal Materials
ILO	International Labour Organization
IMF	International Monetary Fund
IMO	International Maritime Organization
IO	International Organization

ITLOS	International Tribunal for the Law of the Sea
ITO	International Trade Organization
IUCN	International Union for the Conservation of Nature
IWC	International Whaling Commission
MAI	Multilateral Agreement on Investment
MEA	multilateral environmental agreement
MNE	multinational enterprise
MOP	Meeting of the Parties
NAFTA	North American Free Trade Agreement
NATO	North Atlantic Treaty Organization
NGO	non-governmental organization
OAS	Organization of American States
ODIHR	OSCE Office for Democratic Institutions and Human Rights
OECD	Organization for Economic Cooperation and Development
OJ	Official Journal of the European Communities/European Union
OSCE	Organization for Security and Co-operation in Europe
OUP	Oxford University Press
P5	Permanent Five Members of the Security Council
PA	Parliamentary Assembly of the Council of Europe
PCIJ	Permanent Court of International Justice
PISA	Programme for International Student Assessment
PMSC	private military and security company
R2P	responsibility to protect
SA 8000	Social Accountability 8000
SC	United Nations Security Council
SDN	Société des Nations
SPLOS	Meeting of States Parties to the United Nations Convention on the Law of the Sea
TEU	Treaty on European Union
TFEU	Treaty on the Functioning of the European Union
TNC	transnational corporation
UK	United Kingdom of Great Britain and Northern Ireland
UN	United Nations
UNCCD	United Nations Convention to Combat Desertification
UNCLOS	United Nations Convention on the Law of the Sea
UNCTAD	United Nations Conference on Trade and Development
UNDHR	United Nations Universal Declaration on Human Rights
UNECE	United Nations Economic Commission for Europe
UNEP	United Nations Environment Programme
UNESCO	United Nations Economic, Social and Cultural Organization
UNFCCC	United Nations Framework Convention on Climate Change
UNICEF	United Nations International Children's Emergency Fund
UNTS	United Nations Treaty Series
UP	University Press
US	United States of America

US S.Ct.	United States Supreme Court
VCCR	Vienna Convention on Consular Relations
VCLT	Vienna Convention on the Law of Treaties
WEU	Western European Union
WHO	World Health Organization
WIPO	World Intellectual Property Organization
WTO	World Trade Organization

1

Setting the Scene

Jan Klabbers

1. Introduction

Fragmentation, verticalization, and constitutionalization form the holy trinity of international legal debate in the early 21st century, and made a sustained appearance in the well-known *Yusuf* and *Kadi* cases. In September 2005, the Court of First Instance (CFI) of the European Union (EU) came up with these two remarkable decisions, which engaged the CFI in testing the legality of Security Council acts.[1] They spurred the CFI to comment on general international law, and *jus cogens* in particular. They urged the CFI to take a position on the question whether the United Nations (UN) Charter is hierarchically superior to other international institutions, including the EU itself. And those cases, most tellingly, involved the CFI in applying and interpreting classic human rights standards.

The CFI, in all honesty, did not do a particularly good job at most of these issues. It held, somewhat implausibly, that the European Community (EC) was bound to adhere to UN law because, even though not a member itself, all the EC member states were UN members.[2] It seemed to hold that the UN Charter was superior to EC law, but seemed to derive this position from EC law itself which, in a paradoxical move, would rather suggest the supremacy of EC law over the Charter. It engaged in review of Security Council acts, but only after saying it was not competent to do so; and when engaged in judicial review, it limited itself to purported norms of *jus cogens*.[3] And most of all, when interpreting and applying human rights law, it adopted positions that few human rights lawyers would ever think defensible: an intensely political, non-judicial procedure to be removed from a sanctions blacklist was deemed compatible with

---

[1] Case T-306/01 *Yusuf and Al Barakaat v Council and Commission* [2005] ECR II-3533 and Case T-315/01 *Kadi v Council and Commission* [2005] ECR II-3649.

[2] This succession theory had been created in the early 1970s to explain the EC's allegiance to General Agreement on Tariffs and Trade (GATT). Here, though, the succession was far more plausible, as the EC could claim exclusive powers in the field of trade and commerce—it can hardly claim exclusive powers, though, in foreign and security policy. The *locus classicus* is Cases 21/72–24/72 *International Fruit Company and Others* [1972] ECR 1219.

[3] This, too, is implausible, as it would suggest that *jus cogens* norms come with their own jurisdictional components attached.

the right to a fair trial; a freezing of bank accounts was held not to violate the right to property because of its temporary nature; and, more generally, the human rights of suspects of terrorism should be balanced against the number of victims caused by the suspected terrorist acts.

Still, for all their flaws, the *Yusuf* and *Kadi* cases represent a microcosm of some of the most fundamental debates in international law today. Those debates have to do with the specialization that takes place in international law, a process often referred to as fragmentation: international human rights law has become a more or less self-contained system, as has international trade law. International environmental law has become something for specialists, as has international criminal law. International watercourse law has little in common with international refugee law, etc. And indeed, seeing human rights law applied by three judges relatively unfamiliar with the general concepts and norms of human rights law, its general doctrines, and generally unfamiliar with its sensibilities, was perhaps not a happy spectacle.

At the same time, though, many welcomed the idea of some court, however inappropriate, busying itself with reviewing the legality of acts of the Security Council or, in this case, some of its subsidiary organs.[4] For many, the idea that the Security Council is also subject to legal limits is a clear truth which needs no further demonstration, and it is better to have the CFI exercise some scrutiny than to have no scrutiny at all. By the same token, those initial *Yusuf* and *Kadi* decisions demonstrate, however uncomfortably perhaps, the fundamental unity of the international legal order: Even the EC, often thought of as having left the framework of international law behind a long time ago, seemed willing to subject itself to UN law, at least if the CFI is to be believed. And the CFI, moreover, did suggest that even the Security Council is bound to respect *jus cogens* norms—and this, again, suggests a fundamental unity, on the basis of shared and common values. No matter that the CFI got parts of its decisions wrong; what matters, some might say, is that it tried; what matters is that, overall, the CFI suggested that no one is above the law; what matters is that the CFI suggested that there is some legal space hovering over all political activities, containing some untouchable norms which themselves originate in the hearts and minds not of selfish states, but of humanity itself.

As was to be expected, the *Kadi* decision has been appealed against, and Mr Kadi's claims have been by and large upheld by the European Court of Justice (ECJ).[5] Still, the raw originality of those initial two decisions is more closely in touch with the

---

[4] See Christian Tomuschat 'Annotation' (*Kadi* and *Yusuf* cases) (2006) 43 *Common Market Law Review* 537–551.

[5] The co-applicant in *Yusuf* (the trading company Al-Barakaat) also appealed, but Mr Yusuf did not. See Case C-402/05 P, judgment of 3 September 2008. Some of the underlying theory is espoused by the Advocate-General in the case, writing in an academic capacity (and without being very specific about the interaction between international law and EU law). See Miguel Poiares Maduro 'Interpreting European Law: Judicial Adjudication in a Context of Constitutional Pluralism' (2007) 1 *European Journal of Legal Studies* 1–21.

pulse of the time, is more closely in tune with the *Zeitgeist*, than the later appellate decision of the ECJ in *Kadi*. While this, too, is quite a brilliant decision, its brilliance resides above all in shielding the EU from general international law. The ECJ, in its 2008 decision, underlined that it has no business testing the legality of Security Council decisions; and to the extent that such decisions have been transposed into EU law, the resulting EU legislation must conform to EU human rights standards. As a result, this strengthens the position of the EU, but possibly ends up undermining the authority of the UN. The ECJ accepts the fragmentation of international law and global governance, leaving the rest of the world to fend for itself.

2. The Plan of this Book

This chapter aims to describe all these -isms and -izations that came to the fore in the *Kadi* case (fragmentation, verticalization, constitutionalization, and a few others as well) in order to set the scene for the discussion in subsequent chapters, and will inevitably use a fairly broad brush doing so. In order to facilitate the discussion, it is perhaps useful to bear in mind—as a heuristic device rather than an accurate description of reality—that much of the following may be understood in terms of action and reaction, move and counter-move. Thus, globalization calls forth localization, which then, at the same time, by looking like parochialism, may inspire yet other manifestations of the global through de-localization. Likewise, fragmentation may inspire constitutionalism which, however, at the same time, may appear as domination in a different guise and therewith provoke the sort of counter-reaction it was designed to overcome to begin with.

But before going there, perhaps it is useful to first outline our purpose, to illustrate why the broad brush will be used and where this book ought to be situated. It is not a book about international ethics as such: we neither devise a coherent normative global ethics[6] nor do we feel the need to make the point that international law is based on ethical principles.[7] We also do not aim to flesh out a particular vision on the rule of law in international affairs or, which may or may not be the same, the international rule of law,[8] although this already comes closer to what we set out to do (in that constitutionalization and the rule of law are intimately linked ideas). Instead, the idea behind this book is as follows. Many international lawyers talk about the constitutionalization of international law but do not seem to step down from abstract heights: many claim that

---

[6] See, e.g., Charles Beitz *Political Theory and International Relations* (Princeton UP 1999 [1979]).

[7] See, e.g., Stefan Kadelbach 'Ethik des Völkerrechts unter Bedingungen der Globalisierung' (2004) 64 *Zeitschrift für ausländisches öffentliches Recht und Völkerrecht* 1–20.

[8] See, e.g., Jeremy Matam Farrall *United Nations Sanctions and the Rule of Law* (CUP Cambridge 2007); Jeremy Waldron 'The Rule of International Law' (2006) 30 *Harvard Journal of Law and Public Policy* 15–30.

international law is going through a process of constitutionalization, but few work out what this means—or could mean. In essence, the literature takes on two forms. On the one hand, much energy is spent on making the normative case for a better and more just world, and this may well take place under the label of constitutionalism. Lawyers and political philosophers alike conceive of global theories of justice (or theories of global justice),[9] but rarely provide their theories with hands and feet. On the other hand, much energy is also spent on making the empirical case for constitutionalization: politico-legal processes are described under the heading of constitutionalization, suggesting that it is not so much a creature of the academic imagination but that constitutionalization actually exists. And of course, often enough the two go hand in hand. As Werner succinctly puts it, much of the literature on constitutionalism is 'an attempt to explain existing developments in international law in terms borrowed from domestic constitutionalism, with the aim of furthering a normative agenda of internationalism, integration and legal control of politics.'[10]

By contrast, we will adopt a different approach. While we will borrow freely from domestic constitutionalism whenever we feel this is useful and appropriate (while respecting all caveats about the dangers of applying domestic analogies), we will not claim to have found a way to guarantee global justice. Neither will we aim to demonstrate that a process of constitutionalization is actually taking place; instead, we work on the assumption that such a process is indeed taking place, however much in fits and starts perhaps.

Hence, our aim is to see what a constitutional international legal order could look like: we take the idea of constitutionalism and run with it, so to speak. We aim to provide the notion of constitutionalization with some hands and feet, realizing full well that ours are not the only hands and feet possible. Our approach lies somewhere in-between the strictly normative ('this is what things should be like') and the strictly descriptive ('this is what things are like'). We offer neither, but instead offer the empirical parameters within which further normative debate can take place. We sketch how constitutionalism can come to affect central issues such as law-making in the international community, membership of the global community, and dispute settlement. In a sense, borrowing from the US constitutional scholar Laurence Tribe, we aim to make visible what might be called the invisible constitution of the international community.[11] Or,

---

[9] Noteworthy recent examples include Kwame Anthony Appiah *Cosmopolitanism: Ethics in a World of Strangers* (Norton New York 2006); Simon Caney *Justice Beyond Borders: A Global Political Theory* (OUP Oxford 2005); Andrew Kuper *Democracy Beyond Borders: Justice and Representation in Global Institutions* (OUP Oxford 2004); and John S Dryzek *Deliberative Global Politics* (Polity Cambridge 2006).

[10] See Wouter Werner 'The Never-ending Closure: Constitutionalism and International Law' in Nicholas Tsagourias (ed) *Transnational Constitutionalism: International and European Perspectives* (CUP Cambridge 2007) 329–367, at 330.

[11] See Laurence H Tribe *The Invisible Constitution* (OUP Oxford 2008). To be sure, Tribe writes about the US constitution and his main point is that one cannot understand the text of that

more accurate still, we aim to make visible how one could reasonably think about the various elements of a global constitutional order; we aim to articulate what, following Waldron, we could refer to as our 'constitutional instincts'.[12]

But in order to get there, the idea behind the present chapter is to set the scene and discuss a number of developments relating to the international legal and political order which are of relevance. Even if we do not aim to be descriptive, at least we should demonstrate that something is going on worth paying attention to. While we release ourselves from the thick obligation to demonstrate that constitutionalization is taking place, we do feel the need to make clear that all the talk about constitutionalization does not exist only in the minds of academic lawyers. This is a much thinner claim, of course, than demonstrating once and for all that constitutionalization is taking place, but, however thin the claim, it does provide us with some solid ground to justify our project. Hence, this chapter sets out to discuss the constitutionalization of international law and a number of phenomena that, we feel, are somehow related. It aims, one might say, to provide a 'state of the art', situating the process of constitutionalization in its legal, social, and normative context.

That is not a very straightforward task, as all of the key terms are themselves without any clear meaning. Globalization, for instance, is often deemed to refer to economic processes, but also often to much more than that (cultural, social, and technological processes[13]). What adds to the complications is that globalization is hardly a unilinear process, but instead is more dialectical in nature, oscillating between 'dis-embedding' and 're-embedding', to use the language of social scientists,[14] and that far from promoting homogeneity, globalization is sometimes said to thrive on difference and diversity: at least in economic globalization, differences between locations dictate marketing decisions, location decisions, etc.[15] And for some globalization is predominantly an ideology, supported by cosmopolitan elites at the expense of less fortunate people.[16] Likewise, global governance would largely seem to be intangible (it being unclear who exercises it, and how exactly), but nonetheless many would agree it exists in some meaningful way.[17]

---

document without also having an eye to a number of relevant things not directly visible. His approach is therewith different from us, but the concept of an invisible constitution was too good to resist—and at any rate will come back throughout this book.

[12] See Jeremy Waldron *Law and Disagreement* (OUP Oxford 1999), at 51.

[13] For a very accessible overview, see Alex MacGillivray *A Brief History of Globalization* (Robinson London 2006).

[14] This is a central theme in Thomas Hylland Eriksen *Globalization: The Key Concepts* (Berg New York 2007).

[15] The point is forcefully made in John Gray *False Dawn: The Delusions of Global Capitalism* (Granta London 1998), at 57–58.

[16] See Jonathan Friedman 'Globalization' in David Nugent and Joan Vincent (eds) *A Companion to the Anthropology of Politics* (Blackwell London 2004) 179–197.

[17] The very notion of governance, as opposed to government, suggests elusiveness. The seminal volume is James R Rosenau and Ernst-Otto Czempiel (eds) *Governance without Government: Order and Change in World Politics* (CUP Cambridge 1992).

Indeed, constitutionalization and constitutionalism themselves are controversial notions, as the remainder of this chapter will illustrate.

Moreover, it should be borne in mind that many of the things discussed here can also be interpreted differently. By way of example, the rise of international investment arbitration has been seen as evidence of the 'humanization' of international law (it does, after all, allow recourse to international dispute settlement to actors other than states).[18] Equally plausible, though, it can also be seen as eroding public authority for private gains[19]—an altogether less blissful state of affairs. In short, much depends on background assumptions and starting points; much depends on the proverbial 'eye of the beholder'.[20] Still, it is perhaps best to start with a few anecdotal observations.

Observation number one. Walk through the 'constitutional law' section of any law library these days, and one is bound to see works on a wide variety of topics. Thus, a typical section will comprise works on law-making, democracy, and judicial review, but also on a variety of rights, ranging from generic works on fundamental rights to highly specific studies on, say, patients' rights, or transgender rights. There will be studies on the 'pouvoir constituant' and on the conduct of foreign relations, but also on globalization, federalism, or the institution of the ombudsperson. Some of these are what one would expect because they have been treated as constitutional issues for many, many years: this applies to law-making, to judicial review, and to the legal aspects of foreign policy-making, amongst others. Yet, inclusion of some of the other topics seems less obvious: patients' rights may also be covered in a growing section on law and medicine; studies on various categories of rights may be covered by a separate human rights section; while such things as globalization, federalism, or democracy might just as well be covered by the political science department in the same library.

Observation number two. A few years ago, a leading publishing house published a self-styled handbook of legal studies,[21] aiming (it would seem) to provide a comprehensive overview of what law is all about. To some extent, the work is organized along traditional lines, with separate chapters for contract, tort, property, criminal law, and civil procedure. Surprisingly, though, there is no separate chapter on constitutional law. Instead, a large chunk of the book is devoted to 'Citizens and Government', and is further divided in chapters on

---

[18] See Theodor Meron *The Humanization of International Law* (Martinus Nijhoff Leiden 2006) chapter 5.

[19] For an argument to this effect, see Gus van Harten *Investment Treaty Arbitration and Public Law* (OUP Oxford 2007).

[20] Truth, as Kratochwil felicitously puts it, is always 'relative to a frame of reference', adding that this does not imply that truth is arbitrary or even non-existent. See Friedrich V Kratochwil 'Of False Promises and Good Bets: A Plea for a Pragmatic Approach to Theory-building (the Tartu Lecture)' (2007) 10 *Journal of International Relations and Development* 1–15, at 3.

[21] See Peter Cane and Mark Tushnet (eds) *The Oxford Handbook of Legal Studies* (OUP Oxford 2005).

'The Nature and Functions of the State', 'Citizenship', 'Regulation', and 'Judicial Review of Legislation', amongst others. Curiously, though, the same section also includes the chapter on criminal law as well as one on criminology. Yet, the chapter on 'Legislation and Rule-making' is to be found in a different part of the book, under the general heading of 'Processes'. The point is not, of course, to say that the editors got it wrong—far from it. Instead, the point is, as with the anecdotal library, that within domestic settings, the notion of what constitutional law stands for seems to be in flux. Topics traditionally included (think of rule-making) can just as easily be excluded, it seems, whereas topics not usually associated with constitutional law—such as criminal law— may nowadays be mentioned in the same breath. Boundaries between legal sub-disciplines are sometimes seen to be rapidly disintegrating, and the likelihood of works on democracy, federalism, and globalization being located in the Constitutional Law section also suggests that the disciplinary divide between law and the social sciences is in the process of being bridged, or at least renegotiated.

If constitutionalist thought is in flux within domestic orders, it is not too far-fetched to suggest that it is also in flux in international society: the only difference may reside in the direction of the flow. Domestic societies, one could argue, are undergoing a process of de-constitutionalization, partly no doubt as a result of globalization (more on this below).[22] The standard witticism about constitutional law professors, at least in Europe, is that they have nothing left to do: law-making has become the province of the EU, whereas rights protection has become captured by the European Court of Human Rights, and the effect of external sources in the domestic legal order is a topic increasingly left to international lawyers.[23] By contrast, however, the international society would seem to be undergoing a process of constitutionalization.

The previous paragraph underlines the need for some further definitions. How can one speak, for instance, of international society? What does globalization mean? And what do we mean when we speak of constitutionalization? While the former two are less relevant for us to define with any precision (our common sense notions of international society and globalization will do nicely), the notions of constitutionalism and constitutionalization are central to this work. On one level, one could well suggest that the modern international legal

---

[22] In light of our general theme of action provoking reaction, it may well be claimed that domestic constitutional law is re-constitutionalizing, for instance by opening itself up to comparative projects and pioneering the conceptualization of economic and social rights. Examples include Vicki C Jackson and Mark Tushnet (eds) *Defining the Field of Comparative Constitutional Law* (Praeger Westport CN 2002); Tijmen Koopmans *Courts and Political Institutions: A Comparative View* (CUP Cambridge 2003); and Ran Hirschl *Towards Juristocracy: The Origins and Consequences of the New Constitutionalism* (Harvard UP Cambridge MA 2004).

[23] The sentiment is not limited to Europeans, incidentally. See Ernest A Young 'The Trouble with Global Constitutionalism' (2003) 38 *Texas International Law Journal* 527–545, at 545, expressing fears that 'constitutional law may soon cease to exist as an autonomous discipline.'

order has always been a constitutional order, in the sense that since Westphalia that order has been governed by a clear fundamental, constitutive, norm or set of norms: the norm of sovereignty. Hypocritical or not,[24] clearly the international legal order was constituted (in a relevant sense both linguistically and legally) by the idea of sovereignty. Hence, on this line of thinking, to speak of a current process of constitutionalization would, arguably, be wrong.

Still, while plausible, such a use of language is somewhat distorted, as empirical legal sovereignty (the Westphalian type of sovereignty) and legitimate sovereignty need not go hand in hand. Indeed, the ordinary meaning of constitution, or constitutionalization, suggests not only a system constituted by a certain norm or set of norms, but also has a normative dimension: when people think of constitutionalization, or constitutionalism, or any suchlike conjugation, the association is not only with something that is constituted in a technical sense, but also, and predominantly, with something that is constituted in a politically legitimate sense: a constitutional order is a legitimate order, deriving its legitimacy (in part at least) precisely from its constitutional nature.

The above seems fairly uncontroversial: there is more to constitutionalism and constitutionalization than merely the claim that, somehow, a political order or system is 'constituted'. It is no coincidence that when Hedley Bull found world politics to be based on a Grotian notion of order—this referred to an order comprising sovereign states acknowledging the existence of basic rules of law and morality applicable to their interactions—he nonetheless avoided use of the word 'constitutional' to describe this order, sensing the term would be more at home in relation to what he referred to as a Kantian, universalist world order.[25]

This also implies that constitutionalization entails something else than 'legalization'. The latter is an unfortunate term to begin with, in that it presupposes that a legal void is coming to be filled, without properly questioning whether that void existed to begin with.[26] In some of the literature, legalization is used to describe the increasing number of treaties and the creation of ever more courts and tribunals. This may be accurate, as such, but is not the same as constitutionalization: a very dense web of obligations and courts is still compatible with a Westphalian, non-constitutional order.[27]

---

[24] See Stephen D Krasner *Sovereignty: Organized Hypocrisy* (Princeton UP 1999).

[25] See Hedley Bull *The Anarchical Society: A Study of Order in World Politics* (MacMillan Houndmills 1977). Incidentally, this also serves as a warning concerning the facile use of labels: earlier authors would have understood Grotianism to refer to the sort of universalism Bull describes as Kantianism. A nice example is Cornelis van Vollenhoven *De drie treden van het volkenrecht* (Martinus Nijhoff The Hague 1918). And one later writer suggests that Bull, indeed, got his labels wrong. See Andrew Hurrell *On Global Order: Power, Values, and the Constitution of International Society* (OUP Oxford 2007), at 13.

[26] Moreover, the term legalization is also commonly used to advocate that certain practices be rendered lawful, as in the phrase 'legalize marihuana'.

[27] See generally Judith Goldstein, Miles Kahler, Robert O Keohane, and Anne-Marie Slaughter (eds) *Legalization and World Politics* (2000) 54 *International Organization* (special issue).

Many theorists of constitutionalism start from the same premise: somehow, a constitutional order is not just every order, but is something more than a mere factually working order; something more, also, than sheer anarchy. The consensus extends a bit further still: somehow, at least in domestic systems, a constitutional order is one in which '[p]ower is proscribed and procedures prescribed'.[28] A constitutional order has to do with the empowerment of political institutions, and with control of those same institutions, by creating fundamental rights for citizens and a system by which courts and other institutions can keep each other in check. A constitutional order, in other words, is one which helps create public authorities, but at the same time limits the powers of public authorities and sets out proper procedures for the institutions of governance to follow. Thus, constitutions typically will have rules on how laws ought to be made, how disputes ought to be settled, and which institutions shall exist, and will also have rules on the sort of basic values (typically cast in the form of fundamental rights) that no official action may encroach upon. In addition, a constitution will somehow identify what it is constitutive of: what is the political community concerned, and who are included and excluded (and on what basis).[29]

Still, this hardly exhausts the matter, for at least two different broad schools of constitutional thought can be recognized. There is, one the one hand, the classical school, inspired by classical liberalism and working on the assumption that constitutions are a-political (or pre-political), carved in stone, containing transcendental values valid beyond the here and now. Second, there is a more (overtly) politicized brand, which has less faith in the transcendence of values but, instead, emphasizes that constitutions continuously evolve, related as they are to society. In this version, pride of place is given not so much to values, but rather to the purpose and functions of governance; hence, Loughlin speaks of a 'functionalist style'.[30]

It is not too far-fetched to posit that the constitutionalization discussion in international law contains elements of both. In stressing the enduring rule of values and endorsing classical, individual-oriented liberalism, the role of markets

---

[28] See William Andrews (ed) *Constitutions and Constitutionalism* (2nd edn Princeton UP 1963), at 13.

[29] Using a slightly different vocabulary and a rougher prism, Tomkins ascribes two main characteristics to public law: 'It provides for the institutions which exercise political power, and it seeks to hold those institutions to some form of account.' See Adam Tomkins *Public Law* (Clarendon Press Oxford 2003), at 18. In turn, Lane distinguishes four characteristics common to every written domestic constitution: they address the nature of the state; the rights of individuals; the powers of the state; and the process of constitutional change. See Jan-Erik Lane *Constitutions and Political Theory* (Manchester UP 1996), at 110. We shall refrain from addressing constitutional change, and claim that such things as rules on membership or law-making fall under the broader headings of the nature or powers of the state.

[30] See Martin Loughlin 'The Functionalist Style in Public Law' (2005) 5 *University of Toronto Law Journal* 361–403. He speaks of 'style' rather than 'school' because functionalism comprises many different variations.

and the like, some participants can plausibly be typecast as members of the classical school of thought. Others, though, tend to come closer to the functionalist camp: those who stress deliberative decision-making processes or those who advocate control of international public authority might be included. And many will be inspired by a combination of both schools of thought: as will be discussed below, it is by no means uncommon for international lawyers to advocate the testing of public authority against transcendental values. As a result if only because reality is constructed partly by what people write about and how they write about things,[31] any empirical sketch will also contain elements of both: the growth and popularity of investment law, to name but one example, exemplifies a classical approach, while the drive to secure accountability of international organizations comes closer to Loughlin's functionalist style.

We will by and large follow this division, despite its somewhat unfortunate terminology: functionalism in the law of international organizations has quite different connotations—indeed, it is often posited as the polar opposite of constitutionalism.[32] We will ask ourselves throughout this book, informed by the tension between classical and functionalist constitutionalism, what a constitutional world could look like. How can law-making take place in this constitutionalizing world order? How do the institutions of a global constitutional order interact? What values could plausibly be regarded as protected against overzealous attempts at global governance? Before going there, however, it might be useful to discuss where the very idea of constitutionalization comes from, how it relates to other developments in international law, and what theories of constitutionalization abound. This will form the remainder of this chapter, and will owe perhaps more to what should properly be called constitutionalism.

Constitutionalism, as far as we are concerned, signifies not so much a social or political process, but rather an attitude, a frame of mind. Constitutionalism is the philosophy of striving towards some form of political legitimacy, typified by respect for, well, a constitution. This differs from other frames of mind, even those that share with constitutionalism a yearning for legitimacy. For legitimacy, after all, need not be exclusively connected to constitutionalism. Those who insist that political legitimacy derives solely from the effectiveness of decisions cannot lightly be considered constitutionalists; and the same applies to those who feel that legitimacy is first and foremost a matter of efficiency.[33]

To conclude, then, constitutionalization is, to us, a process, inspired by constitutionalist thought. This is even the case where the original ideas are no longer immediately recognizable. A court in, say, Switzerland proclaiming that

---

[31] For a lucid account, see John R Searle *The Construction of Social Reality* (Penguin London 1995).

[32] See Jan Klabbers 'Contending Approaches to International Organizations: Between Functionalism and Constitutionalism' in Jan Klabbers and Åsa Wallendahl (eds) *Research Handbook on International Organizations Law: Between Functionalism and Constitutionalism* (Edward Elgar Cheltenham 2011 forthcoming).

[33] See in more detail below, pp. 37–43.

the prohibition of torture is a matter of *jus cogens* may not intend to be, somehow, constitutional; but it could not reach this judgment without the earlier attempts by international lawyers to constitutionalize international law through the creation, promulgation, and endorsement of the concept of *jus cogens*.[34]

3. Fragmentation, Pluralization, Verticalization (and Privatization)

It is a truism to state, or so it seems, that international law is increasingly starting to look like the sort of legal order we are familiar with from our domestic legal systems. Many international lawyers have made the somewhat panicky observation that international law is engaged in a process of fragmentation: the various aspects of the international legal regime are branching out and gaining some form of quasi-independence, often misleadingly labelled 'self-containment'.[35] The label may be deceptive, but the underlying sentiment is not: just as in domestic law criminal lawyers have little or no time for tax law, and company lawyers by and large do not grapple with environmental law or administrative procedure, so too in international law the various sub-disciplines are increasingly leading a life of their own. And in much the same way as domestic systems are held together by constitutional law (the one area of domestic law which can hardly be practised[36]), so too these various branches of international law are increasingly seen as having some form of constitutional law hovering over it: a general body of rules which, much like domestic law, does not really lend itself to legal practice in quite the same way as contract law or tax law or criminal law do, but which nonetheless is vital for indicating how the various branches hang together. In a justly famous metaphor probably first coined by Oscar Schachter, general international law provides the highways between the otherwise isolated villages of international environmental law, international criminal law, international trade law, etc.[37]

In addition, there is also a dispersion of authority taking place. Where it was undisputed, in yesteryear's world order, that legitimate authority rested with states and states alone, authority now springs from a variety of sources and

---

[34] Leaving earlier natural law theories aside, in its modern form the notion of *jus cogens* was first proposed, it would seem, by Alfred Verdross 'Forbidden Treaties in International Law' (1937) 31 *AJIL* 571–577.

[35] For early analysis, see Bruno Simma 'Self-contained Regimes' (1985) 16 *Netherlands Yearbook of International Law* 112–136. See also Bruno Simma and Dirk Pulkowski 'Of Planets and the Universe: Self-contained Regimes in International Law' (2006) 17 *EJIL* 483–529.

[36] Once more anecdotal: it is surely no coincidence that within law schools, constitutional law and public international law tend to attract the same kinds of students (those with an interest in politics and public affairs), and tend to be viewed somewhat suspiciously by students with a clear interest in practising law: these tend to specialize in criminal law, tax law, or some or other area of private law.

[37] See Oscar Schachter *International Law in Theory and Practice* (Martinus Nijhoff The Hague 1991), at 1. This suggests that for Schachter, general international law played a proto-constitutional role.

institutions.[38] Obviously, legitimate authority may be exercised by international organizations, but these can still be cast as manifestations of statehood (indeed, sometimes organizations are conceptualized as gatherings of states, without an existence of their own[39]) or, at least, as exercising tasks and powers delegated by states.[40] But the same cannot be said for other entities, from liberation movements to non-governmental organizations (NGOs), and from companies to indigenous movements. Nor can it be said about migrant communities and diasporas,[41] or global cities such as New York, Sao Paulo, and Shanghai that are the focal point of some sociological analyses of globalization.[42] It is not just that the circle of subjects of international law is expanding (although it is[43]), but it is first and foremost that those non-state entities have started to compete with states for the scarce resource of politico-legal authority (i.e. the power to set authoritative standards).[44] They do not merely wish to be involved in monitoring international law, as the traditional role of NGOs was, or wish to receive benefits created under international law by states; instead, they increasingly demand a seat at the table.[45]

This authority can also take on all sorts of legal and quasi-legal forms.[46] Cooperation between states may be formalized in legal documents (treaties, decisions of international organizations), but also, and increasingly so perhaps, in instruments claiming a status outside the law (often labelled soft law instruments, informal instruments, or non-legally binding instruments[47]). Such norms may emanate, moreover, not just from regular and formalized meetings, but also from informal get-togethers, or be issued by entities whose standard-setting powers are in doubt.[48] Thus, much authority is exercised by networks of

---

[38] As Loughlin writes: 'The real threat which globalization poses is to traditional structures through which political authority is exercised.' See Martin Loughlin *Swords and Scales: An Examination of the Relationship Between Law & Politics* (Hart Oxford 2000), at 145. For a vivid illustration of the relevance of informal contacts and the informal economy, see Carolyn Nordstrom *Global Outlaws: Crime, Money, and Power in the Contemporary World* (University of California Press Berkeley CA 2007).

[39] An example is G-R Berridge *Diplomacy: Theory and Practice* (Prentice Hall Hemel Hempstead 1995).

[40] See Dan Sarooshi *International Organizations and their Exercise of Sovereign Powers* (OUP Oxford 2005).

[41] See, e.g., Jonathan Friedman 'Diasporization, Globalization, and Cosmopolitan Discourse' in André Levy and Alex Weingrod (eds) *Homelands and Diasporas: Holy Lands and Other Places* (Palo Alto Stanford UP 2005) 140–165.

[42] See, e.g., Saskia Sassen *A Sociology of Globalization* (Norton New York 2007).

[43] See already Hermann Mosler 'Die Erweiterung des Kreises der Völkerrechtssubjekte' (1962) 22 *Zeitschrift für ausländisches öffentliches Recht und Völkerrecht* 1–48.

[44] See generally Jan Klabbers '(I Can't Get No) Recognition: Subjects Doctrine and the Emergence of Non-state Actors' in Jarna Petman and Jan Klabbers (eds) *Nordic Cosmopolitanism: Essays in International Law for Martti Koskenniemi* (Martinus Nijhoff Leiden 2003) 351–369.

[45] See, e.g., Alan Boyle and Christine Chinkin *The Making of International Law* (OUP Oxford 2007). For further discussion, see pp. 225–227.

[46] This will be discussed further in chapter 3 below.

[47] For critical reflection, see Jan Klabbers *The Concept of Treaty in International Law* (Kluwer The Hague 1996).

[48] See in particular Anne-Marie Slaughter *A New World Order* (Princeton UP 2004).

civil servants meeting in all sorts of informal settings—in addition to more formal mechanisms.

If this process of 'legal pluralization' is underway in various manifestations (diffusion of actors as well as forms), it is accompanied by a broader normative pluralization: it is no longer immediately evident (presuming it ever was) that legal authority is the sort of authority to strive for.[49] It might be just as effective —perhaps more effective still—to exercise authority through other ways of standard-setting, and soft law or informal instruments merely form the tip of the iceberg. Commands may come from all sorts of directions: from legal norms, but also from moral norms, cultural norms, or norms internal to entities (think, e.g., of the rules in force within the Catholic church). Thus, to start with the latter, churches may often retain internal archaic rules which are difficult to reconcile with generally accepted legal standards. For example, priesthood may be limited to men, and overt homosexuality may be grounds for discrimination within churches when it comes to appointments and promotions, despite general social or legal norms against discrimination on the basis of gender or sexual orientation. More prominently, perhaps, church officials have also managed to escape from the workings of criminal law under reference to internal rules, or internal disciplinary procedures, in particular in sexual molestation cases. The point here is not to suggest there is anything particularly wrong about the church retaining a measure of autonomy from criminal justice (although such a case could no doubt be made); the point is rather to suggest that it is not immediately self-evident which form of authority should apply in such cases: should law prevail over internal standards, or should it be the other way around? And to what extent can the quest for legal personality (and the grant thereof) be seen as precisely a request (and grant) to be relatively isolated from the workings of the legal order?[50]

The same pluralization can be seen in other settings. Thus, athletes face criminal prosecution for acts of aggression committed on a football pitch, despite having been punished in accordance with the internal rules of their sports.[51] Others find themselves punished by sporting bodies and threaten to appeal to human rights tribunals, thus mixing sporting rules and legal rules, while in some cases sports rules and criminal law intertwine. Yet others commit so-called 'honour killings' in the name of socio-cultural norms within local communities (often immigrant communities), and when a humanitarian intervention in Kosovo proved legally problematic, it was justified under an appeal to

[49] See, e.g., William Twining *Globalization and Legal Theory* (2nd edn Butterworths London 2000); Boaventura de Sousa Santos *Towards a New Legal Common Sense* (Butterworths London 2002), and Brian Z Tamanaha *A General Jurisprudence of Law and Society* (OUP Oxford 2001).

[50] This, at least, is one of the greater benefits usually associated with legal personality: the right to regulate one's own internal affairs. See generally Jan Klabbers 'The Concept of Legal Personality' (2005) 11 *Ius Gentium* 35–66.

[51] As much was confirmed by the Dutch Supreme Court (Hoge Raad) in Case BB7087, judgment of 22 April 2008.

morality.[52] Again, the point is not to condemn or accept any of these practices; instead, the relevant consideration is that norms can emanate from various distinct normative orders, and it is by no means clear how to decide those cases when morality clashes with international law, or when church rules clash with domestic criminal law.

Indeed, it is not too far-fetched to suggest that the fragmentation of international law goes hand in hand with a process of verticalization: the system is no longer exclusively made up, as it still was in earlier days, of independent and sovereign states who famously interact as if they are billiard balls on the green sheet of a pool table.[53] Instead, other actors have come to the fore, including international organizations, multinational corporations, national liberation movements, international NGOs, minority groups, policy-making networks, and even (or especially) individuals, and at least some of these bring their own internal normative ('legal') orders to the table.[54] The previous emphasis on state sovereignty, resulting in the image of international law as a horizontal legal order made up of equals, so the argument goes, is slowly giving way to a conception of international law as more vertically organized. The subsystems that give rise to fears (or hopes) of fragmentation are, in this conception, independently functioning regimes where business is being done, indeed, which are eventually themselves doing the business, overcoming the traditional paradigm of state sovereignty.[55]

Fragmentation, pluralization, and verticalization are very much in the eye of the beholder. As Martti Koskenniemi recently wrote, what looks like fragmentation from one perspective may look more like unity from a different vantage point.[56] More importantly, perhaps, to the extent that these phenomena take place, they take place on two distinct levels. One is the level of international practice, where what matters is what states and other actors do, whereas the other is the level of scholarship. While the two influence each other without a doubt, care should be taken to keep them separate and not mix them up entirely: the circumstance that many academics write about fragmentation as such only means that many academics write about fragmentation, and interpret certain

---

[52] For an insightful discussion of the various debates, see Anne Orford *Reading Humanitarian Intervention* (CUP Cambridge 2003).

[53] Famous as the metaphor is, it has always been plagued by uncertainties concerning the identity of the person or persons wielding the cues, unless it be supposed that the balls move of their own volition.

[54] See generally Neil Walker 'Beyond Boundary Disputes and Basic Grids: Mapping the Global Disorder of Normative Orders' (2008) 6 *International Journal of Constitutional Law* 373–396.

[55] The most sophisticated rendition of this argument is Andreas Fischer-Lescano and Gunther Teubner *Regime-Kollisionen: Zur Fragmentierung des globalen Rechts* (Suhrkamp Frankfurt am Main 2006).

[56] See Martti Koskenniemi 'The Fate of Public International Law: Between Technique and Politics' (2007) 70 *Modern Law Review* 1–30, at 24–5. See also Mario Prost 'All Shouting the Same Slogans: International Law's Unities and the Politics of Fragmentation' (2006) 17 *Finnish Yearbook of International Law* 131–159.

events and trends as indicating fragmentation. While there usually is no smoke without fire, still it does not mean that therewith fragmentation becomes an irreversible fact or trend, and strictly speaking, it does not even imply that fragmentation 'really' exists.

Be that as it may (and it so happens that we do believe that fragmentation, pluralization, and verticalization have some meaning beyond the purely academic), our main interest in the current work is with what international lawyers, political scientists, and theorists do with constitutionalization. What interests us is how international lawyers (and others) construe the world around them, how they come to think in terms of fragmentation, pluralization, and verticalization, and, most of all, how they come to formulate the response that will be central to this study: the constitutionalist response.

For it is not only fragmentation that comes with a constitutionalist response, with general international law taking, in part, the place occupied in domestic legal orders by constitutional law. For pluralization and verticalization too provoke a constitutionalist response: indeed, the very notion of verticalization implies a form of hierarchy. In a vertical order (not unlike the domestic legal order, once more), some rules or institutions may be superior to others. In most states, a formal piece of legislation is deemed to be of higher status than a governmental decree, let alone a departmental memorandum or circular. Likewise, nationwide regulation is to be deemed of higher status than local or regional regulation. Verticalization, by definition, carries a sense of hierarchy with it, and the argument can increasingly be heard that international law is moving in this direction.[57] This is symbolized not least by the emergence of international criminal law as a branch of international law—criminal law, after all, in presupposing the existence of a public order and someone to speak for that public order, presupposes a strong notion of hierarchy to begin with.

In other words, both fragmentation and verticalization, intimately related as they are, come accompanied by some form of constitutionalization or, at least, discussions in constitutionalist language. With fragmentation, much of the constitutional response simply refers to general international law; with verticalization, however, much takes on the form of thinking in terms of the international order having a constitution, or something approximating it. Moreover, increasingly with fragmentation too, the constitutionalist discussion takes on 'constitutionalist' dimensions, if you will, and understandably so: there is a deep-seated anxiety that merely to respond to fragmentation by invoking general international law will be insufficient. Instead, in order to keep fragmented units together, something of a higher status must be involved and invoked, and it is precisely constitutionalism, or constitutionalization, that promises to be able to create some order in what otherwise would be chaos. Fragmentation, in yet other

---

[57] This will be further developed in chapter 2 below.

words, would lose some of its risks because it would, on the constitutionalist view, always be subject to higher imperatives.

What exactly those higher imperatives are remains uncertain. Many would agree, discussing matters on a substantive level, that fundamental human rights might qualify as such: the prohibitions of torture or genocide come to mind. Others would perhaps argue that as a functional matter (and from a much more utilitarian perspective[58]), the whole world would be better off if free trade were the norm: hence, free trade, and all that it entails, takes on constitutional dimensions.[59] And yet others would, surprisingly perhaps, support inclusion of some of the classic norms of the international order as constitutional: the prohibition on the use of force, but also such norms as the sovereign equality of states.[60]

On the more formal level, many invoke notions such as *jus cogens* rules as being of higher status than other rules, or *erga omnes* principles setting other norms aside,[61] or claim that the UN Charter, by virtue of its Article 103, prevails over any other agreement.[62] And yet a different response, inspired in part by the same desire but radically different in elaboration, is to protect local communities from 'intervention' by international law. Examples include the creation of a novel doctrine of dualism in US legal circles, to the effect that joining a treaty regime does not mean also accepting decisions of tribunals giving effect to that very same treaty.[63] Likewise, the ECJ has over the years built a legal wall around the EU, giving priority to EU law over competing considerations, including international legal norms.[64]

Whereas topics such as fragmentation and verticalization have received quite a bit of attention, less well recognized (or less well researched, at any rate) is the circumstance that international law is also confronted with a serious process of

---

[58] Eric Posner goes a long way toward this direction in Eric A Posner 'Human Welfare, not Human Rights' (2008) 108 *Columbia Law Review* 1758–1801.

[59] See, e.g., Ernst-Ulrich Petersmann 'Time for a United Nations "Global Compact" for Integrating Human Rights into the Law of Worldwide Organizations' (2002) 13 *EJIL* 621–650.

[60] This at least is one reading of Jed Rubenfeld 'Unilateralism and Constitutionalism' (2004) 79 *New York University Law Review* 1971–2028. Insightful is also Eyal Benvenisti 'Exit and Voice in the Age of Globalization' (1999) 98 *Michigan Law Review* 167–213. This goes so far as to even worry about finding inspiration in foreign precedent. For a critique, see Lorraine E Weinrib 'Constitutional Conceptions and Constitutional Comparativism' in Jackson and Tushnet (eds), *Defining the Field*, 2002, 3–34.

[61] There are many works on this. Among the more thoughtful ones is Bruno Simma 'From Bilateralism to Community Interest in International Law' (1994/VI) 250 *Recueil des Cours* 217–384.

[62] For a useful discussion of Art 103 see Rain Liivoja 'The Scope of the Supremacy Clause of the United Nations Charter' (2008) 57 *ICLQ* 583–612.

[63] Classic dualism would most likely accept that an authoritative interpretation would be included in self-executing norms, if it would accept the possibility of self-executing norms to begin with: it would not distinguish between the norm and its interpretation. An example of this novel dualism is Mark L Movsesian 'Judging International Judgments' (2007) 48 *Virginia Journal of International Law* 65–118.

[64] The *Kadi* case may be the most prominent recent manifestation, but is by no means the only one.

privatization. Sometimes, manifestations of this come within public view, such as the use of private military companies by US authorities in Iraq, culminating in the Abu Ghraib disgrace. But much more may be going on below the surface. Serious arguments can be made that military occupations and privatization go hand in hand: occupations pave the way for future untrammelled free market operations, and in the process end up creating huge amounts of profitable work in construction and reconstruction of war-torn territories.[65]

At the same time, investment protection has been immensely strengthened in recent years, with the effect that many exercises of domestic public power—whether done with a view to environmental protection or social justice—end up in tension with the internationally recognized rights of investors (some speak, rather evocatively, of an 'International Law of Greed'[66]). The debt crisis is said, by some, to have been created on purpose by cliques of Western banks and the financial institutions,[67] and at any rate, those financial institutions operate in such a way that the poor end up bankrolling the rich: the income of the financial institutions, largely in the form of interest payments, is channelled back to the richer member states.[68] The private sector benefits largely from the anti-terrorism measures taken after 9/11: from the producers of the small Ziploc bags allowed to carry a minimum of liquids and the producers of the sealable bags in common use at the duty free stores, to the companies checking and double-checking passengers and their luggage. And one authoritative source seems to suggest that even NATO's action over Kosovo, in the late 1990s, often heralded as a decent example of a humanitarian intervention, was actually done in order to coerce Serbia into accepting the market economy.[69]

More generally, it seems reasonably clear that globalization is a process driven in large measure by the private sector, with quite a bit of help from the public sector.[70] The banking crisis of 2008 made clear just how much the private sector depends on the public: in many cases, the failure of banks could only be thwarted by pouring public money into them. Indeed, the very point of globalization may well be that the distinction between a public and a private sector is rapidly disintegrating: the public sector operates in the service of the private sector, while the scope of the private sector is expanding and encompassing all sorts of activities once deemed public.[71] The two become indistinguishable.

---

[65] See Naomi Klein *The Shock Doctrine* (Penguin London 2007).

[66] This was the title of a presentation by Professor Sornarajah, one of the leading investment lawyers, during a conference in Heidelberg, in September 2008.

[67] See John Perkins *Confessions of an Economic Hitman* (Ebury Press London 2005).

[68] See Ngaire Woods *The Globalizers: The IMF, the World Bank, and Their Borrowers* (Cornell UP Ithaca NY 2006).   [69] As referred to in Klein, *Shock Doctrine*, 2007, at 328.

[70] See Ulrich Beck *Was ist Globalisierung?* (Suhrkamp Frankfurt am Main 1997).

[71] Therewith bucking the earlier trend of making private things (education, healthcare, even crime and punishment) a matter of public concern. Already Dewey recognized that few things are public by nature. See John Dewey *The Public and its Problems* (Swallow Press Athens OH 1927).

Either way, many of the above-mentioned phenomena (fragmentation, verticalization, pluralization) have something to do with globalization, and it is no exaggeration to claim that constitutionalization is a response to all of them simultaneously. Constitutionalization responds to fragmentation by somehow promising the unity of the global order. Confronted with fragmentation and the concomitant chaos of overlapping and competing regimes, constitutionalization carries the promise that there is some system to the madness after all;[72] there is something which helps keep the system together.[73]

Constitutionalization also offers a response to pluralization: it offers the response of centralization. A constitutional world order is one which has a centre of authority, so the underlying idea goes; in a constitutional global order, it is clear who can issue what norms and standards, and what the effect of such standards will be.[74]

Constitutionalization responds to verticalization in a different manner (indeed, some would claim that verticalization is itself a manifestation of constitutionalization, or more accurate yet, that the various manifestations of verticalization tend to stem from constitutionalist sentiments[75]). The one promise in this respect is, again, the promise of unity, to overcome the varying claims of varying verticalization projects. Where people claim that trade ought to prevail over human rights, or suggest that environmental concerns should trump trade concerns, or have human rights concerns trump environmental considerations, constitutionalization once again promises unity and order: it promises to unify the globe by authoritatively imposing hierarchy between vertical regimes and between norms all vying for prominence. Constitutionalism promises to settle the score once and for all, by giving either *jus cogens* priority, or trade, or human rights, or *erga omnes* principles. Here, then, constitutionalization comes in armed with a clear set of normative commitments, which displays that at least in this guise, constitutionalization is an intensely political process.

Constitutionalization finally also offers a riposte to privatization in two ways. First, it does so by carving out a protected public realm. If there is indeed a risk

---

[72] See Jan Klabbers 'Constitutionalism Lite' (2004) *International Organizations Law Review* 31–58.
[73] One may also conceive of non-constitutional ways of preserving or guaranteeing the unity of the system. Perhaps the best-known of these is the International Law Commission's 'principle of systemic treaty-interpretation'. See Martti Koskenniemi *Fragmentation of International Law: Difficulties Arising from the Diversification and Expansion of International Law. Report of the Study Group of the International Law Commission* (Erik Castrén Institute Helsinki 2007). See also Campbell MacLachlan 'The Principle of Systemic Integration and Article 31(3)(c) of the Vienna Convention' (2005) 54 *ICLQ* 279–320.
[74] This would also seem to be the premise underlying Gavin W Anderson *Constitutional Rights after Globalization* (Hart Oxford 2005). Anderson's approach is, in part, to reject any difference between law and non-law: law can found in the state, but also in universities, churches, and even the family.
[75] Not all manifestations though: it is possible to argue that while *jus cogens* may operate on the basis of *ordre public* thought, it is not by definition constitutionalist.

that the public sphere threatens to be overtaken by the private sphere, constitutionalization appears to put a stop to this; it appears to build a fence around the public, and protect it as well as it can. But, emphasizing that few things are ever what they seem, constitutionalization also helps discipline the public institutions that serve the global marketplace. In its domestic variant, this means that states are subjected to such things as conditionality under supervision of public institutions; on the global level, it suggests that those public institutions themselves guarantee and lock in place the rights of market actors, by introducing '"binding constraints" on the conduct of fiscal, monetary, trade, and investment policies.'[76]

Whether these responses are successful is beyond the scope of this book, but it can perhaps briefly be intimated that no miracles should be expected. It has been suggested that the promise of unity is by and large false, as constitutionalization may well result in cementing fragmented regimes and making cleavages between them more rather than less serious.[77] By the same token, constitutionalization as such, without political input, is unable to decide whether to favour trade or environment, human rights or security, *jus cogens* or anything else. Yet the point of constitutionalization is, often enough, to remove matters from the ordinary political process. And constitutionalization to halt privatization is likely to come to naught without reconsideration of its commitments to the private sector, such as the increased protection of private property rights.

4. On Constitutionalization

Constitutionalism in general has been on the rise in recent years.[78] In a development often associated with the fall of communism, many states have found mechanisms to keep politics in check. This is typified by the creation of rights catalogues, deemed by some to protect the prerogatives of domestic political elites,[79] deemed by others to protect individuals and groups against overzealous majoritarian decision-making.[80]

---

[76] Political scientist Stephen Gill thus speaks of the 'new constitutionalism' although his use of the term constitutionalism would seem to be broader than ours, and perhaps comes closer to juridification. See Stephen Gill 'Globalisation, Market Civilisation, and Disciplinary Neoliberalism' (1995) 24 *Millennium: Journal of International Studies* 399–423, at 412.

[77] See Klabbers, Constitutionalism Lite, 2004.

[78] See Bruce Ackerman 'The Rise of World Constitutionalism' (1997) 83 *Virginia Law Review* 771–797. For a critique, suggesting that sometimes constitutionalism receives more praise than it deserves, see Andrei Marmor 'Are Constitutions Legitimate?' (2007) 20 *Canadian Journal of Law and Jurisprudence* 69–94.

[79] This is the argument in Hirschl, *Towards Juristocracy*, 2004.

[80] But see Frank I Michelman *Brennan and Democracy* (Princeton UP 1999) for the argument that democratic decision-making and liberal rights protection can go hand in hand.

Much the same applies to international constitutionalism. While political theorists have written quite a bit on the prospects for global justice, they only recently started to theorize about international constitutionalism (individual exceptions notwithstanding).[81] Still, there already exists a large variety of studies on the constitutionalization of international affairs by lawyers and others. Some of it is related to constitutionalization within functional regimes, and most often this sector-constitutionalization, as we shall refer to it, takes place at the level of a single international organization. Thus, some work has been devoted to the World Trade Organization (WTO), and quite a bit more to the EU. Yet, even though ostensibly dealing with sector-constitutionalization, often such works take on a broader significance: those writing on the constitutional nature of the WTO often end up discussing the 'world trade constitution',[82] thereby, in the meantime, elevating the norms regulating trade to something of a global constitution. This follows from two lines of argument. One: if there is a world trade constitution, it follows that there can be no other constitution, as the idea of concurrent constitutions seems incoherent. Ergo: trade constitution equals constitution at large. Two: if trade constitution merely refers to the field of trade and helps define that field (while excluding non-trade concerns), then it still claims prevalence, as it is the trade constitution which decides what properly belongs also to other fields: it is the trade constitution that constitutes what qualifies as the human rights field, the environmental field, etc.[83]

More importantly, perhaps, the constitutionalization of the EU has spawned a rich literature on the theory of constitutions beyond the domestic state level;[84] this alone elevates such studies to a significance above and beyond that of the specific organization at issue. One of the more influential articles to speak of the constitutionalization of Europe is Eric Stein's classic in the *American Journal of International Law*. Stein's main point was that within the EC, a process of constitutionalization had been set in motion by the ECJ by its creation of the doctrines of direct effect, supremacy, the notion of European legislation, and implied powers.[85] Hence, without there being a formal constitution, the EC had entered into a constitutionalization stage thanks to the workings of the Court.

---

[81] Most prominent perhaps is Jürgen Habermas *The Divided West* (Polity Cambridge 2006 Cronin trans).

[82] See John O McGinnis and Mark L Movsesian 'The World Trade Constitution' (2000) 114 *Harvard Law Review* 511–605.

[83] For a general discussion of the 'field constitution', see Duncan Kennedy *A Critique of Adjudication {Fin de Siècle}* (Harvard UP Cambridge MA 1997).

[84] A fine collection is Joseph H H Weiler and Marlene Wind (eds) *European Constitutionalism Beyond the State* (CUP Cambridge 2003). See also Zenon Bankowski and Andrew Scott *The European Union and its Order: The Legal Theory of European Integration* (Blackwell Oxford 2000).

[85] See Eric Stein 'Lawyers, Judges, and the Making of a Transnational Constitution' (1981) 75 *AJIL* 1–27.

This has become something of a staple in the literature on the EU constitution, with even the proponents of a written constitution claiming that such a written constitution should respect and codify the 'acquis communautaire constitutionnel', and those less in thrall by the idea of a written constitution warning that such a constitution would inevitably undermine the judicially created constitution.[86]

Part of the discussion has revolved around the question of whether one can meaningfully speak of a constitution and all that entails (e.g. democracy) in the absence of a European collective identity: can there be a constitution without a demos? Answers vary: some have maintained that a demos is indispensable, others have adopted the more laconic stand that a constitution is bound to help galvanize a European demos, in much the same way as state-building may precede the existence of a national sentiment.[87] As the Italian revolutionary Massimo d'Azeglio famously quipped after Italian unification in the 19th century: 'We have made Italy, now we have to make Italians.'[88] Perhaps the bigger problem, as some have observed, is not so much the absence of a demos, but rather of a European public space: there is little or no truly European political debate going on, and chances for such a European public space appear very slender at any rate, given the linguistic diversity in Europe.[89]

An outgrowth of the discussion concerning the EU's constitutionalization debate is that many have come to accept the possibility of multilevel governance,[90] perhaps even of multilevel constitutionalism. The former is empirically not too difficult to verify: the citizens of Paris are simultaneously governed, at the very least, by the Paris municipality, the national French authorities, and the EU. And much the same applies to everyone these days: governance can take place on varying levels, from local neighbourhood to international organization. While not all of these levels will exercise an equally strong impact on everyday life, at least there is the possibility for them to have some impact. Thus, the Parisian may also, on occasion, be confronted with snippets of authority coming

---

[86] This is, by and large, the position adopted by Weiler. See, e.g., Joseph H H Weiler 'In Defence of the Status Quo: Europe's Constitutional *Sonderweg*' in Weiler and Wind (eds), *European Constitutionalism*, 2003, 7–23; Joseph H H Weiler 'A Constitution for Europe: Some Hard Choices' (2002) 40 *Journal of Common Market Studies* 563–580; see also Paul Craig 'Constitutions, Constitutionalism, and the European Union' (2001) 7 *European Law Journal* 125–150.

[87] The very term demos, moreover, is rather ambivalent, as are other manifestations such as 'the people'. Useful on this point is Margaret Canovan *The People* (Polity Cambridge 2005).

[88] As quoted in Eric J Hobsbawm *Nations and Nationalism Since 1780: Programme, Myth, Reality* (2nd edn Canto Cambridge 1992), at 44.

[89] See, e.g., Dieter Grimm 'Does Europe Need a Constitution?' (1995) 1 *European Law Journal* 282–307. In the same vein, Mireille Delmas-Marty *Vers une droit commun de l'humanité* (2nd edn Textuel Paris 2005), at 84.

[90] It would seem that domestically, too, centralized government has by and large been replaced by multilevel governance, leading some to speak of the eclipse of government by administrative law. The point is eloquently made by Sabino Cassese 'Les transformations du droit administratif du XIXe au XXIe siècle' (2002) 41 *Droit Administratif* 6–9, at 9.

from the WTO, or the Organization for Economic Cooperation and Development (OECD), or the French province in which Paris is located, or even her arrondissement.[91]

Multilevel constitutionalism, by contrast, is a bit more difficult: the very possibility depends on one's thoughts about what a constitution means. If the term constitution stands for ultimate authority, then multilevel constitutionalism appears as an oxymoron, since only one authority can be ultimate. The only way out, then, is the sort of distribution of powers which neatly separates one level from the other. It is only in this manner that one can meaningfully say that the citizens of Maryland are subject to multilevel constitutionalism: some things are ultimately governed by the Maryland constitution, others by the US constitution. The one open question then relates to conflict between the two: how is this to be solved?[92]

On a more relaxed definition, however, some have come to accept the possibility of multilevel constitutionalism (albeit perhaps constitutionalism with a small c rather than the capital C). Thus, Pernice defines constitution as 'the legal instrument by which the people of a certain territory agree to create institutions vested with public authority', in particular with reference to their respective rights and their status as subjects. On such a reading, multilevel constitutionalism means little more than multilevel governance.[93]

Still, within the EU the possibility of multiple constitutionalism seems to be reasonably well accepted, at least in scholarship,[94] and at least in the fairly thin sense in which multi-level constitutionalism stands for multi-level governance. And in practical politics, too, it might be argued that the resistance of French and Dutch citizens to the Treaty establishing a Constitution for Europe (which they famously rejected in 2005) owed more to the precise contents of this particular treaty than to its constitutional or quasi-constitutional nature. Put differently, it is possible that French and Dutch citizens were concerned first and foremost about the policies enshrined in the Treaty, rather than the circumstance that the Treaty had constitutional ambitions. On this reading, then, the

---

[91] A useful collection is Andreas Føllesdal, Ramses Wessel, and Jan Wouters (eds) *Multilevel Regulation and the EU: The Interplay between Global, European and National Normative Processes* (Martinus Nijhoff Leiden 2008).

[92] This presupposes that such neat power divisions are possible to begin with. Practice would seem to be a bit less neat, though, with entities, while exercising their own powers, often interfering with the proper exercise of someone else's powers. For an exploration, see Jan Klabbers 'Restraints on the Treaty-making Powers of Member States Deriving from EU Law' in Enzo Cannizzaro (ed) *The European Union as an Actor in International Relations* (Kluwer The Hague 2002) 151–175.

[93] See Ingolf Pernice 'Multilevel Constitutionalism in the European Union' (2002) 27 *European Law Review* 511–529, at 515. For the argument that on the global level, too, a system of multilayered governance is already in place, see Charlotte Ku 'Forging a Multilayered System of Global Governance' in Ronald St J MacDonald and Douglas M Johnston (eds) *Towards World Constitutionalism: Issues in the Legal Ordering of the World Community* (Martinus Nijhoff Leiden 2005) 631–651.

[94] For theoretical reflection, see Neil MacCormick *Questioning Sovereignty? Law, State, and Practical Reason* (OUP Oxford 1999).

defeat of the Constitutional Treaty is not a defeat of multi-level constitutionalism *per se*.

Be that as it may, the precise parameters of this EU debate are unlikely to be reproduced on the global level, if only because no international tribunal, including the International Court of Justice, is capable of exerting anything remotely resembling the ECJ's influence. Still, it does raise two additional issues. First, it raises the question of what to do with exercises of authority that do not neatly fall within a recognized category? Neil Walker offers an insightful discussion of such instruments as administrative decisions adopted under the Good Friday Agreements concerning Northern Ireland: those are neither easily cast as British legal acts, nor as international law instruments, nor as EU law acts. For those, a different category ought to be invented: Walker speaks of 'metaconstitutionalism'.[95]

Second, the entire EU constitutionalization discussion suggests a more common problem: is constitutionalization a spontaneous process, a *bric-à-brac* of decisions taken by actors in a position of authority responding to the exigencies of the moment, or is it rather the result of a top-down process, in which a constituent authority designs a constitution? The latter is unlikely to occur on the global level; the former, almost by default, might be more likely. This is not to suggest that the global constitution will be the aggregate of a number of sector constitutions; it is rather to suggest that the global constitution will be a patchwork quilt, and will most likely be identified rather than written in any meaningful sense: a material rather than a formal constitution. In Hurrell's term, it will be a 'common law constitution' rather than a more continental type of constitution.[96]

With that in mind, discussions on such questions as to whether a global demos exists need not detain us too much. The likely answer is in the negative (with global solidarity being a long way off, let alone a global demos); as a result, it remains an open question who, in international matters, can exercise constituent power.[97] Either way, it is less than plausible to nominate existing treaties as candidate global constitutions. The most famous example is, of course, that of the UN Charter, immortalized by Bardo Fassbender[98] and harking back to a longer tradition, especially, perhaps, in the German-speaking world.[99]

---

[95] See Neil Walker 'Flexibility within a Metaconstitutional Frame: Reflections on the Future of Legal Authority in Europe' in Gráinne de Búrca and Joanne Scott (eds) *Constitutional Change in the EU: Between Uniformity and Flexibility?* (Hart Oxford 2000) 9–30.

[96] See Hurrell, *On Global Order*, 2007.

[97] A useful collection is Martin Loughlin and Neil Walker (eds) *The Paradox of Constitutionalism: Constituent Power and Constitutional Form* (OUP Oxford 2007).

[98] See Bardo Fassbender 'The United Nations Charter as the Constitution of the International Community' (1998) 36 *Columbia Journal of Transnational Law* 529–619. A precursor is Blaine Sloan 'The United Nations Charter as a Constitution' (1989) 1 *Pace Yearbook of International Law* 61–126. See also Pierre-Marie Dupuy 'The Constitutional Dimension of the Charter of the United Nations Revisited' (1997) 1 *Max Planck Yearbook of United Nations Law* 1–33.

[99] Verdross, e.g., would habitually speak in terms of the 'Verfassung der Völkerrechtsgemeinschaft'. An early example of him doing so is the very first, pre-war edition of his well-known textbook.

Less immediately obvious, though, the same would have to apply to other treaties. The global constitution cannot be found in the International Covenant on Civil and Political Rights (ICCPR) (which has also attracted too many reservations for this claim to be plausible), or the Rights of the Child Convention (despite having the largest number of parties of any treaty), or even the Vienna Convention on the Law of Treaties and, in particular, its rules on interpretation. While it is plausible to argue that because the Vienna Convention deals with all sorts of treaties and cannot completely be circumvented when states conclude treaties, what hinders the Vienna Convention's possible claim to constitutional status is that, technically, it only covers treaties concluded between states, and while there is a companion Convention addressing treaties concluded with or between international organizations, that still means that instruments concluded by others (indigenous peoples, liberation movements, private actors) are not covered.[100] Moreover, the Vienna Convention has been ratified by not much more than half the number of existing states,[101] and surely not all of its provisions can be found in customary international law, or, if they can, can not be found having the exact same contents.[102] Finally, and perhaps most relevant for present purposes, many of the Vienna Convention's norms are residual in nature: states are free to devise their own rules on such issues as reservations, interpretation, entry into force, or termination.[103] It is only when they refrain from doing so that the provisions of the Vienna Convention can be invoked. While one might count the Vienna Convention, perhaps, amongst a body of international constitutional law—this seems to be the premise underlying the International Law Commission (ILC) report on fragmentation, assigning a prominent place to the principle of systemic integration in interpretation even though it shuns constitutionalist language—to claim that

---

See Alfred Verdross *Völkerrecht* (Springer Berlin 1937). Another, more recent, is Alfred Verdross *Die Quellen des universellen Völkerrechts: Eine Einführung* (Rombach Freiburg 1973). Influential has also been Mosler's use of the phrase 'constitutional elements', functioning more or less as *Grundnormen* holding international law together rather than as blueprints for its structures. See Hermann Mosler 'The International Society as a Legal Community' (1974/IV) 140 *Recueil des Cours* 1–230, at 31–32.

[100] This 1986 Vienna Convention on the Law of Treaties Concluded With or Between International Organizations, moreover, has yet to enter into force.

[101] As of January 2009, the 1969 Vienna Convention on the Law of Treaties (VCLT) had 108 parties.

[102] One can entertain serious doubts about, at least, the *jus cogens* provision and about the material breach provision (which in practice is applied in marked contrast to the formula used in Art 60 VCLT).

[103] Art 42 aimed to create a vacuum around the Vienna Convention by suggesting that validity of treaties (and termination) were exclusively to be governed by the Vienna Convention. This, however, has proved impossible to achieve, and was unlikely to begin with. For further discussion, see Jan Klabbers 'Reluctant *Grundnormen*: Articles 31(3)(c) and 42 of the Vienna Convention on the Law of Treaties and the Fragmentation of International Law' in Matthew Craven, Malgosia Fitzmaurice, and Maria Vogiatzi (eds) *Time, History and International Law* (Martinus Nijhoff Leiden 2007) 141–161.

the Vienna Convention is the constitution of international society would be fanciful.

Instead of full and comprehensive efforts to achieve a state-like constitutional structure, within quite a few international organizations aspects of constitutionalism have found a place. Perhaps the most prominent idea here is the notion that decision-making within organizations should take place in accordance with internal rules and guidelines. This has resulted, with quite a few organizations, in the creation of departments of internal oversight, the appointment of so-called compliance officers, and in some cases even in the establishment of quasi-judicial bodies, the World Bank Inspection Panel being possibly the most well-known example.

These are all manifestations (as is much of the constitutionalization discussion) of an increasing willingness to submit the exercise of public authority on the international level to closer control. Other emanations of this increased willingness resides in the discussion on the accountability of international organizations, which has kept three august bodies of international lawyers occupied (the Institut de Droit International, the International Law Association, and the International Law Commission) but without much tangible success so far.

Likewise, the debate on the possibilities for judicial review in international law owes much to similar concerns. In particular since the heightened activities of the Security Council following the end of the Cold War, many have suggested that it should be possible to submit resolutions of the Council to review their legality and validity.[104] Sometimes the suggestion is made that such review should be done by the International Court of Justice, but increasingly also other courts are mentioned, including domestic courts.[105]

5. A Pluralist Constitutionalism

If no single instrument can be considered to represent the constitution of international society, it would seem to follow that the notion of constitution will remain contested. Indeed, several ideas about international constitutionalism are floating around. Perhaps the most obvious one, based as it is on classical liberalism, is that which regards international constitutionalism as founded on common and universal values. These, then, in turn, need to be protected against political decision-making.[106]

---

[104] For an overview, see Jan Klabbers 'Straddling Law and Politics: Judicial Review in International Law' in MacDonald and Johnston (eds), *Towards World Constitutionalism*, 2005, 809–835.

[105] See Erika de Wet and André Nollkaemper (eds) *Review of the Security Council by Member States* (Intersentia Antwerp 2003).

[106] Representative samples include Christian Tomuschat 'International Law: Ensuring the Survival of Mankind on the Eve of a New Century' (1999) 281 *Recueil des Cours* 9–438; Pierre-Marie

This strand suggests that there can be little doubt that the international community recognizes some values as universal. These are recognized as *jus cogens* norms and *erga omnes* obligations, and would typically consist of the liberal human rights portfolio and the prohibition of the use of force, in addition to such things as democracy and perhaps, for some, free trade. These values are universally shared, so it is asserted, and therewith manifest the unity of world society. Based on these values, there is indeed an international constitutional order, and unconstitutional behaviour can simply be dismissed, perhaps even prosecuted. Because the order is based on universal values, moreover, there is no need to insist on the consent of individual states as creating legal obligation. On this thick constitutionalist reading, norms come into being when they are necessary to protect the common good and will bind all actors.[107] State consent becomes superfluous, while questions concerning the opposability of rules become stultified: the law applies to each and every one who is affected by it. This is mandatory, moreover: it would be impossible to claim that states are bound by rule X, but that this rule does not apply to other actors.[108]

There are various well-known problems with such a thesis in this particular form. One problem is that it presupposes all too easily that the liberal human rights catalogue is universally shared. Perhaps this is so on a high level of abstraction (although even that is debatable, given the recent popularity of torture in some circles), but surely, on the ground there is widespread disagreement.

An obvious second problem is the determination of what is or is not necessary. Surely, such thick constitutionalism is incomplete without also having thought through the institutional implications: who is the law-maker in such a scenario? Which institution is capable of setting authoritative and legitimate standards, applicable to all, and binding upon all without the need for expressions of consent to be bound? Without an institutional framework, the only plausible answer is to say that this power resides with groups of powerful states. One possible manifestation thereof is the Security Council, but this, as currently composed, suffers from a legitimacy deficit. While eminently equipped for its original task (maintaining and restoring international peace and security), it is far less suitable as a global law-maker.

Not surprisingly, perhaps, in this light, sometimes this thick constitutionalism ends up endorsing judicial review in international law.[109] If

---

Dupuy 'L'Unité de l'ordre juridique international' (2002) 297 *Recueil des Cours* 9–490; Jost Delbrück 'Prospects for a "World (Internal) Law"? Legal Developments in a Changing International System' (2002) 9 *Indiana Journal of Global Legal Studies* 401–31; Erika de Wet 'The International Constitutional Order' (2006) 55 *ICLQ* 51–76.

[107] See, e.g., Jonathan I Charney 'Universal International Law' (1993) 87 *AJIL* 529–551.

[108] It would be different with power-conferring rules: these can differentiate between various actors. Thus, one may well argue that a right of diplomatic protection (if still necessary in a thick constitutional setting) would accrue to states but not to NGOs or indigenous peoples.

[109] See Erika de Wet *The Chapter VII Powers of the United Nations Security Council* (Hart Oxford 2004).

institutions such as the Security Council are engaged in law-making then, so the argument goes, it should be possible to exercise some form of control over them, most likely some form of judicial control. This is almost a knee-jerk reflex: this brand of constitutionalism goes hand in hand with judicial review; or even, influenced by US constitutionalism, tends to be seen as synonymous: judicial review equals constitutionalism.[110] In US discussions, often the topic of constitutionalism is re-cast as judicial review—small wonder then that international lawyers looking to the US for guidance adopt a similar stance. And judicial review does indeed offer some of constitutionalism's benefits, without seeming to be overambitious. For one thing, judicial review aims to tame the beast of politics: it sends the message that no matter what politics may decide, it cannot overstep the bounds of law.

Control is also central to attempts to reform decision-making processes in international institutions, although such debates are rarely conducted by invoking ideas of constitutionalism. On this idea (more closely affiliated with what we have labelled the functionalist approach above), international decision-making processes ought to be more representative, more open to participation of a diversity of actors, and more transparent. The most well-known example is the possible (always possible) reform of the Security Council, aiming to make it more representative, even though it is not always immediately obvious what it should be made to represent. But other discussions also fall under this heading, such as the debate on whether *amicus curiae* briefs should be admissible before WTO panels, or discussions on the proper role of NGOs in the making of international law.[111]

Something of a *via media* is the attempt by Kingsbury *et al* to flesh out a global administrative law. While not as ambitious (or 'conceited', to use Dunoff's term[112]) as full-fledged classical constitutionalism, nonetheless the global administrative law project taps into worries about the exercise of power on the international scene and the absence of accountability. Where the classical school resorts to universal and globally accepted values to prop up the system, global administrative law circumvents the need to do so by concentrating on administrative law principles and standards, in the expectation that such principles and standards, by being largely procedural or technical in character, offer less opportunity for political discord than any proclamation of universal values. Such principles may be borrowed from domestic systems and then applied elsewhere, either in an international context (e.g. to scrutinize the activities of international institutions), or in other domestic settings.[113] Indeed, a key point is to focus on

---

[110] See, e.g., Larry Alexander (ed) *Constitutionalism: Philosophical Foundations* (CUP Cambridge 1998). Many of the essays are effectively essays about judicial review and how best to interpret the (US) constitution.

[111] On this, see Boyle and Chinkin, *The Making of International Law*, 2007.

[112] See Jeffrey L Dunoff 'Constitutional Conceits: The WTO's "Constitution" and the Discipline of International Law' (2006) 17 *EJIL* 647–675.

[113] See also Daniel C Esty 'Good Governance at the Supranational Scale: Globalizing Administrative Law' (2006) 115 *Yale Law Journal* (2006) 1490–1562.

the functioning of actors: on what they do and how they take decisions. While seemingly workable, at the end of the day global administrative law also cannot entirely escape from the question of where its principles and standards derive their legally binding force from: the global administrative law project, for all its merits, still requires a plausible sources chapter.[114]

Another class of approaches focuses not so much on the application of standards (often externally proclaimed but of uncertain pedigree), but rather more on the sort of constitution that the international community ought to have. This group comprises first and foremost legal theorists of varying ilk. Two approaches in particular stand out. First is the one pioneered by Gunther Teubner and his younger colleague Andreas Fischer-Lescano,[115] as a consequence of the social systems approach first developed by the sociologist Niklas Luhman and further developed by Teubner two decades ago.[116] The core of this approach is, as noted, the fragmentation of the world (all spheres of it, really), into distinct realms. Science has become a world of its own, as has, say, education. So too have law, politics, economics, and other walks of life become separated from each other: these have become, in jargon, self-contained regimes (or auto-constitutional regimes, as Fischer-Lescano and Teubner sometimes refer to them[117]), each operating according to a logic of its own, and each operating according to its own internal standards and operating procedures.

In such a setting, the role for a constitution is to keep the system unified and to regulate how conflicts between the various regimes can be settled: much of the relevant law is therefore characterized as 'conflict law' (*Kollisionsrecht*), and indeed, in its methodology, this approach bears a more than passing resemblance to what some call private international law, and others refer to as 'conflict of laws'.[118] The aim is not to overcome conflict once-and-for-all, but rather to mitigate its worst effects through harmonizing, balancing, and similar activities. Much like private international law, *Kollisionsrecht* searches for contextually acceptable solutions on a case-by-case basis. While the critic may denounce this as using plasters to cure cancer, the proponent may retort that at least it avoids the ruinous effects of chemotherapy. *Kollisionsrecht*, in the version developed by

---

[114] See in greater detail also pp.100–102.

[115] See Fischer-Lescano and Teubner, *Regime-Kollisionen*, 2006.

[116] See Gunther Teubner *Law as an Autopoietic System* (Blackwell Oxford 1993 Bankowska and Adler trans).

[117] See Andreas Fischer-Lescano and Gunther Teubner 'Regime-Collisions: The Vain Search for Legal Unity in the Fragmentation of Global Law' 25 (2004) *Michigan Journal of International Law* 999–1046, at 1014–1017. They also on occasion speak of societal constitutions, by which they mean those same regimes.

[118] This is further discussed in the specific context of the EU by Christian Joerges and Florian Rödl 'Informal Politics, Formalised Law and the "Social Deficit" of European Integration: Reflections after the Judgments of the ECJ in *Viking* and *Laval*' (2009) 15 *European Law Journal* 1–19. Note though that at least in this publication, the notion of 'constitutional' carries specific associations as something societal and foundational, rather than formal-legal.

Teubner and Fischer-Lescano and like-minded authors, may not end conflict altogether, but does allow for politically sensible solutions.

Second, and perhaps more overtly normative, is the plea for a pluralist constitutional order. This takes several forms. A first one, instantly recognizable to traditional international lawyers, is that advocated by the political scientist Andrew Hurrell, who sees the global constitution as being predominantly concerned with co-existence between independent entities.[119] What distinguishes his approach from that of many traditional international lawyers, though, is that he is not content with merely developing a procedural approach. Mutual recognition of sovereign entities alone is not enough; this would amount to a return to 19th-century international law, akin to pushing the toothpaste back into the tube. Instead, while accepting the basic division of the world into sovereign entities, Hurrell nonetheless claims that there ought to be additional roles for other actors, and that the pluralist world order should make serious work of reducing inequality. Thus, his pluralism, while on a par with traditional approaches, nonetheless goes a step further, and includes a normative element that is decidedly absent in similar rival conceptions.

Some legal theorists have also come to embrace pluralism, but perhaps in a less state-centric manner. Thus, in line with the recognition that a plurality of values exists (as discussed above), Walker suggests that constitutionalism also comes in a variety of settings, and that observers ought to accept this as a point of departure: there simply is no other plausible conception.[120] More radical still, this pluralism starts from the position that there is no way of determining which validity claims are stronger and weaker: Walker refers to 'epistemic pluralism', on the basis of which 'constitutional pluralism' is founded. And the latter then entails an acceptance of the circumstance that legitimate authority can come from a variety of sources, while there is no shortcut to decide which one to follow in case of conflict. 'The incommensurability of authority claims', so Walker writes, 'means that the idea of a fully consensual "sharing", "pooling" "division" or "co-ordination" of authority between units ... can never be more than an aspiration whose full realisation is frustrated by the resilient distinctiveness and authoritativeness-in-the-last-instance of the units who might pursue it.'[121]

While multilevel constitutionalism often lapses in mere governance, or aims to set a hierarchy, Walker's constitutional pluralism is self-consciously heterarchical; not in search of hierarchy, but accepting that units co-exist side by side and constantly intermingle. That said, Walker proposes a 'metaconstitutionalism' to provide closure in given cases, and in cases of constitutional collisions, metaconstitutionalism could consist of a dialogue between constitutional authorities. This may not 'solve' anything, but at least would promote

[119] See Hurrell, *On Global Order*, 2007.
[120] Neil Walker 'The Idea of Constitutional Pluralism' (2002) 65 *Modern Law Review* 317–359.
[121] *Ibid*, at 338–339.

dialogue and discussion, and make various sites of authority familiar with each other and provide cross-fertilization.[122]

Also inspired by the pluralist literature, but reluctant to insist on constitutionalism and law alone, some authors have come to pay more attention to what Ivor Jennings once called the 'psychology' of government (and by extension governance). Somehow, if it is the case that constitutionalism is a political project, and if it is the case that constitutional norms too tend to be circumvented as soon as the end is calculated to justify the means, perhaps what matters is not so much the very rules that are locked in place, but also, additionally, the mindset of those who do the ruling and governing. Thus, Koskenniemi endorses a re-reading of Kant which stresses Kant's conception of the moral politician (as opposed to the political moralist, whom Koskenniemi associates with many a liberal),[123] following his earlier advocacy of a 'culture of formalism'.[124] The latter phrase is often understood as endorsing formalism (and therewith often the subject of caricature), at the expense of the notion of culture. What matters is, however, the culture prevailing amongst those in positions of power: will they respect existing formalities, or take shortcuts to the good life?[125] Indeed, elsewhere Koskenniemi speaks in terms of a call for 'spiritual awakening and moral purity' as guiding constitutionalist projects, including his own.[126]

Likewise Klabbers has argued for a 'lite' version of constitutionalism.[127] Based more directly on Arendt than on Kant, and inspired to some degree by republican thought and virtue ethics, the point of his exercise is not to diminish the value of more traditional approaches to constitutionalism, or to somehow suggest that international constitutionalism by definition cannot be anything other than 'lite' in comparison to domestic constitutionalism,[128] but rather to urge those in positions of power to behave responsibly, for even the most wonderful constitutional blueprints are defenceless against overzealous governance.[129]

---

[122] *Ibid*, at 358.

[123] See Martti Koskenniemi 'Constitutionalism as Mindset: Reflections on Kantian Themes about International Law and Globalization' (2007) 8 *Theoretical Inquiries in Law* 9–36.

[124] See Martti Koskenniemi *The Gentle Civilizer of Nations: The Rise and Fall of International Law 1870–1960* (CUP Cambridge 2001).

[125] This is strongly emphasized in Martti Koskenniemi 'Formalism, Fragmentation, Freedom: Kantian Themes in Today's International Law' (2007) 4 *No Foundations: Journal of Extreme Legal Positivism* 7–28.

[126] See Martti Koskenniemi 'On the Idea and Practice for Universal History with a Cosmopolitan Purpose' in Bindu Puri and Heiko Sievers (eds) *Terror, Peace, and Universalism: Essays on the Philosophy of Immanuel Kant* (OUP Oxford 2007) 122–148, at 143.

[127] See Klabbers, 'Constitutionalism Lite', 2004 and Jan Klabbers 'Possible Islands of Predictability: The Legal Thought of Hannah Arendt' (2007) 20 *Leiden Journal of International Law* 1–23.

[128] For this reading, see Bardo Fassbender '"We the Peoples of the United Nations": Constituent Power and Constitutional Form in International Law' in Loughlin and Walker (eds), *The Paradox of Constitutionalism*, 2007, 269–290, at 282.

[129] Parts of the public administration literature reach similar conclusions. An insightful critique of thinking in terms of rules alone is Michael Harmon *Responsibility as Paradox: A Critique of*

Such attempts to arrive at a more responsive and responsible form of constitutionalism owe something, in inspiration, to worries about what some refer to as the 'imperialism' of modern constitutionalism. On this line of thought, modern constitutionalism is characterized not so much by openness towards all, but rather by attempts to carve in stone a liberal political project which, like most political projects, tends to be of greater benefit to some than to others.[130] In order to prevent domination under the banner of constitutionalism, constitutionalism would need to be accompanied by a sense of responsibility. This is difficult to capture in legal rules, of course: one cannot order political leaders to 'be responsible'; but that does not render it irrelevant.[131]

6. Forms and Techniques

In the absence of a unitary world state, with a single government in a centralized structure, a constitutional order must somehow find ways of dealing with relations between the whole and its parts. Broadly speaking, two models of constitutionalization can be discerned, accompanied by three distinct techniques. To some extent, these are predominant above all on the level of ideal theory; sometimes they also come with more visible empirical backing.[132]

A first idea is to borrow notions from federalism. While federalism itself is a broad school, encompassing different political systems, the core idea is a division of powers between the whole and its parts, accompanied, often enough, by institutions policing the boundaries between the two.[133] With respect to the international setting, a world federalist movement has been in existence already for a long period of time. Still, despite this impressive pedigree, federalism is not for the fainthearted. Quite a few federal states are born out of necessity rather than intense federal idealism; with respect to Belgium, for example, which resorted to federalism in the early 1990s, it was seen as the most plausible way of preventing a total break-up of the (formerly unitary) state, while Germany's post-war federalism seemed the safest way of preventing the centralization of

Rational Discourse on Government (Sage Thousand Oaks CA 1995); useful on responsible exercises of authority is Larry D Terry *Leadership of Public Bureaucracies: The Administrator as Conservator* (2nd edn Sharpe Armonk NY 2003).

[130] See above all James Tully *Strange Multiplicity: Constitutionalism in an Age of Diversity* (CUP Cambridge 1995), and James Tully 'The Imperialism of Modern Constitutional Democracy' in Loughlin and Walker (eds), *The Paradox of Constitutionalism*, 2007, 315–338.

[131] For an elaboration with respect to judicial decision-making, see Haywood Jefferson Powell *Constitutional Conscience: The Moral Dimension of Judicial Decision* (University of Chicago Press 2008).

[132] The distinction is helpfully elaborated in Beitz, *Political Theory and International Relations*, 1999, at 156–158.

[133] For Wheare, the 'federal principle' is 'the method of dividing powers so that the general and regional governments are each, within a sphere, co-ordinate and independent.' See Kenneth C Wheare *Federal Government* (OUP Oxford 1947), at 11.

political power. Federalism, in other words, can be integrative, but can also be seen as a tool to manage devolution.[134]

Either way, chances for a world federation are not to be overestimated.[135] For one thing, if the pluralists are right in saying that there are fundamentally different values operating across the globe, then it would seem that federalism may remain out of reach. It is one thing to move back to federalism from a unitary position, as Belgium did: this is plausible even in the face of wide disjunctions. But it seems a lot less plausible for a federation to emerge from the ground up and in voluntary fashion in a situation of clashing civilizations. The move to a federal structure would seem to presuppose at least some common ground.

Much the same applies, *a fortiori*, to the creation of a more hierarchical structure. Indeed, on one level, the very idea of hierarchy in international law is difficult to reconcile with the very conceptual foundations of international law: that the system is a system of equal sovereigns. Such a system could not accept, it is often thought, the possibility of a hierarchy of norms, and if the endless discussions on *jus cogens* are anything to go by, it will at least be clear that the creation of a normative hierarchy is not easily accomplished. By the same token, a system of sovereign equals would have problems accepting the supreme position of one or some of these entities. If all are sovereign and all are equal, then it follows that none can be superior, at least not as a matter of principle.

If neither a world federal order nor a hierarchical order are entirely plausible, global constitutionalism has to make use of other, more specific and limited techniques at its disposal. Three such techniques can be identified: subsidiarity, margin of appreciation, and, perhaps most of all, proportionality.

The principle of subsidiarity, historically linked to the Catholic Church,[136] received a new impetus when it was introduced, in the early 1990s, within the EU. According to the Maastricht Treaty, the EU committed itself to live by the idea that decisions ought to be taken at the most appropriate level. Thus, it is not for heads of state meeting in Brussels to decide whether some municipality in the south-east of the Netherlands should add another bicycle lane to its existing network. Conversely, that municipality is not the proper body to decide on the introduction of an EU-wide company statute. In short, subsidiarity is grounded in the intuition that for many political decisions, there is an optimal level at which decision-making should take place: decisions concerning the city

---

[134] See generally Koen Lenaerts 'Constitutionalism and the Many Faces of Federalism' (1990) 38 *American Journal of Comparative Law* 205–263.

[135] For a more optimist appraisal, see Ottfried Höffe 'Vision Weltrepublik: Eine philosophische Antwort auf die Globalisierung' in Winfried Brugger, Ulfrid Neumann, and Stephan Kirste (eds) *Rechtsphilosophie im 21. Jahrhundert* (Suhrkamp Frankfurt am Main 2008) 380–396.

[136] When (re-)introducing it in 1931, Pope Pius XI emphatically used it to safeguard social sectors from state intervention, therewith also conveniently shielding the Church. It is unclear whether Pius XI also intended subsidiarity to apply within the Church hierarchy. The relevant passages of his call are reproduced in the fine article by Paolo G Carozza 'Subsidiarity as a Structural Principle of Human Rights Law' (2003) 97 *AJIL* 38–79, at 42.

should be taken at city level; those concerning the state should be taken at state level; and those concerning the broader entity, be it the EU or some other level, should be taken at the level of that broader entity.

As codified in EU law, the notion of subsidiarity includes a presumption 'that the primary responsibility and decision-making competence should rest with the lowest possible level of authority of the political hierarchy'.[137] This is not always the case though: it has also been observed that the Anglo-Saxon concept of federalism contains the reverse presumption: effective decision-making can only take place at a sufficiently high level of political authority.[138]

Still, there is nothing really wrong with the intuition that there is some optimum level of decision-making as such, except that the notion of subsidiarity itself cannot decide on the appropriate level of decision-making: it can provide a justification, but the justification is always open to discussion. This stems from two circumstances. First, a lot depends on what yardstick to use. As Toth has claimed, subsidiarity within the EU is to be decided upon by having a look at effectiveness of action, and the scale of effects of action. Yet it is perfectly plausible for those two tests to lead to different outcomes: it may well be possible that the most effective way to protect flora in southern Spain, for example, is to take action on the Community level, rather than to leave it to the local Andalucían authorities.[139] Second, subsidiarity assumes that all levels of political authority are in harmony on the goals to be achieved. Yet this will often be open to doubts. And where the different levels are divided in what they want, subsidiarity cannot provide an answer; it is more likely then to serve as veneer for centralized decision-making.[140]

The idea of the margin of appreciation stems from similar concerns.[141] Pioneered in the mid-1970s by the European Court of Human Rights,[142] the underlying idea is that in many cases, local authorities are better placed to make judgements on prevailing sentiments in their communities than authorities located far away. Consequently, local authorities should be given quite a bit of leeway when decisions affecting them are at issue, even if this were to lead (as it did in the pioneering *Handyside* decision) to differentiated applications of the same norm in different places: the Court accepted the proposition that

---

[137] See Nicholas Emiliou 'Subsidiarity: Panacea or Fig Leaf?' in David O'Keeffe and Patrick M Twomey (eds) *Legal Issues of the Maastricht Treaty* (Chancery Law Chichester 1994) 65–83, at 66.

[138] *Ibid*, at 66–67. An illustration is provided by Wheare, whose concept of federalism is a rather centralized one. See Wheare, *Federal Government*, 1947, at 79–80.

[139] See Akos G Toth 'A Legal Analysis of Subsidiarity' in O'Keeffe and Twomey (eds), *Legal Issues*, 1994, 37–48, at 43.

[140] See Gareth Davies 'Subsidiarity: The Wrong Idea, in the Wrong Place, at the Wrong Time' (2006) 43 *Common Market Law Review* 63–84.

[141] For a sophisticated discussion, see Yuval Shany 'Toward a General Margin of Appreciation Doctrine in International Law?' (2005) 16 *EJIL* 907–940.

[142] See European Court of Human Rights, application No 5493/72, *Handyside v United Kingdom*, judgment of 7 December 1976.

something that was generally accepted in Denmark could lead to outrage in the UK. Indeed, it went one step further still, and proclaimed that it might even be possible for different parts of the UK to entertain different standards of morality.

Not surprisingly, perhaps, observers have sometimes criticized the margin of appreciation doctrine for taking the sting out of human rights protection. What good is it to claim that people shall have freedom to express themselves, except when their local communities may come to think the expressions are not desirable? Does this not erode human rights from within? By giving states the right to judge against their own standards, the utility of external standards (such as the European Convention on Human Rights) is drastically diminished: what the left hand gives, the right hand takes away again.[143]

Nonetheless, others praise the margin of appreciation doctrine for its flexibility: it allows for a reconciliation of local practices while also respecting a minimum international standard. Without it, that international standard may be left without many adherents. Thus, the margin doctrine offers states an escape clause: they can be bound by human rights norms, but in such a way as to make those norms responsive to the particular needs of local communities.[144]

Subsidiarity is usually mentioned predominantly in the context of EU law, with perhaps some excursions to the broader field of international trade law. While its possible uses in the context of human rights law have been discussed,[145] it has not been systematically applied to other branches of international law. Likewise, the margin of appreciation doctrine has traditionally been associated with human rights law and not with other branches of the law.

More recent writings, however, put subsidiarity and margin of appreciation in the service of a form of constitutionalism. The beauty of subsidiarity, as Carozza puts it, is that it 'provides a tool to mediate the polarity of pluralism and the common good in a globalized world'.[146] Shany, for his part, strongly suggests that increased use of the margin of appreciation doctrine in appropriate cases will enhance the legitimacy of international law, and therewith help stabilize world order. The question then becomes which those appropriate cases are, and interestingly, among his main contenders are issues of security, despite the circumstance that these are precisely the sort of issues where the law as such is relatively unconditional and leaves little discretion to states.[147] Therewith,

---

[143] One formulation of this point is Marie-Bénédicte Dembour *Who Believes in Human Rights? Reflections on the European Convention* (CUP Cambridge 2006), at 35–37.

[144] One formulation of this point is George Letsas *A Theory of Interpretation of the European Convention on Human Rights* (OUP Oxford 2007), at 90–92.

[145] Carozza, Subsidiarity as a Structural Principle, 2003.   [146] *Ibid*, at 38.

[147] He does so by subtly distinguishing the legal threshold condition ('has an armed attack occurred?') from the state's response ('how shall we react?'). The former would leave little room for discretion, but the latter would, and thus could be subjected to application of the margin of appreciation doctrine. This hinges, though, on the proposition that threshold and response can be neatly separated. See Shany, Margin of Appreciation, 2005, at 937.

Shany inadvertently reveals how easily the margin of appreciation doctrine can be used to paper over uncommendable behaviour.

Although the subsidiarity principle and the margin of appreciation doctrine have thus far been applied in fairly limited settings only, there is one notion which is mentioned in quite a few contexts: the idea of proportionality. While proportionality is related to subsidiarity and margin of appreciation, it is nonetheless different in nature: while subsidiarity and margin of appreciation are 'lopsided', so to speak, ultimately favouring one interest over another whenever they are applied, proportionality aims to prevent this from happening by achieving a balancing of (typically) rights.[148] Therewith, its promise is considerable: it has even been referred to as the 'ultimate rule of law'.[149]

Proportionality analysis can take place in a wide variety of settings.[150] EU lawyers are accustomed to thinking in terms of proportionality when discussing whether a certain domestic administrative requirement that forms an obstacle to intra-EC trade is nonetheless acceptable;[151] trade lawyers within the WTO have for many years discussed much the same when thinking of applying the exceptions laid down in Article XX GATT: is the import restriction really necessary? Are less harmful measures conceivable? But proportionality is also applied in radically different settings. It makes an appearance in human rights law, when decisions must be made on whether limiting practices can be justified. It is arguable that 'domestic jurisdiction' clauses à la Article 2, paragraph 7 of the UN Charter encompass proportionality. It can even be seen to play a role in the law of armed conflict, together with the closely related notion of military necessity; indeed, most international lawyers will first come across proportionality in connection with the right to self-defence which, in the classic Webster formula, must be proportional.[152] As this example suggests, moreover, proportionality does not only enter the picture when it concerns the exercise of power by public authorities; it may also apply where states take unilateral action.[153]

Still, its popularity notwithstanding, the idea of proportionality comes with a handful of difficulties.[154] The most obvious one is this: how to determine the

---

[148] For this reason, Rivers can characterize the margin of appreciation doctrine as a method to soften the impact of applying proportionality. See Julian Rivers 'Proportionality and Discretion in International and European Law' in Tsagourias (ed), *Transnational Constitutionalism*, 2007, 107–131.

[149] See David Beatty *The Ultimate Rule of Law* (OUP Oxford 2004).

[150] Very useful is Alec Stone Sweet and Jud Mathews 'Proportionality Balancing and Global Constitutionalism' (2008) 47 *Columbia Journal of Transnational Law* 72–164.

[151] See, e.g., Case 104/75 *De Peijper* [1976] ECR 613.

[152] See generally Judith Gardam 'Proportionality and Force in International Law' (1993) 87 *AJIL* 391–413.

[153] This may in Kelsenian fashion, be conceptualized as the state exercising a power under international law. For such a conceptualization, see Enzo Cannizzaro *Il principo della proporzionalitá nell'ordinamento internazionale* (Giuffrè Milan 2000).

[154] One of these, which we will not discuss further, is that it entails the risk that courts end up being engaged in law-making. See further Tomkins, *Public Law*, 2003, at 198–9.

yardstick against which to measure whether or not behaviour is proportional? In other words, one must always first ask (and answer) the question: proportional to what? At least two different sets of answers are usually possible. The first set is this: must behaviour must be proportional to the goal to be achieved by the rule concerned, or is the proper test whether the behaviour itself is proportional to its own goal? And second: does each individual act have to be proportional, or can one assess proportionality on a cumulative basis? In the context of the law of armed conflict this translates into the question of whether individual attacks must be proportional, or whether their cumulative effect must meet the proportionality test: the outcomes may differ substantially.[155]

There are deeper worries about proportionality, though. Perhaps the most serious one is that proportionality risks the introduction of an element of consequentialism into otherwise deontic reasoning, and this creates problems of fit and coherence. Put differently, legal rules are, typically, deontic in character: they set standards of behaviour which, quite simply, aspire to be met, and aspire to be met in all circumstances (except when the rule itself specifies otherwise). The rules themselves do not worry too much about the resulting social or economic life—those concerns are deemed to have been solved by the people making the rules. Thus, once a parliament decides that raising taxes is good for the economy because it helps finance large public spending, the new tax rule must be followed, even though it would appear that the rule's effects are the exact opposite. Implementing and applying the rule demands that its consequences are deemed to be irrelevant. Colloquially put: one cannot justify tax evasion by pointing to macro-economic arguments, no matter how correct those arguments may be. Likewise, one cannot justify shoplifting by pointing out that the profits the shop in question makes are obscene, or are used to prop up harmful regimes, or could be more effectively used when more evenly spread. Such arguments are simply not available within deontic logic.

Yet, this is precisely the kind of argument that proportionality invites, by having recourse to the consequences of action. In the rough and tumble world of politics, proportionality will often be considered a useful compromise. The point to note, though, is that the compromise rests on a theoretical (or philosophical) incoherence: the compromise can only be achieved by trading in the rule-based deontic approach for something altogether more dependent on political acceptance, for something which is more in harmony with the prevailing sentiment of the day—and that, arguably, is precisely what a deontic logic operates against.[156]

---

[155] See Gardam, Proportionality and Force, 1993, at 407.

[156] It is no coincidence that discussions of proportionality sometimes adopt the vocabulary of consequentialism, speaking of Pareto-optimal solutions, Pareto-frontiers, and the like. See, e.g., Sweet and Mathews, Proportionality Balancing; Rivers, Proportionality and Discretion.

7. On Legitimacy

Perhaps it is no coincidence that many discussions on global constitutionalism and global governance end up discussing legitimacy. Where it is unclear who holds the global 'pouvoir constituant', where it is unclear who governs, where it is unclear how governance takes place, and according to what mandate, it is probably no coincidence that observers seek refuge in notions of legitimacy. Legality as such does not seem to be too helpful, with governance being conducted through all sorts of formal and informal means and instruments. Where power is being exercised (as it undoubtedly is, at the global level), but it is unclear who exercises it and how exactly this happens, mere legality does not seem to offer much solace. Indeed, sometimes it even gets in the way of community goals: if people are being ethnically cleansed, does one really have to respect the law when it orders restraint in intervening?[157]

Legitimacy therewith has emerged as the *deus ex machina* of global affairs, as the mechanism, in Koskenniemi's scathing phrase, 'to ensure a warm feeling in the audience'.[158] If power cannot be backed up by legality, it needs to be propped up by something else, as Weber already realized. Merely referring to material interests or the righteousness of its exercise is often deemed insufficient: 'Experience shows that in no such instance does domination voluntarily limit itself to the appeal to material or affectual or ideal motives as a basis for its continuance. In addition every such system attempts to establish and to cultivate the belief in its legitimacy.'[159] An important ramification is that different forms of domination may lead to different forms of legitimacy.[160]

A relevant starting point, therewith, would be to distinguish legitimacy from power and authority as such.[161] Legitimacy is not to be equated with power or authority, as it is perfectly possible for power or authority to be illegitimate. The gunman ordering me to hand over my belongings clearly exercises some form of momentary authority over me; it would be difficult to claim this to be legitimate authority though. By the same token, dictators may exercise power, but it is unlikely to be legitimate power.[162]

---

[157] For one example among many of such an approach to legitimacy, see Kenneth Manusama *The United Nations Security Council in the Post-Cold War Era: Applying the Principle of Legality* (Martinus Nijhoff Leiden 2006).

[158] See Koskenniemi, Formalism, Fragmentation, Freedom, 2007, at 16.

[159] See Max Weber *Economy and Society: An Outline of Interpretive Sociology* (University of California Press Berkeley CA 1978 Roth and Wittich eds), at 213.

[160] As pointed out by Steffek: see Jens Steffek 'The Legitimation of International Governance: A Discourse Approach' (2003) 9 *European Journal of International Relations* 249–275, at 258.

[161] On power, one of the classic texts is Steven Lukes *Power: A Radical View* (MacMillan London 1974).

[162] Some discuss the legitimacy of the global order or that of states and governments (or both). Our interest, however, as far as it concerns legitimacy to begin with, resides predominantly with the

Hurd defines legitimacy as 'an actor's normative belief that rule or institution ought to be obeyed'.[163] He explains that it is a subjective notion, dependent on the perceptions (or feelings) of an actor, but that once actors believe a rule or institution is legitimate, they tend to behave in accordance with it: follow its demands, obey its instructions. Properly understood, legitimate rules and institutions help actors to define their interests. The operative aspect, as Hurd puts it, 'is the internalization by the actor of an external standard'.[164]

Others have suggested that a focus on beliefs alone might be misleading: surely, what matters is not only what people believe about power and authority, but depends on more objective factors as well. Beetham in particular presents a more objectified theory of legitimacy: to him, power is legitimate if it conforms to established rules (possesses legal validity); if those rules, in turn, 'can be justified by reference to the beliefs shared by both dominant and subordinate', and if those over whom power is exercised have in one way or another consented to it.[165]

This raises at least two questions: how can rules and institutions achieve legitimacy? And who bestows legitimacy? The former is often answered by reference to two different forms of legitimacy: procedural legitimacy and substantive legitimacy. Procedural legitimacy is often taken to flow from proper procedure: a rule will be considered legitimate if it has been made in accordance with the procedure according to which such a rule must be made; an institution will be deemed legitimate if it has been created in accordance with a procedure made for that purpose. Thus, if a domestic constitution prescribes that all laws shall pass through two chambers of parliament having heard the advice of a Constitutional Council, and a law is enacted in accordance with this procedure, then such a law shall be deemed legitimate: actors believe it ought to be obeyed precisely because it shows no procedural flaws, even if they disagree with the law's contents. A procedurally correctly made rule or institution will exercise, in Thomas Franck's words, a considerable 'compliance pull'.[166] It is no coincidence that this form of legitimacy is often conflated with legality, for on this reading, the differences between the two are marginal.[167]

---

legitimacy of the rules and institutions that make up international law. In other words: we will presume that the global constitutional order is legitimate, otherwise we would not refer to it as constitutional. But that does not mean that all its institutions and rules are therefore legitimate. This sets us apart from, e.g., Allen Buchanan *Justice, Legitimacy, and Self-determination: Moral Foundations for International Law* (OUP Oxford 2004).

[163] See Ian Hurd *After Anarchy: Legitimacy and Power at the United Nations Security Council* (Princeton UP 2007), at 7.

[164] *Ibid*, at 31.

[165] See David Beetham *The Legitimation of Power* (MacMillan Basingstoke 1991), at 15–16.

[166] See Thomas M Franck *The Power of Legitimacy among Nations* (OUP Oxford 1990).

[167] Although it also depends on how legality is defined. If legality is supposed to encompass also substantive concerns (i.e. law is only law if also morally acceptable), then the gap between legality and legitimacy might be bigger.

In international law, a strongly legitimizing role in securing procedural legitimacy is still played by the notion of state consent; in the absence of any general law-making procedure, consent plays a pivotal role.[168] This is visible from the notion that states need to express their 'consent to be bound' to treaties; it is, more subtly, also visible from the circumstance that all bar one of the accepted grounds to declare treaties invalid deal with defects in state consent.[169] Customary international law, too, however implausibly perhaps, is said to be based on state consent (albeit more often implicit consent), and the powers of international organizations are often said to be delegated by states, which, in turn, also presupposes consent. Consent, thus, has an important legitimizing function: a rule that has come into being on the basis of state consent will generally be treated as legitimate. Indeed, even mildly dubious practices, such as the insistence by the EC in some cases on including a disconnection clause in wider treaties, are legitimized by pointing to the consent of the EC's treaty partners.[170]

Substantive legitimacy, by contrast, is more concerned with the contents of rules and institutions: with what they stand for. A procedurally correctly made rule may still lack legitimacy if it asks us to do something obnoxious, something substantively unjustifiable. This plays a far less prominent role in contemporary international law, where states are typically still thought to have an almost unlimited freedom of contract: only the injunction not to conclude treaties going against *jus cogens* reflects a substantive concern.[171] Other than this, the label 'illegitimate' seems to apply first and foremost to omissions. When states refuse to intervene in the face of ethnic cleansing; when the international community refuses to do something about genocide or mass human rights violations or military aggression, it is the omission that is often deemed illegitimate.

This points to yet another aspect of the elusive nature of legitimacy. Legitimacy can refer to rules and institutions, but also to behaviour more generally. A Security Council refusal to intervene in the Rwandan genocide is behaviour by an institution generally held to be legitimate in matters of peace of security (the Security Council[172]) applying a rule generally held to be

---

[168] See Daniel Bodansky 'The Legitimacy of International Governance: A Coming Challenge for International Environmental Law?' (1999) 93 *AJIL* 596–624.

[169] See VCLT, Arts 46–52. The exception resides in the invalidity of treaties incompatible with *jus cogens*.

[170] See, e.g., Koskenniemi, Fragmentation, 2007, at 151. For a general discussion, see Constantin P Economidès and Alexandros G Kolliopoulou 'La clause de déconnexion en faveur du droit communautaire: une pratique critiquable' (2006) 110 *Revue Générale de Droit International Public* 273–302.

[171] Perhaps here one might add the mildly substantive concern inherent in the repeated reference, in the Vienna Convention on the Law of Treaties, to a treaty's object and purpose. Thus, a treaty's object and purpose may not be defeated pending the treaty's entry into force; reservations must be compatible with a treaty's object and purpose, and modifications of a treaty between some parties *inter se* must be compatible with the object and purpose of the treaty concerned.

[172] Arguably, to the extent the Security Council has a legitimacy problem it relates not so much to its responsibilities with respect to peace and security, but rather to its law-making activities.

legitimate (the non-intervention rule), yet the sum total is somehow held to be illegitimate.[173]

This curious circumstance may well be related to another relevant distinction: that between input legitimacy and output legitimacy. Input legitimization refers to such things as transparency and representation of all 'stakeholders'. If all who are affected by a decision have had a chance to have their say, then legitimacy is guaranteed. As Scharpf explains though, this is problematic with any instance of decision-making by majority, for such a scenario is characterized precisely by outvoting some of the stakeholders. Hence, input legitimacy cannot thrive on participation by stakeholders alone; it also needs a fairly thick social basis. It might be easier to accept being outvoted by those with whom one forms a community, than by total strangers.[174]

Output legitimacy, by contrast, taps into the results of policies.[175] Thus, international institutions may derive legitimacy from their work: being able to deliver the goods helps legitimize institutions; being seen to work helps legitimize rules. Here, a 'thin' constituency suffices. Scharpf makes a strong case for the proposition that while input and output legitimacy usually complement (and perhaps sometimes contradict[176]) each other, on the international level the most that can be achieved is output legitimacy. Since the thick constituency on which input legitimacy rests is absent, much of the legitimizing burden[177] is carried by output legitimacy: by such considerations as whether rules or institutions function effectively and efficiently.

From the above it would also seem to follow that legitimacy is not an on/off matter: rules or institutions can be legitimate (or illegitimate) in varying degrees. While a strong claim can be made that law is a binary matter, with behaviour being either legal or illegal but not 'a little legal', and activities either being prohibited or allowed, but not 'a little bit allowed',[178] legitimacy can be

---

[173] A useful discussion of the United Nations' inaction in Rwanda is Michael Barnett and Martha Finnemore *Rules for the World: International Organizations in Global Politics* (Cornell UP Ithaca NY 2004) chapter 5.

[174] See Fritz W Scharpf *Governing in Europe: Effective and Democratic?* (OUP Oxford 1999) 6–10.

[175] None of these elements are mutually exclusive. Kumm's model of constitutional legitimacy, e.g., encompasses input and output legitimacy as well as legality and subsidiarity. See Mattias Kumm 'The Legitimacy of International Law: A Constitutionalist Framework of Analysis' (2004) 15 *EJIL* 907–931.

[176] Think, for instance, of an inclusive entity creating ineffective policies or, more likely perhaps, effective policies being ordained by directorate. These may have output legitimacy, but little input legitimacy.

[177] See Scharpf, *Governing in Europe*, 1999, esp at 11–12. While he limits himself to the case of the EU, the point can be applied more broadly.

[178] At this point, any self-respecting international lawyer will expect a reference to Prosper Weil 'Towards Relative Normativity in International Law?' (1983) 77 *AJIL* 413–442. The point is, however, controversial: the wide acceptance of the notion of soft law amongst international lawyers would suggest that many have abandoned the binary idea of law.

observed along sliding scales: rules and institutions can be more or less legitimate; can be a little bit legitimate, or very legitimate.

Legitimacy is sought in order to buttress rules or institutions, in order to make them acceptable and accepted. It is no surprise then that most often legitimacy is sought by authorities, whether public or private. This can take on unexpected forms, a good example of which is the circumstance that Russian troops, while active in Moldova in the early 1990s, were prone to wear blue helmets, raising the impression that they were associated with UN peacekeeping. Hence, the Russian authorities tapped into the legitimacy of UN peacekeeping, which also suggests, incidentally, that legitimacy is intensely manipulable.[179]

The trickier question, however, is to find out who can bestow legitimacy. Perhaps the easiest answer is to refer to the public at large, but there are a few obvious complications here. Thus, in some cases, judgments on the acceptability of behaviour have been delegated or transferred[180] to international institutions. If and when this is the case, one would expect those institutions to be able to bestow legitimacy on political action. An example is the authority bestowed on the Security Council: most people would agree that military intervention becomes dramatically more legitimate when approved by the Security Council, and this may help explain why the US was keen to seek Security Council approval before invading Iraq in 2003. Yet, the Council is not almighty: as NATO's intervention over Kosovo suggests, military action may also be deemed legitimate without Council approval. Here, then, many held that the action may well have been illegal, but legitimate nonetheless. The difference, obviously, goes back to the distinction between procedural and substantive legitimacy, and the way these two interact.[181]

Thus, it would seem that institutions not only clamour for legitimacy, but are also able to bestow it themselves. Much the same would apply to informal groupings, such as the epistemic communities[182] that social scientists talk about, and interpretive communities[183] including what Schachter once so felicitously referred to as the invisible college of international lawyers.[184] Surely, a controversial action backed by the majority of international lawyers will enjoy

---

[179] As mentioned in Hurd, *After Anarchy*, 2007, at 126.

[180] On the distinction, see Sarooshi, *International Organizations*, 2005.

[181] It may also owe something to the distinction between input and output legitimacy, although this is difficult to substantiate. One could argue that by being located in the western world, the action in Kosovo tapped into the sentiments of a fairly thick constituency, and that its success helped create its output legitimacy. The botched UN action in Somalia, in the early 1990s, would have scored low on both counts.

[182] See, e.g., Peter Haas 'Introduction: Epistemic Communities and International Policy Coordination' (1992) 46 *International Organization* 1–35.

[183] The phrase was coined by Stanley Fish *Doing What Comes Naturally: Change, Rhetoric, and the Practice of Theory in Literary and Legal Studies* (Clarendon Press Oxford 1989).

[184] See Oscar Schachter 'The Invisible College of International Lawyers' (1977) 72 *Northwestern University Law Review* 217–226.

greater legitimacy than the same action generally condemned by international lawyers: again, the US invasion of Iraq or its treatment of prisoners at Guantanamo would seem to illustrate the point.

The above suggests first and foremost that legitimacy is an elusive notion: this may well be part of its attraction. Being difficult to pin down and define with some certainty, legitimacy can be invoked by each and any institution wishing to buttress its authority or the authority of its rules and resolutions. By the same token, legitimacy (or the lack thereof) can also be invoked to contest exercises of authority. Precisely because legitimacy cannot be pinned down, it carves open a space for political deliberation, but also for the exercise of power: those who can claim to have legitimacy on their side have a strong argument that they ought to be followed and obeyed.[185] In that light, it is no surprise that legitimacy has become such a prevalent notion precisely when the boundaries between law and non-law have become porous. Precisely when legal authority is in doubt, legitimacy has made a sustained appearance, and become more relied on than ever before. Or rather, it has become more and more separated from other forms of authority: where in earlier times legal authority was almost by definition legitimate authority, more recently the two have become less obviously related, to the point that in some cases legal authority is deemed to be illegitimate. In such a scenario, moreover, legal authority can easily (legitimately) be cast aside: legitimacy is rated higher than legality.

Still, in order for any political system to be workable, it probably is the case that legal validity creates a strong presumption of legitimacy. The opposite, at any rate, would be unworkable: a political (and thus legal) order cannot function on the basis of a presumption that its rules and institutions are illegitimate until proven to be legitimate.

Finally, there is the issue of how exactly legitimacy is bestowed. For some, consent remains 'by default, the principal source of legitimacy' in international matters. This, in turn, is considered likely to limit the very prospects for international governance, as consent may be hard to achieve.[186] Others, however, disagree, or at least suggest that there is more to legitimacy on the international level than consent alone. Thus, most obviously perhaps, those focusing on output legitimacy may well come to think of expertise and effectiveness as possible sources of legitimacy.[187] Still others suggest, in the footsteps of Weber and Habermas, that legitimacy is a function of a rational discourse among the subjects of rules and institutions. As Steffek puts it in a nuanced manner, '[w]hat creates legitimacy is less the fact of having consented, but rather having

---

[185] The point is forcefully made by Martti Koskenniemi 'Legitimacy, Rights, and Ideology: Notes Towards a Critique of the New Moral Internationalism' (2003) 7 *Associations* 349–373. See also Koskenniemi, Formalism, Fragmentation, Freedom, 2007, at 14–16.

[186] See Bodansky, The Legitimacy of International Governance, 1999, at 624.

[187] An example is Scharpf, *Governing in Europe*, 1999. Ku, Multilayered System, 2005, presents much the same argument, without phrasing it in terms of legitimacy though.

consented to a certain normative reasoning, linking shared values and principles to practice type norms'.[188] On this note, it is not just efficiency that is decisive; in fact, among the most legitimacy-generating institutions may well be the General Assembly of the United Nations, as Steffek suggests. Often derided as 'all talk and no action', it may well represent precisely that which is vital about international governance—the power to bestow legitimacy through talk and rational deliberation.[189]

8. Conclusions: Towards a Legitimate Constitutional Order?

A constitutional world order will have to be a legitimate world order—this much is clear.[190] What is less clear, though, is the amount of work that has to be done in this context by the notion of legitimacy. In a circular way, a constitutional order will need to be legitimate; otherwise it does not deserve the label 'constitutional'. Yet, the reverse is not true: not all legitimate orders are by definition also constitutional in the sense in which that idea is mostly employed, with its connotations of legitimacy. As a result, while considerations of legitimacy will play a role in the next chapters, there are good reasons to be careful with the notion, and not to treat it as a substitute for constitutionalism.

From the foregoing it has also become clear that a constitutional global order needs to be a pluralist global order. This pluralism enters the picture in at least four different ways. First, there is the case for political pluralism: the constitutional global order must respect the position that different people may have different interests and different perspectives on what they hold to be the good life. As an important result, the constitutional global order cannot be based on a single set of values, whether these be the values adhered to by liberals, Marxists, or religious movements. This does not imply the reification of toleration for, as Michael Walzer has pointed out, the Westphalian system itself is a tolerant one: the co-existence of sovereign states in an anarchic order owes much to toleration.[191] Instead, something more is called for than mere toleration, something coming closer to respect perhaps.

Second, the global constitutional order shall be pluralist in the sense that a diversity of actors will need to find their proper place. The classic Westphalian order was an order made by states to regulate relations between states and largely for the benefit of states. Clearly, if the constitutional order claims to be different,

---

[188] See Steffek, Legitimation of International Governance, 2003, at 264.

[189] Klabbers makes the similar point (without invoking legitimacy) that what he calls the agora function of international organizations is no less important than their managerial functions. See Jan Klabbers 'Two Concepts of International Organization' (2005) 2 *International Organizations Law Review* 277–293. [190] This will be further explored in chapter 6 below.

[191] See Michael Walzer *On Toleration* (Yale UP New Haven CT 1997), at 19–22.

it has to move away from this state-centric focus and also accommodate other actors, from indigenous peoples to voluntary associations of individuals, and from intergovernmental organizations to corporations.

Third, the constitutional order shall be pluralist in the sense that it will have come to terms with its own heterarchy. Authority is being exercised from various positions and on various levels. The search for a single centre of global authority is bound to remain fruitless—and that is possibly a good thing too. As has been observed by many, a world government would leave dissenters no place for shelter, and would suppress the pluralism that characterizes humanity. Hannah Arendt once put it with characteristic verve: 'A world citizen, living under the tyranny of a world empire, and speaking and thinking in a kind of glorified Esperanto, would be no less a monster than a hermaphrodite.'[192] This may be unkind to hermaphrodites, but it does raise a strong voice against global hierarchy and the inevitably accompanying homogenization of the human.

Finally, the constitutional global order will encounter normative pluralism. Individuals, states, and other actors act and behave in different webs of normative utterances: we are subjected to law, but also to the internal rules of the religions we adhere to, the rules of the games and sports we play, the standards prevailing in our chosen professions, the customs of the communities we are born in, etc. This, too, is a phenomenon the global constitutional order will somehow have to come to terms with. One cannot simply proclaim the hierarchy of legitimate moral behaviour over anything else—indeed, there might be decent reasons why, in a constitutional order, law and legality might be worthy of *prima facie* deference, even in the face of seemingly conflicting moral imperatives.[193]

All this means that the demands on a constitutional global order are quite heavy: the global constitutional order must respect pluralism in its different guises, and it must be legitimate too. This raises questions of feasibility and reasonableness. In light of the above, for instance, it would be unreasonable to claim that a global constitutional order would need to have a single legislative centre. But if not by means of central legislation, how then can law-making be organized in a global constitutional order? Likewise, how does the global constitutional order, in a reasonable manner, organize itself? How does it come to terms with the demands of democracy? What does it say about membership, and which values does it end up endorsing? It is to these questions that we will now turn.

---

[192] See Hannah Arendt 'Karl Jaspers: Citizen of the World?' in *idem Men in Dark Times* (Harcourt Brace and Company San Diego 1968) 81–94, at 89.
[193] This will be further explored in chapter 3 below.

2

Institutions and Competences

Geir Ulfstein

1. Introduction

International cooperation is first of all necessary in fields that may not be controlled at the national level, such as international security, trade, and climate change. But international organizations are not only empowered to deal with what are unquestionably international issues. They may also interfere with areas traditionally governed by states. The grounds may be that certain issues have been internationalized, such as the protection of human rights.

International empowerment may have cumulative effects. The allocation of state subsidies, formerly a domestic issue, may be internationally regulated to ensure fair trade. Moreover, restrictions on states' freedom may be compensated by more international legislative powers. Strong international courts may also be matched by an empowered international legislator. Finally, empowerment in one area, such as international trade, may require corresponding institutions in another area, such as environmental protection. This means that the distinction between what should be considered international and domestic is becoming irrelevant.

States are formally free to decide whether to join or leave international organizations, but they may in practice have little choice if they want to influence policy-making in issues that may be of vital importance to their interests, to reap the benefits of membership, or to be regarded as an actor of 'good standing' in international society. States may also choose whether or not to implement decisions by international organizations, even if this should result in international legal responsibility. But this freedom may be of limited value in practice if the state wants to retain a meaningful membership in relevant international institutions.

While the substantive scope of international cooperation increases and states feel compelled to participate in such cooperation, the empowerment of international organizations is not an ordinary delegation of national powers. It means that institutions other than the state can make decisions and adopt policies beyond the control of each individual member state. In the absence of national constitutional control, to what extent democratic control of decision-making, guarantees related to the rule of law, and the protection of human rights should be ensured at the international level will be examined. Whether the fragmented international institutional framework should be replaced by a hierarchic constitutional order will also be discussed. Finally, the interaction and respective functions of international and national constitutional organs will be addressed.

2. Organizational Framework

There is a multitude of venues and forms of international cooperation. While traditional bilateral diplomatic exchanges continue to be important, they are supplemented by multilateral collaboration at international meetings and conferences. The meetings of the most powerful nations in the informal Group of Eight (G8) attract no less attention than meetings of the World Bank or the World Trade Organization (WTO). And international conferences can last for several years, as was the case with the United Nations Conference on the Law of the Sea (1973–82).

States may enter into institution-building of a political character such as the Organization for Security and Co-operation in Europe (OSCE) and the Arctic Council. Since they are not based on a treaty, they will be called soft law organizations. States may furthermore enter into treaties establishing organs of different kinds, such as the Conference or Meeting of the Parties (COP/MOP) under the United Nations Framework Convention on Climate Change and its Kyoto Protocol, or the Human Rights Committee under the International Covenant on Civil and Political Rights (ICCPR). These organs will be called treaty bodies. States may finally use the treaty instrument to establish full-fledged international organizations. Such institutions may in its turn provide the basis for cooperation through networks of governmental and international officials. Each of these three forms of cooperation raises different questions in relation to international constitutionalization.

2.1 Formal international organizations

Treaties establishing formal international organizations will define their organs and competences. International organizations will usually have a plenary body, an executive body with limited membership, and an administrative body in the form of a secretariat. They may also include a parliamentary body and a court.[1]

This set-up may look like the one we know from national constitutions: a parliamentary assembly, the executive, and courts. But to the extent that international organizations have legislative, executive, and judicial powers, such

---

[1] Jan Klabbers *An Introduction to International Institutional Law* (CUP Cambridge 2002), at 169–178.

powers will not necessarily be allocated among the organs according to the principles known from national constitutional law. As was stated by the International Criminal Tribunal for the former Yugoslavia (ICTY) in the *Tadic* case:

It is clear that the legislative, executive and judicial division of powers which is largely followed in most municipal systems does not apply to the international setting nor, more specifically, to the setting of an international organization such as the United Nations. Among the principal organs of the United Nations the divisions between judicial, executive and legislative functions are not clear cut. Regarding the judicial function, the International Court of Justice is clearly the 'principal judicial organ' (see United Nations Charter, Article 92). There is, however, no legislature, in the technical sense of the term, in the United Nations system and, more generally, no parliament in the world community. That is to say, there exists no corporate organ formally empowered to enact laws directly binding on international legal subjects.[2]

The UN General Assembly, as the plenary organ, may adopt 'law-making' measures, but only in a non-binding form. The Security Council may, on the other hand, adopt binding measures, but only to prevent threats to or breaches of peace and security. As will be discussed, the Security Council has, however, recently adopted binding measures of a more general character.

Organs of limited membership, such as the Security Council, are not necessarily accountable to plenary organs, like the General Assembly—although the Assembly may exercise some control through its budgetary powers. Furthermore, organs of limited membership may have designated permanent members of major powers, such as the Security Council, or quotas of important states, such as the largest shipping nations in the Council of the International Maritime Organization (Article 17), or appointed by the largest contributing states in the International Monetary Fund (Article 12(3)(b)). The executive powers may also be more politically controlled than is known from the domestic context, as is illustrated by authorization to the use of force by the Security Council. Political organs, such as the Security Council, may also be involved in dispute settlement.

In short, the principle of separation of powers does not apply and the organs of international organizations—at least many of them—may be dominated by the great powers, Furthermore, as will be discussed below, judicial review of international decisions may not be available. There is no reason for arguing that the constitutional principles of international organizations should be similar to those known from the domestic context. What will be discussed is the constitutional features of international organizations in light of the increasing empowerment of such organizations, and the ensuing need for constitutional control of their activities. But first, the constitutional features of treaty bodies and soft law organizations will be examined.

---

[2] *Prosecutor v Dusko Tadic, Decision on the Defence Motion for Interlocutory Appeal on Jurisdiction* Case IT-94-1-AR72 Appeals Chamber of 2 October 1995 paragraph 43.

2.2 Treaty bodies

States may choose to establish treaty bodies rather than formal international organizations. Such treaty bodies come in different forms and serve a variety of functions. The Meeting of States Parties (SPLOS) established by the 1982 United Nations Law of the Sea Convention (Article 319 (2)) elects members of the International Tribunal for the Law of the Sea (ITLOS) and the Commission on the Limits of the Continental Shelf (CLCS), and deals with budgetary and administrative matters of the Tribunal.[3] While ITLOS is an international court, the CLCS has a specific function in making substantive recommendations on the outer limit of continental shelves. The limits established by the coastal state on the basis of such recommendations shall be 'final and binding' (Article 76 (8)). Hence, the CLCS may be considered to have a certain law-making or judicial power by contributing to the binding nature of the outer limit of continental shelves.

The Consultative Meetings (ATCM) of the 1959 Antarctic Treaty has important functions in developing the substantive content of the cooperation in Antarctica, including scientific research and environmental protection. Measures adopted by the ATCM become 'effective'—presumably they may also be legally binding—when approved by the states parties (Article IX (4)).[4] The Conference of the Parties (COPs)—or organs with a comparable denomination—of multilateral environmental agreements (MEAs) have a multiplicity of functions, including the development of new substantive commitments, guidance of sub-organs and the secretariat, and ensuring implementation of states' obligations.[5] Hence, the Commission on the Limits of the Continental Shelf, the Antarctic Treaty System (ATS), and MEAs share the essential function of international organizations in law-making. The formal structure of the cooperation—especially in MEAs—also bears similarities with what we know from international organizations.

On the other hand, the bodies established by treaties on human rights and arms control are essentially limited to one function, i.e. the control of implementation of the relevant treaty obligations by the states parties. Human rights treaties will generally establish two kinds of treaty bodies: a meeting of the parties and a supervisory organ, such as the Human Rights Committee of the International Covenant on Civil and Political Rights. The function of the

---

[3] There has, however, been disagreement on the mandate of the Meeting of States Parties to discuss 'matters of substantive nature relating to the implementation of the Convention' (Report of the seventeenth Meeting of States Parties, paragraph 109, 16 July 2007 (SPLOS/164)).

[4] Sir Arthur Watts *International Law and the Antarctic Treaty System* (Grotius Cambridge 1992), at 25.

[5] Robin R Churchill and Geir Ulfstein 'Autonomous Institutional Arrangements in Multilateral Environmental Agreements: A Little-Noticed Phenomenon in International Law' (2000) 94 *AJIL* 623–660.

meeting of the parties is comparable to that of the United Nations Convention on the Law of the Sea to elect members of the supervisory organ. The supervisory organs, however, entertain important roles in examining state reports, i.e. a form of administrative control; they may adopt 'general comments' about the interpretation of the relevant convention, i.e. a form of law-making; and some of them may receive state complaints, and, more importantly, individual complaints, i.e. a form of dispute settlement.

Arms control agreements have chosen different approaches: the Convention on Chemical Weapons and the Comprehensive Test Ban Treaty each establish an 'Organization', whereas the Ottawa Convention on Land Mines has established a meeting of the parties whose function is to 'consider any matter with regard to the application or implementation of this Convention' (Article 11), i.e. again a form of administrative control function.

Why do states decide to establish treaty bodies rather than a full-fledged international organization? The answer may vary between different subject matters and from case to case. In international environmental law, the emergence of the institutional structures in the 1970s and 1980s coincided with dissatisfaction with traditional organizations because of their cost and bureaucracy. COPs might have seemed less costly and more effective; they avoid difficulties that could arise by using an existing organization with an already fixed membership; and, finally, choosing the location of a new organization is unnecessary.[6] There may have been similar reasons for not establishing a formal international organization in the Antarctic cooperation. But the Antarctic Treaty was adopted in a different political climate, for a continent with a disputed territorial status, which may also explain its design. Its organizational features have been characterized as 'institutional caution, coupled with institutional accretion'.[7] The choice for treaty bodies rather than international organizations in international human rights and arms control is probably due to their limited functions in control of states' implementation of treaty obligations and the election of members to the supervisory organs. It may, however, be difficult to explain why an international organization was established by the Convention on Chemical Weapons and the Comprehensive Test Ban Treaty, but not by the Convention on Land Mines.

The emergence of treaty bodies could be viewed as a form of 'legalization' of political cooperation. The term legalization has been used as a 'particular form of institutionalization characterized by three components: obligation, precision, and delegation'.[8] 'Obligation' is referring to the use of legal commitments, 'precision' means that the obligations are unambiguous, and

---

[6] Churchill and Ulfstein, Autonomous Institutional Arrangements, 2000, at 629–631.

[7] Watts, *International Law*, 1992, at 12.

[8] Kenneth W Abbott, Robert O Keohane, Andrew Moravcsik, Anne-Marie Slaughter, and Duncan Snidal 'The Concept of Legalization' (2000) 54 *International Organization* 401–441, at 401.

'delegation' indicates that third parties are given the authority to 'implement, interpret, and apply the rules; to resolve disputes; and (possibly) to make further rules'.[9]

In our context of constitutionalization it is the latter element that is of importance with treaty bodies: the empowerment of international institutions to undertake functions impinging on the authority earlier regarded as the sole prerogative of national constitutional organs, and the extent to which they in these functions should be controlled by constitutional guarantees comparable to those known from the national level.

It could, however, be argued that the preference for treaty bodies rather than formal international organizations could represent a form of deconstitutionalization. This would be consonant with a concern that international law is being 'deformalized', leaving too much power to experts at the expense of political and judicial control. Treaty bodies like those established by the Climate Change Convention, with its Kyoto Protocol, and the Montreal Protocol for the Protection of the Ozone Layer have been mentioned as examples.[10]

There is, however, nothing in the legal technique of using treaty bodies that in itself provides for more or less political or judicial control. The superior organ in the Antarctic Treaty, environmental treaties, and the Ottawa Convention on Land Mines is the plenary political body. These bodies will determine any regulations applying to member states and the cooperation under the relevant treaty. While there is a need to ensure political control and to avoid expert dominance, this apprehension is known also from formal international organizations (as will be discussed in section 3.1 below). Neither is it obvious that international tribunals are necessarily to be preferred to the use of non-compliance procedures. International tribunals may be preferable in solving disputes between parties, either between states or between states and private parties. But non-compliance procedures may be better suited to deal with collective interests, such as international environmental challenges (see chapter 4). In short, constitutional guarantees designed for the functions exercised should be applied whether international powers are exercised by formal international organizations or treaty bodies.

It could be argued that treaty bodies should be transformed into formal international organizations. One reason would be that the uncertainty of the proper law to be applied to treaty bodies could threaten the need for predictability. But it is difficult to see why the law of international organizations should not be applicable to treaty bodies resembling international organizations in all but name. A reservation should, however, be made to applying international

---

[9] Abbott *et al*, The Concept of Legalization, 2000, at 401 and 415–418.
[10] Martti Koskenniemi 'The Fate of Public International Law: Between Technique and Politics' (2007) 70 *Modern Law Review* 1–30, at 9–13.

organization law *in toto* to treaty bodies with limited functions, such as human rights bodies.[11]

As already mentioned, states may have chosen cooperation through treaty bodies for several reasons: costs, effectiveness, and avoiding the need for choosing the location of a new organization. In the case of single purpose treaty bodies, such as the supervisory bodies of international human rights, the establishment of an international organization for such a purpose seems hardly relevant. But even in a more complex institutional setting, states should be allowed flexibility in designing the format of their cooperation, including the use of treaty bodies when considered appropriate. This would presumably increase the possibilities of finding the institutional structure appropriate for the task at hand. But it is important in our context that to the extent that treaty bodies are given powers like international organizations, they should also be subject to comparable constitutional guarantees, such as political accountability, rule of law, and protection of human rights, as discussed in the following sections.

2.3 Soft law organizations

States may also choose to establish non-treaty based institutions, or soft law organizations, like the former General Agreement on Tariffs and Trade (GATT), the OSCE, and the Arctic Council. In the case of the former GATT, its ambiguous international legal status was a consequence of the rejection by the United States of an International Trade Organization (ITO).[12] The background for this rejection was partly disagreement about the desirability of free trade and the impact of ratification on other foreign policy goals, but also disillusionment with the United Nations and some other organizations established after World War II.[13] GATT gradually developed an institutional structure in the form of a secretariat, a Council, and a system for dispute settlement. It has therefore been characterized as a *de facto* organization.[14]

When the Conference on Security and Co-operation in Europe (CSCE) was transformed into the Organization for Security and Co-operation in Europe (OSCE) in 1995, the parties agreed that the term Organization would not change the status of the cooperation into a legal organization. While several members of the EU had proposed that a treaty should be negotiated, establishing the CSCE as an international organization with international legal personality, the United States was sceptical. There was agreement that the OSCE needed legal capacity and privileges and immunities. A treaty would, however, require

---

[11] Churchill and Ulfstein, Autonomous Institutional Arrangements, 2000, at 658–659.
[12] John H Jackson, *Sovereignty, the WTO and Changing Fundamentals of International Law* (CUP Cambridge 2006), at 94.
[13] Andreas F Lowenfeld *International Economic Law* (2nd edn OUP Oxford 2008), at 28.
[14] Jackson, *Sovereignty, the WTO*, 2006, at 96–97, 137–145.

ratification and could result in some participating states not ratifying the treaty. The view prevailed that a political declaration should be adopted, committing the participating states to grant the OSCE sufficient legal capacity and privileges and immunities in national legislation.[15]

The United States also had difficulties in accepting the Arctic Council as an international organization with legal personality, a position that has been considered 'consistent with a tendency in recent American diplomatic practice to seek an informal cooperative structure when that structure is adequate for the purposes of the issues involved'.[16] It has furthermore been claimed that the advantages of such informal organizations would include the freedom of the participating states to determine to what extent they would pay for the activities of the organization, decisions would tend to be made on the basis of consensus, meetings could be more result-oriented, and it could be easier to handle domestic legislation, including the US presidential constitutional authority to manage foreign policy.[17]

Jan Klabbers has argued that 'if an entity looks like an international organization, functions like one, and is treated by outsiders as one, then it is pretty unlikely that it is, all appearances notwithstanding, something other than an international organization'.[18] But in the case of soft law organizations, the participating states have consciously determined not to establish legally binding international constitutional structures. This distinguishes soft law organizations from formal international organizations. The legal freedom of the participating states has thus been preserved. But, on the other hand, soft law organizations are not empowered to enter into treaties or to adopt legally binding decisions.

It may, however, be asked whether soft law organization should be 'constitutionalized' by transforming their character into a legally formally binding cooperation, either because more international empowerment or more constitutional guarantees are needed.

The OSCE may be taken as an example of considerations relevant for determining whether a soft law organization should be transformed into a formal international organization. A Panel of Eminent Persons to consider possible steps to strengthen the organization proposed that the OSCE's

development from a conference to a full-fledged international organisation must now be completed, finally making 'participating States' into 'member States' ... Participating States should devise a concise Statute or Charter of the OSCE containing its basic goals, principles and commitments, as well as the structure of its main decision-making bodies.

---

[15] Miriam Sapiro 'Changing the CSCE into the OSCE: Legal Aspects of a Political Transformation' (1995) 89 *AJIL* 631–637, at 634–635.

[16] Evan T Bloom 'Establishment of the Arctic Council' (1999) 93 *AJIL* 712–722, at 721.

[17] *Ibid*, at 721–722.

[18] Jan Klabbers 'Institutional Ambivalence by Design: Soft Organizations in International Law' (2001) 70 *Nordic Journal of International Law* 403–421, at 415.

This would help the OSCE to become a full-scale regional organisation ... Participating States agree on a convention recognising the OSCE's legal capacity and granting privileges and immunities to the OSCE and its officials.[19]

However, the disagreement about establishing the OSCE as a formal organization persisted. It was only possible to agree upon the latter element, i.e. on the negotiation of a convention on OSCE's legal capacity and privileges and immunities. But an interpretative statement of the Russian Federation stated that the entry into force of such a convention would only be possible in conjunction with the adoption of a statute or a charter of the OSCE.[20]

An expert group then prepared a draft Convention on the international legal personality, legal capacity, and privileges and immunities of the OSCE. However, the draft contained three footnotes requested by two delegations referring to the need for an OSCE Charter.[21] The draft provided that the OSCE 'shall possess international legal personality' (Article 3) and 'shall possess such legal capacity as is necessary for the exercise of its functions' (Article 4), in addition to provisions on privileges and immunities and dispute settlement. In a decision of the Ministerial Council of the OSCE in Helsinki in 2008, while agreeing upon the need for the OSCE's acquiring international legal status, the Chairman-in-Office was only tasked with pursuing a dialogue on strengthening the legal framework of the OSCE and reporting to the next Ministerial Meeting in Athens in 2009. The decision was accompanied by an interpretative statement by Russia and six former soviet republics to the effect that strengthening of the legal framework also would mean that work on a draft Charter of the OSCE would begin.[22]

The OSCE experience may illustrate that the establishment of a formal international organization is fraught with a complex set of political and legal issues. First, it is a question of how much power should be transferred from the

---

[19] *Common Purpose: Towards a More Effective OSCE* Final Report and Recommendations of the Panel of Eminent Persons On Strengthening the Effectiveness of the OSCE, 27 June 2005 <http://www.osce.org/documents/cio/2005/06/15432_en.pdf>, paragraphs 28–30. See also Marco Odello 'Thirty Years After Helsinki: Proposals for OSCE's Reform' (2005) 10 *Journal of Conflict & Security Law* 435–449.

[20] Decision No 16/06 'Legal Status and Privileges and Immunities of the OSCE' 5 December 2006 (MC.DEC/16/06) and 'Interpretative Statement under Paragraph IV.1(A)6 of the OSCE Rules of Procedure 5 December 2006 (MC.DEC/16/06). See also Sonia Brander and María Martin Estebanez 'The OSCE Matures: Time for Legal Status' (2007) 2–5 *Helsinki Monitor*, at 4–5.

[21] 'Report of the Chair of the informal Working Group at expert level tasked with finalizing a draft Convention on the international legal personality, legal capacity, and privileges and immunities of the OSCE', attached to 'Statement by the Chairman-In-Office of the OSCE at the Closing Session of the Fifteenth Meeting of the Ministerial Council', Madrid, 30 November 2007 (MC.DEL/67/07).

[22] Decision No 4/08 'Strengthening the Legal Framework of the OSCE', 5 December 2008 (MC.DEC/4/08) and 'Interpretative Statement under Paragraph IV.1(A)6 of the Rules of procedure of the Organization for Security and Co-Operation in Europe' 5 December 2008 (MC.DEC/4/08).

national to the international level. This question may differ for major powers and small states, where bigger powers may more easily secure their international interests outside international organizations. There may also be more concrete consideration in relation to each organization. In the case of the OSCE the question has been raised whether the negotiation and ratification process of a new convention may leave some of the participating states out. There is also a concern that some of the OSCE *acquis* developed since the CSCE was established in 1975 may not survive the transformation to a formal organization due to present tensions between the East and West.

The approach chosen by the majority, however, is not without legal difficulties, uncertainties, and inconsistencies. First, it is difficult to understand that the OSCE will not become an international organization proper if it is endowed with international legal personality. Such personality means that there would be a new international legal entity in international law, capable of undertaking such legal acts 'as is necessary for the exercise of its functions', presumably also entering into treaties and having international legal responsibility for its acts. While this would be the assessment under international law, the assessment in domestic law may—or may not—be different.

The OSCE approach is different from what is usual in international organizations in the sense that member states have traditionally been concerned about the internal structure and powers of the organization and the consequences of establishing a treaty framework in these respects, whereas the international legal personality could be based on 'implied powers'. The opposite solution has been chosen in the OSCE: defining the external capacity and leaving the internal structure and powers unregulated by treaty. But this has the peculiar effect of determining such external capacities but not including any binding rules about which organs that may initiate, negotiate, and enter into any such external acts or agreements. It seems that obtaining the benefits of an international organization at the external level without creating an international organization may be insurmountable.

The principal focus in assessing whether or not to establish a formal international organization seems to have been the balancing between, on the one hand, creating an effective international institution through its legal empowerment and, on the other hand, the preservation of national constitutional freedom. As has been illustrated by the OSCE, the assessment of institutional modes to improve effectiveness—understood as the ability to attain the objectives of the cooperation—may be complex. Relevant criteria include legal needs, such as securing necessary privileges and immunities of the institution and its officials; the increased symbolic value of a formal international organization; and the costs and possible disadvantages of transformation. The assessment may depend on the subject matter, the institution, and the political configuration at the relevant time.

But there may also be a need for balancing the preservation of formal national freedom and securing constitutional guarantees, both at the national and international level. Soft law organizations exercising powers that in practice are comparable to formal international organizations should arguably be formalized.[23] Such formalization through a treaty may imply restrictions on the freedom of national legislators. But, on the other hand, it provides an opportunity for national democratic organs to participate in defining the mandate of the international organization, and eventually to accept or reject membership through the ratification process. Furthermore, formalization provides the basis for application of international constitutional guarantees, including binding procedural guarantees in decision-making, the doctrine of *ultra vires* acts as restrictions on such decisions, the international legal responsibility for the organization if it oversteps its competence—and possibly judicial review of its decisions (see pp. 64–67).

3. Constitutional Guarantees

3.1 Political accountability

Democratic control over law-making is fundamental in national constitutions. Likewise, international 'legislation' in the form of decisions binding on member states should ideally be adopted by democratic organs composed of directly elected representatives, and supported by public debate, transparency, and the participation of actors from civil society.

International organs of elected representatives, either directly, as in the European Parliament, or indirectly by national parliaments, as in the Parliamentary Assembly of the Council of Europe are, however, only exceptionally to be found in international organizations, and, if they exist, only with a limited power in decision-making. In the absence of such democratically elected organs, one is left with the participation of states in the political organs of international organizations and the indirect control of such decision-making through the democratically elected national constitutional organs—to the extent that member states are democratic (see chapter 6).

Plenary organs of international organizations are the most legitimate for undertaking legislative activities since this—indirectly—allows for participation by citizens of member states through their representatives ('sovereign equality', see also pp. 271–273). The UN General Assembly is therefore given a broad competence to adopt resolutions on 'any questions or any matters' within the scope of the Charter (Article 10). Such decisions are formally non-binding, but the Assembly has demonstrated its ingenuity both as regards decision-making procedures, especially by applying the principle of consensus, and in the forms

---

[23] See also Klabbers, Institutional Ambivalence by Design, 2001, at 420.

of decisions, in order to increase their political and legal significance, including in the formation of customary international law.

The General Assembly has adopted conventions for subsequent ratification and accession by member states. It has also chosen a more solemn form, i.e. 'declarations', in important substantive decisions, such as the Universal Declaration on Human Rights. In the case of the draft articles on state responsibility adopted by the International Law Commission, the General Assembly took 'note of the articles on responsibility of States for internationally wrongful acts, presented by the International Law Commission, the text of which is annexed to the present resolution, and commends them to the attention of Governments without prejudice to the question of their future adoption or other appropriate action'.[24] The combined effect of adoption by the International Law Commission as an expert organ and the General Assembly as a political organ was to give an authoritative status to these draft articles, and thereby evade the more cumbersome and possibly disruptive process of convening a diplomatic conference to negotiate a treaty on state responsibility.

The legislative activities of the United Nations are supplemented by those of the plenary bodies of more specialized institutions, be they formal international organizations or treaty bodies. Different methods have been developed to overcome—or circumvent—the need for securing state consent. For example, the International Maritime Organization, the International Whaling Commission, and several fishery commissions and environmental treaties permit the adoption of legislative measures by majority decision, but allow member states to 'opt out' by making a reservation to the decision. In this way a balance is struck between effective international decision-making and the preservation of national sovereign freedom. But, in practice, such decisions may place considerable political pressure on states not to make a reservation.

Other examples are that the decisions of the International Maritime Organization may be considered as 'generally accepted international rules and standards established through the competent international organization', allowing coastal states to implement such norms as laws and regulations to prevent pollution from foreign vessels in their 200-mile exclusive economic zones (UN Convention on the Law of the Sea, Article 211 (5)). Finally, the Assembly of the States Parties of the International Criminal Court may by a two-thirds majority adopt 'elements of crimes' which shall 'assist the Court in the interpretation and application' of the crimes within the jurisdiction of the Court (ICC Statute, Article 9 (1)).

It is not to be expected that states will allow the General Assembly as the plenary body to 'legislate' in 'grand' questions like the legality of nuclear

---

[24] A/RES/56/83, paragraph 3.

weapons. It is, furthermore, not obvious that one-state-one-vote is the most democratic principle when considering the variations between the populations in different states. On the other hand, voting rights based on the size of populations may conflict with other possible criteria for allocation of voting power, such as diversity in funding or other resources provided to the relevant organization by different member states. It may thus be difficult to find a proper balance between relevant criteria when agreeing upon the appropriate voting power of member states. Similar consideration may apply also to decision-making in more specialized international organizations.

Although plenary bodies may be the most legitimate when it comes to law-making, there are accordingly difficulties in accepting them as legitimate 'legislators' in the sense of making decisions binding on member states. Different law-making techniques have overcome some of the obstacles presented by the need for individual state consent. It may also be that more specialized organizations should be allowed more powers within their restricted substantive scope. But both the 'democratic deficit' of international institutions and their decision-making procedures should restrict such legislative powers. This is even more the case if decisions are ultimately directed towards individuals rather than states (see pp. 77–80). The principle of subsidiarity may, however, provide some guidance regarding the appropriate allocation of powers between international and national constitutional organs (see pp. 74–77).

The Security Council is an example of an organ with limited membership, and with the special feature of the right of veto by the five permanent members in matters of a non-procedural character. The Council's responsibility has traditionally been seen as keeping peace and security in specific situations. But in recent years it has adopted binding general measures, such as requiring states to take certain measures to prevent financing of terrorism and access to weapons of mass destruction. This has been seen as a new legislating activity by the Security Council.[25]

It may be argued that the five militarily strongest nations should have a special role and responsibility in securing international peace and security. It may also be necessary to accept a certain degree of *realpolitik* in the form of a trade-off between the need for ensuring that major powers do not act outside the UN, especially when it comes to the use of force, and securing certain privileges for such powers. It is, however, difficult to accept that an organ with limited membership, and where three out of five permanent members are Western states, should have law-making powers.[26]

---

[25] Paul Szasz 'The Security Council Starts Legislating' (2002) 96 *AJIL* 901–904 and Stefan Talmon 'The Security Council as World Legislator' (2005) 99 *AJIL* 175–194.

[26] Martti Koskennimi 'International Legislation Today: Limits and Possibilities' (2005) 23 *Wisconsin International Law Journal* 61–92, at 74; Alan Boyle and Christine Chinkin *The Making of International Law* (OUP Oxford 2007), at 115, 161–162.

Reform of the Security Council to better reflect the current geopolitical situation, and not the situation 60 years ago has for long been debated.[27] In the 'World Summit Outcome', adopted by the General Assembly on 16 September 2005, the member states agreed to an

early reform of the Security Council—an essential element of our overall effort to reform the United Nations—in order to make it more broadly representative, efficient and transparent and thus to further enhance its effectiveness and the legitimacy and imple-mentation of its decisions. ... We recommend that the Security Council continue to adapt its working methods so as to increase the involvement of States not members of the Council in its work, as appropriate, enhance its accountability to the membership and increase the transparency of its work.[28]

But even with a more representative membership—which also raises the question of 'representative of what'—and better working methods, the Security Council would continue to be an organ with a far more limited membership than the present 192 United Nations members. This restricts the legitimacy of the law-making role for the Council, especially as it expands the substantive scope of its mandate with respect to its 'primary responsibility' for the maintenance of international peace and security (article 24(1)). There may, however, be imagined ways of involving the General Assembly in law-making relating to peace and security in order to increase the legitimacy of the law-making process.[29]

While international organizations other than the United Nations may not deal with such important matters as peace and security, and do not have the authority to make binding decisions like the Security Council, the legitimacy deficiency of law-making by organs of limited membership may be comparable. It may be argued that there is less ground for concern if the organ with limited membership only can make binding decisions subject to an opting-out proce-dure, or any other way of law-making that does not imply final binding deci-sions. On the other hand, it is difficult to see why such decisions should not involve the plenary organ of the relevant international organization, in order to include all the member states of the organization.

The increased empowerment of international organizations also means em-powerment of its officials. Anne-Marie Slaughter has championed the idea that networks of international government officials have important powers and should be allocated more power. It is even claimed that we in the future could see dis-aggregated government institutions—the members of government networks—as actual bearers of a measure of sovereignty. This would include horizontal networks between governmental officials, but also vertical networks involving officials of international organizations. On the other hand, it is claimed that

---

[27] Hans Corell 'Reforming the United Nations' (2005) 2 *International Organizations Law Review* 373–391, at 381.   [28] A/RES/60/1, paragraphs 153–154.
[29] Boyle and Chinkin, *The Making of International Law*, 2007, at 102 with further references.

such networks need checks and balances and that they would complement rather than replace the existing international institutional framework.[30]

Networks of officials, including legislators, executives, and judges, are positive aspects of internationalization in the sense that they may be able to contribute to the mutual understanding and accommodation between different national jurisdictions, and between the international and the national level. Empowerment of inter-governmental networks may, however, be at the expense of national constitutional organs.[31] To the extent that they also involve officials from international organizations, their activities may also threaten the political control of such organizations. It must be kept in mind that it is the formal organs of international organizations that are primarily accountable for their decisions, not networks as such. Furthermore, the formal organs are composed in a way and are equipped by procedures for decision-making, preferably including transparency and broad participation also from non-state actors, to be trusted to wield power in a responsible way (see pp. 225–235 and 326–330). Hence, international networks should give important input to decision-making organs, but the decisions should be taken by the formal international organs.

3.2 Rule of law

The ideal of the rule of law is well known from national constitutional law (or *Rechtsstaat* in the German tradition and *État de Droit* in French), but its content is not easily defined, and may vary between different jurisdiction. It relates, however, to the regulation of a community based on law and justice, not on power. The idea has been recognized in several treaties and international legal instruments, especially at the European level, such as the preamble of the European Convention on Human Rights (ECHR) referring to the 'common heritage of political traditions, ideals, freedoms and the rule of law'.

While the respect for the rule of law traditionally has been a requirement addressed to the domestic legal order, the relevance of the principle is increasingly acknowledged also as part of international law.[32] It may be argued that the

---

[30] Anne-Marie Slaughter *A New World Order* (Princeton UP 2004), at 4, 10, 13, 17, 18–19, 253–254, and 261.

[31] Kenneth Anderson 'Book Review: Squaring the Circle? Reconciling Sovereignty and Global Governance Through Global Government Networks' (2005) 118 *Harvard Law Review* 1255–1312, at 1310; Boyle and Chinkin, *The Making of International Law*, 2007, at 27.

[32] Brian Z Tamanaha *On the Rule of Law: History, Politics, Theory* (CUP Cambridge 2004), at 127–137. Sir Arthur Watts 'The International Rule of Law' (1993) 36 *GYIL* 15–45; Stéphane Beaulac 'An Inquiry into the International Rule of Law' (2007) 14 *European University Institute Workings Papers MWP*; James Crawford 'Internatonal Law and the Rule of Law' (2003) 24 *Adelaide Law Review* 3–12; Simon Chesterman '"I'll Take Manhattan": The International Rule of Law and the United Nations Security Council' (2009) 1 *Hague Journal on the Rule of Law* 1–7; Jeremy Matam Farrall *United Nations Sanctions and the Rule of Law* (CUP Cambridge 2007); and André Nollkaemper 'The Internationalized Rule of Law' (2009) 1 *Hague Journal on the Rule of Law* 74–78.

rule of law is of less relevance at the international level since obligations will generally not be imposed on states without their consent. But as the decision-making powers of international organizations increase, both formally and in practice, the need for control of such powers increases accordingly.

It may also be argued that the rule of law at the domestic level shall primarily protect individuals, whereas states are the principal legal subjects at the international level. But also states have a need for predictability, and a minority of states or weaker states may need protection from abuse by a majority or by stronger states. Furthermore, to the extent international organizations exercise powers in relation to states, their decisions will ultimately affect individuals, not least if the use of military force is authorized or sanctions are adopted. International decisions are, moreover, increasingly targeting individuals directly, such as smart sanctions and counter-terrorist measures (see pp. 77–80).

The application of the rule of law both at the national and the international level is reflected in the General Assembly's 2005 World Summit Outcome, recognizing 'the need for universal adherence to and implementation of the rule of law at both the national and international levels'.[33] This commitment has been followed up in subsequent General Assembly resolutions, such as resolution 62/70 'The rule of law at the national and international levels', which states in its 4th preambular paragraph:

Reaffirming further the need for universal adherence to and implementation of the rule of law at both the national and international levels and its solemn commitment to an international order based on the rule of law and international law, which, together with the principles of justice, is essential for peaceful coexistence and cooperation among States.[34]

There may be different opinions about the proper elements of the rule of law as applied in international law. But the idea has traditionally been seen to include that no one and no organ is beyond the law, i.e. that the use of power shall be governed by law; the absence of arbitrary power; equality before the law; and protection of rights by independent courts. The following three aspects of this ideal will be discussed below: separation of powers; procedural principles for decision-making; and judicial review.

Separation of powers

We have seen that international organizations will not necessarily have only *one* legislative body—legislative activities may take place in both plenary bodies, like the General Assembly, and bodies with limited representation, like the Security Council. It has been argued above that, as a general principle, international law-making should be undertaken by the plenary body in order to ensure participation by all member states of the international organization.

---

[33] A/RES/60/1, paragraph 134.   [34] A/RES/62/70, 4th preambular paragraph.

But if we turn from general law-making to decision-making in individual cases, there is a need to prevent arbitrariness by ensuring that decisions are taken on the basis of law rather than from political considerations. This can be done by balancing the need for professional executive power and an independent judiciary on one hand, and, on the other hand, ensuring political accountability of executive organs.

If we again take the Security Council, it has an extremely wide discretion both to decide whether there has been a 'threat to the peace, breach of the peace, or act of aggression' according to Article 39 of the Charter and to decide on possible coercive measures under Chapter VII. As already mentioned, there may be a legitimate need for allowing more political control over the taking of coercive measures than at the national level, the reason being the need for having major powers on board and for making use of their military forces.

But, firstly, political organs may adopt general directives for the way in which powers should be exercised, i.e. a form of self-restraint. In the World Summit Outcome in 2005, the General Assembly agreed that the Security Council could apply the 'responsibility to protect' if states are 'manifestly failing to protect their populations from genocide, war crimes, ethnic cleansing and crimes against humanity'[35] (see also pp. 185–186). Such criteria are useful in providing guidance for the use of coercive measures—and may at the same time establish a basis for political accountability.

Secondly, political organs may delegate powers to bodies that are under their general control, but leaving individual decision-making to such bodies. The counter-terrorism bodies under the Security Council, which are responsible for controlling states' implementation of counter-terrorism obligations under defined Security Council resolutions, and for listing and delisting of persons and organizations suspected of financing terrorism, is similarly politically composed as the Security Council. It is, however, difficult to see why decisions on listing and delisting of persons and organizations suspected of financing of terrorism should be taken by a political organ, and not by professional executives accountable to the Security Council.[36]

The General Assembly and the Security Council have even taken decisions which have the character of dispute resolution, like the establishment of a boundary between two states in the case of Iraq and Kuwait.[37] While there may be a need not to exclude the political element in executive functions altogether, but rather to control the use of such powers, binding dispute settlement should

---

[35] A/RES/60/1, paragraph 139.
[36] See <http://www.un.org/sc/committees/1267/information.shtml> (last visited 12 March 2009).
[37] Boyle and Chinkin, *The Making of International Law*, 2007, at 110 and 231. See about separation of powers in the International Criminal Court: Dominic Raab and Hans Bevers 'The International Criminal Court and the Separation of Powers' (2006) 3 *International Organizations Law Review* 93–135.

be left to international tribunals, and not to the discretion of the Security Council (or any other political organ).

Procedural principles

As state consent as a basis for legitimacy becomes more tenuous, alternative bases include not only separation of powers but also due process guarantees in the form of procedural principles.[38] Such principles may serve accountability in relation to international political organs, but may also provide guarantees for entities affected by international decisions, be they states or individuals.

The 2005 World Summit Outcome agreed, as mentioned earlier, that the Security Council should become more transparent and that involvement of states that are not members of the Council should be increased. Such procedures could include the holding of open debates on legislative measures, consultations with non-members of the Council, and review of the resolution after an appropriate time.[39] Procedural requirements should apply to the most intrusive measures, i.e. the authorization of the use of armed force against a state, but also to other coercive measures in the form of sanctions. In relation to the imposition of sanctions it has been recommended that the Security Council should observe requirements of transparency, consistency, equality, due process, and proportionality.[40]

The targeting of individuals should also respect international human rights. The Security Council has been reluctant to accept such restrictions to its activities.[41] Although it has introduced a focal point to receive delisting requests in counter-terrorism and required persons to be informed about their designation on a list and adopted criteria for their removal, it is argued that it has not yet addressed the basic human rights concerns.[42] But, as has been illustrated by the European Court of Justice in the *Kadi* case on counter-terrorism measures, failure to do so may result in their non-implementation at the regional or domestic level (see pp. 77–79).

The need for increased accountability has been the focus for a new field of law, i.e. global administrative law.[43] This legal discipline has been defined as:

comprising the mechanisms, principles, practices, and supporting social understandings that promote or otherwise affect the accountability of global administrative

---

[38] Boyle and Chinkin, *The Making of International Law*, 2007, at 25.

[39] See Simon Chesterman 'The UN Security Council and the Rule of Law' (2008) New York University School of Law, Public Law and Legal Theory Research Paper Series, Working Paper No 08–57 (Recommendation 11).   [40] Farrall, *United Nations Sanctions*, 2007, at 230–241.

[41] E J Flynn 'The Security Council's Counter-Terrorism Committee and Human Rights' (2007) 7 *Human Rights Law Review* 371–384, at 371.

[42] Chesterman, 'I'll Take Manhattan', 2009, at 5–6.

[43] Benedict Kingsbury, Nico Krisch, Richard B Stewart, and Jonathan B Wiener 'Foreword: Global Governance as Administration—National and Transnational Approaches to Global Administrative Law' (2005) 68 *Law and Contemporary Problems* 1–14; Benedict Kingsbury, Nico Krisch, and Richard B Stewart 'The Emergence of Global Administrative Law' (2005) 68 *Law and Contemporary Problems* 15–62; Nico Krisch and Benedict Kingsbury 'Introduction: Global Governance and Global Administrative Law in the International Legal Order' (2006) 17 *EJIL* 1–13.

bodies, in particular by ensuring they meet adequate standards of transparency, participation, reasoned decisions, and legality, and providing effective review of the rules and decisions they make. Global administrative bodies include formal intergovernmental regulatory bodies, informal intergovernmental regulatory networks and coordination arrangements, national regulatory bodies operating with reference to an international intergovernmental regime, hybrid public-private regulatory bodies, and some private regulatory bodies exercising transnational governance functions of particular public significance.[44]

The desirability of pooling these different organs and their activities into one discipline called global administrative law may be questioned—both from a strictly legal and from a normative point of view. It is, for example, difficult to accept that informal intergovernmental networks and private bodies have a law at all. Furthermore, although both international organizations and states should respect the rule of law, they have their distinct legal systems—there is accordingly not *one* global administrative law—and implementation of the principles should respect the plurality of organizational designs and needs.[45] The focus on global administrative law has, however, the positive effect of emphasizing the need for accountability and pointing out relevant procedural standards.

Relevant principles may also be found in the Code of Good Administration adopted by the Committee of Ministers of the Council of Europe in 2007, which includes the principles of lawfulness, equality, impartiality, proportionality, legal certainty, taking action within a reasonable time limit, participation, respect for privacy, and transparency.[46] Admittedly, this recommendation is directed to the exercise of public power at the national, not the international level. But with the increasing powers of international organizations, the principles listed are also becoming of growing relevance at the international level.

The essential point is that procedural safeguards are also needed at the international level, both to serve accountability in relation to the political organs that have delegated such powers and to secure the rights of entities affected by such decisions. Furthermore, no attempt has been made to distinguish between what should be considered constitutional and what should properly be called administrative principles. Some principles may have both a constitutional and an administrative character. While the rule of law is clearly a constitutional idea, its concretization in specific standards should be regarded as being of a more administrative nature.

---

[44] Kingsbury, Krisch, and Stewart, Global Administrative Law, 2005, at 17.

[45] See also Nico Krisch 'The Pluralism of Global Administrative Law' (2006) 17 *EJIL* 247–278.

[46] Recommendation CM/Rec (2007) 7 of the Committee of Ministers to member states on good administration (20 June 2007). See also principles of good governance proposed by the International Law Association Committee 'Accountability of International Organisations' Final Report Berlin Conference 2004 at 8. See <http://www.ila-hq.org/en/committees/>.

Judicial review

The control of public power by courts should be considered an integral part of the rule of law. But its form varies in different domestic contexts, especially as to whether courts have the power of constitutional control of law-making. The purpose of judicial review is both an accountability mechanism, to ensure that the executive power implements legislation loyally, and to protect those affected by relevant decisions. While other mechanisms may serve the purpose of oversight, judicial review of both legislation and executive acts is essential to protect the rights of individuals and minorities at the national level. Likewise, it may be argued that individual states and—increasingly—also individuals may need protection against acts by international organizations.[47]

Decisions of international organizations may be addressed by international courts in different ways. First, the International Court of Justice (ICJ) may be asked for an advisory opinion by the General Assembly or the Security Council, or by other UN organs and specialized agencies authorized by the General Assembly, on 'any legal question', under the UN Charter Article 96. This means that the Court may be asked about the legality of the decisions of any international organ. While the Court has expressed its opinion about decisions by the General Assembly as well as the Security Council,[48] it has also pronounced on a decision by the International Maritime Organization (formerly the Inter-Governmental Maritime Consultative Organization)[49] and the World Health Organization.[50] Since requests for advisory opinions are adopted by a majority, they are, however, not well-suited to the protection of individual states—or individuals—against majority decisions. Furthermore, they are by necessity of a non-binding character.

The legality of decisions by international organizations may also come up as part of contentious cases between two states. The most well-known is the *Lockerbie* case, where Libya claimed that sanctions adopted by the Security

---

[47] Much has been written about judicial review in international law, particularly on the review of Security Council decisions by the ICJ: Mohammed Bedjaoui *The New World Order and the Security Council: Testing the Legality of its Acts* (Martinus Nijhoff Leiden 1995); José E Alvarez 'Judging the Security Council' (1996) 90 *AJIL* 1–39; Bernd Martenczuk 'The Security Council, the International Court and Judicial Review: What Lessons from Lockerbie?' (1999) 10 *EJIL* 517–547; Bardo Fassbender 'Review Essay: *Quis judicabit?* The Security Council, Its Powers and Its Legal Control' (2000) 11 *EJIL* 219–232; Erika de Wet *The Chapter VII Powers of the United Nations Security Council* (Hart Oxford 2004); James Crawford '"Marbury v. Madison" at the International Level' (2004) 36 *George Washington International Law Review* 505–514; and Jan Klabbers 'Straddling Law and Politics: Judicial Review in International Law' in Ronald St John MacDonald and Douglas M Johnston (eds) *Towards World Constitutionalism: Issues in the Legal Ordering of the World Community* (Martinus Nijhoff Leiden 2005).

[48] Such as the *Certain Expenses of the United Nations (Article 17, paragraph 2, of the Charter)*, (advisory opinion) [1962] ICJ Reports 151.

[49] *Constitution of the Maritime Safety Committee of the Inter-Governmental Maritime Consultative Organization* (advisory opinion) [1960] ICJ Reports 150.

[50] *Legality of the Use by a State of Nuclear Weapons in Armed Conflict* (advisory opinion) [1996] ICJ Reports 66.

Council were illegal.[51] In the *Bosnia* case, it was claimed that the arms embargo adopted by the Security Council violated Bosnia's right of self-defence.[52] The ICJ has, however, not finally determined whether it has the competence to undertake judicial review of Security Council decisions. In the *Lockerbie* case it stated that it was not 'at this stage called upon to determine definitively the legal effect of Security Council resolution 748 (1992)'.[53]

In the *Tadic* case, the defendant argued that the International Tribunal for the Former Yugoslavia (ICTY) was illegally established by the Security Council. The Tribunal stated:

There is no question, of course, of the International Tribunal acting as a constitutional tribunal, reviewing the acts of the other organs of the United Nations, particularly those of the Security Council, its own 'creator'. It was not established for that purpose, as is clear from the definition of the ambit of its 'primary' or 'substantive' jurisdiction in Articles 1 to 5 of its Statute. But this is beside the point. The question before the Appeals Chamber is whether the International Tribunal, in exercising this 'incidental' jurisdiction, can examine the legality of its establishment by the Security Council, solely for the purpose of ascertaining its own 'primary' jurisdiction over the case before it.[54]

The Tribunal found that it was properly established by the Security Council.[55]

But testing the legality of international decisions through contentious cases between states has inherent limitations: the case must concern the relations between states (except for international criminal law); the international organization will not have status as a party; and the court's finding will only be part of the reasoning and not the conclusions, in order to determine the respective states' rights and obligations. The question remains, therefore: should states— and possibly individuals—be able to take international organizations to an international court for review of their decisions?

Constitutional review at the domestic level has been confronted by the counter-majoritarian argument, i.e. that democratically unaccountable courts should not have the competence to set aside decisions made by duly elected organs (see pp. 147–148). But the democratic element in international organizations' decision-making is less dominant. Decision-making will generally not be taken by elected organs, but by organs composed of state representatives or

---

[51] *Questions of Interpretation and Application of the 1971 Montreal Convention arising from the Aerial Incident at Lockerbie* (Libyan Arab Jamahiriya v United Kingdom) (preliminary objections) [1998] ICJ Reports 9.

[52] *Application of the Convention on the Prevention and Punishment of the Crime of Genocide* (provisional measures) [1993] ICJ Reports 3.

[53] *Questions of Interpretation and Application of the 1971 Montreal Convention arising from the Aerial Incident at Lockerbie*, at 15.

[54] *Prosecutor v Dusko Tadic, Decision on the Defence Motion for Interlocutory Appeal on Jurisdiction* Case IT-94-1-AR72 Appeals Chamber of 2 October 1995 paragraph 20.

[55] *Prosecutor v Dusko Tadic, Decision on the Defence Motion for Interlocutory Appeal on Jurisdiction* Case 1995 paragraphs 47 and 48.

administrative bodies. In these circumstances the counter-majoritarian argument may be turned upside down in the sense that judicial review may serve as a control of whether the international organization respects its mandate as accepted by the national legislatures in the ratification process.

It has been claimed that judicial review could make the Security Council less effective,[56] which has been countered by the argument that such review could increase the credibility of Security Council decision.[57] The Security Council is furthermore an extremely politicized organ in its enforcement and quasi-legislative powers: it could be argued that a confrontation with the ICJ could possibly discredit both organs. On the other hand, the Council enjoys wide discretion in determining the conditions for the use of force and which measures to apply, a discretion that must be respected by the Court. Possible frictions may also be mitigated to the extent that the ICJ applies a presumption of the validity of the actions taken, in determining their conformity with the Charter, as in the *Certain Expenses* case.[58]

The dangers of such politicized confrontations are less pronounced in the case of judicial review of other organs of the UN, or of the decisions by other international organizations. Moreover, it would seem that the issue should be treated in a more nuanced fashion, by not only focusing on the Security Council, but also on other organs of the UN, such as the General Assembly; other international organizations than the UN; whether the review concerns legislative or executive acts; which courts should be entrusted with review; the standards and intensity to be applied; who should have the right to contest international organization decisions; and the effects of the review.[59]

Judicial review should be available for both law-making and executive acts of international organizations—to the extent that the relevant international organization would have such powers. It is less obvious that judicial review should also encompass non-binding decisions (soft law).[60] Such decisions may, however, form the basis of binding obligations—hard law—if recognized as such by other treaties, such as the 'international standards' referred to in the United Nations Law of the Sea Convention. Non-binding measures may also put a political pressure on states to comply, such as the moratorium on whaling adopted by the International Whaling Commission (IWC), and may furthermore provide the basis for national import restrictions.[61] These effects militate in favour of expanding judicial review to encompass soft law decisions as well.

---

[56] Fassbender, Review Essay: *Quis judicabit?*, 2000, at 224.

[57] Martenczuk, What Lessons from Lockerbie?', 1999, at 547.

[58] *Certain Expenses of the United Nations (Article 17, paragraph 2, of the Charter)* (advisory opinion) [1962] ICJ Reports 151, at 168.

[59] See, Klabbers, Straddling Law and Politics, 2005, at 820.   [60] *Ibid*, at 824 (footnote 71).

[61] Ted L McDorman 'Iceland, Whaling and the U.S. Pelly Amendment: The International Trade Law Context' (1997) 66 *Nordic Journal of International Law* 453–474.

The review should first of all cover the procedural requirements for decision-making.[62] But it should also control that the decisions are within the substantive scope of the relevant organ, possibly also of the international organization, and whether the decisions respect general international law, including *jus cogens* obligations.

Decisions of international organization will (except for a supra-national international organization like the European Community) formally be directed to states, while the ultimate intention may be to direct the activities of private individuals and organizations. States should obviously be accorded the right to instigate judicial review. But affected individuals and organizations should not be left to the mercy of their home states: they should also be given a right to individual complaint.[63]

The effects of judicial review may be invalidity of the regulation or decision in question, its inapplicability in relation to affected states or non-state actors, or a statement of inconsistency—as in the United Kingdom's Human Rights Act.[64] While invalidity may be a too strong measure and a statement of inconsistency too weak, it would seem that the interests of the relevant parties would be well served if the court had the competence to determine the regulation or decision inapplicable in the actual instance.

The legality of decisions by international organizations may arise in contentious cases before different international tribunals. Both the International Tribunal for the Law of the Sea and the WTO Dispute Settlement Body may, for example, need to assess to what extent a decision by the Security Council has set aside rights established by the respective treaties. The ICJ is, however, the only international court with a general competence of adjudication in international law—to the extent accepted between the states parties and not entrusted to specialized international courts. A right of judicial review could be designed for each international organization with a designated international tribunal, either an existing tribunal or a tribunal specializing in dealing with administrative complaints. But the interest of coherence may be best served by generally assigning this responsibility to the ICJ.

4. The Relationship between International Institutions

4.1 The need for consistency

While states' constitutions establish legislative, executive, and judicial organs, and define their respective competencies within a common legal order, the

---

[62] Klabbers, Straddling Law and Politics, 2005, at 813.
[63] Corell, Reforming the United Nations, 2005, at 380.
[64] Klabbers, Straddling Law and Politics, 2005, at 833.

relationship between international institutions is characterized by legal autonomy and functional differentiation.

The United Nations is the global organization with the broadest general competence, but it operates in an institutional architecture with other organizations in such fields as international maritime transport (IMO), international aviation (ICAO), international trade (WTO), and international health (WHO). Some of these organizations are UN specialized agencies with an agreement with the UN, others are not, but none of them are under instructions from the UN. In addition, we have treaty bodies, soft law organizations, and political fora for cooperation, both at the global and the regional level.

This fragmentation of global and regional institutions may be regarded as a threat to international government under international law.[65] But since international organizations have minimal formal law-making power, the potential for legal conflicts between such acts is limited. Conflicts may, however, arise at the political level between the objectives pursued and measures adopted by the multiple institutions. Furthermore, such fragmentation may lead to lack of focus of these institutions and to waste of resources. Hence, there is a need for better consistency in the work of international institutions.

The Study Group of the International Law Commission on the Fragmentation of International Law dealt extensively with the difficulties created by fragmentation in substantive international law, but it decided to leave the institutional issues aside. It was stated that the 'issue of institutional competence is best dealt with by the institutions themselves'.[66] The focus of this section is the opposite: it will not deal with the substantive issues, but rather with the institutional aspects. It will in particular discuss whether constitutionalization would be an appropriate counter-move to institutional fragmentation.[67]

4.2 Principles for organizing the relationship

The most ambitious way of 'constitutionalizing' international governance would be to integrate existing institutions to the extent they overlap or compete. One could also imagine a less grand programme by retaining the institutions, but establishing a hierarchy between them.

However, states show no inclination to move towards such a comprehensive international institutional system, not even within specialized regimes such as international environmental law. The High-level Panel on UN System-wide

---

[65] Martti Koskenniemi 'International Legislation Today: Limits and Possibilities' (2005) 23 *Wisconsin International Law Journal* 61–92, at 81.

[66] Martti Koskennimi *Fragmentation of International Law. Difficulties Arising from Diversification and Expansion of International Law. Report of the Study Group of the International Law Commission* (The Erik Castrén Institute Research Reports 21/2007 Helsinki), at 13.

[67] See Jan Klabbers 'Constitutionalism Lite' (2004) 1 *International Organizations Law Review* 31–58, at 31.

Coherence characterized the United Nations Environment Programme (UNEP) as 'weak, under-funded and ineffective', and suggested that it 'should be upgraded with a renewed mandate and improved funding'.[68] But also the establishment of a World Environment Organization has been proposed.[69]

A World Environment Organization would supposedly contribute to more effective and more comprehensive decision-making, and could even ensure that the environment would speak with 'one voice', particularly in relation to trade interests. However, not much progress has been made. The 2005 World Summit recognized 'the need for more efficient environmental activities in the United Nations system' and acknowledged the need 'to explore the possibility of a more coherent institutional framework to address this need, including a more integrated structure', but in stating that improvements should build on 'existing institutions and internationally agreed instruments, as well as the treaty bodies and the specialized agencies', it did not foresee new institutional structures.[70] Neither has the proposal by the UN High Commissioner for Human Rights for a 'unified standing treaty body' as a substitute for the existing treaty organs recieved much support.[71]

The integration of existing international organizations and treaty bodies might not be desirable from an effectiveness point of view. In international environmental law, for example, the treaties with their Conferences of the Parties (COPs), subsidiary bodies, and secretariats have generally been successful in providing a non-bureaucratic and dynamic framework for environmental cooperation. They have developed decision-making and non-compliance systems designed to accommodate the needs of the different environmental challenges, and represented arenas for mutual learning. It is not obvious that the result would be better in a centralized organization.[72]

---

[68] 'Delivering as One', Report of the High-level Panel on United Nations System-wide Coherence, (A/61/583), paragraphs 37 and 39.

[69] See Julie Ayling 'Serving Many Voices: Progressing Calls for an International Environmental Organisation' (1997) 9 *Journal of Environmental Law* 243–270; Steve Charnovitz 'A World Environment Organization' (2002) 27 *Columbia Journal of Environmental Law* 323–362; Sebastian Oberthür and Thomas Gehring 'Reforming International Environmental Governance: An Institutionalist Critique of the Proposal for a World Environment Organisation' (2004) 4 *International Environmental Agreements: Politics, Law and Economics* 359–381; Frank Biermann and Steffen Bauer (eds) *A World Environment Organization: Solution or Threat for Effective International Environmental Governance?* (Ashgate Aldershot 2005).

[70] World Summit Outcome Resolution 24 October 2005 (A/RES/60/1) paragraph 169.

[71] Concept Paper on the High Commissioner's Proposal for a Unified Standing Treaty Body (14 March 2006) (HRI/MC/2006/CRP.1). See also Michael O'Flaherty and Claire O'Brien 'Reform of UN Human Rights Treaty Monitoring Bodies: A Critique of the Concept Paper on the High Commissioner's Proposal for a Unified Standing Treaty Body' (2007) 7 *Human Rights Law Review* 141–173; Rachael Lorna Johnstone 'Cynical Savings or Reasonable Reform? Reflections on a Single Unified UN Human Rights Treaty Body' (2007) 7 *Human Rights Law Review* 173–201; and Michael Bowman 'Towards a Unified Treaty Body for Monitoring Compliance with UN Human Rights Conventions? Legal Mechanisms for Treaty Reform' (2007) 7 *Human Rights Law Review* 225–251.

[72] Geir Ulfstein 'Treaty Bodies' in Daniel Bodansky, Jutta Brunnée, and Ellen Hey (eds) *The Oxford Handbook of International Environmental Law* (OUP Oxford 2007) 877–889, at 889.

It may moreover more generally be argued that a multiplicity of international organizations may be desirable as it protects the relative autonomy of the respective international organizations and treaty bodies and their constituencies.[73] This means that one regime may not impose its order on another, and that interaction rather would be channelled through dialogue between the regimes. On the other hand, the bargaining power of the respective regimes may be unequal,[74] and they may be supported by enforcement mechanisms of different strengths, as in the case of WTO's court-like Dispute Settlement Understanding and the weaker non-compliance bodies of the environmental agreements. This may call for political, legal, and institutional responses to rectify imbalances.

Furthermore, the integration of international organizations and treaty bodies once established may be difficult to achieve, both for political and legal reasons. First, institutions tend to acquire an identity of their own, and both the institutions and their member states may be reluctant to allow their dissolution. Secondly, amendments or termination of the founding treaties will usually require unanimity and new institutions will require ratification of the respective treaties by the member states. Integration of institutions may also represent difficult processes of transition, and not all member states will necessarily choose to participate in the new institutions.

The establishment of an integrated international institutional framework with a hierarchical order between the different organs would have the benefits of legal clarity and the potential for more focused international governance. But it is not obvious that such an institutional framework would be more effective in solving international problems, and its creation would be fraught with difficulties. Structural adjustments would consequently require concrete assessment of benefits and disadvantages. The need for a more consistent international governance structure would, however, justify caution in establishing new institutions.

A less ambitious strategy to avoid the difficulties involved in a fragmented international institutional framework is to establish arrangements of complementarity. The preamble of the Cartagena Protocol on Biodiversity establishes, for example, that 'this Protocol shall not be interpreted as implying a change in the rights and obligations of a Party under any existing international agreements'. While a principle of complementarity is well-advised, it will not solve the problems entirely, since it is usually impossible to establish clear-cut demarcation of competences, and because cooperation is necessary in closely related subject matters. This leaves us with the more modest strategy of ensuring coordination between the institutions.

---

[73] Krisch, The Pluralism of Global Administrative Law, 2006, at 278.
[74] Koskenniemi, International Legislation Today, 2005, at 81.

The need for cooperation between trade interests and environmental concerns is, for example, acknowledged in the Plan of Implementation of the 2002 World Summit on Sustainable Development (2002) in Johannesburg, which called for efforts to 'strengthen cooperation among UNEP and other United Nations Bodies and specialized agencies, the Bretton Woods institutions and WTO, within their mandates'.[75] The Trade and Environment Committee of the WTO was already established in 1995 and shall serve as forum for dialogue on the impact of trade policies on the environment, and of environmental policies on trade. It has, however, been pointed out that the effectiveness of this Committee suffers from the fact that it is embedded in an organization established to promote trade liberalization and the absence of an institutional counterpart in international environmental law.[76]

4.3 The competence to act at the external level

A closer cooperation between international institutions may be achieved in two different manners: either that member states adjust the founding treaties of the relevant institutions or that such institutions arrange for their mutual relationship through bilateral or multilateral agreement. Although the former approach does not create particular legal problems, it may—as we have already seen—meet with resistance and may be difficult to implement in practice. This means that agreements between international institutions will generally be a more viable approach.

The treaty establishing a formal international organization may explicitly set out the international legal capacity to enter into agreements with other international subjects, including other international organizations. The capacity to enter into treaties with non-member states and other international organizations will not follow exclusively from the founding treaty itself, but from the fact that such common intention by the member states is accepted by customary international law, i.e. that the international organization will have 'objective international personality'.

The doctrine of 'implied powers' accepts, however, that the common intention of the parties need not follow from an express stipulation in the founding treaty, but from the purposes of the international organization. This approach was used by the ICJ in the *Reparation* case to establish the 'international legal personality' of the United Nations:

The subjects of law in any legal system are not necessarily identical in their nature or in the extent of their rights, and their nature depends upon the needs of the community.

---

[75] Plan of Implementation of the World Summit on Sustainable Development, paragraph 154. See <http://www.un.org/esa/sustdev/documents/WSSD_POI_PD/English/WSSD_PlanImpl.pdf>, last visited 18 March 2009.

[76] Richard G Tarasofsky 'The WTO Committee on Trade and Environment: Is it Making a Difference?' (1999) 3 *Max Planck Yearbook of United Nations Law* 471–488, at 486.

Throughout its history, the development of international law has been influenced by the requirements of international life, and the progressive increase in the collective activities of States has already given rise to instances of action upon the international plane by certain entities which are not States. This development culminated in the establishment in June 1945 of an international organization whose purposes and principles are specified in the Charter of the United Nations. But to achieve these ends the attribution of international personality is indispensable.[77]

Generally, formal international organizations should be considered to have the capacity needed to enter into binding agreements with other international subjects, either on the basis of explicit or implied powers.[78] This does not necessarily mean that the international organization may enter into agreement on any substantive issue. While the doctrine of implied powers provides a basis for international legal personality, it also limits the acts international organizations may undertake at the external level in relation to other international subjects, such as states and international organizations, to those necessary to fulfil the purposes of the international organization. This was recognized by the ICJ in the *Legality of the Use by a State of Nuclear Weapons in Armed Conflict* case:

In the opinion of the Court, to ascribe to the WHO the competence to address the legality of the use of nuclear weapons—even in view of their health and environmental effects—would be tantamount to disregarding the principle of speciality; for such competence could not be deemed a necessary implication of the Constitution of the Organization in the light of the purposes assigned to it by its member States.[79]

It is worth mentioning that the ICJ in this Opinion also took into account the wider constitutional context of the relationship between the WHO and the UN by referring to 'the logic of the overall system contemplated by the Charter' and that the competencies of the WHO 'cannot encroach on the responsibilities of other parts of the United Nations system'.[80] In this way, the Court acknowledged the need for allocating different functions between the respective organizations according to what might be deemed a constitutionalist approach.

As long as legal instruments entered into between international organizations respect the substantive scope of the particular organizations, they would consequently have the competence to regulate their mutual relationship and to coordinate their activities. It may, however, be asked whether treaty bodies not organized as formal international organizations would also have the

---

[77] *Reparation for Injuries Suffered in the Service of the United Nations* (advisory opinion) [1949] ICJ Reports 174, at 178.

[78] Chittharanjan Felix Amerasinghe *Principles of the Institutional Law of International Organizations* (2nd edn CUP Cambridge 2005), at 101; see also Klabbers, *International Institutional Law*, 2002, at 284.

[79] *Legality of the Use by a State of Nuclear Weapons in Armed Conflict* 1996, paragraph 25.

[80] *Ibid*, paragraph 26.

international capacity to enter into legally binding agreements with international organizations and other treaty bodies for such purposes.

It should first of all be recognized that such needs may exist. The treaty bodies may want to enter into agreements on practical matters with the institution hosting their secretariat, on privileges and immunities with the host state of the secretariat or meetings by the treaty body, or, what is of particular relevance in the present context, on agreements with relevant international organizations and other treaty bodies on cooperation in substantive issues. The Conference of the Parties of the Climate Change Convention may, for example, need to coordinate with the United Nations and its specialized agencies and programmes, the treaty bodies of the Convention on Biological Diversity and the Global Environment Facility (GEF) of the World Bank. Furthermore, treaty bodies in the environmental field have entered into such agreements in practice. Finally, the reason for establishing treaty bodies rather than formal international organizations was supposedly the need for 'institutional economy' rather than a desire to establish less effective institutions.[81]

Such treaty bodies should therefore be considered to have the legal capacity to enter into legally binding agreements on their mutual relationship. This would also accord with the dynamic approach chosen by the ICJ in the *Reparation* case by pointing out that the 'subjects of law in any legal system are not necessarily identical in nature or in the extent of their rights', that 'their nature depend upon the needs of the community', and that 'the progressive increase in the collective activities of States has already given rise to instances of action upon the international plane by certain entities which are not States'.

It is not obvious, however, that all treaty bodies—for example human rights treaty bodies—should be seen to have treaty-making capacity, in spite of the need to coordinate their activities. Relevant factors in deciding the international legal personality of treaty bodies could include the mandate of the body—is it a law-making or administrative or compliance control organ—and the organizational structure in which it is a part, including its relationship with existing international organizations. To the extent that it resembles a formal international organization in everything but name, it is easier to accept its international legal personality than if it is a separate organ with a specific function served by an existing international organization, such as the supervisory bodies under human rights conventions. Soft law organizations would not have the necessary international legal personality anyway, and would need to coordinate their relationship to other international institutions with informal arrangements, such as memorandums of understanding.[82]

---

[81] Churchill and Ulfstein, Autonomous Institutional Arrangements, 2000, at 647–655.

[82] See Anthony Aust *Modern Treaty Law and Practice* (2nd edn CUP Cambridge 2007), at 20–21 and 32.

The fragmentary character of the international institutional framework is not easily overcome. It has also been pointed out that the diversity of international institutions has its positive aspects. But to the extent that a more consistent—or 'constitutional'—institutional set-up is desirable it is probably a more realistic approach to rely on a network of treaty arrangements between the autonomous international institutions than redesigning the international institutional architecture. It has been shown that formal international organizations and treaty bodies generally have the competence to use the treaty instrument for such a purpose: it is up to these institutions—pushed by their member states—to enter into the necessary arrangements.

5. The Relationship to Member States

The *raison d'être* for allocating powers to international institutions should be the inability of states acting individually or through traditional diplomatic cooperation to deal with relevant problems. But national constitutional organs are still the primary basis for democratic control.

While the distribution of powers between the national and international level are based on the founding treaties of international organizations entered into between member states, not on a formal constitution, the principles by which such powers are distributed would arguably profit from a constitutional perspective.

There is no doubt that international organizations enjoy law-making powers in relation to member states expressly entrusted by way of a treaty. But, as we have seen, international organizations have also been considered to enjoy 'implied powers'. This principle was confirmed by the ICJ most recently in 1996 in its Advisory Opinion *Legality of the Use by a State of Nuclear Weapons in Armed Conflict*:

The powers conferred on international organizations are normally the subject of an express statement in their constituent instruments. Nevertheless, the necessities of international life may point to the need for organizations, in order to achieve their objectives, to possess subsidiary powers which are not expressly provided for in the basic instruments which govern their activities. It is generally accepted that international organizations can exercise such powers, known as 'implied' powers.[83]

The law of international institutions also derives dynamism from the weight it gives to the practice of organs of these institutions.[84] In the *Namibia* case, the ICJ relied on such practice in accepting that abstention by a permanent member

---

[83] *Legality of the Use by a State of Nuclear Weapons in Armed Conflict* 1996, paragraph 25.
[84] Klabbers, *International Institutional Law*, 2002, at 231.

did not prevent the Security Council from adopting decisions under article 27 (3) of the UN Charter.[85]

But, as has been argued by Jan Klabbers, the doctrine of implied powers lends itself to a very wide interpretation of the powers of international organizations, especially in the form used by the ICJ in the *Reparation* case ('necessary implication as being essential to the performance of its duties').[86] In his view, the activities of international organizations would be better controlled by applying the stricter approach as advanced by the minority in this case, Judge Hackworth, to the effect that 'there had to be an explicit power from which the implied power could, quite literally, be implied. The mere "necessity" of some power was insufficient, if only because necessity as such is a blank cheque'.[87] As we have seen, a more restrictive approach may be discerned in the *Nuclear Weapons* case, where the ICJ restricted the powers of the WHO under reference to the principle of speciality.

The democratic legitimacy of the activities of international organizations lies primarily in the consent of states when ratifying their founding treaties (see pp. 271–272 on the problems related to this issue). The national constitutional organs have accepted the treaty text with its allocation of powers to the organs of the relevant institution. This means that it is the expressly stated powers that should be considered binding on states.[88] Furthermore, the conferral of powers to international organizations is a far more significant step than delegating power to different national organs, the reason being that an international organization is an autonomous entity with limited control from individual member states, and it may be politically difficult to withdraw membership.[89] This also calls for caution in extending the powers of international organizations through interpretation. Requiring consent in the form of express authorization in the constitution of the international organizations or some other form of consent is also consonant with the general requirement of consent in international law as a basis for establishing obligations on states.

The need for express authorization for adopting measures binding on member states corresponds to the principle of legality in democratic states.[90] The principle of legality at the domestic level, as expressed in Article 9 of the ICCPR and Article 5 of the ECHR, is aiming at the protection of individuals against the

---

[85] *Legal Consequences for States of the Continued Presence of South Africa in Namibia (South West Africa) Notwithstanding Security Council Resolution 276 (1970)* (advisory opinion) [1971] ICJ Reports 16 paragraph 22.

[86] *Reparation for Injuries Suffered in the Service of the United Nation* 1949, at 182.

[87] Klabbers, *International Institutional Law*, 2002, at 74.

[88] Amerasinghe, *Principles of the Institutional Law*, 2005, at 163–164 and 172.

[89] Dan Sarooshi distinguishes between three types of conferral of powers: agency relationships, delegations, and transfers, see Dan Sarooshi *International Organizations and their Exercise of Sovereign Powers* (OUP Oxford 2005), at 29.

[90] Finn Seyersted *Common Law of International Organizations* (Martinus Nijhoff Leiden 2008), at 5 and 219.

abuse of state power. In the relationship between international organizations and member states the principle would, however, serve a different function, i.e. the protection of democratic values. The principle of legality (or 'conferred powers') is also reflected in the European Community (Article 5 ECT)—although it has not prevented the ECJ from an extensive interpretation of Community powers.[91]

The principle of subsidiarity is also aiming at the protection of national freedom by leaving decision-making to states, unless it is more effectively or efficiently performed at the international level.[92] Subsidiarity has found explicit expression in the EU (Article 5(2) ECT and Article 1 TEU). Article 7 of the UN Charter prohibiting the intervention 'in matters which are essentially within the domestic jurisdiction of any state' may also be seen as a reflection of the principle of subsidiarity. This principle would call for caution in accepting powers of international organizations without express authorization, but could also restrict powers expressly authorized—to the extent that such powers could be better exercised at the national level.

The need for express authorization should, however, not exclude the application of other elements of treaty interpretation, such as effective interpretation (*effet utile*). The rejection of a liberal application of implied powers should accordingly not be turned into the opposite extreme of denying international organizations the possibility of achieving what is needed and expected from the member states. In this restricted sense, implied powers should continue to be accepted.[93] It should also be more legitimate to apply an extensive interpretation of the text to the extent that decision-making of the international organization is controlled by procedural guarantees. Even subsequent practice of the international organization should be considered relevant in determining international organizations' powers, but caution is advised as regards practice by organs of limited representation, unless such practice has been accepted expressly or tacitly by other member states.

The principle of legality should apply to all binding decisions made by international organizations, but there is reason to argue that binding decisions subject to reservation by states should also be covered, the reason being that such decisions may put considerable pressure upon states. It would be more difficult to argue that soft law decisions without legal effect should be covered, even though such decisions may also entail political pressure on states. While there

---

[91] Trevor C Hartley *The Foundations of European Community Law* (6th edn OUP Oxford 2007), at 104–105.

[92] See Isabel Feichtner 'Subsidiarity' *Max Planck Encyclopedia of Public International Law* 2009 (see <http://www.mpepil.com>); Andreas Føllesdal 'Survey Article: Subsidiarity' (1998) 6 *The Journal of Political Philosophy* 190–218; Paolo G Carozza 'Subsidiarity as a Structural Principle of International Human Rights Law' (2003) 97 *AJIL* 38–79; and Mattias Kumm 'The Legitimacy of International Law: A Constitutionalist Framework of Analysis' (2004) 15 *EPIL* 907–931, at 920–24.

[93] Klabbers, *International Institutional Law*, 2002, at 74 and Seyersted, *Common Law of International Organizations*, 2008, at 243.

should be no reason not to include treaty bodies not formally international organizations from the principle of legality, it would be no basis for claiming that soft law organizations should need to respect the principle of legality.

6. Protection of Human Rights

A salient feature of national constitutions is human rights provisions to protect individuals against abuse of government power. While international organizations, like the UN, may have important functions in protecting and promoting human rights, such activities have been directed towards the states. The international organizations themselves, however, have not been considered to exercise such control over individuals that their activities need to be covered by human rights obligations.

The European Community, with its competence to adopt regulations with direct applicability for individuals, may obviously violate human rights obligations.[94] But, as already discussed, decisions of other international organizations are—although formally directed to states—increasingly aimed at private individuals and organizations.[95] This is the case with smart sanctions, such as travel restrictions on key officials of a targeted state or organization, rather than in effect punishing a whole population by sanctions against a country. Individuals and organizations have also been the real addressees of counter-terrorism measures, for example in the form of freezing of their financial assets. To the extent that the United Nations undertake territorial administration in post-conflict situations, the UN may be directly responsible for the rights and obligations of individuals, such as UNTAET in East Timor and UNMIK in Kosovo. It has even been argued that the control exercised by the UN over refugee camps and over prisons, as part of international criminal prosecution, should be covered by human rights protection.[96]

The increased focus on human rights in a regional and an international context has been described as part of an emerging international constitutional order.[97] But while human rights conventions have been widely ratified by states, international organizations are generally not as such able to become parties to these conventions. There has also been reluctance among certain international organizations and their organs to acknowledge their responsibility in the

---

[94] Hartley, *European Community Law*, 2007, at 97–101 and 133–146.

[95] José E Alvarez *International Organizations as Law-makers* (OUP Oxford 2005), at 245.

[96] Frédéric Mégret and Florian Hoffmann 'The UN as a Human Rights Violator? Some Reflections on the United Nations Changing Human Rights Responsibilities' (2003) 25 *Human Rights Quarterly* 314–342, at 333–340.

[97] Erika de Wet 'The Emergence of International and Regional Value Systems as a Manifestation of the Emerging International Constitutional Order' (2006) 19 *Leiden Journal of International Law* 611–632.

protection of human rights, such as the United Nations' territorial administration in Timor and Kosovo[98] and the UN Counter-Terrorism Committee.[99]

The European Community is, however, an example of how human rights may be integrated through an interaction between the judiciary and political action. The European Court of Justice was forced to embrace human rights through the reluctance of German courts to accept the supremacy of Community law over constitutional human rights protection—unless Community law accepted a comparable protection.[100] This was followed up by the adoption of the Charter of Fundamental Rights of the European Union. Human rights are now included in Article 6 (2) TEU. The Lisbon Treaty—also as adapted after the Ireland referendum rejecting the original treaty—integrates the Charter of Fundamental Rights as part of the treaty framework (Article 6 (1)).

If human rights are not protected in the relevant international organization at the international level, other international organizations and member states may find it necessary to ensure their protection by applying dualistic approaches to the relationship between international and domestic law, such as in the *Kadi* case.[101] The European Court of Justice referred in this case to the fact that measures against Kadi were adopted by the European Community pursuant to Security Council resolutions on counter-terrorism on the freezing of assets of suspected individuals. But the Court found that the measures had been imposed without taking into account fundamental rights as part of EU law with respect to the requirements of fair procedure and protection of property. The relevant regulations were therefore annulled.

This judgment is laudable in the sense that it protects human rights. Furthermore, it applies pressure on the UN Counter-Terrorism Committee to emphasize the protection of human rights.[102] But it has also been pointed out that the judgment may put in doubt the status of international law in European Community law, and provide legitimacy to an *à la carte* approach by other states towards the implementation of international law in their national legal system.[103] The protection of human rights by the relevant international organizations, especially the United Nations, is obviously much to be preferred.[104]

---

[98] Mégret and Hoffmann, The UN as a Human Rights Violator?, 2003, at 336–337.
[99] Flynn, The Security Council's Counter-Terrorism Committee, 2007, at 371; Chesterman, 'I'll Take Manhattan', 2009, at 7.
[100] Hartley, *European Community Law*, 2007, at 133–139.
[101] Cases C-402/05P and C-415/05P, *Kadi and Al Barakaat v Council and Commission*, Judgment of the Court (Grand Chamber) of 3 September 2008.
[102] Flynn, The Security Council's Counter-Terrorism Committee, 2007, at 383–384; Chesterman, 'I'll Take Manhattan', 2009, at 6.
[103] Gráinne de Búrca 'The European Court of Justice and the International Legal Order after *Kadi*' Jean Monnet Working Paper 01/09, NYU School of Law (see <http://www.jeanMonnet-Program.org>).
[104] See Report to the General Assembly by the Special Rapporteur on the promotion and protection of human rights and fundamental freedoms while countering terrorism, Martin Scheinin, 6 August 2008 (A/63/223).

The *Saramati/Behrahmi* case[105] also shows the difficulties that may arise in establishing the respective responsibilities of international organizations and member states, but also between different international organizations, in this case the UN and NATO, and France, Germany, and Norway as contributing military forces in Kosovo. The case concerned injuries as a result of remaining mines (Behrami) and illegal detention (Saramati). The European Court of Human Rights found that the acts were attributable to the UN, not NATO and its member states. Since the UN is not a party to the European Convention, it concluded that the case was inadmissible. This case illustrates that territorial administration by international organizations may well be intended to serve the interests of the people concerned. But individuals of this population may not have formal protection against acts by the international organization comparable to their protection against the territorial sovereignty of a state.

Security Council resolutions may even create doubt about whether human rights have been set aside on the basis of the UN Charter Article 103, establishing that obligations under the Charter prevail over other treaty obligations. This was illustrated by the *Al-Jedda* case[106] on the internment of Al-Jedda in Iraq on the basis of Security Council Resolution 1546 (2004), possibly in violation of relevant human rights and humanitarian law obligations.[107]

In dealing with individuals, international organizations have to respect human rights as embodied in customary international law. It may also be argued that it follows from the UN Charter that the UN shall promote human rights and therefore should also be under an obligation to respect such standards.[108] It is, however, difficult to see why international organizations should not also be able to become parties to human rights conventions, and be subject to their supervisory organs, and possibly regional courts. Article 17 Protocol 14 of the ECHR establishes, for example, that the EU may accede to the Convention. Additional protection could be provided through judicial review of human rights obligations, either based on international customary law obligations or human rights treaties entered into by the international organization (see pp. 64–67 on judicial review, above). Strengthened substantive and procedural human rights guarantees against acts by international organizations would represent a further constitutionalization of international law.[109]

---

[105] Admissibility of application No 71412/01 by Agim Behrami and Bekir Behrami against France and application No 78166/01 by Ruzhdi Saramati against France, Germany and Norway (Grand Chamber Decision).

[106] *R (on the application of Al-Jedda) (FC) v Secretary of State for Defence* [2007] UKHL 58 (see <http://www.publications.parliament.uk/pa/ld200708/ldjudgmt/jd071212/jedda-1.htm>, last visited 18 March 2009).

[107] Alexander Orakhelashvili 'R (on the application of Al-Jedda) (FC) v Secretary of State for Defence' (2008) 102 *AJIL* 337–345

[108] Mégret and Hoffmann, The UN as a Human Rights Violator?, 2003, at 317–318.

[109] See also International Law Association Committee Accountability of International Organisations, Final Report, 2004, at 33.

7. Conclusions

International organizations are increasingly empowered to make decisions affecting states and individuals. Such decisions may only to a limited extent be controlled by national constitutional organs. This calls for a more con-stitutionalized control at the international level.

International decision-making will continue to suffer from a democratic deficit in the foreseeable future. It is important to ensure political control through the plenary organs of international organizations. But decision-making also requires other forms of legitimacy. The constitutional guarantees known from the domestic level need not be copied at the international level. But the considerations may be comparable, such as the balance between political control, executive organs with integrity, and an independent judiciary. Hence, most constitutional guarantees known domestically may be relevant at the interna-tional level, such as the separation of powers, procedural safeguards, and judicial review. As international organizations increasingly exercise power over indivi-duals, they should furthermore be subject to human rights standards, including effective remedies in cases of violations. Soft law organizations and treaty bodies that function like formal international organizations should be brought under constitutional control comparable to international organizations.

The international institutional architecture is fragmented and may result in contradictory, inconsistent, and wasteful governance. A constitutionalization of international law could mean integration and a hierarchic relationship between international institutions. Fundamental institutional changes at the international level are, however, not realistic—and may not even be desirable—in the short term. A more modest approach is to establish arrangements for complementarity and cooperation through agreements between the different international orga-nizations. But the burgeoning of international institutions may make it more difficult to restructure the international institutional architecture in the future.

While the powers conferred on international organizations are essential for the accomplishment of their tasks, it is also important to establish the limits for such powers. The relationship between international organizations and states should be based on the principles of legality and subsidiarity. The principle of legality would ensure that international organizations do not go beyond the powers they have been assigned in a democratic ratification process. The prin-ciple of subsidiarity means that international organizations do not exercise more power than is necessary to achieve the objectives of cooperation.

3

Law-making and Constitutionalism

Jan Klabbers

1. Introduction

In the film *A Few Good Men,* much of the drama revolves around the interplay of different norms. The storyline, in brief, is as follows: two low-ranking marines are court-martialed for having killed a fellow marine while giving him a 'Code Red'. Code Red stands for punishment by one's peers for having violated the battalion's code (the death, in this case, was accidental), and is strictly prohibited according to military law: no private justice shall be meted out. Yet, their victim stood accused of whistle-blowing; hence, the battalion commander, as it transpired, had actually ordered the Code Red. The men thus only followed orders, issued to them by their commanding officer.[1]

What makes the film interesting is its mixture of normative utterances. Military law is unequivocal: the Code Red treatment is prohibited. Yet, in the circumstances, it was also clear that the two men were expected to follow orders, even those which they could have reason to regard as illegal. Earlier incidents had suggested that disobeying orders and exercising personal judgment was not tolerated, and would seriously damage any career prospects. In the midst of all this, the morality aspect remains ambivalent: is it morally justifiable to punish a whistle-blower to maintain discipline and morale in circumstances where national security may be at risk, or where the lives of fellow soldiers may be at stake somewhere down the line?[2]

The example, quaint as it is, highlights two related issues of great relevance. First, it underlines that norms come at people from a variety of directions: there may be legal norms, but also moral norms, norms associated with professional practices, the internal rules of organizations and associations, social mores, etc.[3]

---

[1] The film, directed by Rob Reiner, came out in 1992 and starred Tom Cruise, Demi Moore, and Jack Nicholson.

[2] Tantalizingly, the incident is said to have been set in Guantanamo Bay (pre-9/11), consistently depicted as an outpost in enemy territory.

[3] I will use 'norms' as a generic term, encompassing both legal and non-legal utterances. This is not always the case: some use 'norms' to refer exclusively to non-legal phenomena. An example is Peer Zumbansen 'Law after the Welfare State: Formalism, Functionalism, and the Ironic Turn of Reflexive Law' (2008) 56 *American Journal of Comparative Law* 769–808.

Second, it highlights that those norms may well be in competition with each other. It is by no means self-evident which norms should prevail in which situations. Examples abound: state criminal law interferes, on occasion, with sporting rules.[4] Athletes accused of doping may turn—or threaten to turn—to international human rights law arguing that sports rules are not living up to the requirements of fair trials. So-called honour killings are defended by an appeal to community norms, while morality is sometimes used to justify acts which many hold to be against the law.[5] Churches can invoke their internal rules on promotion and appointments, and escape in this way from having to apply state law on gender equality. And military law may conflict with either a code of military conduct, or with the demands of the battlefield—or both.[6]

Individuals are subjected to many forms of norms and commands throughout their lifetime.[7] In childhood, parents will tell their children to eat their spinach, not to play soccer near breakable windows, and to be home before dark. Elsewhere, individuals will be confronted with rules in their workplaces ('Clock in every morning before nine') and their family relationships ('Take out the garbage'). They may also be subjected to church rules, such as the injunction not to have sex before marriage, or, when having sex, not to use contraceptives. In addition, there are the Ten Commandments, including the one not to covet thy neighbour's wife. There are the rules of grammar and spelling ('Don't split your infinitives'), which differ across languages, and even rules of word-processing: the word-processing program used to write this text, influenced by Christianity no doubt, urges me to capitalize 'Ten Commandments', and specifies that 'christianity' is not an existing word (but 'Christianity' is).[8] When playing games, people are expected to follow the rules of those games, whether it be chess, soccer, or cricket. When going out on the town, men are prohibited from simultaneously wearing socks and sandals. There are customary rules within communities, which may range from respecting one's elders to a duty to avenge possible shame brought on the family. And there are rules of morality, such as the oft-posited duty to save a drowning stranger, give to the poor, and not to milk the welfare system. All those can be used to guide behaviour, and all of those can also be used to assess behaviour.[9]

---

[4] See, e.g., the Dutch Supreme Court (Hoge Raad), case BB7087, decision of 22 April 2008, accepting criminal liability for a foul committed during a professional football match. In paragraph 4.5, the Hoge Raad explained (not without circularity, perhaps) that while in principle football is governed by its own set of rules, criminal law may apply in situations where actions are so dangerous that the absence of criminal liability would be out of the question.

[5] The leading example, no doubt, is the intervention by NATO on behalf of Kosovo.

[6] A brief overview of the issues is Jan Klabbers 'Reflections on Soft International Law in a Privatized World' (2005) 16 *Finnish Yearbook of International Law* 313–328.

[7] The same starting point underlies William Twining *Globalisation and Legal Theory* (Butterworth London 2000).

[8] It also tells me that wordprocessing is not a word, though word-processing is.

[9] On the distinction, see Rosalind Hursthouse *On Virtue Ethics* (OUP Oxford 1999).

None of the above examples would clearly qualify as a legal rule. No matter mum's anger if you left your spinach untouched, you would not go to jail over it. No matter the social disgrace befalling unwed mothers, few people would argue that in having sex before marriage they had broken the law. Even the coarseness of wearing sandals and socks would not result in a criminal record; in fact, it would not even result in a fine. And still, to this day, none of the above would be considered by anyone as being law in any meaningful way.[10]

There are other bodies of rules, though, which come a lot closer to being accepted as law these days: where once the borderline between law and non-law was relatively clear, it has become a lot less clear over the years, and the obfuscation has come from two directions. On the one hand, there are constant attempts to think of norms as law, and even try to get them judicially enforced. Codes of conduct relating to companies, for example, have been subject to litigation,[11] and courts have come to accept agreements between relatives ('I shall give you a car if you don't smoke until the age of 18') as contracts, governed by the law of contracts.[12]

From the other end, there have been attempts to shrink the public sphere often associated with law, and even to de-legalize the legal. Thus, governments have demonstrated considerable enthusiasm for governing by contract: what used to be the preserve of legislation became regulated through contractual undertakings, for example in the field of environmental protection or the construction sector.[13] The widespread use of soft law, often substituting for hard law, suggests a blurring of the line between law and non-law. Already the growth of the welfare state has resulted in a move towards general principles, sometimes leaving considerable discretion to administrators.[14] And in some countries (most, probably), even the political process itself is governed by instruments that are supposed to bind the parties, but are not considered enforceable in any legal way: coalition governments often work on the basis of such 'governing agreements',[15] and

---

[10] Although colloquially they might. The Dutch, e.g., have a saying to the effect that 'Mum lays down the law' ('Moeder's wil is wet').

[11] Thus, Wal-Mart has been sued for failing to living up to labour conditions specified in supplier's agreements, while Nike has been sued over statements it has made relating to its production processes. The latter case reached the US Supreme Court as *Nike v Kasky* (Case No 02–572) but was eventually settled. California's Supreme Court had regarded the statements as false and misleading advertising. See Andrzej Mancewicz 'What's Behind the Window Dressing? Legal Ways of Enforcing Multinational Corporations' Human Rights Codes of Conduct' (unpublished master's dissertation, Helsinki/Venice 2007, on file with the author).

[12] See, e.g., Andrew Kull 'Reconsidering Gratuitous Promises' (1992) 21 *Journal of Legal Studies* 39–65.

[13] See F J van Ommeren en H J de Ru (eds) *Convenanten tussen overheid en maatschappelijke organisaties* (Staatsdrukkerij en –uitgeverij The Hague 1993).

[14] A useful discussion is Roberto M Unger *Law in Modern Society: Toward a Criticism of Social Theory* (Free Press New York 1976).

[15] See, e.g., David Kretzmer 'Political Agreements—A Critical Introduction' (1992) 26 *Israel Law Review* 407–437.

the English constitution is made up, to quite an extent, of constitutional conventions.[16]

In international affairs, the array of possible instruments to be used, and the spectrum of ways in which norms are set, ordered, made, or spontaneously emerge, is enormous as well. The combined effects of globalization and privatization mean that it is no longer clear what exactly constitutes international law, and what does not. Sir Robert Jennings already lamented some three decades ago that it was unclear what international law was, and how could one tell when one saw it[17]—and the situation has not improved in the intervening decades. This chapter, then, is devoted to trying to clarify that situation: in a constitutional world order, one might legitimately expect there to be some rules relating to law-making and, in particular, some concept as to what constitutes valid law within that particular constitutional order. Moreover, in a constitutional order one would expect not just that there be some rules relating to law-making, but it also stands to reason that those rules themselves manifest some of the attributes usually associated with constitutional thought, as outlined in the introductory chapter above. Put negatively, a single rule saying 'Those who carry the biggest sticks can dictate the law' or, briefer, 'Might makes right', is not a rule we would consider appropriate for a constitutional global order. A more positive rendition will be fleshed out throughout this chapter.

I will start (in section 2) by sketching the types of injunctions and commands that play a role in the international system. This will be followed in section 3 by a discussion of recent attempts to theorize international law-making. These attempts have remained, by and large, unsatisfactory, and section 4 will sketch a potentially more promising approach. Section 5 will argue that the distinction between law and non-law remains vital. Subsequently, section 6 will outline a presumptive approach to law. Section 7 will address some outstanding issues, while section 8 concludes.

But before proceeding, two general points ought to be made. First, this chapter does not aim to describe the way international law is currently made. Others have done so recently, and have done so very well; hence, there is no particular need to pay too much attention to description.[18] Instead, this chapter will look at the theory of law-making, and will try to answer some more fundamental questions about the making of international law in a constitutionalizing global system.

This then leads to the second general point: a theory of international law-making should address at least three distinct issues. It should address the

---

[16] For a brief discussion, see Adam Tomkins *Public Law* (Clarendon Press Oxford 2003), at 9–12.

[17] See Sir Robert Jennings 'What is International Law and How Do We Tell it When We See it?' (1981) 37 *Schweizerisches Jahrbuch für Internationales Recht* 59–88.

[18] See, e.g., Alan Boyle and Christine Chinkin *The Making of International Law* (OUP Oxford 2007).

question of the basis of obligation: under what circumstances can international law be said to be binding, and on whom? It should address the question of the various forms international law can possibly take: what are the recognized sources of international law in a constitutional order? And most of all, perhaps, it should address the issue as to how to distinguish between law and non-law. The three issues are intimately related and likely often to be indistinguishable in practice. While in the abstract it might be possible to have a legal order that does not distinguish between law and non-law but would still only recognize an exhaustive account of sources, in practice such is extremely unlikely to happen.

In what follows, most attention will be paid to the distinction between law and non-law, for this is, so to speak, the threshold issue: once a system accepts that law can be distinct from non-law, it can start to think about how exactly law can come into being (the basis of obligation) and what forms it can possibly take (the sources issues). Importantly, though, it does not work the other way around: one cannot look at recognized sources and hope to find out how to distinguish law from non-law that way. Moreover, if the system is to be deserving of the label 'constitutional', the distinction between law and non-law is of great relevance, because in such a system law is supposed to substitute for power—to a greater degree than in systems that cannot properly be called constitutional. And it is precisely to distinguish law from power that the threshold question assumes prominence. As a result, much of this chapter undeniably has a theoretical, perhaps somewhat rarefied, flavour; it could hardly have been otherwise.

2. An Infinite Variety[19]

When it comes to law-making, international law faces at least three profound systemic challenges. The first of those relates to the circle of law-makers. It would seem obvious that law-making by states alone has lost some of its legitimacy. As Delbrück poignantly puts it, 'the monopoly of the state as a political actor in the international system has been entirely broken'.[20] Other actors, in particular perhaps international organizations and non-governmental organizations (NGOs), have come to the fore, and have made strong claims to be included in the process of producing normative output. To this may be added the normative output of more or less formal networks of civil servants, or industry representatives. The increased relevance of privatization, moreover, adds yet another dimension here: what to make of the results of the activities,

---

[19] An early comment on the various forms international law can take is Richard R Baxter 'International Law in "Her Infinite Variety"' (1980) 29 *ICLQ* 549–566.

[20] See Jost Delbrück 'Prospects for a "World (Internal) Law?": Legal Developments in a Changing International System' (2002) 9 *Indiana Journal of Global Legal Studies* 401–431, at 410.

spontaneous or organized, of private actors? How, for example, to treat codes of conduct drawn up by companies or industry associations? How to characterize the usages that emerge among people working in the same area of activity: the architects and builders creating their *lex constructionis*, the engineers and computer users creating their *lex informatica*, or the merchants and their *lex mercatoria*? These, after all, as Teubner so elegantly put it, break a 'double taboo': they emerge without state involvement, and they emerge without the blessing of a validity criterion, or so it seems.[21]

Second, the law should somehow come to terms with the activities of actors with recognized law-making capacities who nonetheless may not always use those capacities. In other words, many acts of states take on forms that may not immediately fit into the recognized categories of international law. Instead of treaties, soft law may be created; instead of legally binding rules, states may sometimes, so it seems, agree on norms that are not legally binding but bind under other normative orders. Thus, it has become common to speak of politically binding agreements, or morally binding agreements. This raises deep questions, though, about the limits and possibilities of law: is it really possible to choose between alternative normative orders? Whatever the answer, it is clear that this sort of activity challenges international law, as the aim, often enough, is to withdraw from the law altogether, on the thought that law stands for rigidity and the absence of flexibility.[22]

And third, there is the vexed question of consent. International law is often said to be based on the consent of states. Yet, it is at least arguable that for some situations, this creates unacceptable vetoes. Surely, to stay on the hypothetical level, one cannot give a veritable veto when it comes to topics such as climate change. Likewise, many might find it unpalatable to claim that genocidaires can only be prosecuted if they happen to be nationals of a state consenting to rules outlawing genocide. Such ways of thought, however traditional and however they play with themes of democratic accountability,[23] leave something to be desired.

It is conventional to start discussions on law-making in the international community by referring to Article 38, paragraph 1, of the Statute of the International Court of Justice (ICJ). As is well known, this recognizes as sources of international law mostly treaties and customary international law. It also

---

[21] See Gunther Teubner ' "Global Bukowina": Legal Pluralism in the World Society' in Gunther Teubner (ed) *Global Law Without a State* (Ashgate Aldershot 1997) 3–28, at 10–11.

[22] Taking this a step further, this can be viewed as an example of turning international law into something of mere instrumental value, to be used only when no preferable alternatives exist. For a critique, see Jan Klabbers 'The Commodification of International Law' (2006) 1 *Select Proceedings of the European Society of International Law* 341–358.

[23] If at all, such a position can only be justified by pointing out that democracies need not tolerate international norms unless they have consented to them. Such a strand is visible in some of the US-based literature in particular. An example is Jed Rubenfeld 'Unilateralism and Constitutionalism' (2004) 79 *New York University Law Review* 1971–2028.

mentions general principles of law, and, albeit as subsidiary means, pays deference to judicial decisions and the writings of the most highly qualified publicists of all nations. These, then, are, and have been for a long time, the generally accepted sources of international law.

This is still a useful starting point, but not much more than that, for it leaves two important topics unaddressed.[24] For one thing, this sources catalogue is unclear as to its precise scope: it does not specify whether the list is exhaustive, or whether other sources of international law exist—or can exist. Still, on this point the literature is near-unanimous: there are no good grounds to suppose that the list is exhaustive, and practice would indeed suggest that other types of sources of law can and do exist.[25] Thus, the ICJ has recognized the binding force of a certain kind of unilateral declaration[26] in *Nuclear Tests*,[27] and confirmed as much in the *Frontier Dispute* case.[28] That same court has given its stamp of approval to decision-making practices within an international organization in the 1971 *Namibia* case,[29] and accepted the binding force of decisions of international organizations in other cases, including the (ultimately undecided) *Lockerbie* case.[30]

Yet with all these instruments, there is always some uncertainty as to whether they really constitute additional sources of international law, or whether they should not be somehow captured by the list of Article 38. The practice of decision-making within the Security Council, approved in *Namibia*, is sometimes seen as a new rule of customary international law, replacing the earlier written rule of Article 27, paragraph 3 of the Charter. Such a re-conceptualization is not entirely plausible, perhaps, as the practice is, in effect, only the practice of a handful of states—hardly general practice. But still, it is not entirely implausible either: the practice would seem to have been generally accepted as law and, mindful of the *North Sea Continental Shelf* dictum,[31] the practice is that

---

[24] And arguably a third as well, as it does not distinguish between sources of law and sources of obligation. For a discussion, see Sir Gerald Fitzmaurice 'Some Problems Regarding the Formal Sources of International Law' in F M van Asbeck *et al* (eds) *Symbolae Verzijl* (Martinus Nijhoff The Hague 1958) 153–176.

[25] But see Danilenko, arguing that the list is best seen as exhaustive in practice, even if textually it could be read as open-ended. See Gennadij Michajlovič Danilenko *Law-making in the International Community* (Martinus Nijhoff Dordrecht 1993), at 30–44.

[26] This refers to the kind that can be seen as promises, not to declarations which aim to state facts, express outrage, or aspire to create a new legal situation. A declaration of independence might fall into that category. Still the leading study is Eric Suy *Les actes juridiques unilatéraux en droit international public* (Pédone Paris 1962).

[27] See *Nuclear Tests* case (Australia v France) [1974] ICJ Reports 253.

[28] See *Case Concerning the Frontier Dispute* (Burkina Faso v Mali) [1986] ICJ Reports 554.

[29] See *Legal Consequences for States of the Continued Presence of South Africa in Namibia (South West Africa) Notwithstanding Security Council Resolution 276 (1970)* (advisory opinion) [1971] ICJ Reports 16.

[30] See *Case Concerning Questions of Interpretation and Application of the 1971 Montreal Convention arising from the Aerial Incident at Lockerbie* (Libya v UK), order [1992] ICJ Reports 3.

[31] See *North Sea Continental Shelf* cases (Federal Republic of Germany v Denmark; Federal Republic of Germany v The Netherlands) [1969] ICJ Reports 3.

of the states whose interests are most affected, i.e. the five permanent members of the Security Council (if the practice of an organ can be reduced to the practice of states composing that organ).[32] The point, then, is that it is not immediately obvious what the better view is: both arguments are plausible within their own four corners.

Likewise, the binding force of unilateral declarations may be constructed as a form of treaty. The ICJ has done so explicitly when it comes to declarations accepting its compulsory jurisdiction,[33] but also *Nuclear Tests* can be read as the interplay of offer and acceptance, with the Court underlining the importance both of the intention to be bound on the part of the offeror, and the reliance— or potential reliance—on the offer by the offeree.[34] In both cases, however, there is some element of stretching involved in categorizing unilateral declarations and decision-making practices within international organizations within the accepted sources catalogue of Article 38 ICJ. And things are more awkward still with respect to decisions of international organizations: while, for instance, Security Council decisions derive their binding force from Article 25 UN, one cannot meaningfully say that such a resolution is itself, in one way or another, a treaty or convention in force. While such reasoning may possibly apply to decisions taken by plenary organs by unanimity (as suggested by the Permanent Court of International Justice (PCIJ) in *Railway Traffic*[35]), surely it cannot explain the binding force of resolutions taken by non-plenary organs.

If one issue with Article 38 ICJ is that it is not clear how other possible sources fit in, the second issue is that Article 38 does not provide anything beyond a most rudimentary definition. It is one thing to suggest that treaties or customary international law may be applied by the ICJ, but what exactly is a treaty? What exactly is customary international law? This has given rise to a voluminous literature on both topics: one could fill quite a few bookshelves just with all the writings on what constitutes customary international law, and while the question of what constitutes a treaty has received somewhat less attention, writings on this, too, are fairly numerous. Much of this takes the form of writings on the legal status of General Assembly resolutions or soft law; much of this takes the form of discussions on informal agreements or Memoranda of Understanding. In short, Article 38 provides a useful point of departure, but does not do much more. And arguably, it was never meant to do much more to begin with: it is no coincidence that it is drafted as, merely, a clause listing the

---

[32] On this, see Jan Klabbers 'International Organizations in the Formation of Customary International Law' in Enzo Cannizzaro and Paolo Palchetti (eds) *Customary International Law on the Use of Force* (Martinus Nijhoff Leiden 2005) 179–195.

[33] See *Case Concerning Military and Paramilitary Activities In and Against Nicaragua* (Nicaragua v USA), jurisdiction and admissibility [1984] ICJ Reports 392.

[34] It is instructive to read paragraphs 43 and 46 of *Nuclear Tests* in one sitting.

[35] See *Railway Traffic between Lithuania and Poland (Railway Sector Landwarów-Kaisiadorys)* [1931] Publ. PCIJ, Series A/B, No 42.

somehow thought to be intended not to give rise to legal rights and obligations. A prime example of this is the 1975 Helsinki Final Act, embodying the most important agreement between East and West during the Cold War but somehow, it is often suggested, devoid of legal force.[41] The Final Act contains a clause that it shall not be registered with the UN, which is often taken as a clear indication of an intention on the part of the drafters not to be legally bound. That said, it was clear since 1975 that transgressions would not be taken lightly: clearly, Europe after 1975 was expected to be a different place than Europe before 1975, so something was supposed to happen upon the signing of the Helsinki Final Act. It's just, so the argument goes, that this 'something' had little to do with law; by contrast, the Final Act is often said to give rise to political commitments, or maybe moral commitments.

The reference to moral agreements taps into a long-standing tradition in international law: the existence of gentlemen's agreements which, so the argument goes, bind the individual gentlemen concluding them, but do not bind their states.[42] It has long been accepted that such a category may exist, but typically, in its initial conception in the late 19th and early 20th century, it was also thought to be of extremely limited scope, covering, for instance, agreements between Foreign Ministers on territorial issues, or establishing a framework for cooperation (the Entente Cordiale between Britain and France comes to mind), but not much more, and always on the basis of the thought that somehow, the responsible individuals would not be able to muster domestic political support.

Likewise problematic but, initially, kept small was the possibility of concluding agreements not involving Foreign Offices, so-called administrative agreements. This sparked some interest in the 1920s,[43] quickly leading to the conclusion, though, that these were best seen as binding commitments on the states concerned rather than resting upon the individual agencies actually involved in their conclusion.

A host of other instruments prove to be far more problematic these days. How, for instance, should one look at the Global Compact, an initiative coming from the UN Secretary-General allowing companies to declare that they shall support and respect human rights, labour standards, and environmental principles on a voluntary basis, with the stated aim not so much of laying down rules concerning behaviour per se, but rather to engage companies in learning and

---

[41] See, e.g., Harold Russell 'The Helsinki Declaration: Brobdingnag or Lilliput?' (1976) 70 *AJIL* 242–272. Incidentally, Russell, member of the US delegation at Helsinki, expresses some doubts whether there can be such a thing as non-legally binding agreements to begin with.

[42] A useful discussion is Pierre-Michel Eisemann 'Le gentlemen's agreement comme source de droit international' (1979) 106 *Journal du Droit International* 326–348.

[43] See Ludwig Bittner *Die Lehre von den völkerrechtlichen Vertragsurkunden* (Deutsche Verlags-Anstalt Stuttgart 1924); Jules Basdevant 'La conclusion et la rédaction des traités et des instruments diplomatiques autres que les traités' (1926/V) 15 *Recueil des Cours* 539–643.

sort of things that the ICJ may apply—but it was never inte
constitutional provision on law-making in the global commun

The result of this is that there is uncertainty as to what con
tional law, and how to distinguish international law from
uncertainty has been used to great effect in recent decades by the
the idea of soft law, located somewhere in the space created p
uncertainty and useful, most of all, as a tool for diplomats and p
After all, soft law allows for regulation but without any of the gu
ciated with formal law-making: think of democracy, think of a
think even of legal certainty.[38]

Problems in locating the boundary between law and non-law can
variety of elements, or factors. Doubts may be cast on the legal qua
by virtue of their hortatory language. Sometimes the intention of
regarded as decisive, or at least as a relevant consideration. Someti
legal status of those responsible for normative utterances that is
doubtful: can entities that have no recognized law-making capacity
make law?

Possibly the least problematic cases are treaties, duly signed and
duly authorized national authorities and containing deontic language
this core of legal certainty unravels rather rapidly. One often cited ex
instance, is Part IV of GATT 1947: this part, added in the mid-196
instigation of the less developed countries, contains predominantly
terms in an otherwise binding instrument. An obligation under whic
'shall to the fullest extent possible—that is, except when compelling
which may include legal reasons, make it impossible—. . . accord high
to reducing barriers to market access,[39] is not a very strong obligation,
is said and done. While not meaningless, it is not terribly compelling eitl
indeterminate enough to create uncertainty as to the boundary between
non-law.[40]

If the legal force of GATT's Part IV was subject to some debate, thi
decidedly much more problematic still when instruments are cast in deont
obligatory) language and are duly signed by duly authorized persons, b

---

[36] For a useful overview of the drafting, see Alain Pellet 'Article 38' in Andreas Zimmerman
(eds) *The Statute of the International Court of Justice: A Commentary* (OUP Oxford 2006) 677

[37] Seminal pieces include Christine Chinkin 'The Challenge of Soft Law: Developmen
Change in International Law' (1989) 38 *ICLQ* 850–866, and Tadeusz Gruchalla-Wesiersl
Framework for Understanding "Soft Law"' (1984) 30 *McGill Law Journal* 37–88.

[38] See generally Jan Klabbers 'The Redundancy of Soft Law' (1996) 65 *Nordic Journa
International Law* 167–182.   [39] Art XXXVII, paragraph 1 GA

[40] Indeed, GATT's legal existence generally constituted an intricate play with the bor
between law and non-law: its binding force depended, for close to half a century, on a protoco
provisional application, while its status as an international organization was complicated, in
early years, by the absence of any organs. A fine overview is Bernard Hoekman and Michel Koste
The Political Economy of the World Trade Organization: From GATT to WTO (OUP Oxford 199

dialogue? This is a far cry from traditional forms of regulation, yet is clearly meant to have effects which are indistinguishable from legal effects.[44]

Arguably, the Global Compact has precursors in the forms of earlier codes of conduct for multinational companies, set up by a variety of organizations as sometimes specific, relating to a single issue, or sometimes more generic. An example of the former are the Sullivan principles, designed primarily to dissuade companies from investing in South Africa in the days of apartheid, and the McBride principles, addressing the situation in Northern Ireland. Examples of the latter include the United Nations Conference on Trade and Development (UNCTAD)'s restrictive business practices code, cast in hortatory language and rarely considered to have been a great success, and principles emanating from the Organization for Economic Cooperation and Development (OECD). These OECD principles at least seem to have met with some practical success, having been resorted to in negotiations between companies and employees and having formed the basis of decent compromise.[45]

Likewise, it is by no means clear how banking regulation operates, or even whether it can be said to exist at all in a meaningful way. The current system is an intricate mixture of formal and informal standards set by formal and informal bodies. The formal bodies include the OECD, the International Monetary Fund (IMF), and the World Bank, while the Bank for International Settlements (BIS) hosts some additional standard-setters.[46] But at the same time, banking regulation owes something to the G7, arguably the most high-profile gathering of a select group of states, and to less visible bodies such as the Financial Action Task Force,[47] the Basel Committee, or the Committee on Payments and Settlements Systems, a committee operating under BIS auspices. In addition, some influence is exercised through standard-setting activities by bodies such as the International Forum of Independent Auditor Regulators and the International Organization of Securities Commissions.[48]

---

[44] Its website explains that the Global Compact is 'designed to stimulate change and to promote good corporate citizenship', and participating companies are expected to report on their progress in connection with the principles laid down in the Global Compact. While words such as 'compliance' are studiously avoided, the website does speak of 'integrity measures': see http://www. unglobalcompact.org (last visited 6 February) 2009). A useful early study is Viljam Engström *Realizing the Global Compact* (Erik Castrén Institute Helsinki 2002).

[45] The story is well-told in Ignaz Seidl-Hohenveldern 'International Economic "Soft Law" ' (1979/II) 163 *Recueil des Cours* 165–246.

[46] The latter has always been regarded as a curiosity, in that, as a public organization, it none-theless had private shareholders. A buy-out of those private shareholders resulted in arbitration under the auspices of the Permanent Court of Arbitration, with the arbiters holding that the BIS is best seen as an intergovernmental organization. See *Reineccius et al v Bank for International Settlements*, Partial award, 22–11–2002, at <http://www.pca-cpa.org> (last visited 20 January 2009).

[47] See generally Marie Wilke 'Emerging Informal Network Structures in Global Governance: Inside the Anti-Money Laundering Regime' (2008) 77 *Nordic Journal of International Law* 509–531.

[48] Very useful is Howard Davies and David Green *Global Financial Regulation: The Essential Guide* (Polity Cambridge 2008).

By the same token, environmental protection is something that ought to be achieved through a variety of instruments and approaches. The Rio Conference of 1992 saw the adoption not only of regular treaties, but also of a Declaration on Environment and Development, and a Statement of Principles on forest issues, not to mention scores of other instruments. At the same time, bits and pieces of environmental protection are emanating from (or under the auspices of) the International Maritime Organization, the United Nations Economic, Social and Cultural Organization (UNESCO), the International Atomic Energy Agency (IAEA), and the UN's Economic Commission for Europe, while an important role is also played by the non-governmental organizations such as the World Conservation Union (formerly the IUCN).

Similar pictures emerge with respect to well-nigh all issue areas. The human rights regime is a patchwork of norms: binding conventions and case law, non-binding recommendations, declarations and general comments, interlaced with reservations, interpretative declarations, and even the odd non-self-executing declaration. The security regime relies on the work of several important international organizations (such as the IAEA), again often cast in both binding rules and recommendations. Product safety owes something to the World Trade Organization (WTO), but also to the standards set by bodies such as the Codex Alimentarius and a hybrid such as the International Organization for Standardization (ISO).

Even the field of education is no longer free from international influences. In Europe, the so-called Bologna Process aims to achieve the creation of a European Higher Education Area by means of voluntary harmonization of the duration of studies and translatability of degrees. And the most remarkable phenomenon to date is perhaps the PISA programme run by the OECD. This Programme for International Student Assessment aims to measure the quality of students in a number of states, in order to allow those states to become more competitive. Still, the interesting thing is that PISA aims to do so merely by measuring and ranking: it does not set standards or offer recommendations, much less set binding norms. And still, the potential influence that PISA exercises is huge: anecdotal evidence suggests that schools, educators, and ministries of education take PISA very seriously indeed. Clearly, then, PISA exercises some form of public authority, in much the same way as law does, albeit in unorthodox form; but less clear is how lawyers should approach such exercises of public authority.[49]

Noteworthy is also the possibility of the extraterritorial application of domestic law. Popular when it comes to fighting the operation of trusts and cartels, this entails that state A declares that its laws are also applicable to the behaviour of its citizens or companies abroad, or even to others acting abroad in

---

[49] See Armin von Bogdandy and Matthias Goldmann 'The Exercise of Public Authority Through National Policy Assessment' (2008) 5 *International Organizations Law Review* 241–298.

such a manner as to affect state A. This may create all sorts of practical problems for individuals: bank officers working for US banks may be under subpoena to produce bank records in the US which might simultaneously violate Swiss banking secrecy laws.[50]

Finally, private law, too, is not immune to the pressures of globalization. Many have observed that attempts are made to recast private law, and come to, for example, a European Contract Code, or even to rules that would apply worldwide. While the driving forces here may be academics, nonetheless it would be silly to dismiss their work as legally irrelevant. Tort law is sometimes being used for public purposes across boundaries, in particular to start human rights litigations for violations committed by foreigners abroad.[51] The emergence of the Internet has not only meant that some 'organizational' issues needed regulation (think of the distribution of domain names), but also that the law somehow has to come to terms with activities taking place in cyberspace, be it public activities (exercising free speech), or be it private activities such as the sale of goods or the organization of auctions.[52]

All this means that a constitutionalist perspective on the making of international law must meet a number of difficult challenges simultaneously. More and more 'fields' or 'issue areas' have become internationalized; an increasing number of actors (and an increasing diversity in the kind of actors, it is no longer only about states) can legitimately claim to have an interest in the making of international law; and the techniques that have been created to set standards and regulate at the international level have become highly varied as well, ranging from recognizably legal instruments to soft law documents, and from top-down commands to amorphous non-deontic exercises of public authority.[53]

3. Recent Theorizing

Recent attempts at theorizing about the sources of (international) law in a global world stem, roughly, from two directions. On the one hand, international lawyers have picked up the gauntlet, and have started to discuss how sources

---

[50] The example is gratefully borrowed from David J Bederman 'Diversity and Permeability in Transnational Governance' (2007) 57 *Emory Law Journal* 201–231, at 223.

[51] The seminal work is Craig Scott (ed) *Torture as Tort: Comparative Perspectives on the Development of Transnational Human Rights Litigation* (Hart Oxford 2001).

[52] See generally Tapio Puurunen *Dispute Resolution in International Electronic Commerce* (doctoral dissertation, University of Helsinki 2005).

[53] Weiler distinguishes three broad categories: transactional law, regulatory law, and the law of the community (roughly corresponding to traditional international law, administrative law, and constitutional law, respectively) and suggests that, much as in geology, the three layers stratify: they exist and continue to exist alongside each other. See Joseph H H Weiler 'The Geology of International Law—Governance, Democracy and Legitimacy' (2004) 64 *Zeitschrift für ausländisches öffentliches Recht und Völkerrecht* 547–562.

doctrine somehow needs to be reconfigured so as to do away with the bewildering variety of instruments mentioned above and to do justice to the role of actors other than states. While typically these authors resort to social sciences in their quest for explanations and theory, they have been remarkably reluctant about consulting the work of legal theorists. On the other hand, legal theorists have gone about analyzing new legal phenomena, including self-regulation and spontaneous law, but without necessarily paying much attention to international law or the insights of international lawyers. For many, their intellectual struggles are aimed first and foremost at trying to come to terms with the changing role of the state.[54]

Legal theorists aiming to come to terms with globalization and a multitude of normative instruments tend to look for inspiration in the work of legal pluralists (or, indeed, are themselves leading exponents of legal pluralism).[55] While in earlier years legal pluralism stood for the co-existence of several forms of law—state law, customary law—within the same time-space constellation, and was often geared to describing the relationship between those various forms,[56] more recently legal pluralists have come to celebrate a wide diversity of normative exhortations without trying to capture them in a single model. Indeed, some go so far as to see the divide between law and non-law as disappearing completely—or as irrelevant.

A prominent example is the work of Boaventura de Sousa Santos, a leading legal sociologist and heralded by many as the main representative of post-modern thinking about global law.[57] For Santos, law can come in a variety of settings: in the state, obviously, but also, for example, at work or in local communities. As a result, he has no qualms about describing internal factory rules or local social customs as 'law'. Instead, then, of looking for a criterion to distinguish law from non-law, he is far more interested in probing how norms interact. To Santos, all law is characterized by the complex interplay between rhetoric, bureaucracy, and violence; legal orders where there is little bureaucracy typically depend a lot on rhetoric, whereas those where bureaucracy has taken off and a monopoly on violence established, have less room for rhetoric.[58] State law is one manifestation, characterized by a monopoly on violence and usually a high degree of bureaucratization; traditional international law, by contrast, would score high on the rhetoric element, but less on bureaucracy, and much the

---

[54] A useful overview is Simon Roberts 'After Government? On Representing Law Without the State' (2005) 68 *Modern Law Review* 1–24.

[55] Many legal theorists are more concerned about studying the properties of individual rules. This may well result in brilliant and insightful work, but is of less immediate relevance for our concerns. Hence, the theorists discussed here all have done some work on globalization, however defined.

[56] See, e.g., Sally Falk Moore 'Law and Social Change: The Semi-autonomous Social Field as an Appropriate Subject of Study' (1973) 7 *Law and Society Review* 719–746.

[57] See Boaventura de Sousa Santos *Toward a New Legal Common Sense* (2nd edn Butterworths London 2002). [58] *Ibid*, at 86–88.

same would apply to such legal orders as the mafia (for Santos would not hesitate to qualify mafia rule as 'law'). In the end, the question why non-state law should be characterized as 'law' is met with a shrug of the shoulders and a laconic 'why not?' Comparing law to art or medicine, Santos disputes that there can only be one true specimen, and suggests that attempts to define law in a restrictive sense display a 'politics of definition'.[59]

Much the same applies to Gavin Anderson, who in a recent work devoted to rights after globalization starts from the premise that the 'primary reference point' in explaining law in a globalized era is no longer the nation state, but rather the global economy.[60] As a result, Anderson dismisses traditional state-centric ideas about law, and presents a wide array of sources of legal pluralism, including 'laws made in the family, in the workplace, in indigenous societies, among neighbours'.[61] It turns out that even fundamental rights—the pinnacle of liberal ideology—cannot be guaranteed by state authorities alone without taking other law-producing sites into account. For instance, the right to have an abortion is meaningless if hospitals are unwilling to engage in such procedures,[62] and freedom of expression cannot alleviate internal censorship.[63] Like Santos, in the end Anderson finds that the question 'what is law?' is a political or ideological issue, and dismisses the search for a criterion to distinguish law from non-law as being symptomatic of 'liberal legalism'.[64]

Less insistent on ideological factors—and less keen on identifying them—is William Twining. For him, the definition of what law is, is perhaps best seen as contextual, depending on the purpose of one's activities: for the scholar working in, say, banking law, the question whether Basel Committee guidelines constitute 'law' is less relevant than for the judge asked to apply them. Indeed, he makes the point that lawyers engaged in academic legal disciplines tend to ignore such niceties altogether, and tend to concentrate on what for them are the relevant 'forms of normative and legal ordering'—regardless of whether these formally qualify as law or as non-law.[65]

Where legal theorists by and large seek to come to terms with globalization by adopting and re-thinking legal pluralism, international lawyers have sought refuge in adopting a different perspective: that of the social sciences. This comes in three different forms. First (and not, admittedly, terribly interested in the connections between law-making and globalization per se), some have adopted a

---

[59] *Ibid*, at 91. Berman is by and large in agreement: '... the whole debate about law versus non-law is largely irrelevant in a pluralism context because the key questions involve the normative commitments of a community and the interactions among normative orders that give rise to such commitments, not their formal status.' See Paul Schiff Berman 'Global Legal Pluralism' (2007) 80 *Southern California Law Review* 1155–1238, at 1177.

[60] See Gavin Anderson *Constitutional Rights after Globalization* (Hart Oxford 2005), at 11.

[61] *Ibid*, at 12.   [62] *Ibid*, at 88–89.   [63] *Ibid*, at 94–95.

[64] *Ibid*, at 103, and 40–44, respectively.

[65] See William Twining 'Implications of "Globalisation" for Law as a Discipline' (unpublished paper, on file with the author), esp at 10.

rational choice approach, suggesting that law is based on the interests of states and states, in turn, are rational actors seeking to act so as to maximize their own benefits; those interests, moreover, can be identified on the basis of what states actually do.[66] As a result, the role of law is seriously limited or, at a minimum, becomes difficult to verify: if states only act in accordance with their own interests, then it is difficult to say whether behaviour in accordance with a treaty rule is actually the result of that rule, or whether it would also have taken place in the absence of this rule.

A second approach also zooms in on the behaviour of states, but does so in a much more subtle and engaging way. Alvarez, in his monumental study of international organizations as law-makers, launches the proposition that the normative output of international organizations may well turn out to be 'law', once this output demonstrates having 'normative ripples'.[67] In other words: a resolution adopted by an international organ, if followed by practice in accordance with its terms, may well be classified as law. If practice remains absent, then in all likelihood the resolution can not be considered as law.[68] By the same logic, even decisions on internal matters may radiate externally: a decision of a plenary body, say, to withhold funding may be cast as an internal decision, but will have external effects. Thus, international organizations cannot be said to have only binding powers when it comes to their own internal matters.

A third approach, also having notable social science overtones, is that pioneered by Anne-Marie Slaughter.[69] In an important study, she makes the trenchant observation that much regulatory activity takes place below the level of formal cooperation: in networks of domestic civil servants, transnational dialogues of judges or parliamentarians, or through more or less spontaneous networks, often composed of experts rather than politicians. While she does not confront the question whether the output of such networks constitutes law head-on, she does seem to work on that presumption, treating it as normatively relevant and as 'both a feasible and a desirable response to the globalization paradox'.[70] Indeed, the final chapters of her book include lengthy discussions of issues typically associated with law-making, such as political representation and accountability.

Finally, among recent studies Alan Boyle and Christine Chinkin concentrate more on the role of NGOs and other actors than on the formalities of law-making. For them, it is a foregone conclusion that somehow international law-making can no longer satisfactorily be explained by a state-centric approach. Yet, unlike Alvarez and to some extent Slaughter, they do not offer much by way

---

[66] See Jack L Goldsmith and Eric A Posner *The Limits of International Law* (OUP Oxford 2005).
[67] See José E Alvarez *International Organizations as Law-makers* (OUP Oxford 2005).
[68] *Ibid*, e.g. at 261. Note however that Alvarez also acknowledges that much of the output of organizations can be shoehorned into the categories of Art 38 ICJ: *ibid*, e.g. at 237.
[69] See Anne-Marie Slaughter *A New World Order* (Princeton UP 2004).   [70] *Ibid*, at 17.

of replacement. They advocate recognition of the increased role of non-state actors in global law-making, but hesitate to define law in any conclusive manner, and, indeed, hesitate to posit a theory of the sources of international law.[71]

Where the legal theorists tend to be quick to give up the distinction between law and non-law as somehow being ideological (Santos, Anderson) or, at any rate, not terribly relevant for most practical purposes (Twining), the international lawyers are too keen to reduce law to a sub-branch of the social sciences—which leads to the same result: the distinction between law and non-law becomes very porous. Moreover, this inexorably leads to ignoring the distinction between prescriptive and descriptive rules; it leads to ignoring the distinction between the statement 'thou shalt not kill' and the statement 'as a rule, it snows in February'.[72] Goldsmith and Posner's approach has as a serious consequence the creation of an extremely stultified world, comprising two actors (both of them states) and not much more. They do not address the normative output of international organizations, or the possible contribution to law-making by non-state actors because, for them, such actors do not exist: there is no room for such actors in their rational choice model.[73] While their approach is miles apart from the more subtle and more informed work of Alvarez, it shares with the latter a problematic behaviouralism: both seem to presume that the existence of legal rules can be identified by looking at the behaviour of states. Slaughter and Boyle and Chinkin, by contrast, do not offer much by way of explicit opinion on legality. Both are sensitive to untraditional ways of standard-setting and the role of actors other than states, but are also reluctant to treat the distinction between law and non-law as relevant.

Alternative approaches, while disavowing the behaviouralist perspective, present much the same picture. Brunnée and Toope, for example, have pioneered an 'interactional' theory of international law which builds on the jurisprudential work of Lon Fuller and suggests that 'there is no radical discontinuity between law and non-law'.[74] Indeed, elsewhere they write that 'a search for a single, ultimate basis of obligation is unlikely to elucidate the binding force of law'.[75] Whether this should literally be taken to mean that the binding force of

---

[71] See generally Boyle and Chinkin, *The Making of International Law*, 2007.

[72] See generally Frederick Schauer *Playing by the Rules: A Philosophical Examination of Rule-Based Decision-Making in Law and in Life* (Clarendon Press Oxford 1991).

[73] This is less a problem of rational choice theory as such than a problem of their particular approach: an example of a far more nuanced picture is the one sketched by Ian Hurd, combining rational choice theory with constructivism and suggesting that state interests are influenced also by the existence and work of international organizations. See Ian Hurd *After Anarchy: Legitimacy and Power in the United Nations Security Council* (Princeton UP 2007).

[74] See Jutta Brunnée and Stephen J Toope 'International Law and Constructivism: Elements of an Interactional Theory of International Law' (2000–1) 39 *Columbia Journal of Transnational Law* 19–74.

[75] See Jutta Brunnée and Stephen J Toope 'Persuasion and Enforcement: Explaining Compliance with International Law' (2002) 13 *Finnish Yearbook of International Law* 273–295, at 289.

international law is independent of, or cannot be illuminated by, a theory of obligation, or whether it means that such a theory will have little practical relevance, is uncertain, but it does signify a fluid concept of law.

The picture that emerges, then, both from the work of legal theorists and from the work of international lawyers, is that the distinction between law and non-law has lost much of its relevance. A synthesis of the approaches adopted above, however different in their own right they may be, would probably read something like this: in today's globalized world, what matters is whether and how the subjects of norms, rules, and standards come to accept those norms, rules, and standards. If they treat them as authoritative, then those norms can be treated as such and perhaps, if they ought to be given a name, designated as 'law'. If, however (so the argument continues), the subjects and addressees of normative utterances do not take those norms, rules, and standards very seriously, then the label 'law' would seem to be out of place, or inappropriate. Either way, the label as such would hardly make a difference; instead, norms will be judged on the basis of whether or not they are complied with. Norms, rules, and standards would seem to derive their 'compliance pull', if any, from other considerations: from legitimacy, or effectiveness, or utility, or perhaps from still other considerations.

Yet, such a stand is not unproblematic. In particular when effectiveness or utility are placed on a pedestal, the legal nature of a rule would only appear at some point in the future. Thus, while the rule (i.e. prescription) might guide behaviour on a voluntary basis, it would not contribute to legal certainty: the law's subjects would not know for sure whether they would have to comply with the rule, or whether they would be at liberty to ignore it, circumvent it, reinterpret it in their own fashion, or set it aside. In a domestic setting, such would be unacceptable: it would be deemed to fall short of abidance with the rule of law, for the rule of law, most agree, demands that the subjects of a legal order know what behaviour is expected from them; or at least it demands that subjects are in a position to know what is expected from them. It is from this that the injunction against retroactive legislation springs; and to have citizens be able to arrange their own life also presupposes a relatively stable and clear legal framework, which spells out what the consequences are if one enters into contract or buys property.[76]

Much the same applies when the compliance pull is thought to derive from legitimacy, at least when legitimacy is juxtaposed against legality. In such a case, again, those to whom the law applies have no way of knowing with any reasonable degree of certainty what it is they are supposed to do or refrain from doing. Conceptions of legitimacy being notoriously fluid and dependent on the observer's perspective (where often, and rather magically, legitimacy coincides

---

[76] See generally, e.g., Lon L Fuller *The Morality of Law* (rev. edn Yale UP New Haven CT 1969).

with the observer's political preference), the net result is that, except in those cases where legality and legitimacy run parallel, those to whom the law applies cannot rest assured until well after enactment of a rule or norm.

4. A Functionalist Turn?

Where the legal theorists shrug their shoulders when confronted with the question how to distinguish law from non-law, and many of the international lawyers seek for answers in the social sciences, there is a distinctly different approach which does away with the origins of legal rules altogether, and it echoes earlier developments in domestic public law.[77] The argument goes as follows: with the rise of the welfare state and the increased density of norms regulating society, norm-setting became more and more entrusted to administrative agencies and others, to such an extent that the resulting norms could hardly be related to the will of the legislative sovereign anymore. The King, the Crown, or Parliament had fairly little to do with the norms thus enacted. As a result, it became increasingly difficult to maintain the traditional link between law and sovereign authority in domestic settings, and in the end, as Loughlin writes, 'the authority of an administrative act [was] derived not from its origin but from its purpose'. Laws were to be evaluated not by their source, but whether they could meet their purpose: a thoroughly functionalist perspective.

Something similar can be discerned in some current writings in international law, in particular in attempts aiming to formulate an administrative law for a globalizing world. The argument here is rather similar, if and when it is made explicit. There is increasing recognition of the difficulties of shoehorning all international instruments in the recognized sources of Article 38, paragraph 1 of the ICJ's Statute.[78] For, after all, many instruments are made which cannot meaningfully be equated to treaties; many practices arise for which the label customary international law seems a mite overblown.

Not surprisingly, then, in terms of sources doctrine the category of general principles of law has received a new lease of life. One of the first suggestions to revive general principles of law came in the context of human rights. Having observed that states often enough did not act in accordance with human rights, Simma and Alston found that many of these human rights could not meaningfully be referred to as customary international law without diluting the very idea of customary international law—after all, the element of a consistent practice was often found wanting. As an alternative, however, general principles

---

[77] See Martin Loughlin 'The Functionalist Style in Public Law' (2005) 55 *University of Toronto Law Journal* 361–403, esp. at 372–373. Loughlin explicitly follows the early 20th century French public law theorist Leon Duguit.
[78] So, e.g., Alvarez, *International Organizations as Law-makers*, 2005.

of law would be attractive, as such principles are less insistent on concrete instances of practice. Instead, they would seem to emanate, on a consensual basis, from expressions of moral and humanitarian sentiments.[79] This approach therewith signified that it could be possible to relax the element of actual consent in the formation of international law without doing away with it altogether. Consent was still required, but no longer needed to be concrete; instead, open-ended pronunciations could be taken as sufficient evidence of legally relevant agreement among actors; hence, this approach opened the door for less specific ways to make international law without completely severing the link with consent.

In recent years, a similar line of thought has been picked up especially in connection with the control of the exercise of global administrative authority. This provokes two questions concerning the sources of law utilized. First, where do the norms come from that can be characterized as global administrative action? How, in other words, can such instruments as the Basel Accords emanating from the Basel Committee, be explained in legal terms? How can Security Council resolutions be classified and how can they come to have binding effects on individuals? Second, where do the norms come from that help to control such global administrative action? If it is true that global administration should be transparent, then where does the norm of transparency come from, and why does it bind global administrators?

For Esty, these are fairly straightforward questions. Discussing the desirability of a global administrative law structure and often carefully avoiding the use of legal-sounding notions like rules or principles, he relies on what he refers to as 'a number of administrative law strategies, approaches, and tools...', and builds 'on governance practices in the United States, EU, and elsewhere...'.[80] And when discussing the possible Western bias inherent in his approach, he responds by invoking results: the precise source would appear to be less relevant as long as results can be expected. Likewise, whether these tools and strategies are 'law' to begin with is deemed by and large irrelevant. 'Indeed', so he suggests, 'the weak will benefit most by having functioning international institutions', and the tools he proposes should be universally attractive precisely because they promise results: they promise good governance and accountability, and will thus be highly legitimate.[81]

Another school of thought within global administrative law adopts a more subtle position, and acknowledges that on a fundamental level, the question of sources raises issues that it cannot as yet fully answer. Traditional international law thinking 'cannot account for the origins and authority of the normative

---

[79] See Bruno Simma and Philip Alston 'The Sources of Human Rights Law: Custom, Jus Cogens, and General Principles' (1991) 12 *Australian Yearbook of International Law* 82–108.
[80] See Daniel C Esty 'Good Governance at the Supranational Scale: Globalizing Administrative Law' (2006) 115 *Yale Law Journal* 1490–1562, at 1523.   [81] *Ibid*, at 1541.

practice already existing in the field'.[82] Instead of resorting to a traditional *jus inter gentes*, this school suggests that 'a revived version of *ius gentium*' might be more appropriate—but it remains unclear what such a *jus gentium* would entail, where it would come from, and what its basis of obligation would be.

A third approach self-consciously adopts the language of principles, and suggests that the internal constitutionalization within international organizations might be most promising. On this line of thought, most international organizations develop internal mechanisms of control, be they operational policies, internal guidelines, or even, as with the EU, formal treaty-obligations to respect fundamental rights.[83] This kind of 'internal constitutionalization, based on the founding document of an international institution, would allow for the development of legal procedures, instruments and constraints in tune with the specificities of each regime'.[84] Taken together, this results in 'a pluriverse of general principles of different international institutions, which are, however, interlinked, thereby forming an overarching layer of common legal arguments'.[85]

Within the same tradition efforts have been made to develop a concept of 'standard instruments', which should facilitate analysis. With the help of rules of identification and the definition of the applicable legal framework (e.g. whether the institution adopting it was competent to do so), such standard instruments could take the place of sources doctrine. For such a concept could bring together for analytical purposes all sorts of instruments (resolutions, guidelines, standards, etc.) from the same functionalist perspective, and therewith create a level of transparency in global governance currently lacking. Moreover, it would be of general application: whereas sources doctrine typically only relates to legal norms, the standard instrument analysis could also comprise non-legal instruments. Explicitly borrowed from domestic administrative law (especially German and Italian), this manifests the 'functionalist style' in *optima forma*.[86]

---

[82] See Benedict Kingsbury, Nico Krisch, and Richard B Stewart 'The Emergence of Global Administrative Law' (2005) 68 *Law and Contemporary Problems* 15–61, at 29. See also Carol Harlow 'Global Administrative Law: The Quest for Principles and Values' (2006) 17 *EJIL* 187–214.   [83] See article 6, paragraph 2 TEU.

[84] See Armin von Bogdandy, Philipp Dann, and Matthias Goldmann 'Developing the Publicness of Public International Law: Towards a Legal Framework for Global Governance Activities' (2008) 9 *German Law Journal* 1375–1400, at 1391–1392.

[85] See Armin von Bogdandy 'General Principles of International Public Authority: Sketching a Research Field' (2008) 9 *German Law Journal* 1909–1939, at 1926. For a similar conceptualization of the role and relevance of general principles, see Nicholas Tsagourias 'The Constitutional Role of General Principles of Law in International and European Jurisprudence' in *idem* (ed) *Transnational Constitutionalism: International and European Perspectives* (CUP Cambridge 2007) 71–106.

[86] See Matthias Goldmann 'Inside Relative Normativity: From Sources to Standard Instruments for the Exercise of International Public Authority' (2008) 9 *German Law Journal* 1865–1908. See also von Bogdandy and Goldmann, National Policy Assessment, 2008. For a comment on the former, see Jan Klabbers 'Goldmann Variations' in Armin von Bogdandy *et al* (eds) *The Exercise of Public Authority by International Institutions: Advancing International Institutional Law* (Springer Berlin 2009, forthcoming).

Still, this functionalist turn, focusing on the results to be associated with norms rather than the origins of those norms, does not alleviate the need to distinguish between law and non-law, protestations to the contrary notwithstanding;[87] it is telling indeed that this need comes back in various guises. Thus, discussing the output of international institutions, Armin von Bogdandy distinguishes between authoritative and non-authoritative output, for it remains the case that not all outputs warrant further scrutiny.[88] As he and his co-authors point out, it is only authoritative acts that 'need to be constituted and limited by public law',[89] and in doing so the distinction between law and non-law is brought back in, albeit in a different vocabulary.

Indeed, the functionalist perspective is only capable of papering over the need to separate law from non-law for so long precisely because it marks a shift in perspective: as far as results go, it hardly matters where norms are legal or not, as all norms that are set by authorities aim at generating results[90] and thus, in one way or another, can be said to be binding. It has been widely documented that non-legal norms can be just as effective as legal norms, and that should not come as a coincidence: this can be so precisely because the addressees will realize that some specific behaviour is expected from them, regardless of whether an instrument is formally binding or not. But if the perspective changes to that of public (or private, for that matter) authority aiming to govern with legitimacy, the distinction between law and non-law re-enters, for here issues of competence and procedure play their part. To take a far-fetched example: a declaration of war against Moldova issued by the president of the EU Commission acting on his own will not be considered to have legal effect precisely because of lack of competence (and acting on his own does not help his case either). Yet from Moldova's perspective, it might still be wise to take some precautions and mobilize troops: Moldova cannot be entirely sure that the declaration will be considered invalid.

The law-making perspective thus focuses attention back to considerations that are of constitutionalist relevance, leading to the conclusion that in a constitutional order the functionalist perspective cannot be applied on its own: it needs to be accompanied by the law-making perspective. In domestic administrative law, this circumstance has remained somewhat obscured by having been incorporated automatically, as it were: the idea of an administrative agency taking a decision or setting a standard that would somehow not be binding in law would be highly curious, to say the least, and eventually self-defeating.

---

[87] Thus, for Goldmann, eventually the distinction between law and non-law 'is theoretically elusive and is not a meaningful criterion for a theoretically sound distinction between different kinds of instruments expressing different kinds of commitments'. See Goldmann, Inside Relative Normativity, 2008, at 1907.   [88] See von Bogdandy, General Principles, 2008, at 1917.

[89] See von Bogdandy, Dann, and Goldmann, The Publicness, 2008, at 1381.

[90] Otherwise they are not norms to begin with, but other things: tenders, announcements, invitations.

In the end, current theorizing about law forsakes an important point: the point that law ideally should be cognizable, and should be cognizable as such. This is an insight already formulated by Fuller, albeit with a different goal in mind. For him, secret laws were no good, because not cognizable. But equally, he would accept the proposition that uncertainty about the distinction between law and non-law falls short of the standards set by the internal morality of law. The rule of law demands nothing less.[91]

This may not, admittedly, be of great concern in an international society based, as traditionally often held, on balance of power conceptions. In the anarchical society, so the argument could go, the rule of law has little role to play. That is not to say there are no rules, but rather that those rules' main task is to maintain order—however dictatorial or arbitrary. This is different from the task of rules under any conception of the rule of law, where order is no longer the sole desideratum. Weber has suggested that the very idea of the rule of law was invented to allow the emergence of capitalism: it would be important for a capitalist economy that there be certainty about rules and about the consequences of economic activities.[92] Others would suggest that the rule of law somehow implies an injunction against arbitrariness, an injunction against the maxim that 'might makes right'. This may in turn lead to proceduralist approaches[93] or introduce substantive concerns,[94] but either way, it seems clear that uncertainty over what sort of behaviour is demanded is difficult to reconcile with the rule of law.

In other words, a constitutionalist approach to international law would demand some mechanism for distinguishing between law and non-law, at least (however circular this may sound) as long it is maintained that actors can meaningfully make a distinction between the two—and that is a claim that is often made. If, as many maintain, the choice is in quasi-Shakespearean terms 'to treaty or not to treaty',[95] then it follows that somehow that distinction is given

---

[91] The point also emerges from the case law of the European Court of Human Rights, which allows for exceptions to some rights if (amongst other things) these are prescribed by law. The notion of law employed puts a premium on clarity and cognizability, while encompassing unwritten rules or rules set by professional bodies. For a useful overview, see Clare Ovey and Robin C A White *Jacobs and White European Convention on Human Rights* (3rd edn OUP Oxford 2002) 201–204.

[92] See Max Weber *Economy and Society: An Outline of Interpretive Sociology* (University of California Press Berkeley CA 1978 Roth and Wittich eds). Hayek's enthusiasm for the rule of law undergirding a *laisser faire* economy implicitly confirms much the same. See Friedrich August von Hayek *The Road to Serfdom* (Routledge London 2001 [1944]).

[93] See, e.g., Michael Oakeshott 'The Rule of Law' reproduced in Michael Oakeshott *On History and Other Essays* (Liberty Fund Indianapolis 1999 [1983]) 129–178.

[94] See, e.g., T R S Allan *Constitutional Justice: A Liberal Theory of the Rule of Law* (OUP Oxford 2001).

[95] See Peter H Sand 'To Treaty or Not To Treaty? A Survey of Practical Experience' (1993) 87 *Proceedings of the American Society of International Law* 378–383. Whether this is plausible or not in its own right is an altogether different matter. For a critique, see Jan Klabbers *The Concept of Treaty in International Law* (Kluwer The Hague 1996).

relevance. Otherwise, there is no point in having actors 'intend' to create legally binding or non-legally binding relations.[96] Indeed, it is precisely in a constitutionalist setting that the distinction between law and non-law assumes relevance. The sheer Westphalian system could make do with a theory of power; a constitutional world order, by contrast, in order for the rule of law to be more than an empty phrase, demands some way to separate law from non-law.

On the technical level, as was suggested above, it is important that law be visible and cognizable, so as to give its addressees the chance to act in accordance with its terms and to give officials some idea as to what they are expected to enforce or apply. But, it might be countered, there is no particular reason why this is something only law can achieve: it might be claimed that the legal form can be replaced by some other form which is just as visible and cognizable. Hence, it remains imperative to be able to distinguish between law and non-law.

At least four reasons can be discerned, neatly summed up in Onuf's claim that rules of recognition 'answer the question, on whose behalf, and at whose sufferance, those who make (apply, adjudicate) legal rules exercise their powers'.[97] An advantage law has over at least some of its competitors is that it can be made intentionally, and is therewith suitable for regulation of the future. While legal blueprints are unlikely to be realized to the full and may meet with resistance in the form of existing and strong social customs,[98] nonetheless, to the extent that the future can be steered at all, it can be done only by means of law. By contrast, social customs or mores, or a common culture, or morality, are much harder to steer: even agreement amongst people exercising moral authority that, say, letting a car engine run while not being on the road is immoral in light of climate change, cannot guarantee that people start to think of it that way and will stop letting their engines run while having breakfast.[99] And if it cannot guarantee that people start to accept this as a matter of morality, much less can it guarantee that people actually start to behave in accordance with it. This is relevant for being able to distinguish law from non-law in at least the minimalist sense that it suggests that categories such as 'morally binding agreements' will often be based on a confusion of categories: if it is true that law is unique in being intentional,

---

[96] A radically different conception is offered by Shelton, for whom the blurring of the distinction signifies 'a maturing of the international legal system'. As she explains, states have come to trust one another so much that they no longer need to give their agreements the force of law: lesser force will do just as well. See Dinah Shelton 'Editor's Concluding Note: The Role of Non-binding Norms in the International Legal System' in Dinah Shelton (ed) *Commitment and Compliance: The Role of Non-binding Norms in the International Legal System* (OUP Oxford 2000) 554–546, at 556. Such a position comes frighteningly close to holding that the ideal society is one where law is no longer necessary.

[97] See Nicholas Onuf 'The Constitution of International Society' (1994) 5 *EJIL* 1–19, at 13.

[98] As pointed out by Moore, Law and Social Change, 1973.

[99] As the Dutch sociologist De Swaan pointedly observes, some form of world culture has arrived before Unesco adopted even a single resolution. See Abram de Swaan 'Verdriet en lied van de kosmopoliet' in Abram de Swaan, *De draagbare De Swaan* (2nd edn Bert Bakker Amsterdam 2008) 230–242, at 241.

then it follows that classifying agreements between political actors as 'morally binding' is of little additional value. The moral force of such agreements relate to the idea that as a general rule one should keep one's promises, and in this sense most, perhaps all, agreements are morally binding.[100]

Secondly, law is, potentially, the result of democratically reached agreement between interested actors: the 'mongrel' result of agreements between strangers.[101] While not all law is the result of democracy, most non-law clearly has no basis in democracy. Thus, the rule of a mafia boss may owe something to his closest advisors, but has no democratic pedigree. Relationships within the family typically are top-down, with parents telling children what to do, and hopefully doing so with the best interest of the child in mind. Religion may owe much to the pope or the clergy, but again usually has no democratic pedigree. Morality may owe much to grass roots acts, but also needs education and media for dispersal; and media ownership tends to be fairly concentrated, capable of stifling other voices. The one other set of norms with some democratic pedigree, it seems, are social customs: '... the mundane growth of repeated contact between different humans and different human groups can lay the foundation for the emergence of cosmopolitan norms, in a way that does not necessarily presuppose a formal juridical apparatus.'[102] What makes such norms potentially democratic is that they spring from everyday concerns in the lives of ordinary people. Moreover, a rule resulting from a long and well-established pattern of conduct may well boast a sense of legitimacy absent from expressly created consent-based rules precisely because they are rooted in long-standing practice.[103] Yet here too a word of caution would seem appropriate: at least in some social settings (think of commodity markets), those ordinary people may possess radically diverging power bases. The seller of grain or rice may be able to dictate terms to his many buyers concerning such things as down payments, conditions of delivery, and the like, whereas the opposite is less likely to happen. In other settings perhaps it is buyers or investors who can dictate terms. Either way, it may be difficult to classify such processes as democratic.

Thirdly, since law is rarely the result of unanimity, some vocabulary other than that of law may be useful for criticizing the law. In Benhabib's words: 'If we do not differentiate between morality and legality, we cannot criticize the legally enacted norms of democratic majorities',[104] even if they do things many people

---

[100] See further Klabbers, *The Concept of Treaty*, 1996, at 143–151.

[101] The term stems from Bonnie Honig *Democracy and the Foreigner* (Princeton UP 2001), at 39.

[102] See Jeremy Waldron 'Cosmopolitan Norms' in Seyla Benhabib *et al Another Cosmopolitanism* (OUP Oxford 2006) 83–101, at 94.

[103] See Jeremy Waldron *Law and Disagreement* (OUP Oxford 1999), at 64 (ascribing the point to Bartolus).

[104] See Seyla Benhabib 'Hospitality, Sovereignty, and Democratic Iterations' in Benhabib *et al, Another Cosmopolitanism*, 2006, 147–186, at 158–159; mutatis mutandis, the same would justify distinguishing between law and social norms, law and religion, etc.

would consider immoral. While Benhabib only speaks of law versus morality, the point would allow for broader application: surely, a law which goes against established social customs, or professional standards, may well be scrutinized and criticized from those vantage points. In short, getting rid of the distinctions between law and other normative orders implies deserting alternative vantage points.

Fourthly, law is socially accepted as a justification for the use of violence. Sociologists have long observed that one of the hallmarks of statehood is the monopoly on the use of force; and this monopoly itself is limited, normally speaking, to upholding the law: the state can use violence to uphold the law; it cannot use violence to uphold moral precepts that are not part of the law, or religious commands, or social mores. We would frown at being fined, or even thrown in jail for, say, failing to take off our hats in church, or coveting our neighbour's wife, or not opening a car door for a lady. And where people can meet with justified state-backed violence for such activities, it is in countries where such precepts have been turned into law.[105]

5. Law versus Non-law

If it is indeed correct to state that a constitutional world order needs some theory of legal obligation or some criterion to distinguish law from non-law, then the question arises quite naturally what such a theory ought to look like. This is not the time and place to develop a full-fledged theory of law-making for a globalized world; instead, I will set out a few tentative thoughts.

Law is traditionally thought of as a system of rules. Hart, for example, posited that a legal system mixes primary and secondary rules, and is held together by a rule of recognition.[106] And even where the whole would not make up a system properly speaking (for want of secondary rules or a rule of recognition), it nonetheless would comprise primary rules: rules relating to the sort of behaviour deemed acceptable or desirable in a society. On such a view of law, the distinction between law and non-law is relevant, for legal rules typically have characteristics that distinguish them from other rules: one cannot, for instance, create moral rules or social customs intentionally and with a stroke of the pen. In other words: if rules are to serve as guideposts for what is deemed to be the good life, they need to be intentionally created, and such creation presupposes the

---

[105] Thus, Dutch newspaper *De Telegraaf* reported on 18 December 2008 that a South Korean actress had been sentenced to eight months imprisonment for having committed adultery, explaining that under South Korean law adultery is prohibited, carrying a maximum sentence of two years. See <http://www.telegraaf.nl/buitenland/2820657_Veroordeling_overspelige_actrice_.html> (last visited 1 January 2009).

[106] See H L A Hart *The Concept of Law* (Clarendon Press Oxford 1961).

possibility of law. While law not only covers intentionally made rules, such rules do form an important group.

But also to those who do not think of law as a matter of rules, the distinction between law and non-law remains relevant. Kratochwil is an example. He suggests that law is best seen not so much as a system of rules, but rather as a style of reasoning. As a style of reasoning it is distinct from the reasoning practiced by others (e.g. philosophers), because lawyers receive a different kind of training—legal reasoning differs from practical reasoning or, more accurately, is a subspecies thereof.[107] Yet, this does re-introduce the law–non-law distinction, albeit in a less mechanistic sense: surely, as Kratochwil is quick to acknowledge, legal language differs also from ordinary language. Since people are unable to speak in purely neutral terms about the things they observe, all language comes with a sense of evaluation.[108] Whether to call the structure interjected between the populations of Israel and Palestine a security fence or a separation wall is not a neutral affair, but itself the result of an evaluation. Likewise, whether Osama bin Laden is a terrorist or a freedom fighter depends not only on what he does, but also on how his actions are gauged. The point now is that they cannot be gauged in language that has no legal implications, at least not in legally meaningful ways.[109]

Kratochwil himself put it as follows: 'The main characteristics of legal arguments deal with the finding and interpretation of the applicable norms and procedures, and with the presentation of the relevant facts and their evaluations. Both questions turn on the issue of whether a particular interpretation of a fact-pattern is acceptable rather than "true"...'[110] What then decides on whether or not evaluations are acceptable depends on the legal arguments invoked. These may include articles in formal treaties, but are not likely to include the story of Little Red Ridinghood. While a principle common to most domestic legal orders may qualify, a precept common to most moral systems (such as the injunction against polygamy) may not. And while a practice that is generally accepted as law will, indeed, qualify as law, a practice not accepted as such will not. In short, there is still some room left for the distinction between law and non-law; there is still some role to play for the sources of international law and for a theory of international legal obligation, not so much to determine once and for all what the law says (because chances are that 'the law' as such does not say all that much, or rather says too much, seeing that typically a variety of

---

[107] See also Neil MacCormick *Legal Reasoning and Legal Theory* (Clarendon Press Oxford 1978).
[108] See Friedrich V Kratochwil *Rules, Norms, and Decisions: On the Conditions of Practical and Legal Reasoning in International Relations and Domestic Affairs* (CUP Cambridge 1989), at 229.
[109] This may sound circular, but is meant to convey the idea that classifying things or events or actions can also take place outside the realm of law altogether. One may, for instance, admire the architectural qualities of the wall (or fence) built by Israel, or discuss Osama bin Laden's role as a father and husband. Here too judgments will be made (and in that sense the language used will again be evaluative), but these would seem to have little legal relevance. [110] *Ibid*, at 42.

applicable sources can be invoked), but rather to determine which are acceptable legal arguments and which are not. The distinction between law and non-law is relevant in that it seeks to distinguish between the sort of reasons that are acceptable in legal argument, and reasons that are not acceptable.

Typically, lawyers address the need for the distinguishing criterion in terms of validity: somehow, some criterion must be found that makes it possible to separate law from non-law, and usually that criterion is referred to as a criterion of (legal) validity. A normative utterance in a priest's sermon may be very powerful, but is not usually thought of as law, either because priests lack legislative authority or because sermons are not generally recognized as legal instruments, or both. On the other hand, the statement 'I do' uttered by two lay people in a church during a marriage ceremony may well suffice to have the legal effect of marriage, depending on whether the legal system at hand recognizes the statement as having these effects.[111]

In short, somehow a criterion of legal validity is used—and required. Hypothetically, this can come in various forms. As noted above, some adopt a more or less behaviouralist perspective, according to which the validity of law depends on whether it is complied with or, more subtly, whether it gives rise to 'normative ripples'. This, however, is not a very useful criterion, partly because, as set out earlier, it leaves it unclear to the law's addressees what sort of behaviour is actually expected from them at which moment in time, in addition to there being a fairly obvious distinction between recognizing a norm, and behaving in accordance with it.[112] That is not to say that behavioural studies are no good, for such would be untenable. Law-makers may benefit greatly from studies indicating which norms work, and which do not, and why some are more effective or instrumental than others. But having said that, it bears emphasis to claim that external observation cannot indicate whether a norm is legally valid or not. This misses what Hart has referred to (perhaps following Weber[113]) as the internal aspect of law: the idea that those who are subject to it somehow use it as a standard for their behaviour and for criticizing others.[114]

Leaving behaviour aside as a possible criterion for validity, two other broad categories remain: validity can be determined under reference to the substance of norms, and it can be determined by looking at how the norms in question have

---

[111] The example is inspired by speech act theory. See generally John Langshaw Austin *How To Do Things With Words* (2nd edn Clarendon Press Oxford 1975), and John R Searle *Speech Acts: An Essay in the Philosophy of Language* (CUP Cambridge 1969).

[112] Thus already Hans Kelsen *General Theory of Norms* (Clarendon Press Oxford 1991 Hartney trans), at 44.

[113] On the possible Weberian influence on this point, see Nicola Lacey *A Life of H.L.A. Hart: The Nightmare and the Noble Dream* (OUP Oxford 2004), at 230–231.

[114] See Hart, *The Concept of Law*, 1961, at 86–88. For a useful discussion of the various (including additional) possible perspectives and some of their implications, see Christiane C Wendehorst 'The State as a Foundation of Private Law Reasoning' (2008) 56 *American Journal of Comparative Law* 567–604.

come about. For those who favour substantive considerations, it would be impossible to think of morally obnoxious prescriptions as meriting the label 'law': a rule that specifies that everyone wearing eyeglasses should be killed can never be a legal rule, even if it appears on the books. Likewise, one might reach the conclusion that a rule that allows the use of aggression, or a rule that stimulates mass starvation, cannot properly be considered as 'legal'. The law, on this view, should decline to provide immoral injunctions with the imprimatur of law.

The problems with this view are well-rehearsed. For one thing, it presupposes that there is widespread agreement that aggression or starvation are bad things (which there probably is) and about how they can best be countered. It is particularly here that problems set in: while most people would probably reject aggression in general, most would also like to make an exception for aggression for a worthy cause. A vivid reminder hereof is the General Assembly's Definition of Aggression, which condemns aggression generally, but deems it acceptable in the name of the struggle for national liberation.[115] Equally useful is the reminder that the international community has tried for close to a century to define aggression, without many tangible results:[116] a tell-tale sign is also the lack of definition in the Statute of the International Criminal Court. By the same token, while starvation is a bad thing, it is not easy to agree on what causes it, and on what could or should be done to prevent it. Some would leave it all to the market; others, however, tend to see the market as a contributing factor, leading to exploitation, inequality, and, ultimately, starvation. In short, the view that the validity of norms ought to depend on their substance is fraught with problems relating to the underlying values.

But even so, as Hart has observed, even if we all agree that killing people is a bad thing, there is still a difference between the moral injunction against killing and the legal prohibition of murder, and part of the difference resides in the way they have come about.[117] Morality is transmitted through education, within the family and through the media, and what may start as an activist campaign may well come to be embraced by millions. But morality cannot be created by a stroke of the pen: it cannot be 'legislated'. Moreover, there need not always be a necessary connection between morality and law: surely, morality is rather indifferent to the question of whether to drive on the right side of the road or on the left, or whether the signing of wills should be witnessed by two persons rather than by three.

---

[115] See General Assembly Resolution 3314 (XXIX) of 14 December 1974. It reaches this result by proclaiming that the struggle for independence—by whatever means—shall not be considered as 'aggression'.

[116] See Bengt Broms 'The Definition of Aggression' (1977) 154 *Recueil des Cours* 297–400.

[117] As reported in Lacey, *A Life of H.L.A. Hart*, 2004, at 225.

This would seem to lead, inevitably, into the embrace of a procedural criterion of validity, but here too one ought to be careful. For one thing, a purely procedural criterion would allow nasty, odious law: under a purely procedural requirement, the injunction to kill everyone wearing eyeglasses would be law, its contents notwithstanding, if adopted by the appropriate state organ by means of the prescribed procedure and by the required majority. And being legal, it would need to be obeyed, as part of what it means to live with law is the duty to obey the law. It might be possible to argue that this duty may be set aside in extreme circumstances, but that re-introduces the sort of substantive considerations that refuge into a procedural criterion was meant to prevent: what circumstances would allow for disobeying the law? Again, this may fall prey to more or less subjective standards: I disobey whenever I feel that it is justifiable, or perhaps even imperative, to do so. But even if this may work, there remains the problem of what to do with those who actually obey the odious law: can one find fault with them for refusing to disobey? Only, it seems, where the boundary between right and wrong is very obvious[118]—but then there are situations, as Hannah Arendt has suggested, where that boundary itself becomes unrecognizable: the hallmark of totalitarianism is precisely that the difference between right and wrong is consistently undermined.[119]

Given these formidable difficulties, it is no surprise that much scholarship aims to do away with the distinction between law and non-law altogether. This, however, is unwise, as outlined above. Perhaps another strategy may prove more productive, and this strategy takes two distinct, though related, steps. First, it posits that while law ought to be distinguished from non-law, the distinguishing feature is not that the one emanates from public authority while the other does not. While law may well emanate from public authority (and often does), there is no reason to equate law and the public sector. For, as Tamanaha, amongst others, has suggested, law can also emanate from elsewhere:[120] it is not eccentric to speak of religious law, or of indigenous law. Still, what ought to be borne in mind is that not everything emanating from a religion is therewith religious law, not everything an indigenous people does is therefore indigenous law. In other words: within legal systems, the distinction between law and non-law remains to be discussed.

Secondly, instead of trying to posit procedure over contents, or contents over procedure, it may be more fruitful to try and find a *modus vivendi*, or perhaps a *via media*, between the two. In other words, might it be possible to somehow

---

[118] Or backed up by international commitments: this is the approach taken by the European Court of Human Rights in the *German Border Guards* case. See applications 34044/96, 35532/97 and 44801/98, *Streletz, Kessler and Krenz v Germany*, judgment of 22 March 2001.

[119] See Hannah Arendt *The Origins of Totalitarianism* (Harcourt Brace and Company San Diego 1951).

[120] See Brian Z Tamanaha *A General Jurisprudence of Law and Society* (OUP Oxford 2001), at 224–230.

combine positivist and naturalist concerns and reach a theory of obligation that incorporates both without being completely unworkable? Put like this, the only plausible outcome would be a fairly thin theory of obligation. For, obviously, a thick theory would merely add up the problems of both the procedure and the substance schools.

6. Towards Presumptive Law

Like Hart, Tamanaha utilizes an internal perspective to help distinguish law from non-law: 'A minimum threshold to qualify is if sufficient people with sufficient conviction consider something to be "law", and act pursuant to this belief, in ways that have an influence in the social arena.' Law, as he neatly summarizes, 'is whatever people recognize and treat as law through their social practices'.[121] While this may seem open-ended and could allow for family relations, or mafia rule, to be given the label 'law', Tamanaha himself is not too worried on this score. After all, few people actually label such relations 'law'; few think of the family, or the mafia, as 'law'.[122]

Intuitively, Tamanaha's approach makes some sense with respect to international law. At the very least, international law does not emanate from a single legislative source, and has always had a hard time fitting into the typical paradigm according to which law emanates from a single public authority. Indeed, an approach such as this is, it seems, capable of accommodating the daunting circumstance that international law can possibly be made within a wide variety of international organizations, but also within less institutionalized settings, bilateral and multilateral.

This does not solve all problems, of course, but would seem to be instrumental in a first step: to distinguish legal orders from non-legal orders. On this basis, it may with some confidence be posited that the United Nations can possibly create law, as can the EU, the WTO, the World Bank, and possibly such bodies as the Basel Committee or the G7 (or G8) as well. So too can law possibly be made by states meeting incidentally, and perhaps also involving actors other than states. More to the point, perhaps, it would also serve to suggest that the rules of FIFA (the Fédération Internationale de Football Association) do not qualify as 'law' in quite the same sense: few people would apply the label 'law' to FIFA's rules. And likewise, Papal Encyclicals, or the teachings of the Dalai Lama, may not qualify as 'law', no matter how influential they may be, simply because few people think of them in terms of law.

Admittedly, this is a rather open-ended way of looking at law, and hypothetically at any rate it is subject to change: what was not 'law' half a century ago may

---

[121] *Ibid*, both quotes at 167.   [122] *Ibid*.

well have become 'law' by now, or otherwise might become 'law' in another 50 or 100 years. And this is probably as it should be: with law being a social phenomenon, it only stands to reason that its boundaries are not carved in stone but can ebb and flow in accordance with prevailing social opinion. Thus, the point is at least arguable that at some historical moment, Papal Encyclicals were actually considered as 'law'; however, they have stopped being considered so. This openendedness may disappoint die-hard conceptualists ('essentialists', as Tamanaha call them), but so be it: law has no essence beyond the here and now.

Even so, it obviously does not mean that everything coming out of the UN or the World Bank is 'law', or that all instruments promulgated by the EC or all agreements reached by political leaders are by definition 'law'. For this, a validity test is still needed, and, as mentioned above, both a purely procedural test and a purely contents-based test run into problems. An intermediate approach was launched, some four decades ago and in a domestic setting, by the American legal theorist Lon Fuller. Fuller became known for endorsing what he referred to as 'procedural natural law': he scripted a list of eight more or less procedural requirements which, taken together, would make it extremely unlikely that laws would pass whose substance would be considered as odious. Following Fuller's prescriptions, the law thus created could be expected to be morally acceptable while at the same time being procedurally sound.

Fuller's eight desiderata were, in a nutshell, as follows. Law, he suggested, must consist of norms to begin with; one cannot leave things to be decided on a case-by-case basis only. Second, laws ought to made public, so that people can have an idea what is expected of them. Third, law should not made retroactively (save in certain limited circumstances). Fourth, law should be understandable: a rule to 'water the elephants every seventh Sunday of the month' makes no sense and accordingly cannot be complied with. Fifth, laws should not be made to contradict each other. Sixth, it should be possible to obey the law (thus, the injunction to levitate above the sidewalk would be out). Seventh, the law should not change so frequently as to become unpredictable. And finally (and most importantly perhaps), there should be a reasonable measure of congruence between the rules and the way they are applied by officials.[123]

These eight requirements together should guarantee that anything that passes them will be morally acceptable, and indeed, it is difficult to imagine that perfidious rules can come into being. The earlier example about killing everyone wearing eyeglasses may serve as a case in point: it would be difficult to reconcile with a more general celebration of the right to life, and thus create a contradiction within the system. It is also difficult to imagine official action to follow up with great zeal so as to create congruence. That is not to say nasty enactments are impossible, but, as Fuller maintained, they would be rather unlikely.

---

[123] See Fuller, *The Morality of Law*, 1969, esp. at 39. A fine collection of essays on Fuller's work is Willem J Witteveen and Wibren van der Burg (eds) *Rediscovering Fuller* (Amsterdam UP 1999).

As the example suggests, though, there would seem to be a serious background assumption: the assumption that there is already a substantively decent system in place. For only on such a scenario would the rule to kill all spectacle wearers look out of place. By contrast, if the pre-existing framework is itself nasty, then the introduction of yet another nasty rule will not create any contradictions, and will easily result in official congruence. This, however, does not seem to be a very realistic assumption, and it perhaps serves at best as a limiting condition: Fuller's requirements cannot turn hell into heaven. But that said, the condition of hell seems to be a paper condition: it is difficult to think of a legal system that does not celebrate life, work on the basis of good faith, etc.[124]

Still, a Fullerian perspective alone is not enough. Fuller himself never intended his internal morality to serve as some kind of sources doctrine and was, in effect, positively cavalier when it came to accepting normative utterances as law: like some of the legal pluralists, he utilized a rather broad conception of what law is, and simply did not seem to be overly interested in distinctions between law and non-law to begin with.[125]

So for all its merits, Fuller's list alone will not do the trick: a more formal criterion is still required, for only a formal criterion 'can guarantee that the content of law can be determined in an objective and value-neutral way', as Raz once put it.[126] For much of the 20th century, within the international legal order the notion of state consent functioned as the formal criterion, at least for most practical purposes.[127] While consent cannot explain the binding force of international law as a system (the rule that says that consent creates obligation must itself have been created in the absence of consent), it can—or rather could—explain most individual rules of international law in most individual settings.[128] Treaty-making, as the PCIJ famously held in *Wimbledon*, was an attribute of state sovereignty; treaties—and by extension international law

---

[124] For a jurisprudential exploration of the suitability of using Fuller's internal morality of law as the equivalent of sources doctrine, see Jan Klabbers 'Constitutionalism and the Making of International Law: Fuller's Procedural Natural Law' (2008) 5 *No Foundations: Journal of Extreme Legal Positivism* 84–112.

[125] According to Raz, 'totally uninterested' would have been closer to the truth: Fuller's theory, so Raz states, 'is best seen as an inquiry into some putative features of practical laws generally, whether legal or not'. See Joseph Raz 'The Problem of the Nature of Law' in Joseph Raz *Ethics in the Public Domain: Essays in the Morality of Law and Politics* (rev. edn Clarendon Press Oxford 1994) 195–209, at 196–197.

[126] See Joseph Raz 'Legal Validity' in Joseph Raz *The Authority of Law: Essays on Law and Morality* (Clarendon Press Oxford 1979) 146–159, at 152. See also Martti Koskenniemi 'International Legislation Today: Limits and Possibilities' (2005) 23 *Wisconsin International Law Journal* 61–92, at 89–90.

[127] Earlier, the doctrine of natural rights of states is said to have played that role. See James Leslie Brierly 'The Basis of Obligation in International Law' in James Leslie Brierly *The Basis of Obligation in International Law and Other Papers* (Scientia Aalen 1977 [1928]) 1–67. Brierly himself ends up advocating that international law should be obeyed because there is a moral obligation to obey the law (*ibid*, at 64–67). This may well be true, but is of little help in distinguishing between law and non-law.   [128] So also, eventually, Hart, *The Concept of Law*, 1961, at 220–221.

generally—gained their binding force from being consented to by sovereign states. Again, on the philosophical level this was probably never a tenable proposition, but on the pragmatic level it worked: it managed to hold the system together for much of the 20th century.[129]

It is difficult to imagine the formal validity criterion to be anything other than a consent-like criterion, whether consent be expressed directly or indirectly, as is the case when it comes to binding majority decisions within international organizations.[130] After all, anything else would be dictatorial, and would need a justification in terms of religion, faith, necessity, or *recta ratio*—yet none of these seem plausible. That is not for want of trying: attempts to posit universal values try to do precisely this, but end up meeting with considerable scepticism. The problem is not so much that there might not be universal values; the point is rather, as John Gray puts it, 'to deny that universal values can only be fully realized in a universal regime'.[131] As a result, any attempt to espouse universal values almost automatically carries the suspicion of domination.[132] Hence, in order to prevent domination, some consent-like mechanism is required.

Still, even if consent is limited to the consent of states, it is by no means always clear what states actually consent to. The debate over possibly illegal resolutions of the Security Council and judicial review suggests that while the basic idea may be clear, at least it ought to be possible to counter the legally binding force of Security Council resolutions with good arguments—patently illegal resolutions need not be accepted. It is here that Fuller's list of requirements, discussed above, may be of some help.

Another possibility for organizing a consent-based mechanism (and one which might end up doing greater justice to non-state actors) might be to move to some form of representative decision-making or, alternatively, reform today's version of representative decision-making. Some have suggested that today's system is in fact a form of representative decision-making (representative democracy might be too strong a term): states create law acting with a mandate from their citizens.[133] While theoretically neat, this meets with at least three practical counterarguments. First, with some states, it is highly implausible to claim that they represent their citizens on the international level: this may generally be true with democracies, but is less plausible with non-democracies, except perhaps on the

---

[129] See further Jan Klabbers 'Clinching the Concept of Sovereignty: Wimbledon *Redux*' (1998) 3 *Austrian Review of International and European Law* 345–367.

[130] The latter can be said to be consent-based on the idea that member states express general consent to be bound by future majority decisions when they ratify the organization's constituent document.   [131] See John Gray *Two Faces of Liberalism* (New Press New York 2000), at 21.

[132] For a reading of Kant to this effect, see Martti Koskenniemi 'On the Idea and Practice for Universal History with a Cosmopolitan Purpose' in Bindu Puri and Heiko Sievers (eds) *Terror, Peace, and Universalism: Essays on the Philosophy of Immanuel Kant* (OUP Oxford 2007) 122–148.

[133] A specifically republican version of this argument is made by Mortimer N S Sellers *Republican Principles in International Law: The Fundamental Requirements of a Just World Order* (Palgrave MacMillan New York 2006). See also chapter 6 below.

unpleasant theory according to which people get the leaders they deserve. Second, even if formally all states were democracies, it is still the case that, in many states, international affairs are relatively isolated from democratic control. Parliaments typically have little influence over treaty-making (let alone over the formation of customary international law or decision-making within international organizations), and need not even always be consulted.[134] And typically, where a duty to consult and involve parliament exists concerning treaty-making, states have been keen to circumvent this precisely by claiming to be engaged in the conclusion not of treaties, but of non-legally binding instruments.[135] And third, there remains the problem that even in parliamentary democracies, some interests tend to be better represented than others.

To be sure, these are not problems of principle but empirical problems: it might be possible to devise a better system of representation. Thus, Linklater has argued for increased acceptance of sub-national and supranational entities as being representative, in effect endorsing an increase in the number of subjects of international law.[136] Others, by contrast, would expect more from a global parliament or world assembly in some shape or form.[137] A distinct strand of the literature would expect much from shareholder and consumer activism in order to make global law more representative,[138] and yet others would stress an increased role for international manifestations of civil society, finding comfort, for instance, in the creation of the World Social Forum to counterbalance the World Economic Forum.[139]

An alternative approach would not so much focus on changing modalities of representation, but start from the other end: rethink the way law is recognized. On this view, what matters is how norms are received by their possible addressees. One possible approach might be to propose what can be labelled 'presumptive law': normative utterances should be presumed to give rise to law, unless and until the opposite can somehow be proven. This does not amount to giving up the quest for validity; it merely reverses the burden of proof. In short, it might be productive to think in terms of a presumption of law, a presumption that normative utterances bind as law unless and until rebutted. Thus, a Security

---

[134] For this reason, some endorse global constitutionalism to make up for domestic de-constitutionalization. See Anne Peters 'Compensatory Constitutionalism: The Function and Potential of Fundamental International Norms and Structures' (2006) 19 *Leiden Journal of International Law* 579–610.

[135] See, e.g., Anthony Aust *Modern Treaty Law and Practice* (CUP Cambridge 2000), at 37.

[136] See Andrew Linklater *The Transformation of Political Community: Ethical Foundations of the Post-Westphalian Era* (Polity Cambridge 1998).

[137] See, e.g., Heikki Patomäki 'Rethinking Global Parliament: Beyond the Indeterminacy of International Law' (2007) 13 *Widener Law Review* 369–387.

[138] See, e.g., Robert J Foster *Coca-Globalization: Following Soft Drinks from New York to New Guinea* (Palgrave MacMillan New York 2008).

[139] See, e.g., Teivo Teivainen 'The World Social Forum and Global Democratisation: Learning from Porto Alegre' (2002) 23 *Third World Quarterly* 621–632.

Council resolution should be presumed to be binding; any agreement between states, whether given the name 'treaty', 'convention', or anything else, should be presumed to be binding between them; standards adopted by the ISO should be presumed to be law; decisions of the G7 or G8 are presumed to create law; the *lex mercatoria* is presumed to be law; even resolutions of the General Assembly are presumed to be law.

This is, as such, not nearly as big a step to take as it would appear at first sight: it amounts to a reversal of what seems to be the current presumption (that normative utterances are not law unless somehow that presumption is rebutted), and therewith gives a voice to two fairly classic sentiments. One of these has been the long-standing dissatisfaction with the decision of the PCIJ in the *Lotus* case, which in effect (and in actual wording) laid down a presumption of non-law.[140] Second, it pays homage to the classic maxim *ubi societas, ibi jus*, wherever there is a society, there shall be law, for, eventually, law is the name societies give to the norms they design and want themselves and each other to uphold. A society without law is, quite literally, unthinkable; and a society which has norms but does not refer to them as 'law' is, in the end, merely deceiving itself.

Moreover, the two generally accepted 'hard cases' when it comes to the role of consent in international law-making seem to work on the same basis. The first of these is the process of customary law-making. Here, silence is construed as consent. Customary international law, so the PCIJ intimated in *Lotus*, emanates from the free will of states: their usages are expressions of this free will.[141] And this, in turn, implies that somehow, norms of customary international law, like treaties, can be seen as requiring consent.[142] Yet, it is possible to opt out, by persistently objecting while a norm is in the process of formation and articulation: this is known as the persistent objector rule. Hence, the process can be construed as creating the presumption that one is bound by a customary rule unless there is evidence to rebut the claim.

The second hard case involves state succession.[143] It is often claimed that a new state cannot escape being bound by the norms that bound its predecessor; as such, this would mean that consent cannot always be regarded as decisive. Yet, it also seems that new states may renegotiate many of the primary obligations thus incurred,[144] or may seek classification as 'newly independent states', for in such a

---

[140] See *Case of the SS Lotus*, [1927] Publ. PCIJ, Series A, No 10, at 35: 'The rules of law binding upon States ... emanate from their own free will ... Restrictions upon the independence of States cannot therefore be presumed.'   [141] *Ibid.*

[142] See, e.g., Danilenko, *Law-making*, 1993, at 106.

[143] An excellent recent study is Matthew Craven *The Decolonization of International Law: State Succession and the Law of Treaties* (OUP Oxford 2007).

[144] The reference to primary rules here suggests, loosely, that it may be easier for new states to escape from concrete rules of behaviour than from the rules that relate to the operation of the legal order. It would be awkward, for instance, for new states to claim not to be bound by the rules relating to law-making, whereas it would be perfectly plausible to claim not to be bound by a trade agreement or an extradition treaty upon succession.

case there is widespread agreement that starting with a clean slate may be more appropriate.[145] Hence, this hard case, too, can be construed in terms of presumption and rebuttal.

To speak of a presumption of legally binding force is itself by no means novel: half a century ago, FA Mann proposed much the same, suggesting that, with respect to treaty-making, there could only be two presumptions: either it is presumed to be binding, or it is presumed not to be binding. The latter, however, would be unworkable: 'An agreement governed by no system of law is unthinkable. The presumption would, therefore, always and automatically be rebutted.'[146]

Mann here responded to an article by James Fawcett published a few years earlier, who had proposed that agreements between states are not presumed to be legally binding. This was the case, so Fawcett had held, because international affairs are highly political. In such an environment, political relations may give rise to politically binding agreements, but these can only be deemed legal if accompanied by clear evidence that this is what their drafters intended.[147] Fawcett suggested '. . . that there is no presumption that States, in concluding an international agreement, intend to create legal relations at all, and that this intention must be clearly manifested before a legal character is attributed to the agreement'.[148]

Whatever the merits of Fawcett's argument with respect to the classic Westphalian world order (and according to Mann these merits would have been meagre indeed), it seems that his position is incompatible with the very idea of a constitutional global order. Surely in a constitutional order the starting point cannot be that agreement reached in the body politic does not result in law unless it is clearly intended to. This would be incompatible with staples of constitutionalist discourse such as transparency in governance, legal certainty, predictability, and judicial protection. Hence, if Fawcett's position must be rejected, the only possible presumption, as Mann already saw, is the one according to which agreements reached by politically relevant actors must be presumed to give rise to law.

That said, though, presumptions are only true presumptions if they can be rebutted: a presumption that cannot be rebutted is not a presumption, but a hard and fast rule, while a presumption that is always rebutted is not a rule at all. This

---

[145] See Art 16 of the 1978 Vienna Convention on the Law of Treaties in respect of State Succession.

[146] See Frederick Alexander Mann 'Reflections on a Commercial Law of Nations' (1957) 33 *BYIL* 20–51, at 31.

[147] This may well be an emanation of Thomas Jefferson's sentiment: 'On the subject of treaties our system is to have none with any nation, as far as can be avoided.' As quoted in Michael J Glennon *Constitutional Diplomacy* (Princeton UP 1990), at 192, note 2.

[148] See James E S Fawcett 'The Legal Character of International Agreements' (1953) 30 *BYIL* 381–400, at 385. Fawcett's opinion may have been coloured by what seems to have been his fairly Austinian starting point: only obligations that are judicially enforceable can properly be called law.

raises the question of how, in a constitutional global order, the presumption of law can be rebutted. Here, various broad categories must be discerned. A first has to do with contents; a second with context; a third with origins; a fourth with procedure, and a fifth with topic.

As for contents, an instrument which leaves everything to the discretion of the addressee may well be deemed to rebut the presumption of law. Even if embedded in a legally binding instrument, if there is a clear 'element of non-commitment in the commitment', to quote Glennon with respect to Article 5 NATO, then there can be no law.[149] Obvious as this may sound, examples may be hard to come by: even the vacuity of Part IV of GATT is not entirely devoid of meaningful contents. An obligation to 'accord high priority' to grant market access whenever possible[150] is still decipherable. It may not amount to much, and definitely does not create a corresponding right to market access no matter what, but is still something that can be tested and applied.[151]

Thus put, there will not be many instruments which can escape the workings of the law altogether—at least not on the basis of their contents. Even the softest-phrased provision will at least contain a good faith obligation to seriously consider giving effect to it. But this is, of course, as it should be: domestic legal systems also know many variations in the strength of norms and express these through language.

Second, rebutting the presumption of law may successfully occur when it transpires from the context that no one ever thought of making law. The standard case here refers to political leaders making promises (or what appear to be promises) during press sessions or interviews. When cornered, politicians may say many things, and when they seem to be sincere in promising, for example, to withdraw troops from occupied territory, or to close an army base abroad after human rights abuses, or to prosecute those responsible for those abuses, they may perhaps be held to their word.[152] If, however, they promise to end world poverty in the next week while securing full global disarmament in the process, there might be reasons for not taking them too literally.[153] In the end, though, it bears

---

[149] Glennon, *Constitutional Diplomacy*, 1990, at 214. Note however that Art 5 NATO at least implies a good faith obligation to seriously consider providing assistance to fellow member states subjected to an armed attack, and is thus not entirely non-committal.

[150] As contained in Art XXXVII GATT.

[151] In a similar vein, Jean d'Aspremont 'Softness in International Law: A Self-serving Quest for New Legal Materials' (2008) 19 *EJIL* 1075–1093, esp. at 1084–1087.

[152] As discussed more generally below in terms of powers, an intervening factor here might be whether in speaking on topic A, the politician remains within his sphere of competence. A Defense Minister making promises relating to market access for agricultural products may be taken less seriously than the Agriculture Minister making the same promises.

[153] This builds on the *Frontier Dispute* case, where the apparent promise by the Malian president to accept as binding a boundary running through Mali's capital was deemed not to have been made with legal intentions in mind.

emphasizing that subjective intent alone cannot be decisive; it is, eventually, the law which determines which consequences to attach to which acts.

This may also have a bearing on the law-making powers of international organizations. If states consent to a certain course of action but do so on the understanding that their consent gives rise to recommendations (i.e. non-law) only, then this should be factored in: the context may suggest that legislative intents were absent *ex hypothesi*. This does not, of course, prevent the occurrence of a new rule to the effect that when a recommendation is given a certain designation (e.g. 'Declaration') it may be presumptively law, but such an analysis must be conducted with care.

The category of the origins of norms may be of great utility when it comes to discerning between law and non-law and rebutting the law presumption. Thus, some actors clearly lack any law-making authority in any accepted sense of the term: this relates to parents and their commands, for example, but also to those who make word-processing programs or compile grammar and syntax texts. Whatever the linguistic status of the rule 'Do not split infinitives' may be, it clearly is not a rule of law, if only because no one accepts it as such or speaks of it in those terms.

That is not to say it may be easy to determine, in any given situation, whether an entity or actor actually has some law-making authority. To resort to a formal criterion might be deemed desirable, but will inevitably include entities whose real, material authority might be limited, while excluding entities of great material authority. Thus, a formal criterion—depending on how it would be formulated— might exclude informal actors such as the G7 or the Basel Committee, while including a largely dormant entity such as the Western European Union. In this light, it might be wiser to focus on material evidence of authority: actors who are usually heard and followed will be deemed to have some prima facie law-making capacity. This also suggests that the capacity can develop over time.

This point about the origins of norms also aligns to such issues as concrete powers of actors. While, clearly, a decision emanating from the wrong organ shall not be considered binding on the addressees, it may still be binding on the organ itself. For example: should the G7 decide to alleviate poverty and, to that end, impose a tax on currency transactions, it is well arguable, first, that the tax is invalid (as the G7 lacks the power to legislate), but that the G7 itself would remain under an obligation to do something to alleviate poverty. At the very least, it would be estopped from claiming that poverty is not its concern, and it is arguable that its member states would be estopped from lowering development aid, prohibiting market access for products from developing countries, refusing loans for spurious reasons, and similar acts. This might, of course, have the effect of making the G7 more reluctant to come out with grandiose but eventually unfulfilled promises at its summit meetings; it is far from self-evident, though, that such reluctance would be a bad thing.

Likewise, the powers of all actors are somehow limited by existing international law. States cannot declare war just like that, or apply their own laws extraterritorially, or legislate for third states. Thus, an attempt by Belgium and Germany to create a legal regime applicable to Luxembourg will not survive the rebuttal phase: it will stumble over the third parties rule.[154] An attempt by France to apply French criminal law over something Dutch citizens did in the Netherlands will likewise not be considered legal.

In similar manner the legislative powers of other actors are limited, and are typically limited both by general international law and by their own by-laws, constitutions, and internal rules. Thus, Amnesty International's Statute explicitly prohibits its sections from taking action 'on matters that do not fall within the stated vision and mission' of the organization,[155] and there may well still be an internal rule to the effect that those who resort to violence cannot be supported as prisoners of conscience.[156] Likewise, it is undisputed as a matter of principle that the powers of international organizations are limited to those that have been attributed to them and those that can plausibly be implied from their constitutions, even though the limits of the latter remain disputed.[157]

The third possible ground for rebutting the presumption of law resides in procedure, and it is here that Fuller's 'procedural natural law' comes in. Secret norms or norms that instruct people to do the impossible will not be regarded as law. The same applies to norms that are enacted with retroactive force (unless justifiable, for instance to correct past wrongs) and norms that are incomprehensible, and eventually to norms that are left without execution. Surely, if everyone refuses to abide by a rule, than the presumption that the rule be a legal one will eventually be rebutted.

This also applies to norms that contradict other, existing norms. The latter point merits some specific attention. It is almost generally accepted within Westphalian international law that in case of conflict between norms applicable to the same addressees, the later in time shall normally prevail, as it is this *lex posterior* which reflects the contemporary underlying political sentiments.[158] This is plausible within a Westphalian order, but loses some of its plausibility in

---

[154] The seminal study in Christine Chinkin *Third Parties in International Law* (OUP Oxford 1993).

[155] See Statute of Amnesty International, available at <http://www.amnesty.org> (last visited 15 January 2009), Art 12 (intriguingly, there seem to be two Arts 12. The above refers to the first of these).

[156] For a discussion of this rule as it played out in Amnesty International's early years, see Jonathan Power *Like Water on Stone: The Story of Amnesty International* (Penguin London 2002), at 125–126.

[157] See generally Jan Klabbers *An Introduction to International Institutional Law* (CUP Cambridge 2002) 60–81.

[158] See Art 30, paragraphs 3 and 4 of the Vienna Convention on the Law of Treaties. On treaty conflict generally, see Guyora Binder *Treaty Conflict and Political Contradiction: The Dialectic of Duplicity* (Praeger New York 1988). On specific manifestations, see e.g. Joost Pauwelijn *Conflict of Norms in Public International Law: How WTO Law Relates to Other Rules of International Law* (CUP Cambridge 2003) and Jan Klabbers *Treaty Conflict and the European Union* (CUP Cambridge 2009).

a constitutional order, which places a premium on certainty and predictability, or, in other words, in not giving in too quickly to the whims and caprices of the day. A similar point was made, classically, by Judge van Eysinga in his separate opinion in the *Oscar Chinn* case: where a treaty establishes something beyond *jus dispositivism*, it cannot be departed from too easily.[159] Three quarters of a century ago, Van Eysinga was ahead of his time (yet, curiously perhaps, came across as conservative); in a global constitutional order, though, his approach makes some sense: it should not be possible to change constitutional norms too easily, not even by new constitutional norms.

This category would also have to include participation rights. Fuller never addressed these, as his (hypothetical) model was that of a single legislator; he could thus take representation and participation for granted. It seems obvious, though, that under a constitutional model, law-making cannot be done by a global dictator, or a global directorate, or global empire. The rule can be formulated relatively easily in abstract form: norms made without the involvement of all those entitled to participate shall not qualify as law.[160]

Finally, then, the presumption of law may be rebutted under reference to the topic. This is not a revival of the old quip that amidst the clatter of weapons, the law shall remain silent; it should not be taken to mean that law has no business regulating war and security. Quite the opposite: it refers instead to a *de minimis* rule. For instance, an agreement between political leaders to have a photo session during a summit meeting is not the sort of agreement that the legal system should be bothered with. By the same token, an agreement reached at a conference to have a coffee break at 11.00 does not give rise to legal rights and obligations: the presumption of law shall be rebutted by the circumstance that such an agreement is simply too trivial.

These factors all stand on their own. Each single one will be sufficient to rebut the presumption of law. Thus, the idea of an agreement to have a coffee break will not be law, because it fails the *de minimis* test. Even if cast in compulsory terms, emanating from clear legislative authority following the proper procedure and clear regard for the input of all concerned, it will not be law. While clearly the first element (contents) allows for greater or lesser degrees of intensity, a hortatory declaration will not be rescued by having been adopted by a recognized law-maker. Likewise, an instrument in compulsory terms will not be seen as law if adopted by an entity without law-making powers or capacity.

---

[159] See *The Oscar Chinn Case* (United Kingdom v Belgium), [1934] Publ. PCIJ, Series A/B, No 63, esp. at 133–134 and actually using the word 'constitution' to describe the regime established by the 1885 Berlin Act.

[160] This is a huge topic in its own right, and will briefly be touched upon below, in section 7, and in greater detail in chapter 6.

7. Some Outstanding Issues

The above sketches a possible approach to law-making in a constitutional global order, and provokes more questions than it answers. This is not the place to try and cater to all outstanding issues and questions: the ambition was rather to sketch a general approach which would do justice to the idea of the constitutionalization of international law while at the same time remaining faithful to the notion of consent. For, as outlined above, consent will have to remain the main criterion of validity: the absence of consent by those involved in the law-making process (or those who ought to have been involved) will immediately rebut any presumption of law. At the very least, then, this approach will take consent seriously—and this will represent a welcome change from those approaches that insist that consent has become irrelevant and that, instead, law is whatever is 'necessary', or based on 'shared values'. Briefly put, where the appropriate actors agree in accordance with appropriate procedure that some or other initiative is the appropriate course of action, then the result will presumptively be law.[161]

This puts quite a premium on figuring out who exactly the appropriate actors are. A plausible case could be made that it includes all those who are affected by the possible output. In such a manner, at least the worst perversities of earlier days—such as the carving up of entire continents by European powers—can be prevented. This would imply that the poor (or at least those who meaningfully represent them) have a say in decisions affecting poverty, development, and the like, whether they be located in the institutions of world trade (such as the WTO) or elsewhere (IMF and World Bank, G7, World Economic Forum). Shifting venues so as to exclude the poor would not be acceptable: taking intellectual property rights to a revamped WIPO or some to-be-established new organization will be taken as a circumvention of existing procedure, unless it meets itself with the approval of all those affected. And of course, within the alternative institution the same demand for inclusion applies at any rate.

Some outstanding issues remain on the more technical side. For instance, if the law presumption is rebutted, does that mean that the remaining rule—the residue, so to speak—is invalid? Or shall it be deemed to remain in existence in some universe other than law? And if so, shall it have a normative, though not legal, effect? Probably the better view is to regard everything that does not survive as law as invalid, in much the same way that domestic legislation, if not made in accordance with the right procedure, will typically be seen as invalid,

---

[161] Therewith a presumptive approach may help overcome the problem Weiler sketches so pointedly: that of coming to terms with demcoracy on the international level. See Weiler, The Geology of International Law, 2004.

rather than as existing alongside the law and continuing to make normative demands on its addressees.

It should also be stressed that the above does not mean that universal law-making can all of a sudden take place, unless of course all relevant actors agree. The continued relevance of consent suggests that still, states and others cannot be held bound against their explicit will, but the key word here is explicit. The presumption of law can be rebutted, as can the presumption of being individually bound by an individual rule, by deciding to opt out. But it is fitting, in a constitutional global order, to accept the presumption of law—rather than the presumption of non-law—as the starting point.

One important point remains to be discussed. Granted the possibility of a presumption of law, and granted the possibility that the presumption will be confirmed in given cases, it may still be the case that the law conflicts with other norms. With intra-law conflicts, the law can be expected to formulate its own conflict rules and find legal mechanisms to settle possible disputes. These may include such ideas as the principle of systemic interpretation, endorsed by the International Law Commission to help mitigate treaty conflicts;[162] these may include rules establishing hierarchy, as is the case with Article 103 UN Charter, or these may include jurisdictional rules, allocating jurisdiction along the lines of private international law.[163]

But what to do when legal rules conflict with other norms? What if the legal prohibition of intervention clashes with a moral imperative? Or with a strong social norm? There is a good reason, in line with the above, to presumptively favour the legal norm over the non-legal one. The reason for doing so (set of reasons, really) harks back to the discussion above on why it is relevant to distinguish between law and non-law to begin with: law can be made intentionally and on the express basis of widespread agreement based on some form of democratic legitimation, and this is what other normative systems typically lack. In line with the above, this may well be characterized, as Schauer does, as a 'presumptive positivism': apply the law 'unless particularly exigent reasons can be supplied for not applying it'.[164] The reasons for overriding the law have to be 'particularly strong',[165] precisely because legal rules exist for a reason: they should not be cast aside at the faintest whim or caprice.

---

[162] See Martti Koskenniemi *Fragmentation of International Law: Difficulties Arising from the Diversification and Expansion of International Law. Report of the Study Group of the International Law Commission* (Erik Castrén Institute Helsinki 2007).
[163] See, e.g., Berman, Global Legal Pluralism, 2007; Andreas Fischer-Lescano and Gunther Teubner *Regime-Kollisionen: Zur Fragmentierung des Globalen Rechts* (Suhrkamp Frankfurt am Main 2006). [164] See Schauer, *Playing by the Rules*, 1991, at 203.
[165] *Ibid*, at 204.

8. Conclusions

In the film *A Few Good Men*, the suspects were eventually convicted. After all, by engaging in a Code Red, they had broken the applicable law. The fact that they had been ordered to so by their superiors, and the fact that their superiors had a zero-tolerance policy as far as disobedience of their orders was concerned, was not considered a credible defence—not credible enough to find them 'not guilty', although the circumstances were taken into account in the sentencing.

This conclusion seems right. When confronted with conflicting norms stemming from a variety of normative orders, it makes some sense to give presumptive priority to legal commands, yet somehow also recognize that law does not operate in a tightly sealed vacuum. This holds true especially, it may be postulated, in a constitutional order: if the label 'constitutional' is to have any meaning beyond the rhetorical, it stands for placing a premium on law, over power, but also over other normative orders. After all, as outlined above, law is uniquely valuable in that it can boast a conscious and democratic pedigree.

But placing a premium on law, in a constitutional order, is a two-way street. This not only places burdens on the addressees of law, but also on those who make it: it implies that they follow established procedures, that they do not take shortcuts on the way to what they hold to be the good life, and that they accept the possibility of being held accountable. As Fuller posited long ago (and somewhat against the jurisprudential grain), even legislation properly speaking owes much to reciprocity between law-maker and addressees.[166]

This chapter has sketched the outlines of the sort of considerations that enter the picture with respect to law-making once one starts to take seriously the claim of a constitutional global order. It has done so by trying to find a middle way between community interests and more parochial interests, always insisting that the distinction between law and non-law be respected. This culminated in the notion of presumptive law, embedded within presumptive positivism.

Such a conclusion may well be considered a disappointing conclusion for die-hard universalists. These committed universalists may find that the proposals do not go far enough, do not sufficiently take into account the needs of the global community, the possibility or reality of universal values, or the existence of *jus cogens* as either a precursor or a manifestation of the community interest. To those who think, with Louis Henkin, that sovereignty is a 'bad word',[167] presumptive global law may simply not go far enough in overcoming sovereignty.

Likewise, the above may be disappointing to the confirmed localist. Those who feel threatened by the global and maintain that anything international is

---

[166] See Fuller, *The Morality of Law*, 1969, at 39–40.
[167] See Louis Henkin 'International Law: Politics, Values and Functions' (1989/V) 216 *Recueil des Cours* 9–416, at 24.

bound to be undemocratic and too isolated from any possible moorings in any grassroots society may well feel that the above goes too far, that it pays too much homage to the universal, and does not do enough to protect bounded political communities. And insisting on the distinction between law and non-law is likely to upset quite a few people as well.

Still, things could hardly be otherwise: the toothpaste cannot be placed back in the tube, aspiring to return to a Westphalian world that no longer exists in pure form. Yet, there is considerable merit in protecting the autonomy of bounded political communities, not only those based on territory such as states, but also those founded on other bases, whether they be international organizations, churches, indigenous peoples, or activist groups.

At the same time, it is by no means clear that an overarching hierarchical universal order would be all that attractive, no matter how much certain global issues may need (or may appear to need) forceful solutions. As outlined in the opening chapter of this book, it would seem that some form of pluralism is well-nigh inescapable, both by default (because the alternatives are implausible or undesirable) and positively: because pluralism has its own merits. Coming to terms with pluralism in a constitutionalizing global order in the context of the making of law may be best served by a notion of presumptive law.

4

The International Judiciary

Geir Ulfstein

1. Introduction

A prominent feature of current international law is the increased importance of international tribunals. The President of the International Court of Justice (ICJ) could in her annual statement inform the United Nations General Assembly that 2008 had been the 'most productive year in [the] history' of the Court.[1] But we have also seen the establishment of new inter-state tribunals, like the International Tribunal for the Law of the Sea (ITLOS) and the dispute settlement system of the World Trade Organization (DSU/WTO). There are international criminal courts, such as the International Criminal Tribunals for the former Yugoslavia and for Rwanda (ICTY/R) and the International Criminal Court (ICC). International tribunals for settlement of investment disputes are established under the International Convention on the Settlement of Investment Disputes between States and Nationals of Other States (the ICSID Convention). Furthermore, there are treaty bodies (e.g. the Human Rights Committee) and regional courts (e.g. the European Court of Human Rights) to deal with human rights.

The burgeoning of international tribunals means that ever-more substantive areas of law are brought under international control. This concerns not only traditionally international issues, such as the use of armed force and boundary delimitation, but also fields that have so far been considered national, such as the relationship between the individual and the state, industrial subsidies and environmental protection. On the other hand, foreign policy is no longer the sole prerogative of foreign ministries. Democratic constitutional organs are increasingly taking part in decision-making in such issues as military operations or international trade. This means that international tribunals may interfere in most subject matters of national constitutional concern. The distinction between international and national issues is becoming blurred.

Furthermore, the jurisdiction of international tribunals in essential areas of law—such as international trade, the law of the sea, and, at the regional level,

---

[1] International Court of Justice Press Release No 2008/38, 30 October 2008 (see <http://www.icj-cij.org/presscom/files/5/14825.pdf>, last visited 23 March 2009).

human rights—are increasingly of a legally compulsory character. States are formally free to join or to leave such treaties and their dispute settlement, and they may decide whether they will give effect to international judgments in their national legal system. However, if states want to benefit from a global market or the rights provided in the law of the sea, or be regarded as a nation of good standing in the protection of human rights, or avoid international legal responsibility, they may have no choice but to ratify the relevant treaties with their dispute settlement procedures, and to implement international judgments. The formal freedom of states may thus not be worth much in practice.

A primary function of international tribunals is—as at the domestic level—the settlement of legal disputes. The tribunals deal only with individualized disputes and the judgments are made on the basis of rules adopted (more or less) by the consent of states in the form of treaties and customary international law. But, since international law may be indeterminate and vague, international tribunals have an essential law-making function. International human rights courts are also prone to dynamic—or 'evolutive'—interpretation of treaty obligations, with results that could hardly be foreseen at the treaty's adoption and ratification. Binding dispute settlement by international tribunals means, therefore, the conferral of important sovereign powers.

The combined effects of the wide-reaching substantive scope of international tribunals, their increasingly compulsory character—in law or fact or both—and their law-making function do not mean that alternatives to national constitutions are established, or that international tribunals are national constitutional organs. But it means that these tribunals exercise constitutional functions in the sense that they may interfere significantly with the activities of national legislative, executive, and judicial national organs.

This raises the question whether international tribunals should be subject to democratic control and constitutional guarantees comparable to what is known from national constitutions. First, whether international tribunals should be guided by requirements of independence and other due process guarantees as required for national courts will be discussed. Next, the extent to which the international judiciary should be organized with a hierarchic structure known from the national judiciary will be examined, and furthermore what should be the respective constitutional roles of the international and national judiciary. Then, the relationship between international tribunals and democratically elected organs will be analysed. The protection of international human rights, as an essential constitutional feature, will also be scrutinized.

2. Due Process

The requirement of 'due process of law' has been recognized in international human rights instruments, such as Article 14 of the International Covenant of Civil and Political Rights (ICCPR), and regionally in Article 6 of the European

Convention on Human Rights (ECHR) and Article 8 of the American Convention on Human Rights.[2] Article 14 of the ICCPR requires that parties are 'equal before the courts and tribunals' and that everyone shall be entitled to a 'fair and public hearing' by a 'competent, independent and impartial tribunal established by law'. Additional procedural requirements are established for criminal prosecution.

Admittedly, these instruments lay down the basic requirements for courts at the national level, and not for international tribunals. But the Appeals Chamber of ICTY held in the *Tadic* case that an international criminal court 'ought to be rooted in the rule of law and offer all guarantees embodied in the relevant international instruments'. The rule of law requires that the Court must be established 'in accordance with the proper international standards; it must provide all the guarantees of fairness, justice, and even-handedness, in full conformity with internationally recognized human rights instruments'.[3]

The basic assumption in the following is that international dispute settlement should satisfy certain minimum standards, as reflected in the human rights instruments.[4] It may of course be discussed whether all these standards have a constitutional character. The requirement of independence is well-known as fundamental to the constitutional separation of powers. But it is also essential that courts and tribunals possess the necessary expertise and that they act in an impartial manner, etc., in order to carry out a proper judicial function. Such minimum standards are therefore treated here as being of a constitutional quality. This is supported by the fact that decisions from international courts are generally not subject to appeal. If international appellate bodies are available, as in international criminal courts and in the WTO, the constitutional function would apply to such bodies.

The composition and process of international tribunals should, however, depend on their mandate, the parties, and the specific substantive area they are meant to serve: whether they are civil or criminal courts; the extent to which they can hand down binding judgments or non-binding recommendations; whether they are of an inter-state character or human rights courts open for individuals; global or regional tribunals, etc.

2.1 Expertise

It would be expected that judges possess the necessary legal qualifications. Democratic involvement in the composition of courts is, however, also

---

[2] Manfred Nowak *U.N. Covenant on Civil and Political Rights: CCPR Commentary* (2nd rev. edn N.P. Engel Kehl 2005), at 305.

[3] *Prosecutor v Dusko Tadic, Decision on the Defence Motion for Interlocutory Appeal on Jurisdiction* Case IT-94-1-AR72 Appeals Chamber of 2 October 1995 paragraphs 42 and 45.

[4] See also Paul Mahoney 'The International Judiciary—Independence and Accountability' (2008) 7 *The Law and Practice of International Courts and Tribunals* 313–349, at 317.

recognized in national constitutions, where the final appointment is decided by political organs. In this way a balance may be struck between professionalism and democratic control. Such a balance should also be sought in the election of judges to international tribunals.

The election process of judges to international tribunals has been characterized as highly political. Deals are made between states on mutual support for candidates.[5] The national nomination procedures may also be politicized and opaque. The combined effects of the national and international processes will not necessarily result in the most competent candidates being elected. The High Commissioner for Human Rights suggests that the composition of the global human rights treaty bodies has been 'uneven in terms of expertise and independence, as well as geographical distribution, representation of the principal legal systems and gender balance'.[6] James Crawford claims that the electoral process of the treaty bodies '... (like most such processes within the UN) is haphazard and takes limited account of qualifications'.[7]

We find more elaborate procedures for appointment of members of certain international tribunals. The statute of the International Criminal Court not only requires judges to be chosen from among persons of 'high moral character, impartiality and integrity who possess the qualifications required in the respective States for appointment to the highest judicial offices' (Article 36(3)(a)), but also goes some way to ensure the competence of the candidates by requiring that the nominating states shall specify how their candidate meets the stipulated requirements (Article 36(4)(a)). The Assembly of States Parties may also decide to establish an Advisory Committee on nominations (Article 36(4)(c)).

Another example is the European Court on Human Rights, where each state shall nominate three candidates and election is not performed by the states parties, but by the Parliamentary Assembly (Article 22).[8] The candidates are interviewed by a parliamentary panel composed mainly of legal experts, and its recommendations are almost always followed. The purpose of this procedure is

---

[5] Michael Wood 'The Selection of Candidates for International Judicial Office: Recent Practice' in Tafsir Malick Ndiaye, Rüdiger Wolfrum, Thomas A Mensah, and Chie Kojima (eds) *Law of the Sea, Environmental Law and Settlement of Disputes* (Brill Leiden 2007) 357–368, at 357 and 359. See also Ruth Mackenzie and Philippe Sands 'International Courts and Tribunals and the Independence of the International Judge' (2003) 44 *Harvard International Law Journal* 271–285, at 277 and Daniel Terris, Cesare P R Romano, and Leigh Swigart *The International Judge. An Introduction to the Men and Women who Decide the World's Cases* (OUP Oxford 2007), at 15.

[6] *Concept Paper on the High Commissioner's Proposal for a Unified Standing Treaty Body* (14 March 2006) (HRI/MC/2006/CRP.1) paragraph 22.

[7] James Crawford 'The UN Human Rights Treaty System: A System in Crisis?' in Philip Alston and James Crawford (eds) *The Future of UN Human Rights Treaty Monitoring* (CUP Cambridge 2000) 1–15, at 9.

[8] The appointment procedure has been criticized in Jutta Limbach, Pedro Cruz Villalón, Roger Errera, Anthony Lester, Tamara Morshchakova, Stephen Sedley, and Andrzej Zoll *Judicial Independence: Law and Practice of Appointments to the European Court of Human Rights* (Interrights London 2003), available at <http://www.interights.org/jud-ind-en/index.html>, last visited 23 March 2009.

to promote appointments based on merits, rather than a political bias—and at the same time ensure democratic legitimacy.[9] The Council of Europe has furthermore recommended national procedures that should include a call for candidates through the press, and criteria for their nomination.[10] Procedures for the call and nomination of candidates to international tribunals have been adopted at the national level in some states, such as in the United Kingdom.[11] But the absence of such procedures in other states may subject the international election process to questionable candidates.

Compromises may be needed between specialized knowledge in the special subject area of the tribunal and general expertise in international law—in the national judiciary we also know the representation of lay persons to ensure democratic representation. Panels under DSU/WTO need not be lawyers (Article 8(1) DSU). On the other hand, the Appellate Body shall 'comprise persons of recognized authority, with demonstrated expertise in law, international trade and the subject matter of the covered agreements generally' (Article 17(3)). Human rights treaty bodies may also consist of non-lawyers. The Committee Against Torture (CAT) shall, for example, consist of persons with a 'recognized competence in the field of human rights', but the parties only recognize 'the usefulness of the participation of some persons having legal experience' (Article 17(1)). It may be asked whether a Committee without lawyers would be appropriate in dealing with intricate questions of interpretation of the Convention, especially in individual communication concerning human rights violations—although such decisions are non-binding.

2.2 Independence

The requirement of the judiciary's independence from the legislature and the executive means in an international context independence both from national authorities and from international organizations.[12] International tribunals will generally make final judgments which cannot be overruled by any political or executive body—whether national or international. The need for adoption of WTO Appellate Body decisions by the political Dispute Settlement Body seems purely formal, since non-adoption requires a consensus decision (Article 14 DSU).

The requirement of independence at the international level must, however, be balanced with the need for representativeness of the tribunals' composition. The ICJ statute, for example, sets out that in 'the body as a whole the representation

---

[9] Marie-Louise Bemelmans-Videc 'Chairperson of the Subcommittee on the Election of Judges to the ECtHR' *Economist* 6 December 2008, at 18.
[10] Wood, The Selection of Candidates for International Judicial Office, 2007, at 360–361.
[11] *Ibid*, at 366–368.
[12] See Theodor Meron 'Judicial Independence and Impartiality in International Criminal Tribunals' (2005) 99 *AJIL* 359–369, at 359–360.

of the main forms of civilization and of the principal legal systems of the world should be assured' (Article 9).

The need for representativeness would not in itself threaten the independent character of the Court, but rather bring in useful diversity in experience. It is more difficult to accept a requirement that the judges shall come from desig-nated countries. In regional settings, it has been required that all states should be represented by a judge, such as in the European Court of Human Rights. The judges obviously act in their individual capacity, but their independence may in such circumstances be questioned. This is also the case in the International Court of Justice, where the five permanent members of the Security Council in practice always are represented.[13] The independence of the judges would, however, increase if they were elected for an extended period of time, or were not eligible for re-election, as is the case in the International Criminal Court (Article 36(9)(a)). The new Protocol 14 to the ECHR establishes similarly that judges will be elected for nine years, and may not be re-elected (Article 23(1)).[14]

International arbitration leaves the choice of arbitrators to the disputing parties.[15] The arrangement with the appointment of *ad hoc* judge(s) to the International Court of Justice in contentious cases may also be seen as an aspect of distrust of the professional judges on the bench—although it may provide trust in the ability of the Court to accommodate the interests of the relevant parties in a dispute.[16] It has been argued that this system 'has worked rather satisfactorily'.[17] This system can also be found in the International Tribunals for the Law of the Sea (Article 17(2)). The system with *ex officio* representation of the defendant state in the European Court of Human Rights (Article 27(2)) may be questioned for similar reasons, but it has been claimed that '[l]ittle would be gained, and much lost, by abandoning the requirement of the presence of the national judge'.[18] This is different from dispute settlement in the WTO, where

---

[13] John G Merrills *International Dispute Settlement* (4th edn CUP Cambridge 2005), at 147. Richard Steinberg has stated that the European Communities and the United States exercises a *de facto* veto power in the selection of judges to the WTO Appellate Body, see Richard Steinberg 'Judicial Lawmaking at the WTO: Discursive, Constitutional, and Political Constraints' (2004) 98 *AJIL* 247–275, at 264.

[14] See Meron, Judicial Independence and Impartiality in International Criminal Tribunals, 2005, at 362.

[15] It has been argued that dependent, rather than independent, international tribunals are more effective at resolving international disputes, see Eric A Posner and Jonh C Yoo 'Judicial Indepen-dence in International Tribunals' (2005) 93 *California Law Review* 1–74, with response from Laurence R Helfer and Anne-Marie Slaughter 'Why States Create International Tribunals: A Response to Professors Posner and Yoo' 901–973, and Eric A Posner and John C Yoo, 'Reply to Helfer and Slaughter', 957–973.

[16] See Brian Z Tamanaha *On the Rule of Law. History, Politics, Theory* (CUP Cambridge 2004), at 134–135.

[17] Pieter Kooijmans 'Article 31' in Andreas Zimmermann, Karin Oellers-Frahm, and Chistian Tomuschat (eds) *The Statute of the International Court of Justice. A Commentary* (OUP Oxford 2006) 495–506, at 506.

[18] Lucius Caflisch 'Independence and Impartiality of Judges: The European Court of Human Rights' (2003) 2 *The Law and Practice of International Courts and Tribunals* 169–173, at 173.

citizens of a party to a dispute may not serve as a panellist, except with the agreement of the parties (Article 8(3) DSU), but where no account is taken of the judges' citizenship in establishing the division of the Appellate Body to deal with an appeal (Article 17(1) DSU)).[19]

2.3 Equal access

The right of equality before courts and tribunals, as required by Article 14 of ICCPR, includes the right of equal access. All states have equal access to international tribunals. It may, however, be questioned to what extent the access given to states always ensures an adequate representation of the real interests at stake.

States are regarded in international law as representing the population on a certain territory and would as such be the appropriate entities to appear in cases affecting territorial rights, such as boundary delimitation, the use of force against an aggressor, etc. They have also traditionally exercised diplomatic protection in the interests of individuals and companies injured by other states. But states are probably under no international obligation to exercise diplomatic protection. The International Law Commission has therefore only proposed recommended practices in the form of 'should'—not 'shall'—obligations regarding states' consideration of the possibility of exercising diplomatic protection, of taking into account the views of the injured persons, and of transferring any compensation obtained to such persons.[20]

It is not obvious, however, that individuals and companies should need to rely on the willingness of their home state to protect their rights. The rise in international tribunals provides occasion to question whether these tribunals should not be available to private entities directly affected by the acts of other states. The accessibility by individuals of human rights courts and treaty bodies, and by companies of international tribunals established under the ICSID Convention in investment disputes, should be welcomed. Furthermore, the rights of individuals and private entities should not be restricted to actions against states: they should also be privileged with a right to bring cases against international organizations to the extent they adopt decisions affecting private actors—and other venues are not available (see also p. 67 and pp. 161–166).

Dispute settlement is not only a matter of protection of the interests of individual states, private persons, and companies. Increasingly, international law is intended to protect what should also be regarded as general human interests, be it the protection of human rights, the environment, or international peace

[19] World Trade Organization *A Handbook on the WTO Dispute Settlement System* (CUP Cambridge 2004), at 51 and 69.

[20] Article 19 of the 'Draft Articles on Diplomatic Protection' *Report of the International Law Commission*, 58th Session (2006), 94–100.

and security. International law has acknowledged the need for the use of international tribunals in the protection of collective interests through the notion of *erga omnes* obligations.[21] But the protection of collective interests should not be dependent on actions by individual states. One supplementary approach is international action through non-judicial non-compliance procedures, which are well known in treaties on international human rights, international environmental law, and arms control.[22]

An alternative to the use of international tribunals to protect collective interests through individual states' actions and to the use of non-compliance procedures, however, would be to vest an international organ with the power to bring cases before an international tribunal against states violating multilateral treaty obligations. This would not necessarily be in the form of an international prosecutor and international criminal law—since international law does not know of criminal responsibility for states.[23] But an option is to apply a similar system to the one known in the European Community, where the Commission may bring member states before the European Court of Justice for breach of their treaty obligations (Article 226 EC). This would combine the need for collective action with the possibility of obtaining a binding judgment.

The competence to bring states before an international court for violation of obligations protecting collective interests should presumably be conferred to specialized international organizations as part of their enforcement function— and not to the United Nations as the most general world organization. But the judicial function could be allocated to the ICJ rather than to specialized courts— provided, however, that Article 34 of the ICJ Statute is amended to allow international organizations to seize the Court.

2.4 Fair hearing

It is essential that the parties are allowed to present their case properly, that international tribunals are well-informed about the facts and relevant law pertaining to the case, and that the proceedings are conducted in a transparent manner.

The procedure before international tribunals is based on a combination of oral and written proceedings. It is difficult, however, to apply meaningful questioning of the counsel when the tribunal consists of 15 members as in the ICJ, or 21 members as in the ITLOS.[24] The number of judges of the

---

[21] Christian J Tams *Enforcing Obligations* Erga Omnes *in International Law* (CUP Cambridge 2005).

[22] Geir Ulfstein, Thilo Marauhn, and Andreas Zimmermann (eds) *Making Treaties Work. Human Rights, Environment and Arms Control* (CUP Cambridge 2007).

[23] Yearbook of the International Law Commission, 2001, vol II, Part Two, at 55.

[24] Sir Arthur Watts 'Enhancing the Effectiveness of Procedures of International Dispute Settlement' in Jochen A Frowein and Rüdiger Wolfrum (eds) (2001) 5 *Max Planck Yearbook of United Nations Law* (Kluwer Law International Leiden) 21–39, at 25–26.

tribunals in each case should accordingly be reduced—or chambers used more extensively—to allow for meaningful oral proceedings in addition to the written proceedings.

The Human Rights Committee deals with complaints only on the basis of 'written information made available to it by the individual and by the State Party concerned',[25] and does not allow oral presentations, examination of witnesses or experts, nor independent fact-finding.[26] There is no transparency in deliberations since the complaints are considered in 'closed meetings'.[27] Henry J Steiner has argued that '[a]ll these provisions contrast sharply with characteristic requirements for judges and judicial process'.[28] As the functions of human rights treaty bodies dealing with individual complaints are similar to those of international courts—except for the non-binding character of their findings—they should also apply comparable procedural guarantees.

International tribunals should also be provided with the competence to ensure the availability of the relevant facts of the case. The European Court of Human Rights has from time to time embarked on extensive fact-finding. But a balance has to be found in relation to the role of national courts.[29] This latter aspect may not be as important in subject matters not usually dealt with by national courts, for example the legality of the use of international armed force. But national courts are also increasingly becoming involved in traditionally foreign matters, such as breaches of international humanitarian law or human rights in the use of armed force and territorial occupation.

The interaction between the tribunals and the counsel also merits analysis. It may be somewhat unclear what is to be expected from the tribunals in terms of the responsibility of counsel to present all aspects of a case, and Sir Arthur Watts has suggested that there may be a need for an 'international Bar' to develop common standards for the profession.[30] The proper role of the prosecutor in international criminal cases has also been raised.[31]

---

[25] Optional Protocol to the International Covenant on Civil and Political Rights, Art 5(1).

[26] Henry J Steiner, Philip Alston, and Ryan Goodman *International Human Rights in Context. Law, Politics, Morals* (3rd edn OUP Oxford 2008), at 892.

[27] Optional Protocol to the International Covenant on Civil and Political Rights, Art 5(3).

[28] Henry J Steiner 'Individual Claims in a World of Massive Violations: What Role for the Human Rights Committee?' in Philip Alston and James Crawford (eds) *The Future of UN Human Rights Treaty Monitoring* (CUP Cambridge 2000) 1–15, at 29. See also Geir Ulfstein 'Do We Need a World Court of Human Rights?' in Ola Engdahl and Pål Wrange (eds) *Law at War—The Law as it Was and the Law as it Should Be* (Brill Leiden 2008) 261–272, at 264–265.

[29] Laurence R Helfer 'Redesigning the European Court of Human Rights: Embeddedness as a Deep Structural Principle of the European Human Rights Regime' (2008) 19 *EJIL* 125–159, at 142–144.

[30] Watts, Enhancing the Effectiveness of Procedures of International Dispute Settlement, 2001, at 27–28.

[31] Frédéric Mégret 'International Prosecutors: Accountability and Ethics' (2008) *Working Paper No 18* Leuven Centre for Global Governance Studies (also available at <http://ssrn.com/abstract=1313691>, last visited 23 March 2009).

3. The Need for Consistency

The hierarchical order of national courts shall serve the finality, consistency, and implementation of the courts' decisions, in short the effective constitutional function of the judiciary. The question is to what extent a similar order should be established between different international tribunals, as well as between international tribunals and national courts.

3.1 International tribunals

International tribunals are not organized in a hierarchical order. As it was stated in the *Tadic* case:

International law, because it lacks a centralized structure, does not provide for an integrated judicial system operating an orderly division of labour among a number of tribunals, where certain aspects or components of jurisdiction as a power could be centralized or vested in one of them but not the others. In international law, every tribunal is a self-contained system (unless otherwise provided).[32]

The diversity of the international judicial architecture increases with the rising number of specialized tribunals. There are, however, diverging opinions about the magnitude of the problems represented by the growth of international tribunals. One former President of the ICJ, Gilbert Guillaume, has, for example, argued that the dangers 'may have been underestimated by lawyers'.[33] On the other hand, one of his successors, Rosalyn Higgins, holds that 'we should not exaggerate the phenomenon of fragmentation'.[34]

In the following, it will be discussed what kind of challenges are raised by the fragmented international judiciary and which responses may be considered. The issues will be examined under three headings: the potential of competing jurisdictions between different tribunals; conflicts between and inconsistencies in their decisions; and, finally, the possible threat of the burgeoning of international tribunals to subject matters not endowed with their own judicial institutions.

The jurisdictional problems may be further divided into three categories. They may first of all relate to the risk of overlapping jurisdictions, in the sense that similar cases may run before different courts at the same time, unless such difficulties are prevented by the principle of the *litispendence* (or *lis pendence*) effect of lawsuits. The other difficulty would be that judgments by one tribunal are not given binding legal effect if the dispute subsequently is brought before

---

[32] *Prosecutor v Tadic* 1995 paragraph 11.

[33] Gilbert Guillaume 'The Future of International Judicial Institutions' (1995) 44 *ICLQ* 848–862, at 861.

[34] Rosalyn Higgins 'A Babel of Judicial Voices. Ruminations from the Bench' (2006) 55 *ICLQ* 791–805, at 761.

another tribunal, i.e. whether international judgments are given *res judicata* effects. Thirdly, overlapping jurisdiction could lead to forum shopping by the parties to a legal dispute and to a defensive attitude among international tribunals in order to attract cases.

There are few examples of formally overlapping jurisdiction that may result in conflicting jurisdiction. Such overlap may arise between two tribunals with general jurisdiction, such as between the ICJ and a court of arbitration endowed with general treaty-based jurisdiction, for example a Treaty on Friendship, Commerce and Navigation.[35] Furthermore, it could arise between a tribunal with general jurisdiction and a specialized tribunal. The relationship between a general and a specialized tribunal is, however, usually regulated in the rules of the specialized tribunal. States parties to the UN Convention on the Law of the Sea will, for example, have to choose their preferred dispute settlement mechanism—be it ICJ, ITLOS, or arbitration—as they ratify the treaty (Article 287 UNCLOS).

The specialized courts will have jurisdiction within the treaty system they have been designated to serve. ITLOS, for example, has jurisdiction regarding interpretation or application of the United Nations Convention on the Law of the Sea or an 'international agreement related to the purposes of this Convention, which is submitted to it in accordance with the agreement' (Article 288 (1) and (2)). The DSU/WTO is limited to the 'covered agreements', such as GATT 1994, and disputes concerning the WTO Agreement and the Dispute Settlement Understanding (DSU Article 1 (1)). This means that jurisdictional conflicts between, for instance, the ITLOS and DSU/WTO may hardly arise.

The *Swordfish* cases between Chile and the European Community is an example of cases involving both the DSU and ITLOS.[36] The dispute concerns fishing of swordfish in the South Pacific by EC member states. Chile denied access to its ports. The Community argued that this action violated GATT obligations, whereas Chile referred to obligations concerning conservation of fish stocks in the United Nations Convention on the Law of the Sea. Since the two parties reached a provisional agreement, the process of establishing a WTO panel as well as the proceedings of the special chamber established by ITLOS were suspended. But one of the cases would relate to GATT obligations whereas the other would relate to obligations under UNCLOS. As these are two different treaties, the two cases would, formally, concern different violations. Accordingly, these cases are not examples of jurisdictional conflicts, but different findings under the two treaties could potentially create inconsistencies in the law.

---

[35] Vaughan Lowe 'Overlapping Jurisdiction in International Tribunals' (1999) 20 *Aust. YBIL* 191–204, at 191.

[36] ITLOS Case No 7 *Concerning the Conservation and Sustainable Exploitation of Swordfish Stocks in the South-Eastern Pacific Ocean* Order 2008/1 and DSU/WTO Dispute DS 193 *Chile- Measures affecting the Transit and Importing of Swordfish* (<http://www.wto.org/english/tratop_e/dispu_e/cases_e/ds193_e.htm>, last visited 3 March 2009).

The *MOX* case between the United Kingdom and Ireland concerned the disposal of radioactive waste from recycling of plutonium. Ireland brought the case first before an arbitral tribunal on the basis of the Convention for the Protection of the Marine Environment of the North-East Atlantic (OSPAR Convention) (Article 32).[37] It furthermore instituted proceedings before an arbitral tribunal provided for in Annex VII to UNCLOS. However, this raised the question of whether Ireland had the competence to bring such a case before an international tribunal according to European Community law. The arbitral tribunal deferred its proceedings until the European Court of Justice (ECJ) had expressed its opinion.[38] The ECJ concluded that it had exclusive jurisdiction and that Ireland accordingly had no right to bring the case before the dispute settlement mechanisms of UNCLOS.[39] The relationship between the courts was thus solved through the arbitral tribunal's yielding before the ECJ.

But, formally, the arbitral tribunal would have no competence to determine with binding effect to what extent Ireland had the legal capacity under Community law to bring such a case before the tribunal. A preliminary finding by the arbitral tribunal that it had jurisdiction would not have *res judicata* effect and would therefore not conflict with the ECJ ruling. But it would obviously cause problems of inconsistency. On the other hand, a separate judgment by the arbitral court could be closer to a formal conflict with the ECJ's finding—but even in this situation the competence of the arbitral tribunal would be to determine its own jurisdiction, and not with binding effect determine the content of Community law. As with the *Swordfish* case, there would, however, be a potential for inconsistent jurisprudence if both the arbitral tribunal and the ECJ were to deal with the substantive obligations of the parties.

In conflicts between international courts and treaty bodies, there may be jurisdictional conflicts in respect of parallel proceedings. Such conflicting jurisdiction may be explicitly regulated, as in the ECHR which prohibits the European Court from dealing with matters that 'ha[ve] already been submitted to another procedure of international investigation or settlement and contains no relevant new information' (Article 35(2)(b)). Formally, the findings of international courts will prevail, however, since they are of a binding character. As regards international criminal courts, they deal with the responsibility of individuals, not states, and no conflicting jurisdiction will thus occur, but in relation to treaty bodies and international criminal courts, the result may also be inconsistent jurisprudence.

---

[37] *Dispute Concerning Access to Information under Article 9 of the OSPAR Convention*, Permanent Court of Arbitration, Final Award 2 July 2003 (<http://www.pca-cpa.org/showpage.asp?pag_id=1158>, last visited 27 March 2009).

[38] *The MOX Plant Case*, Permanent Court of Arbitration, Order No 3 24 June 2003 (<http://www.pca-cpa.org/showpage.asp?pag_id=1148>, last visited 27 March 2009).

[39] Case 459/03, *Commission of the European Communities v Ireland*, Judgment of the Court (Grand Chamber) of 30 May 2006.

Overlapping jurisdiction of different international tribunals will thus rarely create problems. But to the extent such overlaps exist, the principle of *res judicata* is an integral part of international law—preventing cases about issues that have already formally been decided by a binding judgment between the parties.[40] On the other hand, it does not seem that the principle of *litispendence* is as firmly embedded in international law[41]—but it is convincingly argued that this principle also applies to international tribunals so as to guarantee the prevention of parallel proceedings.[42] One might also claim that doctrines like abuse of rights (*abus de droit*), comity,[43] and a duty to cooperate in international law[44] may supplement these principles.

The infrequency of parallel jurisdictions suggests also that the possibilities of forum shopping—and a possible 'race to the bottom'—to a large extent are prevented. It may furthermore be added that forum shopping need not necessarily lead to the bottom. It could have the opposite effect in the form of a race to the top, in the sense that international tribunals will compete in providing the best judicial service to the parties by delivering judgments of high quality. That being said, the interest of the parties to a dispute is primarily to win the case, and not the professional skill demonstrated by the tribunal.

The potential problems are therefore largely related not to questions of jurisdiction, but to jurisprudence. Moreover, conflicting jurisprudence in a formal sense may only occur in cases of conflicting jurisdiction, where two (or more) tribunals have come to contradictory results concerning the same legal obligations for the same parties.[45] As this is not likely to occur very often, the focus should primarily be, not on conflicting jurisprudence, but instances of inconsistent jurisprudence. But how big is this problem?

The reasoning of the ICJ in the *Nicaragua*,[46] *Genocide*,[47] and *Democratic Republic of the Congo v Uganda*[48] cases and, on the other hand, the analysis by

---

[40] Chittharanjan Felix Amerasinghe *Jurisdiction of International Tribunals* (Kluwer Law International The Hague 2003), at 200.

[41] Karin Oellers-Frahm 'Multiplication of International Courts and Tribunals and Conflicting Jurisdiction—Problems and Possible Solutions' in Jochen A Frowein and Rüdiger Wolfrum (eds) (2001) 5 *Max Planck Yearbook of United Nations Law* 67–104, at 77; Jasper Finke 'Competing Jurisdiction of International Courts and Tribunals in Light of the *MOX Plant* Dispute' (2006) 49 *German Yearbook of International Law* 307–326, at 317; and Yuval Shany *The Competing Jurisdictions of International Courts and Tribunals* (OUP Oxford 2003), at 244.

[42] Lowe, Overlapping Jurisdiction, 1999, at 203 and August Reinisch 'The Use and Limits of *Res Judicata* and *Lis Pendens* as Procedural Tools to Avoid Conflicting Dispute Settlement Outcomes' (2004) 3 *The Law and Practice of International Courts and Tribunals* 37–77, at 48.

[43] Shany, *The Competing Jurisdiction*, 2003, at 255–266.

[44] Finke, Competing Jurisdiction, 2006, at 318.

[45] Reinisch, The Use and Limits, 2004, at 50–51 and Finke, Competing Jurisdiction, 2006, at 310.

[46] *Military and Paramilitary Activities in and against Nicaragua* (Nicaragua v United States) [1986] ICJ Reports 14.

[47] *Case Concerning the Application of the Convention on the Prevention and Punishment of the Crime of Genocide* (Bosnia and Herzegovina v Serbia and Montenegro) [2007] ICJ Reports 91.

[48] *Case Concerning Armed Activities on the Territory of the Congo* (Democratic Republic of the Congo v Uganda) [2005] ICJ Reports 116.

the ICTY in the *Tadic* case[49] has often been referred to as an example of inconsistent jurisprudence. The ICJ required the standard of 'effective control' over forces in another territory in order to involve the international legal responsibility of the supporting state, whereas the ICTY instead applied 'overall control' to establish the existence of an international character of a conflict. But as pointed out by Rosalyn Higgins, 'given the different relevant contexts, they hardly constitute a drama'.[50] She has furthermore emphasized that the ICJ in the *Genocide* case benefited much from the assessment of factual evidence and law in the case law from the ICTY, and that, on the other hand, the ICJ's considerations in the *Democratic Republic of the Congo v Uganda* may in the future prove useful for the ICC.[51]

While it is generally accepted that international law does not acknowledge binding precedents, there cannot be much doubt that international tribunals will take the decisions by other tribunals into account—in this sense the international judiciary applies a doctrine of precedent.[52] As stated by Thomas Buergenthal: 'But if other courts decide not to follow these precedents, they have an obligation, in my opinion, to distinguish these precedents, that is, to explain why they cannot or need not follow them, and do so by reference to generally accepted methods of international legal analysis and discourse.'[53] Rosalyn Higgins has pointed out 'the tremendous efforts that courts and tribunals make, both to be consistent inter se and to follow the International Court of Justice'.[54] This means that although there may be competition and rivalry between international tribunals, there are also legal doctrines and experiences indicating that the tribunals will strive towards achieving consistency in international jurisprudence.

Furthermore, different interpretations will not necessarily represent difficulties for states' implementation. A state may, for example, be required to respect the strictest standard of 'fair trial' imposed by different international courts. But difficulties may arise when different international tribunals assess reciprocal rights and obligations between two or more states, or balance different human rights differently.

---

[49] *Prosecutor v Tadic* Case IT-94-1-A Appeals Chamber of 15 July 1999.

[50] Higgins, A Babel of Judicial Voices?, 2006, at 795.

[51] Speech by H E Judge Rosalyn Higgins, President of the International Court of Justice, at the 58th Session of the International Law Commission (<http://untreaty.un.org/ilc/sessions/58/ICJ_President(e).pdf>, last visited 23 March 2009).

[52] See Robert Y Jennings 'The Judiciary, International and National, and the Development of International Law' (1996) 45 *ICLQ* 1–12, at 6; Mohamad Shahabuddeen 'Consistency in Holdings by International Tribunals' in Nisuke Ando, Edward McWhinney, and Rüdiger Wolfrum (eds) *Liber Amicorum Judge Shigeru Oda* (Kluwer Law International Leiden 2002) 633–650, at 646; and Anthony Aust 'Peaceful Settlement of Disputes: A Proliferation Problem?' in Tafsir Malick Ndiaye, Rüdiger Wolfrum, Thomas A Mensah, and Chie Kojima (eds) *Law of the Sea, Environmental Law and Settlement of Disputes* (Brill Leiden 2007) 131–141, at 137–138.

[53] Thomas Buergenthal 'Proliferation of International Courts and Tribunals: Is It Good or Bad?' (2001) 14 *Leiden Journal of International Law* 267–275, at 274.

[54] Higgins, A Babel of Judicial Voices?, 2006, at 797.

Finally, the increasing number of international tribunals may be thought to pose a threat to subject matters not endowed with their own judicial institutions, in the sense that such interest will not be represented in cases dealing with issues of relevance for them. The dispute settlement system of the WTO, for example, dealt with international environmental issues in the *Shrimp-Turtle* case.[55] Thus, we may see a snowball effect in substantive areas affected, but not yet covered by such international tribunals. A continued increase in specialized tribunals may partly be based on the 'defensive' need for protection against other specialized tribunals, but also on the 'offensive' interest of the sector's own needs.

The need for such protection may be lessened to the extent international tribunals take into account 'any relevant rules of international law applicable in the relations between the parties', in accordance with Article 31(3)(c) of the Vienna Convention on the Law of Treaties. This approach has been called '-systemic interpretation' by the Study Group of the International Law Commission on the Fragmentation of International Law.[56] Alan Boyle has, for example, concluded that the WTO Appellate Body 'has been rather sensitive to general international law' and 'has posed no threat to the viability of international environmental law'.[57] Furthermore, sectors characterized by a common interest of the international community may not necessarily see their interests best served by establishing international tribunals. International environmental law and arms control would be examples.[58]

It has thus far been concluded that, although the fragmented international judiciary may result in overlapping, conflicting, and inconsistent jurisdiction and jurisprudence, these problems should not be overstated. Now, possible ways to accommodate such difficulties by complementarity and/or horizontal integration and/or a vertical relationship between international tribunals will be discussed.

An approach based on complementarity would be to further define the respective substantive competences of different specialized tribunals. States may also be forced to choose between courts when accepting the jurisdiction of new courts. As we have seen, these methods are already applied—but they will not prevent jurisdictional disputes or inconsistent jurisprudence.

A horizontal integration of different international tribunals and/or a vertical international judiciary comparable to national constitutional structures,

---

[55] *United States—Import Prohibition of Certain Shrimp and Shrimp Products,* adopted WTO Dispute Settlement Body (DSB) 6 November 1998, WTO Appelate Body Report, Doc. WT/DS58/AB/R (1998).

[56] Martti Koskennimi *Fragmentation of International Law. Difficulties Aring from Diversification and Expansion of International Law. Report of the Study Group of the International Law Commission* (The Érik Castrén Institute Research Reports 21/2007 Helsinki), at 243–244 (paragraphs 479–480).

[57] Alan Boyle 'Relationship between International Environmental Law and Other Branches of International Law' in Daniel Bodansky, Jutta Brunnée, and Ellen Hey (eds) *The Oxford Handbook of International Environmental Law* (OUP Oxford 2007) 125–147, at 138.

[58] Ulfstein *et al Making Treaties Work. Human Rights, Environment and Arms Control,* 2007.

presumably with the ICJ at its apex, would represent a more ambitious structure. The ICJ could be established as an appeals court and, furthermore, other courts could be given the possibility of requesting preliminary rulings from the ICJ, comparable to the system between national courts and the ECJ.[59] A less ambitious project could be to pursue a sectoral horizontal and vertical integration. The UN High Commissioner for Human Rights has, for example, proposed replacing the existing human rights treaty bodies with a unified treaty body.[60] It is even possible to imagine a World Court for Human Rights.[61]

A general redesign of the international judicial architecture will, however, hardly find the necessary political support. It should also be pointed out that a diversified international judiciary also has its advantages. It makes it possible to establish new tribunals specially designed to serve the interests of the respective sectors. As has been stated by Martti Koskeniemmi and Päivi Leino, the increasing number of international tribunals 'arise as effects of politics and not as technical mistakes or unfortunate side-effects of some global logic'.[62] Moreover, the plurality of tribunals also has the advantage of increasing the international case law. While this surely may result in inconsistent jurisprudence, it provides in addition the opportunity to examine similar cases from different angles. The result may be a well-informed and consistent international case law, built up step by step.[63]

This may not seem to represent a constitutionalization of international law. It would at the most seem to look like an international 'legalization' or 'judicialization'.[64] But, first, it should be emphasized that the burgeoning of international tribunals should in itself be seen as representing a constitutionalization of international law by its empowerment of the international judiciary. This development means that the international judicial system looks increasingly like what we find in national constitutions. Furthermore, international tribunals exercise constitutional functions to the extent that they interact with national constitutional organs. Finally, they may even be given powers to review decisions by international organizations (see pp. 64–67).

What is more, the dearth of a formal hierarchy does not necessarily prevent international tribunals from acting in a functionally constitutionally manner, i.e.

---

[59] See Shany, *The Competing Jurisdictions*, 2003, at 272–277; Guillaume, The Future of International Judicial Institutions, 1995, at 862; and Oellers-Frahm, Multiplication of International Courts and Tribunals, 2001, at 91–98.

[60] Concept Paper on the High Commissioner's Proposal for a Unified Standing Treaty Body (14 March 2006).   [61] See Ulfstein, Do We Need a World Court of Human Rights?, 2008.

[62] Martti Koskenniemi and Päivi Leino 'Fragmentation of International Law? Postmodern Anxieties' (2002) 15 *Leiden Journal of International Law* 553–579, at 561.

[63] See Jonathan I Charney 'The Impact on the International Legal System of the Growth of International Courts and Tribunals' (1999) 31 *New York University Journal of International Law & Politics* 697–708, at 700. See also *idem* 'Is International Law Threatened by Multiple International Tribunals?' (1998) 271 *Recueil des Cours* 1.

[64] See Judith Goldstein, Miles Kahler, Robert O Keohane, and Anne-Marie Slaughter 'Introduction: Legalization and World Politics' (2000) 54 *International Organization* 385–399, at 389.

as a coherent structure. The existence of multiple tribunals obviously involves a danger of jurisdictional and jurisprudential conflicts and inconsistencies, but, as has been shown, the dangers should not be exaggerated. The difficulties represented by inconsistent jurisprudence may be alleviated by 'systemic interpretation' of the relevant treaties and by mutual acceptance of the precedential value of judgments from other tribunals. The appreciation of the reasoning by different courts is also augmented by the formal and informal contacts between the judges.[65] An increasing professional identity among the 200 international judges in permanent international tribunals may further advance consistency in their rulings.[66]

The respect for the dissimilar roles of different tribunals would further enhance the constitutional functions of the international judiciary. Hence, it could be argued that specialized tribunals should use restraint when addressing issues outside their own domain and covered by other tribunals, for example if the dispute settlement system of the WTO needs to deal with international human rights. Such courts could also use restraint when addressing legal questions of a general nature. General international courts could, on the other hand, show similar restraint when addressing issues falling within the jurisdiction of specialized courts. But it should be kept in mind that both specialized and general courts have a mandate to solve the case at hand in a legally proper way. They should also be considered to have a responsibility to develop international law within their special or general jurisdiction—even at the risk of contributing to inconsistencies between different international tribunals.

3.2 National courts

The questions of overlapping and conflicting jurisdiction and conflicting and inconsistent jurisprudence, as discussed above in relation to international tribunals, may be raised also between international tribunals and national courts. Indeed, Benedict Kingsbury finds that this is perhaps the greatest problem associated with the growth and jurisdiction of international courts and tribunals.[67]

But there is an important formal difference. Whereas international law may be fragmented in different legal fields with their own treaties and institutions, it is still one legal system. On the other hand, the idea of monism between the international and national legal system seems now to have been rejected in favour of a prevailing view of formal dualism, i.e. that international law is

---

[65] Anne-Marie Slaughter *A New World Order* (Princeton UP 2004), at 96–99.

[66] The number of judges is taken from Mackenzie and Sands, International Courts and Tribunals and the Independence of the International Judge, 2003, at 274.

[67] Benedict Kingsbury 'Foreword: Is the Proliferation of International Courts and Tribunals a Systemic Problem?' (1999) 31 *New York University Journal of International Law & Politics* 679–696, at 694.

separate from the different national legal systems.[68] Furthermore, there is no hierarchical structure between international and national law, or between international tribunals and national courts.[69]

This means that even if the same issues are dealt with both by an international tribunal and in a national court, the legal effects of the respective courts' actions would be different. Whereas international tribunals are the supreme rulers at the international level, national courts are supreme at the national level. Therefore, the judgments by international tribunals on the one hand, and national courts on the other, would not formally be in conflict: the international tribunal will make binding findings with respect to international law, whereas the binding effects of decisions of national courts will concern national law (except for supra-national organizations like the European Community). If, however, there should be different findings by the international tribunal and the national court in a legal question referring to the same issue, this may result in the international legal responsibility of the relevant state.

The dualist approach may not, however, provide a realistic representation of the interaction between international tribunals and national courts in practice.[70] First, the number of international obligations increases in different areas—including in areas traditionally considered domestic issues. Furthermore, international law is increasingly becoming part of national law through incorporation in national constitutions, legislation, and case law (the 'veil of dualism' has become more permeable). Finally, as we have seen, international tribunals are multiplying. The combined effects are that the risks of inconsistencies between decisions made by international tribunals and national courts are increasing correspondingly. This may cause confusion among the actors involved, be they states, with their legislative, executive, and judicial branches; international organizations; or non-state actors, including individuals and companies. To the extent that judgments by international tribunals are given internal legal effect in domestic legal systems, they may also become the source of contradictions in national law.

What is more, although there is no formal hierarchy between international tribunals and national courts, in the introduction to this chapter it has been argued that states in practice may feel compelled to accept the compulsory jurisdiction of international tribunals as well as to implement their decisions. On the other hand, international tribunals are dependent on the general allegiance of national courts for their credibility and viability. What should be the appropriate relationship between international tribunals and national courts?

---

[68] Janne Nijman and André Nollkaemper (eds) *New Perspectives on the Divide Between National and International Law* (OUP Oxford 2007), at 341 and Yuval Shany *Regulating Jurisdictional Relations Between National and International Courts* (OUP Oxford 2007), at 81.

[69] See Neil Walker 'Beyond Boundary Disputes and Basic Grids: Mapping the Global Disorder of Normative Orders' (2008) 6 *I•CON* 373–396, at 385–386.

[70] Nijman and Nollkaemper, *New Perspectives*, 2007, at 341 and Shany, *Regulating Jurisdictional Relations*, 2007, at 105–106.

The interface between international tribunals and national courts may be discussed both in respect to jurisdiction and to jurisprudence. But the relevant concerns are somewhat different from those related to the relationship between different international tribunals. As regards international tribunals and national courts, proper account should be taken of the need for decentralized decision-making, i.e. choosing institutions as close as possible to the parties and the circumstances of the case (including evidence and witnesses), and to the public debate about relevant political and legal issues (see pp. 147–148). Both these concerns militate in favour of decisions by national courts, i.e. according to the principle of subsidiarity.[71] On the other hand, there is a need to avoid national bias and to ensure the effective implementation of international law, which may be arguments in favour of international tribunals.

The problems connected with jurisdiction between international tribunals and national courts are regulated in general international law through the requirements of exhaustion of local remedies. There are also treaty arrangements giving effect to the concern of subsidiarity, such as the principle of complementarity or the use of internationalized ('hybrid') courts in international criminal law, and national courts requesting preliminary rulings of the ECJ.[72] Human rights treaty bodies will only give non-binding decisions and thus leave the final decisions to national courts.

Such jurisdictional arrangements can be important in determining the appropriate forum for the litigants: international or national. But they do not remove the risk of inconsistent jurisprudence between international tribunals and national courts. This raises the question whether the implicated tribunals and courts should respect a certain 'code of conduct' in their respective roles of international and national judicial organs.

As regards the respective jurisprudence of international tribunals and national courts, it may be asked to what extent international tribunals should exercise judicial restraint in order to allow more extensive freedom for national courts, or, conversely, whether national courts should exercise restraint—or should both international tribunals and national courts take an active part in the interpretation and development of international law?

The doctrine of a 'margin of appreciation' used by the European Court of Human Rights is a well-known example of an international tribunal exercising restraint in reviewing decisions by national authorities, including national courts. Yuval Shany has argued that a similar approach is also being used by other international tribunals—although the ICJ is reluctant—and, furthermore,

---

[71] See re subsidiarity: Isabel Feichtner 'Subsidiarity' *Max Planck Encyclopedia of Public International Law* at <http://www.mpepil.com>; Andreas Føllesdal 'Survey Article: Subsidiarity' (1998) 6 *The Journal of Political Philosophy* 190–218; Paolo G Carozza 'Subsidiarity as a Structural Principle of International Human Rights Law' (2003) 97 *AJIL* 38–79; and Mattias Kumm 'The Legitimacy of International Law: A Constitutionalist Framework of Analysis' (2004) 15 *EJIL* 907–931, at 920–924.   [72] Shany *Regulating Jurisdictional Relations*, 2007, at 27–36.

that such use is commendable as a more general approach.[73] He claims that the margin of appreciation should have a special role concerning international norms that are legal standards, discretionary or result-oriented.[74] But, as he also points out, an application of a margin of appreciation may be norm-eroding and it may not take into account the problem of externalities, i.e. that adversely affected non-parties to the dispute are not afforded effective protection. The latter factor could justify a distinction between 'inward-looking' and 'outward-looking' norms, with more latitude given to national courts concerning the former norms.[75]

It would seem that this distinction is essential: there is more reason to respect decisions by national courts in matters concerning traditionally domestic issues, such as criminal procedure. Relevant examples from the practice of the ICJ are the review and reconsideration of conviction and sentences by US courts in contravention of the duty to notify defendants of their right to consular assistance. In the *LaGrand* case, the ICJ stated that '[t]his obligation can be carried out in various ways. The choice of means must be left to the United States'.[76] This was later confirmed in the *Avena* case.[77] It should be added that such discretion was permitted by the ICJ without explicit application of a margin of appreciation.

On the other hand, the interpretation of the prohibition against the use of armed force and the right to self-defence should be entirely up to international tribunals to decide, and it is difficult to accept Shany's view that national authorities should be allowed a margin of appreciation in determining what are necessary and proportional self-defence actions.[78] Furthermore, 'inward-looking' norms may also be of fundamental international importance, such as the prohibition against the use of torture—as also accepted by Shany—so that no margin of appreciation should be accepted.

Should national courts be deferential towards decisions by international tribunals? National courts should be cautious in challenging international tribunals' decisions in matters that are primarily of an international character. But as the distinction between issues of an international and national character increasingly becomes blurred, national courts may have an important role to play in many fields of international law. National courts should contribute with national experiences and cultural conceptions, and play a particular role in issues where local knowledge is of importance. They should also actively take part in the interpretation and development of international

---

[73] Yuval Shany 'Toward a General Margin of Appreciation Doctrine in International Law' (2005) 16 *EJIL* 907–940.

[74] Shany, Toward a General Margin of Appreciation Doctrine, 2005, at 914–917.

[75] *Ibid*, at 912 and 924–925.

[76] *LaGrand* (Germany v United States of America), [2001] ICJ Reports, 466 paragraph 125.

[77] *Avena and Other Mexican Nationals* (Mexico v United States of America) [2004] 12 paragraph 141.   [78] Shany, Toward a General Margin of Appreciation Doctrine, 2005, at 937.

legal norms, and not shy away from tensions resulting from different interpretations of such norms.

The international legal system recognizes that national judicial practice is a
relevant source in international law, as reflected in the statute of the ICJ Article
38(1)(d). But the doctrine of precedent should also be applied when national
courts assess the significance of international judgments. In this way the combined practice of international tribunals and national courts would form the
basis for developing more precise international rules. National courts should,
however, bear in mind that international tribunals have the final say at the
international level. They should furthermore consider the risk of international
legal responsibility of the state if binding international judgments are not
respected.

The disrespect of the ICJ's *Avena* judgment by the US Supreme Court in
the *Medellin* case[79] would contribute to undermining a relationship based on
consistency between the international and national judiciary. The *Kadi* judgment[80] is more ambiguous. The ECJ annulled measures adopted pursuant to a
UN Security Council resolution as contrary to the fundamental rights of
individuals under European Community law. Although this case concerned the
relationship between the Security Council and the ECJ, and not the relationship between an international tribunal and a national court, it provides an
instructive example of possible conflicts between the international and national
judiciary.

Non-compliance with an international judgment directed to a state could be
seen as a form of de-constitutionalization, in the sense that the international and
national judiciary system would not work in a functionally integrated manner.
But on the other hand, the endeavour by national courts to provide stronger
protection of human rights than accepted by international tribunals could in
itself be seen as a form of constitutionalization, in the sense that national courts
protect substantive values that traditionally have been considered worthy of
constitutional protection (see pp. 77–79).

There is no indication of a development towards a formally constitutionalized
global judicial system of a supra-national character, like the European Community. The combined effect of the increasing significance of international tribunals and their recognition by national courts mean, however, that the
international and national judiciary work as a more integrated system. To the
extent that international tribunals and national courts acknowledge their
respective functions in the interpretation and application of international law—
although tensions will inevitably arise—the combined international and national
judicial judiciary may in practice work as a constitutionalized system.

---

[79] *Medellin v Texas* 552 U.S. ___ (2008).
[80] Cases C-402/05P and C-415/05P, *Kadi and Al Barakaat v Council and Commission*, Judgment of the Court (Grand Chamber) of 3 September 2008.

4. Democratic Control

Democratic control is a fundamental part of constitutionalism. But majority ruling is restricted by another constitutional principle, i.e. the separation of powers. This means that national courts should be independent of political control in their judicial function. Likewise, international tribunals should be independent of political control of both states and international institutions in their function as tribunals. How should the need for democratic control and the independence of international tribunals be balanced—both in relation to national and international law-makers?

4.1 National legislator

While the national legislature may adjust the law as understood by national courts through law-making, this avenue is not available when it comes to decisions by international tribunals. Furthermore, the composition of the tribunals is the result of collective action by the states, and the possibility of influencing international tribunals through their composition are therefore beyond the control of individual governments.[81]

The 'counter-majoritarian' character of national courts has received much attention in current scholarship.[82] The focus has been particularly on constitutional review of legislation, and the concern that such review is undertaken by democratically unaccountable judges, at the expense of the democratically elected legislators. It could be argued that leaving decisions to international tribunals beyond national control is even more worrisome from a democratic point of view—possibly with the exception of treaty bodies making non-binding findings. The democratic legitimacy of international tribunals has, however, only been the subject of scant consideration.[83]

The counter-majoritarian argument may be most pertinent in matters traditionally considered domestic affairs. In typically foreign policy matters, the

---

[81] Helfer and Slaughter have emphasized the non-formal political and discursive constraints on international tribunals ('constrained independence'), see Helfer and Slaughter, Why States Create International Tribunals: A Response to Professors Posner and Yoo, 2005, at 930 and 942–954.

[82] See Jeremy Waldron 'The Core of the Case Against Judicial Review' (2006) 115 *Yale Law Journal* 1346–1406 and Richard Bellamy *Political Constitutionalism. A Republican Defence of the Constitutionality of Democracy* (CUP Cambridge 2007).

[83] A Norwegian government report on power and democracy concluded that representative democracy was eroding, partly due to conferral of power to international tribunals. See NOU 2003:19 *Makt og demokrati. Sluttrapport fra makt- og demokratiutredningen* (at <http://www.regjeringen.no/en/dep/fad/Documents/ NOUer/2003/NOU-2003-019.html?id=118893>) and Per Selle and Øyvind Østerud 'The Eroding of Representative Democracy in Norway' (2006) 13 *Journal of European Public Policy* 551–568, at 563. See also Tom Campbell, Keith D Ewing, and Adam Tomkins (eds) *Sceptical Essays on Human Rights* (OUP Oxford 2001).

legislature has been more sympathetic to the idea that the executive has a more prominent function, and that negotiations with other states take place on a confidential basis. But as it becomes harder to distinguish between what should be considered foreign and domestic, leaving any issues affecting state interests under the final control of international tribunals may be increasingly difficult to accept.

States enter into treaties because they want to achieve other objectives than those available through national legislation. The objectives may be manifold. One essential purpose is to commit the other treaty parties—be it concerning international trade, human rights, or environmental protection. But there may also be other reasons, such as achieving a status of good standing in the international community. If states were to renege on their international commitments, including the willingness to respect decisions by international tribunals, they would therefore—through weakening of the international commitment—not only frustrate the other treaty parties, but also the objectives sought to be achieved by the committing state itself by entering into the treaty. The achievement of such objectives may provide a democratic legitimacy for restricting states' freedom through treaties establishing international tribunals.

There may also be matters that are considered of such fundamental importance that national policy-makers would see them protected against interference by future national legislators. Treaties and international tribunals may then be used as a form of self-commitment. First and foremost, this applies to human rights—including democratic rights, such as the freedoms of speech and of assembly. A primary purpose of human rights is exactly that individual dignity should be protected against abuses by the majority. One may also envisage other fields to be of such international importance that national policy-makers may want to restrict the national freedom, such as the protection of the environment and international peace and security.

On the other hand, the need for protection against the national legislature is a relative question. The point of departure should be the freedom of the democratically elected national institutions to determine the law of the land. The interference by international tribunals should only be accepted to the extent that this serves genuine international and national needs which require restrictions on national freedom. Furthermore, a distinction should be made between issues of, on the one hand, a fundamentally international character or serving to protect fundamental common values, and, on the other hand, those which are better addressed at the national level. Such criteria may be applied when determining the allocation of jurisdiction to international tribunals, but also as guidelines for the exercise of such tribunals' jurisdiction through their jurisprudence. This militates in favour of such principles as subsidiarity, complementarity, and a margin of appreciation—which have been discussed in relation to national courts above.

4.2 International legislator

The absence of a legislator (or legislator*s*) in international law may be an argument in favour of judicial activism by international courts so that essential legal problems may be clarified, in relying on such judgments as precedents. On the other hand, since a legislator—national or international—may have difficulties in adjusting 'law-making' by international courts, a more cautionary approach could be envisaged in drawing up general rules through jurisprudence. Should international courts take account of the (un)availability of international legislative authorities—either as a basis for judicial restraint or activism?

The European Community may be taken as a model of a legal system combining extensive judicial control with international law-making. The judicial activism of the ECJ may be considered to be based on the mandate of the Community ('ever closer union'). But such activism could also be justified by the existence of an effective Community legislator. On the other hand, the DSU/WTO could be considered less legitimate in judicial activism, partly because of its mandate, since its rulings 'cannot add to or . . . diminish the rights and obligations provided in the covered agreements' (DSU Article 3 (2)), and, furthermore, because of the absence of legislative powers of the WTO.[84] This could be taken as an argument for strengthening the legislative arm of the WTO. It has, however, been maintained that this avenue is currently not very realistic.[85]

The European Court of Human rights is well known for its progressive interpretation, while also taking into account any emerging consensus on human rights standards it finds among member states.[86] The activist role of the Court may be justified by the preamble of the Convention, which refers to the need for achieving 'greater unity' between the member states of the Council of Europe. Furthermore, the Court's function is to protect human rights—if necessary at the expense of the majority view among national legislators. It could be argued that this important task should be undertaken without any political interference whatsoever—or at least only through the cumbersome process of treaty amendment. On the other hand, it could be asserted that the amendment procedure should be comparable to features known from national constitutions, such as qualified majority voting and other threshold barriers. In the international context this could imply a qualified majority vote by the treaty parties and

---

[84] Armin von Bogdandy 'Law and Politics in the WTO—Strategies to Cope with a Deficient Relationship' in Jochen A Frowein and Rüdiger Wolfrum (eds) (2001) 5 *Max Planck Yearbook of United Nations Law* 609–674, at 618 and 647–649 and Joel P Trachtman 'The Constitutions of the WTO' (2006) 17 *EJIL* 623–646, at 625 and 632.

[85] Steinberg, Judicial Lawmaking at the WTO: Discursive, Constitutional, and Political Constraints, 2004, at 274.

[86] Helen Keller and Alec Stone Sweet (eds) *A Europe of Rights. The Impact of the ECHR on National Legal Systems* (OUP Oxford 2008), at 6.

possibly other specified procedures, overcoming the need for unanimity but protecting against quick and frequent amendments.

It may be concluded that extensive empowerment of international tribunals may be necessary in order to achieve what are considered important international objectives—even at the expense of democratic majority ideals. But the tension between international effectiveness and democratic control should have a bearing on how international tribunals exercise their powers.

It should firstly be pointed out that it is generally accepted that international tribunals have a role in developing international law, although the appropriate balance between activism and restraint may be the subject of debate.[87] The application of an expansive or a more restrictive approach should primarily be determined on the basis of the mandate of the relevant tribunal. But it would in addition seem more legitimate to accept expansive interpretations from international tribunals if their power is balanced by an international legislator.

Global integration represented by ever-more restrictive obligations imposed by international tribunals could be outweighed by positive integration through international law-making. More empowerment to international legislators, however, entails its own challenges. First, it should be pointed out that development of legislatures within different treaty regimes may lead to a more fragmented international law. More effective international decision-making may also empower the national executive at the expense of the legislature. Further, there are no clear-cut models for building international democracy (see chapter 6). Finally, more powers to international law-making authorities raise the issue of international constitutional control of such legislation (see pp. 64–67 on judicial review).

5. Conclusions

The increasing number of international tribunals represents an empowerment of international legal organs in the sense that more substantive areas are covered by such mechanisms, including areas traditionally regarded as domestic affairs; these organs have an increasingly compulsory character, either in legal or in political terms, or both; and they undertake important law-making functions. This means that international tribunals in practice exercise functions that earlier were the exclusive domain of national constitutional organs, and these international functions are largely beyond the control of national organs. Hence, the empowerment of international tribunals should in itself be seen as an aspect of international constitutionalization.

[87] See Hugh Thirlway 'Judicial Activism and the International Court of Justice' in Nisuke Ando, Edward McWhinney, and Rüdiger Wolfrum (eds) *Liber Amicorum Judge Shigeru Oda* (Kluwer Law International Leiden) 75–105 and Pieter Kooijmans 'The ICJ in the 21st Century: Judicial Restraint, Judicial Activism, or Proactive Judicial Policy' (2007) 56 *ICLQ* 741–754.

International tribunals should be guided by comparable procedural human rights and constitutional standards as those applicable for national courts in terms of their composition, independence, equality of access, and fair hearing. The nomination and election of judges should be based more on merit; international organizations, individuals, and companies should increasingly be given access to the tribunals; the parties should be given the possibility of presenting their case both in a written and oral form; there should be possibilities for reliable fact-finding; and the proceedings should be transparent.

International tribunals must relate to two constitutional functions, i.e. the judiciary and the legislature, and two levels, the international and national. It has been argued that jurisdictional overlap between different international tribunals has so far not represented a major problem, although it may result in inconsistent jurisprudence. The establishment of a hierarchic international judiciary is not realistic in the short term and may not even be desirable at the present time. The benefits of the current diversity of international tribunals are that the tribunals may be designed according to their specialized functions and that the international case law is enriched. The increasing involvement of national courts in questions concerning international law may also contribute to clarifying and developing international law.

It has, however, been concluded that in the absence of formal rules about the relationship between different courts and tribunals at the international and national level, it is essential that the respective judicial organs act in a constitutionalized manner: they should all be guided by precedents in the sense that decisions by other courts and tribunals are taken into account. Furthermore, specialized tribunals should exercise restraint when addressing issues beyond their special regimes, and general courts should show similar restraint in dealing with issues within the jurisdiction of specialized courts. International tribunals should respect the principle of subsidiarity in relation to issues that should primarily be addressed by national courts. On the other hand, national courts should respect that issues of a primarily international character should be finally decided by international tribunals.

The increasing importance of international tribunals also raises democratic challenges. Unlike the situation in national law, individual national law-makers are not in a position to change the law if they disagree with the decisions of international tribunals. The counter-majoritarian character of international tribunals may thus be more strongly felt than in relation to national courts. It has, however, been argued that the aim of treaties, including those establishing international tribunals, is different from national laws. States accept being bound in order to commit the other treaty parties. The achievement of international objectives as mutually defined by states, but beyond the reach of national legislation, may justify restrictions on the national legislator. Self-commitment may furthermore be justified in certain issues, especially in human rights. Such restrictions on national law-making are more difficult to defend in traditionally domestic affairs and where a final decision by international tribunals is less essential. The increasing empowerment of international tribunals is furthermore an argument in favour of balancing this power with stronger international legislators—with due respect to the principle of subsidiarity.

Finally, the protection of human rights is fundamental both in international and national law. If human rights are not protected at the national level, there are international tribunals to review such violations of the international obligations. But if international tribunals violate international human rights, national courts should not respect such decisions. In these cases, the fundamental constitutional value of protecting human rights should prevail over the significance of respecting decisions by international tribunals.

5

Membership in the Global Constitutional Community

Anne Peters

1. The Constitutional Community

The legal subjects within the framework of the contemporary international legal order are widely conceived as an international community.[1] The international community might be a precondition or, on the contrary, the result of the constitutionalization of the international legal order. The concept might also function as a substitute for a global constitution.

A community can be distinguished from a mere agglomeration on account of the closeness and the common objectives of its component entities. A community is, in short, integrated. It possesses members, and is not made up of only isolated actors. The concept of an international community suggests inclusiveness, and therefore tends to favour rather than to hinder the inclusion of non-state actors. The concept also implies that the mutual relationships are more than bilateral or plurilateral ones. Furthermore, the idea of a *legal* community means that the relationships are governed by law, and not by force. Finally, the concept evokes (rightly or wrongly) some common 'spirit' or identity. The concept of an international community has been criticized as concealing a *de facto* oligarchy. It has been pointed out that there 'is a danger of the implantation in international society of a legislative power enabling certain states—the most powerful or numerous ones—to promulgate norms that will be imposed on the others'. Thus, concepts such as that of the '"international community"

---

[1] See Art 53 VCLT; Art 42 lit. b) and 48 sec. 1 lit. b) ILC-Articles on the Responsibility of States for International Wrongful Acts of 2001 (UN Doc A/CN.4/L.602, Rev.1). In scholarship seminally Hermann Mosler 'The International Society as a Legal Community' (1974/IV) 140 *Recueil des Cours* 1–230, at 11–12: '[I]nternational society is at the same time a legal community which regulates its members' relations with one another and with organized institutions by rules and principles and maxims of conduct.' See for a focus on natural persons as a member of the community René-Jean Dupuy *La Communauté internationale entre le mythe et l'histoire* (Economica Paris 1986), e.g. at 180. See further Christian Tomuschat 'Die internationale Gemeinschaft' (1995) 33 *Archiv des Völkerrechts* 1–20; Andreas Paulus *Die internationale Gemeinschaft im Völkerrecht* (Beck München 2001).

may become code words, lending themselves to all kinds of manipulation, under whose cloak certain states may strive to implant an ideological system of law',[2] says the critique.

I submit that the constitutionalist paradigm is both a useful extension of the concept of the international community and apt to counter the critique of concealed oligarchy. Stating that the international community is a *constitutional* community evokes the constitutionalist principle of democracy and thus offers a leverage for making visible and arguing against the privileges of some states, such as the permanent members of the Security Council. Moreover, constitutionalism provides both a parsimonious explanation for the existing community-like features of the international legal order, and allows the easy extrapolation of these features.

First, the constitutionalist paradigm explains the existence of *erga omnes* norms.[3] Why should certain obligations create rights or at least interests for non-affected actors, and possibly even allow those to apply countermeasures or to raise claims? One answer could be that those actors are members of the constitutional community. A body of (international) constitutional law, even if not codified in one single document, provides some glue to hold actors together, because it sets out common objectives or aspirations, and defines the rules of interaction. This type of integration makes the legal possibility of claims by actors not directly affected much more plausible. On the other hand, the establishment of hierarchical centralized enforcement mechanisms, which would be an important component of an international constitutional order, could also render the concept of *erga omnes* norms superfluous. *Erga omnes* norms seem to be a device to facilitate the protection of community interests in a 'horizontal' manner in the absence of hierarchical enforcement (see on this issue p. 133).

Second, a constitutionalist reading allows overcoming the dichotomy between original, full international legal subjects on the one hand, and derivative and partial legal subjects on the other. This dichotomy was in reality only a reification of the distinction between states as the makers of international law and all other, newer, subjects, such as international organizations or individuals. In opposition to this view, the constitutionalist approach decentres the state. If the international system is conceived as possessing constitutional law, the following argument can be raised: once a constitutional order has been set in place by the global multiple *pouvoirs constituants*, it no longer makes sense to speak of 'original' legal subjects, because all subjects have been transformed into *pouvoirs constitués*. Therefore, the distinction between 'original' and 'derivative' subjects breaks down. The various types of members of a constitutional community have

---

[2] Prosper Weil 'Towards Relative Normativity in International Law?' (1983) 77 *AJIL* 413–442, at 441.

[3] See ICJ, *Legal Consequences of the Construction of a Wall in the Occupied Palestinian Territory*, Advisory Opinion, ICJ Reports 2004, 136, paras 155–157; Art 48 sec. 1 lit. a) and b) ILC Articles.

different rights and obligations, as defined by constitutional law, but there is no categorical distinction between states and all others.

Certainly, the constitutionalist approach does not deny, and to my mind even explains better than traditional approaches, the difference between being (only) able to *have* international rights and obligations (as is currently the case for individuals), and being capable of *making* international law. But while insisting on this categorical difference, the constitutionalist view promotes the future evolution of the international rules on law-making in the direction of an involvement of natural persons in the international law-making process. From a constitutionalist perspective, natural persons should in the long run acquire some kind of limited law-making power.

This leads us to the third and related normative point. The constitutionalist approach offers a new foundation for the view that the ultimate international legal subjects are individuals, as has already been espoused by Georges Scelle[4] and others. Constitutionalism, as I understand it, postulates that natural persons are the ultimate unit of legal concern. Global constitutionalists abandon the idea that sovereign states are the material source of international norms.[5] In consequence, the ultimate normative source of international law is—from a constitutionalist perspective—humanity, not sovereignty.

Fourth, the current trend of the reopening of the circle of members of the global community, so as to now include international organizations, individuals, non-governmental organizations (NGOs), transnational corporations (TNCs), hybrid actors such as public–private partnerships and quasi-governmental organizations (quangos), or even terrorist groups, can be explained from a constitutionalist perspective. It should be recalled that historically international legal relations were restricted to states only in the course of the 19th century. Before, the *jus naturae et gentium* had not dealt with legal relations between independent entities (states), but was concerned with the universal validity of certain rules for all peoples and humans.[6] Because ultimately all law was derived from nature, the *jus gentium* was not distinguished sharply from internal law.[7] Consequently, its actors were also not sharply distinguished. But because in a pluralist world natural law is no viable path, the current trend which reverses the narrowing-down tendency of the 19th century must be interpreted and backed up differently than with a resort to natural law. It can be interpreted and welcomed as a trend towards inclusiveness and towards empowerment, which means a trend towards the realization of basic tenets of constitutionalism.

---

[4] See the references below in note 13.   [5] See also below p. 179.
[6] Ulrich Scheuner 'Die grossen Friedensschlüsse als Grundlage der europäischen Staatenordnung zwischen 1648 und 1815' reprinted in *idem Schriften zum Völkerrecht* (Duncker & Humblot Berlin 1984 Tomuschat ed) 352–354.
[7] Hugo Grotius in *De iure belli ac pacis* (first published 1625) did distinguish between the national law and the *jus gentium* (book I, chapter I, XIV (at 44)). However, Grotius treated numerous legal issues that are today counted as domestic law, such as contracts, rights of persons, promises, donations, and the like within the *jus gentium*.

Finally, the constitutionalist vocabulary can help explain the transnational activities of NGOs and also of TNCs as an emerging global civil society. The concept of a global civil society in turn facilitates the formulation of consistent proposals on the reform of the international legal status of both types of actors (see below pp. 219–262, and also chapter 6).

But while supporting inclusion, the constitutionalist approach prevents abandonment of the distinction between legal subjects and actors devoid of international legal personality, as suggested by adherents of the New Haven School and other authors.[8] A constitutional order defines and determines the law-making processes. It thus introduces a high degree of formalism into the legal process. On the premise that international law includes a body of constitutional rules, the distinction between informal and formal participation in the international legal process must be upheld. One reason for this is the need to safeguard legal clarity and certainty. If all kinds of activities, ranging from lobbying to codifications by interested academics, could without further official acts of public authority create international law, citizens would have no means to recognize and readily identify the law. Ultimately, the rule of law would be undermined, and this runs counter to constitutionalist aspirations. A second reason for upholding the distinction between international legal persons and other actors is that the concept of international legal personality has the 'function of forming an essential link between the international legal system, democracy and the individual',[9] which corresponds to constitutionalist objectives.

While opposing the abandonment of the concept of the (international) legal person, constitutionalist-minded international lawyers tend to favour the formalization of the legal status of those actors who are currently still devoid of international legal personality, notably NGOs and TNCs, although the current discrepancy between the *de facto* influence of those actors and their formal incapacity is, from a constitutionalist perspective, ambivalent. On the one hand, NGOs and transnational corporations should be kept at a distance from the international law-making process. The reason is that civil society actors need to stay outside the formal political and legal process in order to fulfil their watchdog and opposition function. On the other hand, the irregular international status of corporations, and also of NGOs, is pernicious because it leaves space for the exploitation of their power for self-interested goals to the detriment of the public good and of affected individuals. In this respect, the formalization of

[8] See Myres McDougal 'International Law, Power, and Policy: A Contemporary Conception' (1953/I) *Recueil des Cours* 137–259, at 173–174; Rosalyn Higgins 'Conceptual Thinking about the Individual in International Law' (1978) 4 *BYIL* 1–19, at 5. See also Philip Allott *Eunomia: New Order for a New World* (OUP Oxford 1990), at 372: '[I]nternational law must abandon the conceptual category of subjects of international law.'
[9] Janne Elisabeth Nijman *The Concept of International Legal Personality: An Inquiry into the History and Theory of International Law* (TMC Asser Press The Hague 2004), at 27.

the status, e.g. of business actors, would engender legal clarity and containment, which is laudable from a constitutionalist perspective.

To conclude, the constitutionalist account can on the descriptive level rely on legal experience. It offers explanations for important current legal phenomena relating to the international community and saves the trouble of citing controversial philosophical accounts of communitarianism. At the same time, normative constitutionalism as an agenda of legal politics functions as a heuristic device, as a guideline for the (dynamic) interpretation of international law towards a more constitutionalized community. Overall, a dialectical process occurs: the emergence and extension of a global constitutional community is both a manifestation and a driver of global constitutionalism, while the constitutionalization of international law is at the same time an explanation and a promoter of this communitarization. That said, one should keep in mind that the normative and practical power of international law ultimately does not depend on the use of the term international community as such (nor the use of the concept of constitution), but rather on concrete institutions, principles, and rules.[10]

2. Individuals

2.1 Primary international legal persons

In a constitutionalized world order, natural persons are the primary international legal persons and the primary members of the global constitutional community, as will be explained in this section.[11] I have already mentioned that historically speaking private individuals were embedded until far into the 18th century in the 'natural and public international' legal order. Only the gradual emancipation of public international law from natural law (completed only in legal positivism in the 19th century[12]), the personification of the state, and the legal focus on inter-state relations had led to the expulsion of individuals from the realm of public international law. Today, the re-introduction of the individual should not come as natural law in disguise, but should rely on other considerations, and I deem constitutionalist considerations a useful starting point.

The view that individuals are not only the actual beneficiaries of all international law, but even the ultimate or even sole legal persons (or subjects) of this order, was

---

[10] Bruno Simma 'From Bilateralism to Community Interests in International Law' (1994/VI) 250 *Recueil des Cours* 217–384, at 248.

[11] *Cf* Tesón's 'normative individualism', i.e. the insistence 'that our moral concepts should be referred in the last analysis to individual rights and interests'. Fernando Tesón *A Philosophy of International Law* (Westlake Boulder 1998), at 27.

[12] See Albert Zorn *Grundzüge des Völkerrechts* (2nd edn Verlagsbuchhandlung von JJ Weber 1903), at 3: 'Träger völkerrechtlicher Beziehungen sind also niemals Privatpersonen, sondern ausschliesslich Staaten...' See also *idem*, at 26 *et seq*.

espoused by international scholars notably in the inter-war period.[13] The inter-war international legal individualism, which foreshadowed the general recognition and codification of international human rights, was not only a reaction to the human rights abuses of the Great War. It was also strongly motivated by concerns for democracy, and by a fear of the society of the masses. More specifically, the 'individualistic'-minded international lawyers sensed the rise of totalitarianism, and sought to defend human individuality via international law.[14] A second boost for moving individuals to the centre of the international legal system were the Nuremberg trials of 1946, which established the international responsibility and criminal liability of human beings and removed the smokescreen of the state behind which perpetrators of crimes sought to hide.[15] Since then, the *lex lata* has evolved in the direction foreseen by academics in the 1930s. Contemporary international lawyers diagnose a paradigm-shift in international law in the sense that the integration of individuals in the international legal process, far beyond human rights, has become 'the basic axiom' of the international legal order.[16] This has been called a shift 'from the law of nations to the law of the world'[17] or a 'humanization of international law'.[18] From that perspective, '[t]he individual is the ultimate unit of all law, international and municipal'.[19]

2.2 The individual's right to have international rights

The right to legal personality, the 'right to have rights',[20] is acknowledged in international law (Article 6 Human Rights Declaration; Article 16(2) ICCPR).

---

[13] See Hans Kelsen 'Les Rapports de Système entre le Droit Interne et le Droit International Public' (1926/IV) 14 *Recueil des Cours* 231–329, at 281: 'L'idée qu'il y aurait entre l'État et les individus, et par suite d'État à État, des rapports qui ne seraient pas des rapports entre individus est une simple illusion, qui ne s'explique que par l'inadmissible hypostase de l'État en un surhomme.' Bourquin diagnosed 'une poussée, chaque jour plus visible, en faveur de ce qu'on pourrait appeler l'émancipation internationale de l'individu.' (Maurice Bourquin 'Règles Générales du Droit de la Paix' (1931/I) 35 *Recueil des Cours* 5–229, at 46). See notably also Georges Scelle *Précis de Droit des Gens, Principes et Systématique* vol I, Introduction, le milieu intersocial 'en droit international public.' at 42: 'Les individus seuls sont sujets de droit en droit international public.' Also Brierly taught that 'en dernière analyse, seuls les individus sont susceptibles d'être sujets de ce droit-là [i.e. international law]'. (James Leslie Brierly 'Règles Générales du Droit de la Paix' (1936/IV) 58 *Recueil des Cours* 5–237, at 47).
[14] See for an excellent analysis Nijman, *International Legal Personality*, 2004, at 87, 126–127, 130, 147–148, 171, 187, 225 and *passim*.
[15] See below pp. 174–179.
[16] Oliver Dörr 'Privatisierung des Völkerrechts' (2005) 60 *Juristen-Zeitung* 905–916, at 905; see also P K Menon 'The Legal Personality of Individuals' (1994) 6 *Sri Lanka Journal of International Law* 127–156, at 148.
[17] Angelika Emmerich-Fritsche *Vom Völkerrecht zum Weltrecht* (Duncker & Humblot Berlin 2007).
[18] Theodor Meron *The Humanization of International Law* (Martinus Nijhoff Leiden 2006).
[19] Hersch Lauterpacht 'The Grotian Tradition of International Law' (1946) 23 *BYIL* 1–53, at 27.
[20] Hannah Arendt *The Origins of Totalitarianism* (Harcourt, Brace and Company New York 1951), at 287–298, esp. at 294, deploring the plight of persecuted persons and refugees who were often divested of their nationality, stateless, and thus rightless.

Historically, these codifications responded to the practice of totalitarian regimes to divest political opponents of their rights ('civil death'). These provisions have therefore been traditionally interpreted as relating only to the national level, as a guarantee of domestic legal personality. However, in times of globalization and of the intermingling of the national and international spheres of law and governance, the guarantee would be seriously weakened if limited to domestic law. Given the fact that international rules matter for persons' lives, the lack of an international legal status would affect them a similar way as the lack of a domestic legal status in former times affected slaves and outlaws.

From a constitutionalist perspective, the empowerment of individual beings is a core objective of any constitutional order. This premise leads to interpreting the relevant guarantees in a teleological way along the line just drawn. The constitutionalist interpretation of Articles 6 Human Rights Declaration and 16 (2) ICCPR is that these provisions may not reasonably be limited to the domestic legal capacity, but that they enshrine a human right to have international legal personality.[21]

2.3 Individual rights to participation: towards individuals' law-making power

Although individuals already have rights and obligations under international law as it stands, they do not possess the capacity to make international law. They can not conclude treaties, and their behaviour does not constitute relevant practice which could lead to the formation of customary law. On these grounds, some authors conclude that individual persons are therefore still not international legal subjects,[22] or at best merely 'passive subjects'.[23] In this view, individuals are still considered as 'an object on which to bestow or recognize rights, not as agents from whom emanates the power to do such bestowing [,] ... as an object or, at best, as a consumer of outcomes, but not as an agent of process.'[24]

I submit that the characterization of individuals as mere consumers of international law does not do justice to their current standing in the international legal system. Although it is technically correct that states have created the

---

[21] See in this sense also Nijman, *International Legal Personality*, 2004, at 466.

[22] Prosper Weil 'Le droit international en quête de son identité: Cours générale de droit international public' (1924/VI) 237 *Recueil des Cours* 9–370, at 122: individuals are only objects of international law because they do not themselves make international law but are only conferred certain rights and obligations by states.

[23] Robert Kolb 'Nouvelle observation sur la détermination de la personalité juridique internationale' (2002) 57 *Zeitschrift für öffentliches Recht* 229–241, esp. at 236 and 239.

[24] Joseph H H Weiler 'The Geology of International Law—Governance, Democracy and Legitimacy' (2004) 64 *Zeitschrift für ausländisches öffentliches Recht und Völkerrecht* 547–562, at 558. See also Michel Cosnard 'Rapport introductif' in Société française pour le droit international (ed) *Colloque de Mans: Le sujet en droit international* (Paris 2005) 13–53, at 51 '[L]es individus ne sont pas maîtres de leurs droits internationaux'.

international legal status (rights and obligations) of natural persons, this status has allowed and continues to allow individuals to emancipate themselves. They have in legal terms become active legal subjects and in political terms transnational citizens (pp. 296–313).

A first aspect of this emancipation or empowerment are internationally guaranteed rights to participation in the international legal process and in transnational governance. Participatory rights are at least on the halfway point between merely having rights and making law, and blur the line between law-producers and bystanders. Most participation of natural persons in the international legal process happens through NGOs (see below pp. 220–235). There are also other types of participation, which, however, remain quite weak. One type is contained in the safeguard policies adopted by the World Bank since 1997. Although these policies do not refer to international human rights instruments, a number of them foresee participation and empowerment of persons affected by bank-financed projects. For instance, the operational policy on indigenous people requires free, prior, and informed consultation with affected communities about the proposed project throughout the project cycle.[25] The operational policy on involuntary resettlement highlights that '[t]he involvement of involuntary resettlers and hosts in planning prior to the move is critical'.[26] A similar instance are participatory rights in (to some extent transnationalized) settlements on indigenous rights, e.g. fishing rights, between indigenous populations and states. The Human Rights Committee has interpreted the minority rights provision (Article 27 ICCPR) so as to require states to allow representatives of minorities to participate in the process of adopting governmental regulation which affects the rights of that minority.[27] Another example is the 'Equator Principles', a global financial industry benchmark for determining, assessing, and managing social and environmental risk in project financing, adopted by financial institutions in 2006. One of the principles concerns consultation and dialogue. The banks that have committed themselves to the Equator Principles pledge not to provide loans to projects where the borrower, the respective government, has not 'consulted with affected communities in a structured and culturally appropriate way'.[28] These (hard or soft) legal requirements of consultation empower affected individuals and communities

---

[25] Operational Policy 4.10: 'Indigenous People' of January 2005, Art 2.

[26] Operational Policy 4.12: 'Involuntary Resettlement' of January 2001 (the operational policy statement was updated in March 2007), Art 8.

[27] UN Human Rights Committee, *Apirana Mahuika et al v New Zealand*, comm. No 547/1992, CCPR/C/70/D/547/1993 (2000), paras 9.6–9.8.

[28] Equator Principles, Principle 5: 'Consultation and Disclosure'. The principle also states that for projects with significant adverse impact on affected communities, that consulation must 'ensure their free, prior and informed consulation and facilitate their informed participation, as a means to establish, to the satisfaction of the [borrowing financial institution], whether a project has been adequately incorporated affected comunities' concerns.' See <http://www.equator-principles. com>.

only to a very limited extent. They are not entitled to initiate a project themselves, for instance.

The second, more robust, vehicle of emancipation is the individuals' *standing to initiate judicial or arbitral proceedings*, such as under the European Convention on Human Rights (ECHR) or the International Centre for the Settlement of Investment Disputes (ICSID). These claims have given rise to case law which progressively develops the corpus of international law in general,[29] and more specifically fortifies and enlarges the rights and obligations of natural persons. Because international judges enjoy independence, this law-making happens without direct state control. Therefore the individual capacity to claim is a limited functional equivalent to the law-making power of states (see p. 340).

These two factors have empowered individuals under international law, and are contributing to their gradual, yet merely rudimentary transformation into agents, as opposed to mere recipients or consumers of international legal rules. From a constitutionalist perspective, it is desirable that the trend towards individual empowerment continue. This could and should happen first in the context of general rule-making, where democracy is the bridge principle: the international human right to political participation includes, as I will argue in chapter 6, the right to contribute to the creation of international law. Second, the judicial and quasi-judicial claiming options of individuals before international courts and tribunals should be extended against states[30] and against international organizations. That second strategy of empowerment will now be discussed.

2.4 Towards individualized law-enforcement

Significance of individual enforcement power for the international legal personality of the individual

The individual's international legal personality, and thereby its membership in the international constitutional community, does not depend on international procedural enforcement mechanisms. This assertion contradicts the traditional view that individuals were partial and derivative subjects of international law only where and to the extent they could avail themselves of procedural venues before international courts and tribunals and enforce their rights without having to rely on diplomatic protection by their state.[31] The traditional view thus linked substance to procedure.

---

[29] An independent development of substantial law has recently been notably performed by NAFTA (North American Free Trade Agreement) tribunals.

[30] See on the merits and drawbacks of granting business actors access to the WTO dispute settlement mechanism pp. 253–254 below.

[31] Hans Kelsen *Principles of International Law* (2nd edn Holt Rinehart and Winston New York 1967), at 234, and the bulk of contemporary scholarship.

I suggest severing this link.[32] From a constitutionalist perspective, the 'proceduralist' conception of the individual's international legal personality is unpersuasive for several reasons. First, it stands in the positivist tradition of defining law in general, and rights in particular, by sanctions and enforceability. The better view seems to be that law is not defined by sanctions, but rather by certain criteria of (procedural) fairness (see pp. 106–111). A constitutionalist mindset can easily accommodate this insight, because constitutional norms in particular are often not justitiable, while undeniably law. On the other hand, rights should not be confused with mere aspirations. It should be recognized that conflicts determine the very contents of the rights and cannot be defined away.[33] Therefore, rights are meaningful only if they confer entitlements and when there is a remedy ('no right without a remedy'). However, the remedy can take various forms. The enforcement of rights can happen on different levels of governance, on the international and on the domestic level. And it does not necessarily require judicial action, as the 'proceduralist' view of the individual's international legal personality implied.

The old view that rights must be actionable is rooted in the common law, which traditionally defined claims by their actionability through a writ. But this tradition is not universally shared. Most legal systems make a distinction between substance and procedure. While the Roman adage, '*ubi actio, ibi jus*', may be correct, it is not reversible: there can be '*jus*' without *actio*.[34] To tie the existence of substantial individual rights and the individual's legal personality on the availability of procedural remedies against states is particularly inappropriate in the realm of international law, where states are not subject to the compulsory jurisdiction of an international court.

Finally, and most importantly, the 'proceduralist' conception of the individual's international legal personality underestimates the important role of national bodies to enforce international law in a decentralized fashion. In the emerging multi-level constitutional system, the domestic courts are not only a functional equivalent to international courts and tribunals. The constitutional principle of subsidiarity[35] and practical considerations require the domestic institutions to be even the prior forum. This order of priority is particularly well established in human rights practice. Here the international forums are only the last resort and function as a safety valve. Given the important systemic protective function of domestic courts, it is doctrinally inconsistent to make the procedures before international bodies a defining element of the international legal

---

[32] See in this sense already Hersch Lauterpacht 'The Subjects of the Law of Nations (Part I)' (1947) 63 *The Law Review Quarterly* 428–460, at 455. In contemporary scholarship Karl Doehring *Völkerrecht* (2nd edn CF Müller Heidelberg 2004), paras 246–250.

[33] Michael Ignatieff 'The Attack on Human Rights' (2001) vol 80 No 6 *Foreign Affairs* 102–116, at 108–109.

[34] *Cf* PCIJ, *Peter Pázmány University Case*, Ser. A/B, No 61 (1935), at 231: '[i]t is scarcely necessary to point out that the capacity to possess civil rights does not necessarily imply the capacity to exercise those rights oneself.'   [35] See on subsidiarity p. 76.

personality of the individual. Nevertheless, constitutionalists welcome the extension of access of individuals to international courts and tribunals.

Individual enforcement of international law in international forums

It is well known that in the last decades individuals have obtained a variety of procedural options to claim breaches of international law far beyond human rights violations, in numerous judicial, quasi-judicial, or administrative international forums. I leave aside the European Court of Human Rights and those human rights expert committees which can be directly acceded by natural persons. The best-known case beyond human rights are ICSID tribunals which are relevant for business actors (see below pp. 251–252). A further example is the compliance-control of the Aarhus Convention on environmental information. The compliance committee may receive communications brought forward by 'members of the public',[36] with 'public' meaning NGOs and individuals.[37] Finally, in international criminal proceedings before the International Criminal Court (ICC), the victims have the right to participate in the proceedings and enjoy a limited right to be informed of progress of the criminal trial.[38]

Another international complaint mechanism available to individuals is the World Bank Inspection Panel. Groups of two or more natural persons who believe they have been hurt by World Bank-financed projects can request an inspection. The Panel will examine whether a failure of the World Bank to follow its own operational policies and procedures or contractual documents during the design, appraisal, or implementation of a Bank-financed project has adversely affected the material rights or interests of those persons.[39] In these procedures, the private requesters also have participatory rights.[40] But a finding of a violation of these policies does not as such suspend or cancel the lending agreement between the Bank and the borrowing state. And in cases of non-compliance with contractual conditions on the part of the borrower, the Bank—and not the Inspection Panel—has discretion to decide on such

---

[36] UNECE, Decision I/7 *Review of Compliance*, adopted at the first meeting of the parties, Annex 'Structure and Functions of the Compliance Comittee and Procedures for the Review of Compliance', MOP 1 (2002), Doc ECE/MP.PP/2/Add.8 (2004), sec. VI 'Communications from the Public'.

[37] See the definition in Art 2(4) Aarhus Convention (UNECE Convention on Access to Information, Public Participation in Decision-Making and Access to Justice in Environmental Matters of 25 June 1998, (1999) 38 ILM 517–533).

[38] See Art 68(3) ICC-Statute. See ICC Appeals Chamber, *Prosecutor v Lubanga: Decision on Participation of Victims*, (ICC-01/04–01/06 OA 12 of 6 August 2008).

[39] The legal basis is International Bank for Reconstruction and Development and International Development Association, Resolution No IBRD 93–10 and Resolution No IDA 93–6 'The World Bank Inspection Panel' of 22 September 1993, (1995) 34 ILM 520–523. The Operating Procedures (OP) of the Inspection Panel are reproduced in: The World Bank Inspection Panel, 'Accountability at the World Bank—The Inspection Panel 10 Years On', Washington 2003, Annex VIID.   [40] Art 47 Operating Procedures.

measures. So the World Bank inspection procedure is essentially an in-house review system, forming part of the purely internal management review. It does not furnish a judicial remedy. In all mentioned cases, the judicial analogies are more or less weak.

The most obviously insufficient forum from an individual rights' perspective is the focal point within the UN Secretariat for receiving delisting and exemption requests by individuals targeted by Security Council sanctions.[41] The focal point was established after the World Summit Outcome Document of 2005 had called upon the Security Council to ensure that 'fair and clear procedures exist for placing individuals and entities on sanctions lists and for removing them, as well as for granting humanitarian exemptions'.[42] The focal point empowers targeted individuals (whose names figure on a currently 73-page long web-published consolidated list[43]) to act themselves as a petitioner and request delisting, without having to wait for diplomatic protection of their state of nationality. However, the focal point is not much more than a 'revamped letter box'.[44] Its role is mostly that of a clearing house which puts the governments of the designating state and of the state of citizenship or residence in contact with each other, which may then recommend delisting. But the power to decide on delisting remains entirely with the respective sanctions committee and this includes the power of a permanent member of the Security Council to veto a delisting proposal. This mechanism does not constitute an independent review. It is inadequate to safeguard the minimum procedural standards under the rule of law.[45] The ongoing critical debate on the listing process, which has not been silenced by the establishment of the focal point, benefits greatly from a look into the constitutionalist toolbox. The Fassbender study commissioned by the UN Office of Legal Affairs had defined the minimum standards for the required 'fair and clear procedures' as comprising four basic elements, namely the right to be informed, the right to be heard, the right to an effective review mechanism, and a periodical review of targeted sanctions by the Security Council.[46] Moreover, the study qualified the rights of a targeted person as 'subjective rights *vis-à-vis*

---

[41] Established by SC res 1730 (2006). See, e.g., the guidelines of the 1267-sanctions committee, as amended on 9 December 2008, para 7 lit. g) on the focal point.

[42] UN GA res 60/1 (2005), para 109 (emphasis added).

[43] See 'Consolidated List established and maintained by the 1267 Committee with respect to Al-Qaida, Usama bin Laden, and the Taliban and other individuals, groups, undertakings and entities associated with them' (as updated on 24 March 2009). See <http://www.un.org/sc/committees/1267/pdf/consolidatedlist.pdf>.

[44] Michael Bothe 'Security Council's Targeted Sanctions against Presumed Terrorists' (2008) 6 *Journal of International Criminal Justice* 541–555, at 547.

[45] See in this sense explicitly Parliamentary Assembly (PA) of the Council of Europe, PA res 1597 (2008), esp. para 6; see also PA res 1824 (2008).

[46] Bardo Fassbender 'Targeted Sanctions Imposed by the UN Security Council and Due Process Rights: A Study Commissioned by the UN Office of Legal Affairs and Follow-Up Action by the United Nations', repr. in (2006) 3 *International Organizations Law Review* 437–485.

the United Nations that derive from the Charter'.[47] A second study by the Watson Institute suggested various mechanisms for review, either under the authority of the Security Council itself, such as a monitoring team, an ombudsman as an interface with the UN, a panel of experts (following the models of the human rights committee or the anti-torture committee), independent arbitral panels (e.g. under the auspices of the Permanent Court of Arbitration, or hosted by an international organization such as the ICSID tribunals by the World Bank), or finally judicial review (e.g. by a body like the UN Administrative Tribunal).[48]

So far, these recommendations were largely ignored by the Security Council. Nevertheless, I deem it important that here the constitutionalist approach has offered a vocabulary to claim and design improved procedures which move further in the direction of rule-of-law based procedural standards, fair trial guarantees, and review mechanisms. I submit that it is preferable and inevitable to draw on global norms, such as the Universal Declaration on Human Rights with its guarantees of procedural due process (Article 10 UDHR). This approach is compelling if one wants to safeguard constitutional minimum standards without undermining the coherence of the UN system of collective security, as the inward-oriented posture of the European Court of Justice (ECJ)[49] threatens to do.

To conclude, individuals have been empowered to enforce international law beyond human rights in international non-judicial forums. This development has strengthened their international constitutional status. However, these forums are in many respects deficient in the sense that they do not properly safeguard the affected individuals' rights and procedural fairness.

Individual enforcement of international law in national forums: direct application

There seems to be a general trend in real-life litigation practice, and in the accompanying academic discourse, to broaden the areas of international law whose direct applicability by domestic courts acting upon complaints by individuals is an issue. A preliminary question here is whether the question of direct applicability really pertains to domestic law, and is left to the municipal courts to decide for themselves. The traditional answer is positive, based on the argument that the entire matter concerns the application of public international law, and that the modes of application fall within the *domaine reservé*. In contrast, the constitutionalist stance is that the question of direct applicability is

---

[47] Fassbender, Targeted Sanctions, 2006, at 438.

[48] Strengthening Targeted Sanctions through Fair and Clear Procedures: White Paper prepared by the Watson Institute Targeted Sanctions Project, Brown University, 30 March 2006, Appendix B (UN Doc A/60/887-S/2006/331).

[49] ECJ, Cases C-402/05P and C-415/05P, *Kadi and Al Barakaat*, judgment of the Court (Grand Chamber) of 3 September 2008.

first of all a question of the interpretation of a treaty provision, and that the interpretation of an international instrument, even if performed by a national court, must follow international principles.[50] In fact, the practice of municipal courts with regard to direct applicability seems to be guided by some common principles, and does not diverge that much. Municipal judiciaries normally take into account the intentions of the contracting parties and inquire whether the parties wanted to endow a treaty provision with direct effect. National judiciaries also look at the structure of the treaty as a whole, and at the relevant provision's suitability for judicial application, notably at its precision and unconditionality.

Traditionally, the possibility of a direct application (or direct effect or self-executing nature) was basically limited to human rights treaties and to EU law and it has been intensely discussed with regard to World Trade Organization (WTO) law.[51] In recent times, the direct application of international criminal law by municipal criminal courts has become a normal event, at least in an intermediary stage until the international criminal provisions have been formally inserted in wording or substance into the domestic criminal codes. Besides, as will be discussed later, the direct application of norms of international humanitarian law has become a battlefield.[52]

Finally, the invocation of breaches of international law in domestic extradition proceedings has become important. Increasingly, persons facing extradition or criminal trial claim that international legal principles, e.g. respect for another state's territorial jurisdiction, has been breached in the course of their arrest.[53] This tendency is distinct from the parallel global trend to make respect for (international) human rights an integral part of extradition procedures by, for example, refusing extradition to countries where the death penalty or discriminatory proceedings are looming.

Overall, the current trend is one of increasing the options for individuals to enforce international law either in international or in domestic forums. Constitutionalists welcome it. The mere availability of diplomatic protection is insufficient, because it paternalizes individuals and prevents ownership and agency.[54] The process of empowerment is a core element of the constitutionalization of the international legal system.

---

[50] See in that sense already Joe Verhoeven 'La notion d'"applicabilité directe" du droit international' (1980) 15 *Revue Belge de droit international* 243–264, at 258–259.

[51] See references below at p. 207   [52] See below pp. 169–170.

[53] See, e.g., German Constitutional Court, order of 5 November 2003 (BVerfG, AZ 2 Bv R1506/03), paras 39–62, rejecting the claim that international law mandates the staying of criminal proceedings when a person was arrested in violation of the territorial jurisdiction of another state, with references to previous case law of various national courts. Accessible via http://www.bverfg.de. See on this issue also ICTY, *Nicolic*, case No IT-94-2-AR73, decision on interlocutory appeal concerning legality of arrest, of 5 June 2003.   [54] See below pp. 172–174.

2.5 The expansion of international human rights

Under the premise that international human rights are international constitutional rights,[55] the recent expansion of international human rights in various dimensions is a manifestation of the constitutionalization of international law. International human rights have first expanded in substance. Some have been explicitly endorsed in new international human rights treaties, such as the human right against forced disappearance. Others have been acknowledged even without explicit textual foundations in international covenants, such as the right to be free from discrimination on the ground of sexual orientation or of genetic features. Other liberal rights, such as the right to property, were already enshrined in the Human Rights Declaration, but have been concretized and spelled out only more recently, for example due to dense case law by ICSID tribunals. In the field of social and economic rights, much has changed only in the last 15 years. It is meanwhile acknowledged that all human rights must be positively protected, and that the economic and social rights are no second-class rights. Also, new rights without an explicit textual basis, such as the human right to water, are acknowledged. Finally, ecological rights are recognized, especially for indigenous populations.

The circle of addressees of human rights has also widened. International human rights are no longer opposable only to states. It is meanwhile generally admitted that international organizations, such as the United Nations and its peace-keeping operations, are bound to observe international human rights and international humanitarian law.[56] Because the organizations are not formally a contracting party to the relevant conventions, the doctrinal path to construe bindingness is controversial. Especially in this context, the idea that the UN Charter is a constitution is frequently employed as an argument for applying the human rights norms to the UN.[57] However, the use of the term constitution cannot simply conjure up human rights constraints. It would have to be shown concretely that the constitutional quality of the Charter necessarily comprises (unwritten) human rights standards for the organization, which is not very plausible.

International human rights are increasingly held to have at least indirect 'horizontal' effects for other private actors, notably for transnational corporations (see below pp. 243–246). Outside the business context, human rights

---

[55] *Cf* Stephen Gardbaum 'Human Rights as International Constitutional Rights' (2008) 19 *EJIL* 749–768.

[56] See for the UN only August Reinisch 'Developing Human Rights and Humanitarian Law Accountability of the Security Council for the Implementation of Economic Sanctions' (2001) 95 *AJIL* 851–871. See for the EU the Charter of Fundamental Rights of the EU of 7 December 2000 (OJ 2000 C 364, 1).

[57] Nigel D White and Dirk Klaasen 'An Emerging Legal Regime? in *idem* (eds) *The UN, Human Rights and Post-Conflict Situations* (Manchester UP 2005) 1–16, at 7.

standards *de facto* constrain the behaviour of private persons. For example, the principle of *non-refoulement* prohibits states from expelling foreign women who are menaced by domestic violence at home, which means that private perpe- trators' actions are measured at a human rights standard. Along this line, a debate on the human rights obligations of NGOs should be initiated, because, from a constitutionalist perspective, these should be held accountable as well. Overall, the human rights expansion is not only, as stated in the beginning, a manifestation of global constitutionalization, but a constitutionalist approach can dialectically furnish insights and arguments to refine, channel, and limit this process, notably to prevent a human rights inflation.

2.6 Beyond human rights

Another important legal trend which highlights the move of individuals to the centre of the international legal system is the emergence of international indi- vidual rights beyond human rights. The probably best-known 'ordinary' inter- national individual rights are the rights to consular assistance granted to detained foreign nationals by Article 36 paragraph 1 of the Vienna Convention on Consular Relations (VCCR). The relevant provision expressly speaks of 'rights' of arrested or imprisoned persons, and thus cannot be understood to stipulate merely inter-state obligations, as the United States had unsuccessfully argued in the *LaGrand Case*. In that case, the International Court of Justice (ICJ), relying on the clear wording of the provision, held 'that Article 36, paragraph 1 creates individual rights, which, by virtue of Article I of the Optional Protocol, may be invoked in this Court by the national State of the arrested person'.[58] In a different context, the German Constitutional Court found Article 36 VCCR to embody an individual 'subjective' right and the treaty provision to be self-executing and directly applicable in German criminal procedure law.[59]

The individual's rights to communicate with, to have access to consular officers, and to be informed about the former rights are ancillary to the human rights to due process or fair trial. In that sense, the Inter-American Court of Human Rights had stated in a 1999 Advisory Opinion that non-observance of Article 36 VCCR is prejudicial to the guarantees of the due process of law, and that the imposition of the death penalty in such circumstances violates the right to life.[60] Also Germany had argued in the *LaGrand Case* that the right of the

---

[58] ICJ, *LaGrand Case* (Germany v United States of America), ICJ Reports 2001, 466, para 77.

[59] German Constitutional Court, First Chamber of the 2nd Senate, of 19 September 2006, BVerfG, 2 BvR 2115/01, repr. in *Europäische Grundrechte-Zeitschrift* 33 (2006), 684 *et seq*. But see US S.Ct., *Medellín v Texas*, judgment of 25 March 2008, No 06–984, 552 U.S. (2008).

[60] Inter-American Court of Human Rights, Advisory Opinion OC-16/99 'The Right to Infor- mation on Consular Assistance in the Framework of the Guarantees of the Due Process of Law' (of 1 October 1999), para 137, see also paras 124 and 129.

individual to be informed without delay under Article 36 'has today assumed the character of a human right'. But the ICJ did not find it necessary to consider that additional argument.[61] And in the later *Avena* judgment, the Court seemed to find an eventual human rights qualification irrelevant.[62] This view is the better one, because the right to consular assistance is not sufficiently fundamental to warrant the human rights label. It is also no simple emanation of the human right to a fair trial, because consular assistance on the one hand concerns not only accused persons in criminal proceedings but all foreigners, and on the other hand serves only foreign detainees, but not national detainees. In contrast, a human right should benefit all persons who are in a similar situation.

Another case in point are the four freedoms within the European Union which can hardly be understood as human rights. They are—in contrast to human rights—linked to transborder activities, and they are primarily instrumental to the creation of a common market, and not granted for the sake of the individuals themselves.[63] Nevertheless, they are real international (or European) subjective rights. Further international individual rights arguably flow from bilateral investment treaties (see below p. 251). In international humanitarian and criminal law, a similar evolution towards individual ownership is taking place. Antonio Cassese has argued that it would be 'consistent from the viewpoint of legal logic but also in keeping with new trends emerging in the world community' to acknowledge that customary law generates rights which directly accrue to individuals: 'They are entitled to respect for their life and limbs, and for their dignity, hence they have a right not to become a victim of war crimes, crimes against humanity, aggression, torture, terrorism.'[64] Such a customary international entitlement not to become victim of an international crime, deriving from general international rules, would be an international right directed against private persons. The practical consequence of the suggested international direct individual entitlement is that this right is held by persons even if a nation state has not adopted appropriate criminal legislation or has even acted contrary to international law. However, such a conception seems to inflate individual rights, and, in practical terms, might not be helpful.

Specifically in international humanitarian law (IHL), nobody denies that the purpose of most primary norms is to benefit individuals, and that states as parties to a military conflict are obliged to protect natural persons. But according to the traditional view, these obligations were inter-state obligations, owed to the other contracting parties. However, some norms of IHL explicitly mention

---

[61] ICJ, *LaGrand,* para 78.

[62] ICJ, *Case Concerning Avena and other Mexican Nationals* (Mexico v United States of America), ICJ Reports 2004, 12, para 124.

[63] Alexander Schultz *Das Verhältnis von Gemeinschaftsgrundrechten und Grundfreiheiten des EGV* (Duncker & Humblot Berlin 2005), esp. at 107–109, 111, 182.

[64] Antonio Cassese *International Law* (2nd edn OUP Oxford 2005), at 145.

individual rights or entitlements.[65] This wording supports the constitutionalist interpretation that these obligations are owed to individuals and arguably even confer on those individuals the corresponding rights to protection. However, individuals lack standing to enforce IHL before international tribunal or other international bodies, e.g. before a commission under Article 90 AP I. The secondary level of remedies for breaches of IHL is even more controversial. Treaty provisions on the liability to pay compensation for war-related damages, such as Article 91 of AP I, were traditionally understood to foresee only inter-state compensation. From an individualist and emancipatory, in short: from a constitutionalist perspective, these textually open clauses can and should be understood as creating rights for individuals. But even on this premise, the problem remains that an international forum is lacking. The only options are domestic courts. But international treaty law does not prescribe states to establish jurisdiction for processing claims for breach of IHL, and there is no customary law in that sense.[66] A constitutionalist approach would be to develop international law in that direction. For the time being, remedies for violations of IHL are available for individuals only where domestic courts recognize first the individual 'ownership' of rights both on the primary and on the secondary level. Moreover these same courts must also recognize the direct applicability (or self-executing character) of the relevant norms of IHL. I submit that the mounting pressure for the admissibility of municipal civil-law actions for financial compensation for violations of IHL is one manifestation of the overall trend to 'individualize' international law both in terms of substance and procedure, coupled with a strengthening of domestic courts as enforcers of international law. And this in turn demonstrates constitutionalization.

The question arises how to determine whether an individual right is a human right, and thus a constitution-based right, or merely an ordinary, subjective right. A formal approach would be to define as human rights only those rights that carry this official label and have been codified in a Human Rights Convention. Another formal approach would be to look for a universal consensus on a novel human right in form of a General Assembly Resolution.[67] I submit that the criterion for a human right must also be substantial, not only formal in the sense of universal recognition. Only rights that are both universally recognized and of paramount importance for the well-being of individuals can be human rights.[68]

---

[65] See notably common articles 7/7/7/8 of the four Geneva Conventions of 1949.

[66] The authoritative compilation of customary IHL only diagnosed 'an increasing trend of enabling victims ... to seek reparation directly from the responsible State', without confirming the existence of an international customary rule to that effect (Jean-Marie Henckaerts and Louise Doswald-Beck *Customary International Humanitarian Law* vol I, Rules (CUP Cambridge 2005), at 541).

[67] Philip Alston 'Conjuring up New Human Rights: A Proposal for Quality Control' (1984) 78 *AJIL* 607–621.

[68] *Cf* Sinai Deutch 'Are Consumer Rights Human Rights?' (1994) 32 *Osgoode Hall Law Journal* 537–578, at 549 with further references.

Because the world changes and with it the potential threats to human flourishment, human rights can change, and new human rights can emerge as a response to the perceived need for protection arising from novel threats or due to changed societal sensibilities.

The emergence of international individual rights 'below' the level of human rights is a corollary of the constitutionalization of international law first because it refines and intensifies the international status of the individual. Second, it is a corollary of constitutionalization because it contributes to the conceptualization of various levels of international law, namely 'ordinary' international law and international constitutional law. In a constitutionalized international order, human rights form part of the corpus of international constitutional law, whereas other individual rights pertain to the body of ordinary international law.

Third, the recognition of simple international individual rights strengthens the normative power of international human rights, because it works against their inflation. The current proliferation of human rights assertions in the international legal discussion tends to devaluate or debase those very rights, because the attribution of a human rights label to all sorts of claims inadvertently promotes their trivialization.[69] Reserving the human rights seal for rights which are really important helps preserving their pedigree. And this in turn helps to strengthen the idea of global constitutionalism.

2.7 Individuals as creditors of international responsibility

From a constitutionalist perspective, individuals are not only 'owners' of certain primary rights to performance of international obligations, but should in principle also own the correlative secondary rights flowing from international (state) responsibility in the event of a breach of the respective primary international norm, because otherwise their emancipation remains seriously incomplete. Put differently, international state responsibility should move further beyond a purely inter-state responsibility. In the context of human rights law and IHL, the secondary right is called the right to a remedy.[70] The human rights conventions typically foresee that states parties must create effective remedies within their domestic legal order.[71] These provisions have been traditionally interpreted as

---

[69] *Cf* Mary Ann Glendon *Rights Talk: The Impoverishment of the Political Discourse* (The Free Press New York 1991), at 16: '[O]ne must ask whether an undifferentiated language of rights is really the best way to address the astonishing variety of injustices and forms of suffering that exists in the world.' See also Laurence R Helfer 'Overlegalizing Human Rights: International Relations Theory and the Commonwealth Caribbean Backlash against Human Rights Regimes' (2002) 102 *Columbia Law Review* 1832–1911.

[70] See General Assembly, Basic Principles and Guidelines on the Right to a Remedy and Reparation for Victims of Gross Violations of International Human Rights Law and Serious Violations of International Humanitarian Law (UN Doc A/Res/60/147 (21 March 2006).

[71] See, e.g., Art 2(3) ICCPR or Art 13 ECHR.

procedural obligations addressing states, which must then enact appropriate legislation.[72] From a constitutionalist perspective, these provisions should be read as enshrining international (secondary) rights owed by the states directly to individual victims, so as to eliminate their dependency on supportive state activity. This would also mean that individuals possess this right independent of their nationality, and even against their home state. The content of international (state) responsibility towards individuals would then be, according to general principles, cessation, non-repetition, and reparation.[73] Reparation may in principle include restitution, compensation, rehabilitation, and satisfaction.[74]

Notably monetary compensation is problematic and controversial. In the law as it stands, the Human Rights Committee has not interpreted the entitlement to an 'effective remedy' under Article 2(3) ICCPR as encompassing a right to (monetary) compensation. Such an obligation can only be derived from additional sources, such as Article 41 ECHR or Article 75 ICC Statute which obliges the ICC to 'establish principles relating to the reparation to, or in respect of, victims, including restitution, compensation and rehabilitation'.[75]

Notably the current controversy whether victims of violations of IHL have or should have an (internationally grounded) direct personal and individual right to a remedy, including eventual compensation, could benefit from a constitutionalist approach. That approach, with its focus on individual rights, highlights that the underlying issue is similar to that in the field of human rights. It suggests that even in the absence of an explicit right to a remedy codified in the Geneva Conventions and Protocols for violations short of grave breaches, at least a procedural obligation for states to establish domestic civil law remedies against states, government officials, and private perpetrators should be acknowledged. The constitutionalist approach at least supports progressive interpretation of the law in that direction. To conclude, the emancipation of individuals as creditors of secondary obligations is ongoing, and can be furthered through a dynamic, constitutionalist interpretation of the norms on international responsibility.

2.8 Individual agency in the law of diplomatic protection

Another example for the trend towards individual agency in international law, which can in turn be further promoted and bolstered by a constitutionalist approach, is the evolution often called 'humanization' of the international law of

---

[72] For instance, Art 14(1) of the 1984 Anti-Torture Convention does not stipulate a direct international individual right to compensation against states or state officials, but merely obliges each state party to ensure in its legal system that the victim of an act of torture obtains redress and has an enforceable right to fair and adequate compensation.

[73] Arts 30 and 31 ILC-Articles on the Responsibility of States for International Wrongful Acts of 2001 (UN Doc A/CN.4/L.602, Rev.1).

[74] General Assembly, Principles on the Right to a Remedy, 2006, principles 11, 18–23.

[75] That provision is complemented by section III, Victims and Witnesses (rules 85–99) of the Rules of Procedure and Evidence of the ICC, which detail some of the conditions for the granting of compensation to victims (UN Doc PCNICC/2000/1/Add.1 (2000)).

diplomatic protection.[76] The traditional legal fiction that a state exercising diplomatic protection claims a violation of its 'own' rights has been basically given up. But individuals are still not entitled to diplomatic protection under international law, not even in the event of the violation of a *jus cogens* norm. The respective proposition of ILC rapporteur John R Dugard in the first ILC Report on Diplomatic Protection did not meet with approval.[77] ILC draft Article 19 of 2006 now (only) declares that a State entitled to exercise diplomatic protection '*should* ... give due consideration to the possibility of exercising diplomatic protection, especially when a significant injury has occurred'.[78] The rapporteur suggested that, despite the continuing insistence of states on the discretionary nature of diplomatic protection, 'international law already recognizes the existence of some obligation on the part of a State *to consider* the possibility of exercising diplomatic protection on behalf of a national who has suffered a significant injury abroad'.[79] In fact, numerous mostly modern state constitutions enshrine the government's obligation to protect their nationals abroad, and some even contain explicit individual rights, entitlements, or guarantees of protection.[80] Various recent judgments of national and international courts on diplomatic protection have found that citizens abroad are entitled to due consideration and to a fair procedure in processing their request, that governments may be required to furnish reasons for their decisions, that protection may not be refused in an arbitrary fashion, and that legitimate expectations can arise.[81]

---

[76] But see Vasileios Pergantis 'Towards a "Humanization" of Diplomatic Protection?' (2006) 66 *Zeitschrift für ausländisches öffentliches Recht und Völkerrecht* 351–397, arguing that there is not and should not be 'humanization', because an entitlement to diplomatic protection would be inoperational.

[77] John R Dugard *First Report on Diplomatic Protection*, UN Doc A/CN4/506 (of 7 March 2000), Art 4 (1), at 27 with paras 75 *et seq.*

[78] Report of the International Law Commission, Fifty-eighth session (1 May–9 June and 3 July–11 August 2006), General Assembly Official Records, Sixty-first session, supplement No 10 (A/61/10), at 94 (emphasis added).

[79] John R Dugard 'Commentary on Article 19' *ibid* at 96–97 (emphasis added).

[80] E.g. Art 10 of the Croatian Constitution of 21 December 1990; Art 69(3) of the Hungarian Constitution of 20 August 1949; Art 13(1) of the Estonian Constitution of 28 June 1992; Art 61 of the Russian Constitution of 12 December 1993.

[81] See most of all Constitutional Court of South Africa, *Samuel Kaunda and others v President of the Republic of South Africa and others*, 4 August 2004, repr. in ILM 44 (2005), 173, especially Ngcobo, C.J., para 192. See also UK Supreme Court of Judicature—Court of Appeal, Civil Division, *Abbasi v Secretary of State for Foreign and Commonwealth Affairs*, repr. in ILM 42 (2003), 355. Here the English Court of Appeal departed from the traditional position that the exercise of diplomatic protection is a matter beyond the jurisdiction of courts. In that case, the court accepted a complaint by a British detainee in Guantànamo Bay who was dissatisfied with the measures of protection offered by the British government and who sought judicial review to compel representations about the illegality of his detention. Although the court rejected the claim that a general duty to exercise specific protective measures existed, it assumed that legitimate expectations could arise in that context. See also the ECHR, holding that, even in the absence of effective control over the Transdniestrian region, Moldova had 'a *positive obligation under Article 1 of the Convention to take the diplomatic,* economic, judicial or other measures that it is in its power to take and are in accordance with international law to secure to the applicants the rights guaranteed by the Convention'. ECHR, *Ilascu v Moldova* (application No 48787/99), judgment of 8 July 2004, para 331 (emphasis added).

A constitutionalist approach to international law highlights and supports this development, because constitutionalists work on the premise that international law should—if in doubt—be interpreted in a way which empowers individuals. Because the constitutionalist perspective is a comprehensive one, it allows the reconciliation and accommodation of the law of diplomatic protection with the human rights paradigm of a 'duty to protect'. The duty to protect is not limited to protection against harmful private activities, and requires both preventive and remedial action. From a constitutionalist perspective, the duty to protect should in principle include diplomatic protection *vis-à-vis* third states. Moreover, a comprehensive approach requires taking into account the effects of state immunity in the event of lawsuits instituted by individuals against states before domestic tribunals. If state immunity is upheld even in the event of gross human rights violations, this could and should be compensated by a reduction of the discretion of the victim's home state to exercise diplomatic protection for the victim on the international plane.[82]

Finally, constitutionalism is as a general matter concerned with the prevention of arbitrary power and thus with the circumscription and limitation of discretion. So while not denying that diplomatic protection remains a political institution with discretion, constitutionalism claims that under the rule of law, all discretion has limits, and that there are no completely law-free zone of politics. A constitutionalist reading of the current state practice with regard to diplomatic protection therefore leads to acknowledging an international obligation to give due consideration to the possibility of exercising diplomatic protection. At least, constitutionalist-minded lawyers welcome the progressive development of the law of diplomatic protection in this direction.

2.9 International individual obligations

Individuals are increasingly addressed by international law. This is significant for the constitutionalization of international law, not because the international obligations incumbent on individuals are 'constitutional' ones, but because that development contributes to the normalization of the international legal status of individuals. 'Fundamental duties' corresponding to fundamental rights, as enshrined in the African Charter on Human and Peoples' Rights (Articles 27–29) are problematic and will not be discussed here.

The most obvious field where international individual obligations short of 'fundamental duties' seem to exist is international criminal law. However, the traditional pre-Nuremberg international criminal law conventions and the Geneva Conventions on international humanitarian law did not directly

---

[82] François Flauss 'Vers un aggiornamento des conditions d'exercice de la protection diplomatique?' in *idem* (ed) *La protection diplomatique: Mutations contemporaines et pratiques nationales* (Bruylant Bruxelles 2003) 29–61, at 53.

prohibit let alone criminalize individual behaviour. They merely obliged states to enact domestic criminal law and to try individuals in domestic criminal procedures. In particular, the Geneva Conventions' provisions on grave breaches merely address states, and do not suggest that the international norms in themselves can justify criminal punishment. The traditional but nowadays challenged interpretation therefore has been that the respective Geneva law provisions cannot be applied in the internal sphere of states without implementing legislation, and that they are most of all not fit to form the legal basis of a criminal judgment without being supplemented by a domestic criminal statute.[83]

This scheme of only 'indirectly' addressing individuals is still present in modern conventions such as the 1984 UN Convention Against Torture (CAT). Recently, the anti-torture committee stressed that the CAT imposes obligations only on states parties and not on individuals.[84] The same holds true for Security Council resolutions. The important resolutions on targeted sanctions only oblige states to take domestic measures, e.g. to freeze assets, or to prohibit travel.[85] Technically speaking, the individual is here still mediated by the states (or by the EU). Furthermore, numerous Security Council resolutions hold that terrorism (committed by private persons) is a threat to world peace in terms of Article 39 of the UN Charter.[86] But they do not directly impose clear obligations on terrorists. Likewise, the first resolution on weapons of mass destruction in the hands of non-state actors seeks to reduce the risk that non-state actors acquire those weapons, and explicitly formulates that objective,[87] but then goes on to define obligations of states only.

The constitutionalist reading of these and other international norms favours their interpretation as in principle being apt to directly impose obligations on individuals, independently of any intermediating act of a national authority. The Nuremberg judgment against the principal war criminals of 1946 stated this clearly, albeit only with regard to the Nuremberg crimes:[88] 'That

---

[83] Michael Bothe 'The Role of National Law in the Implementation of International Humanitarian Law' in Christophe Swinarski (ed) *Studies and Essays on International Humanitarian Law and Red Cross Principles in Honour of Jean Pictet* (Martinus Nijhoff Dordrecht 1984) 301–312, at 302. But see Kai Ambos *Völkerstrafrecht* (Beck München 2006), at 96: The progressive development of IHL may have modified the meaning of the Geneva conventions. Notably Art 85 of the AP I qualifies the grave breaches as 'crimes'. Ambos concludes that IHL itself is the actual source of the criminalization of the prohibited acts.

[84] CAT, General Comment No 2: Implementation of Article 2 by States Parties (UN Doc CAT/C/GC/CRP.1/Rev. 4 of 23 November 2007), para 15.

[85] Such as UN SC res 1267 (1999) against the Taliban; 1591 (2005) against Sudanese officials.

[86] See, e.g. UN SC res 1368 (2001); 1377 (2001); 1735 (2006); 1757 (2007).

[87] UN SC res 1540 (2004) preamble, para 8.

[88] I.e. crimes against peace, war crimes, and crimes against humanity (as enumerated in Art 6 of the London Agreement for the Prosecution and Punishment of Major War Criminals of the European Axis of 8 August 1945 (concluded between the UK, USA, France, and Soviet Union) with the Charter of the International Military Tribunal (so-called 'Nuremberg-Charter') as an annex of the Agreement (text in (1945) 39 *AJIL* suppl. 257 *et seq.*).

international law imposes duties and liabilities upon individuals as well as upon States has long been recognized. ... Crimes against international law are committed by men, not by abstract entities, and only by punishing individuals who commit such crimes can the provisions of international law be enforced. ... [T]he very essence of the Charter is that individuals have international duties which transcend the national obligations of obedience imposed by the individual State.'[89]

Since then, it is conceded that the prohibitions on committing international crimes in the strict sense, i.e. those enshrined in the ICC Statute and entrenched as custom, are addressed to every human being in the world in his or her private and personal capacity. Not only state officials or agents acting in their official capacity as militaries or politicians, but also private businessmen are under obligation.[90] It is immaterial for the quality as an *international* obligation whether the international norms are enforced by international criminal courts or merely by municipal courts which apply international law either directly or indirectly.[91]

A slightly different matter are the legal consequences of a violation of these international criminal-law obligations, namely criminal punishment. Generally speaking, the issue is one of direct applicability. May a domestic criminal court directly apply international criminal law, or are these provisions too imprecise to warrant criminal conviction? From a constitutionalist perspective, the real reason for the need for implementation is not dualism or justiciability as such, but the principle *nulla poena sine lege*. This principle is guaranteed in international human rights conventions (Article 15(1) ICCPR; Article 7 ECHR) as an underogable right (Article 4 ICCPR, Article 15 ECHR).[92] It is a central achievement of liberal constitutionalism rooted in the idea that the citizen owes obedience to the state only on the basis of clearly codified rules and is otherwise free. The *nulla poena* principle thus has constitutional status as a core element of the rule of law. It requires that criminal laws must in principle be written and precisely worded, including a clear circumscription of the punishment, and these conditions are not always met in international law. The constitutionalist approach highlights that two objectives may be in conflict: on the one hand the targetting of individuals directly, without a state smoke screen, and on the other hand the demand to comply with the *nulla poena* principle.

---

[89] Judgment of the international military tribunal of Nuremberg for the trial of German major war criminals of 30 September/1 October 1946.

[90] US Military Tribunal at Nuremberg, *US v Alfred Krupp et al*, The United Nations War Crimes Commission, Law Reports of Trials of War Criminals, vol X, 1949, 130–159, reprinted in Marco Sassòli and Antoine A Bouvier *How Does Law Protect in War* (ICRC Geneva 1999), at 666; ICTR, *Prosecutor v Kayishema and Ruzindana*, Judgement, Case No ICTR-95-1-T, of 21 May 1999.

[91] Gerhard Werle *Völkerstrafrecht* (2nd edn Mohr Siebeck Tübingen 2007), paras 109–112.

[92] The *nulla poena* principle is also endorsed in domestic constitutions (see, e.g., Art 103(2) German Basic Law. It also forms part of international customary law and applies to international criminal trials, *cf* Arts 22–24 ICC-Statute.

In other areas of international law as well, primary and secondary obligations that are incumbent on individuals are in *statu nascendi*. I have already mentioned the debate on human rights responsibilities of transnational corporations and on civil liability for private violators of IHL. In international environmental law, the civil liability conventions in the field of oil pollution, nuclear damages, transboundary movements, or other carriage of hazardous waste and noxious substances oblige the contracting states parties to ensure liability and payment of damages by business actors. Again, these conventions directly and formally address the states only, which must enact implementing legislation. In substance, however, these conventions target private actors. It has therefore been suggested abandoning the doctrinal distinction between the (directly international law-based) state responsibility and the (but indirectly international law-based) so-called 'civil liability' of firms: 'Plainly stated, the treaties place duties on business not to cause pollution', writes Steven Ratner.[93]

From a constitutionalist perspective, the current evolution and progressive interpretation of international law as comprising both primary and secondary international obligations of individuals[94] is welcome. Individual international legal responsibility should be recognized with the consequence that individuals are saddled with international legal duties to compensate victims for breaches of international law. This evolution on the side of obligations would properly mirror the rise of individual rights beyond human rights, and refine the constitutional status of individuals as the ultimate international constitutional unit.

2.10 By way of conclusion: from *bourgeois* to *citoyens*

In synthesizing the international constitutional status of individuals, I want to highlight three aspects. First, the constitutionalist approach, focusing on the centrality of individuals, unveiled the hidden parallels in the seemingly diverse debates on problems such as criminal punishment based on international law, direct effect, and monetary compensation for violations of IHL. They all revolve around piercing the state veil and empowering individuals.

Second, many, if not all of the new individual rights, such as the rights to consular assistance, rights to due consideration in diplomatic protection, the numerous rights to institute judicial and arbitral proceedings, and finally the right to environmental information and participation,[95] are procedural or procedure-related ones. This corresponds to the general trend, visible in many legal

---

[93] Steven Ratner 'Business' in Daniel Bodansky, Jutta Brunnée, and Ellen Hey (eds) *The Oxford Handbook of International Environmental Law* (OUP Oxford 2007) 807–828, at 814.

[94] Dörr, Privatisierung des Völkerrechts, 2005, at 913–14.

[95] The 1998 Aarhus Convention (UNECE Convention on Access to Information, Public Participation in Decision-Making and Access to Justice in Environmental Matters of 25 June 1998, (1999) 38 ILM 517–533) grants individuals rights to environmental information, to participation in relevant administrative proceedings, and to access to justice.

systems, to care more for procedural safeguards. This trend has a special significance in international law, because it is a strategy to overcome disagreement on substance and on material values, which is normal in pluralist societies, but extreme in the highly diverse global society. Procedural safeguards cannot erase or overcome all dissent in substance, and are no full substitute for agreement on minimal substantial principles. Still, the application of some procedural principles, such as notice and comment by affected persons, can increase the likelihood of fair and acceptable outcomes of those procedures. The proceduralization is to that extent a manifestation of a 'thin' constitutionalization of the international legal system.

The third conclusion to be drawn from this section is that individuals are so far quite firmly entrenched as international *bourgeois*. I also showed that there is a very weak trend towards empowerment of individuals in the international legal process and in global governance, which means a trend towards transnational *citoyenneté*. Expressed in terms of constitutional philosophy, I have discerned an increasing number of elements of a 'jus cosmopoliticum' in a Kantian sense[96] in international law. International law as it stands has already overcome the Hegelian idea that individuals can be free, and a legal subject, only through and in a state.[97]

The individual's ongoing transformation 'from subject of international law to international citizen is (an essential) part of the transformation of the international legal system from a Vattellian inter-state system into a universal constitutional democracy in which the individual is not only imputed with international rights and duties but in which he is (directly) represented and in which he participates in the international institutions that create and apply international law.'[98] A fuller constitutionalization of international law would

---

[96] Immanuel Kant 'Perpetual Peace' in *idem Perpetual Peace, and Other Essays on Politics, History, and Morals* (Hackett Publ Indianapolis 1983 (German orig. 1795) Humphrey trans), section II, third definitive article. See also *idem Die Metaphysik der Sitten, erster Theil, metaphysische Anfänge der Rechtslehre* (orig. Königsberg 1798) in *idem Die Metaphysik der Sitten*, works (Werkausgabe) vol VIII (3rd edn Suhrkamp Frankfurt am Main 1978 Weischedel ed) § 62, at 476 on the 'jus cosmopoliticum' (which Kant did not conceive as a right to political participation).

[97] See Georg W F Hegel *Vorlesungen über die Philosophie der Geschichte, I. Band: Einleitung—Die Vernunft in der Geschichte* (Meiner Leipzig 1920 Lasson ed), at 89–90: 'Dies Wesentliche nun, die Einheit des subjektiven Willens und des Allgemeinen, ist das sittliche Ganze und in seiner konkreten Gestalt der Staat. Er ist die Wirklichkeit, in der das Individuum seine Freiheit hat und geniesst, . . . Im Staat allein hat der Mensch eine vernünftige Existenz. Alle Erziehung geht dahin, dass das Individuum nicht ein Subjektives bleibe, sondern sich im Staate objektiv werde. . . . Alles was der Mensch ist, verdankt er dem Staat; er hat nur darin sein Wesen. Allen Wert, den der Mensch hat, alle geistige Wirklichkeit, hat er allein durch den Staat.' *Ibid*, at 97: 'Gesellschaft und Staat sind diese Zustände, in welchen die Freiheit vielmehr verwirklicht wird.' *Cf* also Christoph Enders *Die Menschenwürde in der Verfassungsordnung: zur Dogmatik des Art. 1 GG* (Mohr Siebeck Tübingen 1997), at 243: 'Wer als frei anerkannt sein will, muss in den staatlichen Zustand treten: Nur dort ist er Person, Rechtssubjekt' (on Hegel).

[98] Nijman, *International Legal Personality*, 2004, at 424.

require a prolongation and reinforcement of that trend. This is the issue of the democratization of the global legal order, which will be discussed in chapter 6.

3. States

3.1 States as *pouvoirs constitués*, not *pouvoirs constituants*

The global constitutional community is dominated by states. States are the most powerful international legal persons. But the narrowed version of international law as pure and exclusively inter-state law, which had been established by Emer de Vattel[99] and had its heyday around the turn of the 19th to the 20th century,[100] has been gradually abandoned since the Second World War. I have already pointed out that the constitutionalist reading of international law relativizes the dichotomy between states as the makers of international law and all other legal subjects, to the extent that all subjects are *pouvoirs constitués*. The various types of members of a constitutional community have differing rights and obligations, as defined by international constitutional law, but there is no categorical distinction between states and all others (pp. 154–155). So the constitutional approach engenders a shift of perspective: the traditional view suggested that the international legal limits on statehood and state action are imposed on the state from the outside (which implied that the state is not constituted by international law). From a constitutionalist perspective, by contrast, states—as international legal subjects—are *constituted by* international law.

Moreover, because, from a constitutionalist perspective, the well-being, interests, needs, and rights of individuals should be the prime concern of all governance arrangements,[101] states should not be conceived as the 'primary' subjects of international law. While states are indeed the principal, though not exclusive, creators of international law, this is a technical status only. The states' international constitutional legitimacy, however, depends on how they serve individuals as members of humanity. It has been argued that only representative and well-functioning states should be acknowledged as 'full' international legal persons.[102] However, there is no central institution which could 'withdraw' the

---

[99] Vattel defined the 'law of nations' as 'the science of the rights which exist between Nations or States, and of the obligations corresponding to these rights' (Emer de Vattel *Le droit des gens ou principes de la loi naturelle, appliqués à la conduite et aux affaires de Nations et des Souverains*, vol I (London 1758), in James Brown Scott (ed) *The Classics of International Law* (Carnegie Institution Washington 1916 Fenwick trans), § 3).
[100] See, e.g., Heinrich Triepel 'Les Rapports entre le Droit Interne et le Droit International' (1923) 1 *Recueil des Cours* 77–121, at 82.   [101] See above p. 157.
[102] 'If a state functions well and its citizens are represented properly by the government, the international legal personality which the state derives from its citizens remains with the state. The state is then the legitimate representative of its citizens at the international level with the authority to pursue their interests. ... The well-functioning state has full international legal personality, but only derived from its citizens.' (Nijman, *International Legal Personality*, 2004, at 473, see also 458).

international legal personality of a failing, collapsing, or oppressive state. By contrast, it is the decentralized recognition of states which serves to acknowledge their international legal personality, and to this I now turn.

3.2 The effectiveness and legitimacy of states

From a constitutionalist perspective, it is significant that the international legal requirement for statehood, namely 'effectiveness', has suffered some modification. To be a state, a political entity traditionally had to satisfy criteria based primarily on effectiveness (territory, people, effective government),[103] but not on the legitimacy of its government.

The concept of effectiveness that used to govern and which is still important for the definition of statehood means that factual capacity is acknowledged as a basis of international entitlements. To some extent, right here follows might. So an entity which as a matter of fact enjoys control over territory and independence from other powers is conceded the right to enjoy that situation. The function of the principle of effectiveness is to integrate the realities of power into law. The underlying rationale is that in the absence of a centralized international law-enforcement agency, international legal subjects must enforce their rights in a decentralized fashion, e.g. by sanctions. If they lack the power to do so, their rights remain hollow. In the long run, such a situation would undermine the international legal order as a whole. This identification of the rationale of the principle of effectiveness allows the realization that this principle is apt to evolve through constitutionalization. The more constitutionalized the international order becomes in the sense of a strengthening of centralized law-enforcement, the less important becomes the rationale of preventing a split between legal claims and their satisfaction through self-help. Put differently, the importance of the principle of effectiveness for the overall stability and normative power of international law diminishes.

Even under the reign of the principle of effectiveness, factual might is only a necessary, but not a sufficient, condition for the acknowledgement of statehood and of a state's rights. The continuing validity of the principle of effectiveness does not prohibit setting up additional requirements for statehood. One set of additional requirements are the standards of international law. Under current international law, a state may not be created in violation of a people's international right to self-determination and through unlawful use of force.[104] A constitutionalist approach suggests extending the scope of this requirement of

---

[103] See for the concept of state in international law the Montevideo Convention on the Rights and Duties of States of 26 December 1933, 165 LNTS 25, Art 1: 'The state as a person of international law should possess the following qualifications: a) a permanent population; b) a defined territory; c) government; and d) capacity to enter into relations with the other states.' In scholarship James Crawford *The Creation of States* (2nd edn CUP Cambridge 2006), at 37–95.

[104] Crawford, *Creation of States*, 2006, at 107. Therefore the Transkei, for instance, was not a state.

international legality so as to cover other peremptory precepts as well. It is unpersuasive to demand the observance of self-determination, but not of human rights which are *jus cogens*, such as basic humanitarian law norms, which may be violated in the course of a secession war.[105] The fact that the acknowledged legal requirements of statehood have something to do with territory does not warrant singling them out as sole conditions for valid statehood.

One discernible aspect of the constitutionalization of statehood is that the principle of effectiveness has been complemented and to some extent even substituted by the principle of international legality and legitimacy in international recognition practice. Although recognition by other states has only a declaratory effect, and therefore *de jure* does not constitute or 'make' a state, it has important practical effects. A political entity that is effective, but recognized by only a few other states, such as the Republic of Northern Cyprus or even Kosovo, may well be a state in theory, but lacks good standing in the international community, because it cannot accede to multilateral treaties and organizations. It is therefore in constitutionalist terms important that the post-1989 practice of recognition of states placed a high premium on standards of international legality and legitimacy. For instance, East Timor's process towards independence was closely monitored by the UN. The new state's constitution of 2002 was signed in presence of the Secretary General's Special Representative and Transitional Administrator, and the relevant UN reports emphasized that the Timorese Constitution provided 'for a unitary democratic state, based on the rule of law and the principle of the separation of powers'.[106] And after the break-up of the Soviet Union and Yugoslavia, new states in Eastern and Central Europe were required by the EC member states to explicitly renounce boundary changes, to guarantee the protection of minorities, and to subscribe to the commitments 'in the Final Act of Helsinki and the Charter of Paris, especially with regard to the rule of law, democracy and human rights'.[107] Most significantly, the 'legitimate', notably democratic, character of a state was apt to compensate for its lack of effectiveness,[108] as in the case in Bosnia Herzegovina in 1995, and to a lesser extent also in Kosovo in 2008. For sure, these recognition 'conditions' have been

---

[105] See on the status of basic rules of IHL as *jus cogens* Alexander Orakhelashvili, *Peremptory Norms in International Law* (OUP Oxford 2006), at 61–64, with references to the case law.

[106] Report of the Secretary-General on the United Nations Transitional Administration in East Timor of 17 April 2002, para 5 (UN Doc S/2002/432); see also UN Doc/S/RES/1480 (2003), para 2 of the Preamble.

[107] European Community, Guidelines for the recognition of new states in Eastern Europe and the Soviet Union of 16 December 1991, repr. in (1992) 31 ILM 1486 *et seq*. See on the post-1989 legitimacy-based international practice of supporting the emergence of legitimate states Jean d'Asprémont 'La création internationale d'Etats démocratiques' (2005) 109 *Revue Générale de Droit International Public* 889–908, concluding that 'nowadays, international administrations of territories entail the creation of democratic institutions. ... it is beyond doubt that whilst the international community cannot entirely control the birth of States, it strives to ... impose a precise type of political regime.' (Quotation from the English abstract).

[108] Jean d'Asprémont *L'Etat non démocratique en droit international* (Pedone Paris 2008), at 140.

applied only selectively. Moreover, they were abandoned in the recent Kosovo secession. Although Kosovo explicitly committed itself to all mentioned international legal principles in its declaration of independence, this could not relieve third states from making them an issue in the recognition process, because the declaration of independence did not bind Kosovo *vis-à-vis* other states.

A different matter is the recognition of governments, not states.[109] Democratic legitimism in the international recognition of governments had been practised notably by the United States and the United Kingdom in the 19th and beginning of the 20th century. This practice was—before 1989—too selective to become customary law. Since 1989, the density of precedents may work towards the emergence of a legal principle embracing substantial conditions for the international recognition of governments beyond the effectiveness test. After the Iraq war, for instance, a Security Council Resolution formulated, albeit implicitly, conditions for the recognition of a new Iraqi government. The Council here encouraged the people of Iraq to form 'a representative government based on the rule of law that affords equal rights and justice to all Iraqi citizens without regard to ethnicity, religion, or gender'.[110]

The discernible trend to complement, not substitute, the principle of effectiveness by considerations of legitimacy which are themselves engrained in international law, such as human rights protection and democracy,[111] is welcomed by constitutionalists. The reason is that global constitutionalism is premised on the respect of those principles and seeks to avoid the mere ratification of the status quo of power constellations by the law. The recognition practice should be consolidated in that direction and governments should take care to avoid double standards.

3.3 Sovereignty

Much of the contemporary debate on sovereignty turns around the potential erosion of sovereignty due to globalization and the ensuing practical necessities. This erosion is not the result of constitutionalization but should rather trigger the quest for constitutionalization. I will discuss now what the shape of sovereignty is in the process of constitutionalization, and how sovereign the states should be in a fully constitutionalized world order.

---

[109] According to the prevailing doctrine, changes of government, including illegal overthrows, leave the identity of a state as a subject of international law intact. The socialist international legal doctrine to the contrary has been discarded. So the recognition of governments has no effect on statehood in the sense of international law.

[110] UN Doc S/RES/1483 (2003). Another example is the treatment of the Taliban government in Afghanistan. In 1996, the Taliban sought international recognition and a representation in the UN. However, the new government was recognized only by Pakistan, Saudi Arabia, and the United Arab Emirates, and was not allowed to send its representative to the UN. Refusal of recognition was explained by reference to the Taliban government's violations of human rights, notably of women's rights.   [111] See pp. 273–277 on democracy as an international legal principle.

Sovereignty as a legal status defined by international constitutional law

From a constitutionalist perspective, the *differentia specifica* of states, their sovereignty, is a legal concept and as such embedded in international law. This view was present *in nuce* in the infancy of our discipline. Initially, public international law was conceived as natural law, applied to states, which were depicted as being in the state of nature (*jus naturae et gentium*). Because natural law was considered as eternal and immutable, this conception entailed the acceptance of legal boundaries for state action. For Jean Bodin, the sovereign was bound by divine and natural law and subject to further legal limits.[112] The theory of the just war, which has lived through a renaissance in the aftermath of the Kosovo intervention of 1999, reflects the acceptance of such boundaries.[113] But already towards the end of the 16th century, the uniform world view rooted in a uniform religious faith and with it the consensus on the substantial 'good' and 'just', was crumbling. In consequence, the theories of the just war increasingly concentrated on the formal element of '*auctoritas*' and marginalized the material elements such as '*justa causa*' and '*recta intentio*'. A war was 'just' if it was conducted among rulers with the proper authorization.[114] From there, it was only a small step to replace the old doctrine of the just war by the focus on sovereignty.[115] So the formal principle of sovereignty (independent of whatever beliefs the sovereign espoused) began to function as a substitute for the lost ideal of material justice. Legal positivism considered the question of a moral justification of war between nations futile, and highlighted that an arbiter to decide that question was anyway lacking. Sovereignty was conceived as absolute.[116] The sovereign's right to wage war, the *liberum ius ad bellum*, became the epitome of sovereignty

---

[112] Bodin's sovereigns were 'subjects aux lois de Dieu, & de nature, & à plusieurs loix humaines communes à tous peuples.' (Jean Bodin *Les six livres de la République*, livre I, chapter 8, reprint of the edition of Paris 1583, first edition of 1576, 122 (Scientia Aalen 1977), at 131).

[113] See Anne Peters and Simone Peter 'Lehren vom "gerechten Krieg" aus völkerrechtlicher Sicht' in Georg Kreis (ed) *Der 'gerechte Krieg'* (Schwabe Basel 2006) 43–96.

[114] This led to the paradoxical situation of a war which was 'just' on both sides ('*bellum iustum ex utraque parte*'). Baltasar De Ayala *De jure et officiis bellicis et disciplina militari libri tres* lib. I, cap. 2, at 5 *et seq.* (Carnegie Institution Washington 1912 (orig. 1581) Westlake ed).

[115] Carl Schmitt *Der Nomos der Erde im Völkerrecht des Jus Publicum Europaeum* (Greven Köln 1950), at 119.

[116] For Thomas Hobbes, 'Power Unlimited, is absolute Soveraignty.' (Thomas Hobbes *Leviathan* (CUP Cambridge 1991 (orig. 1651) Tuck ed), chapter 22, at 155 [115]. For sure, sovereignty for Hobbes existed and lasted only within functional limits: 'The obligation of Subjects to the Soveraign is understood to last as long, and no longer, than the power lasteth, by which he is able to protect them.' *Ibid*, chapter 21, at 153 [114] (emphasis added). But this Hobbesian limitation on sovereignty was ultimately inoperable, because the sovereign was accountable only to God, not to the citizens. See *ibid* chapter 30, at 231 [175]: 'The Office of the Soveraign (be it a Monarch, or an Assembly,) consisteth in the end, for which he was trusted with the Soveraign Power, namely the procuration of the safety of the people, to which he is obliged by the Law of Nature, and to *render an account thereof to God, the Author of that Law, and to none but him.*' (Emphasis added).

in the 19th century.[117] Pushed to its extreme, the concept of sovereignty as *auctoritas* or power led to the idea that the sovereign was by definition above the law, and therefore legally unbindable. This view was correlated with the assertion that public international law was not really law, because it lacked sanctions.[118]

In 20th century domestic constitutional discourse, Carl Schmitt—in a controversy with Hans Kelsen—most prominently framed sovereignty as an extra-legal concept. According to Schmitt, 'he who decides on the state of emergency is sovereign'.[119] The sovereign stands outside the normal legal order because he is competent to decide whether the constitution may be suspended.[120] Building on Schmitt, Giorgio Agamben has construed sovereignty as beyond the law, as a-legal. For Agamben, the paradigmatic expression of sovereignty, understood as the power to suspend the law, is the camp, e.g. Guantànamo Bay. In the camp, each policeman or guard is 'temporarily sovereign' and 'every question concerning the legality or illegality of what happened there simply makes no sense'.[121] This state of affairs is the opposite of constitutionalism.

In contrast to the proponents of sovereignty as extra-legality, Alfred Verdross, the ancestor of global constitutionalism,[122] had already emphasized in the 1920s that sovereignty meant sovereignty *within* public international law.[123] This conception has survived until today and has led to the widely accepted dictum that external sovereignty means (only) that states are not subordinate to other

---

[117] Paul Heilborn *Grundbegriffe des Völkerrechts. Handbuch des Völkerrechts* vol 1 (Kohlhammer Stuttgart 1912), at 23: 'Will ein Staat sein eigenes Selbst einsetzen, so darf er jederzeit Krieg beginnen. Die Gewalt ist also im Staatenverkehr unbedingt gestattet.'

[118] Georg W F Hegel *The Philosophy of Right* (Encyclopedia Britannica Chicago etc. 1952 Benton publ, Knox trans) (*Grundlinien der Philosophie des Rechts* 1821)), addition to paragraph 330: 'Now *since there is no power in existence* which decides in face of the state what is right in principle and actualizes this decision, it follows that so far as international relations are concerned we can never get beyond an "ought"' (emphasis added). Adolf Lasson *System der Rechtsphilosophie* (Guttentag Berlin and Leipzig 1882), at 394 and 402: 'Zwischen den Staaten als souveränen Wesen ist zwar ein eigentlicher Rechtszustand nicht möglich . . . . . . der Charakter eigentlichen Rechtes bleibt . . . dem Völkerrechte . . . für immer entzogen'. See in more detail Adolf Lasson *Princip und Zukunft des Völkerrechts* (Wilhelm Hertz Berlin 1871), at 22; John Austin *Lectures on Jurisprudence* vol I (John Murray London 1911) lect. VI, at 226: '[T]he law obtaining between nations is not positive law: for every positive law is set by a given sovereign to a person or persons in a state of subjection to its author.'

[119] Carl Schmitt *Politische Theologie: vier Kapitel zur Lehre von der Souveränität* (Duncker & Humblot München 1922), at 9 (transl. by the author).

[120] *Ibid*, at 10: '. . . ausserhalb der normal geltenden Rechtsordnung und gehört doch zu ihr, denn er ist zuständig für die Entscheidung, ob die Verfassung in toto suspendiert werden kann.' '*Die Existenz des Staates bewährt hier eine zweifellose Überlegenheit über die Geltung der Rechtsnorm. Die Entscheidung macht sich frei von jeder normativen Gebundenheit und wird im eigentlichen Sinne absolut. Im Ausnahmefall suspendiert der Staat das Recht, kraft eines Selbsterhaltungsrechtes, wie man sagt.*' (*Ibid*, at 13, emphasis added).

[121] Giorgio Agamben *Homo Sacer: Sovereign Power and Bare Life* (Stanford UP Palo Alto 1998 (orig. 1995) Heller-Roazen trans), at 170.

[122] Alfred Verdross *Die Verfassung der Völkerrechtsgemeinschaft* (Springer Wien 1926). See for a recent review Evelyne Lagrange 'Book Review' (2008) 112 *Revue Générale de Droit International Public* 521–565.

[123] Alfred Verdross 'Le fondement du droit international' (1927/I) 16 *Receuil de Cours* 247–323.

sovereign states, but that they are not free from international legal constraints. States are thereby directly subordinate to public international law. This boils down to the common formula that external sovereignty means independence from other sovereigns.

Against this background, the establishment and entrenchment of the international prohibition on the use of military force can be properly appreciated as a (re-)legalization of sovereignty and as a crucial step towards the constitutionalization of the international legal system.[124] The next important achievements are the international human rights guarantees adopted after the Second World War. The human rights limitations are crucial because they compel the sovereign states to observe specific international standards within their own territory and with regard to their own citizens. International (constitutional) law thus affects two facets of sovereignty: territorial and personal jurisdiction. From a constitutionalist perspective, sovereignty is not only 'surrounded' by legal safeguards,[125] but sovereignty exists only within the confines of international constitutional law. 'Sovereignty is the legal status of a state as *defined* (and not only "protected") by international law.'[126]

Sovereign responsibility

Constitutionalists welcome the re-characterization of sovereignty as implying a responsibility to protect (R2P),[127] because the concept of R2P takes human needs as the starting point and shifts the focus from states' rights to states' obligations (or responsibilities), which is a typical constitutionalist concern. The sovereign's responsibility exists for somebody (a principal) and for something (the tasks to be performed). These tasks extend in two directions (external and internal duties): the state must externally respect the sovereignty of other states, and must internally protect its inhabitants against avoidable catastrophes, such as famine, mass murder, and mass rape.[128] The responsible sovereign is accountable to two principals: the population of the state on the one hand, and the international community on the other hand.[129] As far as the 'internal' responsibility is concerned, the R2P to some extent reflects classic, Lockean, liberal constitutionalism, according to which the citizens entrust governments

---

[124] *Cf* Jochen A Frowein 'Konstitutionalisierung des Völkerrechts' (2000) 39 *Berichte der Deutschen Gesellschaft für Völkerrecht* 427–447, at 432–435.

[125] But Hans Joachim Morgenthau *Politics among Nations: The Struggle for Power and Peace* (7th edn McGraw-Hill Higher Education Boston 2005 (orig. 1948) Thompson and Clinton eds), at 337: '[I]nternational law owes its existence to the sovereignty of individual nations. To surround that sovereignty with legal safeguards is one of the main tasks of the rules of international law.'

[126] Bardo Fassbender 'Sovereignty and Constitutionalism in International Law' in Neil Walker (ed) *Sovereignty in Transition* (Hart Oxford 2003) 115–143, at 129 (emphasis added).

[127] International Commission on Intervention and State Sovereignty (ICISS), *The Responsibility to Protect* (2001), <http://www.iciss.ca/pdf/Commission-Report.pdf>. A fuller version of this section, including a detailed discussion of objections against the concept of R2P is contained in Anne Peters 'Humanity as the A and Ω of Sovereignty' (2009) 20 *EJIL* parts 5–7.

[128] ICISS, *Responsibility to Protect*, para 1.35.   [129] *Ibid*, para 2.15.

with sovereign powers, which are consequently intrinsically limited, revocable, and merely in the service of the principals.[130] A difference is that the liberal trust-givers are the citizens (the nation), whereas the responsibility to protect is owed to all persons within the state's territory, including foreigners.[131]

Suspension of sovereignty and residual responsibility in a system of multi-layered governance

The concept of R2P makes room for an argument in favour of humanitarian intervention in two doctrinal steps. First, the concept, as formulated by the International Commission on Intervention and State Sovereignty, explicitly conditions the enjoyment of external state sovereignty on the absence of extreme, conscience-shocking cases of mass atrocities in a state's territory. To the extent that the state's obligation to prevent and combat genocide or crimes against humanity is not fulfilled, the core right flowing from external state sovereignty, i.e. the right to be free from outside intervention, is suspended.[132]

This is a risky path. From a constitutionalist perspective, the prohibition on intervention is, just like sovereignty, ultimately grounded in the well-being of natural persons. Non-intervention protects, first, the inhabitants of potential victim-states (via their states). Additionally and equally importantly, it secures international stability, including the stability of state boundaries, as a whole. Any single intervention, even an illegal one, can be rightly or wrongly referred to as a precedent, and may thereby encourage abusive interventions elsewhere. Therefore, the obligation not to intervene coercively is owed both to individual states (which represent their population) and to the international community as a whole, which includes human beings everywhere. The loosening or abandonment of the prohibition on intervention would lead to a global instability of living conditions and to massive human suffering through interventionist and imperialist wars. Because of its pernicious consequences, non-intervention must be upheld as the rule.

On the premise that the prohibition on intervention is normatively derived from concerns for humanity, the *Lotus* principle does not apply. The starting point of a constitutionalist analysis is not the presumption that states enjoy freedom of action, unless this is prohibited by a norm of international law.[133] The starting point is rather the needs of human beings, notably of potential

---

[130] John Locke argued that 'the legislative being only a fiduciary power to act for certain ends, there remains still in the people a supreme power to remove or alter the legislative, when they find the legislative to act contrary to the trust reposed in them.' John Locke *Two Treatises of Government* (CUP Cambridge 1960 (orig. 1690) Laslett ed) para 149, at 413.

[131] The concept of R2P thus does not rely on, and does not ask for a democratic relationship between the electorate and the elected government. Responsibility is not conceived as political accountability (to be 'enforced' by voters in elections or by the international community through diplomatic representations), but as a humanitarian and nascent legal responsibility.

[132] The ICISS report does not excplicitly speak of 'suspension', but this is what its reasoning boils down to. See ICISS, *Responsibility to Protect*, paras 2.31 and 4.1.

[133] But see PCIJ, *The SS Lotus* (France v Turkey), PCIJ Reports Ser. A No 10 (1927).

victims of mass atrocities. Therefore, the examination of the rules on intervention should not begin, as in the traditional perspective, with an eventual exceptional right of states to intervene in extreme cases, but with the need of human beings for help. For constitutionalists, the relevant question is therefore not the right to intervene, but that of an eventual, though exceptional, *obligation* of third states or (organized) groups of states to intervene in certain extreme situations, notably *vis-à-vis* upcoming mass atrocities. This leads to the second doctrinal step, which is the following.

The ICISS postulated that a residual responsibility to protect falls on the international community. When the state is unable or unwilling to grant the most basal protection against mass atrocities, the international community's fall-back duty to protect is triggered.[134] The constitutionalist approach provides the missing links for this reasoning. The first missing link is the concept of international community, and the concomitant idea that international legal obligations may not only arise between states, but might fall on the international community (and be owed to that community) as such.

The second missing link is the concept of multi-level governance. This concept assumes that the bunch of governance activities is dispersed on various levels, ranging from local over national and regional supra-national units to the global level. The idea is that powers and competences are allocated to the various levels in a flexible manner, depending on considerations of effectiveness, subsidiarity, tradition, and so on. Under this premise, it is consistent that the responsibility to protect naturally falls on the higher level of governance, once the national level has failed.

A third and again different link between the two responsibilities is the idea of the social contract: the acknowledgment of a responsibility to protect could be a kind of social contract between the state and the international community as a whole. The state commits itself to protect its population in exchange for respect of its sovereignty by the community.[135]

Finally, an additional conceptual source of the residual responsibility of the international community is the emerging international legal principle of solidarity.[136] This principle is apt to bolster populations' claims for humanitarian assistance by other states.

The idea of a defeasibility of sovereignty and of a fall-back international responsibility, linked together by the concepts of multi-level governance and

---

[134] ICISS, *Responsibility to Protect*, esp. at paras 2.29–2.33 and 4.1.

[135] Sandra Szurek 'La responsabilité de protéger, nature de l'obligation et responsabilité internationale' in Société française pour le droit international (ed) *Colloque de Nanterre, La responsabilité de protéger* (Pedone Paris 2008) 91–134, at 134.

[136] Seminally Karel Wellens 'Solidarity as a Constitutional Principle: Its Expanding Role and Inherent Limitations' in Ronald St MacDonald and Douglas M Johnston (eds) *Towards World Constitutionalism: Issues in the Legal Ordering of the World Commmunity* (Martinus Nijhoff Leiden 2005) 775–807.

solidarity, taken together lead to the conclusion that under grave circumstances, namely war crimes, genocide, and crimes against humanity, an intervention of outsiders acting on behalf of the international community does not infringe state sovereignty. On the contrary, the international community's residual responsibility to protect even *requires* intervention, albeit under very limited conditions.[137]

Towards an obligation of the Security Council to take humanitarian action

The follow-up questions are under which (narrow) conditions and under observance of which limitations an intervention must and may take place, and—very importantly—who must authorize it. Under current international law, humanitarian interventions may not be conducted outside the framework of the UN Charter, and, conscious of the danger of abuse, I deem this limitation in principle laudable. However, the insight that sovereignty implies responsibility has shifted the focus from rights of states to the needs of humans, and has thus promoted a significant evolution of international law in the direction of a legal obligation of the international community, acting through the Security Council, to protect populations threatened by genocide or by crimes against humanity. But this obligation is triggered only if there is a sufficiently 'just cause' and whilst respecting strict proportionality, including an assessment of the costs of action as compared to the consequences of inaction.[138] The responsibility would especially fall on the permanent members of the Security Council, whose privilege within this body is in a constitutionalized order only justifiable with a view to those members' special military and economic capabilities (see pp. 190–194). The veto power is thus intrinsically correlated with a special responsibility. The endorsement of R2P as a legal principle fully thought through means that a permanent member's exercise of the veto power in an R2P case would be illegal.

For sure, the traditional reading of the UN Charter could hardly accommodate the notion of an illegal veto or of a 'blockage' of the Security Council, because exactly this blocking option was part of the deliberate institutional design of the organization. Initially, the decisions or non-decisions of the Council, including the exercise of the veto, were considered to be in a nearly law-free zone. But this zone has meanwhile been saturated by the rule of law. The rule of law does not only prohibit arbitrary measures of the Security Council as a whole, as stated above, but should also govern the Council members' votes approving of or preventing those measures. I propose that under the rule of law, the exercise of the veto may under special circumstances constitute an *abus de droit* by a permanent member.

---

[137] ICISS, *Responsibility to Protect*, para 2.31.
[138] See for the (constitutional) limits on Security Council humanitarian action 'A more secure world: our shared responsibility', Report of the High-level Panel on Threats, Challenges and Change of 2 December 2004 (UN Doc A759/565), paras 207–209; 'In larger freedom: towards development, security and human rights for all', Report of the Secretary General of 21 March 2005 (UN Doc A/59/2005), para 126; ICISS *Responsibility to Protect*, paras 4.18 *et seq* and 7.26. See also p. 284.

On the premise that R2P is indeed a nascent international norm, the procedural rule of Article 27 paragraph 3 of the UN Charter which foresees unanimity of the five permanent members (P5) could be interpreted systemically, and take into account the responsibility to protect as a 'relevant rule of international law' in the sense of Article 31 paragraph 3 lit. c) VCLT. The systemic interpretation would lead to qualifying an illegal or abusive refusal to concur by a P5 either as legally irrelevant or as a mere abstention which according to established practice cannot prevent a positive decision of the Council. The legal irrelevance of an abusive veto also flows from the general principle that the United Nations may not invoke internal procedural problems to justify its breach of international law.[139] Besides, an illegal veto would trigger the respective member state's international legal responsibility, whose precise relationship to the organization's legal responsibility would still have to be defined. And because the obligation to protect is an obligation *erga omnes*, third states could at least invoke this illegality under Article 48 sec. 1 b) ILC Articles. The Security Council's obligation to intervene, flowing from the obligation to protect, would thus be to some extent enforceable, but only by addressing the Council members individually.[140] So from a constitutionalist perspective, the Council should under very strict conditions have the duty to authorize proportionate humanitarian action to prevent or combat genocide or massive and widespread crimes against humanity.

Responsibility to protect as an emerging global constitutional norm

The co-chair of ICISS qualified the 'responsibility to protect' as 'guiding principle' and as an 'emerging norm'.[141] Indeed, the concept of a responsibility to protect has been *inter alia*[142] endorsed by the UN Secretary General in various reports,[143] by the High-level Expert Panel of 2004,[144] by the member states at

[139] This general principle of international legal responsibility has so far been codified only for the special case of the failure to perform a treaty (*cf* both Arts 27 of VCLT 1969 and 1986).

[140] The fact that even grossly shocking inaction of the Security Council cannot be directly sanctioned, because the Council is merely an organ of the UN, and not a international legal person which can be held liable, and because no dispute settlement institution is available, is a problem from a constitutionalist perspective. It furnishes an additional argument for the supporters of a legal permission of subsidiary unilateral humanitarian interventions, which I reject.

[141] Gareth Evans 'The Responsibility to Protect: Rethinking Humanitarian Intervention' (2004) 98th annual meeting *Proceedings of the American Society of International Law* 78–89, at 83.

[142] For references to further statements of international and regional actors constituting practice apt to contribute to the formation of customary law see Peters, Humanity as A and Ω, 2009.

[143] 'We the Peoples: The Role of the United Nations in the 21st century', Report of the Secretary General of 27 March 2000, (UN Doc A/54/2000), chapter IV, at 48 (paras 217–219); 'In larger freedom: towards development, security and human rights for all', Report of the Secretary General of 21 March 2005 (UN Doc A/59/2005), para 135; 'Uniting our strengths: Enhancing United Nations support for the rule of law', Report of the Secretary General of 14 December 2006 (UN Doc A/61/636-S/2006/980) para 6.

[144] 'A more secure world: our shared responsibility', Report of the High-level Panel on Threats, Challenges and Change of 2 December 2004 (UN Doc A759/565), subchapter 3: 'Chapter VII of the Charter of the United Nations, internal threats and the responsibility to protect' (paras 199–203).

the world summit of 2005,[145] by the Security Council,[146] and in the ICJ case law.[147] The outbreak of ethnic-related violence in Kenya after the elections of 2007 was qualified as a R2P situation by Archbishop emeritus and Nobel Prize winner Desmond Tutu.[148] But during the natural and ensuing humanitarian catastrophe following the cyclone in Myanmar in May 2008, China and Indonesia rejected the French characterization of that situation as an R2P situation. The French president unsuccessfully asked for a Security Council mandate to enforce the access of foreign aid personnel into the country, which had been denied by the government. The situation in Darfur since about 2001 has, according to all evidence, transgressed the threshold of inhumanity that triggers the subsidiary responsibility of the international community,[149] but still the United Nations and the African Union did not take sufficiently robust action to prevent and combat mass atrocities, and thus did not honour the principle here. So the reiteration of the principle of sovereignty as implying a responsibility to protect, and its limited, but partly inconsistent, application in practice has promoted its ongoing process of crystallization into hard international law, which is not complete, however, and remains precarious. In particular, the legal strategies to enforce the Security Council's nascent residual obligation to take humanitarian action still await elaboration. In terms of legal policy, such an obligation is recommendable precisely to obliterate the need for unilateral action and to forestall pretexts of 'humanitarian intervention' by states. The ongoing process of rendering sovereigns responsible is a cornerstone of the current transformation of international law into a constitutionalized system.

3.4 Equality

Proportionate equality of states and their treatment as equals

In a constitutionalist outlook, the principle of equality of states (Article 2(1) UN Charter), even if it is to some extent utopian, works as a regulative idea, and is a basic principle of justice. Such ideals of justice are an indispensable element of any constitutional order which deserves that name and does not content itself with merely sanctioning the established facts. It is therefore significant from a

---

[145] Resolution adopted by the General Assembly, World Summit Outcome, UN Doc A/RES/60/1 of 24 October 2005, para 138.   [146] UN SC res 1674 (2006); 1706 (2006).

[147] ICJ, *Case Concerning the Application of the Convention on the Prevention and Punishment of the Crime of Genocide* (Bosnia and Herzegovina v Serbia and Montenegro), judgment of 26 February 2007, paras 425–450.

[148] Desmond Tutu 'Taking the Repsonsibility to Protect' *International Herald Tribune* of 19 February 2008.

[149] See for an analysis of the human rights situation in Darfur within the framework of the responsibility to protect UN Human Rights Council, Implementation of GA res 60/251, Report of the High-level Mission on the situation of human rights in Darfur pursuant to HRC decision S-4/101 ('Jody Williams report', UN Doc A/HRC/4/80 of 9 March 2007).

constitutionalist perspective that the current multilaterization of treaty relations brings about a pull towards (state) equality: while in bilateral exchange relationships rights and obligations are usually unequal, the novel multilateral, lawmaking 'world-order treaties' basically lay down equal duties for all.[150]

But important exceptions remain. Within numerous international organizations and treaty regimes, member states have unequal rights and obligations. Typical legal distinctions are made with regard to membership fees, weighted voting, permanent seats, and veto rights. The best-known inegalitarian regimes are the UN Security Council with the veto power of its permanent members, the Non-Proliferation Treaty of 1968 dividing the world in haves (the Atomic Club) and the have-nots, and the Bretton Woods Institutions (World Bank and World Monetary Fund) in which the richest states have the greatest voting power. The question arises whether and how these schemes can be legitimized within a constitutionalized world order.

Positivist reasoning justifies the legal inequalities of the members of international organizations by pointing to the member states' prior consent. The founding states may accord to themselves diverging rights and duties. If a state consents to a set of treaty rights and duties which burden itself but which grants legal privileges to other contracting parties, the principle of equality is safeguarded by that consent. The unequal bargaining power of the (founding) treaty parties is in the positivist view an irrelevant, purely political factor outside the realm of the law.

The non-positivist and constitutionalist response is that such reasoning blends out power disparities and thereby risks undermining one of the basic functions of law, which is to protect the weak. Constitutionalists also insist that the spheres of law and politics are distinguishable but should not be artificially isolated from each other. This means, first, that one indispensable legitimating factor of unequal rights and obligations within concrete legal regimes is the absence of unlawful pressure and constraint in the process of negotiating that regime. If grossly unequal bargaining power, especially coercion or threat of economic force (under a broad reading of Article 52 VCLT[151]) is present, the weak state's consent would seem to be vitiated and the resulting legal treaty should in constitutional terms be considered unjustified, if not void.[152]

---

[150] Nico Krisch 'More Equal than the Rest? Hierarchy, Equality and US Predominance in International Law' in Michael Byers and Georg Nolte (eds) *United States Hegemony and the Foundations of International Law* (CUP Cambridge 2003) 135–175, at 152.

[151] For the claim that the *travaux préparatoires* and subsequent practice have established a presumption in favour of the broad reading see Olivier Corten 'Convention de Vienne de 1969, Article 52' in *idem* and Pierre Klein (eds) *Les Conventions de Vienne sur le droit des traités: Commentaire article par article* (Bruylant Bruxelles 2006) paras 19–26.

[152] This statement is not supported by the *lex lata*, but remains a constitutionalist desideratum. Its implementation would require the establishment of an institution to assess the fairness of a treaty making process (and eventually of its contents in the style of an international 'terms control'). See Anne Peters 'Unequal Treaties' *Max Planck Encyclopedia of International Law* (OUP Oxford 2008 online).

Second, unequal rights and obligations in international regimes need a non-formalist substantial justification, such as the following: from a constitutionalist perspective, equality in law is no abstract and absolute claim. Constitutionalism rather requires *proportional equality* (*suum cuique*, not *idem cuique*). This means that a formally differentiated treatment of states, i.e. legal distinctions among states, are permissible if and as long as this is necessary and adequate to fulfil legitimate objectives of the global constitutional community. Put differently, the states' right to have equal rights within a concrete legal regime may be curtailed by countervailing considerations. Formal equality is thus subject to balancing against other concerns, such as concerns for security or of effective peace-keeping.[153]

A different line of reasoning comes to a similar conclusion, namely that in a constitutionalized system, states need not have formally equal rights under all circumstances. Ulrich Preuss[154] has recently argued that the constitutionaliza-tion of international law (understood as the acknowledgment and institutiona-lization of interdependence) implies formal (legal) state inequality, but should safeguard the states' right to be treated as equally valuable members of a con-stitutional community (not equal rights, but equal respect).[155] The starting point of the argument is the insight that in a non-constitutionalized order, states enjoyed independence or sovereignty-autonomy, understood as the direct sub-jugation of states only to international law (and not to other states), which in turn logically implied the formally equal status of states under international law. So as a matter of logic, independence of states meant state equality.[156] The inverse conclusion cannot be drawn: interdependence does not logically imply inequality. All states can become less autonomous due to globalization pressure, but this can theoretically happen to the same degree for all. However, a realistic assessment is that if actors such as states enter into more intense relations which each other, their respective power and resource becomes significant, because this is what their communication and interactions are ultimately all about.[157] On this ground it can be claimed that constitutionalization implies that the states' relations become hierarchized. Ulrich Preuss demands that the inequality which small and weak states are likely to suffer in a constitutionalist international community must be embedded in constitutional arrangements which guarantee

---

[153] Anne Peters 'The Growth of International Law between Globalization and the Great Power' (2003) 8 *Austrian Review of International and European Law* 109–139, at 130–135.

[154] Ulrich K Preuss 'Equality of States—Its Meaning in a Constitutionalized Global Order' (2008) 9 *Chicago Journal of International Law* 17–49.

[155] *Cf* Ronald Dworkin *Taking Rights Seriously* (Duckworth London 1977), at 227 on the 'right to treatment as an equal' as opposed to equal treatment.

[156] 'Equality, too, is nothing but a synonym for sovereignty, pointing to a particular aspect of sovereignty. If all nations have supreme authority within their territories, none can be subordinated to any other in the exercise of that authority. ... International law is law among coordinated, not subordinated, entities. Nations are subordinated to international law, but not to one another; that is to say, they are equal.' (Morgenthau, *Politics among Nations*, 2005, at 320).

[157] Preuss, Equality of States, 2008, at 43.

that they are treated as equally valuable members. This seems to be a different way of expressing what I have called proportionate equality above. The right to equal concern and respect still allows states to be outvoted time and again by a majority. They must be embedded in a device of international constitutional solidarity. This ultimately leads to a constitutional demand for global distributive justice.[158]

Constitutionally permissible grounds for legal distinctions between states

A constitutional scheme of proportional equality of states would have to be more exacting than John Rawls' distinction between five types of domestic societies: 'liberal peoples' and 'decent peoples' (forming together the group of 'well-ordered peoples'), 'outlaw states', 'societies burdened by unfavourable conditions', and finally 'benevolent absolutisms'.[159] It would also have to be more exacting than a rough distinction between 'liberal' and 'illiberal' states.[160] The starting point of the proponents of that distinction is the quite plausible claim that illiberal regimes are structurally less able to fulfil the requirements that international law imposes on states, notably the obligations to observe the prohibition on the use of force,[161] to prevent the proliferation of weapons of mass destruction, and to respect human rights. This structural difference—so the argument runs—justifies treating those regimes differently under international law. This conception can also fuel the claim that those structurally less apt states should enjoy less sovereignty than other states, and that therefore interventions, for example on humanitarian grounds, should be permissible.[162] That approach poses a number of problems. First, the exact criteria for distinguishing between liberal and illiberal states remain obscure. The distinction itself seems essentially contested and currently has no chance of universal approval. In order to build such a consensus, one necessary step would be to verify empirically the asserted link between regime type and structural inability to fulfil international legal guidelines. But the most serious objection to the distinction between liberal and illiberal states is that it lends itself to abuse by the liberal superpower. In fact, the US-American rogue state doctrine appears as a vulgarized and exaggerated political version of that very distinction.

Although the permissibility of legal distinctions among states ultimately depends on the context in which that distinction is made, there is a basic presumption that criteria embedded in the international legal order generally constitute legitimate grounds of distinction for most purposes. It is therefore in

---

[158] *Ibid*, at 45–47.

[159] John Rawls *The Law of Peoples* (Harvard UP Cambridge (Mass.) 1999), at 63.

[160] Anne-Marie Slaughter 'International Law in a World of Liberal States' (1995) 6 *EJIL* 503–538.   [161] On the democratic or liberal peace thesis see pp. 280–283.

[162] I have discussed this problem above and insisted on the prohibition of unilateral intervention, coupled with an obligation of the Security Council to take humanitarian action (see above pp. 186–189).

principle acceptable to evaluate and distinguish states according to criteria documented in the UN system, such as observance of the prohibition on the use of force, respect for the rule of law, and human rights.[163]

Obvious permissible grounds for legal distinctions among states, and thus for deviations from formal equality, are particular burdens stemming from state power or wealth. A special responsibility may require special rules. For instance, a central concern of the international order is security and effective peace-keeping. World peace cannot be guaranteed without the support of the most powerful states. 'Great Powers are thus not given a privileged position because they have acquired it on the strength of their status of power, but they are given a special function when, on account of their relevant special characteristics, they can serve the cause of law in this function.'[164] This reasoning is in principle apt to defend the veto power in the Security Council. But the permanent members' (P5) veto power would additionally have to be shown to be adequate and pro-portionate in relation to the objective of peace-keeping. Moreover, a problem is that the P5's position is owed to particular historical circumstances and is unduly entrenched. The current law does not force the permanent members to 're-earn' their privilege continously by substantial contributions to world peace.

As far as the international finance institutions are concerned, it seems fair that the decisions to lend out money are taken by those who have contributed the money. Because the World Bank and the International Monetary Fund (IMF) need to attract capital, it could be argued that it makes sense to couple voting rights to capital contributions to encourage the rich countries to join and con-tribute to the IMF and the Bank. However, both organizations rely to a large extent on the (poor) borrowing member countries, both for their capital and their running costs.[165] Against this background, the coupling of voting rights to capital contributions is less compelling than it seems at first sight.

The inverse situation is the differential rights and obligations in environ-mental law treaties (based on the principle of common but differentiated responsibility)[166] or under the GATT (General Agreement on Trade and Tar-iffs) Enabling Clause and the Generalized System of Preferences (GSP).[167] These legal distinctions do not privilege the powerful parties, but on the con-trary grant preferential treatment to less developed states. These preferences are

---

[163] *Cf* Lee Feinstein and Anne-Marie Slaughter 'A Duty to Prevent' (2004) 83 No 1 *Foreign Affairs* 136–150.

[164] Pieter Hendrik Kooijmans *The Doctrine of the Legal Equality of States: An Inquiry into the Foundations of International Law* (AW Sijthoff Leiden 1964), at 112.

[165] See in detail Ngaire Woods *The Globalizers: The IMF, the World Bank, and their Borrowers* (Cornell UP Ithaca NY and London 2006), at 194–200 under the heading 'Who pays the Piper?' Woods concludes that 'there are deep flaws in the reasoning that wealthy countries pay for the IMF and World Bank and should therefore run the organization' (at 199).

[166] See e.g. in the UNFCCC Art 3(1), 4(1) and the distinction between Annex I members and other member states.

[167] 'Enabling Clause', decision of the GATT contracting parties of 28 November 1979 (26S/203). See also Art XXXVI (3) GATT.

necessary and legitimate to the extent that they are in substance not privileges, but merely alleviate or temper the factual burdens of poorer states. In the end, these formal distinctions are intended to counteract factual inequality and to bring the regimes more in line with the ideal of the proportionate and material equality of states.

Finally, a state's respect for the most basic human rights might be a legitimate criterion for legal distinctions between states which would leave proportionate equality intact. A concern for human rights, interests, needs, and security is fully engrained in international human rights law and in other parts of international law, and may therefore outweigh the interest in observing formal equality of states. It would therefore in principle be in line with the right to sovereign equality to condition voting rights, for example in the UN General Assembly, on respect for human rights.[168] Distinguishing states by their human rights performance does not imply the creation of fixed categories of states, as in 19th-century international legal doctrine.[169] All states would still enjoy the presumptive right to formally equal treatment, which could, however, in concrete legal contexts, be relativized on account of their disregard for human rights.[170]

To sum up, the concerns for peace, for human rights protection, for development, or other constitutional concerns may outweigh the interest in observing strict equality of states and may justify legal privileges such as more drawing rights, more votes, or exemptions from liberalization obligations. The constitutional grounds for legal distinctions among states which are reconcilable with the principle of proportionate state equality have to be consensually elaborated or confirmed. The starting point of such constitutional debates should be the acknowledged international legal standards. The potential grounds for legitimate distinctions among states should, for consequentialist reasons, leave the principle of non-intervention intact.[171] Finally, all distinctions must be reversible. If the constitutional concerns that carry the distinctions lose weight, an unequal regime may become illegitimate, and must be adapted.

---

[168] Such a measure could be based on an extensive reading of Art 5 UN Charter allowing for the suspension of the exercise of the General Assembly rights of member states against which preventive or enforcement action has been taken.

[169] Notoriously, James Lorimer divided humanity into three concentric zones: 'civilised humanity', 'barbarous humanity', and 'savage humanity', to which three different types of recognition could be awarded, ranging from 'plenary political recognition' over 'partial political recognition' to 'mere human recognition'. 'Barbarous communities' in 'political nonage' did not have a right to recognition, but merely a right to guardianship. Lorimer also assumed that some non-European states were imbecile or criminal and therefore unrecognizable (James Lorimer *The Institutes of the Law of Nations* vol 1 (William Blackwood Edinburgh and London 1883), at 101–103 and 156–162.

[170] This approach, just like sanctions, risks hurting the populations of the target state, and must therefore be used extremely cautiously.

[171] Differentiations arising from suspensions of sovereignty should be only allowed in a very narrow framework of R2P, as discussed above.

Equality of individuals and equality of states

A final criterion for legal distinctions between states might be their population size. This idea is actually compelling on the constitutionalist premise that the ultimate point of reference should be individuals, not states. But should international constitutional law realize the equality of individuals, not of states? Along this line, it has been asserted that the current international system is one of 'stratified, institutionalized legal inequality', which is, however, morally and politically defensible because what matters is equality among individuals.[172] I disagree both with the descriptive and the normative proposition. Current international law is not a system of institutionalized state inequality, but rather a system of overall extreme factual inequality of wealth and power, with only isolated instances of legal inequality of states, as described above.[173] Second, in the law as it stands, the rights of states are not differentiated according to population size, but the legal inequalities are based on completely different considerations. The current system does not fully honour the principle of state equality, but it is certainly much further away from realizing individual equality.

Endorsing natural persons' individual equal rights on a global level as the regulative idea leads to the claim that the rights of states should be commensurate to their population. Given the vastly differing populations of states, this guiding principle leads not only to tolerating, but even to requiring the legal inequality of states. From that perspective, the principle of 'one state–one vote' in the General Assembly is undemocratic.[174] To democratize the UN, the General Assembly would have to introduce a voting scheme which is based on population size, or—and this seems to be the better idea—the General Assembly should be transformed into a second chamber and be accompanied by a peoples' or citizens' chamber which represents natural persons.[175] Ultimately, if one acknowledges that both individuals and their representatives, the states, are important international legal subjects, the tension between state equality and individual equality can not be resolved, but is there to stay.

3.5 The constitutional functions of states in a constitutionalized world order

Global constitutionalism acknowledges the inextricability of law and politics. Therefore the constitutionalist reading of international law seeks to reconcile the

---

[172] Michael Zürn 'Institutionalisierte Ungleichheit in der Weltpolitik. Jenseits der Alternativen "Global Governance" versus "American Empire"' (2007) 48 *Politische Vierteljahresschrift* 680–704.
[173] But see Gerry Simpson *Great Powers and Outlaw States* (CUP Cambridge 2004), at 352, arguing that inequality is legally entrenched in the international legal system through *legal* hegemony and anti-pluralism.
[174] See, e.g, John J Jackson 'Sovereignty-Modern. A New Approach to an Outdated Concept' (2003) 97 *AJIL* 782–802, at 795.   [175] See pp. 319–326 in detail on this issue.

political position of states with their formal status as international legal persons. So which legitimate legal and political role should states occupy in a constitutionalized world order? Politically speaking, the western nation state has been the model of statehood. During a relatively short phase of its history, this type of state came close to monopolizing the provision of the basic goods of peace and physical security, liberty and legal security, democratic self-determination, and economic growth and social welfare. States were held responsible for the delivery of these goods (outcome responsibility), and they also incurred regulatory and operational responsibility in that regard.[176]

Recent empirical research on the evolution of (western) states has shown that states have not lost these regulatory and operational competencies, but the monopoly over their exercise. This remains true, despite the fact that globalization has not only debilitated the states, but has also empowered them (at least some of them). New forms of interaction and new arrangements between the public and the private sector, novel intergovernmental, multilateral, or regional forums have contributed to maintaining or even extending the reach of the state and thus have not only weakened, but also increased the effectiveness of states.[177] Meanwhile, it is a commonplace that the scholarly dismissal of the nation state[178] which had gained strong currency after the collapse of communism and the corresponding deblocage of the United Nations was descriptively false.[179] Proponents of a 'new theory of the state' claim that 'if the 1990s have shown anything, it is the remarkable resilience of the state'.[180] This assessment has gained ground after the global financial crisis of 2008, which triggered intense governmental interventionism and unprecedented quasi-nationalizations of the banking sector. However, the fact remains that nation

---

[176] Achim Hurrelmann, Stephan Leibfried, Kerstin Martens, and Peter Mayer 'The Transformation of the Golden-Age Nation State: Findings and Perspectives' in *idem* (eds) *Transforming the Golden-Age Nation State* (Palgrave Macmillan Hampshire 2007) 193–205, at 193–194.

[177] Linda Weiss 'Introduction: Bringing Domestic Institutions Back in' in *idem* (ed) *States in the Global Economy. Bringing Domestic Institutions Back in* (CUP Cambridge 2003) 1–36, at 10 and 26. For the financial sector see Peter Haegel 'Standard Setting for Capital Movements: Reasserting Sovereignty over Transnational Actors?' in Anne Peters, Lucy Köchlin, Till Förster, and Gretta Fenner Zinkernagel (eds) *Non-state Actors as Standard Setters* (CUP Cambridge 2009) 351–378. With regard to European integration Alan Steele Milward, *The European Rescue of the Nation-State* (Routledge London 1994).

[178] Kenichi Ohmae *The End of the Nation State* (Harper Collins London 1995); Susan Strange *The Retreat of the State: The Diffusion of Power in the World Economy* (CUP Cambridge 1996); Oscar Schachter 'The Decline of the National State and its Implications for International Law' (1997) 36 *Columbia Journal of Transnational Law* 7–23; Martin Albrow *Abschied vom Nationalstaat* (Suhrkamp Frankfurt am Main 1998/1996); Martin van Creveld *Aufstieg und Untergang des Staates* (Gerling-Akademie-Verlag München 1999).

[179] See in more detail Anne Peters 'Privatisierung, Globalisierung und die Resistenz des Verfassungsstaates' in Philippe Mastronardi and Denis Taubert (eds) *Staats- und Verfassungstheorie im Spannungsfeld der Disziplinen* Beiheft Archiv für Rechts- und Sozialphilosophie 105 (Franz Steiner Stuttgart 2006) 100–159.

[180] Wolfgang Drechsler 'On the Viability of the Concept of Staatswissenschaften' (2001) 12 *European Journal of Law and Economics* 105–111, at 108.

states could not tackle that crisis unilaterally, but had to cooperate. So states in the western world have not ceased to be active in providing the mentioned goods such as security, liberty, self-determination, and wealth, 'but they have increasingly lost their autonomy in guaranteeing for these goods' provision'.[181] Apparently, a (self-)transformation of the state has taken place.[182]

This finding is very important for the constitutionalization of the international legal system. The self-transformation of states poses a challenge to international organizations and other arrangements of transnational governance. On the premise that humans need and want the delivery of the basic goods, beginning with peace and physical security over democracy up to social security, and given the fact that states have less autonomy and capacity for their delivery, international institutions must become more effective in furnishing those goods. This includes the provision of legal certainty and democratic self-determination on a level 'above' states and within international institutions. Otherwise, the legitimacy of the international system is seriously challenged, and this is exactly what seems to happen at present. Global constitutionalism with its potential to compensate for the hollowing out of constitutional guarantees on the national level is apt to furnish at least a toolbox for remedies (see p. 347).

In a constitutionalized world order, states fulfil important functions and therefore have a legitimate role to play. While only democratic states are formal representatives of their citizens, all types of states are apt to constitute a crystallization point for (collective) identity, even if this function of states is tempered by the fact that collective identities are multiple and multi-level (see pp. 310–311). States are also and should continue to be a mediator between sub-state and supra-state governance ('sandwich state'[183] or 'multilevel state'[184]).

As far as the states' constitutional function of law-making is concerned, the following should be noted. First, only states, acting directly or via international governmental organizations, 'make' formal international (treaty) law, while non-state actors participate in international formal legal processes in a manner that is qualitatively and quantitatively different from states and inter-state organizations. But this difference may be less important than it seems at first sight. Maybe the legal exclusion of non-state actors from formal international law-making 'misses the political and social reality of their increased participation' and the impact of that participation on subsequent state behaviour. Therefore Alan Boyle and Christine Chinkin have argued that it 'would be myopic to insist on the classical

---

[181] Hurrelmann *et al*, Golden-Age Nation State, 2007, at 200 and 204.

[182] See notably Stephan Leibfried and Michael Zürn (eds) *Transformations of the State?* European Review 13 Suppl. No 1 (CUP Cambridge 2005).

[183] Peter Saladin, *Wozu noch Staaten?* (Stämpfli Bern 1995), at 237.

[184] Arthur Benz, *Der moderne Staat: Grundlagen einer politologischen Analyse* (2nd edn Oldenbourg München 2008), at 320–322.

view of states as the sole makers of international law; rather we must recognize the multi-layered, multi-partite nature of the international law-making enterprise'.[185] But despite the political and sociological blurriness of the international law-making process, it is, from a constitutionalist perspective, for reasons of legal clarity, preferable to insist on the formal distinction between those actors that vote and those that merely have a voice in international law-making.[186]

Second, states increasingly assume the role of a broker in international law-making. Where two groups of global players, namely TNCs and NGOs, typically have conflicting objectives, the state is less the initiator of new rules but rather a mediator between competing forces.[187] The combined action of states with business and civil society organizations, eventually within public–private partnerships, may be apt to neutralize or at least mitigate the danger of one-sided rules, and thus increases the process- and output-legitimacy of the resulting rules and the system at large.

Finally, states often perform a 'formalizing' role in international law-making. State institutions progressively integrate informal transnational rules (adopted, for example, by a global industry branch or a transnational corporation), not only into their domestic legal system, but also into international law. Put the other way round, non-state and private actors' rules and standards may be used to render state and inter-state law operational.[188] For example, the International Financial Reporting Standards (IFRS), adopted by the privately staffed and privately funded International Accounting Standards Board (IASB), are incorporated into EU law.[189] Overall, the role of states in international law-making has undergone important changes which are analysed in detail in chapter 3.

As far as the constitutional function of law-enforcement is concerned, it was shown in chapter 4 that states here occupy an even more important role. Both international judicial and executive action is dominated by states, albeit in collaboration with international organizations and NGOs. Generally speaking, states are and should continue to be a prime locus of political power and

---

[185] Alan Boyle and Christine Chinkin *The Making of International Law* (OUP Oxford 2007), at 97.
[186] See also pp. 225–227
[187] Boyle and Chinkin, *The Making of International Law*, 2007, at 61.
[188] For instance, the Law of the Sea Convention enshrines the right of innocent passage (Art 17 UNCLOS), but does not say how wide or deep the navigable channel must be. The International Navigation Association (PIANC), which represents port, navigation, and shipping interests, sets the necessary standards for shipping channels. Furthermore, 'diagonal' agreements between governments and firms (e.g. investment agreements) frequently refer to standards for products or for behaviour (e.g. in accounting or evaluation practices), to 'best industry practice' or to 'prevailing commercial usage', and thus incorporate these private standards. See in scholarship Vaughan Lowe 'Corporations as International Actors and International Lawmakers' (2004) 14 *Italian Yearbook of International Law* 23–38.
[189] Commission Regulation (EC) No 1725/2003 of 29 September 2003 adopting certain international accounting standards in accordance with Regulation (EC) No 1606/2002 of the European Parliament and of the Council, OJ 2003 L 261/1.

authority. They typically possess the necessary resources and the monopoly on the legitimate use of force inside their boundaries, subject to the limitations of international law. Therefore, they are still the most important guarantor of human security. There is simply no other political institution in sight which would possess a comparable capacity and legitimacy as the state. Weak and failed states which lack the economic and military power to perform their public tasks should in principle continue to benefit from the international prohibition on intervention, unless they manifestly fail to deliver their obligation to protect (see in detail above at pp. 186–188). Overall, the specific power and authority of a state is the reason for its ambivalent role as the most important protector, but also as the most important potential threat to human security. A global constitutional order must take this fundamental ambiguity into account.

3.6 By way of conclusion: the domestic analogy reversed

In the discipline of *ius gentium et naturae*, states were viewed as analogous to individual persons in the state of nature ('domestic analogy').[190] International law was the law of nature, applied to states. Thus states enjoyed natural rights which were incumbent equally on all, and which were inalienable. These fundamental, natural rights were, for example, the right to liberty, security, commerce, and equality.[191] In later romanticist thought, the domestic analogy was supported by the metaphor of the state as a living organism.[192]

---

[190] On the analogy between states and individuals as one of the most decisive features of the teachings of Hugo Grotius see seminally Lauterpacht, Grotian Tradition, 1946, e.g. at 29. For a nuanced treatment see Christian Wolff *Ius Gentium Methodo Scientifica pertractorum* vol II (Frankfurt 1764 Drake trans) in James Brown Scott (ed) *The Classics of International Law* (Clarendon Press Oxford 1934), preface (p. 5 of the translation) and § 2–3 (p. 9); Vattel, *Le droit des gens*, 1758, passim (e.g. préliminaires, para 18; book II, chapter III (at 285); Jean Jacques Rousseau 'Du contrat social' in *idem Du contrat social et autres oeuvres politiques* (éditions Garnier Frères Paris 1954 (orig. 1762)) 235–336, livre I, chapter VII (at 245): 'à l'égard de l'étranger, il [the state] devient un être simple, un individu'. Draft of Abbé Grégoire for a declaration of the rights of peoples of 23 April 1793: '2. Les peuples sont respectivement indépendans et souverains, quel que soit le nombre d'individus qui les composent et l'étendue du territoire qu'ils occupent. Cette souveraineté est inaliénable. 3. *Un peuple doit agir à l'égard des autres comme il désire qu'on agisse à son égard; ce qu'un homme doit à un homme, un peuple le doit aux autres*', repr. in Wilhem G Grewe (ed) *Fontes Historiae Iuris Gentium: Sources Relating to the History of the Law of Nations* vol 2 (de Gruyter Berlin 1988), at 660 (emphasis added).
[191] Wolff, *Ius gentium*, 1764, § 255. Wolff, however, realized that 'since, indeed, nations are moral persons and therefore only subject to certain rights and duties, ... their nature and essence undoubtedly differ very much from the nature and essence of individual men as physical persons' (preface, at 5).
[192] Friedrich Wilhelm Schelling *Vorlesungen über die Methode (Lehrart) des akademischen Studiums* (2nd edn Felix Meiner Hamburg 1990 (orig. 1803)), tenth lecture, end (at 110): 'The state as an unconditional and independent end in itself, as an absolute organism'; Adam Heinrich Müller 'Von der Idee des Staates' in *idem Ausgewählte Abhandlungen* (Gustav Fischer Jena 1921 (orig. 1809)) 3–16. In legal scholarship see Johann Caspar Bluntschli *Das moderne Völkerrecht der civilisirten Staaten als Rechtsbuch dargestellt* (3rd edn Beck Nördlingen 1878), at 3.

The personification of the state promoted the tendency to elevate the state above individuals (as a Hobbesian 'mortal god').[193] However, the domestic analogy does not inevitably lead to the apotheosis of the state. The analogy was—on the contrary—understood by some as a debasement of the state. It was therefore rejected by the most ardent statists, Hegel and his followers, on the grounds that the state could never be subordinate ('*Unterthan*'), was indispensable for human progress, and had a moral priority over individuals.[194]

I suggest following the yet again different approach of Hersch Lauterpacht, who employed the individualist picture of the state in order to strengthen the international legal position of the individual. Lauterpacht did not assert that states are like individuals, but used the metaphor of the individual as shorthand for 'the fact that States *are composed of* individual human beings'. What counted for Lauterpacht was that 'behind the mystical, impersonal, and therefore necessarily irresponsible personality of the metaphysical State there are the actual subjects of rights and duties, namely, individual human beings'.[195] He continued: 'Undoubtedly, international law is primarily—though not exclusively— a body of rules governing the relation of States, i.e., of individuals organized as a State. But this circumstance cannot affect decisively the moral content of international law and of the dictates of reason and of the general principles of law which underlie it. It may be true to say that "after all" States are not individuals; but it is even more true to say that "after all" States are individuals.'[196]

My conclusion on the international constitutional status of states is that states are not ends in themselves, but merely instrumental for the rights and needs of individuals.[197] This *finalité* makes states indispensable in a global constitutionalized order, but also calls for their constitutional containment.

4. International Organizations

4.1 Sectoral constitutionalization

Amidst the global process of the constitutionalization of international law, there is the sectoral constitutionalization of special regimes. I will here only deal with the sector constitutionalization of international organizations, the most

---

[193] Hobbes, *Leviathan*, 1991 [1651], The Introduction, at 9 [1]: 'For by Art is created that great Leviathan called a Common-Wealth, or State, (in latine Civitas), which is but an Artificiall Man; though of greater statute and strength than the Naturall, for whose protection and defence it was intended; and in which, the Soveraignty is an Artificiall Soul, as giving life and motion to the whole body ...'.

[194] Lasson, *Princip und Zukunft des Völkerrechts*, 1871, at 22. *Cf* Hegel, *Grundlinien der Philosophie des Rechts*, 1928 (1821), esp. §§ 257–259 (engl. transl. pp. 80–82)): The state as the 'actuality of the ethical idea', and as being 'absolutely rational', as 'an absolute unmoved end in itself'.

[195] Lauterpacht, Grotian Tradition, 1946, at 27.   [196] *Ibid*, at 28.

[197] See in this sense Charles Beitz *Political Theory and International Relations* (Princeton UP 1979), at 81; Tesón, *Philosophy of International Law*, 1998, at 42.

prominent, but also controversial cases being the evolution of EU law[198] and WTO law.[199] A different issue is the constitutionalization of special branches of law populated by numerous organizations and treaty regimes, such as international environmental law.[200]

By sector constitutionalization of international organizations, I mean the emergence of constitutional and even constitutionalist elements within the primary and secondary law of the organization. A constitutionalist vision of certain international organizations not only considers them as possessing a constitution, but as possessing a *constitutionalist* constitution-in-the-making.

Sector constitutionalization is one of the most tangible aspects of descriptive global constitutionalism, because it is firmly rooted in the case law. Almost all international courts' and tribunals' decisions using a constitutional or even constitutionalist vocabulary concern sector, but not global constitutionalization. But sector constitutionalization raises the spectre of fragmentation. When different organizations have their own constitution, how can they still be members of a global constitutional order? I submit that the various processes of constitutionalization on different levels do not exclude each other. Global constitutionalism is pluralist, and it relates to multi-level governance. It implies nested constitutional orders. This is no anomaly, given the fact that within a constitutional state sub-units, for example states within federal states, or local communities, have their own constitutions. From that perspective, it can be easily accepted that the members of a global constitutional order, notably the nation states and the international organizations, may have their own sectoral constitution. The result is multi-level constitutionalism.

The very idea of multiple and multi-level constitutionalism implicitly gives up the claim to totality raised by proponents of a more traditional notion of constitution. I submit in response that this claim can in any case no longer be satisfied under conditions of globalization. Even state constitutions do not govern or regulate all the effects of governance acts unfolding for their citizens and within their territorial borders. Totality is no relevant element of constitutions any more, if it ever was.

Normative constitutionalism asks for a constitution that satisfies constitutionalist standards. Therefore the debate on the constitutionalization of international organizations stimulates the revelation of legitimacy deficits of the organizations and may provide a toolbox for improvements.[201]

---

[198] See Anne Peters *Elemente einer Theorie der Verfassung Europas* (Duncker & Humblot Berlin 2001).   [199] See Deborah Z Cass *Constitutionalization of the WTO* (OUP Oxford 2005).

[200] See Daniel Bodansky's sceptical 'Is there an International Environmental Constitution?' (2009) 16 *Indiana Journal of Global Legal Studies* 565–584.

[201] See on this issue also Jean Marc Coicaud 'Conclusion: International Organizations, the Evolution of International Politics, and Legitimacy' in Jean Marc Coicaud and Veijo Heiskanen (eds) *The Legitimacy of International Organizations* (United Nations UP Tokyo, New York, Paris 2001) 519–552.

Before entering into the case law, it is necessary to distinguish from sector constitutionalization of international organizations, as discussed in this chapter, the reading of the UN Charter as the Constitution of the world, as supported by Bardo Fassbender,[202] and of the ECHR as the Constitution of Europe, as envisaged by the Strasbourg Human Rights Court.[203] Those are visions of macro-constitutionalization, on a global or regional level. I do not espouse these claims, because I think that much of what belongs to the body of global or regional constitutional law is not codified in those two conventions. The UN Charter says almost nothing about human rights, to name only one typical ingredient of constitutions. The ECHR inversely deals only with human rights. So, as already stated in the introductory chapter 1, there is no international constitution in a formal sense, codified in one constitutional document, but rather a body of global constitutional law, dispersed in numerous instruments.

4.2 Hybridity: treaty-constitutions

The constitutionalist approach moves significantly beyond the older view that the founding acts of international organizations are constitutions. Several founding acts even carry the official title 'constitution'.[204] Similarly, scholars have long used the term. For instance, decades before the creation of the WTO, John Jackson had contemplated the 'constitutional structure of a possible international trade institution'.[205] This vocabulary is in line with the ICJ's view that '[f]rom a formal standpoint, the constituent instruments of international

---

[202] Bardo Fassbender 'The United Nations Charter as Constitution of the International Community' (1998) 36 *Columbia Journal of Transnational Law* 529–619. Note that Fassbender seeks to reconcile his conception with that of a more inclusive global constitutional process, and considers the Charter as one part of that ongoing process (*ibid*, at 616–617).

[203] ECHR, *Case of Loizidou v Turkey* (preliminary exceptions), Series A 310 (1995), para 75: the ECHR as a 'constitutional instrument of the European public order (ordre public)'. See ECHR, *Ireland v United Kingdom,* application No 5310/71 (1978), at 82: 'Unlike international treaties of the classic kind, the Convention comprises more than mere reciprocal engagements between contracting states. It creates, over and above a network of mutual, bilateral undertakings, objective obligations which, in the words of the Preamble, benefit from a "collective enforcement" '. But see in scholarship Evert Albert Alkema 'The European Convention as a Constitution and its Court as a Constitutional Court' in Paul Mahoney, Franz Matscher, Herbert Petzold, and Luzius Wildhaber (eds) *Protecting Human Rights: The European Perspective: Mélanges à la mémoire de Rolv Ryssdal* (Carl Heymans Köln 2000) 41–63, concluding that the Convention's framework is not a constitution.

[204] 'Constitution of the United Nations Educational, Scientific and Cultural Organization' of 16 November 1945 (UNTS 4, No 52); 'Constitution of the World Health Organization' of 22 July 1946 (UNTS 14, No 221); 'Constitution of the International Labour Organization' of 9 October 1946 (UNTS vol 38, No 583); 'Constitution of the Food and Agricultural Organization of the United Nations' of 16 October 1946 (UNYB 1946–47, 693); 'Constitution of the International Telecommunication Union' of 22 December 1992 (UNTS vol 1825, No I-31251).

[205] John H Jackson *World Trade Law and the Law of GATT* (Bobbs Merrill Indianapolis 1969), chapter 304 'The Constitutional Structure of a Possible International Trade Institution', at 780–785.

organizations are multilateral treaties, ... their character ... is conventional and at the same time institutional'.[206] In the same sense, the ECJ argued that the EC Treaty, despite being concluded in the form of an international agreement, represents the constitutional charter of a legal community.[207] In these judicial awards, the founding documents of international organizations are conceived as having a hybrid character as treaty-constitution. Doctrinally, this qualification could build on the French and Italian institutionalist theory of the mid-20th century.[208] In practice, the hybridity was made explicit for the first time in the official title of an organization's founding Act in the Treaty Establishing a Constitution for Europe of 2004.[209]

That rather traditional understanding of international organizations' founding document as a hybrid treaty-constitution did not rely on any material, value-loaded (constitutionalist) principles, but merely on the fact that the founding treaties established institutional structures, delineated the competences of the organization, and defined the terms of membership. The doctrinal merit of this understanding of the law of international organizations was to overcome the outdated dichotomy between contract or treaty (as a 'horizontal' *inter partes* legal act[210]) and constitution (as a 'vertical' *erga omnes* legal act).[211] But the traditional institutional–constitutional topos did not introduce a *constitutionalist* approach to the law of international organizations. The constitutionalist approach—by contrast—seeks to identify and to advocate the application of constitutionalist principles, such as the rule of law, checks and balances, human rights protection, and possibly also democracy, to the law of international organizations.

---

[206] ICJ, *Legality of the Use by a State of Nuclear Weapons in Armed Conflict, Advisory Opinion*, ICJ Reports 1996, 66, para 19.   [207] ECJ, opinion 1/91, *EEC*, ECR 1991-I, 6079, 6102, para 21.

[208] 'Sous ce profil, l'acte institutif d'une Organisation déterminée est bien un traité international, fondé, en tant que tel, sur la volonté des contractants et donc soumis, au moment de sa formation, à leur volonté, mais il est par ailleurs destiné à devenir la constitution, c'est-à-dire l'acte de fondation de l'Organisation, auquel celle-ci se rattache tout au long de son existence. On pourrait dire, par conséquent, que l'acte institutif revêt *la forme du pacte, mais possède la substance de la constitution: né sur la base d'une convention, il dépasse, avec le temps, son origine formelle, jusqu'à devenir une constitution* de durée indéterminée dont le développement déborde le cadre à l'intérieur duquel elle avait été initialement conçue'. Riccardo Monaco 'Le caractère constitutionnel des actes institutifs d'organisations internationales' in *Mélanges offerts à Charles Rousseau, La communauté internationale* (Pédone Paris 1974), at 154 (emphasis added).   [209] OJ 2004 C 310/1.

[210] But see AB, *Japan—Taxes on Alcoholic Beverages* (4 October 1996) WT/DS8/AB/R, WT/DS 10/AB/R, WT/DS11/AB/R, p 15: 'The WTO Agreement is a treaty—the international equivalent of a contract. It is self-evident that in an exercise of their sovereignty, and in pursuit of their own respective national interests, the Members of the WTO have made a bargain. In exchange for benefits they expect to derive as Members of the WTO, they have agreed to exercise their sovereignty according to the commitment they have made in the WTO Agreement.'

[211] On this dichotomy and its relevance for the debate on the legal nature of the EU Treaties see Anne Peters 'The Constitutionalization of the European Union—Without the Constitutional Treaty' in Sonja Puntscher Riekmann and Wolfgang Wessels (eds) *The Making of a European Constitution* (VS Verlag für Sozialwissenschaften Wiesbaden 2006) 35–67.

It is probably a sign of the fragmentation of international legal scholarship that the two major debates on sector constitutionalization, concerning the WTO and the EU, have been largely led in clinical isolation from one another. Pulling the debates together, one can identify several general indices of sector constitutionalization.

4.3 Constitutional principles containing member states

One indicator and promoter of sector constitutionalization might be the endorsement of constitutional rights and principles such as human rights, rule of law, democracy, and solidarity in the law of international organizations. However—and this is important—in the existing founding treaties of the most important organizations these principles are typically addressed not at the organization itself, but exclusively or primarily at the member states. For instance, the UN Charter states that it is the purpose of the United Nations to promote human rights (Article 2(3) UN Charter), and this means in the member states. In a similar fashion, the prohibition on the use of force and the conferral of a quasi-monopoly on the Security Council to authorize military action works to contain member states, not the United Nations itself.

In the EU, the basic freedoms (free movement of goods, workers, services, residence, and capital) which limit member states' regulation are likewise principles which limit member states' policies, and are increasingly pictured as 'fundamental rights' of the citizens.[212] Also the International Labour Organization (ILO) can be said to be constitutionalized along this line. The ILO Declaration on Fundamental Principles and Rights at Work of 1998 declares that 'all members, even if they have not ratified' the conventions adopted by the ILO 'have an obligation arising from the very fact of membership in the organization, to respect, promote, and realize, in good faith and in accordance with the Constitution, the principles concerning the fundamental rights which are the subject of those Conventions' (Article 2). The declaration thus seeks to contain and bind member states against, or at least independent of, their concrete acceptance of specific conventional rules, merely by appealing to the members' subjection to the ILO constitution.[213]

The most discussed case of constitutionalization consisting in a containment of member states is the WTO. In the WTO, the traditional trade law principles of most-favoured nation and national treatment, which bind the member states, are increasingly viewed as two facets of a constitutional principle of non-discrimination ultimately benefiting the ordinary citizens (importers, exporters,

---

[212] *Cf* Thorsten Kingreen's sceptical view in *Die Struktur der Grundfreiheiten des Europäischen Gemeinschaftsrechts* (Duncker & Humblot Berlin 1999).
[213] For a trenchant critique of this approach see Philip Alston '"Core Labour Standards" and the Transformation of the International Labour Rights Regime' (2004) 15 *EJIL* 457–521.

producers, consumers, tax-payers).[214] GATT was established to provide a forum in which one member would challenge the protectionist policies of another member. Such protectionist policies are widely seen to result from an undue influence of rent-seeking groups whose lobbyism is apt to flaw the domestic democratic processes. Against this background, the WTO's core function is to neutralize the domestic power of protectionist interests. Thereby, the WTO law helps to overcome the domestic political process deficiencies.[215] This is a typically constitutional function, which in the domestic realm is served by fundamental rights guarantees and by judicial protection through constitutional courts.

WTO constitutionalists have highlighted the need to integrate human rights concerns into world trade law, not only through the interpretation of existing agreements, but also through the building of new common institutions. In fact, a constitutionalist approach is apt to provide a vocabulary, a theory, and institutional building blocks to satisfy the quest for coherence among trade law and human rights law. The rights-based constitutionalist school submits that human rights have become guiding principles of international economic law. Proponents suggest endorsing a general maxim of interpretation of the GATT-obligations of WTO members (and the relevant exception clauses) in the light of human rights guarantees.[216]

The rights-based constitutionalist reading of WTO law has (to some extent erroneously) been perceived as narrow. It has been criticized for marginalizing social rights and environmental principles and for focusing on economic and property rights. Early constitutionalist scholarship was therefore criticized as masking a radically economically libertarian free-trade agenda. In fact, the old GATT law has neglected social and environmental issues, and was geared towards negative integration by eliminating trade barriers. Today, TRIPS, Article VI GATS, the TBT- and the SPS-Agreement, the Antidumping Agreement and Agreement on Agriculture seek to realize positive integration through common standards, even if only very few of those standards marginally relate to the environment, and hardly relate to social aspects.

In defence of constitutionalism, it can be claimed that the constitutionalist reading of WTO law precisely supports the quest for the adoption of such

---

[214] The most ardent proponent of this view is Ernst-Ulrich Petersmann, see, e.g. Ernst-Ulrich Petersmann 'Multilevel Judicial Governance of International Trade Requires a Common Conception of Rule of Law and Justice' (2007) 10 *Journal of International Economic Law* 529–552, at 533: 'the WTO guarantees of freedom, non-discrimination and rule of law—by enhancing individual liberty, non-discriminatory treatment, economic welfare, and poverty reduction across frontiers—reflect, albeit imperfectly, basic principles of justice.'

[215] John McGinnis and Mark Movsesian 'The World Trade Constitution' (2000) 114 *Harvard Law Review* 511–605, at 521–530.

[216] Ernst-Ulrich Petersmann 'Time for a United Nations "Global Compact" for Integrating Human Rights into the Law of Worldwide Organizations: Lessons from European Integration' (2002) 13 *EJIL* 621–650, at 645–646.

standards. Moreover, trade liberalization normally triggers a demand for positive integration. However, the WTO, as opposed to the EU, currently lacks the institutions and means to complement the ongoing negative with positive integration.[217] Also, a large part of the membership opposes the WTO having any social agenda; and unlike the EU, the WTO does not have decision-making structures that easily allow for a variable geometry.

To conclude, the 'constitutional' WTO principles directed at the WTO members are too incomplete to found the claim of constitutionalization in a substantive (not only procedural) sense. Further constitutionalization of the WTO could be realized by political actors and promoted by doctrinal arguments along the following lines: in substance, the libertarian tilt of the nascent WTO constitution should be rectified by strengthening the legal relevance of non-trade issues such as environment and social concerns, and the constitutional principle of solidarity should be implemented by promoting liberalization in sectors in which poor countries can compete.

Procedurally, the subjection of member states to the rules and principles of an international organization can be realized along the route of the direct application of the organization's rules by national courts. Direct applicability serves to contain member states as follows: when private actors invoke an international organization's norm which prohibits certain domestic, e.g. protectionist, policies, and when the national judiciary then declares illegal the relevant domestic act for violation of that international norm, domestic law is deprived of effect by virtue of the organization's law. (Another aspect of constitutionalization through direct effect is that the capacity of self-interested natural persons to enforce international rules before domestic courts empowers individuals and elevates them to the quality of an active legal subject of the relevant regime's legal order). So far, direct effect is acknowledged by national courts mainly for human rights treaties, and the possibility of a direct effect is also accepted with regard to EU primary and secondary law.[218] By contrast, a direct effect of GATT is rejected by most domestic courts, by the European courts,[219] and by the WTO dispute settlement institution itself.[220] So a constitutionalization along that line is present only with regard to the human rights treaty regimes and the EU, but not in respect to other international organizations.

---

[217] Robert Howse and Kalypso Nicolaidis 'Enhancing WTO Legitimacy: Constitutionalization or Global Subsidiarity' (2003) 16 *Governance* 73–94, at 84–85.

[218] Case 6/64 *Costa v ENEL* [1964] ECR 1251.

[219] Case C-149/96 *Portuguese Republic v Council of the European Union* [1999] ECR I-8395, paras 34–52; Case C-377/02 *Léon Van Parys NV v Belgisch Interventie-en Restitutiebureau* [2005] ECR I-1465, paras 38–54; Case T-174/00 *Biret International SA v Council* [2002] ECT II-17, para 62.

[220] WTO Panel, *US—Section 301–310 of the Trade Act of 1974*, WT/DS152/R (27 January 2000), not appealed, para 7.72: 'Neither the GATT nor the WTO has so far been interpreted by GATT/WTO institutions as a legal order producing direct effect [i.e. as creating enforceable rights and obligations for individuals].' It would be better to speak of an 'indirect effect' of GATT (para 7.78).

The constitutionalist agenda suggests empowering individuals and providing an additional check on international bodies. Both objectives would be promoted by a more ready acceptance of a direct effect of suitable provisions, notably of WTO law. But as the application of international norms by domestic courts bears the risk of diverging case law, this would ideally have to be accompanied by a system of referral to the international adjudicative organs for preliminary rulings in order to harmonize the interpretation of the respective international organizations' law.

4.4 Autonomy as a proxy for sovereignty and as trigger for constitutionalist demands

The 'autonomy' of an organization's legal order is a central topos in the debate on sector constitutionalization. Without making this explicit, the discussants seem to consider the 'autonomy' of an entity as a corollary of its possession of a constitution. The ICJ explained the constitutional status of the World Health Organization (WHO) Charter by saying that this Charter creates a legal subject, the WHO, 'endowed with a certain autonomy'.[221] Likewise, the ECJ judgment *Van Gend & Loos*, the point of departure of the constitutionalization of the EU, held that 'the Community constitutes a new legal order of international law'.[222] In EU-legal scholarship, the expression 'new legal order' was quickly understood as 'autonomous legal order'. This concept has since been used to demonstrate (erroneously in my view) a categorical distinction between EU law and public international law (ultimately in order to preclude the member states' power to decide for themselves how to incorporate and rank EU law in relation to the domestic legal order, as they do with public international law). Second, 'autonomy' may denote the originality and non-derivability of the organization's law, its 'autonomous' basis of validity. Third, and in practical terms most importantly, 'autonomy' refers to the ongoing relationship between the organization and its member states. In this third meaning, the extent of an organization's 'autonomy' can be diagnosed by looking at various aspects: the conferral of broad competences to an organization and a more generous reading of the principle of speciality and the prohibition of *ultra vires* acts denotes more autonomy, as does majority voting. On the other hand, easy exit options for member states seem to denote a lower degree of organizational autonomy.

Particularly for the EU, typical structural features that in the EU debate are considered as indicators of a sector constitutionalization, such as the direct effect of many provisions of the primary and secondary EU law, the fact that member states need not, and are even prohibited from, specifically transposing certain types of secondary law into their domestic law, and finally the supremacy of EU law over the domestic law of the member states, additionally manifest a certain

---

[221] ICJ, *Legality of the Use by a State of Nuclear Weapons in Armed Conflict, Advisory Opinion*, ICJ Reports 1996, 66, para 19.   [222] Case 26/62 *Van Gend & Loos* [1963] ECR 3, at II.B.

'autonomy' of the EU. These structural features are largely absent in the law of other international organizations.

Autonomy is notably associated with judicial *Kompetenz-Kompetenz*. In this regard, it matters, for example for the WTO, that, despite the important legalization of the dispute settlement mechanism, a key element of judicial or interpretive autonomy is absent: neither the WTO itself nor non-governmental parties can act as monitors of compliance (unlike the situation in the EU with the Commission acting as guardian of the treaties).

As far as 'autonomy' is concerned, it would be short-sighted to concentrate on the classical international organizations only. These are by far outnumbered by 'secondary' international organizations, agencies, and various kinds of complex institutions which have not been created directly by states, but by international organizations (or by states and organizations), either through treaties, through resolutions, or through hybrid instruments.[223] Here the states have lost control to a significant degree, and the entities' will does not simply express the sum of the member states' positions. The traditional image of the states as masters of the treaties is inadequate to describe that complex reality.[224]

Often, the procedures for revising an organization's founding treaty are considered the litmus test for the constitutionalization of the respective treaty regime. Indeed, sophisticated amendment procedures may be a way of entrenching the constituent treaty and thereby conferring on it the status of 'higher' law. However, the procedures for amending the charters of international organizations normally facilitate amendments in comparison with ordinary international law-making. Amendments sometimes require less than unanimous consent or need only majority ratification to enter into force for all parties. A different aspect of amendment procedures is that amendments often require the participation of the organs of the organization itself. This is a typical feature of federalist amendment procedures.

Another issue is that ordinary treaties can, under customary law, be revised informally at any time, even if the treaty stipulates a special procedure for revision. The reason is that the contracting parties can always agree to informally abolish those procedures.[225] But if the founding document of an organization is said to be a constitution, it may only be amended according to the procedures proscribed in the very document. The circumvention of the written amendment procedures by reliance on a subsequent new consensual decision of the member states to leave aside those procedures is not permitted in a constitutionalist perspective. The reason is that constitutions are imbued by the principles of legal security and clarity and are therefore hostile towards unwritten and necessarily

---

[223] See Cheryl Shanks, Harold K Jacobson, and Jeffrey H Kaplan 'Inertia and Change in the Constellation of International Governmental Organizations, 1981–1992' (1996) 50 *International Organization* 593–627, esp. at 594 with data.

[224] Chiara Martini 'States' Control over New International Organization' (2006) 6 *The Global Jurist Advances* 1–25.   [225] *Cf* Art 39 VCLT.

imprecise customary law.[226] But the deepest reason for the importance attached to revision procedures is the putative link to 'autonomy'. Under the premise that a constitution is characterized by the 'autonomy' from its creators, the power to amend a constitution should not lie with the founders (the *pouvoir constituant*), but is a prerogative of the *pouvoir constitué* (the organization itself). However, in all three international organizations whose constitutionalization is discussed most vividly, the amendment procedures display only a small degree of autonomy from the founders.[227]

So what significance does 'autonomy' exactly have for the constitutionalization of an international organization? In the usual debates as summarized above, and without openly admitting and maybe without even realizing it, 'autonomy' is used as a proxy by the observers for the sovereignty of the organization. The question for an organization's autonomy is a different way of asking: who is the 'master' of the organization's law? The organization itself and its bodies, or the member states? Just like sovereignty, autonomy can be conceived as a graduated or as an all-or-nothing concept. Espousing the graduated view, I find that in terms of autonomy, the EU is strongly constitutionalized, whereas the WTO and the UN enjoy a limited degree of autonomy.

However, I think that the postulated link between autonomy and constitutionalization should be reconsidered. In the traditional discourse, autonomy is perceived as a precondition of constitutionalization. The underlying premise is that only sovereign entities can possess a constitution. In contrast, I submit that autonomy is not a notional or conceptual prerequisite for having a constitution, but should trigger the normative quest for accountability and thus for constitutionalization: the more autonomous an international organization is, the more it *needs* to be constitutionalized. This leads us to the core of sector constitutionalization.

4.5 Accountability of international organizations towards citizens

Constitutionalized international organizations must be accountable. In a constitutionalist framework, there is legal accountability (mainly through judicial review), and political accountability realized through the democratic process. The question is, however, what the proper accountability forum is. In the traditional view, international organizations are accountable to their member states. One problem in this context is that some organizations do not grant equal rights to member states (the most conspicuous example being the veto power of the five permanent Security Council members and the weighing of votes in the

---

[226] Fassbender, UN Charter as Constitution, 1998, at 600.
[227] See for the EU Art 48 EU Treaty, for the WTO Art X WTO Agreement. Under Art 108–109 UN Charter, amendments can come into force *for all member states* after ratification of two-thirds of the member states, including the P5.

Bretton Woods Institutions).[228] A related problem is that even organizations whose members have formally equal voting rights practise informal decision-making (e.g. in the notorious WTO 'green rooms') which effectively marginalizes or completely excludes less powerful states.

From this traditional perspective, the main accountability problem of international organizations is the 'runaway' or *'Zauberlehrling'* phenomenon, that is the danger that an organization escapes control by the member states and acquires too much institutional and bureaucratic independence. This can happen on account of 'mission creep' (dynamic expansion of competencies) or overlong chains of responsibility. A slightly different problem is that of potential capture (e.g. the World Bank by 'global capital'), which also distances the organization from its rightful 'shareholders'.

In order to improve accountability, the International Law Association's (ILA) report on the accountability of international organizations recommends a host of rules and practices of a constitutionalist nature, such as participatory decision-making processes, transparency, institutional balance, stating reasons, procedural regularity, and impartiality.[229] Empirical researchers have investigated to what extent international organizations fulfil these and other accountability requirements. Contrary to popular opinion, international organizations are relatively accountable in comparison with TNCs and NGOs.[230] Knowledge about the structure and the functioning of accountability principles as available in constitutional scholarship and practice can contribute to operationalizing the accountability further.

But from a constitutionalist perspective, a deeper problem exists. Constitutionalists claim that the ultimate accountability forum for international organizations should be the (global) citizens, not states. In doctrinal terms, the claim is that individuals should be full and active legal subjects of the respective organization's legal order.

It is therefore significant that the ECJ in its seminal judgment *Van Gend & Loos* stated that the 'subjects' of the Community legal order 'comprise not only member states but also their nationals'.[231] In contrast, a WTO panel considered individuals as merely passive beneficiaries of the WTO legal order, and not as subjects: first it stated that 'it would be entirely wrong to consider that the position of individuals is of no relevance to the GATT/WTO legal matrix. Many of the benefits to Members ... depend on the activity of individual economic operators in the national and global market places. ...[I]indeed one of

---

[228] See above pp. 190–191.

[229] International Law Association, First report on the Accountability of International Organizations, Report of the 71st conference held in Berlin, 16–21 August 2004.

[230] Hetty Kovach, Caroline Nelligan, and Simon Burall *The Global Accountability Report: Power without Accountability?* (One World Trust London 2003), at 31–32 on the basis of a case study of selected international organizations.

[231] ECJ, case 26/62, *Van Gend & Loos* [1963] ECR 3, at II.B.

the primary objects of the GATT/WTO as a whole, is to produce certain market conditions which would allow this activity to flourish.' But then the panel deliberately distinguished the WTO regime from the EU and the *van Gend & Loos* conception by highlighting that 'the GATT/WTO did *not* create a new legal order the subjects of which comprise both contracting parties or members and their nationals'.[232]

This panel report thus reflects the traditional position that citizens are represented by their nation states, and should therefore be entirely 'mediated' by their states in international organizations. But that position is—in the eyes of constitutionalists—flawed. As far as political accountability (the democratic aspect) is concerned, the lines of accountability to the citizens are too long and indirect to allow for effective accountability. Moreover, many member states of international organizations are not democratic, and can therefore not rightfully claim to act for their citizens. As far as legal (notably judicial) accountability is concerned, the incapacity of individuals to institute judicial or administrative proceedings against organizations renders them hostage to their nation states' considerations of high politics.

To remedy the state of relative unaccountability of international organizations towards citizens, organizations should be subject to the rule of law and bound to respect human rights, and citizens should be entitled to participate, at least indirectly, in law-making. I will turn to both strategies for securing the legal accountability of international organizations in the next section, whereas political accountability of international organizations through democratic law-making is treated in chapter 6.

4.6 Rule of law and human rights responsibilities of international organizations

The classic theme of constitutionalism is to contain political power. Constitutionalism thus requires that international organizations themselves are subject to the rule of law, and that their powers are bound by legal principles. It is therefore important from a constitutionalist perspective that the internal law of international organizations forms a hierarchy: all acts adopted by the organizations, including all secondary law, must be in conformity with the primary law, the founding act. Because the principles laid down in the founding act thus perform a containing function, that document works as a constitution, and the internal hierarchy of the law of the international organizations can count as a feature of sector constitutionalization.[233]

---

[232] WTO Panel, *US—Section 301–310 of the Trade Act of 1974*, WT/DS152/R (27 January 2000), not appealed, paras 7.73 and 7.72.

[233] *Cf* Finn Seyersted *Common Law of International Organizations* (Martinus Nijhoff Leiden 2008), at 72–77.

Another constitutional issue arising with the increased activity of international organizations is delegation. With respect to enforcement measures under Article 42 UN Charter, for example, there is a tension between safeguarding central oversight and ultimate responsibility on the one hand, and the practical necessity of employing the military apparatus of the UN member states. The legal tool to deal with this tension between centralization and decentralization is the doctrine of delegation. Constitutionalist reflections on the requirements for a proper delegation of competences, as elaborated in the national state context, can be employed as a source of inspiration to define limits of delegation and resolve questions of the attribution of responsibility. Therefore, the doctrine of delegation has an important 'constitutional function' in the law of international organizations.[234]

To be effective, the constitutional limits to the activity of an international organization must be enforceable. The acts of the organization itself must be subject to judicial or to a functionally similar review which controls whether the constitutional principles are observed and sees that the constitutional limits are respected by the organization itself. This review would in short be a constitutional review, and it could be performed either by international or by domestic courts.

Currently, only the EU possesses this—in my view—crucial constitutionalist feature. The European courts are competent to control the legality of the acts of the organs and institutions themselves. The ECJ judgment *Les Verts* of 1986 highlighted the constitutional significance of this type of judicial control. Here the question was whether acts of the European Parliament could be attacked in an annulment procedure, although the respective treaty provision did not mention these acts. By pointing out that the European Community is a 'legal community' whose Treaty is a 'constitutional charter', the Court was able to argue that neither the acts of the member states nor those of the institutions could escape judicial control, and could therefore draw the conclusion that parliamentary acts deploying legal effects must be subject to judicial review even without an explicit treaty basis.[235]

Judicial or quasi-judicial review as a means of securing the legal accountability of organizations not only towards their member states but also to individuals is currently available only in the EU. Under limited conditions individual persons can institute judicial action before the European courts and can claim the illegality of European institutions' activity. It would significantly increase the accountability of other international organizations, e.g. the United Nations, if judicial review were made available against them for individuals.[236] Along this

---

[234] Robert Kolb *Ius contra bellum: le droit international relatif au maintien de la paix* (2nd edn Helbing Lichtenhahn Basel 2009) 128–141, quote at 137.

[235] Case 294/83 *Parti Ecologiste 'Les Verts' v European Parliament* [1986] ECR I-1339, para 23.

[236] For practical suggestions to realize judicial actions of individuals against international organizations see Karel Wellens *Remedies against International Organizations* (CUP Cambridge 2004), at 255–261.

line, the ILA report on the accountability of international organizations considered the possibility of remedial action against international organizations by private persons. However, the report assumed that remedies can only originate from contractual or tortious acts of the organization.[237] In contrast, it did not envisage a constitutional, notably human rights responsibility of international organizations at all. I submit that a constitutionalist sensibility would broaden the approach here. From a constitutionalist perspective, international organizations should also be held accountable towards individuals for administrative and constitutional illegality. The creation of judicial actions for individuals on these grounds would constitute a significant step of further constitutionalization.

An important issue in this context is whether international organizations must not only respect legality in general, but more specifically human rights, which form the core of modern constitutional law. So far the founding documents of the most powerful international organizations do not explicitly state that the organizations themselves must respect human rights. Full fledged human rights guarantees against EU acts have been only gradually granted, in a dialectical process triggered through opposition by the member states. Still there is criticism that the ECJ's human rights protection is rather weak, that it gives too much weight to the interests of European integration, and that it too generously allows human rights restrictions on that ground.

A parallel process has been set in motion with regard to the UN Security Council. A milestone in this regard is the *Tadic*-judgment of the International Criminal Tribunal for the former Yugoslavia (ICTY). The argument of the appellant Tadic had been that the Tribunal was illegal or not duly created by law, because it had been established only by a Security Council resolution and not by an international treaty. In order to refute the interlocutory appeal on jurisdiction, the Appeals Chamber resorted to constitutional arguments. In a section of the judgment entitled 'Question of constitutionality', the Chamber examined whether Chapter VII, notably Article 39 of the UN Charter, could form a legal basis of the tribunal. It emphasized that the Security Council is subject to the principle of legality, and is not a purely political organ. It is not '*legibus absolutus*'.[238] However, the legal (or constitutional) limits of Security Council action are barely enforceable, in any case no judicial action is available against the Council as such. The constitutional limits identified in *Tadic* thus remain largely virtual. This problem has gained salience with the Security Council's comprehensive sanctions against Iraq since 1991 and its more recent targeted sanctions against individuals, which risk violating notably social rights, procedural rights, and property. As was the case for the EU, the threat of non-compliance by outside courts might push the United Nations to clearly subject

---

[237] International Law Association, First Report on the Accountability of International Organizations, Report of the 71st conference held in Berlin, 16–21 August 2004, at 38.
[238] ICTY, case No IT-94-1-AR72, *Prosecutor v Dusko Tadic, Decision on the Defence Motion for Interlocutory Appeal on Jurisdiction*, Appeals Chamber of 2 October 1995, paras 26–28.

the Security Council itself to human rights standards, to increase the level of human rights protection, and to create an institution to monitor compliance.

In the WTO, this dimension of sector constitutionalization is completely absent. Although it could be argued that certain WTO policies potentially, even if only indirectly, affect or even infringe social or indigenous rights, especially in developing countries, these policies are not subject to any human rights review. Neither are the relevant standards agreed upon, nor are monitoring bodies available. The WTO dispute settlement bodies have no jurisdiction over the WTO institutions themselves. This difference between the (quasi-)compulsory jurisdiction of the WTO dispute settlement mechanism and the EU courts is, from a constitutionalist perspective, crucial. The constitutionalist agenda requires that judicial review against all international institutions itself must be made available to individuals.

To conclude, the EU is a constitutional and constitutionalist system on the ground that individuals enjoy constitutional protection against the organization itself, and are empowered to enforce them. In contrast, individuals are not yet sufficiently empowered *vis-à-vis* the UN or the WTO to warrant the claim that these two organizations have been constitutionalized along that line.

4.7 (Judicial) constitutionalization of and through adjudication

The constitutionalization debate on the WTO concentrates on the judicialization of dispute settlement. In the EU-related debate, the compulsory and extensive jurisdiction of the European courts as a driver of constitutionalization are likewise the centre of interest. In contrast, the United Nations has not been analysed through these lenses at all.

In institutional terms, it matters that the EU possesses a full-fledged compulsory judicial system and that the WTO has progressively entrenched quasi-compulsory and quasi-judicial proceedings which lead to judgment-like reports.

A different element of the constitutionalization of dispute settlement lies in the growing participation of non-state actors. Individuals are empowered to institute judicial proceedings only within the EU. The involvement of NGOs in dispute settlement will be discussed below (at pp. 227–233).

A further different facet of constitutionalization relates to process and substance of adjudication. Specifically for the WTO, it has been argued that the case law of the panels and Appellate Body 'is beginning to display some characteristics ordinarily associated with constitutional case-law'.[239] The dispute settlement institutions have indeed borrowed constitutional doctrines, such as the

---

[239] Deborah Z Cass 'The Constitutionalization of International Trade Law: Judicial Norm-Generation as the Engine of Constitutionalization' (2001) 13 *EJIL* 39–77, at 42. Cass distanced herself from this statement in her later book (Cass, *Constitutionalization of the WTO*, 2005).

proportionality analysis.[240] They take into consideration non-trade issues such as human rights and environmental protection, and apply the constitutional technique of balancing to determine which of the conflicting interests should prevail in the concrete case. This has been called 'constitutionalism in a modest sense', 'an attitude and a framework capable of reasonably balancing and weighing different, equally legitimate and democratically defined basic values and policy goals'.[241]

But that vision of WTO constitutionalism is under heavy critique. A first objection is that by taking the principle of trade liberalization as a constitutional norm, the trade-off between the obligation to liberalize and the protection of non-trade concerns inevitably ends in a preference for free trade. Competing values enter into the picture only as narrow and carefully policed exceptions, and the onus is on the party which invokes the exception.[242] However, an important strand of WTO constitutionalism exactly seeks to counter this order of priorities. In that perspective, the competing values are not just exceptions to trade liberalization, but are provisions to protect legitimate policy goals, which form an integral part of a well-balanced multilateral trading system, and which should be acknowledged to have the same status as other constitutional principles.

Also, the celebration of balancing as constitutionalization risks falsely dignifying the judicial balancing process, instead of admitting its political character. When a WTO panel invalidates an environmental protection scheme, constitutionalists tend to view this as the enforcement of higher (namely constitutional) law (of free trade). In reality, however, says the critique, such invalidation is a political decision which is presumably illegitimate because it replaces the policy balancing of domestic democratic institutions with the panel's own policy.

This objection brings us to the heart of the matter. The entire sector constitutionalization has so far been adjudicative rather than deliberative. Notably the WTO's capacity for legislative response to judicial constitutional engineering is muted by the unanimity- or qualified majority-requirement for Treaty revision and by the consensus practice for decision-making. This again fuels the fundamental objection against the constitutionalist reading of international law, namely that this reading condones an impoverished, legalist (judicially made),

---

[240] See for a balancing approach to the 'necessity'-requirement of Art XX(d) GATT, which grants an *a priori* equal rank to the conflicting objecives: AB, WT/DS161/AB/R, WT/DS169/AB/R, 11 December 2000, *Korea—Measures Affecting Imports of Fresh, Chilled and Frozen Beef*, para 162: 'The more vital or important those common interests or values are, the easier it would be to accept as "necessary" a measure designed as an enforcement instrument.' See in scholarship Alec Stone Sweet and Jud Mathews 'Proportionality Balancing and Global Constitutionalism' (2008) 47 *Columbia Journal of Transnational Law* 72–164.
[241] Thomas Cottier 'Limits to International Trade: The Constitutional Challenge' in The American Society of International Law (ed) *International Law in Ferment: A New Vision for Theory and Practice, Proceedings of the 94th Annual Meeting* (Washington DC 5–8 April 2000), at 221.
[242] Howse and Nicolaidis, Enhancing WTO Legitimacy, 2003, at 75.

a-political conception of constitution.[243] A balance of powers should be established by improving the possibility of a 'legislative response' to adjudication. This can be done only by streamlining the current decision-making procedures within international organizations, including the introduction of majority voting (but see pp. 289–290 and 335–338 for the democratic problems of majority voting). Specifically with regard to the WTO, a stronger law-making branch is needed to bring about positive integration, which is not yet ingrained in the WTO treaties and which can therefore not be effected by the judiciary alone. Effective international legislation is needed to counter the problem of a presumably illegitimate government of judges.

4.8 The constitutionalization of organizations as judicial self-empowerment

The suspicion of a *gouvernement des juges* is confirmed by the insight that all international courts and tribunals, be it the ICJ, the ICTY, the ECHR, or the ECJ have employed constitutional and constitutionalist arguments only in one context, namely in the context of judicial control or review. In every single case, the underlying issue was the power and the autonomy of the respective court. Each time, the result of the constitutionalist reading of the treaty at issue was to preserve, defend, confirm, or even enlarge the competence of the court. Whether self-empowerment was the hidden agenda of the courts or only a side effect, it was always the outcome.

The most obvious decisions are those of the ECJ. Already the judgment *Les Verts* had the consequence of enlarging the competences of the Court by submitting acts of the European Parliament to judicial control, although the Treaty at that time did not include these acts.[244] Also in the opinion on the European Economic Area (EEA),[245] the competences of the ECJ were at issue. In the first version of the EEA Treaty, to be concluded between the EC and third states, it was foreseen that the ECJ should be accompanied by a new EEA court. This scheme would have menaced the autonomy and the monopoly of the ECJ as the ultimate interpreter of the Community legal order. It looks as if the Court invoked the constitutional character of the EC Treaty in order to preserve its monopoly. Finally, the ECJ's opinion on the accession of the EC to the ECHR was on the same line. Here the Court found that the European Community was not competent to accede to the ECHR, because the general clause of Article 308 (then 235) EC did not provide a sufficient legal basis. The reason why the general clause was not deemed sufficient was that the accession to the Human Rights Convention would 'entail a substantial change of the present regime ...

---

[243] See on this pp. 349–351.
[244] Case 294/83 *Parti Ecologiste 'Les Verts' v European Parliament* [1986] ECR I-1339, para 23.
[245] ECJ, opinion 1/91, *EEC* [1991] ECR I-6079, 6102, para 21.

in that it would entail the entry of the Community into a distinct international institutional system … '. Such a move would—according to the ECJ—'be of constitutional significance and would therefore be such as to go beyond the scope of Article 235'.[246] The insertion into a distinct institutional system meant in clear text to submit the ECJ to the ECHR, or at least to force it to cooperate in some formalized way. Faced with this prospect, the ECJ qualified the issue as one of constitutional change which could not be effected without an explicit treaty basis, therefore had to be given up, and thus saved the autonomy of the ECJ for the time being.

For many academics and judges, the qualification of a treaty as a constitution has a practical consequence for its interpretation.[247] The ICJ and the ECHR concluded that *because* of a given treaty's constitutional quality (in that case the WHO Charter and the ECHR), the appropriate method of interpretation was teleological and dynamic rather than historical and static.[248] The underlying assertion is that the teleological interpretation is the quintessential method of constitutional interpretation. But this view is not generally shared. For instance, a core methodological principle of Swiss courts is the 'unity of methods of interpretation' for the judicial interpretation of laws and of the Swiss constitution.[249] A particular and distinct method of interpretation for the constitution is explicitly rejected in Swiss law. So the idea that constitutions must be interpreted teleologically requires a justification which would have to rely on particular features of constitutional texts, e.g. on their typical openness.[250] The appropriate method of interpretation cannot simply be deduced from the qualification of a text as a constitution, as the ECHR and the ICJ did. The consequence or side effect of the courts' resort to teleological interpretation was, of course, to grant the interpreting institution itself more leeway, and thus to increase its political and institutional standing. So again one witnesses an instance of judicial self-empowerment.

The *Tadic* judgment of the ICTY Appeals Chamber also dealt with the competence of the Tribunal. Besides confirming that a Security Council Resolution can be a sufficient legal basis for the Yugoslavia Tribunal, the *Tadic* Chamber approached the question from a human rights perspective. Every person is entitled to access to a court which has been established by law (see, e.g.

---

[246] ECJ, opinion 2/94 of 28 March 1996, *Accession by the Community to the European Convention for the Protection of Human Rights and Fundamental Freedoms* [1996] ECR I-01759, paras 34–35.

[247] See notably Tetsuo Sato *Evolving Constitutions of International Organizations: A Critical Analysis of the Interpretative Framework of the Constituent Instruments of International Organizations* (Kluwer The Hague 1996), esp. at 229–232.

[248] ICJ, *Legality of the Use by a State of Nuclear Weapons in Armed Conflict, Advisory Opinion*, ICJ Reports 1996, 66, para 19; ECHR, *Case of Loizidou v Turkey* (preliminary exceptions), Series A 310 (1995), para 71.

[249] Swiss Federal Tribunal, see only BGE 116a I a 359 E 5c (1990), BGE 131 I 174 E. 4.1. (2005).   [250] See in this sense Fassbender, United Nations Charter, 1998, at 595–598.

Article 14 ICCPR or Article 6 ECHR). These provisions relate to domestic courts and are addressed to national legislators. The new move of the *Tadic* judgment was to apply the underlying principle also to an international tribunal. In that situation, the legal basis can obviously not be a parliamentary law. The *Tadic* Chamber deemed it sufficient that the international tribunal is 'in accordance with the rule of law', and named the relevant requirements, such as guarantees of equity and impartiality. It concluded that these conditions were met in the case of the Yugoslavia Tribunal.[251] In consequence, unsurprisingly, the Tribunal was legal and competent. Again, a judicial institution here raised the constitutional sceptre to confirm its own jurisdiction and to defend and even enlarge its political place. However, this strategy is not improper, given the fact that judicial review is a core quest of constitutionalism.

5. Non-governmental Organizations

It is significant from a constitutionalist perspective that non-governmental organizations (NGOs) *de facto* play an increasingly important role in the international legal process. This role should be reflected, but also steered and contained by global constitutional law. In a constitutionalized world order, NGOs are important members of the international community, because they represent the global civil society. NGOs are non-governmental in the sense that they are not established by governments. They are—at least formally—free from government interference, and do not wield governmental powers.[252]

The constitutionalist approach allows the reframing of the doctrinal debate on the international legal personality of NGOs. The question should not be whether NGOs are (partial) subjects of international law or not, but which precise fundamental rights and obligations they possess and should possess in a constitutionalized world order. These rights and obligations should be suited to their functions. The functions of NGOs in the constitutional community are to represent special or global interests, to enhance the knowledge base for global governance, to ensure transparency, to support international secretariats, to

---

[251] ICTY, case No IT-94–1-AR72, *Prosecutor v Dusko Tadic, Decision on the Defence Motion for Interlocutory Appeal on Jurisdiction*, Appeals Chamber of 2 October 1995, paras 45–47.

[252] 'Non-governmental organizations' lack a generally accepted definition in international law. The Council of Europe's Fundamental Principles on NGOs of 2002 characterize their object as follows: '1. NGOs are essentially voluntary self-governing bodies and are not therefore subject to direction by public authorities. . . . 2. NGOs encompass bodies established by individual persons (natural and legal) and groups of such persons. They may be national or international in their composition and sphere of operation; 3. NGOs are usually organisations which have a membership but this is not necessarily the case; 4. NGOs do not have the primary aim of making a profit. . . . 5. NGOs can be either informal bodies or organisations which have legal personality. They may enjoy different statuses under national law . . .': Council of Europe 2002, *Fundamental Principles on the Status of Non-governmental Organisations in Europe and Explanatory Memorandum* of 13 November 2002.

shape a global public opinion, and thereby to globalize values and preferences. The political role of NGOs for the formation of a global democracy will be discussed at pp. 315–318. The most important legal tasks of NGOs, which will be analysed in this chapter, are their participation in international law-making and law-enforcement. For the sake of the rule of law and predictability and legal certainty, this role should not be left purely to the discretion of the international bodies, but should not be straight-jacketed either.

5.1 Towards a principle of openness

Under current international law, many multilateral conventions provide for the 'participation' of, 'cooperation' or 'consultation' with, or 'information' sought by NGOs.[253] Moreover, many international conferences, organizations, and bodies such as Conferences of the Parties (COPs) and committees, allow for the accreditation of NGOs, with notable exceptions being the WTO[254] and the United Nations as a whole.[255] A general observer or participatory status for NGOs at the UN or in the General Assembly had already been envisaged after the 1992 Rio conference and was again suggested by the Cardoso Report of 2004,[256] but not realized. NGO involvement with the General Assembly and the Security Council remains ad hocish.[257]

---

[253] See the following treaty provisions in the field of economic law: Art 12 c) OECD-Convention (1960); Art 13(2) Convention Establishing the WIPO (1967); Art V.2. WTO Agreement (1994). See in international environmental law Art XI(7) CITES Treaty (1973); Art 6(5) Vienna Convention on the Protection of the Ozone Layer (1985); Art 11(5) of the Montreal Protocol on Ozone Depletion (1987); Art 15(6) Basel Convention on the Transboundary Movement of Hazardous Waste (1989); Art 10(5) Aarhus Convention (1998); Art 22 (7) UN Convention to Combat Desertification (UNCCD, 1994); Art 23(5) Biodiversity Convention (1992); Art 29(8) Cartagena Protocol on Biosafety (2000); Art 7(6) UNFCCC (Framework Convention on Climate Change, 1992); Art 13(8) Kyoto Protocol (1997), and the secondary law and rules of procedures within the treaty regimes.

[254] See for the WTO the Guidelines for arrangements on relations with Non-Governmental Organizations, WT/L/162, Decision of 18 July 1996. WTO Director General Supachi Panitchpakdi had established two informal advisory bodies to the WTO secretariat in 2003, as a platform for dialogue between the Director General and business organizations and NGOs. The subsequent Director General discontinued these informal bodies. See in scholarship Pieter van den Bossche 'NGO Involvement in the WTO: A Comparative Perspective' (2008) 11 *Journal of International Economic Law* 717–749.

[255] Within the UN, NGOs can be accredited to the ECOSOC, whose accreditation procedure has been a model for numerous other international bodies. See UN ECOSOC 1996, res 1996/31—*Consultative relationship between the United Nations and non-governmental organisations* (UN Doc A/RES/1996/31), 49th plenary meeting of 25 July 1996.

[256] United Nations, *We the Peoples: Civil Society, the United Nations and Global Governance, Report of the Panel of Eminent Persons on United Nations-Civil Society Relations* ('Cardoso Report'), UN Doc A/58/817 (11 June 2004), paras 123–128 and proposal 19.

[257] For instance, the General Assembly organized two days of interactive hearings with civil society on 23 and 24 June 2005 in preparing the 2005 World Summit (see 'Organization of the informal interactive hearings', UN Doc A/Res 759/291 (2005), Annex III). Since 1992, the Security Council admits NGO input in informal meetings of Council members under the so-called Arria formula.

Traditionally, the NGO status resulting from accreditation was called 'observer' or 'consultative' status. But with a view to the increasingly active role of NGOs as a partner rather than as a passive observer of the inter-governmental institutions, the observer paradigm seems outdated. It is more appropriate to speak of a 'participatory status', such as in the new Council of Europe rules,[258] or of 'cooperative' or 'official working relations' with the civil society organizations, as foreseen in the Organization of American States.[259] That novel terminology does not necessarily strengthen the position of NGOs by adding new rights or privileges, but reveals a paradigm shift in the working method towards an enhanced dialogue, and towards a certain reliance on self-policing of NGOs.[260] This paradigm shift, from a constitutionalist perspective, is welcome, because constitutionalism suggests an active, not merely passive role of NGOs in law-making and -enforcement.

There are three sets of constitutional questions here. First, what is the constitutional significance of the existing accreditation schemes? Should accreditation, which prevents global civil society actors from accessing global governance fora freely, be upheld? Second, if yes, should the existing procedures be more streamlined and more formalized? Who should be the gate keepers, and which conditions for accreditation should be imposed? And third, what are and what should be the exact consequences, rights, and obligations flowing from such an accreditation? Once duly accredited, what are the concrete conditions of participation for NGOs? In this section I will discuss the first set of questions, and turn to the other questions later.

Accreditation creates a formal status for the NGO, either within an entire organization or related to specific conferences or other bodies. A constitutional question is now whether—under the law as it stands—NGOs are entitled to participate in global governance activities without such accreditation or other admission procedure. Indeed some authors assert that NGOs already have, as a matter of customary law, or as a general principle distillable from the existing law and rules of procedure, a general entitlement to participate (as 'observers' or 'participants') within inter-state institutions.[261] Such an NGO right to participate would come to bear in institutions which do not foresee admission at all, such as

---

[258] Council of Europe, *Participatory Status for International Non-governmental Organisations with the Council of Europe*, res (2003) 8 of 19 November 2003, adopted by the Committee of Ministers at the 861st meeting of the Ministers' Deputies.

[259] Permanent Council of the Organization of American States (OAS), Review of the Rules of Procedure for Civil Society Participation with the OAS, 31 March 2004, CP/CISC-106/04.

[260] Emanuele Rebasti 'Beyond Consultative Status: Which Legal Framework for an Enhanced Interaction between NGOs and Intergovernmental Organizations?' in Pierre-Marie Dupuy and Luisa Vierucci (eds) *NGOs in International Law: Efficiency and Flexibility* (Edward Elgar Northampton 2008) 21–70, at 59.

[261] See in this sense Steve Charnovitz 'Nongovernmental Organizations and International Law' (2006) 100 *AJIL* 348–372, at 368–372 and 370; *contra* Dinh Nguyen Quoc, Patrick Daillier, and Alain Pellet *Droit international public* (LGDJ Paris 2002), at 653; Boyle and Chinkin, *The Making of International Law*, 2007, at 57; Stephen Tully *Corporations and International Lawmaking* (Martinus Nijhoff Boston and Leiden 2007), at 328–330.

the UN Security Council, or in institutions which have only deficient special rules of procedures on NGO involvement. However, a customary right of NGOs to participate freely in the international legal process does not yet exist. Practice and *opinio iuris* has not evolved in that direction, but has on the contrary upheld the requirement of prior accreditation or admission to conferences and committees. NGOs do not enjoy a general 'right' to participate unconditionally without any screening in a conference or committee which does not admit NGOs.

It has been argued that accreditation is an outdated paradigm which should be altogether abandoned.[262] The proposal is, in other words, to allow unconditional and completely free access of NGOs to global government fora. But this proposal is unworkable. If only for practical reasons, NGO involvement in global governance must be channelled, otherwise the system would collapse. Self-policing of NGOs to that effect is laudable, and may be a complementary tool, but is not sufficient. It is therefore necessary to maintain accreditation in principle.

Descriptively, it can be stated that a general legal principle of openness is emerging. The principle of openness means that global governance fora are no longer presumed to be *a priori* closed. They are no longer allowed to categorically exclude NGO access without any justification. They must at least give consideration to the possibility of NGO access, and must provide some type of admission procedure or justify why they do not apply such a procedure. This means that, correspondingly, NGOs have the right to apply for an accreditation and be duly considered. Such a principle of openness has not yet fully crystallized into law, but is nascent. The principle emerges out of the practice that more and more fora admit NGOs on a regular basis and under similar conditions and the accompanying conviction that this is due to NGOs. *De lege lata*, an option of applying for admission should be granted to NGOs even by those bodies where admission procedures do not yet exist at present, e.g. in the General Assembly. Put differently, the nascent principle of openness should be doctrinally acknowledged and further entrenched as a constitutional principle of international law. The principle would not imply unrestricted participation of NGOs in law-making and -enforcement. It would merely imply that inter-state institutions must provide a proper procedure or mechanism which applies reasonable substantive criteria for the admission of NGOs, whose application may lead to the involvement of (some) NGOs.

5.2 A constitutionally appropriate accreditation of NGOs

I now turn to the second set of questions, namely to the appropriate procedures and criteria for admission of NGOs under the constitutional principle of openness. From a constitutionalist perspective, the formalization of NGO status

---

[262] Math Noortmann 'Who Really Needs Art 71?' in Wybo P Heere (ed) *From Government to Governance: The Growing Impact of Non-state Actors on the International and European Legal System* (TMC Asser Press The Hague 2004) 113–120.

through accreditation (and monitoring and evaluations) is ambivalent. While it secures the clarity and operationality of governance, the accreditation requirement makes states the gatekeepers of NGO involvement. And intensified streamlining and further formalization of accreditation procedures by governments risk endangering the NGOs' independence, which is one of their primary elements of legitimacy. In fact, one of the most salient problems of the existing accreditation procedures is their undue politization, especially in the United Nations Economic and Social Council (ECOSOC). In this body, which mostly deals with human rights NGOs, both the accreditation and its suspension or withdrawal have at times been handled disregarding the codified criteria, based on pure national interests of certain governments.[263]

In order to cut back abuses and illegitimate political considerations, the task should be removed further from the states (which are represented in bodies such as the ECOSOC committee on NGOs), but should be entrusted to the secretariats of international organizations which are more distanced from governments. This move has already been realized in the Council of Europe.[264] With regard to the United Nations, a 'depoliticization' of the accreditation procedure was one of the main proposals of the Cardoso Report on UN civil society relations,[265] but did not meet with approval in the General Assembly.

The question arises whether one uniform and standardized accreditation procedure (and ensuing standard forms and conditions of participation) can and should be designed for all international institutions. In fact, the exiting variety of accreditation procedures, the uneven standards, and the confusing procedures have so far hampered NGO involvement in global governance.[266] A uniform and standardized procedure would satisfy the quest for legal security and transparency, and is to that extent, from a constitutional perspective, laudable. But there is a tension between improving legal clarity and the need for tailoring the mechanisms to specific bodies and their roles and procedures. The functions, working methods, and objectives of the different international institutions vary so much, that a one-fits-all-accreditation procedure with identical criteria seems neither realistic nor desirable, as it would be dysfunctional.

Still, some core criteria seem to be recommended from a constitutionalist perspective. An important guideline for new accreditation criteria is that those must not endanger the independence of the NGOs, and that the criteria must

---

[263] See on these cases Olivier de Frouville 'Domesticating Civil Society at the UN' in Pierre-Marie Dupuy and Luisa Vierucci (eds) *NGOs in International Law: Efficiency and Flexibility* (Edward Elgar Northampton 2008) 71–115, esp. at 100–110.

[264] See Council of Europe, *Participatory Status for International Non-governmental Organisations with the Council of Europe* (res (2003) 8 of 19 November 2003) (adopted by the Committee of Ministers at the 861st meeting of the Ministers' Deputies), paras 12–14: The decision to grant participatory status is here taken by the Secretary General with a no-objection procedure by governments.   [265] Cardoso Report, 2004, paras 120–122.

[266] *Strengthening of the United Nations: An Agenda for Further Change*, Report of the Secretary General (UN Doc A/57/387 (2002), para 139.

themselves be independent from the national level (i.e. they must be genuinely international). Finally, the criteria must be transparent and must be applied even-handedly. It is appropriate to require that the NGO seeking accreditation must possess a minimum degree of expertise or display activity in the relevant field, because furnishing information is one of the prime objectives of NGO involvement. Because of the logistical problems resulting from NGO participation and the need to manage the sheer number of potential participants, it is also justified to require that NGOs be sufficiently representative, however difficult this is to measure and verify.

But it seems inappropriate to require an 'international' character of the NGOs in the sense of having offices in various countries, because the spheres of national and international politics are increasingly blurred.[267] Also, registration by a national body should not be mandatory for NGOs, because international law must remain independent from domestic law. Moreover, the gist of NGO activity may be precisely to counteract governmental policies, and oppositional NGOs may have problems being registered in their states.

Explicit requirements on the transparency, accountability, or internal democracy of NGOs are problematic from a constitutionalist perspective. I will explain at pp. 315–318 that NGOs need not be organized in a democratic fashion, as long as other forms of accountability exist. But too strict accountability requirements could hamper the participation of smaller NGOs and thus restrict NGO input by placing a burden on them that is disproportionate to the expected, rather uncertain, and probably limited benefits. Such requirements should therefore be formulated only with caution and must not have a prohibitive effect.

Similarly, an obligation on NGOs to support the objectives of the international bodies to which they seek accreditation is in constitutional terms ambivalent.[268] On the one hand, the principle of democracy requires that critics and 'enemies' of an organization must also be allowed to participate in the deliberations. On the other hand, obstruction of the work must be prevented. The constitutional concept of a 'robust' democracy here offers some guidance. It is permissible and recommended to ask NGOs to subscribe to basic constitutional principles, such as the inviolability of human rights, but it is not appropriate to compel NGOs to declare adherence to concrete policies.

To conclude, in a constitutionalized world order, some form of accreditation of NGOs that desire to become involved in global governance remains indispensable. But the accreditation procedure must observe due process guarantees, and the substantive criteria for accreditation must be reasonable. The mechanisms should be moderately streamlined, under due regard for the specific needs of the concrete institutions. The international institutions themselves, not governments as such,

---

[267] Sebastian Oberthür *Participation of Non-governmental Organisations in International Environmental Co-operation: Legal Basis and Practical Experience* (Schmidt Berlin 2002), at 229.
[268] Currently, the ECOSOC, the Commission on Sustainable Development (CSD), and UNCTAD require accredited NGOs to be supportive of the UN Charter.

should become the principal gatekeepers. Notably, concerned states should not have a veto in accreditation procedures. Procedures to withdraw the participatory status must likewise be clear and fair. As long as accredited, the participatory status of NGOs will be an intermediate one between exclusion of NGOs and their parity with states. I turn now to the precise contours of this status, which depends on the constitutional function at hand, law-making or law-enforcement.

5.3 NGO participation in international law-making: 'voice', not 'vote'

There are different types of NGO involvement in international law-making which raise the question of the precise conditions of the participation of civil society groups. First, especially since the 'participatory revolution' of Rio 1992, NGOs have been engaged in the elaboration of ordinary inter-state international conventions. Here NGO involvement is largely informal. NGOs either lobby at inter-governmental conferences or hold NGO forums parallel to and separate from the intergovernmental conferences. So NGOs do not have any negotiating role whatsoever here, but their activities can still be crucial.[269] The second type of norm-production occurs within international organizations or quasi-organizations, in particular in the framework of the highly institutionalized multilateral environmental agreements. Here, the governmental bodies or conferences of the parties create secondary law for the implementation of the respective regimes, and NGOs participate therein.[270]

How can the *lex lata* of NGO participation in law-making be summarized? Overall, despite the multiple NGO activities and their often forceful presence, 'states retain a tight grip on the formal law-making processes'.[271] Even in those areas where NGOs have had greatest impact, states control the agenda and access to the law-making arenas, in particular through the accreditation procedures mentioned above. As far as secondary law-making within international institutions is concerned, the current procedural provisions regulating the position of accredited NGOs in organizations and conferences are diverse.[272] Nevertheless, typical features can be discerned. Accreditation (admission) usually entails only a qualified allowance of the accredited NGO to be invited, to sit in meetings, to

---

[269] They have, for instance, been a decisive factor in the adoption of important recent multi-lateral treaties. Notably, the Anti-Torture Convention of 1984, the Landmines Convention of 1997, and the ICC Statute of 1998 would probably not have come into being without the intense work of transnational NGO coalitions. Inversely, NGO resistance was a crucial contribution to the failure of the projected Multilateral Agreement on Investment (MAI) in 1998.

[270] Besides, NGOs sometimes draft private texts or propose norms (often in conjunction with academics), such as codes of conduct and guidelines, interpretative treaty commentaries, or principles, in the hope that they will be adopted by other international actors. This activity happens outside the framework of governmental institutions, and does not touch the question of partici-pation.   [271] Boyle and Chinkin, *The Making of International Law*, 2006, at 88–89.

[272] The most detailed procedures can be found in CITES (Convention on International Trade in Endangered Species of Wild Fauna and Flora) (2000), enshrined in rules of procedure for the Convention, and in procedural rules for CITES' committees.

obtain information (agendas, drafts), speaking time, being allowed to distribute documents, and eventually to raise agenda items. Usually these allowances are conditioned upon the absence of objection of a specified number of state parties (e.g. one third of the parties present), so that NGOs do not enjoy unconditional rights in that regard. The crucial feature of the existing procedural rules on NGO involvement in secondary law-making is that the written procedures deny voting rights to NGOs.[273] A comparative look at the rules of procedures of conferences and bodies shows that the mentioned formal participatory conditions are well settled. It can be argued that they constitute a common international procedural law for conferences and international law-making bodies.[274] Put another way, these procedural principles exist, as a matter of an emerging customary common procedural law of international governing bodies, independent of codification in written rules of procedure. If this is correct, the common principles can be extrapolated and would also apply to conferences whose rules fall short of them.

This finding has a consequence for the status of NGOs. I submit, in line with earlier scholarship, that NGOs already enjoy a *legitimate expectation* that—*when accredited*—the participatory conditions will entail four core components: prior notification of meetings and agenda items, automatic and continuous admission to meetings, the option to distribute documents, and being allowed to address the conference upon explicit permission.[275] This would mean concretely that NGOs, once accredited with an international body, should not only be allowed to sit in the relevant meetings, but have the legitimate expectation that they will additionally enjoy (clearly defined and limited) rights to make written (and upon permission) oral statements (voice)—even if the written rules of procedure are silent on this. Admitting that such an expectation or nascent conditional right to active participation in law-making (and eventually also in global administrative decision-making) exists, does not obliterate the need to identify which concrete NGOs can or must be consulted, at what stage, and by what means. The NGO's right to participation would still be subject to restrictions, e.g. for reasons of security or privacy.

---

[273] The standard formula in the rules of procedure of COPS or MOPs of modern multilateral environmental agreements is that NGOs may, upon invitation of the President, participate without the right to vote in the proceedings of any meeting in matters of direct concern to the body or agency they represent unless at least one-third of the parties present at the meeting objects. Exceptions are the ILO where employers' and workers' organizations participate, on a equal footing with governments and with a vote, in the elaboration of conventions and recommendations (tripartism), and the ISO, where business actors dominate technical standard setting. As an example of a law-making conference see the ICC Rules of the Assembly of the States Parties, rules 93 and 95 (ICC-ASP/1/3, at 178–179).

[274] *Cf* Robbie Sabel *Procedure at International Conferences* (2nd edn CUP Cambridge 2006), at 57–58.

[275] *Cf* Tully, *Corporations and International Lawmaking*, 2007, at 233 and 327–328; also Anna-Karin Lindblom *Non-Governmental Organisations in International Law* (CUP Cambridge 2005), at 526; Oberthür, *Participation of Non-governmental Organisations*, 2002, at 206.

It may also be curtailed by a conference's or committee's secretariat due to practical constraints of time and space, but only in a non-discriminatory fashion.

So what would be the precise legal implications of accredited NGOs' legitimate expectation to participate in international law-making processes under the mentioned principles? A constitutionalist approach can draw on the well-known mechanisms of consultation procedures. First, an institution's refusal to admit an accredited NGO to a meeting or to allow oral and written submissions by such an NGO would have to be specifically and concretely justified by the international body. The institutions must give reasons for their decisions concerning NGO participation, especially for negative decisions. Next follows a good-faith procedural obligation for the institutions *viz.* its governmental members or participants to duly take into account the input of NGOs. This is, from a constitutionalist perspective and for reasons of procedural fairness, imperative, because otherwise allowing NGOs to raise their voice does not make sense. So NGOs would be entitled to a summary acknowledgment of receipt and a response which shows that the content of their submission has been considered. Finally, in order to make real and effective the potential rights of accredited NGOs, some review mechanism would have to be established in order to sanction undue refusals, e.g. an NGO ombudsman. Inversely, sanctions for abuse of the participatory status by NGOs must be available, too.

On the premise that a legitimate expectation with the legal consequences just sketched out already exists, the NGOs' participation in law-making, their 'voice', can be qualified as a constitutional function. And because of this constitutional function of NGOs' participation, there is, for the sake of legal clarity and under the rule of law, a need to legally structure it.

To conclude on the role of NGOs in international law-making, there is a need to reconcile the conflicting objectives of inclusiveness and transparency on the one hand with the preservation of the authority and ultimate responsibility of states. Granting NGOs a voice in law-making but not a vote strikes an appropriate balance here. The governments must maintain and exercise their filtering function. They must assess and weigh competing interests, both private and public ones. The ultimate regulatory responsibility, if only residuary, falls on states, but these must be obliged by global constitutional law to listen to the voices of civil society actors in the law-making process.

5.4 NGO participation in law-enforcement

The second formal constitutional function of NGOs is their participation in the enforcement of international law through judicial or quasi-judicial proceedings, treaty monitoring, and verification processes.[276]

---

[276] See on this issue Tullio Treves, Marco Frigessi di Rattalma, Attila Tanzi, Alessandro Fodella, Cesare Pitea, and Chiara Rani (eds) *Civil Society, International Courts and Compliance Bodies* (TMC Asser Press The Hague 2005).

NGO involvement in (quasi-)judicial compliance control

The degree of openness of judicial or arbitral bodies for NGOs is one of the clearest indicators for the retreat of an international order based on inter-state relations and for the emergence of an international order in which individual values and claims can be firmly defended.[277] It is thus an indicator of constitutionalization. In principle, there are two forms of participation in international judicial or arbitral proceedings for NGOs: direct involvement as parties to a dispute and indirect involvement as interveners, notably as *amici curiae*.

In current international law, NGOs are rarely granted standing before international courts and tribunals. Under Article 34 ECHR, they can complain about violations of their own freedom of association. But the more important political and constitutional function of NGOs seems to be to raise concerns that affect a great number of persons (e.g. workers), or impersonal concerns, such as environmental ones. The latter function could be fulfilled by admitting an *actio popularis*, such as under the Article 24 ILO Constitution, under the European Social Charter,[278] and under the American Convention on Human Rights.[279] This strategy is problematic, as will be explained below, and has been rejected by the EU courts.[280] A yet different strategy is to require from the side of international law an NGO involvement in domestic judicial procedures, such as under the EU Racial Discrimination Directive.[281]

Permitting NGOs to file complaints raises a number of problems. Actual litigation might curtail the lobbying power of NGOs and might paradoxically limit their manoeuvring space. However, this should not be of concern for the constitutional designer, but should be left for the NGOs themselves to decide. Furthermore, NGO complaints risk increasing the workload of already over-burdened compliance and monitoring systems, and this is a serious

---

[277] Luisa Vierucci 'NGOs before International Courts and Tribunals' in Pierre-Marie Dupuy and Luisa Vierucci (eds) *NGOs in International Law* (Edward Elgar Northampton 2008) 155–180, at 157.

[278] ESC Additional Protocol of 9 November 1995, ETS No 158 (1995). Trade Unions and international NGOs with consultative status at the Council of Europe can 'submit complaints alleging unsatisfactory application' of the European Social Charter/ESC, 1961) at an experts committee.

[279] Art 44 American Convention on Human Rights (Pact of San José, Costa Rica) of 22 November 1969. The Inter-American Commission on Human Rights is explicitly empowered to receive petitions submitted by any NGO that is legally recognized in at least one member state of the OAS 'on their own behalf or on behalf of third persons.' (Art 23 Rules of Procedure of the Inter-American Commission on Human Rights).

[280] Case T-585/93 *Greenpeace v Commission* [1995] ECR II-2205, paras 48–52.

[281] See Council Directive 2000/43/EC of 29 June 2000 implementing the principle of equal treatment between persons irrespective of racial or ethnic origin (OJ 2000, L 180/ 22). Under Art 7 (2), member states shall ensure that associations, organizations or other legal entities, which have a legitimate interest in ensuring that the provisions of this Directive are complied with, may engage, either on behalf or in support of the complainant, with his or her approval, in any judicial and/or administrative procedure provided for the enforcement of obligations under the Directive.

constitutional problem. Finally, NGO complaint options might unfairly discriminate against those categories of victims who do not have access to potent NGOs.

In a constitutionalized world order, the different members of the constitutional community should not be treated as categorically different when it comes to access to court. The basic principle that rights holders can—as a rule—claim only the infringements of their own rights before courts and tribunals should be upheld. This basic principle translates into the *jus standi* requirements such as the victim-requirement in human rights proceedings.

Granting standing to NGOs and allowing NGOs to become a party and to claim in this quality the rights of *others* or of the public would be a paradigm shift. Even a limited extension of the *locus standi* only to those NGOs which have a formal status (accreditation, consultative, or participatory status) with the monitoring body, such as before the African Court of Human Rights,[282] already constitutes such a paradigm shift and abandons the idea of a personalized protection of rights. That limited solution greatly increases the value of accreditation for NGOs. Hence appropriate and fair, notably depoliticized, accreditation procedures for NGOs become all the more important.

However, I would argue that such a paradigm shift is not recommended in a constitutionalized order, because it risks flooding the complaints system and fostering a system of tutelage and paternalism by NGOs over personally affected groups. It is also not needed, because structurally disadvantaged rights holders, such as victims of human rights violations, can be sufficiently protected through NGO counselling. NGOs can here act as legal representatives of the victims and claim the rights of those victims without themselves becoming a party to the dispute.

In a system of personal claims, the genuine role of NGOs in judicial action would be to defend public goods, such as environmental goods, concerns of future generations that are otherwise unrepresented, and rights with a typical collective dimension, for instance economic and social rights.[283] Only in these limited fields, popular or class actions, typically conducted by NGOs, seem adequate and necessary. Here a *jus standi* to instigate these special forms of action could be envisaged for those NGOs that can show their interest and their competence.

The indirect participation of NGOs in international law-enforcement can be realized through *amicus curiae* briefs. There is a clear, though cautious trend in

---

[282] Art 5(3) of the 1998 Protocol to the African Charter on Human and Peoples' Rights of the Establishment of an African Court on Human and Peoples' Rights of 10 June 1998, entered into force on 25 January 2004, grants standing to such NGOs that are 'relevant' to the case and that enjoy observer status before the African Commission on Human Rights, but only if the involved state has specifically accepted the competence of the Court to receive such a case.
[283] *Cf* Vierucci, NGOs before International Courts, 2008, at 161.

international adjudication, arbitration, and quasi-judicial treaty monitoring to admit such briefs by NGOs, e.g. in North American Free Trade Agreement (NAFTA)[284] and ICSID proceedings.[285] Under Article 36(2) ECHR, the president of the Court may, in the interest of the proper administration of justice, invite 'any person concerned who is not the applicant to submit written comments or take part in the hearings', and the Court under this rubric has occasionally heard NGOs.[286] The ICC prosecutor can request information from NGOs.[287] The ICJ statute refers to 'international organizations' as providers of information or as commentators in advisory proceedings.[288] A constitutionalist interpretation of the expression 'international organization' in those provisions suggests also including NGOs.[289]

The forum best known for indirect NGO-participation in adjudication is the WTO. After *amicus curiae* briefs by NGOs had been admitted by the panel and Appellate Body in the *Shrimp* case,[290] the WTO member states reacted with strong criticism. In consequence, the dispute settlement institutions have taken a restrictive posture in this regard, and admit *amicus curiae* briefs only when they are taken up in the parties' submissions.[291] The spreading practice relating to *amicus curiae* submissions and the borrowing of the various international

---

[284] See NAFTA Tribunal, *Methanex Corporation v United States of America*, decision of the tribunal on petitions from third persons to intervene as 'amici curiae' of 15 January 2001. The tribunal grounded its power to accept *amicus curiae* briefs on Art 15(1) of the Arbitration Rules of the UN Commission on International Trade Law which empowers an arbitral tribunal to conduct the proceedings 'in such manner as it considers appropriate'. Under the rules for ICSID tribunals, the tribunal shall ensure that 'both parties are given an opportunity to present their observations on the non-disputing party submission', but have no veto (rule 37(2) ICSID rules of procedure for arbitration proceedings (arbitration rules), amended and effective as of 10 April 2006).

[285] *Aguas Argentinas, S.A., Suez, Sociedad General de Aguas de Barcelona S.A. and Vivendi Universal S.A v Argentine Republic* (ICSID case No ARB/03/19), order in response to a petition for transparency and participation as *amicus curiae* of 19 May 2005; *Aguas Provinciales de Santa Fe S.A., Suez, Sociedad General de Aguas de Barcelona S.A. and Interagua Servicios Integrales de Agua S.A. v Argentine Republic* (ICSID Case No ARB/03/17), order in response to a petition for participation as *amicus curiae* of 17 March, 2006. The tribunals based their power to decide on the admissibility of *amicus* briefs from suitable non-parties in appropriate cases on Art 44 ICSID Convention.

[286] See Nina Vajic 'Some Concluding Remarks on NGOs and the European Court of Human Rights' in Tullio Treves, Marco Frigessi di Rattalma, Attila Tanzi, Alessandro Fodella, Cesare Pitea, and Chiara Rani (eds) *Civil Society, International Courts and Compliance Bodies* (TMC Asser Press The Hague 2005) 93–104 with a list of proceedings before the ECHR where NGOs intervened either as a third party or by representing applicants at 101–102.

[287] Art 15(2) and Art 44(4) ICC Statute. See also Art 103 of the Rules of Procedure and Evidence of the ICC (ICC-ASP/1/3 at 20 *et seq.*).   [288] Art 34(2) and 66 ICJ Statute.

[289] It is in line with this interpretation that the Court's rules allow NGOs to submit written statements or documents only for advisory proceedings, but not in contentious jurisdiction (ICJ, Practice Direction XII of 7 February 2002, as of 6 December 2006). NGO-submissions do not become part of the file, but are treated as 'publications readily available'.

[290] WTO Appellate Body, *United States—Import Prohibition of Certain Shrimp and Shrimp Products*, AB-1998-4 WT/DS 58/AB/R (12 October 1998), paras 79–110. The panels' competence to accept *amicus curiae* briefs is based on Art 13(2) DSU.

[291] WTO AB, *US—Softwood Lumber*, WT/DS277/R (22 March 2004), at 88, n. 75.

adjudicators from each other and from national courts has given rise to a common approach to this issue. These commonalities, however, have not (yet) led to a set of hard and fast rules applicable to all tribunals. This means that a general entitlement of NGOs to file *amicus* briefs has not yet emerged as a matter of international customary law, but may be in the process of formation,[292] although the WTO experience rather speaks against such a development.

The indirect participation of NGOs in law-enforcement through *amicus curiae* interventions has important benefits which are apt to improve the constitutional function of law-enforcement. NGO input contributes to the legitimacy of courts and tribunals, which flows to a great part from the capacity of these institutions to listen. More technically speaking, information furnished by NGOs contributes to better informed and therefore potentially better and more acceptable judgments.

But NGO *amicus curiae* interventions also raise problems. Those who have the financial resources to prepare a submission are advantaged. The filing of briefs may be motivated by a hidden agenda, such as merely making publicity for the NGO and attracting additional funding. However, as long as the briefs do not flood the judicial bodies, such motives are not pernicious as such. The much more serious problem seems to be the risks for the rights of the parties to the dispute, especially the threat to party autonomy and to the equality of arms. From a constitutionalist perspective, these rights are core elements of fair trial, which is in turn a crucial emanation of the rule of law, and must therefore be taken seriously. The equality of arms may be endangered by the fact that *amici* do not have to prove the veracity of their briefs, in contrast to the parties who have to substantiate their factual allegations. So the onus of rebuttal falls exclusively on the party whose position is undermined by the *amicus curiae* brief. However, this danger for the equality of arms can be forestalled by a requirement that *amicus curiae* briefs be substantiated just as parties' submissions.

Generally speaking, the inevitable tension between the admission of *amicus curiae* briefs and the 'ownership' of a dispute by the parties cannot be eliminated. A greater formalization of *amicus curiae* interventions could help here. There is a need to devise rules of participation which allow the striking of a fair balance between the partially conflicting objectives of increasing the information basis for the court on the one hand and safeguarding the parties' right on the other. Also, these rules must on the one hand be foreseeable for NGOs, but on

---

[292] Ruth Mackenzie 'The *Amicus Curiae* in International Courts: Towards Common Procedural Approaches?' in Tullio Treves, Marco Frigessi di Rattalma, Attila Tanzi, Alessandro Fodella, Cesare Pitea, and Chiara Rani (eds) *Civil Society, International Courts and Compliance Bodies* (TMC Asser Press The Hague 2005) 295–311, at 310–311; Vierucci, NGOs before International Courts, 2008, at 174 with note 63 and further references.

the other hand leave the courts enough flexibility to adapt NGO input to the needs of the concrete case at hand.

The form or level of regulation of NGO interventions could in theory consist in mere self-policing of NGOs. However, this seems insufficient for judicial and quasi-judicial procedures, because these to a large extent draw their legitimacy from strict formalization. At the other end of the spectrum, the most formal type of regulation would be to endorse the rules in the statutes of international courts, tribunals, or in the international conventions establishing human rights monitoring bodies. The definition of the rules would thus be left for the states parties, and would become difficult to change. A middle-ground approach would be to leave it to the controlling bodies themselves to enshrine the relevant norms in their own rules of procedure.[293] This level of regulation for NGO participation seems most appropriate, last but not least because the issue pertains to the sphere of autonomy of the monitoring bodies which those bodies need to safeguard their independence. At the same time it allows for flexibility through relatively easy amendment.

Overall, I conclude that the benefits of a (conditional and) indirect NGO participation in international adjudication, notably through *amicus curiae* briefs, outweigh its risks. The potential dangers of NGO participation are less great than they seem at first sight, because there is one institution which is in charge of securing respect for the rights of the parties, namely the judge himself.[294] The judge, tribunal, or panel itself must determine the need for NGO participation. The judges are able to decide on the appropriateness of the case and the suitability of the non-party to intervene. They would have to assess whether the submission will further the interests of justice, whether the public interests warrant a submission, and whether the NGO possesses expertise in the field. NGO *amicus curiae* briefs seem especially appropriate where *erga omnes* obligations are at stake.[295] The judges can also decide what weight to accord to a submission. However, under the rule of law, these decisions may not be ad hoc, but need to be regulated so as to allow predictability.

In line with the current legal trend, and in order to facilitate NGO participation further, I endorse the suggestion of recognizing a presumption of admissibility of *amicus curiae* briefs. The judges should be obliged to explain satisfactorily the reasons for rejecting *amicus curiae* briefs.[296] Reasons for refusal may be the lack of particular expertise of the NGO and a lack of a potential

---

[293] See, e.g., Art 33 of the ECHR Rules of Court (as of December 2008) on the public character of documents deposited by any third party in connection with an application, in accordance with arrangements determined by the Registrar.
[294] Vierucci, NGOs before International Courts, 2008, at 180.
[295] Dinah Shelton 'The Participation of Nongovernmental Organizations in International Judicial Proceedings' (1994) 88 *AJIL* 611–642, at 627.
[296] Vierucci, NGOs before International Courts, 2008, at 179.

public interest with regard to the concrete proceedings.[297] These conditions should be laid down in autonomous rules of the adjudicatory bodies. Such a presumption would further constitutionalize international adjudication, because it would increase its transparency and public control without unduly curtailing the right of the parties.

NGO involvement in non-judicial compliance control

From a constitutional perspective, compliance control occupies the functional space of the 'third branch' of government and must therefore also be subject to public scrutiny. This constitutionalist objective can be and is already realized through NGO participation. For instance, the efficiency of human rights monitoring to a large extent depends on NGO support, e.g. in the form of shadow reports submitted to the treaty bodies.[298] The involvement of NGOs with the Human Rights Council is manifold and comprises *inter alia* the possibility of submitting complaints to the Council.[299] Furthermore, NGO participation is particularly developed in environmental non-compliance proceedings.[300] Notably the proceedings under the two UNECE Conventions, the Aarhus Convention and the Protocol on Water and Health, are very open towards NGO participation.[301]

Again, two types of NGO participation with a different impact are conceivable. First, NGOs can be vested with the power to trigger non-compliance proceedings. This is so far only the case under the Aarhus Convention.[302] Here

---

[297] For instance, in the NAFTA *Methanex* proceedings, the public interest in the arbitration proceeding arose from its subject matter, namely public access to drinking water (*Methanex Corporation v United States of America*, decision of the tribunal on petitions from third persons to intervene as 'amici curiae' of 15 January 2001, para 49).

[298] See on the involvement of NGOs in international human rights protection the World Summit Outcome, UN GA res 60/1 of 24 October 2005, para 172. See for concrete treaty regimes for example Art 45 lit. a) CRC (1989) and rules 44, 47 and 83 of the CEDAW-committee.

[299] On the principle of involvement of NGOs with the Human Rights Council, see HRC res 60/251 (2006), para 11. The forms of participation are spelled out in Human Rights Council, *Institution Building of the UN Human Rights Council* (2007), Annex to res 5/1, UN Doc A/HRC/21: NGOs may participate in the universal periodic review (para 3 lit. m)); they may nominate candidates as special procedure holders (para 42); they shall interact with the HRC advisory committee (para 82); they may submit communications on human rights violations in the HRC 'complaint procedure' (para 87 lit. d)); they can contribute to a HRC special session (para 125); and they may participate as observers of the HRC (rule 7).

[300] See Cesare Pitea 'The Legal Status of NGOs in Environmental Non-compliance Procedures: An Assessment of Law and Practice' in Pierre-Marie Dupuy and Luisa Vierucci (eds) *NGOs in International Law* (Edward Elgar Northampton 2008) 181–203.

[301] Art 15 Aarhus Convention of 25 June 1998 ((1999) 38 ILM 517–533) and and Art 15 of the Protocol on Water and Health to the 1992 Convention on the Protection and Use of Transboundary Watercourses and International Lakes of 17 June 1999 foresee that the arrangements for compliance control 'shall allow for appropriate public involvement'.

[302] Aarhus Convention MOP Decision I/7 on review of compliance of 23 October 2002, sec. VI. 'Communications from the public', paras 18–24, rules 5(2)(e) and 6(2) of the rules of procedure of the Aarhus MOP (Decision I/1).

NGOs can even nominate candidates for the compliance committee itself. This option led to the election of members with an NGO background in the compliance committee. The historical reason for extensive NGO powers in the Aarhus compliance control regime seems to be that the Convention entrusts NGOs themselves with substantive rights, which are consistently mirrored on the procedural level. But the experience that NGOs are more likely to root out the cases of non-compliance and are less likely to remain silent on them for reasons of diplomacy suggests reconceiving the rationale for NGO involvement as enhancing the regime's effectiveness rather than as an extrapolation of the convention's substance onto the procedural level. Upon this reasoning, the Aarhus triggering mechanism should be taken as a model for other environmental compliance mechanisms.[303]

The second, minor role of NGOs is to submit information to the compliance control committee, as a functional equivalent to *amicus curiae* briefs. NGOs may even be allowed to participate in the discussion before the compliance committee. This type of involvement has so far been accepted by states more readily.[304]

A potential problem of NGO participation in compliance control procedures is that this might undermine the cooperational and non-adversarial features of those procedures which are their main strength. Still, experience has shown that the non-confrontational characteristic is more endangered by the uncooperative attitude of states parties than by NGOs. But extensive NGO involvement might overburden the committees and increase the costs of the proceedings. These risks must be balanced against the expected benefits of a better information basis. In any case, the risk of an abuse of the proceedings through irresponsible and undisciplined NGO activism has not been confirmed by the first years of the work of the Aarhus committee. The danger of a conflict of interests arising for NGOs, e.g. due to involvement in business affected by the environmental issue at stake, could be met by strict disclosure requirements accompanied by sanctions. The attitude of mistrust of developing states towards NGOs, especially in the environmental field, must be countered with special measures in favour of 'southern' NGOs (on this problem see pp. 237 and 240).

---

[303] Jeremy Wates 'NGOs and the Aarhus Convention' in Tullio Treves, Marco Frigessi di Rattalma, Attila Tanzi, Alessandro Fodella, Cesare Pitea, and Chiara Rani (eds) *Civil Society, International Courts and Compliance Bodies* (TMC Asser Press The Hague 2005) 167–185, at 184.

[304] See e.g., the procedures and mechanisms relating to compliance under the Kyoto Protocol (Decision 27/CMP.1, annex, sec. VIII(4): 'Competent intergovernmental and non-governmental organizations may submit relevant factual and technical information to the relevant branch.' (Doc FCCC/KP/CMP/2005/8/Add. 3, 92–103). Information may have to be channelled through a state party, such as under the Basel Convention's mechanism for promoting implementation and compliance. Under para 17 of the compliance mechanism, 'a Party may also consider and use relevant and appropriate information provided by civil society on compliance difficulties'. (Basel Convention on the Transboundary Movement of Hazardous Wastes and their Disposal (1989), COP decision VI/12, Doc UNEP/CHW.6/40, at 45–60).

A generous admission of factual and scientific information by NGOs in non-compliance procedures is warranted, because the know-how of NGOs is needed especially in the increasingly technical and complex field of environmental and climate protection. In theory, the current lack of regulation of the NGO status in environmental compliance control proceedings is not an absolute barrier to their participation. Provisions on the competences of the compliance committees which either grant them broad discretional power in carrying out their mandate or even specifically empower them to seek advisers' and experts' opinions provide a sufficient legal basis for the allowance of NGO input. However, the lack of rules on NGOs have already resulted in controversies over their participation, e.g. under the Espoo Convention on Environmental Impact Assessment in a Transboundary Context of 1991. The Espoo committee decided that considering unsolicited NGO information was not part of its mandate.[305] From a constitutionalist perspective, for the sake of legal certainty, the role of NGOs in environmental non-compliance proceedings should be clarified. Their status and their procedural options should be defined in the rules of the committees themselves. *De lege lata*, accredited or otherwise qualified NGOs with demonstrated expertise in the relevant field should be allowed to trigger non-compliance procedures especially in environmental law. Experience has already shown that the states are very reluctant to file complaints in order not to cause political tensions. In environmental law, self-interested individual petitioners, as in human rights law, are absent. NGOs are in principle suited to step in to fill the gap. In order to prevent flooding and abuse, triggering of the procedure should eventually be channelled through the conventions' secretariats. A quasi-prosecutorial role for NGOs would render environmental non-compliance systems more effective, and would thus serve the public interest. Both objectives have high priority in a constitutionalist perspective.

5.5 The legitimacy and accountability of NGOs

Global constitutionalism as a normative agenda calls for a legitimate international order. NGOs deserve a constitutional role in law-making and law-enforcement only if their contributions enhance the legitimacy[306] of these

---

[305] Doc MP.EIA/WG.1/2004/3 (2003), paras 7–10 and Doc MP.EIA/WG.1/2004/4 (2004) paras 5–8.

[306] 'Legitimacy' is on the one hand a social concept (to be legitimate here means in fact to be accepted or recognized), and on the other hand a normative concept (to be legitimate here means to be worthy of being recognized). Legitimacy as a social concept can be measured empirically, whereas legitimacy as a normative concept is assessed on the basis of a value judgment. Both concepts are analytically independent from each other. The normative legitimacy of an actor, e.g. an NGO, depends on the metric or yardstick that is applied. There are basically three types of yardsticks: moral, legal, and even factual ones. NGOs enjoy normative legitimacy under all three yardsticks. See on NGO legitimacy Anton Vedder (ed) *NGO Involvement in International Governance and Policy: Sources of Legitimacy* (Martinus Nijhoff Leiden 2007).

processes and their outcome. In international law-making and in law-enforcement, NGOs are apt to furnish information, offer expertise, vocalize interests,
act as opposition and counter-power or even as quasi-prosecutors (see also pp.
314–315). All this generally helps to improve the quality of the debates, of the
law-making procedures, of the international rules themselves, and might also
facilitate their effective application. In short, NGO involvement is generally apt
to improve both input- and output-legitimacy of global governance.

Legitimacy

From a constitutionalist perspective, the obvious objection against NGO
involvement in international law-making and -enforcement is that NGOs are
undemocratic and therefore potentially illegitimate. A related concern is that
NGOs pursue partial and special interests. I will address and try to alleviate these
concerns at pp. 315–318, and will argue there that NGOs do not need a
democratic mandate by the global citizenry, because they are in functional terms
the global opposition. However, the onus is on them to show that they can still
be legitimate without being internally organized in a democratic fashion. So to
what extent and under which conditions are NGOs legitimate political actors?
NGOs possess legalist legitimacy through their international accreditation. They
enjoy moral legitimacy depending on the worthiness and credibility of their aims
and mission. Their social legitimacy derived from acceptance is visible in a large
membership and broad donorship. These factors vary with the type of NGO.
For activist and service NGOs working, for example, in disaster relief or environmental protection, the effective performance of their tasks (their output) is an
important source of legitimacy. Advocacy NGOs can in theory also enjoy output
legitimacy with the caveat that drawing causality and attributing tangible success
in advocacy is very difficult. The probably more important legitimacy factor of
advocacy NGOs is therefore their credibility.

A different legitimacy problem is the blurring of the governmental sphere and
civil society:[307] 'Quangos' (quasi-governmental organizations) are emerging, and
ECOSOC increasingly accredits NGOs which are sponsored and controlled by
government and which are thus not independent.[308] This governmentalization
is most relevant for service organizations. For instance, a considerable amount of
governmental development aid is delivered via NGOs. It is not entirely clear
that this policy leads to efficiency gains. In some cases, reliance by governments
on NGOs, especially when they *de facto* become part of national bureaucracies,
may mask the inactivity of governments, and actually weaken the output
legitimacy of governance. More important even is the outright abuse of the
NGO garb by governments, especially in the human rights field. Numerous
NGOs, such as Chinese para-state mass organizations in the Human Rights

---

[307] On the blurring of the civil society and the business sphere see below p. 250.
[308] Cardoso Report, 2004, para 127.

Council, only serve their state of origin or registration by constantly praising and imitating it in general or in country-specific debates. These NGOs form a 'servile society at the UN'.[309] This type of illegitimacy can only be combated through strict requirements of independence in the screening and accreditation procedures.[310]

Probably the most serious legitimacy problem of NGOs as a group is the dominance of the north in international institutions. NGOs originating from or based in the rich industrial countries have a far disproportional impact on global law-making and -enforcement. And universal NGOs, such as Amnesty International, mostly do not have governance mechanisms to ensure that the make-up of the executive is geographically representative of the organization as a whole.

Accountability

NGO involvement can contribute to the accountability of international institutions towards citizens, and thereby enhance their legitimacy. However, constitutionalism asks for the accountability of all actors participating in the fulfilment of constitutional functions, including the NGOs themselves. NGOs are legally accountable to their 'chartering' governments, and also subject to reputational and financial accountability. As they operate in a market for donors and supporters, NGOs could not exist without social acceptance, anyway. However, financial accountability in particular is ambiguous as a source of NGO legitimacy. The mechanism of holding an organization to account through funding or rather non-funding favours NGOs which advocate 'sexy' issues, or those which attract potent, notably industrial, donors, and these are not necessarily the most urgent problems.

Only to a limited extent, NGOs satisfy cross-cutting accountability principles such as transparency, participation, evaluation, and complaint and response. They are thus only weakly accountable along those lines. In particular NGO transparency is often restricted in important areas. As a group, NGOs provide less information about their activities than international organizations and TNCs.[311] Notably the beneficiaries are rarely informed about how the money is spent.

As far as the accountability forum is concerned, many NGOs have a too broad and undefined constituency, which precludes accountability towards that constituency. For instance, many NGOs make broad claims to speak on behalf of 'the oppressed', 'the excluded', or 'youth and nature'. These NGOs cannot refer back to their 'constituency' for guidance. The beneficiaries cannot agree or disagree with certain actions or language on their behalf. Even more

---

[309] See the case-studies by Frouville, Domesticating Civil Society at the UN, 2008, 71–115.

[310] *Cf* CoE 2002, *Fundamental Principles on the Status of Non-governmental Organisations in Europe and Explanatory Memorandum* (November 2002) para 10: NGOs must be free to take positions contrary to stated government policies.

[311] Kovach *et al*, *Power without Accountability?*, 2003, at 33.

importantly, there is no clear way to resolve differences in views between two NGOs that each claim to 'represent' an equally broad constituency.[312]

Self-policing is not well developed with NGOs. It seems most advanced for humanitarian NGOs, which as a group were confronted with criticism concerning their response to the Rwandan genocide. A group of concerned NGOs developed several mechanisms of accountability: a code of conduct, a humanitarian charter, a set of technical standards, and a 'quasi-ombudsman' called the Humanitarian Accountability Project (HAP), a learning network for sharing the lessons learnt from humanitarian operations, and other mechanisms.[313]

Specific guidance on NGO accountability can be gathered from the influential ECOSOC resolution of 1996,[314] and from the more recent principles and rules of the Council of Europe.[315] The ECOSOC states as one principle to be applied in the establishment of consultative relations that the accredited NGOs shall have 'a representative structure and possess appropriate mechanisms of accountability to its members, who shall exercise effective control over its policies and actions through the exercise of voting rights or other appropriate democratic and transparent decision-making processes'.[316] In reality, however, many NGOs are accredited with the ECOSOC which do not conform to this principle.

The Council of Europe's principles state that NGOs 'structures for management and decision-making should be sensitive to the different interests of members, users, beneficiaries, boards, supervisory authorities, staff and founders'.[317] The Principles also contain provisions on 'transparency and accountability', which hold that NGOs should generally 'have their accounts audited by an institution or person independent of their management.'[318] According to the Explanatory Memorandum to the Principles, it is 'good practice' to submit an annual report on accounts and activities.[319]

However, many formal accountability requirements create additional costs for NGOs, which disproportionately burden NGOs from the global south. This fact is all the more important as the under-representation of the southern NGOs

---

[312] Riva Krut *Globalization and Civil Society: NGO Influence in International Decision-making* (United Nations Research Institute for Social Development Geneva 1997), at 25.

[313] Further references in Hugo Slim 'By what Authority? The Legitimacy and Accountability of Non-governmental Organisations' (2002) *The Journal of Humanitarian Assistance.*

[314] UN ECOSOC, *Consultative Relationship between the United Nations and Non-governmental Organizations* (UN Doc A/RES/1996/31) (resolution passed at the 49th plenary meeting of 25 July 1996).

[315] CoE, *Fundamental Principles on the Status of Non-governmental Organisations in Europe and Explanatory Memorandum* (November 2002).

[316] UN ECOSOC, *Consultative Relationship between the United Nations and Non-governmental Organizations* (UN Doc A/RES/1996/31), para 12.

[317] CoE, *Fundamental Principles,* 2002, para 46.

[318] CoE, *Fundamental Principles,* 2002, paras 60–65.

[319] CoE, *Fundamental Principles, Explanatory Memorandum,* 2002, paras 66–68.

is currently one of the main legitimacy problems of NGO involvement in global governance. So here the different, partly antagonist, factors of accountability and legitimacy must be balanced against each other.

5.6 By way of conclusion: NGO voice as a constitutional condition of global governance

In a global constitutional order, NGOs can replace neither states nor international organizations. They do not have the identical legitimacy and do not perform the identical functions. Therefore, their rights and obligations should differ from those of states.

There is currently a gap between the factual activity of NGOs and the legal framework regulating that activity.[320] The consequence of the thin or absent regulation is that bigger and stronger NGOs have an advantage. Formalization with regard to the selection and accreditation of the civil society interlocutors, the definition of the modalities of their participation, and concerning the monitoring of NGO activity would help the weaker civil society actors, notably those of the south, and thereby increase the legitimacy of NGO activism as a whole. Besides, a moderate harmonization of the respective mechanisms would serve the constitutional objective of legal clarity. With such steps, a proper constitutional framework of NGO participation in global governance would be established.

With a view to modernizing and harmonizing the accreditation mechanisms, the 2002 Council of Europe Principles form a useful guideline. These Principles represent the most sophisticated and up-to-date account of what an international organization expects from NGOs; they were adopted after a long period of consideration, and are supported by almost 50 states.[321] They are therefore apt to function as a model for the elaboration of a universal minimum on accreditation procedures. Such accreditation procedures should be complemented by NGO self-regulation. As a complementary, but not in itself sufficient device, self-policing can improve the legitimacy and the accountability of NGOs. Sectoral NGO codes of conduct can be devised for different areas.[322]

Non-governmental participation is strongly emerging as a parameter of good governance for international organizations.[323] I submit that it is also a parameter of the constitutional legitimacy of the activity of international organizations. But increasing NGO participation in international organizations is costly in terms of

---

[320] Rebasti, Beyond Consultative Status, 2008, at 32.
[321] Menno T Kamminga 'What Makes an NGO "Legitimate" in the Eyes of States?' in Anton Vedder (ed) *The Involvement of NGOs in International Governance and Policy: Sources of Legitimacy* (Martinus Nijhoff Leiden 2007) 175–195, at 180.
[322] An example is the Code of Good Practice for relief and development agencies. 'People in Aid: Code of Good Practice in the Management and Support of Aid Personnel' (2003), elaborated by relief and development NGOs.   [323] *Cf* Rebasti, Beyond Consultative Status, 2008, at 66.

time and money. Unless the value of outreach, inclusiveness, and participation exceeds these costs, global governance would be weakened, not strengthened, and thereby its output legitimacy reduced.[324] This is an additional reason for focusing, streamlining, and eventually limiting the participation modes for civil society actors.

In order to improve two decisive factors which increase the legitimacy of global governance, namely inclusiveness and broad participation, measures to counteract the skewed impact of NGOs from the north are needed. Additional financial and technical support should be given to southern NGOs, for instance through a trust fund.[325] In contrast to such targeted capacity building, quota systems such as foreseen in the African Union[326] seem problematic. They tend to hinder the bottom-up emergence of NGOs for new issues and thereby run counter to the NGO-involvement's early warning and oppositional function. Finally, coalition building, as happened, for example, with the 'Coalition for an International Criminal Court'[327] is a means of strengthening the legitimacy of NGO input in global governance, because this increases the diversity, the social acceptance, and the effectiveness of the NGO input.

From a constitutional perspective, NGOs should be given more opportunities to raise their voice for the reasons discussed in this chapter. Within the emerging global, so far more deliberative and contestatory than formal and parliamentary democracy, to which I turn in chapter 6, the NGO voice is a limited functional equivalent to the formal law-making power of international legal subjects. However, NGOs do not need and do not deserve a vote in law-making and law-enforcement, as long as they are not in themselves democratically organized and representatives of a global citizenry.

6. Business Actors

6.1 The international economic constitution as a framework for business actors

Business actors form part of the global constitutional community and are embedded in an economic constitutional framework. Transnational commercial activities have been a crucial factor for the development of international law.

---

[324] *Cf* Cardoso Report, 2004, para 25.   [325] *Cf ibid*, para 143.

[326] Quotas for NGOs representing gender and geographical concerns are foreseen in the African Union's Economic, Social and Cultural Council (ECOSOCC) statutes, adopted by the AU General Assembly with decision Assembly/AU/Dec. 42 (III), Decision on the Economic, Social and Cultural Council of 8 July 2004. The ECOSOCC is composed of 150 representatives of civil society organizations.

[327] See res ICC-ASP/2/ res 8 (2003) 'Recognition of the coordinating and facilitating role of the NGO coalition for the International Criminal Court.'

The freedom of the High Sea was proclaimed by the Dutchman Hugo de Groot with a view to Dutch mercantile interests. Trading companies such as the East India Company were vested by their nation states with broad governmental and administrative authority, and established 'titles' to territory by conquest and occupation for their home country. The entire law of diplomatic protection was developed through cases concerning transborder business activities and foreign investment.

During most of the 20th century, two basic regime types were known in the world: market economy or capitalism on the one hand, and planned economy or socialism on the other. Modern national constitutions typically contain provisions relating to the economy and lay down broad governmental responsibilities in promoting welfare. Thereby, the national constitutions give more or less clear indications which economic regime is adhered to by the state. For instance, constitutions of nations with a market economy normally contain guarantees of private property and entrepreneurial freedom as fundamental rights, and they may also endorse free competition as a constitutional principle. To that extent, national constitutions also endorse a (national) constitution of the economy.

It is more difficult to identify an international economic constitution, because ideological divisions and antagonistic interests persist among the nations of the world. It should be recalled that in the 1960s and 1970s, when many new nation states emerged from decolonization, those new states attempted to establish a 'New International Economic Order', which placed a premium on solidarity and cooperation, transfer of technology, compensatory inequality, and sovereignty over natural resources. But this paradigm met resistance by the old and rich states, and only isolated elements of it became part of international hard law. With regard to questions such as compensation for expropriations, open dissents remained and prevented the formation of universal customary law.

Although after the break-up of the Soviet Union the socialist block more or less crumbled, there are still states which reject market economy and endorse planned economy without necessarily naming it as such, for instance North Korea and Cuba. Additionally, the north–south divergence persists. The attitudes and interests concerning the proper role and place of private business espoused by rich industrialized states on the one hand and poor, developing, rather agricultural states on the other hand, differ in many respects.

Still, some basic tenets can be identified today. The quasi-universal WTO which now has 153 members firmly entrenches the principle of national treatment and the most favoured nation clause and thereby established a regime of free trade. However, free trade as such hardly amounts to a global constitutional principle, *inter alia* because agricultural states do not benefit that much from it. In theory, trade liberalization among nations does not require market economy within the states, but can also be realized by state economies. In practice, however, accession conditions fuelling reform in the direction of a liberal market economy have been imposed by the WTO. The most important recent case is the PR China, which has been obliged to introduce far-reaching reforms on transparency (publication of laws) and judicial review by impartial and independent tribunals.[328] Also, the basic GATT principles of non-discrimination and the most favoured nation clause constrain governments whose decision-making processes are structurally biased in favour of well-organized and powerful protectionist interests, and in that regard perform a constitutional function as well.[329]

The second economic constitutional principle is the guarantee of private property (at least for foreigners). For ideological reasons, the property guarantee of Article 17 UNDHR was neither endorsed in the original ECHR nor in the UN Human Rights Covenants. However, a human right to private property is guaranteed in all world regions except Asia by Article 1 of the 1st Protocol to the ECHR, Article 21 ACHR, and Article 14 African Charter of Human Rights. Although important states still do not, or only in a very limited fashion, protect the private property of their own citizens in domestic law, there is a clear tendency in that direction, which is promoted by the United Nations.[330] Thus, the guarantee of private property seems to be crystallizing into a customary law-based universal minimum for every person independent of transborder activity. In any case, the protection of foreign property forms part of international law. It is in principle recognized in international customary law, and full compensation for infringements and expropriations is guaranteed through a dense web of bilateral investment treaties whose contents reflect the interests and the superior bargaining power of the capital-exporting states.

The trend to privatization and liberalization within nation states, which had already begun in western industrial countries in the 1980s, has been fully endorsed by those international organizations which are dominated by western states. Thus, the World Bank, under the heading of 'good governance' and with its instrument of conditioned loans, has incited and supported reforms in the direction of market economy and liberalization in numerous countries.

Overall, there is a rudimentary international constitutional order which embeds transnational business. The ensuing question, to which I turn now, is which constitutional status transnational business actors have and should possess within this global economic constitution.

---

[328] Part I, 2. (C) and (D) of the Protocol on the Accession, endorsed by decision of the Ministerial Conference of 23 November 2001 (WT/L/432) on the Accession of the People's Republic of China. See Jiangyu Wang 'The Rule of Law in China: A Realistic View of the Jurisprudence, the Impact of the WTO, and the Prospects for Future Devleopment' (2004) *Singapore Journal of Legal Studies* 347–389.   [329] See p. 205–206.

[330] General Assembly *Respect for the right of everyone to own property alone as well as in association with others and its contribution to the social and economic development of member states* (res 45/98 (1990)).

6.2 Rendering business actors responsible

Today, many firms have higher revenues than the budgets of poor states. In times of liberalization and privatization, they often perform functions which have previously been considered as 'public'. Their business activity touches upon the interests and rights not only of employees, but also of consumers, tax payers, contractors, and of other groups affected by business operations.

Against this background, it has long been debated whether TNCs[331] (or multinational enterprises, MNEs)[332] enjoy or should enjoy international legal personality.[333] The first argument in favour is that powerful business actors deal with states on an equal footing and have therefore in functional terms been internationalized. The proponents' second argument relies on the extensive practice of state contracts between states and firms. By concluding a state contract with a firm, so the argument goes, the contracting state implicitly recognizes the private party as an international legal subject. This debate resembles the parallel one on NGOs as potential subjects of international law. As there, I suggest shifting the perspective. The two doctrinal arguments just mentioned are not really convincing, but the intention behind them is praiseworthy: it is to render transnational business actors responsible under international law by transforming them into addressees of international legal obligations.

The same intention underlies the discussion on human rights obligations and responsibilities of transnational enterprises. Soft regulation to that effect has

[331] The broad term 'transnational corporation' is used within the UN family, and denotes a variety of cross-border arrangements and alliances, independent of their precise legal form.

[332] The term 'MNE' is used in the OECD. See the OECD Guidelines on Multinational Enterprises of 2000, which apply to: 'companies or other entities established in more than one country and so linked that they may co-ordinate their operations in various ways. While one or more of these entities may be able to exercise a significant influence over the activities of others, their degree of autonomy within the enterprise may vary widely from one multinational enterprise to another. Ownership may be private, state or mixed.' OECD Guidelines for Multinational Enterprises of 8 November 2000 (DAFFE/IME(2000)20), concepts and principles, para 3.

[333] For the minoritarian position that TNCs (already) are international legal persons see Georg Dahm, Jost Delbrück, and Rüdiger Wolfrum *Völkerrecht* (2nd edn de Gruyter Berlin 2002) vol I/3, at 531; Matthias Herdegen *Internationales Wirtschaftsrecht* (3rd edn Beck München 2002), at 234; Waldemar Hummer in Hans-Peter Neuhold, Waldemar Hummer, and Christoph Schreuer (eds) *Österreichisches Handbuch des Völkerrechts* (4th edn Manz Wien 2004) vol 1, at 238; Pierre-Marie Dupuy *Droit international public* (7th edn Dalloz Paris 2004), at 263. For a subtle analysis concluding that TNCs presumptively enjoy international legal personality see Karsten Nowrot 'Nun sag, wie hast du's mit den Global Players? Fragen an die Völkerrechtsgemeinschaft zur internationalen Rechtsstellung transnationaler Unternehmen' (2004) 79 *Die Friedens-Warte* 119–150; Karsten Nowrot *Normative Ordnungsstruktur und private Wirkungsmacht: Konsequenzen der Beteiligung transnationaler Unternehmen an den Rechtssetzungsprozessen im internationalen Wirtschaftssystem* (Berliner Wissenschaftsverlag 2006), at 562–595.

been worked out,[334] but no international convention has been agreed on. There is a tendency, especially in the recent reports of the Special Representative of the Secretary General on the issue of human rights and transnational corporations and other business enterprises, to obscure the legal basis of potential human rights obligations of business actors, and instead to postulate that business is somehow responsible.[335] A constitutionally informed approach to the issue can here contribute clarity. By applying the domestic constitutional construct of a '*Drittwirkung*' (third-party effect)[336] of fundamental rights in a parallel fashion to international law, human rights as enshrined in the international covenants could be made opposable also to private actors. However, such a direct third-party effect risks violating the private autonomy of business actors which has a constitutional value itself. Most importantly, this construct probably releases states too easily from responsibility. A merely indirect third-party or horizontal effect and the corresponding governmental duty to protect human rights holders from private threats is a more appropriate doctrinal approach, taken directly from the constitutional toolbox. Indirect third-party effect means that firms will not directly be bound by human rights covenants to whom they are not a party, but that all states parties' have the specific and heightened obligation to enact and enforce domestic law which guarantees that the result will be to hold firms fully liable for falling short of similar standards as those established by the Covenants. This construct offers the systematic or doctrinal advantage of respecting that firms are not themselves parties to the human rights instruments, and of not releasing governments from their responsibility, while being sufficiently strict to protect workers and populations from obnoxious business activity.[337] The crucial problem of this construct is, however, the situation of firms acting in weak or failing states which will not enact and enforce the appropriate regulation. Here, the residual inter-governmental duty to protect must come into play. Specific and targeted international action must hold

---

[334] See the OECD Guidelines for Multinational Enterprises of 27 June 2000 (DAFFE/IME/WPG (2000)15/FINAL) and the ILO's Tripartite Declaration of Principles Concerning Multinational Enterprises and Social Policy of 17 November 2000 ((2002) 41 ILM 186 *et seq.*). See for the UN the following documents: Norms of the Responsibilities of Transnational Corporations and Other Business Enterprises of the UN Sub-Commission on the Promotion and Protection of Human Rights (UN Doc E/CN.4/Sub.2/2003//12/Rev.2 (2003) of 13 August 2003); Report of the United Nations High Commissioner on Human Rights on the responsibilities of transnational corporations and related business enterprises with regard to human rights (UN Doc E/CN.4/2005/91 of 15 February 2005).

[335] *Promotion and protection of all human rights, civil, political, economic, social and cultural rights, including the right to development* ('Ruggie report', Human Rights Council Doc A/HRC/8/5 of 7 April 2008) with Addendum (Human Rights Council Doc A/HRC/8/5/Add. 2, of 23 May 2008).

[336] See Evert A Alkema 'The Third-Party Applicability or "Drittwirkung" of the European Convention on Human Rights' in Franz Matscher and Heinrich Petzold (eds) *Protecting Human Rights: The European Dimension (Studies in Hounour of Gérard J Wierarda)* (Carl Heymanns Verlag Köln 1988) 33–45.

[337] See in that direction also John H Knox 'Horizontal Human Rights Law' (2008) 102 *AJIL* 1–47.

business actors responsible if, but only if, host states do not live up to their regulatory responsibility.

A similar question of ultimate responsibility arises in the field of international humanitarian law, which risks being undermined by 'corporate warriors'.[338] The privatization of security (military and police) has a specific constitutional dimension for two reasons: first because conducting war has traditionally been a core 'public' activity, generally reserved to states, and second, because the privatization of the military and police function (within states and across borders) potentially erodes the monopoly on the legitimate use of force (both nationally and transnationally). Against this background, the recent international code regulating the activities of private military and security companies (PMSCs), the 'Montreux Document',[339] has a constitutional dimension. The Montreux Document resulted from an international process launched by the ICRC and the Swiss government and is so far supported by 31 states. While endorsed by the Security Council and the General Assembly and published as a UN document, the press releases accompanying this publication make clear that the Montreux Document is legally non-binding. It thus manifests the trend towards non-legal forms of global governance described in chapter 3. The Montreux Document consists of a restatement of the existing pertinent international legal obligations of states relating to PMSCs, and of a set of good practices. Its objectives are to hold states responsible and to prevent them from shirking their obligations under international humanitarian law through privatization. The decisive anchor for holding all involved states (contracting states, territorial states, and home states of the PMSCs) responsible in this context is the states' duty not only to respect, but also to 'ensure respect' for international humanitarian law as prescribed by common Article 1 of the Geneva Conventions. This provision has here been interpreted dynamically so as not only to reach out to third states as a kind of *erga omnes* obligation,[340] but to encompass a governmental duty to protect persons against private actors, e.g. by stringent licensing procedures and strict monitoring of private military companies. Although the companies' employees on the ground are themselves obliged to comply with international humanitarian law, and may incur international (criminal) responsibility for violations, the initiators of the Montreux process obviously deemed this to be insufficient to guarantee effective compliance with international humanitarian law. The Montreux Document is an example of the insistence of international law on hard and even intensified state obligations, even where the actual performance of previously public functions has been outsourced.

---

[338] Peter W Singer *Corporate Warriors: The Rise of the Privatized Military Industry* (Cornell UP Ithaca NY 2003).

[339] Montreux Document of 17 September 2008, Annex to UN Doc A/63/467-S/2008/636 (2008).   [340] *Erga omnes obligation* in its pre-Barcelona Traction meaning.

To conclude, in both fields just discussed, international human rights law and international humanitarian law, the responsibilities of states have not disappeared but have been refocused on delegation and supervision, and have thus been transformed into a duty to protect. This design satisfies the constitutional quest for containment of political or quasi-political power by non-state actors while securing the ultimate responsibility of states.

6.3 International partnerships, outsourcing public functions, and constitutional limits

The international institutions acknowledge economic corporations as political actors and seek to engage them in 'public' activity. This phenomenon constitutes to some extent a kind of privatization of global governance which mirrors the domestic trend towards privatization. After the global political seismic shift of 1989, the United Nations started to undertake great efforts to cooperate with the private sector. The Johannesburg Summit on Sustainable Development of 2002 envisaged 'type 2 outcomes', i.e. voluntary targets and agreements between industry, governments, and NGOs[341] to complement the inter-governmental commitments ('type 1 outcomes'). Secretary General Kofi Annan (1997–2006) proclaimed that the interests of business converge with the fundamental principles of the United Nations, namely peace, development, and equity.[342] He therefore urged business to assume responsibility and to engage not only in sustainable development, but also in areas which are seemingly unrelated to business activity, such as conflict prevention. The Secretary General also launched the Global Compact, an instrument which calls on business leaders to subscribe to ten internationally acknowledged principles in the areas of human rights, labour, environment, and anti-corruption.[343]

A conspicuous field in which the UN attempts to involve business is military conflict and peace-building. This is noteworthy because it relates to the very core of the UN mandate. At least under Annan, it was the UN's official position that while the principal responsibility to prevent military conflicts rests with governments, this subject also concerns business. Private enterprises produce and sell the necessary military material. They are involved in the exploitation of

---

[341] Johannesburg Plan of Implementation, revised version of 23 September 2002 (Doc A/CONF.199/20), para 49.

[342] Press Release SG/SM/9256 SC/8059 'Role of Business in Armed Conflict can be Crucial'— 'for good and for ill'. Remarks of the Secretary General before the Security Council on 15 April 2004.

[343] <http://www.globalcompact.org>. See in scholarship Oliver F Williams (ed) *Peace through Commerce—Responsible Corporate Citizenship and the Ideals of the United Nations Global Compact* (University of Notre Dame Press 2008).

natural resources around which many recent military conflicts turn.[344] On the other hand, firms need a stable environment to conduct their business. The argument was that because violent strife disturbs or prevents commercial activities in the concerned regions, economic actors have an interest, and also the capacity to contribute to conflict prevention and to post-conflict peace building, complementary to governments.[345]

A 2005 report of the Secretary General heralded 'partnerships' between the United Nations and business as a novel policy instrument.[346] Because such private–public partnerships are intended to contribute to the realization of important public functions, while at the same time raising problems of accountability and transparency, they have a constitutional significance.[347] The report enumerates four functions of partnerships: to perform advocacy, to develop norms and standards, to share and coordinate resources and expertise, and finally to harness markets for development. It asks for a 'partnership mainstreaming' of the United Nations. Most importantly, the Secretary General here presents the partnerships as a catalyst of institutional reform and innovation of the United Nations itself in the direction of a more outward-looking, more impact-oriented organization, as a stimulus for the diffusion of improved management practices and for enhancing a performance-based thinking.[348] This approach copies the administrative reforms that have been pursued within western nation states since the 1980s under the label of 'new public management'. From a constitutional perspective, this approach is quite risky, because the price of more flexibility and more effectiveness-orientation may well be losses in terms of the rule of law (principle of legality and precise attribution of competences and responsibilities). Also, national constitutional and administrative experience has shown that the effectiveness-gains through New Public Management are less great than initially expected.

The question here arises whether constitutionalism places some intrinsic limitations on the 'commercialization' of public institutions and on the transfer

---

[344] For instance, an expert panel mandated by the Security Council established a link between the (illegal) exploitation of natural resources in Congo by private enterprises and the war in the region. *Final report of the Panel of Experts on the Illegal Exploitation of Natural Resources and Other Forms of Wealth of the Democratic Republic of the Congo* (UN Doc S/2002/1146 of 16 October 2002).

[345] See various publications of the Global Compact Office: *Business Guide for Conflict Impact Assessment and Risk Management* (2002); *Enabling Economies of Peace: Public Policy for Conflict-Sensitive Business* (2005). In scholarship Allan Gerson 'Peace Building: The Private Sector's Role' (2001) 95 *AJIL* 102–119; Andreas Wenger and Daniel Möckli *Conflict Prevention. The Untapped Potential of the Business Sector* (Lynne Rienner Boulder 2003).

[346] UN General Assembly 2005, *Enhanced Cooperation Between the United Nations and All Relevant Partners, in Particular the Private Sector. Report of the Secretary General* (A/60/214). The report gives numerous examples of partnerships between business actors and UN sub-organizations or programmes. The UNDP has a 'Partnership Bureau' with a 'Private Sector Division'.

[347] The Secretary General's report realizes that the conflicting objectives of action and impact-orientation must be balanced against securing accountability (*ibid* para 14).

[348] *Ibid* paras 32, 60, 62, 63.

of previously governmental responsibilities, notably core responsibilities such as peace and security, onto business actors. Put differently, the question is whether there is a kind of governmental reserved domain. But such a *domaine reservé* is hard to identify and to circumscribe. The ideas about which tasks or functions are 'public' and therefore are inevitably incumbent on states, and may not be left to the private sector, have dramatically changed through the history of the nation state. Theoretical models and political implementation have ranged from the 18th century police and welfare state with extensive powers in all areas of life, to the minimal state of the 1990s. The dividing line between public and private functions rather seems to depend on tradition, habit, and political choice. Even hard core state functions, linked to the use of physical force, such as waging war, police, jails, and customs administration, have in recent years been privatized.

The most promising approach to identify intrinsic state functions seemed to be the theory of public goods. Public goods are non-rivaled and non-exclusive, therefore free riders cannot be prevented, and no market price emerges. According to the theory, public goods by definition cannot be furnished by markets and must therefore be provided by states. If the theory worked, it would thus provide a clear intrinsic barrier against privatization which could be relied on by constitutionalism. However, the scope and application of the theory of public goods has recently been highly restricted by many economists. In practice, even prime cases of seemingly public goods, such as clean air and biodiversity, have been more or less successfully marketized, as the Kyoto Protocol-based carbon emissions trade and the market mechanisms of the Biodiversity Convention show. So it seems as if no intrinsic limits to privatization exist, but that those limits can only be established normatively, relying on historically contingent value judgments about what is incumbent on states. I submit that these value judgments should be derived from constitutionalism. Privatization, also on the international level, must not undermine the rule of law and democracy. If a mechanism to secure constitutionalist values can be found, outsourcing is in order.

6.4 International law-making with business actors

The most important formal constitutional functions are law-making and law-enforcement. I will now discuss how business (through companies, branch associations, and through professionals and experts) does and should participate therein.

Business actors have become 'regulatory entrepreneurs' in various ways[349] (on this also see chapter 3). First, business lobbies the elaboration of international

---

[349] This section greatly benefitted from Nowrot, *Normative Ordnungsstruktur*, 2006; Tully, *Corporations and International Lawmaking*, 2007.

conventions. This mainly happens on the national level, where companies influence the prior negotiating position of home states, and also the subsequent implementation of conventions. Examples for intense lobbying by business actors, probably with a real impact on the outcome of the treaty negotiations, are the United Nations Convention on the Law of the Sea (UNCLOS), the Convention on Bio-Diversity, the Vienna Convention on the Protection of the Ozone Layer, and the Framework Convention on Climate Change (UNFCCC).

Besides, business engages in various forms of more or less soft regulation. Economic private actors are participating in the elaboration of the *lex mercatoria,* which oscillates between private and public, and between hard and soft law. Firms adopt technical, product, and professional standards, often in joint private–public standard-setting, where transnational private standardizers are closely supervised by public authority. Companies also create company or multi-stakeholder codes of conducts, notably in the field of labour, environment, and human rights. Increasingly, multinational corporations conclude 'agreements' with international organizations.[350] From a formal legal perspective, neither type of corporate self- and co-regulation produces ordinary hard (international) law. However, all these shades of hybrid regulation are functionally equivalent to state or inter-state hard law when they do influence behaviour and are complied with. This observation suggests, from a constitutional perspective which asks for secondary rules on law-making, not to leave the respective business activity completely unregulated.

The participation of business actors in rule-making raises similar problems to the involvement of NGOs which was discussed on pp. 225–227, and additionally some specific ones. In business, there is a north–south cleavage in the same way as there is one with regard to civil society actors. Participation tends to be limited to corporations which are registered or have their headquarters in industrial states. States of the global south, which are generally jealous of their sovereignty *vis-à-vis* business, are additionally concerned about this northern dominance. A remedy would be to bring the International Chamber of Commerce (ICC) to facilitate greater participation in international rule-making by corporations from developing states.[351]

A specific concern which is particularly salient for business involvement in international law-making is the problem of 'double-dipping'. Non-state actors (but only those who possess the necessary resources) may present their views on upcoming regulation both on the national and on the international policy level. Corporations rather than NGOs have these resources and can utilize well-established lobbying techniques. It is criticized that the impact of business is

---

[350] See for an early example the Atlanta Agreement of 14 February 1997 concluded between the ILO, UNICEF, and the Sialkot Chamber of Commerce and Industry. The Agreement seeks to eliminate child labour in the soccer ball industry in the Sialkot disctrict in Pakistan, which produces nearly 75% of the world's hand-stitched soccer-balls.

[351] Tully, *Corporations and International Lawmaking,* 2007, at 337.

thereby in an unfair way doubled. But this critique can be dismantled by unveiling its underlying assumption, namely the assumption that private actors should be entirely mediated on the international plane by their state. Given the blurring of the international and the domestic sphere, this view is no longer appropriate. In multi-level governance, all actors, both the governmental and the non-state ones, do and should be allowed to play the multi-level game.

In the current legal framework on the participation of non-state actors in international law-making, the societal and market sphere are blurred. The accreditation rules of international organizations, bodies, and conferences normally do not differentiate between public interest-oriented, non-profit organizations (genuine NGOs), and 'BINGOs' (business interest organizations). For instance, the ICC enjoys general observer status under Article 71 UN Charter and the 1996 ECOSOC rules. This allow firms to masquerade as NGOs and thus to participate in law-making. The ICC can have itself represented by firms, which resulted in waste traders participating as ICC members in negotiations on the Basle Convention on the Transboundary Movements of Hazardous Waste, and producers of ozone-depleting substances representing the ICC in issues relating to the Montreal Protocol. Also, TNCs have been involved in Codex alimentarius standard setting where they seek to use the Codex to legitimize standards, definitions, and the composition of their own products.[352]

From a constitutional perspective, this state of the law is too undifferentiated. As a constitutionally informed observer, I would prefer international law to reflect the three-sector model in which—besides the state—civil society and business pertain to different spheres. Admittedly, there is no watertight distinction between the three spheres. Some NGOs are commercialized and *de facto* professional service agencies,[353] and some firms act as corporate citizens. Nevertheless, it still matters that civil society actors ideally pursue primarily public interests, while business actors are mainly profit-driven (and legitimately so). If one accepts the three-sector model, NGOs and business should not enjoy the identical participatory conditions in the elaboration of international law. Although the consultation ('voice') of business actors prior to international law- and decision-making, e.g. through business expert groups or advisory committees, may in principle be appropriate for certain types of rule-making, screening and transparency requirements must be stricter than for NGOs in order to prevent corruption. In contrast to NGOs, business does not yet and should not acquire any legitimate expectation to participate in international law-making

---

[352] All three examples from Riva Krut *Globalization and Civil Society: NGO Influence in International Decision-making* (United Nations Research Institute for Social Development Geneva 1997), at 24.

[353] For instance, AI has been criticized for a 'trade with human rights violations', because the Danish section of AI sells to investors information on the human rights situation in potential host countries.

unless the business actors specifically demonstrate their commitment to the public interest.

6.5 The enforcement of international hard and soft law by business actors

The most prominent entirely 'privatized' enforcement mechanism of international hard law by business actors is the ICSID scheme. Under ICSID, private investors can sue host states for breach of the host state's investment-related treaties with the investor, and for breaches of inter-state bilateral investment treaties (BITs) before international arbitral tribunals. The BITs typically contain guarantees of investment protection which go beyond property rights. In doctrinal terms, it is still controversial whether these inter-state treaties create material legal relations between the host state and the foreign investor. The traditionalist view has been that that BITs only protect investors' interests and thus grant third-party benefits, whereas the actual treaty obligations are not owed to the private investors, but to their state of origin.[354] That understanding relied on the traditional complete mediation of individuals by their states and on the availability of diplomatic protection. From a constitutionalist perspective which favours individual agency, the BITs should be interpreted as bestowing substantive international rights, not merely benefits, on private (moral or natural) persons. The true 'owners' of these rights are the investors, and not the contracting state party.[355] The doctrinal debate just mentioned (states' rights or investors' rights?) reflects the policy dualism of investment protection which is both 'private' and 'public'. The objective of BITs and of the ICSID scheme is not only to protect the private interests of investors in secure investment conditions, but also to allow an accommodation of the regulatory interests of host states. The facilitation of capital flows is itself a public interest of host states and capital exporting states. Moreover, the flow and protection of capital, which is thus both a private and a public concern, must be balanced against other, potentially conflicting regulatory objectives such as environmental protection.

From a constitutionalist perspective which seeks to reconcile private liberty with the public interest, one problem is that both BITs and state contracts between investors and host states constrain the policy options of host states

---

[354] See in this sense, e.g., German Constitutional Court (BVerfG), 2 BvM 1/03 order of the second senate of 8 May 2007, para 54, engl transl available via <www.bverfg.de>. The Court pointed out 'that private individuals are able to complain as claimants of the violation of an international agreement concluded between states. In terms of content, therefore, the violation of an obligation is complained of which *is owed not directly to the private applicant, but to his or her home state*, although the protective purpose of the agreement targets the interests of private investors.' (Emphasis added).

[355] See in this sense Zachary Douglas 'The Hybrid Foundations of Investment Treaty Arbitration' (2004) 74 *BYIL* 151–290, at 160–184 under the heading: 'To Whom are Investment Treaty Obligations Owed?'.

without establishing international (inter-state) institutions that regulate corporations. Therefore the host states themselves remain the repository of regulatory authority. The wide acceptance of the ICSID scheme does not imply that states have sacrificed all other governmental priorities for the sake of facilitating capital flows, but only shows that states have accepted a forum which reviews the relevant policy choices. However, by granting (only) private investors the possibility of suing host states, it is entirely left to the investors rather than to the states parties to enforce the investment protection guarantees. The ICSID scheme has thus laid public interests partly in private hands. This does not necessarily 'skew' the system in favour of business interests against the community as a whole, but carries the risk of marginalizing the specifically (global) public interests, which are also involved.[356]

The public law, as opposed to private law features of the ICSID scheme of international investment arbitration have recently been highlighted by Gus van Harten.[357] Investment arbitration is distinct from traditional commercial arbitration, mostly because its context is a regulatory one, and because the main remedy available is state liability. Also, ICSID differs from commercial arbitration where two private parties agree freely on arbitrators, because in ICISD, the state's consent is prospective, and because the arbitration can be triggered only by the investor. These insights can be translated in a constitutionalist language, and gain salience from that perspective. I submit that, due to the public law character of the entire scheme, the adjudication should satisfy constitutional standards. But here deficits are visible. The investment arbitrators are not sufficiently accountable, as there is no judicial review of their decisions. Next, the system does not satisfy the standard of openness. It also lacks coherence because there is no appellate body as, for example, in the WTO. Finally and most critically, the arbitrators are financially dependent on two powerful actors: the executive officials of host states and prospective claimants.[358] The overall conclusion is that the privatization of dispute settlement effected by ICSID is partly inappropriate. Arguably, independent and tenured judges would be better suited to satisfy basic standards of judicial decision-making in a democratic society. The ICSID method of adjudication is thus 'tainted' and 'fails to deliver on the promise of the rule of law'.[359] The recommendation is that—last but not least because of the regulatory and genuinely public interests at stake—investment disputes should rather be entrusted to an international investment court.

---

[356] See Tai-Heng Cheng 'Power, Authority, and International Investment Law' (2005) 20 *American University International Law Review* 465–520 for the argument that international investment law as it stands shifts power and authority from states to investors and tribunals. The paper recommends modifications to secure both inter-state equities and investor-state equities and thereby to 'promote global well being'.

[357] Gus van Harten *Investment Treaty Arbitration and Public Law* (OUP Oxford 2007), esp. at 95–96.   [358] *Ibid*, at 167–175.

[359] *Ibid*, at 153.

In contrast to ICSID, another corpus of international rules which *inter alia* protect business interests, namely WTO law, has so far remained within the traditional inter-state mode of law enforcement. Because the WTO regime ultimately concerns importers and exporters, the constitutionalist perspective of empowerment seems to suggest a paradigm shift. Would it not be appropriate, as a matter of a constitutional design of a fair judiciary, to grant private (business) actors direct access to WTO dispute settlement? This seems all the more desirable as long as the functionally equivalent route, namely traders' access to domestic courts with the complaint that WTO law has been breached, remains barred.[360] Such a direct access of private parties would liberate business actors from the tutelage of their governments which are often reluctant to institute WTO proceedings. The governmental choices to bring or not to bring a particular WTO case to the dispute settlement forum are often not guided by the importance and merits of the issue, but are influenced by diplomatic considerations on the general relations with another country, by an eventual desire to maintain a legal question undecided, or by the lobbying power or weakness of an industry sector. These policy considerations are neglectful of the rule of law, and they lead to unequal treatment of business actors.

The privatization of WTO dispute settlement would remedy these problems and better respect the rule of law and equal protection. Because self-interested commercial actors have a strong incentive to sue, it would moreover strengthen the GATT by terminating underenforcement. It would finally relieve governments through the avoidance of political tensions.

But such a privatization may go too far. Given the fact that the military option is largely foreclosed, economic and trade regulation is nowadays the main foreign policy instrument of governments. Just like investment protection, the regulation of trade flows is intrinsically dualist: it concerns both the public and private interests. Governments litigating before the WTO dispute settlement institutions are therefore often counselled by the interested business actors.[361] This duality should be more clearly acknowledged and regulated under due consideration for the public and private concerns at stake. For instance, it could be questioned to what extent the interest in business secrecy, which is protected through the non-disclosure of business confidential information by the litigating states parties,[362] really outweighs the public interest in the transparency and publicity of the proceedings.

---

[360] As shown at p. 207, the direct effect of WTO law is currently generally rejected by the states parties and by domestic courts (including the ECJ), basically in order to maintain reciprocity among the contracting parties.

[361] For example the WTO dispute raised by the USA against Japan concerning photographic film and paper has for this reason been perceived as a '*Kodak v Fuji*'-dispute, see *Japan—Measures Affecting Consumer Photographic Film and Paper*, WTO Doc WT/DS44/R (1995).

[362] WTO, *Canada—Measures Affecting the Export of Civilian Aircraft*, panel report WT/DS70 (1999), para 9.68 and Appellate Body Report, WT/DS70/AB/R, paras 141 *et seq.*

Ultimately, it must be kept in mind that the public and the private interests at stake need not coincide. The appropriate constitutional design of WTO dispute settlement therefore seems not to remove it completely from governmental control, but to uphold it as a basically inter-state system while greatly increasing and formalizing the participatory opportunities of private actors,[363] and in parallel reconsidering the direct effect of WTO law.

A final example of potential privatized implementation of international hard law is the Kyoto Protocol. It is currently debated whether companies can participate in the Clean Development Mechanism independent of the ratification of the Protocol by their home state.[364]

A yet different matter is the enforcement of business self- and co-regulation. The *lex mercatoria* is created and enforced entirely through commercial arbitration, and professional standards are often monitored and enforced by professional associations. Such enforcement action has at some point been authorized by states, but this authorization is very distant. It is hardly meaningful to ascribe governmental delegated authority to those private enforcers.

Transnational industry standards and codes of conduct are normally enforced entirely through soft mechanisms, namely through monitoring and certification, evaluation of compliance, but not by courts. The mechanisms may be either purely internal (self-evaluation), or performed by governments, NGOs, or experts. Examples of certification schemes with independent accredited certifying bodies are the forest management standards set by the Forest Stewardship Council (FSC),[365] or 'Social Accountability 8000 (SA 8000)'.[366] But even third-party evaluations, auditing, monitoring, and certification may be too lenient, depending on who the evaluators are. In particular, local auditors and certifiers may be insufficiently independent, due to conflicts of interest, financial ties, or corruption. Under the premise that international constitutional law should strike a balance between respecting business' private autonomy and bringing powerful business actors to comply with international standards, self-regulation

---

[363] See Gregory Shaffer *Defending Interests: Public-Private Partnerships in WTO-Litigation* (Brooking Institution Press Washington DC 2003).

[364] Martijn Wilder 'Can Companies or Entities from a Non-Party to the Kyoto-Protocol Participate in a Flexible Mechanism?' in David Freestone and Charlotte Streck (eds) *Legal Aspects of Implementing the Kyoto Protocol Mechanisms: Making Kyoto Work* (OUP Oxford 2005) 249–262.

[365] <http://www.fsc.org/>. See in scholarship Stéphane Guéneau 'Certification as a New Private Global Forest Governance System: The Regulatory Potential of the Forest Stewardship Council' in Anne Peters, Lucy Koechlin, Till Förster, Gretta Fenner Zinkernagel (eds) *Non-state Actors as Standard-Setters* (CUP Cambridge 2009) 379–408. FSC-International establishes principles and criteria of compliance and accredits independent third party certification bodies. The accredited certifying bodies then check whether individual operators comply with the FSC forest management standards and, if so, issue a certificate guaranteeing compliance. Certification bodies can also certify operators against indicators drawn up by national FSC initiatives if these are recognized by FSC-International.

[366] SA 8000 was in 1997 establishd by the NGO 'Council on Economic Priorities and Accreditation Agency' (CEPAA), today 'Social Accountability International'. The SA 8000 standards relate especially to labour rights <http://www.sa-intl.org/-data/n_001/resources/live/2008 StdEnglishFinal.pdf>.

should be encouraged, but rendered enforceable. To this end, international courts and tribunals are not available. Rather, the most appropriate forums seem to be domestic courts, acting upon product liability claims or deceit liability by consumers and competitors, and litigation based on employment contracts.

Concluding the discussion of law-enforcement through business actors, it might be highlighted that privatization is in this area least advanced. But it is also the least recommended in constitutional terms, because a separation of powers between the objects, subjects, and enforcers of regulation should be maintained.

6.6 The legitimacy of business actors

From a constitutionalist perspective, business actors are *prima facie* not legitimized to perform (global) governance functions, because they do not enjoy any democratic mandate. Law-making and law-enforcement differs from the usual business activity of concluding contracts on a horizontal basis, because norms with a general scope address and bind not only the norm-creators themselves (like a contract), but third parties who are not the authors of these norms. Private autonomy and consent cannot justify business' international law-making activity, let alone its enforcement.

A different basis of legitimacy for governance by business could be delegation by governments. If the states had permissibly delegated the law-making (and even law-enforcement) authority to private actors, these standards would be presumptively legitimate, because of the overall legitimacy and authority of states to produce norms. However, is the extensive and highly dynamic and private (global) governance really merely a delegated exercise? The delegation perspective is just the beginning, not the end of the question for the basis of legitimacy of privatized governance.

It can be said that the involvement of business in global legal processes is apt to increase the effectiveness of the processes, and thus their output legitimacy. Particularly in the highly complex context of global economy, national governments lack the information and the capacity to regulate issues which transcend the nation state. The involvement of global business actors might compensate for this loss of regulatory capacity. Business actors bring in their expertise and their skills to design economically viable solutions. In fact, governmental and inter-governmental regulation has arguably become dependent upon the economic data and technical solutions offered by firms. Further, the involvement of TNCs in law-making creates a sense of ownership and therefore facilitates the subsequent implementation of norms. Finally, their more formalized inclusion could eliminate the informal attempts to influence global governance processes, such as the tobacco industry's campaign against the UN and WHO.[367]

---

[367] See WHO, *Tobacco Company Strategies to Undermine Tobacco Control Activities at the World Health Organisation: Report of the Committee of Experts on Tobacco Industry Documents* (Geneva 2000).

On the other hand, business' involvement can also make law-making less effective, because it protracts, delays, or distorts standards, or may offset initiatives by others. But the most obvious danger of the participation of TNCs in law-making and especially in law-enforcement is that this amounts to making the fox guard the henhouse. TNCs are primarily profit driven, and their novel role as 'corporate citizens' is at best a secondary one. Firms do not per se pursue any however defined (global) public interest, but first of all seek to make money. As UNICEF Executive Director Carol Bellamy pointed out in response to the then UN Secretary General Kofi Annan's far-reaching proposals to engage the United Nations more with business: '[I]t is dangerous to assume that the goals of the private sector are somehow synonymous with those of the United Nations, because they most emphatically are not.'[368] TNCs are interested in cooperating with international institutions in global governance not for the common good, but because global standards will minimize trade barriers resulting from national regulation, because they hope to influence global rules in their favour, gain prestige ('bluewash'), and finally because they can use the international forums to directly sponsor their own products. TNCs also seek to embed 'best practices' to squeeze out competitors. This fact blurs the line between agreements on standards among firms and unfair anti-competitive understandings.

Nevertheless, even corporate profit-driven activity may have beneficial spillover effects for the public: it satisfies consumer needs, gives employment, and increases wealth. It is therefore also in the global public interest not to subject business to standards that kill off their incentive to make profit. Also, the dangers of TNCs' involvement in global governance, notably the danger of capture by profit interests, is to some extent mitigated by the fact the global business is by no means a monolithical block with uniform objectives. For instance, during the negotiations of the Kyoto Protocol, which was quite intensely lobbied by business, the energy sector and the insurance sector had opposing interests,[369] which meant that their antagonist inputs contributed to a more balanced solution. But all considered, there is still the real danger that global governance is unduly commercialized through business involvement.

6.7 The accountability of business actors

Accountability is a core value of constitutionalism. Firms now generally assume a (limited) accountability towards external stakeholders. This extension of the accountability forum is justified, because firms have become political actors, as discussed above. However, the extension so far remains an abstract matter of principle. The precise degree and form of accountability *vis-à-vis* those broader

---

[368] Carol Bellamy 'Public, Private, and Civil Society' Speech of 16 April 1999.
[369] Nowrot, *Normative Ordnungsstruktur*, 2006, at 235 with further references.

groups of stakeholders depends entirely on the national laws and practices, and varies from company to company.

So the main accountability mechanism for industry currently comes down to the threat of governmental regulation.[370] This means an accountability deficit for those companies which operate transnationally and which can therefore relatively easily escape national regulation. There is also a serious accountability gap with regard to those global corporations operating in weak or failing states, or in 'neo-patrimonial' states which are captured by politicians as a source of private rents,[371] in 'shadow states',[372] or in 'criminalized states'.[373]

Due to the weaker legal accountability of firms acting on the global level, market and reputational accountability becomes all the more important. But reputational accountability seems to hold well mainly for firms which depend on brand name products. It is doubtful whether consumption choices really function as 'purchase votes' and as an effective sanction, because the people who are most directly negatively affected by the activities of a TNC are often not able to exert much consumer power. Moreover, boycotts require considerable consumer awareness and presuppose a real choice of products.[374]

Global accountability standards in this regard are only nascent. Thus, the OECD Principles of Corporate Governance of 2004 ask for 'disclosure and transparency'.[375] They also mention stakeholders (without defining them), and notably employee participation, but refer back to the 'laws and practices of corporate governance systems'.[376] In collaboration with international organizations and NGOs, business has progressed towards accountability through self-policing. For instance, the Global Reporting Initiative (GRI), founded in 1997, is a multi-stakeholder initiative which seeks to provide a framework, i.e. the 'Sustainability Reporting Guidelines' for sustainability reporting which can be used by businesses of any size, sector, or location.[377] Also, the Global Compact, initially conceived as a learning platform for global business, has matured into a rudimentary accountability regime for TNCs.[378] Since 2003, firms participating in the Global Compact are expected to demonstrate their commitment to the

---

[370] Virginia Haufler *A Public Role for the Private Sector: Industry Self-regulation in a Global Economy* (Carnegie Endowment for International Peace Washington DC 2001), at 119.

[371] Examples are former Zaire and Sierra Leone. See Gero Erdmann and Ulf Engel 'Neopatrimonialism Revisited: Beyond a Catch-all Concept' (2006) 16 *German Institute of Global and Area Studies Working Papers*.

[372] In shadow states, office holders have turned the state into a shadow of other interests. Shadow states maintain an official system of governance, with law and public institutions as a façade hiding the private, often economic or even illict agenda of those who are in power.

[373] Jean-François Bayart, Stephen Ellis, and Béatrice Hibou (eds) *The Criminalization of the State in Africa* (James Currey Oxford 1999).

[374] Kovach *et al, Power without Accountability?*, 2003, at 15–16.

[375] OECD Principles of Corporate Governance of 2004, Principle V.

[376] *Ibid*, Principle IV with annotation at 47.   [377] <http://www.globalreporting.org>.

[378] Karsten Nowrot *The New Governance Structure of the Global Compact: Transforming a 'Learning Network' into a Federalized and Parliamentarized Transnational Regulatory Regime* (Beiträge zum Transnationalen Wirtschaftsrecht 47 Universität Halle 2000).

Global Compact by 'Communications on Progress' in which the outcomes are measured using, as much as possible, indicators such as the GRI guidelines.[379] A more formalized complaint procedure for handling complaints on 'systematic or egregious abuse of the Global Compact's overall aims and principles' has been introduced in 2005.[380] To become full members of the global constitutional community, transnationally active business actors should be held more accountable to stakeholders through international instruments, however difficult it is to define the relevant groups and the accountability mechanisms.

6.8 By way of conclusion: towards trilateral partnerships with governmental residual responsibility

At first sight, the marketization of international law and global governance engendered through business involvement seems the opposite of constitutionalization, because it risks creating legitimacy and accountability gaps. The shift of previously public functions and competencies on private actors entails a loss of control and responsibility. Private actors are not bound by principles such as legality, impartiality, and due process. One way to compensate for legitimacy and accountability deficits engendered by marketization and outsourcing of governance is to make sure that the process of developing and implementing international law is a shared endeavour among (inter-)governmental institutions, business, and NGOs.[381] Put differently, the strategy of partnerships should be exploited further. Existing forms of partnerships include the already well-established 'public-private partnerships' (so-called PPPs, among business and governments)[382] and the less well-known 'private-private partnerships' (business with NGOs), such as the Forest Stewardship Council[383] or the

---

[379] UN Global Compact, Policy for 'Communications on Progress', as of 13 March 2008.

[380] See the 'Note on Integrity Measures' of 29 June 2005. Despite apparent quasi-judicial features of the complaint mechanism (e.g. the complaint will be forwarded to the participating company concerned, requesting written comments), the Global Compact Office stresses that it 'will not involve itself in any way in claims of a legal nature'. The office may, in its sole discretion, offer good offices, ask the regional office to assist with the resolution of the complaint, refer the complaint to one of the UN entities guarding the Global Compact principles, and reserves the right to remove the incriminated company from the list of participants in the Global Compact. (Attachment 1 to the report by the Global Compact Office 'The Global Compact's Next Phase' of 6 September 2005, part 4).

[381] Haufler, *A Public Role for the Private Sector*, 2001, at 119; Peter Muchlinski *Multinational Enterprises and the Law* (2nd edn OUP Oxford 2007), at 550.

[382] On PPPs see Klaus Dingwerth 'The Democratic Legitimacy of Public-Private Rule Making: What Can We Learn from the World Commission on Dams' (2005) 11 *Global Governance* 65–83; in a political science perspective Tanja Börzel and Thomas Risse 'Public-Private Partnerships: Effective and Legitimate Tools of International Governance?' in Edgar Grande and Louis W Pauly (eds) *Complex Sovereignty: Reconstituting Political Authority in the 21st Century* (University of Toronto Press 2005) 195–216.

[383] The FSC is governed by a board of directors representing nationally diverse actors from different forestry backgrounds (environmentalists, forestry companies, and indigenous peoples' organizations), but not governments. The FSC sets forest management standards.

Ethical Trade Initiative (ETI).[384] These and similar partnerships should be expanded to become 'trilateral' public-private partnerships, composed of the business sector, civil society organizations, and governmental actors.

The classical example of trilateral law-making is the creation of labour standards within the ILO which dates from 1919. In its law-making body, the international labour conference, each member state of the organization is represented by a delegation consisting of two government delegates, an employer delegate, a worker delegate, and their respective advisers. The ILO has been fairly successful in adopting global labour standards. The labour conventions have to be formally ratified by governments, and member states are obliged to undertake ratification within 18 months and to report back to the Director General in the case of non-ratification (Article 19(5) ILO Constitution). However, the level of ratification for the more than 180 labour conventions (beyond the eight most important ones) remains relatively low.[385]

A new example of a trilateral transnational governance partnership is the Kimberley Process which was set in motion to combat the war-escalating effects of the trade with 'blood diamonds' in Angola and Sierra Leone. Here the UN General Assembly,[386] the Security Council, diamond producers, traders, manufacturers,[387] governments, and NGOs were engaged. When prohibiting the trade in diamonds originating from the war-struck countries, the Security Council directly addressed the 'diamonds industry' and 'companies involved in trading rough diamonds'.[388] A certificate of origin scheme was established in order to exclude the 'blood diamonds' from the market.[389]

---

[384] The ETI elaborated an 'ETI Base Code of Workplace Standards' in cooperation with various NGOs, such as Oxfam and Christian Aid, see <http://www.ethicaltrade.org>.

[385] See the ratification status at <http://www.ilo.org/ilolex/english/newratframeE.htm>.

[386] *Cf* UN GA res 55/56 (2001), esp. para 5 on 'close collaboration with the diamond industry and taking into account the views of relevant elements of civil society'. See also UN GA res 56/23 (2002).

[387] Industry in 2000 created the World Diamond Council (later International Diamond Council) in order to develop, implement, and monitor a tracking system for the export and import of rough diamonds to prevent their exploitation for illicit purposes. The Council has been in communication with governments and NGOs.

[388] UN SC res 1306 (2000) para 10: 'Encourages the International Diamond Manufacturers Association, the World Federation of Diamond Bourse, the Diamond High Council and all other representatives of the diamond industry to work with the Government of Sierra Leone.' Para 11 '[i]nvites States, international organizations, *members of the diamonds industry and other relevant entities in a position to do so* to offer assistance to the Government of Sierra Leone'. Para 13: '*Welcomes the commitments* made by certain members of the diamond industry not to trade in diamonds originating from conflict zones, including in Sierra Leone, *urges all other companies and individuals* involved in trading in rough diamonds to make similar declarations in respect of Sierra Leone diamonds, and underlines the importance of relevant financial institutions encouraging such companies to do so' (emphasis added). See also UN SC res 1343 (2001) para B.16.

[389] See the World Federation of Diamond Bourses/International Diamond Manufacturing Association's Resolution 'Industry System of Self Regulation' of 29 October 2002.

In trilateral public-private-private partnerships, governmental, NGO, and business contributions could outweigh each others' deficiencies. Notably international organizations and NGOs can derive mutual legitimacy from each other. The NGO allegiance gives an aura of independence and credibility while the affiliation to an international organization gives NGO reports weight and authority. However, the simple 'borrowing' of credibility from NGOs by companies or even by governments is not enough. Legitimacy is gained through joint governance only when the parties remain independent from one another and sufficiently distant, because only then capture and collision is ruled out. So the proper balance between inclusion and distance must be found. Moreover, even if PPP governance is more inclusive and in that regard presumably more legitimate than purely (inter-)governmental steering activity, it still suffers from the lack of formal accountability. Generally, PPPs are rather intransparent and selective. One of the major legitimacy problems of PPP activity is probably the choice (and risk of exclusion) of relevant stakeholders, and the weighting of the stakeholders who should be involved in rule-making and -implementation. And as far as the effectiveness or output legitimacy of PPP governance is concerned, PPP activity can result in mere problem shifting or lead to the lowest common denominator.

A core objective of constitutionalism is to contain power. The claim that this should apply not only to state power but also to other, 'private' forms of power, notably economic power, is as old as industrialization itself. But that old demand has probably gained salience in times of globalization. The rise of global corporations makes it more important to also address to them the central questions of constitutional law, namely who should exercise power, on what terms, and subject to which conditions and limits.[390] This agenda has been in theoretical terms bolstered by legal pluralism. The legal pluralist view, as framed notably by Gunther Teubner and followers, not only seeks to apply constitutional limitations to private actors, but moreover acknowledges private authority as a source of law, including constitutional law. In that view, there are diverse sites of production of constitutional laws which may amount to an auto-constitutionalization of the 'private' sphere.[391] On a meta-level of analysis, legal pluralists also assert that the controversy about competing concepts of constitutional law should be kept open and thus propagate a cognitive pluralism.

---

[390] Gavin W Anderson *Constitutional Rights after Globalization* (Hart Oxford and Portland 2005), esp. at 145. Anderson suggests a 'legal pluralist constitutionalism' in order to hold private power more effectively to account.

[391] Based on general systems theory and the idea of autopoiesis, Teubner argues that private actors and groups, within the states and transnationally, have been constitutionalizing and possess 'civil constitutions' that are in no way derivative of or subordinate to 'public' constitutions. Gunther Teubner 'Societal Constitutionalism: Alternatives to State-Centred Constitutional Theory?' in Christian Joerges, Inger-Johanne Sand, and Gunther Teubner (eds) *Transnational Governance and Constitutionalism* (Hart Oxford and Portland 2004) 3–28.

Independent of the epistemic merits and flaws of the theory of autonomous civil constitutions, I submit that in normative terms a complete constitutionalization of the private sector is not desirable. A constitutionalist approach to international law and global governance assumes that government, society, and economy are different, albeit interrelated and not completely separate spheres. In order to preserve individual liberty, these sectors should not be merged. There are functional equivalents to constitutionalism in corporate and private law, such as management accountability, stakeholder involvement, and contractual liability. These legal, political, and economic mechanisms can and should be improved in order to heighten corporate responsibility.

It might be useful to transfer some principles and instruments of constitutionalism to the economic sphere, but only with due respect for the own logics of that sphere. For instance, one constitutional value is coherence. Attention to coherence calls for remedying the pigeonholing of particular features of corporate behaviour. Labour rights are institutionalized within the ILO while environmental and corruption issues are left to the Global Compact. This state of the law fragments the corporate responsibility. One answer to the problem of fragmentation could be the constitutionalization of the business sphere in order to realize coherence. Beyond this aspect, however, it is a question of constitutional policy, not of constitutionalism as such, how strictly the position of business actors should be regulated, and which global public tasks should be entrusted to them. A constitutional imperialism is not needed to hold private power to account.

To conclude this chapter, it might be said that the members of the constitutional community form a transnational community of responsibility.[392] From a constitutional perspective informed by normative individualism, individual human beings are the ultimate unit of the international (constitutional) community. I have left out the constitutional status of minorities, peoples, and indigenous populations. These also belong to the community, but demand and deserve a more detailed discussion than possible here.

Because the quest for a constitutionalized world order implies a search for a legitimate scheme of global governance, the legitimacy of the governing actors stands in the foreground. Because states are as yet the only formal representative of citizens, are still—as a group—the most powerful global actors, and are (in most areas of the world) important repositories of political, social, and cultural identity, international law and global governance must remain, in order to preserve a sufficient level of legitimacy, linked to states. The regulatory fall-back option is and should stay with states. The ultimate responsibility for governance should not be transferred to non-state actors and

---

[392] Nowrot, *Normative Ordnungsstruktur*, 2006, at 673–675.

certainly not to business actors. However, the involvement of non-state actors in law-making and law-enforcement can be an important additional source for the legitimacy of global governance. It should consequently be broadened, structured, and formalized.

6

Dual Democracy

Anne Peters

1. Democracy as a Principle of the Global Constitutional Order

The democratic deficit of international law and global governance has been called 'one of the central questions—perhaps the central question—in contemporary world politics'.[1] The deficit is crucial because it delegitimizes international law and offers a reason for states not to apply and observe international law.[2] The constitutionalist response to this problem is that the issue of democracy in the international sphere should not be bracketed as unrealizable, but that all should be attempted to make the global order democratic both at the state and at the supra-state level. However, domestic democratic procedures cannot simply be zoned up. The type, shape, and procedures of democracy cannot and need not be identical on both levels of governance. Moreover, the complementarity and interaction of various levels of governance inevitably transforms the domestic ways of democracy as well. Finally, the designers of a global constitutional order must be prepared to give the concept of democracy a new meaning without, however, diluting it to the extreme, and without selling undemocratic procedures as democratic. This book devotes one chapter to the constitutional principle of democracy, not because it is more important than other constitutional principles such as the rule of law, due process, and the protection of fundamental rights and of minorities, but because democracy is more conspicuously absent in global

---

[1] Andrew Moravcsik 'Is there a "Democratic Deficit" in World Politics? A Framework for Analysis' (2004) 39 *Government and Opposition* 336–363.

[2] John O McGinnis and Ilya Somin 'Should International Law be Part of our Law?' (2007) 59 *Stanford Law Review* 1175–1248, at 1246 (suggesting to reject application of what the authors call 'raw international law', notably customary law because of its democratic deficits). For the proposition that international treaties are not 'law', because they do not rest on popular sovereignty see John R Bolton 'Is There Really "Law" in International Affairs?' (2000) 10 *Transnational Law and Contemporary Problems* 1–48, at 3–4. From a philosophical perspective see Allen Buchanan and Russell Powell 'Constitutional Democracy and the Rule of International Law: Are they Compatible?' (2008) 16 *Journal of Political Philosophy* 326–349, concluding that 'the piecemeal, incremental development of increasingly robust international law—which, outside the European Union context, occurs without anything resembling public constitutional deliberation and popular choice—is highly problematic from the standpoint of the values that underlie constitutional democracy' (at 329–330).

governance, and because it seems particularly difficult to build in democratic elements in the design and operation of global governance.[3]

1.1 The duality of global democracy

Global constitutionalism requires dual democratic mechanisms. These should relate both to government within nation states and to governance 'above' states, thus to multiple levels of governance. The result should be a multi-unit democracy, built with domestic and international building blocks.

A fully democratized world order first of all rests on democratic nation states, thus on democracy *within* states. International processes and institutions can hardly be democratized if their constituent units do not themselves know and apply democratic internal procedures. More specifically, domestic democracy is needed in order to secure a transitive democratic basis for global governance, and as a guarantee for the promotion of global goods such as peace and security.[4] For these two reasons, the spread and support of national democracies constitutes a kind of indirect global democratization. It already is and should be further encouraged by international law (see in detail below pp. 273–277). Because of its fundamental and systemic importance, the requirement of democracy within states should be acknowledged as a global constitutional principle.

'*Above*' and among states, both the production of primary international law and the international institutions and their secondary law-making can and should be democratized on two tracks. On the one hand, citizens should continue to be mediated by their states which act for them in international relations (statist track). On the statist track, states as principals of international institutions should be reasserted and their influence improved. But because the ultimate reference point of democracy are natural persons, such a state-mediated democracy is present only to the extent that states really are the representatives of their citizens. Put another way, global governance is transitively democratically legitimate only to the extent that international bodies are accountable through states to citizens. It follows that we can meaningfully speak of an indirect democratization of the global order on the statist track only when all states have realized domestic democratic government. As long as not all states are democratic, a large number of people are not represented in a democratic sense by their states in the international institutions.

However, even if all states of the world became democracies, this would not in itself suffice to attain a meaningful degree of global democratic legitimacy for reasons which will be explained below (pp. 286–296). Therefore citizens, as the ultimate source of political authority, must be enabled to bypass their

---

[3] For an argument in favour of at least striving for the democratization of global governance, and not to bracket this question see Gráinne de Búrca 'Developing Democracy Beyond the State' (2008) 46 *Columbia Journal of Transnational Law* 102–158.   [4] See pp. 278–283.

intermediaries, the states, and take direct democratic action on the supra-state level (individualist track). It is necessary, as Eric Stein has put it, to 'inject the voice of individual citizens into the exclusively state-based structures'.[5]

The two-track model does not imply a complete shift of the international institutions' accountability to natural persons, but merely suggests bringing in the global citizens as principals *besides* states where appropriate. The accountability of the global governance institutions is extended and duplicated. The institutions will not be accountable only to states, but additionally (and sometimes competingly and conflictually) become accountable directly to citizens. The result is a dual accountability of international institutions to a dual constituency: states and citizens.[6]

1.2 The meanings and merits of democracy

Democracy, both as a constitutional principle and as a political process, has been loaded with various, even competing meanings, and has undergone important changes throughout its history.[7] Abraham Lincoln once defined democracy as 'government of the people, by the people, and for the people'.[8] Put another way, democratic government requires that the citizens can give their input to decisions of law and policy, and that political processes produce outputs in the interests of the citizens.[9] Necessary elements of democratic governance are, on the one hand, political equality, participation, inclusion of all governed, and, on the other, responsiveness and accountability of the governing actors to the governed. An essential element of democracy are mechanisms which allow the citizens to evaluate and eventually to sanction the performance of the

---

[5] Eric Stein 'International Integration and Democracy: No Love at First Sight' (2001) 95 *AJIL* (2001) 489–534, at 533.

[6] This conception is inspired by the work of David Held and Daniele Archibugi who suggested 'the creation of a democratic community which *both involves and cuts across democratic states*'. The two authors have advocated 'a model of political organization in which citizens, wherever they are located in the world, have a voice, input and political representation in international affairs, *in parallel with and independent of their own governments*' (Daniele Archibugi and David Held 'Editors' Introduction' in Daniele Archibugi and David Held (eds) *Cosmopolitan Democracy: An Agenda for a New World Order* (Polity Press Cambridge 1995) 1–16, at 13, emphasis added). For implicit and not fully sketched out two-track models see Derk Bienen, Volker Rittberger, and Wolfgang Wagner 'Democracy in the UN System, Cosmopolitan and Communitarian Principles' in Daniele Archibugi, David Held, and Martin Köhler (eds) *Re-Imagining Political Community: Studies in Cosmopolitan Democracy* (Polity Press Cambridge 1998) 287–308; Richard Falk and Andrew Strauss 'On the Creation of a Global Peoples Assembly: Legitimacy and the Power of Popular Sovereignty' (2000) 36 *Stanford Journal of International Law* 191–220.

[7] For the numerous concepts and theories see Manfred G Schmidt *Demokratietheorien* (4th edn VS Verlag Opladen 2006).

[8] Abraham Lincoln 'Gettysburg Address' of 19 November 1863, reprinted in Lincoln *His Speeches and Writings* (World Publishing Cleveland 1946 Basler ed), at 734.

[9] Democracy should ultimately be tied to citizens, and not to a collective, such as a people, because human collectives are in normative and conceptual terms secondary to individuals. See also pp. 302–307.

power-wielders. A system is democratic only if it allows the citizens to disempower and 'throw out' politicians, normally through elections. An important enabling condition for this mechanism is the transparency of governance.

Democracy has become a slogan nearly as powerful as human rights. Practically all governments of the world boast that they are democratic, although they often practice forms of 'democracy' that do not allow the citizens to hold power-wielders accountable, and are therefore not democratic in the sense just defined. But these distortions of democracy only demonstrate how strong the pull of the principle is.

The traditional western defence of democracy, formulated by Jean Jacques Rousseau, is that democracy best reconciles individual freedom and equality with life in society.[10] A new justification of democracy specifically accommodates the basic facts of diversity, disagreement, and cognitive bias, and is therefore particularly relevant for the global scale. Thomas Christiano has argued that political institutions should be designed so as to advance equally the interests of persons who are affected by those institutions. Because the diverse interests and backgrounds make people cognitively biased towards their own interests, the objective of equally advancing affected persons' interests can only be realized through an equal say.[11] This reasoning is especially pertinent for global decision-making, because on a global level there is particularly strong disagreement about how the world should be shaped. This calls for a global collective decision-making process which grants each human an equal say in decisions affecting him or her.

Democratic governance has not outlived itself. 'Post-democracy', as diagnosed and deplored by Colin Crouch, is no good option. Crouch has pointed out that, while the norms of democracy remain fully in place and are actually even strengthened, 'politics and government are increasingly slipping back into the control of privileged elites in the manner characteristic of pre-democratic times; and . . . one major consequence of this process is the growing impotence of egalitarian causes'.[12] Crouch does not acclaim but criticizes the depolitization of lives, privatism, and consumerism in developed western democracies. Propagating post-democracy would be Eurocentric and risks defaming democratization processes outside Europe. In many states in Africa, the Near East, and South East Asia, democratic procedures have just come into being and need to take root. For all these reasons, democracy still seems to be, as Winston Churchill put it, the worst form of government, except all others.[13]

---

[10] Jean Jacques Rousseau 'Du contrat social' in *idem Du contrat social et autres oeuvres politiques* (éditions Garnier Frères Paris [orig. 1762]) 235–336, esp. chapter VI, at 243.

[11] Thomas Christiano *The Constitution of Equality* (OUP Oxford 2008), at 4 and 9.

[12] Colin Crouch *Post-Democracy* (Polity Cambridge 2004), at 6.

[13] 'Many forms of government have been tried, and will be tried, in this world of sin and woe. No one pretends that democracy is perfect or all-wise. Indeed, it has been said that democracy is the worst form of Government except all those other forms that have been tried from time to time', Speech of 11 November 1947 in the House of Commons, reprinted in Winston Churchill *His Complete Speeches 1897–1963* (Chelsea House Publishers New York 1974) 7563, at 7566.

1.3 The democratic deficits of global governance

Global governance[14] is undemocratic even by modest standards. Surely, one must not measure global governance at an ideal of democracy, but at concrete democratic procedures within nation states. This comparative assessment must take into account that the democratic systems in many nation states are undergoing fundamental transformations which to some extent undermine the rule of the people or the functioning of parliaments within nation states.[15] Nevertheless, even if we do not apply a too demanding standard of 'ideal' democracy to global governance, but a realist one, the (comparative) democratic deficits of international governance can not be denied. The deficits lie in the institutional design of the international organizations and bodies themselves, they result from the way states are integrated into the system of global governance, and finally they concern the relationship between citizens and international institutions. Overall, global governance has been aptly termed as '[g]overnance without government and without the governed'.[16]

This state of affairs fuels current reservations against international law and global governance. While these reservations were traditionally phrased in terms of the national interest, they are nowadays couched in terms of democracy, with sovereignty reconceived as popular sovereignty.[17]

Democratization of international law and global governance is all the more urgent as governance has become a multilevel process. The substance of politics has been migrating to the international level, mainly due to the globalization of issues and problems that must be tackled and solved by politics, ranging from trade and finances over migration, climate, and diseases, to terrorism. The result is that while political decisions within national boundaries are still

---

[14] By global governance, I understand all governance activity relating to issues that concern more than one state, by national and even local authorities and by international ones. This encompasses the conclusion of international treaties, the creation of secondary international law (both general norms and concrete decisions) within international organizations, the formation of customary international law, and finally judicial activity by international courts and tribunals and other mechanisms of dispute settlement and compliance control.

[15] Widespread phenomena are the rise of the executive branches, the dominance of specialized, non-democratically elected technical experts in all subject areas of legislation, the spread of para-legislation in the form of compacts, codes of conduct, or agreed standards and principles, which do not result from formal democratic procedures, and finally the circumvention of parliaments by individuals and other interest groups with the help of new technologies of direct communication and networking. Some of these phenomena are linked to globalization and will be discussed at pp. 295–296.

[16] Joseph H H Weiler 'The Geology of International Law—Governance, Democracy and Legitimacy' (2004) 64 *Zeitschrift für ausländisches öffentliches Recht und Völkerrecht* 547–562, at 560.

[17] See, e.g., Jed Rubenfeld 'Unilateralism and Constitutionalism' (2004) 79 *New York University Law Review* 1971–2028, esp. at 2020: 'The whole point of international law, in its present form, is to supersede the outcomes of political processes, including democratic processes. If, therefore, Americans remain committed to self-government, they do in fact have reason to resist international governance today.'

formally taken democratically, national entities undergo a process of *de facto* de-democratization and are less effective (see in detail at pp. 295–296). On the premise that all rule over persons should be democratic, and that the hollowing out of domestic democracy should be compensated as far as possible, the democratization of global governance is inescapable.[18] Because a stand-still or roll-back of global governance is unfeasible, and therefore no way to re-invigorate democracy, a new design to enhance global democracy is needed.

1.4 New types of democracy for the global level?

The implementation of democracy on a global scale seems to require new forms of political action of citizens and civil society organizations. These novel global practices might both manifest and promote an evolution of the concept of democracy. The transformative potential was implied in the UN-commanded expert report on the organization's relations to civil society (Cardoso Report), which argued that the UN could 'reshape' democracy to make it more relevant to today's global realities and needs.[19] Three new shapes are debated, all of which depart from the vision of 'formal' democracy with voting, elections, and representation of citizens on a territorial basis. The first, '*deliberative democracy*' is used with different meanings by numerous authors.[20] John Dryzek so far most explicitly applied deliberative democracy to the international level.[21] According to Dryzek, the essence of democracy itself is 'deliberation, *as opposed to voting*, interest aggregation, constitutional rights, or even self-government'.[22] Deliberative democracy, thus understood, is more at home in the international system than aggregative 'formal' models of democracy. On the basis of this understanding of democracy, it is sometimes argued that 'a highly democratic albeit *nonelectoral*, system of transnational governance' is possible or even already in place.[23] A major reason for the suitability of deliberative democracy on the

---

[18] Seminally David Held 'Democracy, the Nation-state and the Global System' in David Held (ed) *Political Theory Today* (Polity Press Cambridge 1991) 197–235, at 232: 'Democracy within a nation-state requires democracy within a network of intersecting international forces and relations. This is the meaning of democratization today.' David Held *Democracy and the Global Order: From the Modern State to Cosmopolitan Governance* (CUP Cambridge 1995), at 23: '[N]ational democracies require an international cosmopolitan democracy if they are to be sustained and developed in the contemporary era. Paradoxically, perhaps, democracy has to be exended and deepened within and between countries for it to retain its relevance in the future.'

[19] United Nations, *We the Peoples: Civil Society, the United Nations and Global Governance, Report of the Panel of Eminent Persons on United Nations-Civil Society Relations* ('Cardoso Report'), UN Doc A/58/817 (11 June 2004), para 37.

[20] For a new account see Steven Wheatley *The Democratic Legitimacy of International Law* (Hart Oxford 2010).

[21] John Dryzek *Deliberative Democracy and Beyond: Liberals, Critics, and Contestations* (OUP Oxford 2000), esp. chapter 5: 'Transnational Democracy: Beyond the Cosmopolitan Model.'

[22] Dryzek, *Deliberative Democracy*, 2000, at 1 (emphasis added).

[23] Ann Florini *The Coming Democracy: New Rules for Running the World* (Island Press Washington DC 2003), at 209.

international level is that deliberation and communication can cope somewhat more easily with fluid boundaries than voting. Voting means to aggregate preferences or interests of a specific group (normally the 'demos'). However, the boundaries of the relevant groups are very hard to specify in international politics. 'But while aggregation across boundaries is hard to conceptualize, deliberation across boundaries is straightforward', says Dryzek.[24] This is correct, but does not give the full picture of deliberative democracy. In order to be legally relevant, deliberation must be structured. Structured deliberation still needs a circumscription of those entitled to raise their voice. So we face the problem of delimitation here as well.

A related conception is *'participatory democracy'*. '[T]he notion of a participatory society requires that the scope of the term "political" is extended to cover spheres outside national government.'[25] Those who participate are citizens and other members of civil society, notably non-governmental organizations (NGOs). 'Participative democracy' is frequently contrasted with 'representative democracy'.[26] In that perspective it implies, just like deliberative democracy, a turn away from elections. Participatory democracy alongside representative democracy has been favoured by the Cardoso Report. According to the Report, traditional democracy aggregates citizens by communities on neighbourhood (their electoral districts), whereas in a participatory democracy, citizens aggregate in communities of interest. And thanks to modern information and communication technologies, these communities of interest can be global as readily as local, says the Report optimistically.[27] Article 11 of the Treaty on European Union of 2007 spells out the ingredients of 'participatory democracy', namely: notice, hearing, and comment; an open, transparent, and regular dialogue; broad consultations with concerned parties; and finally the citizens' initiative.[28] The purpose of this provision is 'to provide a framework and content for the dialogue which is largely already in place between the institutions and civil society' in Europe.[29] So, overall, participatory democracy involves two shifts: from 'vote' to 'voice', and from territorial communities (electoral districts) to communities of interest ('functional' constituencies). However, the delineation of those 'functional' constituencies is exceedingly difficult.

---

[24] Dryzek, *Deliberative Democracy*, 2000, at 116.

[25] Carol Pateman *Participation and Democratic Theory* (CUP Cambridge 1970), at 106. Pateman and others mainly advocated democratic participation in industry and education. The concept has later been applied to the international sphere.

[26] See the headings of the European Constitutional Treaty of 29 October 2004 (OJ 2004 C 310/1): Art I-46 'representative democracy'; Art I-47 'participatory democracy'. The official headings have been purposely abandoned in the Treaty of Lisbon, while the substance of those two provisions remained largely identical (now Arts 10 and 11 of the Treaty on European Union (TEU)).

[27] Cardoso Report, 2004, at 8, also para 37.

[28] Art 11 Treaty on European Union (TEU) of 13 December 2007 (OJ 2008 C 115/13).

[29] European Convention's Praesidium's comment on the draft of the forerunner provision in the aborted Constitutional Treaty, CONV 650/03, at 8.

'*Contestatory democracy*' is the third conception of democracy which seems to be suitable for transfer to the global level.[30] Proponents of contestatory democracy point out that democracy can hardly be based on an alleged consent of the people, because explicit consent is inaccessible, and implicit consent is empty. Therefore democracy is consensual only in a vanishingly weak sense.[31] Democracy should rather, so the argument goes, be based on the contestability by the people of everything the rulers do. The important thing to ensure is that political action is fit to survive popular contestation, not that it is a product of popular will. In this perspective, the essence of democracy is that ordinary people have 'systematic possibilities' to contest, and 'the right to challenge and to resist indeed constitutes the people as sovereign'.[32] Normally, within the democratic state, challenge occurs through elections. But challenge, resistance, and protest outside the governmental structures become especially important when elections are not available, as in the global sphere. In fact, the actions of the nascent global civil society have until now mainly been 'contestatory' in the form of transnational coordinated or parallel protest (e.g. against the Iraq War in February 2003), consumer boycotts (e.g. against the South African Apartheid regime), or mass action against international conferences (such as the disruption of the World Trade Organization (WTO) ministerial conference in Seattle in 1999). The idea of contestatory democracy allows the description of these features in the current international legal process as democratic in an embryonic sense. Moreover, contestatory techniques could probably be more easily realized on the global level than traditional democratic mechanisms, i.e. voting.

However, all three types of democracy, which place emphasis on 'informal' action, especially deliberation, as opposed to 'formal' voting and elections, have serious drawbacks. Open deliberation does not as such guarantee the congruence between decision makers and those who are affected. Participation (in deliberations or in protests) still needs some kind of structure, and a definition and delimitation of the participants. Otherwise the louder (better financed, better organized) voices will have undue influence. It must therefore be clear beforehand who will select which concerned parties. A skewed selection may even be used to give a misleading impression of popular support. A different point of critique is that discourse and contestation are not enough. The ideas of deliberation and contestation lack a clear account of how the powerless are able to entrench their claims institutionally. Deliberation and contestation is not what the powerless require. To conclude, deliberation, participation, and contestations are no real substitute for formal democracy. These mechanisms would ideally have to be linked to voting at some point. However, the existing conceptions leave open the crucial question of how this should be done. Strictly

---

[30] Seminal is Philip Pettit *A Theory of Freedom and Government* (Clarendon Oxford 1997); for an application to global politics see Lawrence Quill *Liberty after Liberalism: Civic Republicanism in a Global Age* (Palgrave Macmillan Basingstoke and New York 2006).

[31] Pettit, *Theory of Freedom*, 1997, at 184–185.   [32] *Ibid*, at 277–278.

speaking, participatory, deliberative, or contestatory 'democracy' alone may be too weak to deserve the label democracy. However, these forms of engaging citizens in global governance are important first steps on the path of democratization.

2. First Track: The Democratization of International Governance via Democratic Nation States

2.1 States as democratic mediators

It is often claimed that the current international legal order can be understood as an 'inter-state' democracy, and should be developed further in the direction of an association of democratic states. The underlying assumptions are first an analogy between states and natural persons, and second the idea of a transitive, delegated legitimacy of global governance with states as democratic mediators. These accounts and proposals explicitly or implicitly take state sovereignty as the basis of legitimacy of international law, and claim that this ultimately, after a due democratization of all states, should imply popular sovereignty. Based on the analogy between states and natural persons, the general application of the principle of sovereign equality of states can be seen as the international community's analogue of democracy.[33] In the 1994 Agenda for Peace, the Secretary General stated: 'Democracy within the family of nations ... is a principle that means affording to all States, large and small, the fullest opportunity to consult and to participate.'[34] 'Just as legitimate national governments derive their authority from the consent of the governed, so legitimate international institutions derive their validity from the consent of the governments involved.'[35] The legal consequences to draw are that law-making should be inclusive and consensual, that states should participate in treaty-making on an equal footing, and that they should have equal votes within international organizations, notably for creating secondary law.

The inter-state paradigm further relies on transitive legitimacy. In that view, 'in the legitimacy of national regimes resides the legitimacy of the international regime'.[36] As long as the states, the main actors, the primary and original legal subjects, and the principal creators of international law, are in themselves legitimate, they indirectly legitimize international law and global governance, so the argument runs. And because democratic governance is nowadays the 'gold

---

[33] Arthur Watts 'The International Rule of Law' (1993) 36 *German Yearbook of International Law* 15–45, at 32.

[34] UN Secretary General, *Agenda for Development* (UN Doc A/478/935 (of 6 May 1994)), para 134.

[35] Mortimer Sellers 'Republican Principles in International Law' (1996) 11 *Connecticut Journal of International Law* 403–432, at 413.

[36] Thomas Franck 'Legitimacy and the Democratic Entitlement' in Gregory H Fox and Brad R Roth (eds) *Democratic Governance and International Law* (CUP Cambridge 2000) 25–47, at 31.

standard of legitimacy',[37] states must be democratic. In this state-centred view, the spread of democracy within states is understood to lead to an indirect or transitive democratization of international law and global governance. From that perspective, the future of global governance is domestic, democratic, and deliberative.[38]

The essence of democratic global governance, understood in that way, consists of delegation from democratically governed states. Global institutions are democratic to the extent that they are accountable to states which are accountable to their citizens. Notably international treaties, ratified by national parliaments, can and should serve as a 'transmission belt' of accountability to the national electorates. The Lisbon Treaty of 2007 expresses this idea quite precisely in Article 10 of the Treaty on European Union: '1. The functioning of the Union shall be founded on representative democracy. 2. Citizens are directly represented at Union level in the European Parliament. Member States are represented in the European Council by their Heads of State or Government and in the Council by their governments, themselves democratically accountable either to their national Parliaments, or to their citizens.'[39]

Indeed, the accountability of international organizations and regimes to democratic nation states are a *conditio sine qua non* for democratic global governance. States are indispensable as members of the global constitutional order (see also pp. 196–200). Doing away with states would imply a single global polity, which would be remote from the citizens, inevitably inflexible, and complicated, in short not operational. States and other local political units possess more knowledge about local issues than global institutions, and can act quicker. But states are needed not only for effective political action and as crystallization points of collective political and cultural identity, but also for democratic reasons. They are formally constituted political representatives of identifiable groups (nations). They are mediators between six billion people and global institutions. Therefore the global constitutional order should, *inter alia*, rest on state sovereignty, expressing popular sovereignty as a basis of legitimacy. All this means that the global constitutional order should not be a democracy without states, but must rely on states, and that these states should be democratized. Democratic states can contribute to global democracy on two levels: within states, decisions must be taken democratically; and on the international level, the democratic states represent their citizens. I will now turn to the first level, the internal democratization of states.

---

[37] Allen Buchanan and Robert O Keohane 'The Legitimacy of Global Governance' (2006) 20 *Ethics and International Affairs* 405–437, at 416.

[38] Steven Wheatley 'Democratic Governance beyond the State: The Legitimacy of Non-State Actors as Standard-Setters' in Anne Peters, Lucy Köchlin, Till Förster, and Gretta Fenner Zinkernagel (eds) *Non-state Actors as Standard Setters* (CUP Cambridge 2009) pp. 215–240.

[39] TEU of 13 December 2007 (OJ 2008 C 115/13). Paras 3 and 4 of Art 10 deal with participation, transparency, and European political parties.

2.2 Towards a global constitutional principle of domestic democracy

The promotion of democracy within nation states is a central principle of global constitutionalism not only because domestic democracy is the foundation of a transitive global democracy, but also because domestic democracy promotes global goods. This central principle is to some extent already endorsed in international law as it stands, as will be shown in the next section.

Towards an international legal requirement of domestic democracy

International law is evolving towards a requirement that states must be democratic. This nascent legal requirement should be endorsed by a concomitant global constitutional principle. Thomas Franck had already argued in 1992 that an international legal right to democratic governance was emergent.[40] Since then, international law has evolved greatly in the direction of a principle of domestic democracy, based *inter alia* on state practice. According to the Freedom House index of 2008, 121 of 193 states of the world are electoral democracies, and 90 of them are 'free'.[41] The principle of democracy, as emerging in customary law, in case law, and in other legally relevant texts after 1989, is no longer so indeterminate as to allow all rhetorical variants of 'democracy'. One-party 'elections', which had prevailed in socialist regimes of 'peoples' democracies' no longer satisfy the international legal standard.

UN Secretary General Boutros-Ghali has interpreted the UN Charter's preamble's 'We the Peoples' as invoking popular sovereignty, and thus as envisaging democratic member states.[42] Both the Secretary General and the General Assembly have, especially after the demise of the socialist block, promoted democracy as good governance.[43] The 2005 World Summit Outcome has again venerated the 'tryptichon'[44] of human rights, rule of law, and democracy, which are 'interlinked and mutually reinforcing'. It asserted that 'democracy is a universal value. ...[W]hile democracies share common features, there is no single model of democracy, ... *it does not belong to any country or region*, ...'. The governments renewed their

---

[40] Thomas Franck 'The Emerging Right to Democratic Governance' (1992) 86 *AJIL* 46–91. Linos-Alexandre Sicilianos described domestic democracy as an international nascent obligation, implying a novel conception of sovereignty (Linos-Alexandre Sicilianos *L'ONU et la démocratisation de l'Etat* (Pedone Paris 2000)).

[41] <http://www.freedomhouse.org>. For instance, the state of Bhutan has recently been democratized from above. Elections have been imposed by the king in 2008, despite the preference of the people for monarchy.

[42] UN Secretary General, *Supplement to Reports on Democratization* (Annex to UN Doc A/51/761 of 20 December 1996), para 28. On democracy as an implicit principle and objective of the UN see e.g. the preamble of GA res 50/133 (1996) and notably the Cardoso Report of 2004.

[43] UN Secretary General, *Agenda for Development* (UN Doc A/478/935 (1994)), paras 118–138 on 'democracy as good governance'. For the more recent position of the General Assembly see *Promoting and Consolidating Democracy* (UN Doc A/55/96 (2001)); *Implementation of the United Nations Millennium Declaration*, Part V: 'Human rights, democracy and good governance' (UN Doc A/57/270 (2002) paras 82 *et seq*). [44] Sicilianos, *L'ONU*, 2000, at 249.

'commitment to support democracy by strengthening countries' capacity to implement the principles and practices of democracy'.[45] Implementation of the democratic principle in practice is sought through election monitoring[46] and other
assistance funded, *inter alia*, through the UN Democracy Funds established in 2005.
Other organizations, such as the Inter-Parliamentary Union,[47] NATO,[48] and
regional organizations in Europe,[49] America,[50] and Africa[51] endorse democracy, but
regional associations in the Near East and Asia do not.[52]

The entrenchment of an international principle of domestic democracy is
visible in the following legal domains: the right to participate in the conduct of
public affairs and the right to vote in elections is a universally and regionally
recognized human right.[53] Properly understood, the internal aspect of the

[45] UN Doc A/60/1 of 24 October 2005, paras 119 and 135–136 (emphasis added). On the other
hand, the World Summit, as previous pro-democratic General Assembly Resolutions, dialectically reaf-
firmed 'the necessity of due respect for sovereignty and the right of self-determination' (*ibid*, para 135).

[46] On 'periodic and genuine elections' as an indispensable element of democracy see notably GA
res 45/150 (1990); GA res 46/137 (1991).

[47] *Universal Declaration on Democracy* (adopted without a vote by the Inter-Parliamentary
Council at its 161st session (Cairo, 16 September 1997), para 1: 'Democracy is a universally
recognized ideal as well as a goal, which is based on common values shared by peoples throughout
the world community irrespective of cultural, political, social and economic differences'.

[48] Preamble of the NATO-Treaty of 4 April 1949.

[49] Preamble of the Statute of the Council of Europe of 5 May 1949; Arts 9–12. TEU Lisbon;
CSCE-Charter of Paris for a New Europe of 21 November 1993.

[50] Democratic government was initially no condition for membership of the Organization of
American States (OAS). But since the Washington Protocol of 14 December 1992, which was
adopted in reaction to the coup d'état in Haiti, Art 2b of the OAS Charter proclaims as an essential
purpose of the OAS 'to promote and consolidate representative democracy.' Art 9 foresees the
suspension from the OAS bodies of any member state whose democratically constituted government has been overthrown by force. See also OAS Interamerican Democratic Charter of 11 September 2001 (text in (2001) 41 ILM 1289); further the Declaration of the OAS General Assembly
of Santiago on *Democracy and Public Trust: A New Commitment to Good Governance for the
Americas* (OAS Decl. AG/DEC. 31 (XXXIII-O/03) of 10 June 2003). See for the Mercosur Arts 4
and 5 of the Protocol of Ushuaia of 24 July 1998, under which the disruption of democracy in a
member state may lead to the suspension of that state's right to participate in the Mercosur organs.

[51] ECOWAS Protocol A/SP1/12/01 on Democracy and Good Governance, supplementary to
the Protocol Relating to the Mechanism for Conflict Prevention, Managment, Resolution,
Peacekeeping and Security of 21 December 2001, in force since 2005.

[52] See for the state of democratization in the Arab region Khalil Shikaki, Mudar Kassis, and
Jihard Harb (eds) *The State of Reform in the Arab World 2008* (The Arab Reform Initiative and the
Palestine Center for Policy and Survey Research April 2008).

[53] Art 21 Universal Declaration of Human Rights, Art 25 ICCPR. See also UN Commission on
Human Rights, *Promotion of the Right to Democracy* (res 1999/57 of 27 April 1999), *Promoting and
Consolidating Democracy* (res 2000/47 of 25 April 2000), preamble and para 1(d). For the world regions
except Asia see Art 3 Prot. 1 ECHR; Art 23(1) ACHR, Art 13(1) African Charter on Human and
Peoples' Rights. In order to satisfy the international legal standards of genuine, free, and fair elections,
these must take place at reasonable periodic intervals, with universal and equal suffrage, secret ballot,
absence of discrimination of voters, multiple parties, and monitoring by independent electoral authorities. Gregory H Fox 'The Right to Political Participation in International Law' (1992) 17 *Yale Journal
of International Law* 539–607, at 570; Gregory H Fox 'The Right to Political Participation in International Law' in Gregory H Fox and Brad R Roth (eds) *Democratic Governance and International Law*
(CUP Cambridge 2000) 48–90, esp. at 69; Steven Wheatley 'Democracy in International Law: A
European Perspective' (2002) 51 *ICLQ* 225–247, at 238 with references to the case law.

collective right to self-determination implies democratic governance. Otherwise self-determination would be prevented for future generations and would thus not be sustainable.[54] The right to self-determination moreover allows a people to secede from a multinational state when its political representation and participation are persistently denied.[55]

The requirement of internal democratic government is a regional customary norm in Europe.[56] The Strasbourg case law evidences that '[d]emocracy is without doubt a fundamental feature of the European public order' and a conceptual and legal foundation of the European Convention on Human Rights (ECHR).[57] The European Court of Human Rights requires member states to uphold a pluralist democracy, in which freedom of expression is guaranteed.[58]

For some years,[59] there seems to exist a universal customary obligation for all states, including 'old' ones, to work progressively towards democratization.[60] However, certain persistent objectors remain, especially China and states of the Middle East and South East Asia.

Moreover, a prohibition of retrogression is incumbent on democratic states. A violent coup d'état against a democratic government is an internationally illegal act of the new regime.[61] After 1989, the United Nations regularly denounced forcible repudiations of the democratically expressed will of a people. Third states' recognition of governments emerging from a coup d'état to the detriment of a democratic government tends to be withheld.[62] A different case is when a people decides in formally correct democratic procedures to abolish democracy,

---

[54] Anne Peters *Das Gebietsreferendum im Völkerrecht: Seine Bedeutung im Licht der Staatenpraxis nach 1989* (Nomos Baden-Baden 1995), at 387–396. Wheatley, Democracy, 2002, at 230–232 references numerous state reports to the Human Rights Committee which reflect the understanding of self-determination in Art 1 ICCPR as coterminous with the right to democratic government.

[55] Friendly Relations Declaration, UN GA res 2625 (XXV) of 24 October 1970, ILM 9 (1970), 1292, para 7 *e contrario*; Supreme Court of Canada, *Reference Secession of Quebec*, (1998) 2 S.C.R. 217, paras 111–138. See also Allen Buchanan *Justice, Legitimacy, and Self-Determination: Moral Foundations for International Law* (OUP New York 2004) chapter 8 (331–400). The secession of Kosovo from Serbia in 2008 is a case in point.

[56] Jean d'Asprémont *L'Etat non démocratique en droit international* (Pedone Paris 2008), at 293.

[57] ECHR, *United Communist Party of Turkey and others v Turkey*, application No 133/1996/752/951, judgment of 30 January 1998, para 45.

[58] ECHR, *Case of Socialist Party v Turkey*, application No 20/1997/804/1007, judgment of 25 May 1998, para 41; ECHR, *Case of Freedom and Democracy Party v Turkey*, application No 23885/94, judgment of 8 December 1999, para 37; ECHR, *Case of Refah Partisi (the Welfare Party) and others v Turkey*, Grand Chamber, application Nos 41340/98 and 41342–4/98, judgment of 13 February 2003, para 89.

[59] In 1996 still, the United Nations Secretary General highlighted that 'individual societies decide if and when to begin democratization' (*Supplement to Reports on Democratization* (Annex to UN Doc A/51/761 of 20 December 1996, para 4).

[60] All types of regimes express an *opinio iuris* in that sense. Notably non-democratic states constantly affirm that they desire, aspire, and make efforts to become (more) democratic. D'Asprémont, *L'Etat*, 2008, at 269–293. Detailed examination of the *opinio iuris ibid*, at 275–285 with numerous references. [61] Sicilianos, *L'ONU*, 2000, at 286.

[62] D'Asprémont, *L'Etat*, 2008, at 149–150 with references from state practice.

and elects a totalitarian regime. In that situation, non-elected groups sometimes attempt to prevent such an act of popular self-disempowerment. So far, no clear rules of international law have emerged with regard to these complex constellations.

But recent international law seems to require *new* states, such as the successor states of the Soviet Union or of Yugoslavia, East Timor, and the DR Congo, to be democratic. Moreover, post-conflict regime-building with international support has always been democratic, also in the event of state continuity.[63] In particular international territorial administration, such as in Bosnia-Herzegovina or in Kosovo, has been understood as necessarily leading to a democratic state and it must itself be democratic.[64] Third states and international organizations involved in the (re-)construction of a state seem to be obliged to endow that state with a democratic regime.[65] Although democratic government is no formal condition of admission to the United Nations, the internationally supervised processes of 'making' new states such as East Timor or Montenegro had guaranteed that those states were indeed democratic.

The recent practice of recognition of governments and of states is ambiguous. On the one hand, effective control is no longer the sole and maybe not even the decisive criterion. On the other hand no clear pattern of democratic legitimism has emerged (see in detail pp. 80–182).[66] It is doubtful whether this rich international practice has already coalesced into an international norm of democratic governance for various reasons. First, the international bodies' texts do not clearly indicate whether they purport to state the *lex lata* or are merely suggestions *de lege ferenda* or political statements. Second, some definitional debate over the content of the democratic principle persists. Third, the observance of democracy norms varies significantly among the world regions. Finally, an international norm of domestic democracy cuts deep into domestic jurisdiction. UN assistance in election processes has so far regularly operated with the consent of the concerned states, and there is no indication that states have relinquished their right to refuse assistance in this field.[67] But despite the remaining uncertainty over an international hard and fast prescription of domestic democracy, current international law 'indicates a progressive and irreversible movement to a world community

---

[63] *Ibid*, with examples and references to the international documents concerning Lebanon, Cambodia, Afghanistan, Burundi. Not once has the international community proposed that a post-conflict government be chosen in any other way than through democratic elections, normally with international assistance.

[64] Mariano J Aznar Gòmez *La Administración internacionalizada del territorio* (Atelier Barcelona 2008), at 192 and 198.   [65] D'Asprémont, *L'Etat*, 2008, at 75–79.

[66] Brad Roth argued in 1999 that the effective control test must not be seen as a repudiation of the popular sovereignty norm, but rather as 'an application of it in circumstances of ideological pluralism' (Brad R Roth *Governmental Illegitimacy in International Law* (Clarendon Press Oxford 1999), at 414). He admitted that respect for popular will was important, and that the effective control doctrine could be a 'presumptive guide' to it (*ibid*, at 419).

[67] Gregory H Fox, 'Democracy, Right to, International Protection' *Max Planck Encyclopedia of Public International Law* (OUP Oxford 2009), paras 5–7 and 35–37.

of democratic states'.[68] I submit that this trend is one manifestation of the constitutionalization of international law, and should be pushed further.

Facing the critique of a global constitutional principle of domestic democracy

The claim that international (and even international constitutional) law should require states to be democratic has long been attacked on grounds of prudence, principle, and practice. A standard objection to democracy as a universal constitutional principle has been that the concept of democracy is too indeterminate to have any prescriptive power.[69] Democracy has also been criticized as a potential vehicle of neo-colonialism, imposing a specific western world view and government design on the rest of the world, and as a tranquilizer against political revolution.[70] Democracy has further been accused of carrying with it an intrinsic tendency to inter-state violence, a point which will be discussed in detail below.

Furthermore, established legal principles such as states' sovereign equality, non-intervention, and the self-determination of peoples seem to stand against an international constitutional prescription of domestic democracy. In the classic era of constitution-blindness of international law, the choice of a state's government was fully in its *domaine reservé*. Thus in 1912, Oppenheim's International Law stated: 'The Law of Nations prescribes no rules as regards the kind of head a State may have. Every State is, naturally, independent regarding this point, possessing the faculty of adopting any Constitution it likes and of changing such Constitution according to its discretion'.[71] Even in 1986, the International Court of Justice (ICJ) held that in the absence of a specific legal obligation there is no commitment on the part of states to hold free and fair elections.[72] However, the *domaine reservé* is relative and shrinks with the development of international norms. The principle of state sovereignty is notoriously open, and in recent years has been reconstructed as requiring popular sovereignty.[73] Finally, the principle of self-determination can and should also be read in a democratic way. Self-determination cannot expend itself in one

---

[68] Wheatley, Democracy, 2002, at 234.

[69] Classically, Henry Steiner 'Political Participation as a Human Right' (1988) 1 *Harvard Human Rights Yearbook* 77–134, at 89.

[70] *Cf* Martti Koskenniemi 'Intolerant Democracies: A Reaction' (1996) 37 *Harvard International Law Journal* 231–235, at 234. Susan Marks *The Riddle of All Constitutions: International Law, Democracy, and the Critique of Ideology* (OUP Oxford 2000), esp. at 109–119 and 151, suggests maintaining the revolutionary character of a 'principle of democratic inclusion' which seeks to acknowledge democracy's metapolitical appeal, while also recognizing democracy's value as a transformative tool of political struggle.

[71] Lassa Oppenheim *International Law*, vol I (6th edn Longmans, Green and Co New York 1912), at 425. Hersch Lauterpacht deleted the second sentence in the 7th edition of 1948 that he edited.

[72] ICJ, *Case Concerning Military and Paramilitary Activities in and against Nicaragua* (Nicaragua v United States of America) merits, ICJ Reports 1986, 14, para 261.

[73] Commission on Global Governance *The Report of the Commission on Global Governance, Our Global Neighbourhood* (OUP Oxford 1995), at 60: 'Sovereignty ultimately derives from the people. It is a power to be exercised by, for, and on behalf of the people of a state.'

single act of constitution-making or choice of government. To be sustainable, self-determination must be a continuous process. The establishment of an autocracy or the abolishment of democracy by a popular vote would destroy the self-determination of future generations, and therefore cannot be an admissible exercise of the collective right. Any non self-defeating concept of internal self-determination thus invariably implies democracy.

Another problem for an international constitutional principle of domestic democracy is that the social, economic, and cultural prerequisites for a functioning democracy are lacking in many regions of the world. Historic and current experience, e.g. in Afghanistan, Iraq, or Bosnia-Herzegovina, shows that a polity can only be democratic when broader segments of the population dispose of a minimum income and education, when there are no permanent ethnic, religious, or cultural deep cleavages, and when a viable civil society (political parties, free media, citizens' engagement, and associations) exist. This is a valid point, because all law, especially international constitutional law, may be counterfactual only to a certain degree if it is not to be irrelevant or even counterproductive. However, democracy is a matter of degree, and there is no bright line between premature and timely democratization. UN politics, e.g. through the UN Democracy Funds, seeks precisely to address the democratic infrastructure problems. Boot-strapping is to some extent possible: the democratic process itself can in turn promote and fortify the enabling conditions in a positive loop.

Domestic democracy promotes global goods

It is in the interests of the international community to foster democracy within nation states because of the instrumental value of democracy. Democratic governance should be acknowledged as a global constitutional principle because it promotes global goods as follows.

Domestic democracy, human rights, and development

While a state's transition to democracy is typically an unstable and precarious phase, it is also a potent impetus to membership of international organizations.[74] It is an empirically demonstrated fact that states tend to accede to international organizations in order to fortify internal democracy.[75]

Once well-established and mature, national democratic procedures have a stabilizing effect (although strong repressive regimes may be stable as well). The

---

[74] Edward D Mansfield and Jon C Pevehouse 'Democratization and International Organizations' (2006) 60 *International Organization* 137–167.

[75] Although, on the other hand, international organizations may also shield dictatorships. Also, with respect to many treaty regimes, evidence does not support a liberal/non-liberal distinction with respect to the decision to be bound, the level of compliance after ratification, or the likelihood of peaceful dispute resolution when treaty disputes arise. José Alvarez 'Do Liberal States Behave Better? A Critique of Slaughter's Liberal Theory' (2001) 12 *EJIL* 183–244, at 209.

UN Secretary General stressed that democracy provides a long-term basis for managing competing ethnic, religious, and cultural interests in a way that minimizes the risk of violent internal conflict.[76] Internal stability is an international concern, because internal strife and civil war are today one of the most important causes of gross human rights violations.

In addition, domestic democracy reinforces respect for human rights.[77] Historically, it was the lack of a democratic culture in Germany and the resulting war leading to massive human rights abuses which motivated the establishment of international and regional human rights regimes. The Vienna Human Rights Conference of 1993 highlighted that '[d]emocracy, development and respect for human rights and fundamental freedoms are interdependent and mutually reinforcing'.[78] Democracy, if bound up with formal or informal schemes of minority protection, is best equipped to ensure that peoples' basic human rights are protected and their substantive interests furthered, because the democratic accountability mechanisms prevent elites from exercising power in a way that disregards the interests of large segments of the population. Inversely, human rights guarantees are a precondition for democracy. In particular, free speech and freedom of association are 'absolutely basic to a liberal-democratic constitutional order', as the German Constitutional Court famously put it in an important decision not long after the foundation of the German Federal Republic on the ruins of the national socialist regime.[79] In international law, the interdependency between democracy and human rights is most explicit in the framework of the ECHR: according to the Strasbourg case law, democracy is the only system of government compatible with the Convention.

Furthermore, processes of democracy and development are interrelated.[80] A certain level of material development (including food and education) is a precondition of a functioning democracy, because starving and illiterate citizens have no energy and capacity for political participation. Historical examples also show that economic prosperity may generate the quest for democratization.[81] As people become richer, they tend to demand more democracy and civil rights to protect their wealth from arbitrary actions of government: the *bourgeois* reclaim the status of *citoyens*. However, empirical research has so far not established any

---

[76] Report of the UN Secretary General *Agenda for Development* (UN Doc A/48/935) of 6 May 1994, para 120. See also Boutros Boutros-Ghali 'Democracy: A Newly Recognized Imperative' (1995) 1 *Global Governance* 3–11.

[77] Secretary General, *Supplement to Reports on Democratization* (Annex to UN Doc A/51/761/ (1996)), para 3.

[78] Art 8 of the Vienna Declaration and Programme of Action, World Conference on Human Rights of 14–25 June 1993 (UN Doc A/CONF.157/23) of 12 July 1993.

[79] German Constitutional Court, *Lüth* case (BVerfGE 7, 198, at 208 (1958)), engl. translation in Norman Dorsen, Michel Rosenfeld, András Sajó, and Susanne Baer *Comparative Constitutionalism, Cases and Materials (American Casebook)* (West Publishing Co. St. Paul (Minn.) 2003), at 824 (826).

[80] UN Secretary General, *Agenda for Development* (UN Doc A/478/935 (6 May 1994)), para 118. [81] See Milton Friedman *Capitalism and Freedom* (Chicago UP 1962).

causal link between economic growth and democratization,[82] and the economic boom of some Asian autocracies for the moment seems to belie any causality. But while development perhaps promotes democracy, the inverse is also true. The stabilizing effects of democracy are crucial for development, because civil conflict and war prevent and seriously throw back development. Democracy provides incentives to protect the capacity, reliability, and integrity of core state institutions, including the civil service and the legal process, and is to that extent a factor of development.[83] Moreover, freedom of the press and democratic competition among political parties can protect against hunger and other frustrations of basic needs, because the governmental response to the suffering of people often depends on the pressure that is put on the government through the exercise of political rights (voting, criticizing, and protesting).[84]

In international law, the concept of (human) development includes a strong participatory component and has in that regard been itself 'democratized'. Notably the international regimes of environmental protection require or encourage public participation, with the objective of better realizing the primary objective of environmental protection,[85] which is in turn a factor of sustainable development. To conclude, both in fact and in law, development and democracy are positively mutually conducive.

Domestic democracy and world peace

World peace is the primary objective and principle of the international constitutional order. This objective is furthered through the potentially pacifying effects of domestic democracy. The United Nations Secretary General has claimed that democratic rules and procedures within states are 'minimizing the risk that differences or disputes will erupt into armed conflict or confrontation'.[86] If this 'democratic peace thesis'[87] is correct, domestic democracy should also be an international constitutional principle for this reason. Proponents of the

---

[82] For empirical studies on the relationship between political and economic freedom see Eberhard Scholing and Vincenz Timmermann 'Der Zusammenhang zwischen politischer und ökonomischer Freiheit: Eine empirische Untersuchung' (2000) 136 *Schweizerische Zeitschrift für Volkswirtschaft und Statistik* 1–23; Bruce Bueno Mesquita and George W Downs 'Development and Democracy' (2005) 84 *Foreign Affairs* 77–86, concluding: 'As events now suggest, the link between economic development and what is generally called liberal democracy is actually quite weak and may even be getting weaker.'

[83] UN Secretary General, *Agenda for Development* (UN Doc A/478/935 (6 May 1994)), para 128.

[84] Amartya Sen *Development as Freedom* (Knopf New York 1999) chapter 6 'The Importance of Democracy' (146–159). Also Amartya Sen 'Property and Hunger' (1988) 4 *Economics and Philosophy* 57–68.

[85] Convention on Access to Information, Public Participation in Decision-Making and Access to Justice in Environmental Matters of 25 June 1998 (Aarhus Convention), (1999) 38 ILM 517–533.

[86] UN Secretary General, *Supplement to Reports on Democratization* (Annex to UN Doc A/51/761 of 20 December 1996), para 17.

[87] Seminally Michael W Doyle 'Kant, Liberal Legacies, and Foreign Affairs' (parts 1 and 2) (1983) 12 *Philosophy and Public Affairs* 205–235 and 323–353.

democratic peace thesis rely on Immanuel Kant, who had demanded that 'the civil constitution of every state should be republican'. Kant had argued that this would lead to world peace, because 'if the consent of the citizens is required in order to decide that war should be declared (and in this constitution it cannot but be the case), nothing is more natural than that they would be very cautious in commencing such a poor game, decreeing for themselves the calamities of war'.[88]

The democratic peace thesis is confronted with the thesis of the 'liberal-democratic jihad'[89] and of (liberal-)democratic imperialism.[90] Proponents of this thesis argue that, far from constituting a departure from liberal principles, interventionism is fundamentally rooted in them.[91] Indeed, prominent liberal authors have more or less explicitly favoured pro-democratic interventions.[92] The historical record, especially the recent wars waged by the USA, seem to bolster the claim that liberal democracies intrinsically tend to military intervention based on moral claims, and thus escalate inter-state violence. Nations who believe that their form of government and social organization embodies the Truth and the Good might seek to share that—by force, if necessary.[93] If the prevention of genocide and/or the spread of democracy are a part of the role or identity of liberal democracy, inter-state military violence might be used in defence of the process of civilization, and thus appear as a kind of perverted self-defence.[94] In that perspective, the Kovoso war of 1999 is 'the quintessential liberal war of our time'.[95]

Specifically *democratic* war-escalating factors may be election cycles and a concomitant resort to war as diversion manoeuvre. Another specific escalating factor may be the suspicion of (liberal-)democratic states against undemocratic/

[88] Immanuel Kant 'Perpetual Peace' in *idem Perpetual Peace, and Other Essays on Politics, History, and Morals* (Hackett Publ Indianapolis 1983, German orig. 1795 Humphrey trans), section II, first definitive article for perpetual peace.   [89] Roth, *Governmental Illegitimacy*, 1999, at 424.
[90] See notably Anna Geis, Harald Müller, and Wolfgang Wagner (eds) *Schattenseiten des demokratischen Friedens* (Campus Frankfurt and New York 2007).
[91] Doyle, Kant, 1983, part 2 (chap. VI, 323–337); John Vasquez 'Ethics, Foreign Policy and Liberal Wars' (2005) 6 *International Studies Perspectives* 307–315, at 311; Beate Jahn 'Kant, Mill, and Illiberal Legacies in International Affairs' (2005) 59 *International Organization* 177–207, at 180.
[92] John Rawls *The Law of Peoples* (Harvard UP Cambridge MA 1999), at 81: 'All peoples are safer and more secure if such states change, *or are forced to change*, their ways.' (Emphasis added). *Cf* also Charles Beitz *Political Theory and International Relations* (Princeton UP 1979), at 92 on interference in unjust states that does not exclude military force. John Stewart Mill recommended interventions in barbarous or 'semi-barbarous', culturally inferior civilizations. See the excellent analysis by Jahn, Kant, Mill, and Illiberal Legacies, 2005, esp. at 194 *et seq.*
[93] For instance, US President George W Bush declared before the American invasion in Iraq: '[B]y acting, we will signal to outlaw regimes that, in this new century, the boundaries of civilized behaviour will be respected. . . . Members of our armed forces . . . know that America's cause is right and just: liberty for an oppressed people and security for the American people. . . . Free people will keep the peace of the world.' Speech of 26 February 2003, available via CBS News.
[94] Anna Geis, Lothar Brock, and Harald Müller 'Demokratische Kriege als Antinomien des Demokratischen Friedens: Eine komplementäre Forschungsagenda' in Anna Geis, Harald Müller, and Wolfgang Wagner (eds) *Schattenseiten des demokratischen Friedens* (Campus Frankfurt and New York 2007) 69–91, at 82.   [95] Vasquez, Ethics, 2005, at 311.

illiberal ones. Because the latter do not share the same values and institutions, they are expected to be aggressive, and easily become targets of 'missionary' politics. However, such suspicion will hardly suffice to trigger a war. The US-led intervention in Iraq in 2003, for instance, was not primarily justified with the 'rogue nature' of the state, but with the regime's refusal to cooperate with the verification authorities. A final factor increasing the risk of war may be foreign investment. Private property and free enterprise abroad calls for protection by the state. However, the risk of war on these grounds has been greatly reduced by the privatization of investment disputes through the International Centre for the Settlement of Investment Disputes (ICSID), and is also counterbalanced by the pacifying effects of mutual cross-border trade relations. Overall, the causal links between democracy and war are weak at best.

I therefore conclude that interventionism is not inscribed in democracy, and is not a specific problem of democratic government.[96] It might, however, be a problem of legitimism *tout court*, understood as the belief that certain political regimes are morally and socially superior to others. The assertion is that democratic legitimism is implicitly interventionist because 'legitimism *in any form* is inherently aggressive'.[97] But this assertion is not borne out by the facts. The decisive variable for resorting to military violence does not seem to be legitimism, but rather additional factors which promote interventionism. These factors are a state's readiness to pit legitimacy *against* legality (as in NATO's Kosovo war), intolerance and militarism, a failure to honour the fundamentally liberal principle that even desirable ends do not justify any means, and finally, huge power imbalances which can exacerbate the risk of war. To conclude, the 'democratic jihad' thesis is unconvincing.

It is rather the democratic peace thesis which constitutes a viable starting point for global constitutionalism. The 'dyadic' version of the democratic peace thesis contends that liberal democracies do not wage war *against each other*.[98]

---

[96] Unlike nazism, fascism, and communism, 'democratism' does not explicitly seek to realize world rule or world revolution by military means. In fact those ideologies have in the past been extremely aggressive.

[97] Roth, *Governmental Illegitimacy*, 1999, at 426 pointing to the Holy Alliance and the Breshnev, Reagan, and Bush doctrines.

[98] This contention is corrobated by data, although some claim that the data correlations are not significant. Other criticism is that the normative and institutional causal logic applied to explain democratic peace are flawed, that, after 1945, peace rather seems to be caused by American preponderance (Sebastian Rosato 'The Flawed Logic of Democratic Peace Theory' (2003) 97 *American Political Science Review* 585–602 and Sebastian Rosato 'Explaining the Democratic Peace' (2005) 99 *American Political Science Review* 467–472). The democratic peace thesis might neglect other potentially peace-promoting variables such as bipolarity, nuclear deterrence, or alliances (Errol A Henderson *Democracy and War: The End of an Illusion?* (Lynne Riener Boulder 2002)). It has also been argued that the thesis is Eurocentric and ahistoric by leaving out the Europeanness and historical transformations of core categories such as state, democracy, and war (Tarak Barkawi and Mark Laffey 'Introduction: The International Relations of Democracy, Liberalism, and War' in Tarak Barkawi and Mark Laffey (eds) *Democracy, Liberalism, and War: Rethinking the Democratic Peace Debate* (Lynne Rienner Boulder 2001) 1–19.

One explanation of the peace-promoting quality of national democracy is institutional: because democratic governments have to account for their international actions, they must reckon with being answerable in a domestic controversy on whether the decision to go to war was justifiable, lawful, and in the country's best interest. The democratic public is very sensitive about the victims and other costs of a war. If the rulers give a poor answer to the public's questions, they will suffer electoral defeat, and this deters them from waging war. However, this explanation begs the question why the institutional constraints do not prevent wars against non-democratic states. So we should take note of the variances of democracies and of the ambivalence of democracy towards war we have just seen. Further factors seem to raise the probability of peaceful behaviour, notably economic interdependence through trade, and shared membership in international organizations. Democracy, trade, and international cooperation, through positive feedback loops, decrease the likelihood of military inter-state conflict.[99] Because domestic democracy is one element of this virtuous circle, it should be acknowledged as a core principle of global constitutionalism.

Constitutionally admissible means of enforcing domestic democracy

The international (and potentially constitutional) requirement of domestic democracy is breached when a democratic state falls back into an authoritarian regime[100] through a violent coup d'état, such as in Haiti in 1994 or in Sierra Leone in 1997. International (constitutional) law is also infringed by irregular or fraudulent elections and referendums, such as in Belarus and Uzbekistan.[101] I submit that it is consistent to establish a requirement of democratic states, while clearly limiting the means of implementing this principle. Global constitutionalism allows only non-military responses to these constitutional problems, such as unilateral and collective persuasion and incentive, for instance through conditionalities for aid. Other options include sanctions. The principle of domestic democracy is an aspect of the right to self-determination and arguably shares the *erga omnes* character of the latter principle.[102] Therefore third states are allowed to invoke the international legal responsibility of a state which fails to comply with the global (constitutional) requirement of domestic

---

[99] Bruce Russett and John R Oneal *Triangulating Peace: Democracy, Interdependence and International Organisations* (Norton & Company New York 2001).

[100] Also, the creation of a new, non-democratic state, e.g. after a break-up of China, would violate international constitutional law, but such a case seems unlikely in the forseeable future.

[101] With regard to the Uzbekistan parliamentary elections of 26 December 2004 and the presidential elections on 21 December 2007, the OSCE/ODIHR limited observation mission concluded that the elections failed to meet many of OSCE commitments and other international standards for democratic elections. See OSCE final report on parliamentary elections in Uzbekistan of 7 March 2005; OSCE final report on presidential election in Uzbekistan of 23 April 2008. See in this sense also EU Council Presidency statement on the presidential elections in Uzbekistan on 21 December 2007 (PC.DEL/30/08 of 17 January 2008).

[102] ICJ, *Case Concerning East Timor* (Portugal v Australia), ICJ Reports 1995, 90 para 29.

democracy (Art 48 sec. 1 lit. a) and b) ILC Articles). On the premise that all states have a legal interest in compliance with international constitutional law, all, or at least those states which are 'specially affected', should be allowed to impose unilateral, non-military, and proportionate countermeasures against those states which breach the prohibition of retrogression.[103] In fact, the European Union has imposed a visa ban and frozen funds of certain officials of Belarus after that state's parliamentary elections and referendum of 17 October 2004 and the presidential elections of 19 March 2006 had been qualified as unfree by the OSCE/Office for democratic institutions and human rights (ODIHR) limited election observation mission.[104] Third states are not only entitled, but even obliged to protest and not to recognize an illegal situation resulting from the abolishment of democracy in another state.[105]

It is in a constitutionalist perspective permissible and legitimate for the UN Security Council to qualify the violent overthrow of a democratically elected government as a threat to the peace and security of a region, as it has done in the cases of Haiti and Sierra Leone.[106] After such a determination, the Security Council may authorize economic measures under Chapter VII, such as the travel bans and embargoes for Sierra Leone.

However, military measures of the Security Council, such as its authorization of a multinational force for Haiti in order to restore democracy, are problematic from a constitutionalist perspective. Even if the Security Council is the proper institution to authorize military intervention, a violent overthrow of a democratic regime does not seem to constitute a sufficiently serious cause for military measures.[107] Moreover, a military response to democratic irregularities is presumably disproportionate. In a constitutionalized world order, the legal requirements of just cause and proportionality, including a balancing of means and ends and an assessment of the costs of action as compared to the costs of inaction, also bind the Security Council[108] (see also p. 188).

---

[103] Art 54 ILC Articles speaks of 'lawful countermeasures' and thereby leaves open the question of whether affected states may enact countermeasures against an internationally illegal act. The restrictive position which requires 'special affectedness' draws on an analogy to Art 60(2)(b) VCLT. In favour of the narrow reading see James Crawford 'Multilateral Rights and Obligations in International Law' (2006) 319 *Recueil des Cours* 325–482, at 442–451.

[104] EU Common Position 2006/362/CFSP and Council Regulation (EC) No 765/2006 of 18 May 2006 (OJ 2006 L 134/1)).

[105] Cf mutatis mutandis ICJ, *Legal Consequences of the Construction of a Wall in the Occupied Palestinian Territory*, Advisory Opinion, ICJ Reports 2004, 136, paras 154–159.

[106] UN SC res 940 (1994); UN SC res 1132 (1997).

[107] Cf *The Responsibility to Protect* (2001), <http://www.iciss.ca/pdf/Commission-Report.pdf> paras 4.25–4.26. However, the report does not clearly state that this limitation should also govern Security Council mandated action under Chapter VII.

[108] See 'A More Secure World: Our Shared Responsibility', Report of the High-level Panel on Threats, Challenges and Change of 2 December 2004 (UN Doc A759/565), paras 207–209; 'In larger freedom: towards development, security and human rights for all', Report of the Secretary General of 21 March 2005 (UN Doc A/59/2005), para 126; 'International Commission on Intervention and State Sovereignty' (ICISS) paras 4.18 *et seq* and 6.27.

These considerations play all the more for unilateral military action. Very importantly, a democratic regime may not be enforced unilaterally by military means. Pro-democratic interventions are illegal and should remain illegal in a fully constitutionalized world order.[109] Neither does the democratic principle entitle a state or groups of states to enforce the prescription by military action under the pretext of invoking Articles 51 or 53 of the UN Charter. The constitutional prohibition of pro-democratic intervention can be defended with a number of arguments. John Stuart Mill's classic argument is that a democratic regime imposed from outside is not sustainable, because the people has not fought for it and is therefore not fit for it.[110] However, the distinction between home-grown democracy and imposed democracy is in reality not clear cut. Japan and Germany are examples of imposed democracies that function. So Mill's argument is unconvincing.

The second argument against pro-democratic intervention is a cultural-relativist one. It is claimed that the concept of pro-democratic intervention is self-defeating, because it negates the value it purports to protect, namely the consent of the governed, by imposing democracy on a foreign people.[111] It should be respected—so the argument goes—that a people may prefer to be ruled by an undemocratic, even repressive government, e.g. because the inhabitants judge rebellion to be imprudent, because they are accustomed to a government, or because they are personally loyal to their leader.[112] This is a relatively weak argument, because the 'consent' of the governed under a dictator is unlikely to be genuine. Only after the liberation of the population from repression it can be determined what citizens, or the majority of them, really want. This observation undermines the cultural-relativist argument against pro-democratic intervention. However, the focus on a genuine consent of the governed in an undemocratic state does not support pro-democratic intervention either, because it highlights that the prospects of success of such an operation can not be determined *ex ante* and from the outside. The US-led intervention in Iraq of 2003, which led to the removal of the dictator Saddam Hussein, but brought about protracted civil war, counsels against repetition.

This leads to the prudential and consequentialist arguments against pro-democratic interventions. One insight is that any military intervention inevitably causes immediate harms while its chances of making a higher number of peoples' lives better off are highly uncertain. Moreover, a constitutional

---

[109] See only d'Asprémont, *L'Etat*, 2008, at 94, 322 and 326. But see in favour of pro-democratic intervention Fernando R Tesón *Humanitarian Intervention: An Inquiry into Law and Morality* (2nd edn Transnational Publishers New York 1997), esp. at 16 and 141–146.

[110] John Stewart Mill 'A Few Words on Non-Intervention (1859)' in *The Collected Works of John Stewart Mill vol 21 (1984), Essays on Equality, Law and Education* (University of Toronto Press Toronto and Routledge and Kegan Paul London 1963–1991) 111–124, at 122.

[111] James Crawford *Democracy in International Law* (CUP Cambridge 1994), at 20.

[112] Michael Walzer 'The Moral Standing of States: A Response to Four Critics' (1980) 9 *Philosophy and Public Affairs* 209–229, esp. at 214.

principle allowing such intervention would be inherently prone to abuse. The reason is that democracy is such a complex phenomenon that objective judgments on the quality of democracy are difficult. In consequence, measuring the degree of compliance with the international constitutional requirement of democracy is difficult as well. Political manipulation of compliance control is easy, and has already happened, e.g. in the US assessment of autocracies in Latin America in the 1980s.[113] Non-compliance could thus be easily claimed to licence intervention. Therefore, to erode the constitutional principle of non-intervention in an effort to further worldwide democratization would be reckless. Hence all states should unambiguously renounce the use of unilateral, or even regional military force to compel compliance with the democracy requirement. Such a specific renunciation of unilateralism is crucial for the acceptance and thus for the legitimacy of the international constitutional principle of domestic democracy.[114]

The preceding sections have shown that domestic democracy is warranted as a basis for the transitive democratization of global governance, and because it promotes global constitutional values, notably peace. It was also demonstrated that international law as it stands already demands fulfilment of the international constitutional ideal of a community of democratic nation states, while strictly limiting the means of enforcing the spread of domestic democracy. Although the application of the democratic prescription remains selective, the quest for domestic democracy in the international *lex lata* is an indicator of the constitutionalization of international law.

2.3 Persisting problems of the statist track of democratization

Domestic democracy is, as the preceding section showed, indispensable for global democracy, but not sufficient. An exclusively state-focused view of global democracy is flawed on various grounds which relate to the inter-state relations, to the states' control of global governance institutions, and to the internal democratic structures in states. Most fundamentally, the inter-state paradigm alone cannot lead to a democracy whose ultimate unit of concern are citizens.

Inter-state oligarchy

The current system of international governance resembles more an oligarchy than an inter-state democracy. It is in many respects a rule of the few, as opposed to the rule of the majority. A rule of the few violates two basic mediating principles of democracy: inclusiveness and equality. The problem of formal inequality of member states in international organizations (such as the veto power of the permanent members of the Security Council, the two-class system

---

[113] Roth, *Governmental Illegitimacy*, 1999, at 420–421, 427 (with references).
[114] Franck, Democratic Governance, 1992, at 84–85.

in the Non-Proliferation Treaty, and the weighted voting in the Bretton Woods institutions), and also the problem of substantial inequalities among states have already been discussed at pp. 190–196. In a constitutionalized order, a certain amount of corrective action would be appropriate in order to realize the constitutional community's members' treatment as equals.

Specifically with regard to the UN Security Council, the existence of *permament* members, which are irremovable from office, is a clearly anti-democratic element. Radical democrats have therefore long asked for the election of all members of the Council on a regular basis by the General Assembly.[115] Such elections would bring the Security Council closer to a government in the style of a French *directoire* or the Swiss *Bundesrat*. Of course, this scheme carries the calculated risk that powerful states would not be elected. This risk would constitute an accountability mechanism but would at the same time most likely disable the entire regime, because it is not sufficiently rooted in the realities of power on which global governance depends. The contemporary debate on political reform on the Security Council is therefore much less ambitious and does not call into question the existing permanent seats. Proposals are, *inter alia*, to add permanent members without veto, to increase the number of elected members, and/or to readjust the geographical distribution. All current reform proposals focus on broadening the representativeness and inclusivity of this body and to that extent reflect democratic concerns.[116] A different strategy on the non-state track would be to grant consultative status at the Security Council to non-state actors such as members of a new UN Parliamentary Assembly.

Given the fact that voting alone does not suffice to guarantee democratic procedures, the deliberative deficits in the international legal processes are a democratic problem as well. An analysis of the deliberations in the Security Council leading to recent resolutions embodying quasi-legislation and/or quasi judicial action showed that they are deficient. The deliberative deficit in the Council could be brought down by introducing inclusive consultations and public justification, improvements which would not require formal institutional reforms.[117]

---

[115] For the League of Nations' Council see Walther Schücking 'Le développement du Pacte de la Société des Nations' (1927/V) 20 *Recueil des Cours* 349–458, at 387–388.

[116] In the World Summit Outcome Document (UN Doc A/60/1 of 24 October 2005), para 153, the UN member states supported reform of the Security Council as an essential element of the 'overall effort to reform the United Nations in order to make it *more broadly representative, efficient and transparent and thus to further enhance its effectiveness and the legitimacy* and implementation of its decisions' (emphasis added). See *Report of the Open-ended Working Group on the Question of Equitable Representation on and Increase in the Membership of the Security Council and other Matters Related to the Security Council* (UN Doc A/62/47 (2008). General Assembly decision 62/557 of 15 September 2008 transferred the debate under the same heading from a working group to the General Assembly. The first substantive meeting was in March 2009.

[117] Ian Johnstone 'Legislation and Adjudication in the UN Security Council: Bringing down the Deliberative Deficit' (2008) 102 *AJIL* 275–308, analysing SC res 1373, 1540, 1267.

Another manifestation of oligarchy is the outright exclusion of some states from participating meaningfully in relevant regimes. This happens mostly through informal mechanisms. Obvious examples are closed clubs such as the G8. But also formal organizations with open membership, such as the WTO or the UN, possess informal oligarchic structures. WTO decision-making should, according to the WTO Agreement (footnote 1 at Article IX WTO Agreement), be based on the consensus practice, but important decisions are taken in the notorious green rooms, which effectively excludes weak and poor member states. Also, the practice of vote-buying in international organizations, an open secret in the International Whaling Commission, at least in some constellations curtails the freedom of poor states' voting behaviour, and therefore undermines inter-state equality within those organizations. Moreover, the widespread practice of abstaining from formal voting and taking decisions by consensus, especially in the UN General Assembly or in the WTO General Council, favours oligarchy, because the powerful member states' pressure on weak members is more effective in this atmosphere. Numerous gentlemen's agreements between influential states regulate the composition of bodies within international organizations, and secure positions for powerful states. For instance, the President of the World Bank is appointed on the basis of a gentlemen's agreement between the rich Bank member states, which reserves the World Bank Presidency to an American, and the position of the IMF Managing Director to a European. So the top officers are neither chosen democratically nor are they representative of all member states of the Bretton Woods organization.

A final example of international oligarchy is the Antarctic regime. Under the Antarctic Treaty, only those contracting parties may participate in the frequent consultative meetings 'during such time as that Contracting Party demonstrates its interest in Antarctica by conducting substantial scientific research activity there, such as the establishment of a scientific station or the despatch of a scientific expedition'.[118] The result is that only a few wealthy states are able to participate in the Antarctic Treaty meetings. The wording of the treaty, although on its face neutral, effectively excludes poor states. Only if the treaty requirement of a material (and costly) evidence of the member states' 'interest in Antarctica' is deemed as reasonably related to the objectives of the Treaty, is this exclusion justified. Otherwise it would have to be qualified as an indirect discrimination against less affluent contracting parties.

Ending oligarchy in these and other regimes requires plenary organs in which all member states are allowed to deliberate and to participate in any voting with an equal vote, and non-plenary organs whose composition seriously and fairly reflects the requirements of an 'equitable' or 'balanced' geographical

---

[118] Art IX 2 of the Antarctic Treaty of 1 December 1959 (UNTS vol 402, No 5778, 71–85).

distribution, or the representation of specific interests.[119] Such inclusiveness or representativeness would not prejudice how to reach decisions on the basis of those votes. Both unanimity voting and majority voting are perfectly compatible with the principles of inclusion, fair representation, and equality. The choice of the voting modus depends on other considerations, which will be discussed now.

The conundrum of state unanimity versus majority voting

The idea of an inter-state democracy insinuates that state consent, i.e. the unanimity principle which governs treaty making and still large areas of secondary law production, is democratic.[120] I doubt this. The idea is premised on an understanding of democracy as a mechanism to safeguard the autonomy and self-determination of the actors in collective decision-making. When the actors are states, the objective is to safeguard their sovereignty. Indeed, the sovereignty-autonomy of every member of a collective is perfectly safeguarded by the consent principle, because new rules cannot be imposed on a member without the member's agreement. But this view neglects the point that the realistic scenario in any collective is a divergence of interests (be it only due to the members' cognitive bias) and the persistence of reasonable disagreement on political and legal decisions to be taken. In this basic condition, which is not one of pre-stabilized harmony, the consent principle is undemocratic. It is undemocratic because it allows the tyranny of one member of a political community over the others, and allows a small minority to block collective action. With the argument that no greater consensus should be required for a negative action than for a positive one, Francisco de Vitoria had already acknowledged the simple majority to be the most democratic decision-making rule.[121] A non-decision is also a decision, because the simple lapse of time brings about changed circumstances to which the old policies and rules no longer fit. The cementation of the status quo is therefore a no less intensive infringement of autonomy than its change.[122] A veto power of a minority of states within an international organization appears all the more undemocratic when one acknowledges

---

[119] See Art 23 UN Charter; Art 24 WHO; Art 50 ICAO; Art 13 WMO; Art 6A IAEA. However, a deplorable side effect of the concern for geographical diversity is that it has so far quite effectively hindered an equitable representation of the sexes in international organizations. As long as the regional affiliation or nationality of candidates is the most important selection criterion both for the bureaucratic and the political offices within international organizations, the relevant regional pools of qualified women remain too small to permit women as a global group to advance.

[120] For a lucid analysis of unanimity and majoritarian decision-making in a constitutional economics perspective see Joel P Trachtman 'Constitutional Economics of the WTO', part 2 in Jeffrey L Dunoff and Joel P Trachtman (eds) *Ruling the World: Constitutionalism, International Law and Global Governance* (CUP Cambridge 2009).

[121] Francisco de Vitoria 'On Civil Power' in *idem Political Writings* (CUP Cambridge 1991, orig. 1528, Pagden and Lawrance eds) 1–44, at 30 (§ 14).

[122] But see James MacGill Buchanan and Gordon Tullock *The Calculus of Consent* (University of Michigan Press Ann Arbor 1962), at 256–260, concluding that the mere ability to prevent change by a minority with help of the veto is no real power or government.

that autonomy-sovereignty, which is supposed to be protected by democratic decision-making rules, is not only negative or defensive (a right to be left alone), but also active, and includes the right to influence the behaviour of others. Inaction notably curtails the positive autonomy and self-determination of those members of an international organization who seek to bring about law and policy reform. For example, because the European Constitutional Treaty of 2004 required unanimous ratification by all member states of the EU, two states out of 27, representing only a tiny minority of European citizens, could block the adoption of that Treaty. Leaving aside the fact that the remainder of the European citizens did not even get the chance to express their voice, this was an infringement of the positive autonomy of the majority of member states (and of European citizens). The situation is less evident outside the framework of an international organization. For instance, the non-ratification of the ICC Statute by the USA did not prevent other states from establishing the International Criminal Court (ICC). However, all considered, the inter-state unanimity requirement cannot be called democratic, and therefore the current international system cannot be called democratic, even in the statist paradigm of an inter-state democracy. In a constitutionalist perspective, one could even argue that the unanimity principle means no constitution at all, because all decisions still depend on each member's own determination. The only 'constitutional' rule involved is *pacta sunt servanda*.

So should we therefore, in a constitutionalist perspective, call for an expansion of majoritarian decision- and law-making in the international legal order? State majoritarianism would, besides superficially appearing more democratic, improve the effectiveness of global decision-making. Although decision- or rule-making as such does not guarantee that those decisions and rules will be complied with, the acts are a *conditio sine qua non* for effective global governance and thus contribute to output legitimacy of the system. In fact, the scope of the consent principle in the formation of international law seems to shrink continuously: persistent objection is accepted less readily and status treaties deploy some effects for third parties. The practice of voting by consensus is spreading, which means that 'weak' objections not formally voiced will be passed over. More and more decisions in numerous treaty bodies and organs of international organizations are taken by majoritarian vote. Some institutions even produce general and binding rules in majoritarian procedures, such as the Council of Ministers of the EU (under limited conditions). An important extension of state majoritarianism would lie in acknowledging General Assembly Resolutions, adopted by majority vote, as binding international law. However, the extension of inter-state majoritarianism does *not* lead to global democracy either, if we take natural persons as the ultimate unit of democratic procedures. The reasons are the disproportionate populations' sizes and the overruling of democratically formed preferences within one state. These two problems will be treated below at pp. 333–338.

Weak democratic foundation of foreign politics

Another problem of the transitive democratic justification of global governance is that, even within democratic states, the democratic foundation of foreign policy is traditionally weak. International treaties are negotiated, signed, and ratified by members of national executives, who enjoy less direct democratic legitimacy than national parliaments. In democratic states, parliaments are involved in the conclusion of treaties, but often in a late stage when the text is already fixed. They can for the most part only take or leave the treaty and have no creative power to introduce amendments or carve out single articles. As far as customary law is concerned, democratic parliaments are not at all involved in its formation, and also cannot prevent its emergence. Customary law arises primarily from the practice of the executives.

The democratic weakness of the 'transmission belt mechanisms' could be overcome by democratic reforms of the foreign policy instruments on the national level. The need for speed, uniformity, and confidentiality which has made parliamentary involvement difficult in the past, should be put in its place as only one balancing factor among others. The extension of parliamentary input into foreign policy decisions of states could hook onto a current trend in democratic states. For instance, the German, French, and the British parliaments' powers in deciding on military action abroad were recently strengthened and formalized in new laws.[123] Another suggestion would be to allow members of the legislatives (and eventually representatives of the private sector) to participate (maybe only indirectly and only under strict conditions) in the negotiation of international treaties. By strengthening the role of parliaments and citizens in the domestic procedures of treaty making, in decisions on sanctions and on the use of military force abroad, and in all other measures which relate to global governance, the democratic legitimacy of global governance would be indirectly increased. The prolongation of national reforms in that direction thus constitutes one building block of global democratization and hence of constitutionalization. However, these reforms on the national level will not solve serious structural problems of the transitive model of democratic legitimacy of international law, which will be discussed next.

Undemocratic international organizations

International organizations have been called 'islands of non-democracy',[124] and 'bureaucratic bargaining systems'.[125] They have, despite their variety, one thing

---

[123] See for Germany the *Parlamentsbeteiligungsgesetz* of 18 March 2005, BGBl. I 2005, 775 on the participation of Parliament in the decision of deploying armed forces abroad. See for the UK the Constitutional Renewal Draft Bill (introduced in the House of Lords in 2009) (HL Bill 34, Part 3, Sec 24. See for France the revised Art 35 of the Constitution (loi constitutionnelle no 2008–724 of 23 July 2008).

[124] Steve Charnovitz 'WTO Cosmopolitics' (2002) 34 *New York University Journal of International Law and Politics* 299–354, at 310.

[125] Robert A Dahl 'Can International Organizations be Democratic?' in Ian Shapiro and Casiano Hacker-Cordón (eds) *Democracy's Edges* (CUP Cambridge 1999) 19–34, at 33.

in common: they are not organized the way democratic states are.[126] The institutional balance only roughly realizes a functional separation of powers and only faintly secures checks and balances. From a democratic perspective, the main feature of international organizations is their executivist tilt. Member states' representatives belong, even if formally elected or appointed by an organ of the organization, to the member states' bureaucracy, or they have been nominated by the governments, but not by the member states' parliaments or citizens. Where Parliamentary Assemblies exist, such as in the Council of Europe, these are not parliaments in a constitutionalist sense (the EU Parliament being a notable exception).[127] Conferences of the parties, treaty bodies, and informal meetings and regimes do not fare better. They are also, roughly speaking, unelected and executivist.

Another democratic problem is the selection of office-holders in international organizations.[128] The replacement of office-holders (secretary general, executive director, or any other leadership positions, such as high commissioners) normally should be an accountability mechanism. But the current battles of member states in international organizations over appointments of leadership positions more or less openly hinge on nationality, thus on the candidates' expected national loyalty or even bias. Merit, expertise, or experience of a candidate play a smaller role. Criteria guiding selection are seldom specified clearly, and reappointment generally does not require a formal review of top management. These practices hardly allow member states, let alone citizens, to hold office-holders to account.

Additionally, in international organizations such as the WTO, where strong adjudication is not matched by an effective mechanism for treaty reform and the adoption of secondary law, there is an imbalance between judicial and legislative power. This aggravates the democratic deficit, because the international adjudicators are even less democratically legitimate than the international regulators.

A further characteristic of global governance is its relative non-transparency. To give but one example, important food standards are set by the Codex Alimentarius Commission, a sub-entity of the Food and Agriculture Organization of the United Nations (FAO) and the WHO, by simple majority decision taken in secret vote and behind closed doors. Non-transparency is on the one hand the consequence of complexity, multi-layeredness, and size, which makes governance much more complicated and makes it difficult to see through and to attribute responsibility. Non-transparency is also the side-effect of the

---

[126] The salience of the organizations' democracy deficits and the level of regional and international integration are correlated. In organizations where the consensus system prevails and where technical issues with little impact on lives of citizens are treated, the democracy deficits are felt and debated less. But the more 'high' politics is internationalized, the more important the democratic deficiencies become.   [127] See in detail pp. 322–326.

[128] On this problem see Miles Kahler 'Defining Accountability Up: The Global Economic Multilaterals' (2004) 39 *Government and Opposition* 132–158.

diplomatic modes of decision-making, because negotiations and bargaining need a certain degree of confidentiality. Non-transparency is anti-democratic, because it prevents public critique, control, and informed consent. Only if governance is public can civil society assume the role of a democratic actor that cushions the functional deficiencies of parliaments. More transparency will therefore be a pre-condition for the democratization of global governance.[129]

International organizations, e.g. the United Nations, would be indirectly democratized if membership or representation in the plenary organ were conditioned on democratic government. In the two-track model, such a membership condition would be a step on the first track. But such a condition would not make any practical difference for newly created states applying for membership, because current international law obliges new states to be democratic (see above pp. 273–277). A democracy condition would have practical effects only when applied to old undemocratic states. But if these states are already members, they have a legitimate expectation that the membership conditions will not be changed. Therefore such a provision could not be applied to them, and would thus run dry. The positive symbolic value of such a clause would be neutralized by the fact that it would be evidence of the current double standards of international law with regard to the democratic requirements on states.

The blank cheque problem

Another undemocratic feature of global governance is the blank cheque phenomenon. This problem in theory not only concerns the purely transitive democratic foundation of international law and global governance via the democratic nation states, but in practice arises here. States lack control over international law and global governance because many international treaties are not precise and static but general and dynamic. This is most obvious for treaties establishing international regimes or organizations with bodies which monitor behaviour, interpret imprecise and incomplete texts, and which develop new norms (adjudicatory and/or quasi-legislative activity), especially if such secondary law directly addresses individuals, and thus to some extent replaces domestic legislation and administrative acts (global governance properly speaking).

Here it is of little relevance that states have consented to the original treaty. For democratic states, this means that the involvement of national parliaments does not secure democratic legitimacy, because the states' approval of these treaties is a too-general blanket-permission to constitute informed consent in a meaningful sense. The international bodies are so far away and independent from the governments and from citizens that they are *de facto* autonomous. The idea of a democratic vote of states, let alone of a democratic mandate by citizens

---

[129] See in detail below pp. 326–330.

is here rather fictitious. The exit options of states are in most cases illusory, because complex interdependence counsels against ever exercising them, and are therefore no real democratic safeguard.

A remedy against the blanket permission problem would be to demand a continuous and renewable consent, e.g. through sunset clauses in international acts. This is already the practice of the Security Council. Since the experience of not being able to lift the economic sanctions against Iraq because of US opposition, the Security Council has adopted measures under Chapter VII only for limited periods. A similar technique for international treaties would tighten national control (and would thus better secure the internal democratic choices of the contracting states parties' citizens), but would render international cooperation much more precarious.

Another way for nation states to retain or regain (democratic) control seemingly lies in mere informal governmental cooperation, such as in the G8. However, this is, in democratic terms, a double-edged sword. While informal cooperation allows participating states to opt out more easily, and permits the powerful partners to press for the policies their domestic electorate prefers, it tends to be less democratic overall, because it is executive-based and less transparent, and of course because it excludes many states. In the same vein, unilateralism, that is the lonely pursuit of states' national interests, seems to be a way to implement the collective preferences of that state's people. However, unilateralism seems an option only for the few powerful states. And even for those happy few, the option becomes more illusionary, because globalization, financial crises, and terrorism also compel superpowers to cooperate. So unilateralism is only a very limited strategy to safeguard domestic democracy, and it is certainly no way to secure a global multi-unit democracy.

Wrong constituencies

The core concept of transitive democratic global governance, namely the parallel accountability chains from the officials and government representatives within international organizations or other international bodies to the member states, and from the member states to the citizens, which ostensibly secures the democratic link between international institutions and citizens, is a legal fiction that has little to do with reality. Multilevel governance complicates and obscures straightforward 'chains of delegation' (citizens—parliaments—executives—international officers) and makes it hard to identify principals to which institutions would have to account.[130] Normatively speaking, the idea of transitive accountability via states unduly compartmentalizes accountability into national boxes, while neglecting the *dédoublement fonctionnel* of states' agents acting within international institutions. The governmental representatives in

---

[130] Arthur Benz, Carol Harlow, and Yannis Papandopoulos 'Introduction' (2007) 13 *European Law Journal* 441–446, at 444.

international bodies, e.g. in the UN General Assembly, the WTO General Council, or in the Human Rights Council, are in that function not exclusively defenders of the national interest and thus representatives of their home citizens, but also act and vote in the interests of the organization and its objectives.[131] Politics and law resulting from this collective action cannot be explained as the mere result of competition and compromise between conflicting national interests, because the global public interest (which may, but need not always coincide with enlightened national interest) comes into play. The duality of roles is different only in degree for international experts, such as members of the various human rights committees or judges on international courts and tribunals. Although experts and judges should ideally be independent from their governments, the international system reckons with some national bias. For this reason, regional and national diversity is required and practised in filling these posts. The normative consequence of the *dédoublement fonctionnel* of state agents is that an accountability relationship should be required not only between the governmental representatives and their own voters, but also between the former and a global citizenry. The idea of delegation by and accountability to separate national constituencies leaves out this factor. Put another way, it matters whether citizens have the chance to elect and vote out the members of a Global Peoples' Assembly, or whether domestic audiences elect and vote out their government which sends somebody to the General Assembly. The sum of national constituencies does not make a proper global constituency. Thus the parallel chains of accountability to parallel domestic constituencies do not generate an appropriate accountability to the combined citizenry of all the states involved, the global constituency. This also means that the sum of national mechanisms for monitoring and controlling the respective national representatives acting in international bodies does not result in full oversight.

Domestic democracy impaired by globalization

There is a final fundamental reason why an association of democratic states, with states acting on the international plane as representatives of their nationals, is not enough to realize global multilevel democracy. Even if all states of the world became perfect democracies, and even if the international institutions were perfectly responsive to the member states (which they are not, as was shown), this would not lead to a satisfactory situation of global (multi-unit) democratic governance. The reason is that the democratic substance of states is being

---

[131] Conflicts between the national and the global public interest must be solved under due consideration of both spheres. Even if government representatives often negotiate and vote primarily in the national interest, they must justify this before the peers and the public, and thus cannot simply blend out the institution's objectives and policies.

impaired through globalization and through the concomitant zoning-up of governance functions.[132]

This impairment is basically three-fold. First, the reduced capacity of nation states to tackle and solve political problems by themselves reduces the self-determination of citizens within their national polity, hence the democratic output. Second, in the age of global interdependencies, state activities have become further-reaching and more extraterritorial. This means that political decisions produce externalities by affecting people across state borders. The classic example is the utilization of nuclear power. The installation of a nuclear weapon system, the construction of a nuclear power plant, and the performance of nuclear tests may crucially affect persons residing in neighbouring states. Other decisions such as tax reductions or the raising of environmental standards give rise to similar transnational effects. The democratic difficulty lies in the fact that the affected individuals have not elected the decision-makers and can in no way control them. Thirdly, complexities of globalization increase the influence of unelected experts ('technocracy'),[133] and parliamentarianism is additionally undermined by new means of communication, which offers citizens new options of voice without mediation and intervention by parliaments.

All this means that a globalization-induced mismatch between the governing institutions, the governed persons, and the substance of governance weakens the democratic legitimacy of states. Or, put more starkly, it is no longer possible for democratic states to be fully democratic in a non-democratic international system. This observation counsels against channelling legitimation exclusively through the nation states. To conclude, the intrinsic (both conceptual and practical) problems of the state-channelled democratization of international law and global governance justify the quest for a complementary non-state track of democratization. Besides improving the statist track, it seems imperative to pursue, as far as possible, the second individualist track of direct democratization of global governance.

3. Second Track: Citizenship as the Basis of a Non-state Democratization of International Governance

On the second track of non-state democratization, democratic relationships should be established between global citizens and international institutions via schemes of

---

[132] Seminally, Karl Kaiser 'Transnational Relations as a Threat to the Democratic Process' (1971) 25 *International Organization* 706–720. See also Anne Peters 'The Globalization of State Constitutions' in Janne Elisabeth Nijman and André Nollkaemper (eds) *New Perspectives on the Divide between National and International Law* (OUP Oxford 2007) 251–308, at 278–285. For a case study on Switzerland see Oliver Diggelmann *Der liberale Verfassungsstaat und die Internationalisierung der Politik: Veränderungen von Staat und Demokratie in der Schweiz* (Stämpfli Bern 2005). See for a UN view Human Rights Commission res 2003/35 preamble paras 13 and 14.

[133] Frank Fischer *Technocracy and the Politics of Expertise* (Sage Publications Newbury Park Cal. 1990); Gottfried Rickert *Technokratie und Demokratie* (Peter Lang Frankfurt am Main 1991).

participation and representation that cut across nation states. Global citizens should have an input into international law-making independent of their states.

3.1 Transnational citizenship

The political side

In a constitutionalized world order, citizenship would be globalized. This is conceivable without taking sides with particular liberal or republican concepts of citizenship. Both concepts, be they more rights-focused and 'atomized' as the liberal version, or placing more emphasis on the active, participatory, and responsible facet, as the republican version, can accommodate global constitutionalism.[134] Suffice to say that citizenship encompasses political rights and duties, and implies membership of persons in a collective.

Corresponding to the two-track democratization strategy via democratic nation states and through direct global action of citizens and other civil society actors, natural persons have various political roles. We witness their *multiplication fonctionnelle* as citizens of their nation state, of local, regional, and eventually functional polities, and as citizens of the global polity. Martha Nussbaum, referring to Diogenes the Cynic to whom the term 'cosmopolitanism' is ascribed, described this as follows: '[E]ach of us dwells, in effect, in two communities—the local community of our birth, and the community of human argument and aspiration.'[135]

The two-track model precludes the idea of a solely global citizenship. In any case, this would be neither practicable nor desirable. An exclusive global citizenship would ignore the special ties and attachments to one's local and national communities, it would be too abstract to generate the moral and emotional energy needed to live up to its austere imperatives, it could easily become an excuse for ignoring the well-being of the nearer communities, and it provokes reactive nationalism.[136]

Still, the equation between citizenship and nationality is no longer taken for granted. National citizenship is confronted with a dual challenge, from the 'outside' by globalization, and from the 'inside' by multiculturalism.[137] The

---

[134] Although the liberal versions may be more prone to cosmopolitan extensions, republican approaches espouse cosmopolitanism as well. See, e.g., Lawrence Quill on 'cosmorepublican citizenship' and 'republicanism in a global age'. (Quill, *Liberty*, 2006, esp. at 88, 134, 150). See generally and usefully April Carter *The Political Theory of Global Citizenship* (Routledge London 2001).

[135] Martha C Nussbaum 'Patriotism and Cosmopolitanism' in *idem* (ed) *For Love of a Country: Debating the Limits of Patriotism* (Beacon Press Boston 1996) 3–17, at 7. It seems that we are nowadays dwelling not only in two but in multiple communities.

[136] Bhikhu C Parekh 'Cosmopolitanism and Global Citizenship' (2003) 29 *Review of International Studies* 3–17, at 12.

[137] See on this point Paul Magnette *Citizenship: The History of an Idea* (European Consortium for Political Research (ecpr) Colchester 2005), at 168.

outside challenge is the following. With states becoming less (or differently) sovereign than they used to be, a citizenship confined to the nation state seems out of focus with the real places of power. Since citizenship is supposed to be an instrument of self-determination, and since self-determination can be fully exercised only by transboundary cooperation, it follows that citizenship must be exercised at a higher level than within the nation state: no globalization without global participation. The simultaneous challenge to citizenship from inside in the name of multiculturalism is plausibly even causally linked to the outside challenge. Two key aspects of globalization are migration with its ensuing growing diversity of populations, and an uniformization (or Americanization) of lifestyle, which triggers the psychological desire to remember and to revive cultural-specific heritages and traditions of subgroups within nation states.

Both challenges to citizenship ultimately raise the same question: how 'thin' can a viable citizenship be? What is the minimal threshold of rights and duties that must be imposed on persons to preserve the coherence of a political community? There is no abstract and universal answer to this question, and the reason for this seems to lie in the *conditio humana*, as James Tully points out. On the one hand we aspire to be free from the ways of one's culture and place, but on the other hand we long to belong to a culture and place. 'The tension between these two goods cannot be resolved or transcended, and it cannot be overcome by a rootless cosmopolitanism on the one side or a purified nationalism on the other.' Given this basic condition, Tully suggests 'a form of constitutionalism and a spirit of citizenship in which these two human-all-too-human longings can be voiced and conciliated over time'.[138] This spirit of citizenship might be called 'transnational' citizenship.[139] Transnational citizenship is not just an additional layer, but an attitude that modifies the citizenship anchored in nationhood. If citizenship can exist on local, national, regional, and global levels, the transnational or global orientation may be contained within all expressions of citizenship while at the same time transcending them. Transnational citizenship applies dynamic political reasoning to the question of identity, as Paul Magnette explains: by creating a permanent confrontation between national identities and common principles, the parochialism of national polities is eroded, while their capacity of resistance against dangerous trends is strengthened. This might help to break the vicious circle which leads from local prejudice to abstract universalism and from abstract universalism to a rebirth of xenophobic reactions. If the multiple types of identity become permanent

---

[138] James Tully *Strange Multiplicity: Constitutionalism in an Age of Diversity* (CUP Cambridge 1995), at 32.

[139] Magnette, *The History of an Idea*, 2005, at 177. Parekh, Cosmopolitanism, 2003, at 12 calls it 'globally oriented' citizenship. Gerard Delanty 'Theorising Citizenship in a Global Age' in Wayne Hudson and Steven Slaughter (eds) *Globalisation and Citizenship: The Transnational Challenge* (Routledge Abingdon 2007) 15–29, at 16 and 27 speaks of 'multilevelled' citizenship.

features of social groups, their peaceful confrontation at least offers a negative substitute for an ideal form of membership.[140]

Transnational citizenship implies that individuals have a democratic relationship not only with their home state, but also with international organizations, and arguably even with other states. Correspondingly, individuals form part of various constituencies, and realize the various components of citizenship (rights and duties) differently on the various levels of governance. So a crucial feature of transnational citizenship is its non-hierarchical multiplicity. The multiple political affiliations and the ensuing rights and obligations are not exclusive, and not necessarily competitive, but in principle complementary. This is accurately expressed in the Treaty on the Functioning of the European Union, which states that 'citizenship of the Union shall be additional to and not replace national citizenship' (Article 20 TFEU Lisbon).[141] Of course conflicts of loyalty may arise for individuals from multiple allegiances. But the solution of such conflicts is a personal matter which should not be patronized. A person who possesses participation rights on the subnational, national, and global levels of government, decides—if need be—to grant priority to the interests of the one or the other community, and will exercise his or her rights accordingly.[142]

But there is still the problem of stimuli for acting responsibly within those functional constituencies. Why should any member of a functional constituency behave as a responsible citizen, rather than merely voting according to his personal or sectoral interest? If members have no reason to expect that they will be called upon to decide things together in the future, they will not act as responsible citizens, because they do not depend on others behaving responsibly at the next occasion, too.[143] The guarantee of reciprocity as a motivational factor for responsible citizenship is a kernel of truth embodied in the idea of the nation as a 'community of fate'. Surely, the regulatory all-inclusiveness of states has been perforated through the transfer of competences to international organizations. But these transfers do not mitigate the problem of lacking reciprocity among citizens of the world, because the competences are not bundled on a higher level, but are dispersed onto various organizations. None of the organizations' constituencies thus constitutes a 'community of fate'. It is therefore indispensable to strengthen motives other than reciprocity for the responsible exercise of citizenship on the global level. The only way seems to be to engrain and train citizenship in smaller communities, within national borders, and hope that these civic virtues can carry across to wider constituencies.

---

[140] Magnette, *The History of an Idea*, 2005, at 179.

[141] Art-17(1) EC): 'Citizenship of the Union shall complement and not replace national citizenship.'

[142] By contrast, the coordination of collective preferences, expressed in institutional decisions on various levels of governance, is more difficult (see pp. 333–338).

[143] Miller, *Citizenship*, 2000, at 95.

Finally, the question arises which types of global political rights and responsibilities natural persons must generally assume in order to speak meaningfully
of a transnational citizenship. This will be discussed next.

The legal side

The entitlement of the worlds' citizens to direct democratic action on a global
scale as demanded by global constitutionalism can be bolstered by a broader
interpretation of the right to political participation as guaranteed in Article 25
ICCPR. I submit that—under conditions of global governance—the right to
democratic participation should not only be directed against states, but that it
should be generally exercisable across borders and also opposable to those international organizations which rule over people's lives and affect their interests.

The doctrinal consequence of the citizens' right to political participation in
global governance—which is in constitutional terms desirable—is that individuals are upgraded from mere passive international legal subjects (as holders of
human rights and bearers of criminal responsibility) to active international legal
subjects, to co-law makers. The legally relevant difference is that passive subjects
are only capable of having rights, whereas active legal subjects are capable of
creating law. But an active international legal personality of natural persons does
not mean that individuals would have the capacity to sign up and ratify international treaties, just like states. Neither does it inevitably imply the establishment of
a global parliament, elected by the world's citizens, which would pass global laws.
International legal personality can encompass different sets of rights.[144]

For the world's citizens, active international legal personality could mean first
of all a right to be heard in formalized notice-and-comment procedures ('voice')
in treaty-making, such as employed in the drafting of the European Constitutional Treaty of 2004. Eventually, direct global democratic mechanisms, such as
punctual (consultative) referendums of the world's citizens on transnational
issues could be envisaged.[145]

Citizens' voices could instead or additionally be channelled through the various international organizations. However, the establishment of direct democratic relations between individuals and international organizations is fraught
with difficulties. The members of international organizations are states. Because
of their lack of territory and their limited competences, international organizations are not akin to federal states. It does not make sense to consider the
nationals or inhabitants of their member states as 'indirect' citizens of the
organizations via the member states. This means that, *in theory*, the constituencies of international organizations are not spatially, but functionally
defined. However, it is doubtful whether democratic citizenship practices can

---

[144] ICJ, *Reparation for Injuries Suffered in the Service of the United Nations*, Advisory Opinion,
ICJ Reports 1949, 174, at 178: 'The subjects of law in any legal system are not necessarily identical
in their nature or in the extent of their rights.'   [145] See below pp. 318–319.

really work within such functionally defined (both multilevel and sectoral) constituencies. Take development policies as performed by the United Nations as an example. First, the relevant constituency must be defined. It must be determined who has a relevant interest in a certain development policy measure. In times of globalization, almost everybody in the world is affected by some decisions taken at any other place on the globe, especially in the fields of finance, economy, and the environment. Not every remote affectedness should be allowed to trigger a person's right to democratic participation in that decision. A threshold would have to be defined, which is difficult.[146] The problem of undue influence of bystanders would, however, be mitigated if the participatory rights are limited to voice and fall short of vote. Still, a remaining problem of 'functional representation' on the basis of affectedness is that such a scheme could not guarantee that every person is represented only once, because everyone has multiple interests. This could be said to violate the principle of equality.

The more feasible strategy for allowing for political participation of global citizens to some extent independent of and besides their states seem to be peoples' or parliamentary assemblies. Their membership is *not* based on (varying) 'affectedness' but is determined by the fact of states' membership of the organization: citizens who are not nationals of a member state are not represented here and cannot participate, even if they may have material interests at stake. This means that in practice this type of representation is still in a way 'territorial'. That is a somewhat flawed compromise but seems to be inevitable until more precise criteria of purely 'functional' representation on the basis of 'affectedness' have been defined.

Concretely, the active international legal personality of individuals would here mean that citizens directly (or indirectly via national parliaments) elect non-state delegates who have (at least) a consultative status in international forums. Such a forum might be a Global Parliamentary Assembly at the United Nations.[147] Because such assemblies would not replace the governmental representation in international organizations, the member states would remain the co-principals of the international organizations beside the global citizens.

With regard to *alien states*, democratic rights of citizens are difficult to design,[148] although the 'nation state failure' in the form of extraterritorial effects

---

[146] A 'functional' and interest-based delineation of rights and obligations is hardly comparable to the personal delineation of legal regimes as used before the establishment of the territorial nation state. In those times, membership of a legal community was based on personal grounds, and specific legal orders for the various tribes and peoples, Jews, or the clergy, existed. But the standard question of Carolingian judges, 'Quo iure vivis?' ('Under which law do you live?') was relatively easy to answer, whereas the question: 'Who has a legitimate interest in a specific issue based on affectedness?', is not.   [147] See below pp. 324–326.

[148] In political terms, globally oriented citizens should take an active interest in affairs of other countries, they should have a duty to protest if one's own government performs harmful policies *vis-à-vis* third states, and they should be committed to create a more just world order, albeit mainly with the help of their own state. Parekh, Cosmopolitanism, 2003, at 13.

and negative externalities[149] in principle calls for such a design. A rather radical idea is reciprocal representation in form of exchanging parliamentarians among states in parliamentary sessions on transnational issues. The foreign parliamentarians could then be allowed to participate in the debate on issues which affect their country. However, it seems difficult to grant persons (or their delegates) voting rights in other states with regard to those affairs which concern or affect them, because a threshold of intensity can hardly be defined in any operational way. A more moderate procedure would be not voting rights, but 'voice' for non-nationals (or their delegates). This could take the form of notice and comment procedures accompanied by a procedural obligation to take the interests and concerns of non-nationals into account in national democratic decision-making.[150] Although the problem of defining the groups of 'affected' persons does not disappear when it comes to granting voice, the blurriness going with it is less serious because the legal consequences of voice are less decisive than in the case of voting.

3.2 'Who speaks of humankind cheats'?[151]

Many people doubt or vehemently deny that the personal (collective) basis for democratic mechanisms exists or can ever emerge on a global scale.

Demos and equal liberty

A number of arguments surrounding the global collectivity of humans ultimately boil down to the statement that democratic mechanisms independent of nation states cannot realize the equal liberty of persons, and will therefore be unfair and undeserving of the name democracy.

The old version of the argument views democracy and the nation state as intrinsically correlated. It has intellectual roots in the political philosophy of Hegel, according to which the individual can be free only in and by means of the state.[152] Currently, this argument is espoused by some strands of republicanism: 'Republicanism, in contrast to political cosmopolitanism, sees the state as essential to the construction of liberty.'[153]

My response is that, although nation states have historically been the ordinary locus of democracy, there is no logical or necessary link. Democratic procedures

---

[149] See pp. 295–296.
[150] *Cf* Christian Joerges 'Re-Conceptualizing the Supremacy of European Law: A Plea for a Supranational Conflict of Laws' in Beate Kohler-Koch and Bernhard Rittberger (eds) *Debating the Democratic Legitimacy of the European Union* (Roman & Littlefield Lanham MD 2007) 311–327, at 319.
[151] 'Wer Menschheit sagt, will betrügen.' Carl Schmitt *Der Begriff des Politischen* (Duncker & Humblot Berlin 1932), at 55, referring to Proudhon.   [152] See p. 178 n. 97.
[153] Steven Slaughter 'Cosmopolitan Citizenship and Republican Citizenship' in Wayne Hudson and Steven Slaughter (eds) *Globalisation and Citizenship: The Transnational Challenge* (Routledge Abingdon 2007) 85–99, at 97.

are currently not reserved for states, but are applied in different forms to all kinds of societal structures (or parts of them), ranging from schools, sports clubs, and factories to supra-state entities such as the EU. If the assertion of a necessary link between democracy and the state wants to be more than *Begriffsjur-isprudenz*, it would have to demonstrate unique qualities of the state as the sole form of political or social organization capable of securing the equal freedom of natural persons. Current experimenting with novel forms of political organiza-tion besides states renders the claim of such exclusivity implausible and shifts the burden of proof onto Neo-Hegelians.

The weaker version of the Hegelian position asserts that democratic decision-making can only happen in a human collective that would be at least similar to a people of a nation state. In this view, democracy among the world's population is impossible because this collective does not form a global demos. But this position is flawed by the fact that there is no global consensus on what the decisive characteristics of a global demos as a necessary 'carrier' of a global democracy are. On the contrary, there are widely divergent philosophies about what makes 'a people'. The stereotypical French tradition focuses on a common political will to respect basic political ideals (*liberté, égalité, fraternité*). As Ernest Renan put it: '*Une nation est une âme, un principe spirituel*'.[154] The competing 'German' view of a 'people' rather relies on ethnic origin and on common cul-ture. Because that conception rests on elements which are given rather than on elements which can grow and which can be acquired, it is more deterministic and closed than the (ideal-typical) 'French' one. There is not the slightest chance of identifying or building a global people in a 'German' sense. But even if we rely on an ideal-typical 'French' conception of a 'people', it is difficult to discern a global demos in *statu nascendi*.

However, the people from whom democratic government in theory emanates has in reality never been a pre-political, natural entity. It has not been the origin of polities, but often a product of deliberate nation-building.[155] Particularly in states created through decolonization, the inhabitants became 'instant' demoi. So it would be a-historical to ask for a historically consolidated global 'people' as a pre-condition of a global democracy.

A modern formulation of the fundamentalist objection is that a global democracy independent of nation states is impossible because citizens of the world do not have equal stakes in worldwide problems. Therefore, so the argument goes, democratic decisions on a global scale in which every single

---

[154] Ernest Renan 'Qu'est-ce qu'une nation? in *idem Oeuvres complètes* I (Calmann-Lévy Paris 1947, orig. 1882) 887–906, at 903.

[155] See Ernest Gellner *Nations and Nationalism* (Basil Blackwell Oxford 1983), at 55: 'It is nationalism which engenders nations, and not the other way round.' See also Benedict Anderson *Imagined Communities* (Verso London 1983) and Eric John Hobsbawm *Nations and Nationalism since 1780: Programme, Myth, Reality* (2nd edn Canto Cambridge 1992), chapter 3 on a kind of nationalism from above.

person has an equal vote would amount to treating persons as unequals in that context and would therefore be unfair.[156]

But this critique does not effectively discredit all types of transnational citizens' participation, because it applies similarly to voting within nation states. Under the globalizing forces, nations resemble less than before 'communities of fate' which were united by the fact that a large set of important issues arose for every human member. In the heydays of the nation state, the state's extensive regulatory competences and monopolized enforcement powers brought about an overall national package of regulation over time, which resulted in roughly equal stakes for every citizen. However, due to the transfer of public functions to non-state or supra-state actors on the one hand, and migration, tax evasion, and other forms of partial or total transborder mobility of citizens and their goods on the other hand, this regulatory 'package' has become increasingly subject to pick-and-choose. This means that within nation states, citizens may be affected to highly differing degrees by national laws and politics. The stakes of citizens within nation states have thus become increasingly unequal. Inversely, the traditional way of distributing democratic rights within states (allowing all nationals, but only nationals to participate) is increasingly recognized as unfair in certain contexts. This is why electoral rights for foreign residents have been introduced in numerous states, notably in EU member states.[157]

It is not possible, and not even necessary, to begin a futile search for a global community of fate, a global demos. If one recognizes humanity as a novel political subject, it would not be a unitary one, but a plural one, consisting of multiple demoi. Transnational participatory structures are in that perspective a 'demoi-cracy' rather than a democracy.[158] But this is less unusual than it might seem at first sight. Already within states, democracy has been 'decentered'. The sheer variety of mechanisms and processes that constitute political decision-making in states has called into question the ideal of one line of accountability to one demos. The multiplicity of interlocking levels of governance from cities to federal states to international regimes has a similar effect, and likewise implies a shift from demos to demoi. To conclude, the non-state democratization of global governance does not need a monolithical global demos. Participation and accountability can be realized among dispersed demoi in a multi-unit polity.

---

[156] Thomas Christiano 'Democratic Legitimacy and International Institutions' in Samantha Besson and John Tasioulas *Philosophy of International Law* (Oxford OUP 2010) 119–137. This reasoning is familiar from anti-discrimination law. A law which applies formally and equally to everybody (e.g. a housing statute) may disproportionately burden some groups (e.g. Roma) and may therefore constitute illegal indirect discrimination.

[157] However, even these new electoral rights are limited to local and regional elections and decisions and are clearly defined by the territorial criterion of residence. See Jo Shaw *The Transformation of Citizenship in the European Union: Electoral Rights and the Restructuring of Political Space* (CUP Cambridge 2007).

[158] James Bohman *Democracy across Borders: From Demos to Demoi* (MIT Press Cambridge MA 2007), at 126.

Historicity and homogeneity

Obviously, the world population is in cultural, linguistic, economic, political, and social terms highly inhomogeneous. This diversity seems to be one reason for an at best very thin collective identity of humankind. Many consider this to be a major obstacle to global democracy, and to the possibility of transnational citizenship. I will in this section summarize some related points of criticism, and respond in the next section.

One strand of critique pits the abstract and artificial concepts of humanity and cosmopolitanism against the ostensibly natural and organic concepts of nationhood and statehood. According to the 'organics', humankind, being an artificial construct, cannot form the basis of a global political, let alone, democratic, system. Worse, even, any reference to humankind merely camouflages other political, e.g. imperialist, motives.

A modern formulation of this old critique is that political cosmopolitanism neither builds upon existing sentiments, nor does it automatically evoke the social solidarity needed to entertain democratic institutions. Free (democratic) institutions are—so the argument runs—not a bright idea that can be construed on the drawing board and voted in: they must expand upon or restore some traditional institution, and must build on the existing foundations.[159] Only the historically shaped sense of common responsibility by citizens for their state is sound enough for carrying democracy, says the critique.

A similar categorical stance is that citizenship is intrinsically tied to the nation state and cannot exist in larger spaces, what David Miller calls 'bounded citizenship'. Bounded citizenship implies that the practice of citizenship must be confined within the boundaries of national communities. Proponents of bounded citizenship reject transnational or global citizenship as an empty term.[160] The methodological starting point of that objection against transnational citizenship is plausible. Indeed, citizenship is not only a term, but a social practice that can not be simply conjured upon *ex nihilo*. Purely theoretical citizenship, unsupported by a shared public culture, would indeed be empty. Mutual trust and assurance is required for assuming responsibility, and without responsibility, citizenship would remain hollow. However, to conclude that a shared national identity is the basis for citizenship, and that 'inventing in theory cosmopolitan forms of citizenship ... undercut the basis of citizenship proper'[161] just begs the question.[162]

---

[159] S Slaughter, Cosmopolitan Citizenship, 2007, at 94.   [160] Miller, *Citizenship*, 2000.
[161] *Ibid*, at 96.
[162] Miller's answer to this question seems to be that citizenship implies equal rights, including equal social rights. However—so the argument goes—equal social rights require wealth distribution, and this in turn presupposes a thick solidarity, which is out of reach on the global scale. But this problem of social rights and 'social' citizenship goes beyond the issue of democracy. On solidarity see below pp. 311–312.

A different but related problem is that of the lack of homogeneity of the global population. Traditional democrats used to cherish homogeneity as a pre-condition of democracy. Alexis de Tocqueville, in his essay on democracy in America, claimed that 'a homogeneity of civilisation', i.e. the situation 'that men see many things in the same way and have the same opinions about many subjects', is indispensable for democratic government of a state.[163] John Stuart Mill particularly highlighted the need of a common language. In his 'Considerations on Representative Government', Mill asserted that '[f]ree institutions are next to impossible in a country made up of different nationalities'. 'Among a people without fellow-feeling, especially if they read and speak different languages, the united public opinion, necessary to the working of representative government, cannot exist . . . . The same books, newspapers, pamphlets, speeches, do not reach [the different sections of the country] . . . The same incidents, the same acts, the same system of government, affect them in different ways . . .'[164]

A modern writer explains that a democracy must be 'homogeneous' to be stable, because only then 'all (or at any rate the vast majority) of the people share a commitment to the state and its democratic regime form, they are tied to their fellow citizens through an understanding of the commonality of their fate and the recognition of equal liberties, and they rank these commitments and loyalties higher than the various cleavages that divide national society.'[165]

The idea of homogeneity overlaps with the quest for a societal 'basic consensus'. The basic consensus is—so to speak—the uniformity of opinions on the foundational principles of society. It has traditionally been considered as a prerequisite of a viable democracy, because the basic consensus guarantees the stability of institutions, serves as a guideline for deciding controversial issues, discharges politics on those issues where no vote is needed, and generally triggers the diffuse support of the system by its citizens.

An overlapping question is that of global solidarity. Global solidarity might be a prerequisite of a viable global democracy, especially when it comes to redistributive policies. The critical stance is that once solidarity is globalized and universalized, it becomes zero. The empty term of global solidarity is, according to its deniers, just an exercise field for the bad conscience, exploited by the mass media and by humanitarian NGOs.[166]

---

[163] Alexis de Tocqueville *Democracy in America* (The Library of Amercia New York 2004, orig. 1835–1840 Goldhammer trans) vol 1, part I, chapter 8 (190) and vol 1, part II, chapter 10 (431).

[164] John Stewart Mill *Considerations on Representative Government* (Indianapolis 1958, orig. 1861 Shields ed) chapter 16 (230–231). Numerous other commentators have considered linguistic diversity to be an especially important barrier to the evolution of a common identity. This assertion is, however, based on an outdated theory, which exaggerates the role of language amongst the multiple factors of identity-formation. Hobsbawm, *Nations and Nationalism*, 1992, passim.

[165] Claus Offe ' "Homogeneity" and Constitutional Democracy: Coping with Identity Conflicts through Group Rights' (1999) 6 *The Journal of Political Philosophy* 113–141, at 119.

[166] Herfried Münkler 'Enzyklopädie der Ideen der Zukunft: Solidarität' in Jens Beckert, Julia Eckert, Martin Kohli and Wolfgang Streeck (eds) *Transnationale Solidarität: Chancen und Grenzen* (Campus Frankfurt am Main 2004) 15–28, at 22.

Today, a prominent sceptic of the global democratization thesis, Robert Dahl, doubts that international organizations can be elevated above any acceptable threshold of democratization, essentially because of the global diversity. According to Dahl, the highly diverse world population, with little agreement on substantive criteria, and without some generally agreed boundaries as to rights, liberties, and minimal standards of justice, will not accept procedural solutions and a majority decision as sufficient; and determining the general good becomes highly problematic in this setting.[167]

To sum up the critique, a weak collective identity of humankind, the extreme diversity, and the thin global solidarity, all these factors create the risk that rules issued by global governance institutions, awards rendered by international courts, and sanctions imposed by bodies such as the Security Council will be perceived by their addressees as illegitimate forms of 'outside' or 'alien' interference, and will thus not be loyally accepted.

3.3 Looking forward: the globalization of citizenship

My response to the concerns around the lack of global collective identity and the ostensible impossibility of global solidarity and citizenship is guided by methodological individualism and normative pluralism. Methodological individualism does not consider political collectives as given, but as grown or as constructed by individuals, whose rights and needs are at stake. From that perspective, the ultimate unit of legal concern is the individual. Normative pluralism means welcoming 'reasonable disagreement' in a Rawlsian sense, admitting that the citizens of the world may have contradictory views on moral and political questions which may be equally reasonable.[168]

It is also worth recalling that the imagery of artificial, functional, cold, mechanistic, and therefore undesirable institutions, as opposed to natural, grown, and organic ones was employed in 19th-century romanticism to discredit enlightenment, and at that time went hand in hand with political reaction against constitutionalism, rule of law, and democracy. Realizing that the organic objection had already been raised against the attempt to democratize nation states, but was ultimately defeated by the course of history, suggests the need to scrutinize it carefully this time around.

A conversation in international terms

A first question is whether humankind can ever be a socially relevant community. George Herbert Mead taught his students that 'it is the ability of the person to

---

[167] Dahl, International Organizations, 1999, esp. at 26.

[168] John Rawls *Political Liberalism* (expanded edn Columbia UP New York 2005), at 36. But see Thomas Nagel *Equality and Partiality* (Oxford UP New York 1991), at 168–171 arguing that particularly on a global scale some disagreements can make agreement on conditions of justice for their resolution impossible. Nagel concludes that 'a legitimate government of the world is not possible'.

put himself in other people's place ... that gives to the man what we term ... his citizenship, from a political standpoint'. Mead argued that we possess 'membership in the society of human beings', and that this membership was 'becoming more real to us'. 'The question of whether we belong to a larger community is answered in terms of whether our own actions call out a response in this wider community, and whether this response is reflected back into our own conduct. Can we carry on a conversation in international terms?'[169] Under that standard, humanity is, albeit under rare circumstances, a relevant social community.

Granted, the absence of a common language, as highlighted by John Stuart Mill quoted above, makes the conversation in international terms difficult. Democracy's functioning depends on communication between citizens and the governing institutions, and on public debate and participation. However, a uniform language is no *conditio sine qua non* for this. What matters is a uniform space of communication, not of language. The space of communication and the space of a common language are not necessarily identical. Even a single-language community does not guarantee a common discourse, because of different media consumption habits among different social groups. Conversely, a single space of communication can encompass various languages, as multilingual democracies such as India demonstrate. More important than a common language seems to be a common media scene in which global issues are reported and discussed without focusing exclusively on the extent to which a certain policy favours or prejudices one's own country.

Democracy built on diversity

The homogeneity discourse has been thoroughly discredited by history. The quest for homogeneity bears the danger of homogenization through unacceptable means, such as assimilation or exclusion. The infamous dictum of Carl Schmitt in this regard is well known: according to Schmitt, democracy 'necessarily needs, firstly, homogeneity, and secondly—eventually—the exclusion or destruction of heterogeneous elements ... The political power of a democracy manifests itself in the fact that it can extinguish or keep away the alien and unequal, which threatens homogeneity.'[170] The quest for homogeneity emphasizes distance to the 'other' and ultimately boils down to Schmitt's distinction of friend and foe.[171] Its ultimate consequence can be 'ethnic cleansing'.

These dangers inherent in the uniformity approach suffice to break with constitutionalism as 'the empire of uniformity'[172] and to reconceptualize it so as

---

[169] Mead's answer was positive—already in the inter-war period. George Herbert Mead *Mind, Self and Society* (The University of Chicago Press 1934), at 270–271.

[170] Carl Schmitt 'Der Gegensatz von Parlamentarismus und moderner Massendemokratie' in *idem Positionen und Begriffe im Kampf mit Weimar—Genf—Versailles 1923–1939* (Duncker & Humblot Berlin 1988, orig. 1926) 52, at 59 (translation by the author).

[171] Schmitt, *Der Begriff des Politischen*, 1932, at 14.

[172] Tully, *Strange Multiplicity*, 1995, at 58.

to 'recognize and accommodate cultural diversity', as James Tully put it in his seminal work.[173] Tully denounces the presupposition of shared, implicit norms as 'manifestly false' in culturally diverse societies.[174] He asks for a new constitutionalism which 'requires that the citizens affirm diversity itself as a constitutive good of the association'.[175] This should be done in negotiations in which the negotiators recognize their differences. The constitution should be seen as an activity, as an inter-cultural dialogue.[176] Any presumption of an implicit consensus would mis-identify the telos of this type of constitutional dialogue, and would wrongly filter out the diverse similarities and the differences the speakers try to voice.[177] Tully's quest for the accommodation of multiplicity within constitutional communities is relevant for global constitutionalism and democracy.

Starting from diversity allows us to assess the prerequisites for the acceptability of majority decisions by defeated members of a political community differently. A motive for acceptance may be the hope of gaining the majority on another occasion. This is possible only if affiliations to groups (e.g. to ethnic, religious, and economic groups) are not too dominant. If group affiliations are so dominant that they determine the preferences of the group members over all issues, the result is a strictly segmented society which will not be democratically viable. So what matters for the functioning of democracy is not uniformity, but the absence of fixed segmentation—the two are not identical.

Of course, the global citizenry is divided by strong national affiliations. But this is not the only divide. There are changing coalitions and overlapping memberships of citizens in and between different groups, defined by nationality, wealth, gender, political philosophies, and religion. On the inter-state level, a major dividing line runs between the rich industrial states and the global south, but there are also other groups and coalitions which are not fully congruent with the former, such as industrial and agricultural states, interventionist states and others, ecologically active states and others, and so forth. Consequently, there are many sub-cultures which overlap (both on the level of persons, and of states). The breakdown of the socialist block which terminated the world's political bipolarity was, so considered, an enabling condition for global democracy. A further aspect is that the more global policy-making proliferates and the more it covers diverse subject matters, the more improbable the permanent marginalization of a specific group becomes. With diversity as a starting point, the idea of a basic consensus as a prerequisite for democratic procedures can also be assessed afresh. In a pluralistic society, a basic consensus cannot mean agreement on absolute and ultimate values. The basic consensus can at best be general and provisional. It is necessarily vague and only partially articulated. Often it is only a negative consensus, meaning that there is agreement about what is not

---

[173] *Ibid*, at 1.   [174] *Ibid*, at 131.   [175] *Ibid*, at 177.   [176] *Ibid*, at 184.
[177] *Ibid*, at 131.

acceptable. A basic consensus of this type is more easily conceivable on a global scale.

Globalized identities

The irony is that all cultural and socio-psychological factors relating to collectives, notably uniformity, identity, fellowship, solidarity, etc., have typically been exploited by non-democratic regimes. Clearly the sense of belonging does not necessarily lead to democratic politics, but on the contrary lends itself to abuse. Democratic government must be designed so as to satisfy the apparent human desire for belonging, and not leave this for exploitation and manipulation by the opponents of democracy.[178] This means that culturally imbued collective identity must be creatively appropriated by global political institutions as a source of motivation to make at least some sacrifices for the global political community, but its tendencies of aggression and exclusion must be curbed. Global democracy must 'pull off the trick to preserve cultural identity as a part of its substratum while using its own overlay of values and institutions to select only the best and discard what is worst in cultural identity'.[179] This confirms the claim that a global democracy can only grow out of national democracy, because only democracy within the state can draw on the necessary motivational forces.

In this context it is worth noting that politico-territorial identities, such as being a Berliner, a German, and a European, are not ranked in a fixed hierarchy. The actual weight of the respective identity depends on the concrete circumstances. In some instances, self-perception as a citizen of the world may be more important than national identity; in other situations the opposite will be true. Global and regional identities do not grow at the cost of national identity, because the shifting and interaction of identities is no zero-sum-game, but can lead to the transformation and enlargement of identities.

Anthropologist Arjun Appadurai has argued that new resources for a globalized identity lie in the social force of 'imagination', understood as 'a space of contestation in which individuals and groups seek to annex the global into their own practices of the modern'.[180] The twin forces of mass migration and electronic mediation impel (and compel) the work of imagination, which can build a delocalized 'transnation' that retains 'a special ideological link to a putative place of origin but is otherwise a thoroughly diasporic collectivity'.[181] Postnational politics can be built around this cultural fact. It is time, says Appadurai, to rethink '"monopatriotism", patriotism directed exclusively to the hyphen between nation and state',[182] and time to define other attractive ideals ('new patriotisms'). Patriotism itself could become plural, serial, contextual, and

---

[178] *Cf* Christopher Lord and Erika Harris *Democracy in the New Europe* (Palgrave Houndmills Basingstoke Hampshire 2006), at 182–183.   [179] *Ibid*, at 183.

[180] Arjun Appadurai *Modernity at Large: Cultural Dimensions of Globalization* (University of Minnesota Press Minneapolis 1998), at 4.   [181] *Ibid*, at 172.

[182] *Ibid*, at 176.

mobile, and its objects may be susceptible to transformation. This resembles what Dolf Sternberger had called 'constitutional patriotism'.[183]

Any potentially emerging global collective identity of the world's citizens will be far thinner, more tentative, and more contested than the collective identities we are used to. How thick a collective identity must be so as to carry global democratic procedures, and how this can be measured is a question that cannot be answered with legal methods.

A solidarity of difference

Solidarity between states, as a legal principle, arguably forms part of the global constitutional order.[184] Global solidarity as a socio-psychological fact,[185] as a form of societal reaction to social inequality, and as a precondition of democratic mechanisms, is and will remain thin. It cannot flow from pre-political factors such as language or culture, but must be politically gained. Still there is a potential for global solidarity, because it is not in quality different from national solidarity. Solidarity as presumed in domestic democratic politics is not 'natural', but had to be learnt. It is not, in reality, *fraternité* within a family, arising out of personal ties in a small group. National solidarity is solidarity among strangers. In this context, it is useful to recall the famous 1845 dictum of the 'two nations' by Benjamin Disraeli. Disraeli described the division among the social classes in Britain with the strongest metaphor for alienation he could find, namely as '[t]wo nations, between whom there is no intercourse and no sympathy; who are as ignorant of each other's habits, thought, and feelings, as if they were ... inhabitants of different planets'.[186] This metaphor is a good illustration of the paradox that national solidarity is on the one hand the most powerful instance of political solidarity, but on the other hand by no means automatically granted. The gradually and slowly emerging global solidarity will not be less artificial than national solidarity. Finally, within modern national societies, individualization and cultural hybridization modify and even undermine

---

[183] Dolf Sternberger 'Verfassungspatriotismus' (1982) in *idem Schriften*, vol X (Insel Verlag Frankfurt am Main 1990 Haungs, Landfried, Orth, and Vogel eds) 17–31.

[184] Numerous international legal institutions, such as collective security in the UN Charter, collective self-defence, *erga omnes* norms, the obligation to admit humanitarian assistance in armed conflict, the system of refugee law, or the environmental law principle of common, but differentiated responsibility, can be reconstructed as manifestations and emanations of an emerging global constitutional principle of solidarity. See Karel Wellens 'Solidarity as a Constitutional Principle: Its Expanding Role and Inherent Limitations' in Ronald St MacDonald and Douglas M Johnston (eds) *Towards World Constitutionalism: Issues in the Legal Ordering of the World Community* (Martinus Nijhoff Leiden 2005) 775–807.

[185] For a sociological perspective see Angelika Poferl's useful 'Solidarität ohne Grenzen? Probleme sozialer Ungleichheit und Teilhabe in europäischer Perspektive' in Martin Heidenreich (ed) *Die Europäisierung sozialer Ungleichheit* (Campus Frankfurt and New York 2006) 231–252.

[186] Benjamin Disraeli *Sybil, or the Two Nations* (Thomas Nelson London 1845) book I, chapter 5, at 85.

national solidarity. It would be anachronistic to insist on a conception of solidarity that is also vanishing within states.

Against this background, global solidarity can be best understood as flowing from reciprocal respect. Reciprocal respect also seems crucial for democratic (majoritarian) procedures. Ronald Dworkin put this as follows: I am bound by the democratic decisions of a political community, when 'its act is in some pertinent sense *my* act, even when I argued and voted against it, … under no other assumption we can intelligibly think that as a member of a flourishing democracy we are governing ourselves.' This mechanism presupposes that the political process of the community 'must express some bona fide conception of equal concern for the interests of all members'. Members will accept majority decisions as legitimate when they know that the other members of the community take their interests seriously.[187] Along this line, Nancy Fraser has defined (global) solidarity as flowing from recognition of the other as a member of a global community in a dual sense: recognition as respect and as acknowledgment of the connectedness of every member's social existence.[188] Such a 'solidarity of difference' may be a basis for a global democracy.

Building citizens' capacities through institutional boot-strapping

Given the conceptual vagueness of collectives' characteristics, it is analytically more helpful to focus on citizens' capacities. Collective identity is not in itself the enabling factor of democratic culture, but the virtues which ostensibly flow from it are, namely responsibility, solidarity, a willingness to compromise, trust, and tolerance. The growth of these virtues is surely facilitated by a however defined common identity, but it does not logically or psychologically depend on it. Solidarity, for instance, not only emerges via the opposition of 'Us' and 'Them', but from compassion for the well-being of other individuals.

Ultimately, the question of the factual underpinnings of democracy (demos, homogeneity, collective identity, language, solidarity, and the like) is a chicken-and-egg problem, which cannot be definitely solved. 'No chicken, no egg' is not the right answer.[189] Although the importance of cultural and social elements as enabling factors of democratic procedures should not be underestimated, these still interact with the legal (democratic) institutions. None of these factors is a natural, absolute, *a priori* of democratic governance which would have to be present in full before democratic processes could begin. One may reckon with their evolution within and through democracy. This is most obvious for the carrier of democracy, the demos. Global democracy need not be founded upon a

---

[187] Ronald Dworkin *Freedom's Law: The Moral Reading of the American Constitution* (Harvard UP Cambridge MA 1996) 15–26, quotes at 22 and 25 (emphasis added).

[188] Nancy Fraser 'From Redistribution to Recognition?' in Stephen Seidman and Jeffrey C Alexander *The New Social Theory Reader* (Routledge London and New York 2001) 285–293.

[189] *Cf* Joshua Cohen and Charles Sabel 'Global Democracy?' (2005) 37 *New York University Journal of International Law & Politics* 763–797, at 767.

pre-existing people, but on peoples who become continuously more conscious of their common destiny.[190] Bootstrapping is also possible for the other cultural and social factors. Although democratic institutions to some extent presuppose, as just said, certain civic capacities and virtues, these are not clearly pre-institutional and independent from democratic legal structures, but are shaped by and emerge through functioning (democratic) institutions. While the citizens' cognitive and ethical capacities enhance and support the functioning of the institutions, those institutions are in turn apt to improve the democratic capacities of the citizens. Moreover, citizens normally become involved only when they realize that engagement makes sense. Therefore it can be expected that citizens will become interested in the global institutions and seek information about them when these acquire real political power. Global partial publics relating to a range of transnational issues are more likely to emerge if citizens have a voice in global affairs. Thus a global public is not only an enabling factor of a global democratic discourse, but at the same time a possible consequence of the institutionalization of such a discourse, and of the empowerment of global citizens. In short, all social and cultural factors are dynamic and the existing deficiencies are no absolute impediment to a global multilevel democracy.

To conclude, the argument that there can be no global democracy because there is no global identity, solidarity etc. has the same vicious quality as the argument that women could not be citizens, because they had no understanding of public affairs. Women did not have understanding of public affairs, because they did not enjoy citizens' rights, had no place in the *civitas*, but were confined to the private sphere. It was possible to break out of the vicious circle only through political action, by daring to release women into the public sphere. A similar experiment has to be ventured in global constitutional politics in order to continue the path towards global democracy.

4. Second Track: The Role of Civil Society Actors in Global Democracy

4.1 Global civil society

Any democracy needs a civil society, because otherwise no political discourse over the common good takes place, and elites would rule without any serious check on their powers. But what does 'civil society' mean? No fully consented definition exists—which is actually what civil society is about. I understand by civil society a sphere which neither pertains to the state, nor exclusively to the market, and which is public as opposed to private. I do not categorically exclude business actors from civil society, because these increasingly assume societal

---

[190] Pascal Lamy *La démocratie-monde. Pour une autre gouvernance globale* (Seuil Paris 2004), at 59.

responsibility and engage in civil regulation, e.g. in form of environmental and labour codes, even together with NGOs. These developments, encapsulated in the idea of 'corporate citizenship', blur the line between the *citoyen* and *bourgeois*.[191] The public sphere within states is constituted and populated by political parties, NGOs, pressure groups, and activists. News media and constitutional guarantees of freedom of the press and freedom of association are necessary conditions to public debate, and thus constitutive of a civil society.

The concept of civil society is no 'western' one, but was reinvented as a counter-concept to totalitarianism in the Eastern European transition states of the 1990s and in Latin America. It is applicable to global democracy.[192] A global democracy cannot work if global publicity and a global civil society have not surpassed a minimal stage of development. The question is whether this threshold is already reached or whether on a global level, civil society is too disaggregated and consists merely of a 'phantom public'.[193]

Historically, social movements such as the anti-slavery, the pacifist, the feminist, and ecological movements, always had a transnational thrust. In the past decade, the role of civil society in global governance has been acknowledged at the 'We the Peoples Millennium Forum of 2000'[194] and at the 2002 Sustainable Development Summit.[195] The Cardoso Report of 2004 highlighted that public opinion and the involvement of actors from civil society and the private sector have been key factors of effective action on global priorities.[196] So civil society has gone global to some extent. Of course, individuals necessarily remain located in states, and their civic engagement depends on the respective governments' willingness to tolerate or foster NGOs and other forms of associations. Despite this inevitable element of territoriality, civil society action is much less confined within the borders of nation states than some decades ago. The main reasons for the globalization of civil society seem to be the availability of information technology and of targets around which transnational networks can coalesce.

The role of global civil society is mostly one of opposition and contestation. Civil society organizations have elicited greater accountability of global

---

[191] The role of genuinely private actors in global governance, and the privatization proper of global governance, constitutes a challenge for democracy. On business actors as members of the global constitutional community see pp. 240–262.

[192] Seminally, Ronnie Lipschutz 'Reconstructing World Politics: The Emergence of Global Civil Society' (1992) 21 *Millennium: Journal of International Studies* 389–420; see also Ann Florini *The Coming Democracy: New Rules for Running the World* (Island Press Washington DC 2003); Mary Kaldor *Global Civil Society: An Answer to War* (Polity Press Cambridge 2003); Jan Aart Scholte 'Civil Society and Democratically Accountable Global Governance' (2004) 39 *Government and Opposition* 211–233.   [193] Bohman, *Democracy across Borders*, 2007, at 70–71.

[194] Civil society organizations' 'We the Peoples Millennium Forum Declaration and Agenda for Action, Strengthening the UN for the 21st Century' of 26 May 2000. See in this document notably Part F: 'Strengthening and democratizing the United Nations and international organizations' (UN Doc A/54/959).

[195] In the Report of the World Summit on Sustainable Development, Johannesburg, South Africa, 26 August–4 September 2002 (UN Doc A/CONF.1999/20), partnership with 'civil society' was a lead theme.   [196] Cardoso Report 2004, paras 11–27.

governance by increasing its transparency, by monitoring and reviewing global policies, and by seeking redress for mistakes and harms attributable to global regulatory bodies. Besides being a watch-dog, civil society organizations are also agenda setters in global politics. The NGO meetings accompanying the world conferences of the 1990s have so far culminated in the Millennium NGO Forum of May 2000, but it is not clear whether this 'new diplomacy' will continue.

Civil society is also a catalyst for the formation of international law, relating to all traditional legal sources. The classic example is the Martens clause of international humanitarian law, which refers to 'the principles of humanity and the dictates of public conscience'[197] to fill lacunae in the law of armed conflict. And the new human right to be free from forced disappearance, enshrined in the 2006 convention,[198] was triggered by the protests of the *Madres de Argentinia*. Furthermore, the 'opinion of civil society ... cannot be completely discounted in the formation of customary international law today', as dissenting judge Van den Wyngaert stressed in the *Arrest Warrant* case.[199] Overall, global civil society institutions constitute a kind of democratic infrastructure. However, it is not clear whether this global network is already dense enough to allow for a minimum global non-state democracy.

4.2 Democratic benefits of NGO involvement

Direct action of citizens at a transnational level through NGOs is in democratic terms ambiguous. It is a response to the lack of global formal democratic structures. But it might also manifest a different type of global democracy, which would be non-representative, more deliberative (with NGOs contributing information, arguments, and values), and more contestative (with NGOs organizing protest).[200]

However, the claim that NGO activism generates a novel type of global democracy is controversial. The first objection is that NGOs are only a 'surrogate public', and act mainly as opposition. This sort of oppositional influence does not, so the critique goes, by itself make a regime democratic, because 'counterpublics' do not rule.[201] Second, while NGO participation in the decision-making of international organizations must be channelled, the

---

[197] Art 1(2) Protocol I Additional to the Geneva Conventions of 1977, recasting the slightly different formula in the preambles of the Hague Conventions of 1899 and 1907.

[198] *International Convention for the Protection of all Persons from Enforced Disappearance* (GA res 61/177 of 20 December 2006).

[199] Diss.op. judge ad hoc van den Wyngaert, ICJ, *Case Concerning the Arrest Warrant of 11 April 2000* (Democratic Republic Congo v Belgium), ICJ Reports 2002, 3, at 155, para 27.

[200] April Carter 'Transnational Citizenship and Direct Action' in Wayne Hudson and Steven Slaughter (eds) *Globalisation and Citizenship: The Transnational Challenge* (Routledge Abingdon 2007) 127–136, at 127. See on deliberative and contestatory democracy above pp. 268–271.

[201] Bohman, *Democracy across Borders*, 2007, at 66.

screening and accreditation is in a certain tension with the principles underlying democracy, namely equality and inclusiveness. The relevant organization,
e.g. the WTO, will be a gatekeeper and inevitably also a supreme cognitive
arbiter. This could limit the NGOs' capacity to criticize the system from the
outside. It has therefore been concluded that NGO participation is 'no viable
strategy for overcoming the democratic deficit'.[202] The third critique is that
NGO involvement in global governance is not only unhelpful, but even anti-
democratic, because NGOs do not enjoy any democratic mandate by (global)
citizens, but are self-appointed. A fourth and related democratic legitimacy
problem is that many NGOs lack an internal democratic structure. The United
Nations Economic and Social Council (ECOSOC) guidelines, which have
been the most influential model for participatory schemes with other UN
bodies and for organizations outside the UN, postulate that consultative relations can only be established with NGOs having 'a democratically adopted
constitution'.[203] However, this requirement is not enforced by the ECOSOC's
accreditation committee. In reality, only a handful of the more than 2,700
NGOs currently accredited with ECOSOC could be said to be democratic.[204]
The newer Council of Europe 'Principles on the Status of NGOs in Europe'
state that while the management of an NGO must be in accordance with its
statutes and the law, 'NGOs are otherwise sovereign in determining the
arrangements for pursuing their objectives'.[205] According to the Explanatory
Memorandum to these Principles, the internal structure is 'entirely a matter for
the NGO itself'.[206] The Principles thus do not require NGOs' internal
democracy for participation in the Council of Europe.

   I submit that the involvement of NGOs in international law-making is not
undemocratic *tout court*. The democratic function of NGOs is not to be
representatives in a parliamentary sense. By contrast, NGOs pursue single
issues or special interests. They speak (or claim to speak) for minorities, for
vulnerable groups, or for otherwise voiceless entities, such as nature. In most
cases, NGOs have been founded precisely in order to counter the will of the
majority, and to act as opposition. A democratic mandate by a global citizenry
would not serve, but would actually run counter to this function. So a
democratic legitimacy of NGO voice does not require representativity in

---

[202] Falk and Strauss, Creation of a Global Peoples Assembly, 2000, at 215.
[203] UN ECOSOC 1996, *Consultative Relationship between the United Nations and Non-governmental Organizations* (UN Doc A/RES/1996/31) para 10.
[204] Menno T Kamminga 'What Makes an NGO "Legitimate" in the Eyes of States?' in Anton
Vedder (ed) *The Involvement of NGOs in International Governance and Policy* (Martinus Nijhoff
Leiden 2007) 175–195, at 186.
[205] CoE 2002, *Fundamental Principles on the Status of Non-governmental Organisations in Europe*
(November 2002), para 45.
[206] CoE 2002, *Fundamental Principles, Explanatory Memorandum*, para 33.

terms of a democratic mandate conferred by a (more or less virtual) global society.[207]

Likewise, I do not consider the lack of internal democracy in many NGOs as a decisive delegitimation factor, and defend this with two arguments. First, numerous non-democratic states also have the right to vote on international standards. Why should requirements for NGOs be stricter? The formalist answer is that states are the direct addressees of international law, and are obliged to implement and enforce it. Therefore, so the argument goes, they have a legitimate interest in influencing those rules, and should be entitled to co-determine them, independently of their internal government structure. In contrast, NGOs are no international legal persons, therefore no legal duties arise for them from international law, and therefore NGOs do not have an intrinsic legitimate interest in shaping the rules that will bind others, not them. However, this 'state privilege' in law-making is premised on the idea that the state is analogous to a natural person, and as such entitled to self-determination which translates into participation in rule-making. This analogical premise is problematic, because states are no unitary actors, and do not enjoy rights for their own sake, which would be morally comparable to natural persons' fundamental rights to political participation. Therefore, the formalist answer is unsatisfactory. It follows that NGOs should not be treated more strictly than states.

Second, there are viable substitutes for internal democratic control. Donors 'vote' with their cheque book, and members can—unlike the citizens of a state— easily realize their exit option and thereby bring their opinions on the NGO-policies to bear. For these reasons, NGO participation in law-making is legitimate, independently of their internal structure.

The contestatory function of NGOs requires giving them a voice, but not necessarily a vote in the decision-making processes. Voice is the modus of deliberation. The impact of voice on the outcome of the process is informal and less weighty. It correspondingly needs less formal legitimacy, but is sufficiently justified by the reputational and moral legitimacy of NGOs. It is precisely a feature of pluralist law-making processes to offer interest groups the opportunity to participate and give input into the process without requiring any democratic mandate.[208] The NGO voices will complement and contradict each other,

---

[207] Sebastian Oberthür *Participation of Non-governmental Organisations in International Environmental Co-operation: Legal Basis and Practical Experience* (Schmidt Berlin 2002), at 219; Emanuele Rebasti 'Beyond Consultative Status: Which Legal Framework for an Enhanced Interaction between NGOs and Intergovernmental Organizations?' in Pierre-Marie Dupuy and Luisa Vierucci (eds) *NGOs in International Law: Efficiency and Flexibility* (Edward Elgar Northampton 2008) 21–70, at 43.

[208] In Switzerland, the legislative process includes, for all federal bills, a mandatory hearing of associations in the relevant field ('*Vernehmlassung*'); Art 147 of the Federal Constitution and the Law on Consultation of Interested Parties (*Vernehmlassungsgesetz* of 20 December 1968, SR 172.061). See along the same line for law-making in the EU: 'Towards a reinforced culture of consultation and dialogue—General principles and minimum standards for consultation of interested parties by the Commission', COM (2002), 704 final, Communication from the Commission of 11 December 2002.

and will thus contribute to pluralist global deliberations, albeit not to a parliamentary democracy. However, these deliberations are not self-evidently fully democratically legitimate. Who is authorized to define the interests and weigh them, if this does not happen in a formal democratic process? Moreover, besides the usual prevalence of better organized and more powerful interest groups, the geographical imbalance (dominance of 'northern' NGOs) decreases the inclusiveness and equality, and thus the democratic legitimacy of the global deliberative process.

NGO votes, in contrast, would not contribute to the democratic legitimacy of global governance, first, because of the NGOs' lacking democratic mandate, and second, because NGOs' typical selectivity of interests and one-issue character makes them, unlike governments, which pursue and balance a host of competing interests, unfit for package deals or compromises in decision-making. Put differently, NGOs are structurally ill-suited to participate in the governance modus of bargaining. Granting them a vote would therefore hamper the process and thus decrease its democratic legitimacy.

To conclude, as long as NGOs only have voice in decision-making, but not a vote, the lack of formal democratic credentials of NGOs (and likewise of technical experts, professional associations, TNCs, and various public-private or private-private partnerships) does not de-legitimize their participation in global governance. The absence of internal democratic organization can be compensated by other forms of accountability. The legitimacy gains of NGO involvement are apt to outweigh the legitimacy problems. Overall, a further democratization of the international legal order requires that the participation of NGOs in law-making and law-enforcement be strengthened. However, it should remain on the lines of 'voice, but no vote'.

5. Second Track: Institutional Design for a Non-state Democratization of Global Governance

Having established that global non-state democratization is desirable, that transnational citizenship is conceivable, and that NGOs have a legitimate role to play in global democracy, the question is how the international institutions should be designed to pursue the second track. There is no one-fits-all recipe for engaging citizens with diverse institutions and regimes, ranging from treaties, international organizations, and secondary international law to hybrid and more or less formalized regimes, such as treaty bodies, COPs, agencies, and public-private partnerships. I will concentrate on some cross-cutting issues.

5.1 Transnational referendums and consultations

Citizens could be *directly* engaged in global governance through referendums, consultations, and notice-and-comment procedures. A seemingly relatively feasible referendum variant might be *national* referendums on genuinely global issues, such as climate change, in which people over the world have similar stakes. The United Nations could be empowered to request member states to realize this. However, the legitimatory power of such national referendums would be limited, even if the outcomes were analysed both per states, and per capita, as long as the procedures and the embedding conditions of such referendums are very diverse. Such national referendums would therefore be no real progress in terms of global democracy.

It seems more appropriate to envisage genuinely *transnational* referendums, under the auspices of the United Nations, for a narrow range of transnational issues about which a transnational political deliberation is possible (i.e. issues which are not very technical, have a strong moral component, and do not risk violating human rights), about which global voters know enough, and where they all have a legitimate interest in a decision. In principle, such popular votes could also relate to draft international treaties whose substance meets the above-mentioned criteria.[209] Such referendums could as a first step or even in the long term be only consultative. Consultation or consultative referendums would realize the participatory modus of voice, not vote. A not state-bound direct democracy would not require worldwide referendums among the entire world citizenship, but rather referendums for groups of persons who are affected by certain issues, such as a dam project, a nuclear plant, or the disposal of waste, without limitation to the population of one nation state. The problem of lacking information and knowledge on the side of the voters about such transnational issues is mitigated by the worldwide rise in literacy and the enormous spread of information through the internet. Today, average people in a Swiss village can easily and cheaply find out more details about politics, society, and culture in China, than they could ever know about a neighbouring valley 200 years ago, when democracy was introduced on a federal level in Switzerland. However, due to censorship and/or poverty, citizens of totalitarian and underdeveloped states may be much less well informed about political and social events in other parts of the world. This observation is a reminder that the development and democratization of nation states is indispensable for the realization of a global two-track democracy.

5.2 Modes of citizens' representation

Within international organizations and on a more regular and permanent basis, citizens would have to be represented by delegates. The most straightforward

---

[209] The EU Lisbon Treaty was probably not suited for submission to a popular vote because of its extreme technicality. The Irish population which rejected this Treaty in a national referendum felt to a large extent uninformed. According to a study on behalf of the Irish Department of Foreign Affairs, Millward Brown IMS, *Post Lisbon Treaty Referendum Research Findings*, September 2008, '[t]he main reason for voting No was "lack of knowledge/information/understanding" at 42%. There can be little doubt that this emerged as the primary reason for people voting No.' (at ii). Many voters believed that the Treaty would erode Irish neutrality, would end Irish control over abortion, and would lead to conscription into a European army.

way to engage the world citizens with global governance would be the creation of a world parliament, directly elected by the world's citizens. This is one of the old cosmopolitan dreams and was notably ventilated for the League of Nations. For Walther Schücking, it would have been 'le couronnement d'une SDN démocratisée'.[210] In the UN context, the proposal has been called a *Peoples' Assembly* (or *Citizens' Chamber*).[211] A regional model is the Parliament of the EU.

In theory, a genuinely bottom-up process, normatively founded in global popular sovereignty, could lead to the installation of a Global Peoples' Assembly without resorting to a formal treaty process. However, this vision overestimates the power of global civil society in its present stage of development to take concerted action. Also, elections to the Global Peoples' Assembly would pre-suppose the establishment of electoral districts throughout the world. This would need a formal basis which is unlikely to be created. Most importantly, numerous governments would not allow elections in their countries.

Apart from the mode of its creation, the competences of a Global Peoples' Assembly would have to be considered. True parliamentary powers, namely the adoption of global laws which would complement or replace inter-state treaties, are utopian. A less far-reaching competence would be the adoption of texts which would still be subject to ratification by states. But the International Labour Organization (ILO) experience shows that this scheme leads to paper tigers that are rarely ratified. A different strategy would be to start with merely consultative powers, and to wait for an incremental acquisition of law-making powers through time.[212] However, the extensive academic and political debate on the normative status of General Assembly resolutions has shown how difficult it is to justify a law-making power in the absence of a formal legal basis. Overall, a Global Peoples' Assembly is only a long-term objective.

A different model, which reflects more the concept of participatory democracy than 'formal' electoral democracy is the involvement of interest groups, notably professional associations, in global decision-making. Such

---

[210] Schücking, Le développement du Pacte, 1927, at 396–397. But see the harsh critique by Georges Scelle *Une crise de la société des nations* (Presses universitaires de France Paris 1927), at 139–141.

[211] Otfried Höffe *Demokratie im Zeitalter der Globalisierung* (2nd edn Beck München 2002 (1st edn 1999)). Falk and Strauss, Creation of a Global Peoples Assembly, 2000; Richard Falk and Andrew Strauss 'Toward Global Parliament' (2001) 80 *Foreign Affairs* 212–220, at 220; Stein, International Integration, 2001, at 533. Along the same vein, Vaclav Havel, then president of the Czech Republic, at the Millennium Summit, suggested that the UN should reform itself into a 'joint institution for each inhabitant of this planet . . . which would have to rest on two pillars'. Besides the present General Assembly, there should be 'an organ consisting of a group elected directly by the globe's population, in which the number of delegates representing individual nations would roughly correspond to the size of the nations.' (Press Relase GA/9758 8th meeting, 8 September 2000).

[212] If the basis of legitimacy of the Global Peoples' Assembly is the global civil society, it is consistent to put the question whether it should have binding law-making power to the global citizenry in a referendum, as Falk and Strauss, Creation of a Global Peoples Assembly, 2000, at 218 propose.

participation has been realized with the tripartism of the ILO (see p. 259). A 'représentation professionelle internationale', covering not only employers and employees, but the agricultural sector, the liberal professions, and other groups, was recommended by Georges Scelle for the democratization of the League of Nations as a more realistic alternative to a world parliament. Scelle placed high emphasis on the possibility of the expression of diverse interests and the development of a world public opinion through this process.[213] He thus foreshadowed participatory and deliberative democracy on the global scale. However, ILO tripartism has so far not proven to be an encouraging example which would recommend itself for a transfer to other international organizations. Although, or maybe precisely because the norms produced in participation with non-state actors who have not only a voice, but a vote in that process, the ratification status of many ILO conventions remains woefully low.[214] ILO type powers for interest group representatives should therefore not be introduced to the decision-making bodies of other international organizations.

A yet different strategy would be not to create a new assembly for citizens but to bring citizens' weight to bear within the existing state assemblies, notably within the UN General Assembly. To this end, the member state delegates, who are now appointed by governments, could be in part directly elected (e.g. one out of the five delegates to the UN General Assembly). It could also be made a condition that the national parliamentary opposition is represented. The size of member states' delegations could be differentiated, or member states' votes could be weighted according to a composite index which includes population (and eventually also national income). Or the voting scheme could strike a middle way between state equality and citizens' equality, such as the double majority in EU Council.[215] Such weighted voting and similar devices are familiar not only in international organizations, but are also used in domestic constitutional law for the composition of the second parliamentary chamber in some federations (e.g. for the German *Bundesrat*). The disadvantage of this type of scheme is that it mixes up the state track and the individualist track of democratization. It seems clearer to visualize the two tracks in two separate bodies.

Subtle and not over-ambitious forms of engaging the UN with national parliaments have been suggested by the Cardoso Report of 2004.[216] The expert

---

[213] Scelle, *La crise*, 1927, at 142-146 and 157.

[214] For the ratification status of the ILO conventions see <http://www.ilo.org/ilolex/english/newratframeE.htm>. See in more detail on the problems of tripartism in a globalized world Francis Maupain 'L'OIT, la justice sociale et la mondialisation' (1999) 278 *Recueil des Cours* 201–396, at 331–386.

[215] Art 238 Treaty on the Functioning of the EU (TFEU) of 13 December 2007 (OJ 2008 C 115/47) (Article 205(1) and (2) TEC).

[216] Cardoso Report, 2004, proposals 13–18 and Part VI, 'Engaging with elected representatives' (national parliaments), notably by an elected representatives liaison unit (paras 101–152, also in summary pp 10 and 19–20).

report recommended a four-pronged strategy for the democratization of the UN: take UN issues to national parliaments more systematically; ensure that parliamentarians coming to the UN events have more strategic roles at those events; link parliaments themselves with international deliberative processes; and provide an institutional home in the UN for engaging parliamentarians.[217] To that end, the Cardoso Report suggested two novel institutions. First, 'global public policy committees' should be created within the UN, as a global equivalent to national parliamentary standing committees. Such committees should comprise up to 30 parliamentarians (from the relevant national functional parliamentary committees) and be regionally representative. An initial approach might be to invite countries serving on the General Committee of the General Assembly to participate. The function of the global public policy committees would be to forward policy proposals and scrutinize progress on past agreements. It would submit reports to the Secretary General. This could incrementally lead to globally representative committees on all global priorities, with the right to submit policy recommendations and progress audits to the UN and to member states. Additionally, the Secretary General should form a small elected representatives' liaison unit (akin to the existing non-governmental liaison service). Its function would be to inform members of national parliaments, and to suggest topics for parliamentary debate.[218] The Cardoso Report proposals were modest and reasonable. Unfortunately, they were not adopted by the General Assembly. In its debate on the Cardoso Report, the Assembly did not discuss in any detail the liaison with national parliaments and approached the issue of civil society participation very cautiously, emphasizing the inter-governmental nature of the United Nations.[219]

5.3 Parliamentary assemblies

The most powerful organizations, such as the UN, the Bretton Woods Institutions, and the WTO, where parliamentary assemblies are conspicuously absent, should be parliamentarized. Parliamentary assemblies exist currently in 45 international organizations in all world regions, and there is also the Inter-Parliamentary Union (IPU). The existing assemblies under the law as it stands are not parliaments in a constitutionalist sense, because their members are not

---

[217] Cardoso Report, 2004, para 102.

[218] Moreover, the Cardoso Report asked the UN to routinely encourage national parliaments to hold debates on major matters coming up in the UN, and to make the relevant documents available to the parliaments. In that way, national parliaments could debate General Assembly issues in advance, the General Assembly might take note, and this would widen the policy options (proposal 13). Also, member states should more regularly include members of parliament in their delegations to major UN meetings, while taking care to avoid compromising the independence of parliamentarians (proposal 14).

[219] General Assembly Plenary Debates of 4 and 5 October 2004 (press releases GA/10268 and GA/10270).

directly elected by citizens, they do not have law-making and budgetary powers, and do not elect the organizations' 'executive'. The assemblies have members ranging from 27 (in the East African Assembly) to 2000 parliamentarians or former members of national parliaments. They are normally not composed according to the scheme of one state–one vote, but under consideration of the population size of the member states.

The least powerless assembly so far is the Assembly of the Council of Europe.[220] The Hague Congress of 1948 had demanded 'as a matter of real urgency, the convening of a European Assembly' designed 'to stimulate and give expression to a European public opinion'.[221] The Statute of the Council of Europe named this body 'Consultative Assembly', but the assembly has called itself 'Parliamentary Assembly' since 1974. After the end of the Cold War, the assembly began to influence the policy of admission of new member states to the Council of Europe from Eastern and Central Europe and to perform an assessment of the internal political and legal system of candidate states. The Assembly thus benefitted from the transition period to increase its political weight in the institutional balance, although its formal competencies were not extended. This power gain was probably facilitated by the existence of relatively clear legal standards for membership to the Council of Europe, and by the strong incentive for (Eastern) European states for accession to the organization. A new parliamentary assembly, e.g. in the WTO, might acquire a similar role if accession conditions and incentives are similarly clear.

The question is whether the establishment of parliamentary assemblies and/or the strengthening of the powers of the existing ones is a viable strategy to democratize international organizations.[222] One objection is that this strategy overstates the significance of parliaments for democracy. Due to email and internet, with their networking options for active citizens, and due to dependency on experts, parliaments may be in decline.[223] Also, the limited political impact of the existing parliamentary assemblies counsels against over-expectation. Another shortcoming is that citizens whose states do not have a parliament, or whose parliament does not emerge from free and fair elections, will not be represented in the respective parliamentary assembly.

If new assemblies, e.g. to the WTO and UN, were modelled on the existing ones, which under current law cannot directly influence the organizations' decision-making processes, they would not produce a tangible democratic output. But even merely consultative assemblies perform the typical mediating function

---

[220] Arts 22–35 Statute of the CoE of 23 October 1954.

[221] Political Resolution at the Hague Congress (7–10 May 1948), (leading to the foundation of the Council of Europe), para 8(a). Congress of Europe: The Hague May 1948: Resolutions, London and Paris: International Comittee of the Movements for European Unity (no date), at 7–5, available via <http://www.ena.lu>.

[222] See a sceptical view in Stefan Marschall *Transnationale Repräsentation in Parlamentarischen Versammlungen* (Nomos Baden-Baden 2005), at 334.   [223] See above p. 296.

of parliaments, create transparency, and organize interests. Due to their 'parliamentary' quality, even purely consultative assemblies can open public debates or make public statements for which diplomats are not prepared, they can pave the way for negotiations (or disturb them), and they can promote a political dialogue at the level of parliaments, political parties, and civil society. For instance, during the Iraq crisis of 2003, transnational interests were articulated in the NATO parliamentary assembly and the WEU parliamentary assembly.

Moreover, even consultative parliamentary assemblies may strengthen the role of national parliaments in foreign policy. This functions when communication between the parliamentary assembly and the national parliaments is good. Another condition of success is that the national parliaments must have competencies in foreign politics, or must at least be able to influence policies through their spending power. The impact of parliamentary assemblies makes a difference especially in the field of security policy, because this domain is traditionally most closed for domestic parliaments. Here parliamentary assemblies can ruin the two level games played by governmental representatives and prevent scapegoating by providing information on the actors and their political positions. The dual mandate of parliamentarians (who are at the same time members of their national parliaments and of the international assembly) is important here, because it creates a specific 'two-level capacity' which can compensate for the lack of formal powers of the assembly. Overall, even consultative parliamentary assemblies can contribute to the democratization of global governance in this indirect way via national parliaments.

Proposals to create a Parliamentary Assembly in the WTO have been sponsored by the IPU and the EU Parliament, but have been opposed by the USA and many developing countries.[224] With regard to the United Nations, the idea of a Global Parliamentary Assembly has been supported by the EU Parliament,[225] by the Parliamentary Assembly of the Council of Europe,[226] and by the civil society organizations' Millennium Forum.[227] In 2007, a civil society network of NGOs, parliamentarians, activists, and academics, among them

---

[224] See the parliamentary conference on the WTO convened by the EU Parliament and IPU calling for a parliamentary dimension to the WTO (final declaration of 18 February 2003). See in scholarship Gregory Shaffer 'Parliamentary Oversight of WTO-Rulemaking? The Political, Normative, and Practical Contexts' (2004) 7 *Journal of International Economic Law* 629–654; Erika Mann 'Parliamentary Dimensions in the WTO—More than Just a Vision?' (2004) 7 *Journal of International Economic Law* 659–665.

[225] The EP invited the UN Secretary General and the UN's political bodies to extend cooperation with the EU Council and Commission to the European Parliament by jointly launching 'a network of parliamentarians' (Resolution on the Relations between the EU and the UN (2003/2049 (INI)) of 29 January 2004, para 39).

[226] Rec. 1476 (2000) of 27 September 2000 of the Parliamentary Assembly of the Council of Europe, 'encourages the UN to start developing, in close co-operation with the Inter-Parliamentary Union, a parliamentary dimension' (para 13).

[227] 'We the Peoples Millennium Forum Declaration and Agenda for Action, Strengthening the UN for the 21st Century' of 26 May 2000, Part F, para 6: The Forum urges the UN to consider the creation of a consultative parliamentary assembly (UN Doc A/54/959, at 16).

former UN Secretary General Boutros-Ghali,[228] launched the Campaign for a United Nations Parliamentary Assembly of about 800 delegates.

Such a UN Parliamentary Assembly could be established as a subsidiary organ to the General Assembly by a decision of the General Assembly under Article 22 UN Charter and would require no amendment of the Charter.[229] Deputies would be either members of national parliaments (dual mandate) or would be specifically elected by the parliaments. The number of deputies would be roughly proportionate to the population of the UN member states, with minority protection for small states.[230] Once installed, the Parliamentary Assembly could, on the basis of the implied power doctrine, arguably even develop proposals for direct elections by the world's citizens.[231]

The creation of an additional Parliamentary Assembly besides the General Assembly would be in institutional terms more incisive than the Cardoso Report proposals. But in contrast to the Peoples' Assembly as discussed above it would be a middle strategy, because it still relies on inter-state structures. It is more realist but still has the advantage of translating the dual basis of international law, states and citizens, into a visible institutional structure. The model of two assemblies in the UN has a federalist ring.[232] In a global federalist scheme, the General Assembly as the member states' chamber would become a 'second' chamber.

The UN Parliamentary Assembly would in the foreseeable future not acquire the traditional parliamentary competences of law-making and creation and control of the government. A competence to enact binding decisions or to adopt treaties is currently even denied to the states' chamber, the General Assembly, and at the moment seems out of the question for a new Parliamentary Assembly. Also, the ILO scheme for the adoption of binding instruments with votes of non-state delegates functions badly. Even if the Security Council were conceived as an analogy to a UN government, this 'government' is—under the law as it stands—not elected and unaccountable to the General Assembly or to a potential UN Parliamentary Assembly. The creation of an elected and accountable Security Council seems out of reach, just as parliamentary control in the form of a motion of censure. The UN Parliamentary Assembly might share budgetary power with the General Assembly (Article 17 UN Charter). This seems to be a classical parliamentary power. But the analogy

---

[228] Campaign for the Establishment of a United Nations Parliamentary Assembly, <http://www.unpacampaign.org>. A list of signatures is available on the website.

[229] The formal status as a subsidiary organ would not adequately reflect the Assembly's political and symbolical significance, but seems the only realistically attainable one.

[230] For instance, in a total assembly of 560 members, China would have 31 seats, countries up to one million inhabitants would have one seat, Daniele Archibugi 'From the United Nations to Cosmopolitan Democracy' in Daniele Archibugi and David Held (eds) *Cosmopolitan Democracy: An Agenda for a New World Order* (Polity Press Cambridge 1995) 121–162, at 142.

[231] An example for such an evolution is the EU Parliament which was initially composed of parliamentarians and only in a second stage based on direct elections.

[232] Actually, the whole idea of a two-track democracy implies a transnational federal polity, which is not, however, and should never become a federal state.

is misleading as long as the budget rules are not radically changed. Because—in the law as it stands—the UN budget is comparatively small, because the regular budget does not cover important positions, notably peace-keeping forces, and because the organization depends on the payment morals of the member states, the General Assembly (and a potential UN Parliamentary Assembly) lacks the political power associated with budgetary control in democratic states. Potential functions of the Parliamentary Assembly could consist of the following: it would be consulted by the General Assembly and by other UN organs; major draft resolutions would be read before they were voted on by the General Assembly; the Parliamentary Assembly would convey opinions and have a procedure for questioning the principal organs; it could request that policies adopted by the General Assembly be extended or amended; and it could propose new policies.[233] The greatest short-term potential of a UN Parliamentary Assembly lies in the parliamentary function of socialization and mediation, and in the strengthening of national parliaments as described above. The Parliamentary Assembly would inform national parliaments about UN and world policies and vice versa. To that end, delegates of the UN Parliamentary Assembly should have access to Security Council meetings and to inter-governmental conferences.

Even with such limited powers, an additional UN Parliamentary Assembly would be more democratic than the current UN General Assembly for basically three reasons. First, parliamentarians are closer to the citizens than the members of the executive and diplomats who represent the member states in the UN General Assembly. Second, the population size would be taken into account for fixing the number of delegates per state. Third, the delegates to the UN Parliamentary Assembly would reflect the political composition of the national parliaments and include members of the opposition. The initially only consultative competences of the Assembly would—as opposed to law-making competences—exactly reflect the idea of a citizens' voice, not vote on a global level. To conclude, the establishment of parliamentary assemblies in the Bretton Woods Institutions, the WTO, and the UN seems worth trying as a first and relatively modest building block of a democratization of global governance.

5.4 More transparency

The transparency of global governance should be improved in order to assume those very constitutional and in particular democratic functions transparency performs in domestic law. In modern democratic states, both the legislative process and its results, Acts and Statutes, are public. Publicity here allows

---

[233] Erskine Childers and Brian Urquhart *Renewing the United Nations System* (Dag Hammarskjöld Foundation Uppsala 1994), at 179.

citizens' participation, critique and control of the legislature, and is thus ultimately a prerequisite of accountability. Transparency is therefore an element both of the rule of law and of democracy within nation states.[234]

Until recently, transparency in the international sphere has remained limited. Transparency requirements have been a tool to ensure compliance by states with their international legal obligations,[235] but were not directed at the international institutions themselves. The traditional mode of international governance, namely diplomacy, has relied on secrecy and confidentiality. The reason seems to be that non-publicity is an enabling condition for compromises, bargaining, and consensual decision-making. In fact, transparency in treaty negotiations may lengthen the bargaining process, may give interest groups a strong influence on the treaty design which might lead to the treaty's rejection by powerful states, and might thus prevent outcomes with net social benefits. These potential costs of transparency cannot be defined away by constitutionalism, but should not be exaggerated either; they call for empirical investigation.

Moreover, the primarily 'secret' mode of international governance, negotiating and bargaining, is increasingly complemented by modes of deliberation and arguing, e.g. in global summits and forums. This mode of governance is intrinsically 'public' and thus calls for transparency. That trend towards transparent deliberations should be prolonged and would constitute an element of the constitutionalization of the international legal process.

Point One of US President Woodrow Wilson's famous 14 Points, presented as 'the only program of the world's peace' after World War I, was: 'Open covenants of peace, openly arrived at, after which there shall be no private international understandings of any kind, but diplomacy shall proceed always frankly and in the public view.'[236] Along this line, the Inter-Parliamentary Union[237] and the League of Nations[238] already sought to eliminate the traditional practice of 'secret treaties'. Today, Article 102 UN Charter and Article 80 VCLT stipulate that every international treaty shall be submitted to the UN Secretariat for publication. However, the traditional view is that publication is no requirement of a treaty's validity, and there is no customary law obligation to

---

[234] For rule of law reasons, the activity of the third branch, the judiciary, has long been open to the public. In contrast, the working of the executive branch, both on the level of high politics and in the day-to-day administration, has much longer been partly secret. Only in the second half of the 20th century, have numerous states enacted legislation on freedom of information and on 'government in the sunshine'.

[235] The classic fields of international law in which disclosure and reporting obligations are compliance mechanisms are the fields of arms control, disarmament, and nuclear energy. Transparency here fulfils two important functions: it establishes trust and builds confidence among parties, and it can drive parties into compliance by exercising pressure on them. In human rights law, the state reporting systems, visiting schemes, and special procedures likewise seek to induce compliance through publicity, which allows peer and public control.

[236] President Wilson in the US Congress joint session of 8 January 1918.

[237] The Interparliamentarian Union (IPU) was founded in 1889 specifically as a counterbalance to the secret diplomacy of governments. [238] *Cf* Art 18 of the League Covenant.

publish treaties.[239] In a constitutionalist mindset, the growing significance of multilateral treaties as global legislatory instruments invites a readjustment of the relative weight accorded to the values of discreteness and confidentiality of diplomatic treaty negotiations and treaties on the one hand, and the interests of third parties and the global public on the other hand.

The principle of transparency is gaining ground in dispute settlement as well. The WTO Panel and Appellate Body hearings are public, and reports are published *ex officio*. A summary of the confidential submissions of the parties to a dispute is disclosed to the public on request of a WTO member state.[240] In 2006, the ICSID Rules of Procedure were amended to create more transparency, and ICSID awards are now generally published.[241]

WTO law- and policy-making has also been rendered more transparent. In 1996, the WTO General Council agreed on guidelines for arrangements on relations with NGOs which seek 'to improve transparency' and to 'ensure more information about WTO activities in particular by making available documents which would be derestricted more promptly than in the past'.[242]

The most obvious extension of international transparency with a view to democratizing governance has occurred in international environmental law. Under Article 1 of the 1998 Aarhus Convention[243] '[e]ach Party shall ensure that, subject to the following paragraphs of this article, public authorities, in response to a request for environmental information, make such information available to the public, within the framework of national legislation ...'. The Convention thus created an individual right of access to environmental information, which has a democratic function.

Recently, the UN Security Council has not only acted as an executive body, but also as a rule maker. It is therefore in democratic terms all the more deplorable that the body's procedures are still quite non-transparent. Although theoretically the rule is that there should be public meetings, the Council has unfettered discretion to close a meeting.[244] Overall, the decision- and rule-making process is

---

[239] Art 102(2) UN Charter merely holds unpublished treaties as uninvocable before UN organs.

[240] Art 18(2) of the WTO Dispute Settlement Understanding.

[241] Art 48(4) ICSID Rules of Procedure provides that the ICSID Centre shall, after rendering of the award, promptly publish excerpts of the legal reasoning of the tribunal, but only with the consent of the parties. Art 48(4) of the Rules of Procedure corresponds to Art 48(5) of the ICSID Convention and can thus only be amended by consent of all parties to the convention.

[242] Guidelines for arrangements on relations with Non-Governmental Organizations, WT/L/162, Decision of 18 July 1996, II and III.

[243] Art 4 and 5 of the Convention on Access to Information, Public Participation in Decision-Making and Access to Justice in Environmental Matters of 25 June 1998 (Aarhus Convention), (1999) 38 ILM 517–533.

[244] See chapter IX ('Publicity of Meeting, Records') of the Security Council's 'provisional', but *de facto* permanent Rules of Procedure, as amended on 21 December 1982. The Security Council's Rule 48 states that 'unless it decides otherwise, the SC shall meet in public'. Under Rule 54, '[t]he official record of public meetings of the Security Council, as well as the documents annexed thereto, shall be published in the official languages as soon as possible'. For private meetings, the record may be made in a single copy alone, which is kept by the Secretary General (Rule 51).

opaque and the final outcome is often determined by confidential negotiations carried out well beyond the reach of public scrutiny. Recently, a group of small states tried to incite more transparency by suggesting in particular that a Permanent Member of the Security Council using its veto should explain the reason for doing so.[245] In the responding 63-point declaration, the members of the Council expressed their intention to increase the transparency of the body's work.[246] From a constitutionalist perspective this is highly welcome.

The prime example for the opening up of a non-state regime is the EU. The non-transparency of European law-making and law-enforcement had long been a major concern. Since 1992, Article 1 TEU speaks of a Union 'in which decisions are taken as openly as possible', and the European White Paper on Governance of 2001 highlighted 'open governance' as a major principle of governance.[247] Several novel provisions were enshrined in the 2007 Lisbon Treaty in order to make Union governance more transparent.[248] Article 15(3) TFEU (Article 255 TEC) and Article 42 Charter of Fundamental Rights grant EU citizens and residents an individual comprehensive right of access to documents of the Union institutions.[249] From a democratic perspective, the most important type of transparency is the transparency of the legislative process and of legislation. Under Article 297(1) TFEU (Article 254 EC), all legislative acts must be published in the Official Journal. Only with the Lisbon Treaty has the legislative process itself been fully publicized, and the debates in the European Parliament and in the Council are now public.[250] Although the EU is a very special case of international governance, its transparency reforms indicate the proper direction for other international institutions.

To conclude, there is a clear tendency towards transparency in global and supra-state regional governance. This can be taken as a manifestation of constitutionalization. In the interests of further democratization of the international

---

[245] UN Doc A/60/L.49 of 17 March 2006. Members of the groups were Costa Rica, Jordan, Singapore, and Switzerland.

[246] Declaration of 19th July 2006, Annex to the Note by the President of the Security Council, S/2006/507, para 10.

[247] European Commission, *European Governance: A White Paper*, COM (2001) 428 final, OJ 2001 C 287/1, 25 July 2001, Section II. The White Paper summarizes reflections on the reform of European governance since 2000.

[248] See Arts 10(3) and 11(1), (2) TEU; Art 15(1) TFEU, both of 13 December 2007 (OJ 2008 C 115/13).

[249] The relevant principles are specified in regulations and in the institutions' rules of procedures. See notably the Regulation (EC) No 1049/2001 of the European Parliament and of the Council regarding public access to European Parliament, Council, and Commission documents (OJ 2001 L 145/43).

[250] See for the EP Art 232–233 TFEU (Art 199–200 TEC); for the Council Art 16(8) TEU: 'The Council shall meet in public when it deliberates and votes on a draft legislative act. To this end, each Council meeting shall be divided into two parts, dealing respectively with deliberations on Union legislative acts and non-legislative activities.' See before the entry into force of the Lisbon Treaty for the proceedings in the Council Art 207(3) TEC. Only the Commission's contributions to law-making remain somewhat opaque due to 'comitology' proceedings.

legal process, transparency should be improved further. Sessions of the international institutions, particularly the rule-making sessions, should become public as a rule (with due exceptions for security, business, and privacy reasons). Documents of global governance including drafts should be publicized via the internet, without confusing citizens and hiding important information through overflow. The facilitation of technical access to the internet in disadvantaged world regions should be a high priority of UN politics. However, governance designers must be aware of the audience costs created by more transparency. Most importantly, transparency in itself does not bring about democracy. It is only, but importantly, a pre-condition for democratic procedures.

5.5 Impracticalities of non-state democratization

The non-state track of democratization of international law and global governance is fraught with numerous practical problems. The global consultations, elections, or referendums suggested in the preceding section may be impossible to organize.[251] Electoral representation on a global scale may lead to representatives of very high numbers of persons and may render representation largely symbolical. A global parliamentary body such as the UN Global Parliamentary Assembly might be too large to function, and it may be next to impossible to secure minority representation on that scale. The information asymmetry between the global governance institutions and the citizens of the world may be too great. A particular problem is the thin democratic infrastructure on a global scale. Genuinely global media besides the internet are scarce, and a global public sphere barely exists.[252] So would not global participation opportunities of the world's ordinary citizens be diminished to vanishing point?

The persuasive power of the objections pointing to the missing enabling conditions hinges on normative and empirical assessments. All depends on how salient and on how lacunary the conditions *really* are. But it is factually controversial how strong the global civil society actors and networks already are, and it is normatively controversial how powerful they must be in order to constitute a sufficient democratic infrastructure. Furthermore, given the dynamics of constitutionalization, statements about global democracy will depend on one's assessment of the development potential of the enabling conditions. Pessimists will underestimate the potential for further democratization, while optimists will exaggerate it. Optimists will argue that global democratic reform is in principle possible, but needs political decision, enough money, and good management.

---

[251] For practical problems in implementing the European citizens' initiative see Michael Dougan 'Direct Democracy and the European Union . . . is that a Threat or a Promise?' (2008) 45 *Common Market Law Review* 929–940.

[252] Although media and a public sphere are not preconditions of democracy in an absolute or logical sense, they are enabling factors in the sense of 'the more, the better'. The problem of lacking enabling conditions for democracy on a global scale seems to be mainly one of degree.

One major problem is that a global democracy might be unworkable because of its sheer size. Global democratic institutions would be hard to manage, they would be remote from citizens, difficult to communicate with, and potentially unresponsive. The necessary delegation would be extensive, the territory covered huge. There is also the spectre of a tyrannical centralized power, which is largely removed from oversight. Here quantity might at some point result in a qualitative turn. The problem of the size of a democratic unit may be not only gradual. A worldwide constituency might be simply too large, and might move a global political system beyond a democratic threshold. The existence of six billion voters might create an intrinsic, insurmountable obstacle to realizing democracy on a global scale detached from the democratic representation via the nation states. However, it is not clear why the management of six billion voters would be categorically different from managing the one billion voters of India.

One particular aspect of size is democratic representation. Even if the global governance institutions exactly duplicated the system in democratic nation states, they would still be less democratic than the individual states. This is so because the impact of each citizen's vote is diminished in relation to the whole, and because the relationship between citizens and their representatives changes when one delegate represents a much greater number of individuals. However, a difference in kind seems to exist only between those very small communities in which a popular assembly can decide and larger ones which require a system of representation. Within a representative system, no simple line can be drawn between large and 'too large.'[253] Moreover, the problem relates only to the issue of formal representation, whereas the evolving democracy on a global scale has less representative but rather participative and deliberative elements.

The 'size' objection against global democracy is one-sided because it reduces democracy to democratic input. But democracy does not only result from citizens' participation in decision-making procedures (their 'input'), but also from the fact that decisions are effective and have an impact on their lives (the democratic 'output'). While the citizens' input is diminished in larger entities, effective democratic output may require a larger entity which can specialize and may have more options for action. In any case, neither the aspect of democratic input, nor the aspect of democratic output result in an ideal size for a democratic polity.[254] The sheer size of a polity may even be a democratic advantage, because minority-protection and conflict-management are in some respects easier in a larger unit. In large democracies, conflicts are not so personalized. This means that although there are more conflicts, they are less apt to polarize society.[255]

---

[253] Robert A Dahl *Democracy and its Critics* (Yale UP New Haven 1989), at 217.

[254] Robert A Dahl and Edward Tufte from a detailed empirical study draw the conclusion that the positive effects work only when the units are *very small* (in Sweden communities of less than 10,000 inhabitants (Robert A Dahl and Edward Tufte *Size and Democracy* (Stanford UP 1973), at 41–65, 108–109, 135, 138.

[255] This is Madison's 'faction theory'. James Madison 'Federalist No. 10' in Alexander Hamilton, James Madison, and John Jay *The Federalist Papers* (New York 1961, orig. 1788, Rossiter ed), at 83.

Overall, the 'small is necessary' position can hardly identify an exact threshold beyond which bigger units cannot possibly be democratic. Moreover, such a threshold is likely to move upwards with the shrinking of the globe due to cheap and quick communication and travel. Size is not an absolute barrier to global democratic mechanisms beyond nation states. However, it can seriously call their viability into question. But the potential practical obstacles to the realization of a direct democratization of global governance might be neutralized or outweighed by the practical benefits which will be discussed in the next section.

5.6 Practical benefits of non-state democratization

Practical considerations justify the call for additional direct democratic participation of citizens in global governance without the mediation of states at suitable places. Even after full 'horizontal' democratization of all nation states, global direct democratic mechanisms remain important for individuals from small, weak, or failed states. Global direct democracy can thus mitigate the unfair effects of power imbalances among states. Another aspect is that state officials may be more nationally biased and more prone to strategic oscillations than their citizens, which may hamper decision-making in inter-governmental institutions.[256]

Global direct democracy could also correct the misfortune of persons living under a national government that is illegal under global constitutional standards of democracy as sketched out above. But this remains theoretical, because the citizens' participation in global non-state democratic mechanisms (second track) can quite effectively be prevented by undemocratic states. (This is another reason why democracy on a global scale cannot function if the state 'basis' is not democratic.)

A related aspect is that genuinely global political deliberation would presumably be promoted by global direct democratic elements. In the current multilevel system, democratic discourse takes place primarily within states and through national media. The inter-governmental discourse among state representatives is not a broad democratic debate, but is technical, closed, and non-transparent. This means that even deliberation on transnational issues (climate, finance, terrorism, migration, diseases, etc.) is still to a certain extent compartmentalized along state borders. A more intense participation of citizens and civil society actors directly in international legal and political processes would potentially be accompanied by more global deliberation, which would in turn contribute to a less fragmented, and thus fuller, assessment of problems and eventual solutions.

Overall, the two-track global democratization strategy would resemble the usual mix of direct and representative democracy within nation states. In

---

[256] Charnovitz, WTO Cosmopolitics, 2002, at 317–318; Falk and Strauss, Creation of a Global Peoples Assembly, 2000, at 211.

domestic politics, the inclusion of elements of direct democracy (such as popular initiatives and referendums for a more or less limited range of questions under differently strict conditions) into otherwise representative systems invigorates democracy and strengthens citizenship. Citizens' direct democratic rights here are a counterweight to the representatives' bureaucratic power. The mere availability of the tools of direct democracy may have a deterrant effect. Their actual use may counteract and correct the governing actors' institutional bias. All these considerations also work for global politics as well.

6. Tensions between the Two Tracks

In the world as it is now, where international law is *not* adopted in democratic procedures, conflicts between domestic law and international law increasingly cause national disrespect of international law which is justified or camouflaged with the argument that a conflicting international rule violates domestic democracy. An example for the tension between national democratically shaped preferences and international law is the issue of cannabis. Due to changed popular attitudes, many European nations strive for new democratic legislation that would liberalize drugs, but are prevented from doing so by the strict UN drug conventions of the 1960s. Because denunciation of the treaties is difficult and has its costs, some contracting parties are inclined to breach the conventions.

The tension between international obligations and domestic democracy is most obvious when a national sovereign decides directly by way of referendum. In Switzerland, for instance, a popular initiative led to the adoption by the Swiss people of a new constitutional provision according to which a sex offender or violent offender who is regarded as extremely dangerous and whose condition is assessed as untreatable, must be incarcerated until the end of his life, with early release excluded.[257] This constitutional provision violates the internationally recognized right to have one's detention scrutinized by a court as guaranteed in Article 5(4) of the ECHR. Moreover, lifelong detention without any chance of release arguably constitutes inhuman treatment in terms of Article 3 ECHR. Nevertheless, the incarceration prescription is now constitutionally entrenched in Swiss law. Another recent example is the quarrel about a modern bridge to be built near the UNESCO protected valley of the Elbe around the German city of Dresden. The population voted for the bridge in a local referendum in order to solve traffic problems. However, the construction would lead to the loss of the UNESCO status, and might even breach the 1972 UNECSO Convention

---

[257] Art 123a *Bundesverfassung* (Swiss Federal Constitution), adopted by the Swiss people on 8 February 2004.

on World Cultural Heritage. The High Administrative Court of Saxonia framed the issue as a conflict between direct democracy and compliance with an international treaty, and dryly held that direct democracy must prevail.[258] (It is not without irony that the Tribunal pointed to the need to avoid a repetition of the national socialist experience, in which democratic rights of citizens were not respected, to justify its disregard for international law, whereas most analysts depict the international legal commitments of post-totalitarian states as a lock-in mechanism for preventing backsliding into totalitarianism.)

In fact, if one takes only national citizenship and national popular sovereignty as a reference point, international law and global governance prevents the government by 'the people' and instead installs a government by 'the foreigner'.[259] However, this assertion simply assumes without justification that the 'will of the people' should not be constrained so as to take into account the interests of those outside their (national) polity[260] or global interests, such as the cultural common heritage of mankind or the principle of human dignity.

Non-compliance with international law could no longer be justified with the democratic deficits of that body of law if the international legal processes were democratized. However, the dualism of the inter-state paradigm complemented by a non-state track of global direct democratization, as suggested here, will *not* end conflicts that give rise to compliance problems. The two-track global democracy will remain in perpetual internal tension. The reason is that the ultimate reference point of democracy are natural persons, while in a multi-polity world, those natural persons remain partly mediated by their states. These tensions between the statist track and the individualist track pose problems for the rules for decision-making. There are two aspects to this: the incompatibility of state equality and citizens' equality, and between unanimity and majority voting.

Once it has been acknowledged that the international constitutional community has members other than states, notably natural persons, it is no longer clear that the equality of states increases the democratic legitimacy of the order for the following reason: the individuals of the world have, as political agents, multiple identities.[261] In their political role as national citizens and as members of a national polity, they own democratic rights which are on the international level safeguarded by granting their home state

---

[258] *Sächsisches Oberverwaltungsgericht* (provisional measures) order of 9 March 2007 (Az. 4 BS 216/06) at 26–27. Not admitted for constitutional complaint by the German Constitutional Court, BVerfG, order of 29 May 2007 (2 BvR 695/07).

[259] *Cf* Antonin Scalia 'A Conversation between US Supreme Court Justices' (2005) 3 *I Con* 519–554, at 522.   [260] *Cf* Buchanan and Keohane, Legitimacy, 2006, at 434.

[261] To avoid complicating things further, I concentrate only on two levels, the national and the universal one and omit the regional ones below and above the nation states.

one voice. But in their political role as global citizens, persons are not fairly represented by the scheme 'one state—one vote' in treaty making and for the production of secondary international law. Because states contain vastly different sizes of populations, there is no correlation between states' votes and citizens' votes. The equality of states results in the inequality of citizens (as global citizens), and the representation of the citizens is skewed. For instance, a simple majority of UN member states in the General Assembly, made up of the least populated states, represents less than 5 per cent of the world's population. By contrast, a majority of humankind can be reached by aggregating the populations of just six states (around 3 per cent of all states), namely the People's Republic of China, India, the United States of America, Indonesia, Brazil, and Pakistan.[262] In that perspective, state majoritarianism is an impediment to the effective institutional expression of equal consideration of natural persons. So even if all states, 'large and small', could perfectly fairly participate on an equal footing in global governance, and were in themselves perfect democracies, this would not mean democracy in the sense of global citizens' rule on the basis of equality.

The second issue, unanimous versus majoritarian decision-making, arises in the world of multiple polities (democratized states and international organizations) as follows. In order to realize global governance for problems which require global responses, the political action of these units has to be coordinated at least in some fields. But coordination among the (more or less democratic) polities presupposes compromise decisions which will frequently contradict democratic choices made within other democratic units of the global network of polities. Inter-state majoritarianism, from the *inter-state* perspective, is democratic because simple majority voting prevents a rule of a minority.[263] However, the current trend to inter-state majoritarianism, from the individualist perspective, is problematic because it risks forestalling the democratic formation of collective preferences within the nation states. We then face a paradox. From the inter-state perspective, it seems illegitimate and undemocratic that a minority (one state) can block a treaty. On the other hand, such a veto power seems necessary to preserve the democratic decision-making on the 'lower' level, within the smaller community. For example, the political majority in Brazil might legitimately decide not to ratify an international treaty protecting the rain forest—at least if Brazil's domestic democratic system contains suffcient safeguards for protecting minorities', especially indigenous populations', rights. In that perspective, an extension of the inter-state majority principle *aggravates* the democratic deficit. The majoritarian adoption of secondary law in international organizations with undemocratic members raises the additional question why the citizens of a democratic member state should be bound by a majority decision taken with the

---

[262] See for a good discussion Wheatley, *Democratic Legitimacy of International Law* (Hart Oxford 2010), chapter 1. [263] See above pp. 289–291.

support of undemocratic member states. Preventing this type of objection to international law is one additional reason for a global constitutional principle of *domestic* democratization. But even if all involved state parties are democracies, the problems remain that in a system of inter-state majority voting, the defeated nation's collective preferences (which have been ideally determined through a democratic procedure) are completely ignored. Moreover, a state delegate defeated in the vote in an intergovernmental regime cannot be held to account at home.[264] When the defeated nations' choices are based on the will of democratic majorities that are properly constituted according to the rules of their domestic arena, the decisions from 'above' will be experienced as undemocratic, even though in their own terms they were perfectly formally democratic.[265]

But in a multi-polity world, upon further democratization of global governance, how should conflicts between the various (more or less) democratically reached collective preferences be solved? The traditional doctrinal answer was hierarchy. Most textbooks of international law and occasional decisions of international tribunals asserted that international law enjoys supremacy over domestic law. However, this simple solution was a matter of pure theory in a time when international law was relatively unobtrusive. With international law becoming denser and more regulatory, conflicts with domestic law have increased. In reaction to this, a growing body of current international legal scholarship is calling into question the unconditional supremacy of international law over domestic law, notably in the event of a conflict with domestic constitutional values.[266] Even protagonists of a constitutionalist approach to international law specifically insist on the non-hierarchic relationships between the multiple constitutions on the national and global level.[267] As a general matter, the need for a hierarchical

---

[264] Another aspect is that, if a minority of states protects human rights better than others, increasing the scope of majoritarianism means a setback for the protection of human rights (as Buchanan, *Justice*, 2004, at 318–319 points out), and is for this additional reason from a constitutionalist perspective not recommended.

[265] On this problem see Pascal Lamy 'Emergence des preferences collectives dans le champ de l'échange international: Quelles implications pour la regulation de la mondialisation?' Speech of 15 September 2004; Lord and Harris, *Democracy in the New Europe*, 2006, at 179.

[266] See, e.g., Mattias Kumm 'Democratic Constitutionalism Encounters International Law: Terms of Engagement' in Sujit Choudhry (ed) *The Migration of Constitutional Ideas* (CUP Cambridge 2006) 256–293; Peters, Globalisation of State Constitutions, at 306–307; André Nollkaemper 'Rethinking the Supremacy of International Law' (2010) 65 *Zeitschrift für öffentliches Recht* 65–85. For the relationship between EU law and domestic law of the EU member states see Miguel Poiares Maduro 'Contrapunctual Law: Europe's Constitutional Pluralism in Action' in Neil Walker (ed) *Sovereignty in Transition* (Hart Oxford 2003) 501–537; Joerges, Re-Conceptualizing the Supremacy, 2008, 311–328. See also p. 348.

[267] Jean Cohen 'A Global State of Emergency or the Further Constitutionalization of International Law: A Pluralist Approach' (2008) 15 *Constellations* 456–484, at 473; also Konrad Lachmayer 'The International Constitutional Approach: An Introduction to a New Perspective on Constitutional Challenges in a Globalising World' (2007) 1 *Vienna Journal on International Constitutional Law* 91–99, at 97–98.

conception of law has been denied and a network model of law has been suggested as an alternative to the legal pyramid.[268] In parallel, most analysts of global governance agree that the multiplicity of political entities on the globe is not properly described as a hierarchy, and should not be transformed into one. In contrast, the scene is depicted as a polyarchy or heterarchy.[269] The absence of hierarchy is accompanied by the absence of a single authority to decide on eventual conflicts of norms. It has even been argued that the openness of the question 'who decides who decides' and the lack of ultimate authority is a constitutionalist achievement, because it constitutes an additional mechanism for limiting power.[270] However, it seems more likely that legal openness tends to result in the political dominance of the more powerful actors.

Although the democratization of international law along the lines suggested here is apt to alleviate reservations against international law on the grounds of its thin legitimacy, the democratic conundrum described above, namely the irresoluble tension between state equality and citizens' equality and between the democratic choices in the various political units, remains. This insight is an additional policy argument in favour of recent pluralist,[271] non-hierarchical, network-type reconceptualizations of the relationship between international and domestic law (and between international constitutional and domestic constitutional law), based on discourse and mutual adaptation. The task ahead is to devise mechanisms for the adjustment of competing claims of authority in order to realize what Mireille Delmas-Marty has called a 'pluralisme ordonné'.[272] For instance, it must be acknowledged that national courts are at least under a *bona*

---

[268] François Ost and Michel van der Kerchove *De la pyramide au réseau: pour une théorie dialectique du droit* (Facultés universitaires Saint-Louis Bruxelles 2002).

[269] Even the concept of multilayered governance does not necessarily imply a hierarchy with a normative prevalence of the 'higher' level. See Sol Picciotto 'Constitutionalizing Multilevel Governance?' 6 (2008) *I Con* 457–479, at 461.

[270] Poiares Maduro, Contrapunctual Law, 2003, at 522.

[271] The pluralism meant here does not refer to the pluralism of legal orders but is situated on a meta-level. It refers to perspectives and denies the existence of an absolute external observation standpoint ('God's eye-view') from which to decide where the rule for deciding a conflict sits. In this specific pluralist perspective, there is no legal rule to decide which norm should prevail. Different legal actors, e.g. courts, necessarily belong to one of the various orders, therefore necessarily speak from their own perspective, and can only apply a rule of priority residing in their own legal system. In the absence of an overarching, institutionalized power which could decide a conflict, the different actors' perspectives are—in legal terms—equally valid and consistent. Conflicts therefore cannot be decided by legal argument, but must be solved politically. In the words of Neil Walker 'Beyond Boundary Disputes and Basic Grids: Mapping the Global Disorder of Normative Orders' (2008) 6 *Journal of International Constitutional Law* 373–396, at 392: '[W]e must acccept that the disorder of orders, considered as an accomplished and ongoing state of affairs, concerns the absence of transunit agreement in the presence of multiple competing candidate metaprinciples about how we should best resolve the relations between the different units of legal, political, and moral ordering in the world.' On this 'pluralisme cognitif' see also Loïc Azoulay 'La constitution et l'integration: Les deux sources de l'Union Européenne en formation' (2003) 19 *Revue Française de Droit Administratif* 859–875, at 866.

[272] Mireille Delmas-Marty *Le pluralisme ordonné* (Seuil Paris 2006).

fide obligation to take into account international law, must interpret national law consistently with international prescriptions as far as possible, and must give reasons for non-compliance. On the other hand, the international bodies should grant a margin of appreciation to national decision-makers with a strong democratic legitimation.[273] These suggestions are only seemingly minimalist or even subversive for global governance. They might, together with further democratization of international law, provide a flexible and sustainable response to counter nationalist tendencies and non-compliance with international law.

7. Complementary Mechanisms of Legitimacy and Accountability

Global governance need not, and cannot, become a perfect double of national democratic government. Although democracy is, according to historic experience within nation states, the best type of rule for protecting people's rights and interests in the long run, global governance may have its own logic of legitimacy. Also, public international law consists of different layers which are not equally suited and recommended for democratization.[274] For instance, a democratic basis of 'contractual' bilateral treaties seems to be less urgent, and secondary international law might again be a special case.

The overall situation might be comparable with other systems of rule, such as churches or business. These institutions have initially not been democratic at all, but have drawn on other sources of legitimacy. Even in our era, where the pull of democracy has become so powerful, they are not expected to function in a fully democratic manner. There is a clear tendency to introduce democratic elements also into those systems, but other mechanisms of control (e.g. consumer boycotts on business and exit from churches) still remain in place. In a comparable fashion, the democratic deficit of global governance might be mitigated (not fully compensated) by complementary non-democratic mechanisms of public control, which would also perform the normative key function of rendering global governance institutions more accountable. To a limited extent, the non-democratic accountability mechanisms might thus be a functional, partial equivalent to democracy as long as an elected global law-making body is out of sight.

The currently best-trodden path is that of *inclusion and participation* of civil society actors and business. NGOs are being formally integrated into the international legal process through accreditation, participatory status, and voice (see pp. 219–235 and 315–318). Some observers consider these forms of

---

[273] ECHR, *Hatton v UK*, application No 36022/97, judgment of 8 July 2003, para 97: 'The national authorities have a *direct democratic legitimation* and are, as the Court has held on many occasions, in principle better placed than an international court to evaluate local needs and conditions.'(Emphasis added). See more particularly on the relationship between international and national courts pp. 142–146.   [274] Weiler, Geology, 2004, at 549–550.

participation as constituting a 'deliberative democracy'. I insist that presence, observation, notice and comment, and hearing fall short of democracy, because these rights do not allow the participants to block a decision or to disempower the law- and policy-makers. However, informal protest (in the form of petitions, lobbying, public meetings, boycotts, strikes, peaceful blockades, and the like) may contribute to holding those wielding power accountable to the global public.

An alternative to democratic legitimacy might be *expertise* as a source of legitimacy of international law and global governance. The presence of independent experts in international bodies, such as environmental compliance committees, human rights committees, and international courts and tribunals, contributes to the legitimacy of the regimes monitored by them.[275] But this fact is not apt to alleviate the democratic deficit of global governance, because democratic procedures are wanted most of all in the process of law-making, i.e. in the establishment of abstract and general norms which prospectively govern the behaviour of all community members. In contrast, the role of independent experts lies mostly in the field of law enforcement (or compliance control), including (quasi-) judicial activity, and in administrative-type activity (routine application of the law to concrete situations).[276]

Along a similar vein, *independence* has been celebrated as a source of legitimacy of political actors that can be held to account by diffuse and non-electoral mechanisms. Giandomenico Majone wrote: 'What is required to reconcile independence and accountability are richer and more flexible forms of control than the traditional methods of political and administrative oversight. Statutory objectives, procedural requirements, judicial review, budgetary discipline, professionalism, expertise, monitoring by interest groups, even inter-agency rivalry, can all be elements of a pervasive system of control which only needs to be activated. When the system works properly no one controls an independent agency, yet the agency is "under control" '.[277] My response is that independence and expertise are no substitute for democratic accountability. Experts typically operate in the shadow of democratic accountability. Insulation from majorities will by itself not make independent experts more likely to be responsive to the urgent needs of minorities—rather than simply more responsive to their own interests or those of powerful stakeholders or vetoplayers. To conclude, rule by

[275] Rüdiger Wolfrum 'Legitimacy of International Law from a Legal Perspective: Some Introductory Considerations' in *idem* and Volker Röben (eds) *Legitimacy in International Law* (Springer Berlin 2008) 1–24 at 24.

[276] Exceptions are, e.g., the Codex Alimentarius Commission or the numerous technical, financial, or accounting standard-setting bodies, where experts participate intensly in rule-making. These international and transnational standards are *de facto* norms but not formal international law.

[277] Giandomenico Majone 'Independence versus Accountability? Non-Majoritarian Institutions and Democratic Government in Europe' (1994) 1 *The European Yearbook of Comparative Government and Public Administration* 117–140, at 118.

technical (including legal) expertise or, as Robert Dahl called it, 'guardianship',[278] cannot compensate for the democratic deficits in global governance. Technocracy is not democracy.

A yet different type of legitimacy is *output legitimacy*. Outputs 'for the people' form an essential part of democratic governance as well. But good outputs are often generated outside democratic procedures. Output alone is therefore no indicator for democracy at all. From a democratic perspective, outputs which benefit the world's citizens cannot be a substitute for their input in democratic procedures, because democracy is premised on the foundational idea that only the individuals themselves are authorities on their needs and interests. This means that the governing cannot legitimately claim to know (best) the needs and interests of the governed, without individuals being able to articulate those need and interests in the political and legal process. So output cannot be played out versus input. The output must be controlled as well and is controversial. Therefore—to be democratic—the output must be linked to input by the governed. A benevolent world dictatorship may be legitimate under certain standards, but this is not democracy.

A quite popular idea is to alleviate the democratic deficit of global governance through *strengthening judicial review*. This could be done by establishing new tribunals, e.g. a universal human rights tribunal, and by broadening the scope of compulsory adjudication. Standing before international courts and tribunals could be extended and granted to more actors. For instance, international organizations could be admitted as plaintiffs to the ICJ, individuals as complainants under the WTO dispute settlement mechanism, or NGOs as plaintiffs in their own right before environmental chambers. On the passive side, more actors, notably international organizations, could and should be subjected to the jurisdiction of courts. All these are reform proposals in their own right, and are discussed at pp. 64–67, 132–133 and 213–215.

But the question is whether improved judicial protection against international legal acts can compensate for deficiencies in the international law-making processes. I submit that this is not the case, because the type of accountability created by courts and tribunals differs in significant respects from democratic accountability. Accountability through complaints—as opposed to accountability through elections—functions only *ex post*, not *ex ante*. It is necessarily rights-based and cannot take into account interests without a legal basis. It concerns individual cases, not general policies. So complaints are hardly a functional equivalent to democratic elections, referendums, or prior consultations, and cannot substitute those participatory devices. This means that independent (in extremis judicial) review is best understood not as an element of democracy, but rather as a complement to democratization.

---

[278] Dahl, International Organizations, 1999, at 33.

An overlapping issue is the proposal to allow more often for a *direct effect* of international treaties and of secondary international law. Thereby, so the argument goes, individuals would be recognized as stakeholders with individual rights derived from international law, enforceable by the domestic judiciary. However, the fact that individuals can invoke international law against their own states is at best a minimal punctual exercise of citizens' rights. Despite the international legal progress which can be triggered by important cases, litigating is essentially the action of private persons and is no public activity. The extension of direct effect would thus be at best a tiny building-block of transnational citizenship, and thereby co-constitute global democracy.

There is one serious drawback, though. Promotion of judicial protection reinforces the lopsidedness of the constitutionalization of international law. This process has so far been adjudicative rather than deliberative. This is most visible in the WTO and the related sector-constitutionalization debate. What has been identified by some scholars as a constitutionalization of the WTO boils down to the legalization of the dispute settlement mechanism, judge-made principles, and constitutional techniques applied by the panels and Appellate Body, such as balancing (see pp. 215–217). The structurally embedded preponderance of judicial engineering is not limited to the WTO, but also concerns the constitutionalization of the international legal system as a whole. It gives rise to the fundamental objection against the constitutionalist reading of international law, namely that this reading foists an impoverished, legalist (judicially made), a-political conception of a constitution. So exclusive focus on the improvement of judicial protection in international law is not only a foul trick to define away the democratic deficit, but might moreover undermine the persuasiveness of the constitutionalist reconstruction of international law.

To conclude, none of the suggested alternative mechanisms of accountability in global governance can in themselves be considered 'democratic'. At best, a combined formula of the procedures and mechanisms discussed in this section which would be in themselves normatively deficient might create an overall accountability which is functionally equivalent to democratic deliberation, consultation, votes, and elections.

7

Conclusions

Anne Peters

The preceding chapters have shown that the constitutionalist paradigm does some analytic work, generates additional insights, but is also apt to elicit objections.

1. A Paper Tiger?

The term 'constitution' might be a misnomer when applied to the international sphere. Therefore, says the critique, the very terms on which the constitutionalization debate takes place are erroneous. One aspect is that international law lacks the symbolic-aesthetical dimension which is inherent in national (constitutional) law. It could be argued that constitutions have the prime function of storing the meaning of a political community. They embody revolutionary ideas not in an abstract fashion, but by (physical) sacrifice. Consequently, a constitution is genuinely 'owned' by a people mainly because its meaning is transported by the sacrifice made for it.[1] But because all this is lacking on the international plane, the idea of international constitutional law is—so the argument goes—a sham. However, this criticism places a premium on (bloody) revolutions and war. It risks overstating the importance of irrational and mythological foundations of constitutional law.

A more important objection is raised by realists. The constitutionalist paradigm became popular after the final demise of the socialist bloc, in a period marked by an excess of optimism.[2] Realists point out that international law must content itself with a more or less 'symbolic constitutionalization',[3] or that any international constitution is in any case only nominalist as opposed to really effective. The gist of this critique is that the constitutionalist reading of

---

[1] Ulrich Haltern 'Internationales Verfassungsrecht' (2003) 128 *Archiv des öffentlichen Rechts* 511–556, esp. at 533–534, drawing on Benedict Anderson *Imagined Communities* (Verso London 1983).
[2] Sandra Szurek 'La Charte des Nations Unies Constitution Mondiale?' in Jean-Pierre Cot, Alain Pellet, and Mathias Forteau (eds) *La Charte des Nations Unies: commentaire article par article* vol 1 (Economica Paris 2005) 29–68, at 32.
[3] Marco Neves *Symbolische Konstitutionalisierung* (Duncker & Humblot Berlin 1998).

international law is not grounded in and backed by a real common political will and corresponding power structures and sanctions at the international level, which would allow the international constitution to be enforced. The constitutionalist reading, so the argument goes, is too idealistic, and does not adequately reflect the realistic calculus of governments. In the event of a problem or conflict, any constitutionalist attitude will be given up, says the critique.[4] For instance, (western) governments do not advocate universal protection of human rights because they believe that it is a good thing, but because they are exposed to internal pressures by their constituencies to observe human rights standards, and they simply want to prevent other states' competitive advantages by not being themselves restricted by human rights concerns. Likewise, the United Nations (UN) and other international organizations are, for most member states, only a means of realizing their national interests.

The agents of constitutionalization seem to be primarily scholars, not political actors. Empirical findings do not confirm an all-encompassing global trend of constitutionalization. Empirical evidence rather points to uneven processes of constitutionalization, differing in terms of various constitutional dimensions and world regions.[5] All this suggests that global constitutionalism may be a paper tiger.

The danger of blowing up an academic paper tiger is very real, although in theory academic reconstructions do not depend on moral attitudes which governments do or do not share. A good idea does not become bad if politicians do not accept it. However, law and legal constructs and arguments are supposed to have an impact on the exercise of power. This is what law is about. The specific practical function of law to organize society and to structure governance mandates that lawyerly (re-)constructions be palatable to the relevant political actors. So global constitutionalism as an academic agenda should follow the middle path between merely self-dignifying the status quo on the one hand and hanging onto pipe dreams on the other. In order to gain acceptance in the political realm, global constitutionalists might highlight the current situation of global interdependence. With such a state of affairs, national and global public interests tend to converge more and more, national interests and universal idealism are not necessarily in opposition. Given this convergence of global and national, an 'idealist' global constitutionalism which promotes global interests, may even, at least in the long run, further national economic and political interests as well, although some states benefit more than others.

---

[4] Walter Kälin 'Der Menschenrechtsschutz der UNO: Ein Beispiel für die Konstitutionalisierung des Völkerrechts?' in Walter Kälin and Thomas Cottier (eds) *Die Öffnung des Verfassungsrechts: Symposium zum 65. Geburtstag von Prof. Jörg Paul Müller* (recht Sonderheft 2005) 42–49, at 47 and 49.

[5] Klaus Armingeon and Karolina Milewicz 'Compensatory Constitutionalism: A Comparative Perspective' (2008) 22 *Global Society* 179–196.

A related strand of criticism insinuates that an important function of global constitutionalism is to symbolize a simplified, compact order in a world that, in reality, is complex and amorphous. From this perspective, the myth of the unity of the constitution has to be rejected: instead a spontaneous self-coordination of interests must be chosen as starting point, legally anchored in individual liberties (human rights) and the cognitive 'social capital' anchored within it. 'The constitutional concept then remains an (imaginary) reference point for a nation-state like past . . .'[6] However, the term 'constitution' has never been exclusively reserved for state constitutions. Today, the notional link between constitution and state has further been loosened in everyday language and in the legal discourse (and thereby the meaning of 'constitution' may have been broadened). It is therefore not *per definitionem* impossible to conceptualize constitutional law beyond the nation or the state. Global constitutionalism advocates non-state constitutional law, and tends to de-mystify the state and the state constitution.

2. Sneaking into Legitimacy?

The constitutionalist reading of international law might raise dangerously seductive over-expectations.[7] The vocabulary makes it virtually impossible to escape from the assumptions that go with it. And 'social legitimacy is being artificially constructed through the use of constitutional language'.[8] So the constitutionalist reconstruction might fraudulently create the illusion of legitimate global governance. Constitutionalist language—in the eyes of the critique—abuses the highly value-laden term 'constitutionalism' in order to reap profit from its positive connotations and to dignify the international legal order through it. However, the danger that one of us raised some years ago, namely that constitutionalism may be misunderstood 'as a mechanism that can instantly bestow legitimacy'[9] does not seem so real anymore. International and constitutional lawyers are meanwhile discerning enough to realize that 'constitutionalism' is not a ready-made answer, but—on the contrary—a perspective which might help the right questions of fairness, justice, and effectiveness to be asked. I will come back to this below.

---

[6] Thomas Vesting 'Constitutionalism or Legal Theory: Comments on Gunther Teubner' in Christian Joerges, Inger-Johann Sand, and Gunther Teubner (eds) *Transnational Governance and Constitutionalism* (Hart Oxford and Portland Oregon 2004) 29–39, at 35.

[7] Ronald MacDonald and Douglas M Johnston 'Introduction' in *idem* (eds) *Towards World Constitutionalism: Issues in the Legal Ordering of the World Commmunity* (Martinus Nijhoff Leiden 2005) xiii–xviii, at xvii.

[8] Cf Deborah Z Cass *Constitutionalization of the WTO* (OUP Oxford 2005), at 208 and 237, relating to the WTO.

[9] Jan Klabbers 'Constitutionalism Lite' (2004) 1 *International Organizations Law Review* 31–58, at 48.

3. Unpacking Global Constitutionalism?

Another concern is that the concept of international constitutionalism suffers from oversell and vagueness. International law, politics, and economics are being mixed, if not confused. Indeed, there is the danger that reliance on constitutionalism is actually counterproductive because it may postpone rather than encourage concrete debates on concrete problems, such as decision-making in the World Trade Organization (WTO), the composition of the UN Security Council, or how to liaise national parliaments to the UN. Daniel Bodansky has lucidly asked whether it would not be better to consider both the descriptive and the normative claims associated with constitutionalism on their own merit.[10] For instance, judicial review and a diminished role for state consent could be descriptively analysed and normatively propagated without introducing the concept of 'constitutionalism'. Because the meaning of 'constitutionalism' is so unclear, it may not really be a helpful short-hand, but on the contrary may be confusing.

Indeed, it would be detrimental to use the constitutionalist vocabulary for the description of the current international system in an inflationary matter. If all (international) law is somehow 'constitutionalized' and becomes more or less 'constitutional' or constitutionally infused, then nothing is constitutional. The explanatory power of the concept would thereby be reduced to zero.

However, the added value of the constitutionalist paradigm might lie in its comprehensive nature. The normative claim is that the different features of constitutionalism are not merely additive, but that the whole is more than the sum of its parts. Bodansky remains sceptical about this holistic claim. He prefers to unpack the concept of constitutionalism into its component elements and then consider the proper role of each in international governance.[11] In contrast, I suggest that the various constitutionalist features, such as more inclusive and transparent decision-making and judicial review, should go together, and that in combination they take on a special normative significance. If this is true, the constitutionalist reconstruction does possess an additional explicative and prescriptive value. It reminds us of the interlinkage of the various features of constitutionalism, and calls for complementing the existing constitutional features of international law (such as judicial review of governmental acts) with missing ones, such as democracy and judicial review of acts of international organizations. To some extent, there is indeed constitutionalist bootstrapping.

[10] Daniel Bodansky 'Is there an International Environmental Constitution?' (2009) 16 *Indiana Journal of Global Legal Studies*, 565–584. [11] *Ibid*, at 582.

4. Constitutional Pluralism

Another concern is culturalist. The constitutionalist reading of international law may be genuinely anti-pluralist. It may have a uni-civilizational, notably European, bias built into it. The interests and distinctive cultural traditions of developing countries may be eroded by the evolution of such a system.[12] In response, the numerous constitutionalist stories that are currently being told within international legal scholarship might be pointed out; a single, uniform, generally accepted constitutionalist approach does not exist. While constitutionalist thought has in historic terms been developed in Europe, it is a reaction to the universal experience of domination by humans over other humans. In 18th- and 19th-century Europe, constitutionalism was asserted *against* the dominant culture and the establishment, and can thus hardly be called a product of that culture. A 'moderate' constitutionalist reading in no way implies a uniform, coherent world constitution, and certainly does not imply the quest for a world state. Besides, international constitutionalization must necessarily differ from national constitutionalism, and it is therefore not possible to copy one or a few constitutions. The idea is not to create a global, centralized government, but to constitutionalize global (polyarchic and multi-level) governance. This project must indeed take more fully into account the needs and interests of developing countries and their populations.

A related concern makes the point that if Europeans acquire disproportionate leverage on the workings of a more highly constitutionalized global system, the constitutional model of international law is unlikely to command American allegiance, especially if it is promoted as the paramount aspect of the global community.[13] However, reliance on cultural specificity often risks over-simplification. Even within the European academia of international law the constitutionalist approach is frequently criticized, notably by French and British scholars. This criticism is not automatically aligned with a 'pro-US-American' political attitude. The constitutionalist approach is directed against the disregard of the international rule of law. Even if, on average, European academics probably espouse a more international 'legalist' position than average US-American ones, opposition between Europe and US-American academic discourse appears simplistic; important impulses towards global constitutionalism have come from US-American scholars such as Richard Falk, Thomas Franck, or Anne-Marie Slaughter.

---

[12] Carol Harlow 'Global Administrative Law: The Quest for Principles and Values' (2006) 17 *EJIL* 187–214, at 189.

[13] *Cf* Douglas M Johnston 'World Constitutionalism in the Theory of International Law' in Ronald MacDonald and Douglas M Johnston (eds) *Towards World Constitutionalism: Issues in the Legal Ordering of the World Commmunity* (Martinus Nijhoff Leiden 2005) 3–29, at 20.

5. Compensatory Constitutionalism

The constitutionalist reconstruction of international law might be a reasonable strategy to compensate the de-constitutionalization on the domestic level which is effected by globalization and global governance.[14] Globalization puts the state and state constitutions under strain. Global problems compel states to cooperate within international organizations, and through bilateral and multilateral treaties. Previously typical governmental functions, such as guaranteeing human security, freedom, and equality, are in part transferred to 'higher' levels. Moreover, non-state actors (acting within states or even in a transboundary fashion) are increasingly entrusted with the exercise of traditional state functions, even with core tasks such as military and police activity.[15] All this has led to governance which is exercised beyond the states' constitutional confines. This means that state constitutions can no longer regulate the totality of governance in a comprehensive way. Thereby, the original claim of state constitutions to form a complete basic order is defeated. National constitutions are, so to speak, hollowed out; traditional constitutional principles become dysfunctional or empty. This affects not only the constitutional principle of democracy, but also the rule of law, the principle of social security, and the organization of territory.[16] In consequence, if the basic principles of constitutionalism are to be preserved, one must ask for compensatory constitutionalization on the international plane.

6. Global Constitutionalism as a Hermeneutic Device

The constitutionalist reading of international law contributes fresh arguments to an old controversy which recently popped up again, namely the controversy whether international law is real 'law'. The new deniers of international law (*Völkerrechtleugner*) justify the ostensibly non-legal character of international law with the absence of hard enforcement mechanisms and with the democratic deficit of international law. The constitutionalist approach helps to overcome the narrow focus on sanctions and on top-down enforcement. In most countries, domestic constitutional law is not enforceable. Typically, many constitutional provisions are not justiciable in the sense of being directly applicable by courts. This is especially the case in states that do not have a constitutional court, but

---

[14] See Anne Peters 'Compensatory Constitutionalism: The Function and Potential of Fundamental International Norms and Structures' (2006) 19 *Leiden Journal of International Law* 579–610.

[15] In US-occupied Iraq, employees of federal contractors and sub-contractors (Blackwater USA, Kroll Inc., Custer Battles, the Titan corporation, and others) worked as mercenaries, police, guards, prison officers, and interrogators.

[16] Anne Peters 'The Globalization of State Constitutions' in Janne Nijman and André Nollkaemper (eds) *New Perspectives on the Divide between National and International Law* (OUP Oxford 2007) 251–308.

is generally true for constitutional provisions with a programmatic, hortatory character. Despite this feature, nobody denies the character of constitutional law as law for this reason alone. This observation supports the view that international law, resembling constitutional law in this respect, is indeed law.

Also, the interpretation of particular norms and structures as 'constitutional' may provide an interpretative guideline. For instance, a constitutionalist approach to reservations to human rights treaties leads to admitting them only restrictively by interpreting Article 19 lit. c) VCLT extensively: reservations will presumably contravene the 'object and purpose' of such a treaty, whose purpose is to protect human rights effectively. They will therefore be presumptively inadmissible and also severable from the treaty, which should remain in force and fully bind the parties without that reservation.

A constitutionalist-minded international lawyer will, to give another example, determine the supremacy of international law over domestic constitutional law in a non-formalist way.[17] She will pay less attention to the formal sources of law, and more to the substance of the rules in question. In a constitutionalist perspective, the ranking of the norms at stake must be assessed in a more subtle manner, according to their substantial weight and significance. Such a non-formalist, substance-oriented perspective suggests that provisions in state constitutions of minor significance would have to give way to important international norms. Inversely, fundamental rights guarantees should prevail over less important norms (independent of their locus and type of codification). Admittedly, this approach does not offer strict guidance, because it is debatable which norms are 'important' in terms of substance, and because it does not resolve clashes between a 'domestic' human right on the one side and an 'international' human right on the other. However, the basic idea is that what counts is to look at the substance, not at the formal category of conflicting norms. Such a flexible approach appears to correspond better than the idea of a strict hierarchy to the current state of global legal integration, notably in human rights matters. These examples are not meant to imply that every constitutionalist interpretation of an international norm or concept signifies a turn to substance as opposed to formalism, because form can be important to safeguard values such as democracy or predictability. I will come back to this below.

7. The Problem and Promise of Politics

Another objection is that global constitutionalism conveys a false necessity and false rigidity that it is too a-political or pretends to be above politics.[18] And a

---

[17] Peters, Globalisation of State Constitutions, at 306–307; André Nollkaemper 'Rethinking the Supremacy of International Law' (2010) 65 *Zeitschrift für öffentliches Recht* 65–85.
[18] Joel P Trachtman 'The Constitutions of the WTO' (2006) 17 *EJIL* (2006) 623–646, at 623.

'constitutionalist imperialism' performed by the participants in the legal and political process would stifle the ordinary legal process.[19] As far as the academic observers are concerned, the constitutionalist agenda might be a scholarly attempt to channel or minimize politics. In short, constitutionalism can be criticized for embodying an unrealistic 'promise of the end of politics'.[20] This is what Jeffrey Dunoff has aptly called 'constitutional conceits'.[21] My response is that law and politics should not be viewed as distinct realms, but rather as deeply intertwined. Law is both the product of political activity, and an organizer and limiter of political action. In particular, constitutional law is a branch of law which is very close to politics. In consequence, constitutionalism is also a political, not simply an a-political, project (although it does suggest that there is a sphere 'above' everyday politics). So paradoxically, and in my mind laudably, the call for constitutionalism triggers precisely the contestation and politics it is said to pre-empt. The evolutionary dynamics of constitutionalism leads both to the legalization of politics and to a stronger politicization of law.[22] Even if any legalization of political problems (regarding constitutionalization as a special type of legalization) modifies the debate surrounding those problems by introducing a different, juridical logic, the underlying issues are thereby not totally, but only partly de-politicized. Such a relative de-politicization of international relations is not a disadvantage, but a plus, because international relations are as a general matter rather too politicized. The introduction of legal and even constitutional principles contributes to the stability of expectations, legal certainty, and equal treatment of the relevant actors.

A related objection against the constitutionalist reconstruction of international law is that this reading condones an impoverished, legalist (judicially made), a-political conception of constitution. This objection is raised by those who place a premium on popular sovereignty, democracy, and institutions directly accountable to the people. Those critics ask for 'democratic constitutionalism'[23] or for a more 'political constitutionalism'.[24] Political constitutionalism assumes that persons reasonably disagree about substantive outcomes, that the democratic process is more legitimate and effective than the judicial one, and that therefore not rights, but the democratic process is the core of constitutionalization. In contrast, legalist constitutionalism assumes that society can come to a rational consensus, and that this consensus is best expressed in basic rights, and that these are best protected by courts. The problem with global constitutionalism is, in the eyes of the critique, that it is too legalist in that sense. Along the same vein, concern about a global

---

[19] Szurek, La Charte, at 49 (para 26).   [20] Klabbers, Constitutionalism Lite, at 47.
[21] Jeffrey Dunoff 'Constitutional Conceits: The WTO's "Constitution" and the Discipline of International Law' (2006) 17 *EJIL* 647–675.
[22] *Cf* Martin Loughlin *Sword and Scales: An Examination of the Relationship Between Law & Politics* (Oxford Hart 2000), at 209.   [23] *Cf* Johnston, World Constitutionalism, 2005, at 19.
[24] For the national level see Richard Bellamy *Political Constitutionalism. A Republican Defence of the Constitutionality of Democracy* (CUP Cambridge 2007).

juristocracy has been voiced.[25] It is feared by some that unrepresentative international judges will be called upon to adjudicate disputes over the interpretation of a constitutional text. This concern duplicates the traditional British objection to a written, 'rigid', constitution.

Admittedly, the constitutionalization of international law has been lopsided. The process has so far been adjudicative rather than deliberative. This is most visible in the WTO and the related sector constitutionalization debate. What has been identified by some scholars as a constitutionalization of the WTO boils down to the legalization of the dispute settlement mechanism, judge-made principles, and constitutional techniques applied by the panels and Appellate Body, such as balancing. The WTO's capacity for legislative response is muted, last but not least by the consensus practice in WTO decision-making. Such a structurally embedded preponderance of judicial engineering is not limited to the WTO, but concerns the macro-constitutionalization of the international legal system as a whole.

However, this critique, although it may be formulated as a critique of global constitutionalism, is not in fact genuinely concerned with the constitutionalist reading of international law. The pertinent point is rather that global governance suffers from democratic deficits and—to some extent correspondingly—from too powerful courts. I submit that the danger of a global government of judges is so far exaggerated. Although the constitutionalization of international law has been court-driven, and although global constitutionalism even calls for the strengthening of judicial review, the establishment of an international constitutional court with compulsory jurisdiction over constitutional matters is unlikely. An 'imperfect' international constitution, backed by selective judicial control, would constitute progress, not peril.[26] Most importantly, global constitutionalism unveils precisely those deficits by introducing the constitutional vocabulary. The constitutional paradigm also inspires and eventually facilitates the search for remedies. In my view, the remedy against a too 'legalist' and too 'judicial' process of constitutionalization is not to stop that process, but to democratize it.

A constitutionalist approach to international law helps to prevent uncontrolled deformalization,[27] in the sense of resorting to some 'higher' legitimacy arguments in opposition to and in violation of international legality, as, for example, in the Kosovo crisis.[28] Although constitutionalism is a value-loaded

---

[25] Harlow, Global Administrative Law, 2006, at 213–214.

[26] It could also be pointed out that, as long as international law enjoys only weak and indirect democratic legitimacy, the counter-majoritarian difficulty of constitutional review is lesser on the international plane than in the domestic legal order. However, two wrongs do not make a right. The better course to take is to introduce more judicial review, and also more democratic decision-making.

[27] *Cf* Jürgen Habermas 'Does the Constitutionalization of International Law Still Have a Chance?' in *idem The Divided West* (Polity Cambridge 2006 Cronin ed and trans) 115–210, at 116.

[28] The Expert Commission with Richard Falk and others qualified the Kosovo-intervention as illegal, but legitimate (Independent International Commission on Kosovo *The Kosovo Report: Conflict, International Response, Lessons Learned* (OUP New York 2000), at 185–198, esp. at 186).

concept, it is nevertheless a legal approach in which consideration for the rule of law in a formal sense, for legal stability and for predictability, plays a part, and which acknowledges that legality itself can engender a type of legitimacy.[29] Seen in this light, constitutionalism is a juridical alternative to moralizing on the one hand, and to power politics on the other.

8. Global Constitutionalism's Critical Potential

The core reproach of the new deniers of international law, the legitimacy and notably democratic deficit, must be taken seriously. But also in this regard, global constitutionalism is helpful, because it provokes the pressing question of the legitimacy of global governance. But beware, the intrinsic link between constitutionalism and legitimacy cuts in many ways. Constitutionalism may legitimize the international system, but it may also challenge its legitimacy. On the one hand, the danger is that 'things formerly called institutional are being legitimized with the mantle of constitutionalization'.[30] This is unhelpful in analytic terms and dangerous from a normative perspective. On the other hand, ideas borrowed from global constitutionalism are used by some scholars with the opposite intention, namely to call into question international law as a whole,[31] and as a pretext for non-compliance. Again, the best path seems to be the middle one. Neither should global constitutionalism be used apologetically to bestow false legitimacy on international law. Nor should the complaint of the lack of legitimacy of international law undermine the authority of international law as such. Rather, the constitutionalist reading should clarify that the legitimacy of norms and of political rule does not depend on the structures of government or governance being exactly state-like. Global constitutionalism should and could help rather than hinder the revelation of existing legitimacy deficiencies in this body of law, without, however, throwing the baby out with the bathwater.

---

[29] *Cf* Rudolf von Ihering *Geist des römischen Rechts auf den verschiedenen Stufen seiner Entwicklung* part II (5 th edn von Breitkopf und Härtel Leipzig 1898), at 471: 'Die Form ist die geschworene Feindin der Willkür, die Zwillingsschwester der Freiheit. Denn die Form hält der Verlockung der Freiheit zur Zügellosigkeit das Gegengewicht, sie lenkt die Freiheitssubstanz in feste Bahnen, dass sie sich nicht zerstreue, verlaufe, sie kräftigt sie nach innen, schützt sie nach aussen. Feste Formen sind die Schule der Zucht und Ordnung und damit der Freiheit selber und eine Schutzwehr gegen äussere Angriffe—sie lassen sich nur brechen, nicht biegen.'

[30] Cass, WTO, at 245 with regard to the debate on the constitutionalization of the WTO.

[31] For a clear statement (although probably not with the intention to justify non-compliance) see Mortimer Sellers 'Republican Principles in International Law' (1996) 11 *Connecticut Journal of International Law* 403–432. Sellers argued 'that purportedly international laws and institutions bind and should influence republican governments only to the extent that they reflect republican procedures of politics and legislation.' (*Ibid*, at 404). '[I]international institutions deserve political legitimacy and obedience only to the extent that they conform to republican standards of popular sovereignty and pursuit of the common good.' (at 428). 'Republican govenments support the United Nations Secretariat only to the extent that it maintains high standards... the separate republican governments must themselves independently decide whether this is the case' (at 431).

Martti Koskenniemi sees the 'virtue of constitutionalism in the international world' in its 'universalizing focus', allowing extreme injustice in the world to be not only shown but also condemned.

[S]omething like constitutional vocabulary is needed to articulate it as a scandal insofar as it violates the equal dignity and autonomy of human beings. ... The use of the constitutional vocabulary, ... transforms individual suffering into an objective wrong that concerns not just the victim, but everyone. ... In a secular society, it is the political business of constitutionalism to endow such events with the sacredness or with a symbolic meaning that lifts them beyond their individuality.[32]

Indeed, there is, as Neil Walker put it, a 'responsibilising' potential in the constitutional discourse and imagination in the development of a polity.[33] Those who wish, for whatever motives, to make a plausible claim to constitutional elements in international law, must at least be seen to take these values seriously. So although constitutionalism may be invoked as a way of closing the debate, it in practice often has the opposite effect, namely that of opening up a richer and more productive normative debate. The reason is that the tradition of constitutionalism remains the best-stocked reservoir from which responsible politics may draw and the most persuasive medium in which it may be articulated.[34] So global constitutionalism deploys, and this is crucial, a constructive, not obstructive, critical potential.

---

[32] Martti Koskenniemi 'Constitutionalism as a Mindset: Reflections on Kantian Themes about International Law and Globalization' (2007) 8 *Theoretical Inquiries in Law* 9–36, at 35–36.
[33] Neil Walker 'The EU and the WTO: Constitutionalism in a New Key' in Gráinne de Búrca and Joanne Scott (eds) *The EU and the WTO: Legal and Constitutional Issues* (OUP Oxford 2001) 31–59, at 53–54.   [34] *Ibid*, at 57.

Epilogue: Debate on EJIL Talk! Blog

In July and August 2010, the EJIL Talk! blog (www.ejiltalk.org) hosted an online symposium on *The Constitutionalization of International Law*, to which both the authors and a number of expert commentators contributed. The debate that ensued is reproduced here.

In addition to posts by the authors summarising the ideas in the book (parts 1–5 of the epilogue), the exchange included comments by Jeffrey Dunoff (Temple University), Joel Trachtman (Fletcher School, Tufts University); Dan Bodansky (Arizona State Unversity), Steven Wheatley (University of Leeds) and Jean L. Cohen (Columbia University). The authors then responded to critique and submitted final remarks (parts 11–13).

1. Constitutionalization and International Law-making

Jan Klabbers

The main question underlying the recent book by Anne Peters, Geir Ulfstein and me— *The Constitutionalization of International Law*—is this: presuming that international law is indeed, as many contend, constitutionalizing, then what would international law come to look like? Given that there are a number of issues constitutional regimes usually address (political institutions of the community, membership, judicial organization, law-making, and procedures for the making of decisions), we wondered how these would, could or should be addressed in a constitutionalizing international legal order. Our aim was not to demonstrate that constitutionalization is actually going on—we simply presume it is, and leave the demonstration to others. Nor did we set out to sketch an ideal global constitutional order: this is a task perhaps best left to moral philosophers. Instead, we decided it might be interesting to take the claim of constitutionalization seriously and try to figure out what its consequences would be for international law.

The book's first chapter is dedicated to 'setting the scene'. It discusses globalization and a number of other current and related phenomena, such as the fragmentation of international law. One of the main points of the opening chapter is to establish that, in a world of well over 6 billion people, divided into 200 states and a handful of major religions, cultures, and ethical traditions (not to mention their widely divergent situations, giving rise to widely diverging interests), full agreement on all political topics is unlikely. In other words: the chapter recognizes that we live in a world of value pluralism, which entails that constitutionalism has to be pluralist as well: it has to respect and accommodate pluralism.

Second, a constitutional order needs to be a legitimate order. Now, legitimacy is a term which has been, and is, much abused, and while the chapter tracks the legitimacy debate to some extent, the main point for present purposes is simply this. Hypothetically, a constitutional order can be ran in many fashions—depending on one's definition of constitutionalism, there may be no inherent contradiction between constitutionalism and enlightened dictatorship or rule by aristocracy, or even foreign rule or empire. Yet, these are not versions of constitutionalism we would subscribe to. Instead, the idea of a constitution carries overtones of political legitimacy: a constitutional order is a legitimate order, and a legitimate order is one where all relevant stakeholders are involved in governance, in one way or another.

The above has important implications when it comes to law-making. After all, if the starting point of value pluralism is correct, then it seems unlikely that international law can be made on the basis of the unanimous agreement of all states or, more problematic still, all the relevant stakeholders (including actors other than states). And if the notion that the constitutional global order be legitimate—however defined—is to be taken seriously, then it follows that no norms can just be imposed on actors (this is without prejudice to sanctions following wrongful conduct). Hence, consent remains a necessary element of law. This immediately suggests that earlier ideas about universal international law are less than plausible, e.g. Charney's notion of law based on necessity was always vulnerable to the critique that not all actors share the same idea as to what exactly is necessary.[1] Yet, some room needs to be made for law-making by majority: the global constitutional order would need to be able to make law binding all, and not just make law only binding on those who consent. For if left at that, there is no reason to speak of constitutionalization; in such a case, the current vocabulary will serve well enough. In other words, a global constitutional order is one where universal law is at least a possibility, even though it leaves unaffected the possibility of recognizing more limited consent-based instruments as legally valid.

What adds to the complexity is that international law, these days, comes in an 'infinite variety', not always immediately recognizable as law: indeed, that is often the reason behind the conclusion of soft law instruments, non-legally binding agreements, or Memoranda of Understanding. These may look like law and are supposed to operate like law but, somehow, without actually being law. And to make matters more complicated still, there is a wide variety of other norms demanding attention and respect. States and others are not just supposed to follow the law. They are also supposed to adhere to moral injunctions (think of the responsibility to protect, which arguably has yet to become law). Soldiers on the battlefield need to respect humanitarian law, but also military practices and commands and perhaps even notions of chivalry. Traders need to follow international trade law, certainly, but also more spontaneous usages, assembled under the heading of *lex mercatoria*. WHO officials will be subject not just to legal demands, but sometimes also to professional medical standards. In short, individuals and other actors alike are confronted with a wide array of normative injunctions, some of them law, some of them non-law, and quite a few operating in a grey area in-between. In those cases, two questions present themselves. First, how is law to be recognized? Second, what to do in case a legal injunction is in conflict with a moral command, or a professional standard? Should law prevail? Or should preference be given to other normative orders?

Typically, in recent years the question of how to recognize valid law has been approached, under influence of the study of international relations, as a behavioural issue: if actors act in accordance with a norm, then the norm must be legal, for otherwise these actors would not have done so. This, however, misses the point, in two ways. It fails to recognize that actors may respect norms for a variety of reasons (including self-indulgence), and still does not help to separate legal from other injunctions. This

---

[1] See Jonathan I Charney, 'Universal International Law' (1993) 87 *AJIL* 529–551.

approach, eventually, ignores what Hart has referred to as the internal perspective, inquiring not only into the behaviour of the subjects of law but also the beliefs of those who are supposed to apply it.[2]

The challenge, eventually, for a constitutionalized law-making regime is that it must bow to two masters: it needs to be based on consent (anything else would be dictatorial, and would thus be just as unacceptable as doing away with democracy in domestic settings), and yet it must be possible to make law binding for all. Moreover, ideally it would also allow not only for the consent of states (as agents for their citizens), but the consent of all those involved (the poor and disposed included), and consent would have to be real, not nominal: consent procured under threat of withholding development assistance is not consent, and only delegitimizes the outcome.

The one way of achieving this, chapter 3 of the book suggests, is to find inspiration in existing opting-out procedures (and jurisprudentially, to some extent, in Lon Fuller's ideas about 'procedural natural law') and to work on the basis of the presumption that normative utterances are legally valid and legally binding, unless and until it can be demonstrated that they are not.[3] Factors that may help rebut the presumption reside, e.g. in the identity of the would-be law-makers, or whether law-making bodies exceed their competences, or whether putative law violates existing law.

All this may look more eccentric at first sight than it really is. In effect, it merely reverses the burden of proof that exists on paper but has already been reversed in much practice: the position outlined here codifies and makes explicit what is, in effect, already the dominant position. In today's not-yet-constitutionalized international legal order the formal presumption is, in many cases, that normative utterances do not bind unless the opposite can be demonstrated. This presumption is historically understandable (it flows from strong concerns about state sovereignty), but conceptually a bit silly: a presumption that agreements are not binding will always and automatically be rebutted, because no legal system can operate on such a basis. Indeed, the capitalist economy cannot work on a presumption of non-bindingness of contracts until the opposite is proven; and the global capitalist economy cannot operate on the presumption that treaties are not law, and do not give rise to obligations, either. Thus, in practice the historical presumption is already reversed: it is just that the sovereignty cum non-law presumption is reverted to whenever it is deemed politically expedient.

These considerations are strengthened by the demands of constitutionalism. A presumption of non-bindingness is not just unworkable, it is also difficult to reconcile with constitutionalist staples such as transparency, legal certainty, predictability, and judicial protection. No practical legal order can accept that normative utterances are, presumptively, not law; if that legal order is to be considered as constitutional, a presumption of non-law becomes an exercise in bad faith.

Should law conflict with other normative utterances, then a decent case can be made to give law priority. Law generally, in constitutional orders, is created democratically, unlike religion or morality. Law is cognizable and transparent, unlike social usages, or notions such as chivalry. And law is (ideally, at any rate) mindful of competing interests, unlike most professional standards, which are typically more single-minded. In such circumstances, one may perhaps resort to 'presumptive positivism': the law should be applied, unless there is a really, really good reason for not doing so. And that in itself captures the spirit of constitutionalism in a nutshell.

---

[2] H L A Hart, *The Concept of Law* (Oxford Clarendon Press 1961).
[3] Lon L Fuller, *The Morality of Law* (New haven CT Yale 1969, rev. edn).

2. Empowerment and Constitutional Control

Geir Ulfstein

International institutions exercise more and more power. This is not limited to foreign policy issues, such as international security or trade, but increasingly also to issues traditionally under exclusive domestic control, such as the relationship between states and their citizens. Furthermore, the distinction between what should be considered international and domestic is becoming irrelevant.

International lawyers have traditionally focused on the need for effective international institutions. This is no less important today. But with increased international powers comes the need for control. The original consent in the form of ratification to treaties establishing international institutions is seen as insufficient to justify their power. A constitutional approach emphasizes the relationship between empowerment and control.

This is not to say that treaties are formal constitutions. Treaties, including those establishing international institutions, are agreements, and states are free to choose whether to become parties or not. But states may in practice have little choice if they want to influence policy-making in the institutions, to reap the benefits of membership, or to be regarded as an actor of good standing in the international society. Neither should the claim to superiority be seen as a necessary part of a constitutional order. Furthermore, the focus should not only be upon formalized rules in the form of treaties. Also legal practice forms part of a legal order.

A fundamental question relates to 'translation': to what extent is it useful to apply constitutional principles developed for domestic legal orders to international institutions? A response would be that since such institutions exercise powers comparable to, and partly at the expense of, national constitutional organs, they should be subject to comparable control. This does not mean that the constitutional principles should be imported whole cloth. But certain fundamental principles such as democratic control, rule of law and the protection of human rights are also relevant for the international institutional order. It is of course possible to examine the way in which international institutions respect each of these requirements separately. Such an approach misses, however, the need to see the interaction between the principles.

Constitutionalism can be of a descriptive and normative character. It can be used to legitimize international institutions that do not deserve it. More important is, however, the critical potential of constitutionalism. A constitutional approach can be used to hold international institutions to account in requiring that they fulfill certain basic requirement when they exercise their powers. In the following, international organizations and courts will be examined from a constitutional perspective (chapters 2 and 4 of *The Constitutionalization of International Law*).

International organizations

In the absence of democratically elected organs in international organizations, one is left with participation of states in the political organs of international organizations, and the indirect control of such decision-making through the democratically elected national constitutional organs—to the extent that member states are democratic. A democratic approach would militate in favour of plenary organs as the locus for undertaking legislative activities. Accordingly, decisions of legislative character by the UN, whether they concern preventing the financing of terrorism or access to weapons of mass destruction, should be adopted by the General Assembly rather than the Security Council.

Methods have been developed to circumvent the need for decision-making by consensus, such as leaving a possibility of reservation against majority decisions. We also find models of weighted voting. This may strike a balance between effective decision-making and the need for securing state consent. But the democratic deficit in international law-making may limit the powers from a normative point of view—and thereby the effectiveness of the international system to solve urgent international problems.

It has been argued that the rule of law is less relevant to international law since it is based on the consent of states. But as the role of consent becomes more tenuous it is increasingly acknowledged that this principle has a role also in international law, whether to protect a minority of states or individuals against majority decisions. The principle requires that decisions in individual cases should be based on law rather than on political considerations. This may be achieved through the principle of separation of power. While it is difficult to separate decisions to use military force from political considerations, the listing of terrorist organizations is an example of decisions that should be sheltered from such considerations. Due process guarantees in the form of procedural principles become also more important. International organizations increasingly exercise power over individuals, including in territories under international administration. Such powers should be subject to respect for international human rights. Finally, a constitutional approach would call for increased judicial review of international decisions.

A constitutional system means that the different organs have defined competencies in a hierarchic organization. The international legal system is, however, fragmented. The absence of formal binding powers alleviates the difficulties represented by this fragmentation, but it makes it difficult with consistent policy-making. The fragmentation could be overcome by integrating different institutions, establishing a hierarchy between them, or defining their respective responsibilities (complementarity). States show, however, little inclination to embark on such processes. The diversity of international institutions may also have its benefits in allowing the possibility to design the institutions to the task at hand. This could be seen as arguments in favour of arrangements for coordination between the institutions—rather than a formal constitutionalization of their respective powers.

A constitutional system would also require that the international and national system work in a consistent way. As already stated, the focus has so far mostly been on the need to establish effective international institutions. Hence, the focus on the implied powers of such institutions and their possibility to develop their competencies through their practice. But with more extensive powers it is time to revisit also the limits for such powers. The principle of legality requires that the powers of international institutions are exercised on the basis of the consent of states through their ratification on the founding treaty. This means that this treaty also establishes restrictions for their powers. Furthermore, it should be acknowledged that the primary democratic legitimacy is found at the national, not the international level. This means that the principle of subsidiarity should be respected. Accordingly, decisions should not be taken at the international level unless the effects cannot be achieved through national decisions. This is, however, not an argument against effective interpretation of the treaties establishing international institutions.

International tribunals

There is an ever-increasing number of international courts, in more substantive areas, and they increasingly have a compulsory character. They may interpret vague international rules in a dynamic way, and issue binding judgments. The international tribunals are probably the most advanced part of international law when it comes to empowerment.

The empowerment of international tribunals should also require comparable constitutional guarantees. First of all, it should be ensured that the judges have the necessary expertise and independence. The current elections procedures have been characterized as highly political. This would call for more elaborate nomination and election procedures. Improved procedural guarantees in the form of both written and oral proceedings, transparency and fact-finding procedures may also be required.

The hierarchical order of national legal systems shall serve the finality, consistency, and implementation of the courts' decisions, in short the effective constitutional function of the judiciary. The diversity of the international judicial architecture increases, on the other hand, with the rising number of specialized tribunals—with no supreme court.

There are, however, only a few examples of problems related to competing jurisdiction between international tribunals. Such jurisdictional problems may also be alleviated through the principles of litispendence and *res judicata*. Conflicting jurisprudence may only occur in situations of competing jurisdictions. A more actual danger is inconsistent jurisprudence. But this may be lessened to the extent that international tribunals use judgments by other tribunals as precedents.

Thus, the problems with a fragmented judiciary should not be overstated. Possible ways to deal with this include, as with international organizations, integration of different international tribunals, a hierarchic relationship, or complementarity in their respective substantive scope. A general redesign of the international judicial architecture will, however, hardly find the necessary political support. And, as with international organizations, it should also be pointed out that a diversified international judiciary has its advantages. The burgeoning of international tribunals should in itself be seen as an aspect of constitutionalization. What is more, the dearth of a formal hierarchy does not necessarily prevent international tribunals from acting in a functionally constitutionally manner.

The relationship between international and national courts is characterized by formal dualism. International tribunals are supreme at the international level whereas national courts have the final decision in the domestic system. Dualism is, however, not a good description of practice. International law is increasingly becoming part of national law.

There is no sign of a constitutionalized global judicial system of supranational character. But the system may still work as an integrated system in practice. This requires, however, that both the international and national judiciary define their respective roles. International tribunals should, while upholding the effectiveness of international obligations, respect the principle of subsidiarity as regards the relationship between states and their citizens. National courts should neither be too defensive or antagonistic when it comes to respecting international judgments, but rather take active part in the interpretation and development of international law. To the extent that international tribunals and national courts acknowledge their respective functions in the interpretation and application of international law—although tensions will inevitably arise—the combined international and national judicial judiciary may in practice work as a constitutionalized system.

How should the need for democratic control and the independence of international tribunals be balanced—both in relation to national and international law-makers? There has been criticism of constitutional review by national supreme courts (the counter-majoritarian argument). Since treaties are more difficult to amend than constitutions, it could be argued that it is even more reason to be sceptical of international tribunals restricting national democratic freedom. International tribunals are furthermore not elected by national constitutional organs and are not accountable to such organs. This criticism may be valid even though judgments by international tribunals are only binding at the international level.

But, first, international regulation requires restrictions on national freedom. Such mutual restrictions have been accepted through states' ratification. There may also be matters that are considered of such fundamental importance that national policy-makers would see them protected against interference by future national legislators, i.e. a form of self-binding. But international tribunals should take due account of the principle of subsidiarity, while ensuring respect for international obligations.

Finally, the absence of an international legislator may be taken both as an argument for and against international judicial activism. Since we do not have an effective legislator, there is more need for international tribunals to develop international law. On the other hand, there is no legislator to control the activities of such tribunals. The objectives of the treaty establishing the tribunal may, however, justify a dynamic interpretation by the tribunals, e.g. if the treaty shall contribute to more unity among the states parties, or protect human rights. It could be argued that the negative integration between states represented by international restrictions, increasingly specified by international tribunals, should be compensated by positive integration through international law-making powers. States are, however, reluctant to accept increased international law-making.

3. Membership in the Global Constitutional Community

Anne Peters

In Chapter 5, it is argued that there is a global constitutional community which is made up by individuals, states, international organizations, NGOs, and business actors. From a constitutional perspective, individual human beings are the ultimate units of that community. But states are officially held to be the legal representatives of citizens on the international plane (however fictitious this might be for some states), are still—as a group—the most powerful global actors, and are (in most areas of the world) important repositories of political, social, and cultural identity. Therefore international law and global governance must remain, in order to preserve a sufficient level of legitimacy, linked to states. The ultimate responsibility for governance should not be transferred to non-state actors and certainly not to business actors. However, the involvement of non-state actors in law-making and -enforcement can be an important additional source for the legitimacy of global governance. It should consequently be broadened, structured, and formalized.

In a constitutionalized world order, natural persons are the primary international legal persons and the primary members of the global constitutional community. Individuals are so far quite firmly entrenched as international *bourgeois*, i.e. as passive beneficiaries of largely unenforceable rights. They have been granted more and more international rights and obligations beyond human rights, such as the right to environmental information, procedural rights in various international forums, or secondary rights to reparation. Individuals may also incur criminal liability flowing directly from international law. This trend contributes to the creation of different layers of rights (those of constitutional significance and others), and thereby manifests constitutionalization in the sense of an emergence of a specific layer of constitutional law besides (possibly 'above') ordinary international law.

There is a very weak trend towards the inclusion of individuals in the international legal process through hearings, giving opportunities to comment, and other types of participation. Individuals are thereby in political terms empowered. The doctrinal consequence of the citizens' right to political participation in global governance—which is in terms of constitutional policy desirable—is that individuals are upgraded from mere passive international legal subjects (as holders of human rights and bearers of criminal responsibility) to active international legal subjects, to co-law-makers. The legally relevant difference is that passive subjects are only capable of having rights, whereas active legal subjects are capable to create law. This empowerment could be described as a trend towards transnational *citoyenneté*.

States—as international legal subjects—are constituted by international law. As a prerequisite of statehood, the legal principle of effectiveness has in state practice been complemented by standards of legality properly speaking. A territorial entity established through unlawful use of force or in violation of the international principle of self-determination is not a state in the sense of international law (not an international legal person). Respect of basic human rights or of democracy is no precondition for valid statehood. But the abandonment of exclusive reliance on effectiveness has opened a window of opportunity for taking into account further standards of international legality for the assessment of whether a political entity is a state or not.

In a constitutionalized world order, state equality is proportional equality. The concerns for peace, for human rights protection, for development or for other constitutional values may outweigh the interest in observing strict formal equality of states and may justify legal privileges such as more drawing rights, more votes within an international organization, or exemptions from contractual liberalization obligations. But state quality stands in a tension with individual equality which can ultimately not be resolved as long as there are states with vastly differing population sizes. The inhabitants of less populated states will always be overrepresented in a decision-making setting where each state has one vote.

From a constitutionalist perspective, state sovereignty is a legal concept and as such embedded in international law. Constitutionalists welcome the re-characterization of sovereignty as implying states' responsibility to protect their populations from international crimes.

Ultimately, the international constitutional status of states is instrumental for the rights and needs of individuals. This *finalité* means that states remain indispensable in a global constitutionalized order, as crystallization points for (collective) identity, as primary law-makers and law-enforcers, and mediators between conflicting societal actors. But this *finalité* also calls for the constitutional containment of states.

A sectoral constitutionalization is taking place within international organizations. The constitutionalist approach moves beyond the description of the founding treaties of international organizations as constitutions in the sense of basic texts defining organs and their competences, but looks for and propagates constitutional values such as human rights and democracy, within international organizations. It also seeks to overcome the traditional focus on the autonomy of international organizations, where autonomy is usually implicitly taken as a proxy for sovereignty. The constitutionalist argument is that autonomy is not a pre-condition of constitutionalization but on the contrary should trigger the demand for constitutionalization. The more autonomous an international organization is in a sociological sense, the more it needs to be constitutionalized. Finally, it is worth highlighting that sectoral constitutionalization has so far been largely effected through international judges, and goes hand in hand with judicial self-empowerment.

Further members of the constitutional community are NGOs. A principle of openness of global governance forums for NGOs is emerging as a constitutional principle. This means that standard setting conferences, meetings or conferences of treaty parties, and other international bodies must at least consider in good faith whether to grant NGOs access and must justify refusal. A constitutionally appropriate accreditation procedure for NGOs must be relatively distant from states, and it must observe due process guarantees and apply reasonable substantive criteria.

The proper constitutional modality of NGO participation in international law making is voice, not vote. Once accredited, NGOs enjoy a legitimate expectation that the participatory conditions will entail some core components—even if the written rules of procedure are silent on this. Among these components is the (clearly defined and limited) right to make written and (upon permission) oral statements in the forum, which must be duly taken into account.

The second formal constitutional function of NGOs is their participation in the enforcement of international law. The benefits of conditional and indirect NGO participation in international adjudication, notably through *amicus curiae* briefs, outweigh its risks. Therefore, a presumption of the admissibility of *amicus curiae* briefs should be acknowledged. In non-judicial compliance control, NGOs' role needs clarification, to be laid down best in the rules of the committees themselves. *De lege ferenda*, qualified NGOs should be allowed to trigger certain non-compliance procedures themselves.

To conclude, NGO involvement can contribute to the legitimacy of global governance through inclusion and participation, but only if this participation is to some extent formalized and streamlined and if attention is paid to the skewed impact of NGOs from the north.

Finally, business actors are members of the international constitutional community. Constitutionalism might be a source of inspiration for resolving current issues such as the human rights responsibilities of business actors. For example, the acknowledgement of an indirect third party effect of Human Rights Covenants (as opposed to direct human rights obligations imposed on business) would strike a balance between respect of entrepreneurial freedom on the one hand and containment of powerful economic actors on the other, while ascribing the ultimate responsibility to states.

Although it is correct that the core objective of constitutionalism, the containment of power, is, especially in times of globalization, highly relevant with regard to economic power, a complete constitutionalization of the private sector in the sense that private actors would be subject to the full panoply of (international) constitutional standards, just like public actors, is not desirable. It might be useful to transfer some principles and instruments of constitutionalism to the economic sphere, but only while respecting the own logics of that sphere.

The important recent phenomenon of outsourcing public functions has no intrinsic or natural limits. Limits must be established normatively, and the value judgements should derive from constitutionalism. Consequently, the involvement of business actors in law-*making* should reflect the three sector model in which business participants are treated distinctly from civil society actors. As regards law-*enforcement* through business actors, this is least advanced but also least recommended in constitutionalist terms, because a separation of functions between the objects, subjects, and enforcers of regulation should be maintained.

One way to compensate for legitimacy and accountability deficits engendered by the marketization and outsourcing of governance is to make sure that the process of developing and implementing international law is a shared endeavour among (inter-)governmental institutions, business, and NGOs. But legitimacy is gained through joint governance only when the parties remain independent from one another and sufficiently distant, because only then capture and collision is ruled out.

Overall, the legitimacy of governance by business actors might derive from delegation or from beneficial outputs. But all considered, there still is the real danger that global governance is unduly commercialized through business involvement. To become full members of the global constitutional community, transnationally active business actors should be held more accountable to stakeholders through international mechanisms, however difficult it is to define the relevant groups and the procedures.

4. Dual Democracy

Anne Peters

Overview of the argument of chapter 6

Global governance is undemocratic even under a modest standard. The deficits lie in the institutional design of the international organizations and bodies themselves, they result from the way states are integrated into the system of global governance, and finally they concern the relationship between citizens and the international institutions.

On the premiss that all rule over persons should be democratic, and that the globalization-induced erosion of domestic democracy should be compensated as far as possible, the democratization of global governance is inescapable. Because a stand-still or roll-back of global governance is unfeasible, and therefore no way to re-invigorate democracy, a new design to enhance global democracy is needed.

Global constitutionalism requires dual democratic mechanisms. These should relate both to government within nation states and to governance 'above' states, thus to multiple levels of governance. The result should be a multi-unit democracy, built with domestic and international building blocks.

A fully democratized world order first of all rests on democratic nation states, thus on democracy within states. The spread and support of national democracies constitutes a kind of indirect global democratization. It already is and should be further encouraged by international law. Because of its fundamental and systemic importance, the requirement of democracy within states should be acknowledged as a global constitutional principle.

'Above' states, both the production of primary international law and the international institutions and their secondary law-making can and should be democratized on two tracks. On the one hand, citizens should continue to be mediated by their states which act for them in international relations (statist track). On the statist track, states as principals of international institutions should be reasserted and their influence improved. But because the ultimate reference point of democracy are natural persons, such a state-mediated democracy is present only to the extent that states really are the representatives of their citizens, and when additionally the concerns of non-citizens (such as migrants) also are taken care of in state politics. It follows that we can meaningfully speak of an indirect democratization of the global order on the statist track only when all states have realized domestic democratic government and protect 'new' minorities who lack citizenship. As long as not all states are democratic, a large number of people are not represented in a democratic sense by their states in the international institutions.

On the other hand, even if all states of the world became democracies, this would not in itself suffice to attain a meaningful degree of global democratic legitimacy, because national democracy itself is undermined for various reasons. Therefore natural persons, who are in their role as citizens the ultimate source of political authority, must be enabled to bypass their intermediaries, the states, and take direct democratic action on the supra-state level (individualist track). The individualist track can be realized through various institutional mechanisms. The start could be to introduce parliamentary assemblies in more international organizations, and to expand their so-far merely consultative powers.

The two-track model does not imply a complete shift of the international institutions' accountability to natural persons, but merely suggests bringing in the global citizens as principals besides states where appropriate. The accountability of the global governance institutions is thus extended and duplicated. The institutions will not be accountable only to states, but additionally (and sometimes competingly and conflictually) become accountable directly to citizens. The result is a dual accountability of international institutions to a dual constituency: states and citizens.

First track: the democratization of international governance via democratic nation states

It is often claimed that the current international legal order can be understood as an 'inter-state' democracy, and should be developed further in the direction of an association of democratic states. The inter-state paradigm relies on transitive legitimacy. In that view, the legitimacy of the international regime resides in the legitimacy of national regimes. As long as the states, the main actors, the primary and original legal subjects, and the principal creators of international law, are in themselves legitimate, they indirectly legitimize international law and global governance, so the argument runs.

Indeed, the accountability of international organizations and regimes to democratic nation states is a *conditio sine qua non* for democratic global governance. States are indispensable as members of the global constitutional order. Doing away with states would imply a single global polity, which would be remote from the citizens, inevitably inflexible and complicated, and already for these reasons undemocratic.

All this means that the global constitutional order should not be a democracy without states, but must rely on states, and that these states should be democratized. Democratic states can contribute to global democracy on two levels: within states, decisions must be taken democratically, and on the international level, the democratic states represent their citizens.

The promotion of democracy within nation states is a central principle of global constitutionalism not only because domestic democracy is the foundation of a transitive global democracy, but also because domestic democracy promotes global constitutional values, e.g. by reinforcing respect for human rights, fostering development, and finally by reducing the likelihood of war.

International law is evolving towards a requirement that states must be democratic, while strictly limiting the means to enforce the spread of domestic democracy. Although the application of the democratic prescription remains selective, the quest for domestic democracy in the international *lex lata* is an indicator of the constitutionalization of international law.

But while domestic democracy is indispensable for global democracy, it is not sufficient. An exclusively state-focused view of global democracy is flawed on various grounds which relate to the inter-state relations, to the states' control of global governance institutions, and to the internal democratic structures in states.

Finally, even if all states of the world became perfect democracies, and even if the international institutions were perfectly responsive to the member states (which they are not), this would not lead to a satisfactory situation of global (multi-unit) democratic governance. The reason is that the democratic substance of states is being impaired through globalization and through the concomitant zoning-up of governance functions. The substance of politics has been migrating to the international level, mainly due to the globalization of problems that must be politically tackled and resolved, ranging from trade and finances over migration, climate and diseases to terrorism. The result is that while political decisions within national boundaries are still formally taken democratically, national entities undergo a process of *de facto* de-democratization and are less effective. This is the final fundamental reason why an association of democratic states, with states acting on the international plane as representatives of their nationals, is not enough to realize global multilevel democracy. This observation counsels against channelling legitimation exclusively through the nation states.

Second track: global direct democracy

Citizenship

On the second track of non-state democratization, democratic relationships should be established between global citizens and international institutions via schemes of participation and representation that cut across nation states. Global citizens should have an input into international law-making independent of their states.

Under conditions of global governance the right to democratic participation, as guaranteed in Article 25 CCPR, should not only be directed against states, but should be understood as exercisable across borders and also opposable to those international organizations which rule over persons' lives and affect their interests. However, the establishment of direct democratic relations between individuals and international organizations is fraught with difficulties linked to the idea of a purely functional, not spatial representation on the basis of 'affectedness'.

Many people doubt or vehemently negate that the personal (collective) basis for democratic mechanisms exists or can ever emerge on a global scale. The arguments surrounding the global collectivity of humans ultimately boil down to the statement that democratic mechanisms independent of nation states cannot realize the equal liberty of persons, and will therefore be unfair and undeserving of the name democracy.

It is not possible, but not even necessary to begin a futile search for a global community of fate, a global demos. If one recognizes humanity as a novel political subject, it would not be a unitary one, but a plural one, consisting of multiple demoi. Transnational participatory structures are in that perspective a 'demoi-cracy' rather than a democracy.

Another objection is that a weak collective identity of humankind, the extreme diversity, and the thin global solidarity create the risk that rules issued by global governance institutions, awards rendered by international courts, and sanctions imposed by bodies such as the Security Council will be perceived by their addressees as illegitimate forms of 'outside' or 'alien' interference, and will thus not be loyally accepted.

My response to these concerns points to humankind as a socially relevant community, to diversity as a constitutive good of political association, to existing resources for globalized identities, and to solidarity flowing from reciprocal respect.

Ultimately, the question of the factual underpinnings of democracy (demos, homogeneity, collective identity, language, solidarity, and the like) is a chicken-egg-problem. Although the importance of cultural and social elements as enabling factors of democratic procedures should not be underestimated, these still interact with the legal (democratic) institutions. None of these factors is a natural, absolute, a priori of democratic governance which would have to be present in full before democratic processes could begin. One may reckon with their evolution within and through democracy. Bootstrapping is to some extent possible.

Civil society actors

Global civil society institutions constitute a kind of democratic infrastructure. However, it is not clear whether this global network is already dense enough to allow for a minimum global non-state democracy. As long as NGOs only have a voice in decision-making, but not a vote, the lack of formal democratic credentials of NGOs (and likewise of technical experts, professional associations, TNCs, and various public-private or private-private partnerships) does not de-legitimize their participation in global governance. The absence of internal democratic organization can be compensated by other forms of accountability. The legitimacy gains through NGO-involvement are apt to outweigh the legitimacy problems. Overall, a further democratization of the international legal order requires that the participation of NGOs in law-making and law-enforcement be strengthened. However, it should remain on the line 'voice, but no vote'.

Institutional design for a non-state democratization

Citizens could be directly engaged in global governance through referendums, consultations, and notice and comment procedures. Transnational consultative referendums could realize the participatory modus of voice, not vote.

Within international organizations, citizens would have to be represented by dele-gates. A World Parliament, the involvement of interest groups, notably professional associations along the lines of the ILO, or bringing to bear citizens' weight within the existing state assemblies, or engaging the UN with national parliaments have been sug-gested and could be tried out. The most powerful organizations, such as the UN, the Bretton Woods Institutions, and the WTO, where parliamentary assemblies are con-spicuously absent, should be parliamentarized. Even merely consultative assemblies might perform the typical mediating function of parliaments, and they create transpar-ency and organize interests.

Tensions between the two tracks

The two-track global democracy will remain in perpetual internal tension. The reason is that the ultimate reference point of democracy are natural persons, while in a multi-polity world, those natural persons remain partly mediated by their states. These ten-sions between the statist track and the individualist track pose problems for the rules for decision-making. There are two aspects to this: the incompatibility of state equality and citizens' equality, and the shortcomings of both inter-state unanimity and majority voting.

The individuals of the world have, as political agents, multiple identities. In their political role as national citizens and as members of a national polity, they own demo-cratic rights which are on the international level safeguarded by granting their home state one voice. But in their political role as global citizens, persons are not fairly represented by the scheme 'one state—one vote' in treaty-making and for the production of sec-ondary international law. Because states contain vastly different sizes of populations, there is no correlation between states' votes and citizens' votes. Equality of states results in the inequality of citizens (as global citizens), and the representation of the citizens is skewed.

The current trend to inter-state majoritarianism is from the individualist perspective problematic because it risks forestalling the democratic formation of collective pre-ferences within the nation states. In the inter-state perspective, it seems illegitimate and undemocratic that in a consensus system a minority (one state) can block a treaty. But if this is 'cured' through the introduction of a system of inter-state majority voting, the defeated nation's collective preferences (which have been ideally determined through a democratic procedure) will be completely ignored. The national veto power seems necessary to preserve the democratic decision-making on the 'lower' level, within the smaller community. The persistence of this democratic conundrum is an additional policy argument in favour of pluralist, non-hierarchical, network-type reconceptualiza-tions of the relationship between international and domestic law (and between inter-national constitutional and domestic constitutional law), based on discourse and mutual adaptation.

Other mechanisms of legitimacy and accountability of global governance such as inclusion and participation, expert supervision, and judicial review by international and domestic courts, are not really 'democratic'. At best, a combined formula of the proce-dures and mechanisms which would be in themselves normatively deficient might create an overall accountability which is functionally equivalent to democratic deliberation, consultation, votes, and elections.

5. The Pros and Cons of the Constitutionalist Reading of International Law

Anne Peters

Chapter 7 discusses the pros and cons of the constitutionalist paradigm. Critics of global constitutionalism doubt the empirical reality of the phenomenon called constitutionalization, call into question the analytic value of constitutionalism as an academic approach, and fear that the discourse is in normative terms dangerous. The chapter counters these objections.

The term 'constitution' might be a misnomer when applied to the international sphere. Also, the danger of blowing up an academic paper tiger is very real. Global constitutionalism as an academic agenda should follow the middle path between merely self-dignifying the status quo on the one hand and hanging onto pipe dreams on the other. In order to gain acceptance in the political realm, global constitutionalists might highlight the current situation of global interdependence. With such a state of affairs, national and global public interests tend to converge more and more; national interests and universal idealism are not necessarily in opposition. Given this convergence of global and national, an 'idealist' global constitutionalism which promotes global interests, may even, at least in the long run, further national economic and political interests as well, although some states benefit more than others.

The constitutionalist reading of international law might raise dangerously seductive over-expectations. The vocabulary makes it virtually impossible to escape from the assumptions that go with it. Social legitimacy might be artificially constructed through the use of constitutional language. The response is that 'constitutionalism' is not a ready-made answer, but—on the contrary—a perspective which might help the right questions of fairness, justice, and effectiveness to be asked.

Another consideration is that the concept of international constitutionalism suffers from oversell and vagueness. International law, politics, and economics are being mixed, if not confused. Indeed, there is the danger that reliance on constitutionalism is actually counterproductive because it may postpone rather than encourage concrete debates on concrete problems, such as decision-making in the WTO, the composition of the UN Security Council, or how to liaise national parliaments to the UN. However, the added value of the constitutionalist paradigm might lie in its comprehensive nature. The normative claim is that the different features of constitutionalism as a whole are more than the sum of its parts. More inclusive and transparent decision-making and judicial review should go together, and in combination they take on a special normative significance. Therefore the constitutionalist reconstruction does possess an additional explicative and prescriptive value. It reminds us of the interlinkage of the various features of constitutionalism, and calls for complementing the existing constitutional features of international law (such as international monitoring of state activity) with missing ones, such as democracy and judicial review of acts of international organizations.

Yet another concern is culturalist. The constitutionalist reading of international law may be genuinely anti-pluralist. It may have a uni-civilizational, notably European, bias built into it. In response it might be pointed out that while constitutionalist thought has in historic terms been developed in Europe, it is a reaction to the universal experience of domination by humans over other humans. Even in 18th- and 19th-century Europe, constitutionalism was not a confirmation of European culture, but asserted *against* the dominant culture and the establishment.

A 'moderate' constitutionalist reading in no way implies a uniform, coherent world constitution, and certainly does not imply the quest for a world state. The idea is not to create a global, centralized government, but to constitutionalize global (polyarchic and multi-level) governance. This project must indeed take more fully into account the needs and interests of developing countries and their populations.

The constitutionalist reconstruction of international law might be a reasonable strategy to compensate the de-constitutionalization on the domestic level which is effected by globalization and global governance. Globalization puts the state and state constitutions under strain. Global problems compel states to cooperate within international organizations, and through bilateral and multilateral treaties. Previously typically governmental functions, such as guaranteeing human security, freedom, and equality, are in part transferred to 'higher' levels. Moreover, non-state actors (acting within states or in a transboundary fashion) are increasingly entrusted with the exercise of traditional state functions, even with core tasks such as military and police activity. All this has led to governance which is exercised beyond the states' constitutional confines. This means that state constitutions can no longer regulate the totality of governance in a comprehensive way. Thereby, the original claim of state constitutions to form a complete basic order is defeated. National constitutions are, so to speak, hollowed out; traditional constitutional principles become dysfunctional or empty. This affects not only the constitutional principle of democracy, but also the rule of law, the principle of social security, and the organization of territory. In consequence, if the basic principles of constitutionalism are to be preserved, one must ask for compensatory constitutionalization on the international plane.

The constitutionalist reading of international law contributes fresh arguments to an old controversy which recently popped up again, namely the controversy whether international law is real 'law'. The new deniers of international law (*Völkerrechtsleugner*) justify their qualification of international law as non-law by pointing to the absence of hard enforcement mechanisms and to the democratic deficit of international law. The constitutionalist approach is useful here because it helps to overcome the narrow focus on sanctions and on top-down enforcement.

Also, the understanding of particular norms and structures as 'constitutional' may provide an interpretative guideline. For instance, a constitutionalist approach to reservations to human rights treaties leads to admitting them only restrictively by interpreting Article 19 lit. c) VCLT extensively: reservations will presumably contravene the 'object and purpose' of such a treaty, whose purpose is to protect human rights effectively. They will therefore be presumptively inadmissible and also severable from the treaty, which should remain in force and fully bind the parties without that reservation. A constitutionalist-minded international lawyer will, to give another example, determine the supremacy of international law over domestic constitutional law in a non-formalist way. She will pay less attention to the formal sources of law, and more to the substance of the rules in question. In a constitutionalist perspective, the ranking of the norms at stake must be assessed in a more subtle manner, according to their substantial weight and significance.

A further objection is that global constitutionalism conveys a false necessity and false rigidity, that it is too unpolitical or pretends to be above politics. My response is that law and politics should not be viewed as distinct realms, but rather as deeply intertwined. Law is both the product of political activity, and an organizer and limit of political action. In particular, constitutional law is a branch of law which is very close to politics. In consequence, constitutionalism is also a political, not simply an unpolitical, project (although it does suggest that there is a sphere 'above' everyday politics). So paradoxically, and in my mind laudably, the call for constitutionalism triggers precisely the contestation and politics it is said to pre-empt.

A related objection against the constitutionalist reconstruction of international law is that this reading condones an impoverished, legalist (judicially made), unpolitical conception of constitution. Admittedly, the constitutionalization of international law has been lopsided. The process has so far been adjudicative rather than deliberative.

However, this critique, although it may be formulated as a critique of global constitutionalism, is not in fact genuinely concerned with the constitutionalist reading of international law. The pertinent point is rather that global governance suffers from democratic deficits and—to some extent correspondingly—from too powerful courts. Global constitutionalism unveils precisely those deficits by introducing the constitutional vocabulary. The constitutional paradigm also inspires and eventually facilitates the search for remedies. In my view, the remedy against a too 'legalist' and too 'judicial' process of constitutionalization is not to stop that process, but to democratize it.

The core reproach of the new deniers of international law, the legitimacy and notably the democratic deficit, must be taken seriously. But also in this regard, global constitutionalism is helpful, because it provokes the pressing question of the legitimacy of global governance.

Neither should global constitutionalism be used apologetically to bestow a sham legitimacy on international law. Nor should the complaint of the lack of legitimacy of international law undermine the authority of international law as such. Rather, the constitutionalist reading should clarify that the legitimacy of norms and of political rule does not depend on the structures of government or governance being exactly state-like. Global constitutionalism should and could help rather than hinder the revelation of existing legitimacy deficiencies in this body of law, without however throwing the baby out with the bathwater. Although constitutionalism may be invoked as a way of closing the debate, it in practice often has the opposite effect, namely that of opening up a richer and more productive normative debate. The reason is that the tradition of constitutionalism remains the best-stocked reservoir from which responsible politics may draw and the most persuasive medium in which it may be articulated. So global constitutionalism deploys, and this is crucial, a constructive, not obstructive, critical potential.

6. The Lotus Eaters

Jeffrey Dunoff and Joel Trachtman[4]

In *The Constitutionalization of International Law* ("*CIL*"), Jan Klabbers, Anne Peters, and Geir Ulfstein have produced a valuable addition to the burgeoning literature on

[4] Professor Jeffrey Dunoff is Charles Klein Professor of Law and Government at the Beasley School of Law, Temple University. Professor Joel Trachtman is Professor of International Law at the Fletcher School, Tufts University

international constitutionalization. Their important volume presents an admirable overview of many of the major debates in this area as well as a distinctive vision of constitutionalization's features and virtues. In this short post we wish to highlight an important dimension of their argument; raise some questions about their analysis; and briefly outline an alternative approach to understanding international constitutionalization.

CIL's account of constitutionalization is notable for the way that it subverts many standard international law dichotomies. While it is difficult to summarize their subtle arguments in a brief post, we might capture *CIL*'s constitutionalist approach by contrasting it with the vision of international law encapsulated in the PCIJ's landmark *Lotus* decision.

Lotus famously held that '[i]nternational law governs relations between independent States. The rules of law binding upon states therefore emanate from their own free will. . . . Restrictions upon the independence of States cannot therefore be presumed'. CIL's version of constitutionalization turns virtually every element of these claims inside out.

First, *Lotus* both presupposes and reifies a state-centric world-view. States are the primary subjects of international law; they are the creators of international rules, bearers of international legal rights and duties, and operators of international legal processes. International law is hence centrally concerned with the reciprocal rights and duties of States.

In *CIL*'s vision of a constitutionalized international order, the state is no longer the primary actor on the international legal plane. Rather, as Anne Peters emphasizes, '[i]n a constitutionalized world order, natural persons are the primary international legal persons and the primary members of the global constitutional community'. As a result, constitutionalization transforms individuals from mere recipients or consumers of international legal rules into active agents empowered to participate in international lawmaking activities and to initiate judicial or arbitral proceedings to vindicate their rights (p. 161). Hence, one way that *CIL*'s constitutional vision flips the *Lotus* world-view is that the state is decentred, and individuals are the hub around which international law revolves. Notably, *CIL*'s focus on the individual is not the normative and methodological individualism that forms the basis for conventional economic thought, but a juridical claim regarding the relevant actors in international law.

Second, *Lotus* presupposes a certain understanding of the sources of international law. International legal norms 'emanate' from the 'free will' of states. The *Lotus* world, in short, is a highly positivist world, where law is rooted in state consent. Hence, international law can be ascertained and identified by examining the actual methods that states use to give effect to their wills, primarily through treaty and custom.

In contrast, *CIL*'s constitutionalized world order includes many types of processes and forms of normative pronouncements that do not fit easily into the traditional categories of international law. Behaviour ranging from the informal efforts of international networks of civil servants to industry codes of conduct and private merchants' *lex mercatoria* can be considered legislative, and the category 'law' should be expanded to include 'soft law instruments, non-legally binding agreements, or Memoranda of Understanding'. In addition, *CIL*'s constitutionalized world flips *Lotus*'s positivist world based on state consent. Although *CIL* recognizes the continuing relevance of consent, it also, as Jan Klabbers' post emphasizes, opens the door to 'law making by majority' and other forms of non-consensual law. Jurisprudentially, then, *CIL*'s constitutionalized legal order is a decidedly 'non-positivist' legal order (p. 191).

Finally, the *Lotus* presumption that states retain freedom of action unless there is a positive law restriction (what *CIL* calls the 'presumption of non-law' (p. 116)) is flipped on its head. As Klabbers notes, under a constitutionalized international order, the operative 'presumption [is] that normative utterances are legally valid and legally binding, unless and until it can be demonstrated that they are not.'

Thus, *CIL* sets out a distinctive vision of international constitutionalization, one that in many ways is premised upon inverting the conceptual apparatus that supported *Lotus*.

For international lawyers, then, *Lotus* stands for a series of propositions about the nature of the international legal order. For those with a more literary bent, the lotus will have different associations.

In Book IX of *The Odyssey*, strong winds blow Odysseus' vessel off course, toward the 'land of the Lotus Eaters'. Unsure of the reception his crew might find, Odysseus sends three crewmembers to explore the island. The men are well received; the natives 'did them no hurt, but gave them to eat of the lotus, which was so delicious that those who ate of it left off caring about home, and . . . were for staying and munching lotus with the Lotus-eaters . . .; nevertheless, though they wept bitterly I forced them back to the ships and made them fast under the benches. Then I told the rest [of the crew] to go onboard at once, lest any of them should taste of the lotus and leave off wanting to go home, so they took their places and smote the grey sea with their oars'. (Homer, *The Odyssey*, Book IX, lines 82–104 (Butler Translation)).

Juxtaposing the associations of these two understandings of lotus raises a series of provocative questions: might *CIL*'s inversion of the *Lotus* principles in the service of international constitutionalization tend to promote a form of idleness and lethargy in its readers? Is it possible that the invocation of international constitutionalism acts as a narcotic in the sense of diverting relevant actors from the hard work necessary to advance the values that *CIL* associates with constitutionalization? More specifically, might constitutionalization's narcotic effects deprive those who consume it of constructive energy and free will?

CIL employs a heroic conception of the power of law; indeed at one point CIL claims that 'to the extent the future can be steered at all, it can be done only by means of the law' (p. 104). And *CIL*'s constitutionalized international legal order is even more heroic; constitutionalization is associated with a variety of desired outcomes, including peace, legitimacy, rule of law, respect for human rights, accountability, and transparency.

Notably, however, *CIL* fails to establish two critical causal links. First, what will cause constitutionalization? Second, and even more important, *CIL* does not explain how constitutionalization will cause these desired outcomes. Constitutionalization is for *CIL* indeed a *deus ex machina* that can come from above and solve all problems. In this sense, the authors seem to pre-empt a set of discussions and decisions that should be the result of global political processes.

Presenting constitutionalization in this way significantly downplays the critical role of political action in achieving and sustaining the outcomes *CIL* associates with constitutionalization. Specifically, this vision of constitutionalization misleads by eliding the hard work and political engagement necessary to generate outcomes like the rule of law and respect for human rights. It is a mistake to think that the enactment of positive law, even constitutionalized law, automatically leads to these results. Instead, as Jutta Brunnee and Stephen Toope emphasize in *Legitimacy and Legality in International Law*, the enactment of positive law can usefully be considered a starting point, rather than a culmination. Alternatively, the enactment of positive law may punctuate social developments. A participatory process for production of positive law allows participants, including states and other persons, to evaluate for themselves each step. A scholar's insistence on a particular step is undemocratic in the most fundamental sense; indeed it evidences the soft paternalism exercised by Odysseus when he decides, on behalf of his crew and against their wishes, to pull his men away from the Island of the Lotus Eaters. Only the social roots that are built through participatory processes enable law to exist and to endure. Thus, we wonder whether *CIL*'s treatment of the *Lotus*, and its understanding of constitutionalization, might produce a euphoria that distorts vision and obscures the need for the pragmatic, ongoing efforts required to make outcomes like rule of law and respect for human rights concrete achievements.

The arguments presented in *CIL* downplay the role of politics in another way as well. The volume places individuals at the centre of the constitutionalized global community. Since individuals are rights-holders, *CIL* naturally devotes substantial attention to individuals' ability to enforce those rights judicially and, more broadly, to the role of international courts. However, for a book that celebrates global democracy, the emphasis on global courts is paradoxical. *CIL* recognizes that 'international adjudicators are even less democratically legitimate than the international regulators' (p. 292) and that the 'accountability created by courts and tribunals' cannot compensate for a lack of democratic accountability (p. 340). *CIL*'s reliance on courts to produce and enforce normatively desirable constitutional outcomes underemphasizes the ways in which those outcomes can only be sustainably produced by ongoing political activity.

CIL is just one of various recent efforts to describe international constitutionalization. Elsewhere, we've presented an alternative account that can be usefully contrasted with *CIL*'s. Our account does not presuppose a normatively desirable set of outcomes. Instead, it provides states and other relevant legal actors with a roadmap for how to achieve outcomes that they choose to pursue. Perhaps for this reason, we focus much less on judicial processes than *CIL* does, and much more on international legislative processes. Finally, we highlight the role of international politics in achieving anything close to a constitutionalized international legal order.

We do so by detailing a 'functionalist' account of international constitutional norms. Notably, our 'functionalism' is not the functionalism that *CIL* criticizes for obscuring the distinction between legal and non-legal norms (pp. 99–106). Rather, our functionalism focuses on what constitutional norms do, the roles they play, in response to the actually expressed needs of states and other international legal actors. Our functionalism, then, is very much of the 'bottom up' variety, and is usefully contrasted with the 'top down' identification of constitutional desiderata found in *CIL*. *CIL* asserts that the constitutionalization it envisages is 'bottom up' by virtue of its reliance on individuals as the central actors. However, the best evidence of individuals' actual wishes today is still derived inductively from state action, not deductively by scholars. Because the principles inherent in the *Lotus* world-view are rooted in and rely upon actual practice, they have a greater foundation in normative methodological individualism than those proposed by *CIL*.

Our purpose in highlighting these differences is less to argue that one approach is better than another than it is to underscore some of the ways that *CIL* helps to clarify and advance debates over international constitutionalization. *CIL* presents a challenging vision of constitutionalization that can be understood as reversing the vision of international law associated with *Lotus*. The question is whether, by eliding the sustained political efforts needed to produce outcomes such as rule of law and respect for human rights, *CIL* embraces an overly heroic vision of law and correspondingly downplays the hard work of making these aspirations a concrete reality.

7. The Constitution of Constitutionalism

Daniel Bodansky[5]

The recent appearance of two new books on international constitutionalism—Jeff Dunoff and Joel Trachtman's *Ruling the World* (the subject of an earlier EJILTalk symposium) and the volume by Jan Klabbers, Anne Peters and Geir Ulfstein that is the subject of this symposium—suggests that constitutionalism is becoming the latest concept *du jour* in international law, following on the heels of legitimacy, legalization, and fragmentation. Both books are the fruits of multi-disciplinary, international collaborations: *Ruling the World* includes contributions from more than a dozen scholars from the US and Europe; likewise, *The Constitutionalization of International Law* grew out of an international conference in Kandersteg, Switzerland, organized by Anne Peters, involving lawyers, political scientists and economists, which was the subject of a special issue of the *Indiana Journal of Global Legal Studies*. Both books involve top international law academics and are enormously valuable contributions to the field. The newfound interest in international constitutionalism raises many questions:

- First, there are conceptual questions about the meaning of constitutionalism generally and international constitutionalism more specifically. What is a 'constitution,' what is 'constitutionalism,' and what is the relation between the two? How might constitutionalism translate to the international sphere? What would an international constitution look like? Here it is useful to distinguish a thinner and thicker sense of a 'constitution'. On the thinner view, a constitution is simply the body of law that sets forth the fundamental (that is, superior and more difficult to change) rules of a political community. A constitution both constitutes and constrains political power, by creating and setting limits on the basic institutions and decision-making processes of a regime. The thicker view—embraced by Klabbers, Peters, and Ulfstein—associates constitutionalism with a number of more specific procedural and substantive limits that reflect liberal political values, including democracy, separation of powers, fundamental human rights, and judicial review.

[5] Professor Daniel Bodansky is Lincoln Professor of Law, Ethics and Sustainability at Arizona State University's Sandra Day O'Connor College of Law. Previously, he was Emily and Ernest Woodruff Chair in International Law and Associate Dean for Faculty Development at the University of Georgia. In 2009 and 2010 he was a Visiting Fellow at the Smith School of Enterprise and the Environment at the University of Oxford.

- Second, there are explanatory questions about the causes and effects of constitutionalism. For example, what are the social preconditions of constitutionalism and are they present internationally? Is constitutionalism possible only when there is a political community with a common history, language, and 'public space'? What explains the sudden upsurge of interest in constitutionalism among international lawyers? Does this reflect actual changes in international relations, for example, an actual growth in constitutionalism as a mode of governance? Is it a reaction to increased concerns about fragmentation and illegitimacy in international law—an attempt to put international law on a stronger normative footing? Can it be explained as an effort by European lawyers to extrapolate or generalize from the EU experience to global politics more generally? Or does it have some other explanation?

- Third, there is the descriptive question: Is there, in fact, an international constitution? Or, at least, is international law becoming more constitutional? Is it developing constitutional aspects or dimensions?

- Finally, there are normative questions about the proper role of constitutionalism in international law. Should there be an international constitution? If so, what should an international constitution look like? How well does existing international law measure up when evaluated against the standards of constitutionalism? And what changes are needed?

Of these various questions about constitutionalism—conceptual, explanatory, descriptive, normative, and meta—which do Klabbers, Peters, and Ulfstein address? In his introductory chapter, Jan Klabbers says that *The Constitutionalization of International Law* doesn't aim 'to demonstrate that a process of constitutionalization is actually taking place' (p. 4), nor is it a book about international ethics. Instead, he suggests that the aim is largely conceptual, namely, to examine what a constitutional international order would be like—or, as he puts it, to 'provide the idea of constitutionalization with some hands and feet' (p. 4).

But this modest self-description notwithstanding, the book in fact has many things to say about the full range of issues concerning constitutionalism, even if not always explicitly. For example:

- Klabbers states that all of the talk about constitutionalization doesn't exist only in the minds of lawyers (p. 5), that 'the international society would seem to be undergoing a process of constitutionalization' (p. 7) and that the book aims to 'make visible what might be called the invisible constitution of the international community' (p. 4). In a more limited fashion, Peters argues that 'a sectoral constitutionalization' is taking place within international organizations' and that 'a principle of openness of global governance forums for NGOs is emerging as a constitutional principle'. These are descriptive claims about what is actually taking place in the world.

- Peters takes a largely normative approach, arguing (among other things) for proportional rather than equal voting by states in international organizations and giving NGOs greater voice (but not votes), including through the presumptive right to make written statements, file *amicus curiae* briefs, and trigger certain non-compliance procedures. Similarly, Ulfstein makes a variety of normative claims, including that:

  ○ 'decisions of legislative character by the UN . . . should be adopted by the General Assembly rather than the Security Council' (symposium introduction)

- ○ 'decisions in individual cases should be based on law rather than on political considerations' (*ibid*)
- ○ international tribunals should play a bigger role in developing international law, but need better election procedures and due process guarantees (*ibid*).

- Klabbers partially explains the interest in constitutionalism as a response to concerns about fragmentation and legitimacy (chapter 1, section 3), which I think is no doubt true. As international institutions exercise more and more power, there is a greater need for checks and balances. As Ulfstein notes, because a constitutional approach emphasizes the relationship between empowerment and control, it is attractive as a potential means of legitimizing the growing authority of international institutions.

The authors' views on the full range of issues raised by constitutionalism are very welcome. My only concern here is that, because the authors don't always keep the different types of issues distinct, it is not always clear what kind of argument they are making. For example, in her chapter on 'Membership in the International Community,' Anne Peter states: 'In a constitutionalized world order, natural persons are the primary international legal persons and the primary members of the global constitutional community'. Is this intended as a descriptive statement and, if so, what empirical evidence would count in favour or against it? Is it a normative statement about how international relations should be ordered? Or is it a conceptual statement about what international constitutionalism would entail? I think Peters is intending to make a conceptual claim, combined with a normative assessment that such a constitutional order would be a good thing. But, if so, it would be useful to make the conceptual and normative arguments more explicit.

Similarly, Klabbers identifies the requirements of a constitutional world order. It 'must respect pluralism in its different guises, it must be legitimate too', and it will 'have to come to terms with its own heterarchy' (p. 44). But what is the nature of these requirements? Are they required as a normative matter, a conceptual matter, an empirical matter (given the existing nature of the international community), or some combination of the three?

The growing interest in constitutionalism reflected by the publication of *The Constitutionalization of International Law* raises the 'meta' question: what is the value-added of analyzing international law from the perspective of constitutionalism? Is 'constitutionalism' a helpful category in studying international law? How does it compare with global administrative law (and to a lesser degree legalization) as a perspective for assessing and legitimating international governance? In what ways do these perspectives differ and which is most relevant for international lawyers?

Peters argues for the value of a constitutionalist perspective, suggesting that it allows us to ask 'the right questions of fairness, justice and effectiveness' (p. 344), and provides 'the best stocked reservoir from which responsible policies may draw and the most persuasive medium in which it may be articulated' (p. 352).

The problem, however, is that constitutionalism is such a protean concept, with so many different interpretations, that it does not provide clear answers to many questions. Consider, for example, judicial review of Security Council actions. In the United States, which is usually considered to have a strong constitutionalist tradition, courts have refused to review many types of decisions, including those relating to the use of force, on the ground that they are 'political questions'. So constitutionalism, in itself, doesn't necessarily dictate judicial review of all important issues. Rather than argue whether judicial review of Security Council actions is a necessary feature of 'constitutionalism', we might do better to argue the pros and cons of judicial review directly. Similarly, in considering the role of democracy in international governance, it might be preferable to argue the normative issues directly, rather than answering the question through the association of democracy with constitutionalism.

These concerns notwithstanding, *The Constitutionalization of International Law* represents a very thoughtful and valuable contribution to an important topic. We need to understand better what constitutionalization could and should mean internationally, the degree to which it is taking place, the obstacles to its achievement, and the most promising ways forward. The *Constitutionalization of International Law* advances our understanding of all of these issues.

8. Constructing the Global Constitutional Community—Observations on Chapter 5: Membership in the Global Constitutional Community

Steven Wheatley[6]

It is a pleasure to comment on this publication and especially the arguments developed and summarized on EJIL Talk! by Professor Anne Peters, whose writings are constantly illuminating and provocative in their analysis of the emergent patters of international law and concern for the establishment of political legitimacy for global regulation.

The focus of Chapter 5—'Membership in the Global Constitutional Community'— is the increasingly significant distinction in the theory and practice of international law between the concepts of an international community of sovereign states and international community of state and non-state actors. The analysis highlights the shift in international law from a system of inter-state contract to one of global governance in which regulatory norms are no longer exclusively established by an expression of sovereign will (the 'Westphalian' paradigm). States retain a pre-eminent role in the regulation of world society, which is justified by their roles as representatives of citizens and guarantors (through the coercive instruments of government power) of the rights of the individual. States are not the only actors in global regulatory settings: individuals, international organizations, international non-governmental organizations, and business organizations are increasingly recognized as possessing a legitimate 'voice' in the development of international law norms and in the design of regulatory mechanisms and measures.

The inclusion of non-state perspectives might not present a revolutionary or constitutional 'moment' in the regulation of world society; it is, after all, an example of the

---

[6] Steven Wheatley is Professor of International Law at the University of Leeds, and author of *The Democratic Legitimacy of International Law* (Oxford Hart 2010).

better, more inclusive, forms of law-making familiar to advanced democracies. The argument here, though, extends beyond conceptions of 'best practice'. The Global Constitutional Community includes both sovereign states and a plurality of non-state actors, all of which are instrumentally valuable to the extent that they represent the interests of individuals and allow for the avoidance of domination over and injustice against persons. The shift from an international community of states to a Global Constitutional Community suggests that the legitimacy and validity of global law norms must depend, at least in part, on the establishment of law-making processes that allow for the representation of the plurality of interests and perspectives of individuals in global political debates and discourses—as global citizens; as citizens of democratic states; and as political actors with 'self-interested' and 'other-regarding' positions. Two questions arise: the extent to which it is meaningful in theory or practice to speak of a global political community defined by the authority of international law and whether the constitutionalist concern to establish political legitimacy is undermined by an analysis that constructs the world of law in a particular way—without reference to legitimation by any constituent power.

In relation to the first point, there are any number of ways in which a group of individuals can constitute a community (or think of themselves as a community). What then is the 'Global Constitutional Community'? TheGlobal Constitutional Community, as a legal community, is constituted by a system of global law which might be defined in terms of the foundational norms of general 'international law', created by states, for states—with limited exceptions in relation to humanitarian law and human rights; the laws of the United Nations, which remains an international organization of states, although permitting different levels of engagement by non-state actors on different issues; or the various, fragmented, regimes of global governance—together understood as 'international law'. In relation to general international law and United Nations law, it is not clear that individuals conceive of themselves or are conceived by regulators as co-members of a global community of fate defined by reference to a system of public international law, and, in relation to the fragmented systems, it is difficult to conclude that the plurality of regulatory regimes construct, even hypothetically, a Global Constitutional Community. The question then arises as to the ways in which the re-description of the complexities of the extant conditions of global regulation as a Global Constitutional Community are helpful in making sense of the analytical concept or practical application of international law.

The idea of world society as community does emerge in relation to international human rights law and those norms concerned with the establishment of political legitimacy. Human rights and democracy are amongst the basic constitutional values recognized within the discipline of international law, reflecting the ideological imprint of a liberal discourse. Human rights, the rule of law and democratic procedures for the establishment of valid law norms are assumed to be inherent in the constitutionalized idea of international law, with the agreed norms and principles of the Global Constitutional Community imposed on state societies. This is problematic. Whilst the language and metaphors of constitutionalism suggest a realm of 'neutral' and 'objective' discourse that sits above (and constrains) domestic and international politics, the taken-for-granted understandings of the requirements for a constitutionalist understanding of international law are in fact the result of political discussion, discourse and will. If we accept that the supreme democratic right is the right to establish and restructure the constitutional order (the idea of *self*-determination), then we must accept that the Global Constitutional Community has the right to restructure the global constitutional settlement; if this is not the case, one of two conclusions follow: either the fundamental norms identified by the constitutionalist analysis are inherent in the exercise of legitimate political authority through law (see here Steven Wheatley, 'A democratic rule of international law' *European Journal of International Law*, (forthcoming 2011)); or we must regard arguments for reading-in human rights, rule of law, and democratic procedures into the practice of global governance as imposing a liberal paradigm on the idea of international law—a conclusion which is both problematic and paradoxical given that the liberal project is concerned with the avoidance of domination by elites and the subjection of political authority to the 'will of the people'.

9. Thinking Politically about Global Constitutionalism

Jean L. Cohen[7]

I was asked to respond to the chapters of Anne Peters in the new volume, *The Constitutionalization of International Law*. Peters' work is comprehensive, diligent and impressive in its erudition and scope. It gives a good overview of the arguments on all sides. Nevertheless I have retained some serious doubts about global constitutionalism. I'll summarize the general thesis and make some remarks along the way and in conclusion.

Peters' chapter 'Dual Democracy' must be situated in the cosmopolitan camp. Her thesis is that global constitutionalism requires democracy and that democracy must be dual: i.e. it must operate on two tracks: one statist, the other individualist, the former relating to governance within states, the latter to governance 'above' states. While it is not clear to me why global constitutionalism requires democracy (much could depend on the concepts of constitution and constitutionalism which are not examined in these chapters. But whatever conception one works with, surely it is not convincing to equate constitutionalism and democracy: rather their interrelation requires serious theoretical and perhaps historical reflection).Obviously the real thrust of the chapter is about imagining a feasible utopia of democratic global governance. There's no need to repeat the arguments as to the non-democratic character of international law-making or of global governance institutions. Clearly the issue of legitimacy arises due to the expanded scope and reach of international/global law and governance. For Peters, legitimacy means democratic legitimacy. She usefully canvasses all the usual suspects in the democratic camp and comes up with her own distinctive position. The strength of her position is that it avoids the substitutionalism of many models—cosmopolitan democracy does not replace democracy within states, global civil society does not replace domestic or global government, mechanisms of direct democracy do not replace mechanisms of representation or accountability. Nor does her approach simply rest on the domestic analogy: she tries not to simply ratchet up democratic arrangements and mechanisms developed in democratic states to the globe or to international organizations (IOs) or in today's parlance, global governance institutions (GGIs). To be sure, she works with a strong

[7] Jean L Cohen is Nell and Herbert Singer Professor of Political Theory and Contemporary Civilization at Columbia University.

conception of democratic principles—political equality, participation, inclusion of all governed, responsiveness and accountability of the governing actors, and the sanction power of citizens to throw out politicians normally through elections. But the dualistic conception is contrived to mesh with the dualism of the world order—i.e. as one that is and will remain composed of both states and individuals. Thus against substitutes like theories of deliberation, participatory democracy or competitive democracy (ascribed to Dryzek, Pateman, and Pettit respectively) that allegedly should replace formal electoral democracy, she rightly argues that these do not on their own merit the label, democratic, unless they hook up with formal, i.e. electoral democratic mechanisms.

How then to resolve the democratic deficit of international law? Dual democracy apparently provides the answer involving a process of constitutionalization and democratization which must occur on two distinct tracks.

1. First the constitutionalization of international law (or global democracy) requires that all states be democratic. It seems obvious that if the democratic deficit of international/global law-making is to be rectified and if states continue to be international law-makers (treaties, custom) and the key actors making global law (in IOs or GGI's) then their own internal systems would have to be democratic for the claim of delegated democratic representation to get off the ground. In a somewhat confusing blur of the empirical, analytical, and the normative levels of analysis, Peters argues that there already is an international legal democratic entitlement and that this is a key feature now, of the constitutionalization of international law. It is unclear just what this may mean since there are many non-democratic states belonging to GGIs/IOs and making international law and I don't know if she thinks they should be excluded from the former or barred from the latter: not a very attractive or feasible idea in my view. I am not convinced about an international legal requirement of domestic democracy apart from requirements for joining very specific types of polities like the EU, or apart from the possibility of expulsion in case of an anti-democratic military coup as in the OAS. Of course we all want all states to be democratic but no one can seriously contemplate excluding China from the UN or stripping it of its sovereign equality as a subject of international law. If we are speaking of ideal theory, then it would certainly be preferable logically and normatively that in democratic global governance—in which states as states have a key role, indeed in which as members of IOs or GGIs there is voting by majority (instead of unanimity)—ideally the states themselves should be internally democratic and enjoy democratic legitimacy. But this is not a feasible requirement in today's world.

2. Even if every state was democratic and the world order was really based on sovereign equality of states this would apparently be insufficient. In a constitutionalized world order (again constitutionalized=democratized in her view), as all cosmopolitan theorists unfailingly remind us, natural persons, not states are the ultimate unit of moral concern and this to Peters means the ultimate unit of democratic procedures. So voting by state or law-making even by democratic states violates the allegedly core principle of democracy: simple majority rule. Even majority voting by states instead of unanimity violates the principle of one person one vote. Apparently simple majority voting rules rather than compound majority rules are the only real democratic formula. (I am far from convinced by this argument even as it pertains internally within states since one would maintain that all majorities are compound

and thus in some important areas voting by supermajority ensures a broader consensus as in constitutional amendment rules or in federal states or federal polities). However Peters' point that unless GGIs or IOs are also democratized, given their role and scope in the 21st century, then democracy on the level of states will be insufficient to counter oligarchy, power on the global level and will itself be at risk the more the global institutions decide and the more they penetrate the black box of the state and constrain state organs and individuals is compelling. The transitive model of democratic legitimacy that relies on delegation from citizens to their states' political organs to IOs is certainly no longer convincing in many contexts. In other words the old principal/agent model for GGI's and IOs won't do in today's world of complex, pervasive global governance and law-making. The lack of accountability and responsibility in many IOs and GGIs to any democratic instance or to any citizenry is certainly a serious issue today.

For Peters this means that the second track of dual global democracy has to be based on the equal consideration of natural persons and she insists on active legal personality for natural persons such that ideally they become active individual law-maker's not just rights bearers or law-takers. Democratization means that the second track of dual democracy would have individuals as co-subjects of international law-making. Transnational citizenship has to complement domestic citizenship. Why? Because in a constitutionalized (i.e. democratic) world order, citizenship would have to be globalized such that the two relevant communities are taken into account: the local community of our birth (I assume by this she means the state) and the 'community of human argument and aspiration'. I am not convinced that the latter is more than a moral or symbolic community, surely it is not homologous to the demos or political community of a state so the question is what this means institutionally.

Peters proposes a range of institutions to concretize this community of humanity on the second track: including peoples' parliaments within the WTO, the UN and the Breton Woods organizations; mechanisms for the voice and presence of civil society organizations and for their full access to information for all citizens; publicity of decisions and decision-making; referenda regarding important global issues held nationally or globally, and so on. Happily she does not propose the principle of one person one vote for the second track since she knows this is infeasible (although her normative conception seems to require it). Nor does she propose to replace existing institutions such as the General Assembly by a global parliament but to supplement as already indicated. Moreover she sees that the 'all affected principle' allegedly the core democratic principle is not translatable in functional organizations due to problems of delimitation: everyone is affected by everything, of course. But GGIs or global functional organizations like the WTO or the UN are not federal states: she states that it does not make sense to consider inhabitants of member states as indirect citizens of IOs via the member states. The 'flawed compromise' she proposes is one in which membership in parliamentary assemblies tracks states' membership meaning that voting by individuals for representatives to GGI's (who would have initially consultative roles) be determined by state membership. Ultimately the argument for why global parliaments even if they are only (at first) consultative are not only needed to supplement, e.g. the General Assembly in the UN but also more democratic turns on the claims (p. 326) that (elected) parliamentarians are closer to citizens then members of executives and diplomats who represent member states since population size would be taken into account, individual equality (the core democratic principle) would be respected, and finally if delegates are elected from domestic parliaments they would include members of the opposition. The consultative role of such bodies internal to GGIs, if complemented by a similar rule for civil society organizations would be a major step toward their democratization.

In my view the problems start here where the analysis ends. For what is lacking is any reflection on political form which should track differentiation among the types of non-state political formations to which the discourse of democratic constitutionalization is applied, not to mention the problem of how to get there, who would have the incentive and will to push in this direction and so on.

In short, it is utterly unclear what political form the 'human community' could or should or does consist of and what makes it a legal or political community comparable to the legal and political communities into which 'individuals are born', namely, states. We are told that the political community would be organized into multiple demoi. But in a chapter of nearly 80 pages the most obvious analogy, namely federalism is referred to in one short footnote (p. 325, n. 232) in a passage in which she states that her middle strategy which still relies on inter-state structures yet translates the dual basis of international law into a visible institutional structure such as the model of two assemblies in the UN (representation of states, representation of individuals) has a federalist ring (p. 325). In the footnote Peters says as an afterthought: 'Actually, the whole idea of a two-track democracy implies a transnational federal polity which is not, however, and should never become a federal state'.

Indeed. But this is where the crucial critical and reflective inquiry should begin, not where it should end. What is a federation of states and peoples that is not itself a state? Are there different versions of such beasts and could/is the EU, a non-state polity a federation, should it become one, and could a (reformed) UN or WTO be one as well? If a federal polity is not a state and I quite agree that there have been and could again be non-state federations for which the EU is my first candidate, then what are its core features? Does the constitutionalization of international law mean rendering the external internal? In what way? The transnational citizenship of the EU clearly involves federal principles but must a federal polity (a constitutionalized transnational legal and political order) involve direct representation of individuals in its internal organs in order to be constitutional? Not necessarily. What about direct effect? I argue that the discourse of the constitutionalization of international law cannot avoid the issue of political form and after all the endless normative arguments and ideal theorizing about design feasible or infeasible utopias, this is where we should now spend our energies. In short, is there an object suitable to constitutionalization in which the word constitutionalism still has some sense? Return to federal thinking is the first step to answering this question.

10. Democracy Beyond the State and the Problem of too Much Democracy—Observations on Chapter 6: Dual Democracy

Steven Wheatley

In chapter 6, 'Dual Democracy', Anne Peters engages with the challenges presented by regulation by non-state actors and the reduction in the importance of sovereign consent in international law to the practice of domestic democracy. The two-track solution depends on the democratization of domestic political systems (democracy within the state) and the democratization of international organizations and other non-state actors, principally through the introduction of parliamentary assemblies and consultation mechanisms (democracy beyond the state).

International parliamentary assemblies might provide a useful addition to the global institutional architecture, but they would not ensure the democratization of global governance. The establishment of a legislative assembly does not provide democratic legitimacy in the absence of a political community constructed by the exercise of political authority through law. The principal advantages of international assemblies lie in their ability to ensure the representation of the plurality of dominant political opinions within states and to compensate for the democratic deficit that results from the application of the principle of sovereign equality in international law-making (one-state; one vote, irrespective of population size). The most significant contribution would be in establishing an institutional mechanism to monitor the governance activities of global regulators and providing a locus for informed democratic debate on the appropriateness (or otherwise) of global law norms.

Professor Peters concludes that, in developing the idea of global democracy, it is not meaningful to refer to the idea of a global demos (although the conclusion sits uneasily with the idea of a Global Constitutional Community, in which the individual is the ultimate unit of concern). The relationship between international organizations and individuals is established by an application of the principle of 'affectedness' ('those affected' by global regulations have the right to participate in the formation and review of international law norms). There are, however, a number of problems in relying on the 'all affected' principle to establish lines of accountability for the exercise of political authority 'beyond the state'. First, the idea is invariable defined by reference to (international) human rights or material and financial considerations, reflecting particular ways of seeing the world (and particular value systems). Second, reliance on the 'those affected' principle leads to shifting boundaries of political constituency on policy issues, with non-state actors finding themselves accountable to different constituencies on different questions of policy (with different requirements for representation). Third, given that it is often possible for an individual to claim (and demonstrate) that they have in some way been affected by a global regulatory norm, the principle is invariably reformulated to include only those who are 'significantly affected' (etc.), with the test for inclusion (the claim to be 'affected') becoming both (more) indeterminate and subjective.

The argument that the hypothetical political communities of global regulators are defined by the 'those affected' principle is common in the literature, drawing on arguments in domestic settings, where 'those affected' are a subset of 'those subject' to the law (all of whom, *ceteris paribus*, have the right to a vote and voice in deliberations about political law norms and the conditions of domestic justice). The establishment of political law norms is the right and responsibility of all members of the political community ('citizens' in the nomenclature of the state), with a particular concern for those subjects that will bear the burden of the regulatory measure ('those affected'). In other words, the idea of 'affectedness' is defined in terms of an actor being subject to the normative authority of another: 'those affected' are those whose normative position is determined by the authority. This is a question of legitimate authority and not a moral argument for recognizing our responsibilities for all those persons whose lives our decisions impact upon. The political community of an international organization is defined by the principle of 'subjectedness': an autonomous international law order establishes its own jurisdictional boundaries and enters into an accountability relationship with those subject to the legal order. The exercise of political authority by international organizations and other non-state actors defines 'those subjected', who have the right to participate in decision-making processes, directly or through representatives.

The Westphalian settlement, according to the positivist orthodoxy, constructed the modern political world, establishing the sovereign territorial state and dividing the idea of law along a strict binary line: (internal) state law in accordance with a self-given constitutional law order and (external) inter-nation law that relied on sovereign consent for the establishment of international law norms. Within the state, it is now accepted that the legitimacy of law depends on the institutionalization of democratic procedures. The legitimacy of positive international law is provided by the requirement of sovereign consent, constructing an ideal in which political legitimacy rests on an expression of sovereign will and the consent of all subjected states. The two-track model of democratic legitimacy (democratic within the state and sovereign will for the establishment of international law norms) establishes a counterfactual ideal in which the democratic legitimacy of 'Westphalian' (domestic and international) law rests on an expression of sovereign will (in accordance with the will of the people).

The globalization and fragmentation of regulatory functions and reduction in the centrality of sovereign consent for the establishment of law norms means that it is no longer possible for the concerned citizen to seek to influence 'the law' that regulates the conditions of social, economic, and political life through state governments. The analysis developed by Anne Peters concludes with the requirement for a 'multi-unit democracy, built with domestic and international building blocks'. It raises two important (and related) questions: why is it that 'all rule [through law] over persons should be democratic' and how to we make sense of the counterfactual ideal in which the democratic norms of global governance systems conflict with the democratic law norms of the state —the problem of too much democracy? The solution to the 'democratic conundrum', following the *telos* of the constitutionalist argument ('the core objective of constitutionalism [is] the containment of power'), suggests 'an additional policy argument in favour of pluralist, non-hierarchical, network-type re-conceptualizations of the relationship between international and domestic law (and between international constitutional and domestic constitutional law), based on discourse and mutual adaptation'. Systems of law must recognize and accommodate the realities of global legal pluralism, in which overlapping and conflicting legal orders (defined by reference to a basic norm or rule of recognition), which are not organized in accordance with a global constitutional settlement, norm or principle, recognize their own autonomy and possibility of a legitimate claim to authority by other systems of law.

The meta-analysis of the unstructured form of the global constitutional order is compelling, but leaves open the question as to how democratic systems of state law should react to the jurisdictional assertions of systems of global regulation (see, for an example, judgment of the German Federal Constitutional Court on the Acts approving the Treaty of Lisbon: *Bundesverfassungsgericht* (Treaty of Lisbon), BVerfG, 2 BvE 2/08 of 30 June 2009). The argument can be reformulated in terms of (legitimate) authority: law must have authority. For a global regulator to determine the normative situation of others, it must be a legitimate authority; that is, following Joseph Raz (*The Morality of Freedom* (Oxford: Oxford University Press, 1986)) it must regulate in accordance with the interests that the subjects of the legal regime already possess. In relation to the citizens of democratic states, it seems reasonable to conclude that individuals will only accept that those reasons can be determined through engagement with citizens through democratic procedures (the came conclusion does not apply in relation to all communities; consider for example the customary laws of indigenous peoples).

The following conclusions suggest themselves in relation to international organizations and other non-state ('non-sovereign') actors: (1) the exercise of authority by global regulators cannot be justified by reference to global public goods (the interests of international peace and security, a globalized economy, etc.), it must be justified by reference to the interests of the subjects of the regulatory regime; (2) those interests cannot be asserted by experts, or any other institution or persons, they must be established through democratic procedures—a global regulator must engage in democratic procedures to ensure the inclusion of the interests and perspectives of those subject to the regime in any law-making processes; (3) regulatory norms must be established through a process of public reasoning that determines the content of authority directives in accordance with the interests and perspectives of those subject to the governance regime, requiring the establishment of representative, deliberative bodies and formal consultation mechanisms to engage with subjects; (4) in the absence of democratic procedures, a global regulatory body does not enjoy legitimate authority: it cannot legislate international law norms.

The conclusions provides the basis for beginning to think about the structuring of the legal orders that together constitute the modern world of law (including state law orders and the legal orders of global governance): each (autonomous) legal system should structure its relationships with other legal systems in accordance with the idea of democratic authority. On this understanding, three issues will influence the attitude of the democratic state to conflicting assertions of jurisdiction by global governance regimes: its constructed identity as a sovereign state (it will understand itself as being bound to comply with international law norms established through an exercise of sovereign will); its rational self-interest in complying with global regulatory norms; and a revised understanding of the idea of democratic authority in conditions of global legal pluralism. The rule of international law creates a presumption for the authority of international law norms (properly so-called) that can be refuted (1) where a global regulator does not enjoy legitimate authority (where a non-state actor is not accepted as an authority, it cannot legislate valid international law norms); and (2) where the political legitimacy of state law, established through democratic procedures, 'trumps' that of the international law norm. Where the claim to democratic legitimacy of the international law is stronger, the international norm is to be preferred.

The analysis suggests a multi-track approach to democratic legitimacy for 'law' in the modern age, following the globalization and fragmentation of regulatory functions: an international community of democratic states; deliberative forms of diplomacy in the practice of international law, with a particular focus on international law-making through international conferences that allow for the participation of state and non-state actors ('those subjected') and the development of the modern form of customary international law; democratic legitimacy for the global regulatory activities of non-state actors; and a conflicts of law regime that focuses on the question of democratic authority.

11. The Genre of Constitutionalization?

Jan Klabbers

So far, the blogging concerning *The Constitutionalization of International Law* has been fairly sedate. Of course, it was summertime; of course, there was a soccer tournament to focus on; of course, the ICJ's opinion on Kosovo occupied the international legal community; and perhaps there is a certain idleness and lethargy to be associated with constitutionalism these days, as Jeff Dunoff and Joel Trachtman merrily suggest. But it may also be the case that the approach we espouse gives rise to some unease on the part of readers and therewith elicits few responses, for our approach is difficult to pigeonhole. The kind and generous comments published on EJIL: Talk! suggest as much: they display a certain puzzlement at what it is we aim to do, and some seem to have difficulties in identifying the genre we work in.

That is not surprising, as our genre is indeed uncommon. We do not aim to engage in descriptive sociology—ours is not an enterprise to establish that constitutionalism exists, in some real sense and as a matter of positive international law. Nor do we engage in idealist normative theory *pur sang*: we do not aim to suggest that constitutionalism is, as a way of organizing the globe, superior to alternatives. Likewise, ours is not a conceptual study in any strict sense of the term: we do not aim to establish the (or, more modestly, a) concept of global constitutional law. We do not aspire to make an argument *de lege ferenda* about constitutionalization. And emphatically, we never set out to study the causes of constitutionalism, no matter how much Dunoff and Trachtman might have expected us to.

What we engage in, instead, is a different genre, perhaps most closely related to conceptualism (without, it is hoped, lapsing into *Begriffsjurisprudenz*) but nonetheless distinct. As the book makes clear—or should have made clear—we ask ourselves what a constitutional world order could look like. This comes with at least two elements which may cause some confusion. First, in light of the circumstance that there are many versions of constitutionalism circulating, it meant that we had to adopt some form of constitutionalism as the one we were interested in exploring. We could have opted for a Stalinist version, but felt such would be silly, as few people would willingly adopt such a version and, more to the point, because it is not the sort of constitutionalism that international lawyers have come to talk about over the last decades. By the same token, while the realist school of global politics may claim that a Westphalian order is a constitutional order (in that it can be said to constitute global order), we nonetheless did not see the need to explore this version, again largely because it is not what occupies the invisible college of international lawyers. Hence, we took as our starting point the sort of constitutionalism usually invoked by international lawyers, from Verdross to Tomuschat, and from Dupuy to De Wet. This is quite obviously a liberal, western, elitist version of constitutionalism, but for our purposes that is hardly relevant. Or rather, more accurately, it is relevant in the sense that this liberal version is what seems to dominate the debates; hence, there is merit in exploring the possible ramifications of precisely this version, in much the same way as people with an interest in space activities will focus on the US or Russia rather than, say, Austria or Tanzania.

Second, we needed to give some hands and feet to this version of constitutionalism which, in much of the literature, tends to remain remarkably abstract. A brief look at some western liberal constitutions persuaded us that such constitutions tend to come these days with provisions on the institutions of governance and their competences, on law-making, on the judiciary, on membership of the community, and on democracy: as a result, these issues were what we set out to explore, without however claiming that this would exhaust the matter. Moreover though, and relating to the earlier point as well, the very talk of constitutionalism comes with a certain baggage. Constitutionalism is, in one sense at least, a vocabulary with all sorts of connotations, and we felt we could ignore this only at our peril. It is for this reason that we connect constitutionalism to legitimacy: not so much because we feel that the two go hand in hand empirically, or should go hand in hand normatively, but because those who speak the language of constitutionalism tend to mention legitimacy in the same breath: those who invoke constitutionalism tend to suggest that constitutionalism is itself legitimate, and that it helps legitimate governance. It is on this ground that we claim that 'a constitutional world order will have to be a legitimate order' (at p. 43). This does not so much express a normative preference (although we would hardly prefer an illegitimate order) but merely finishes the thought, so to speak—any other construction, however sensible in its own right it may be, would miss the very discussion we aim to contribute to.

That is not to say that there is not some overlap between our genre, such as it is, and other genres. Dan Bodansky is surely correct when claiming that we do not always keep ours neatly separate from others, and that sometimes empirical or normative statements creep in. Correct as this critique is, though, one may wonder whether there are any viable alternatives. What would be the point of studying something that exists only in the minds of international lawyers but with no basis in reality—any reality? In this sense, the conceptual, the normative and the empirical are notoriously difficult, perhaps impossible, to disentangle without lapsing into sterile discussions. Mathematics may work in such a manner, but in the social sciences and humanities this is not an option. John Searle perhaps put it best when denying the comprehensiveness of social constructions: '… there has to be something for the construction to be constructed out of'.[8] In our context, it would be surprising, and not a little arrogant, to claim that all the talk about constitutionalization has no basis in any reality, and is without normative merit.

While our commentators have focused on our discussions on democracy and the role of the judiciary in particular, they have paid remarkably little attention to the chapter on law-making, with the exception of Dunoff and Trachtman claiming that the 'presumptive law' endorsed in that chapter would 'flip' the classic *Lotus* position. This, however, is not really the case: the pertinent chapter underlines that consent remains a serious requirement, and remains the basis of obligation. It is just that in a constitutional order, the expressions of consent can often be presumed, perhaps only to be rebutted. But the very possibility of rebuttal leaves the relevance of consent intact. Instead of turning *Lotus* on its head, the chapter aims to adapt it to constitutionalist thought, in full realization of the continued relevance of the *Lotus* doctrine.[9]

Some of the commentators suggest that ours is an uncritical embrace of liberal, top-down constitutionalism. This, however, is mistaken. As explained above, to some extent descriptive, normative, and conceptual aspects cannot be kept neatly compartmentalized.

---

[8] See John R Searle, *The Construction of Social Reality* (London Penguin 1995), at 190.

[9] Ironically, as the author of the law-making chapter as well as quite a few works on the concept of treaty and soft law, I am often accused of being rather too faithful to the *Lotus* doctrine.

More importantly though, there is no inherent tension in writing about constitutionalization, even sympathetically, while simultaneously being critical.[10] At the heart of our book is the idea of taking the ball and running with it: the ball is not of our making, and the trajectory of the run is more or less pre-determined: we set out to explore what constitutionalization could entail, and which direction it could go, if taken seriously. This does not imply a full embrace of constitutionalization; instead, it takes an ongoing discussion and explores its ramifications. We understand that in a scholarly community where human rights lawyers tend to be pro-human rights, and trade lawyers pro-trade, keeping a normative distance from the object of research is perhaps less common than it should be. However, the implicit suggestion that keeping some distance is so uncommon as to invite criticism is decidedly troubling.

12. Constitutionalization: What is the Value Added?

Geir Ulfstein

First of all: thanks for the thoughtful comments by Daniel Bodansky, and Jeffrey Dunoff and Joel Trachtmann. As I read them, they are not rejecting constitutionalization as a useful approach to the study of international law. This does not, however, mean that they subscribe to everything that is said in *The Constitutionalization of International Law*. I will take up some of their main concerns and objections—which do not commit my co-authors.

I have emphasized the public law character of international constitutionalization, i.e. that empowered international institutions should be under constitutional control, in the form of democratic guarantees, rule of law, and protection of human rights. Our book is a thought experiment in asking how a constitutionalized world might look. There is an underlying assumption that the world is becoming more constitutionalized. But the book does not represent an empirical study of this process and its causes. It is more concerned with the normative issues: what kind of constitutional guarantees should balance the increasing empowerment of international institutions?

This does not mean that we are fully occupied with enjoying the Lotus garden at the expense of hard work, as Dunoff and Trachtman suggest. First, the development of a constitutional perspective and its possible consequences represent in itself hard work. This is what we have tried to do in the book. But, second, although we have not undertaken an empirical study in this book, this does not mean that we dismiss the value of such studies. On the contrary, empirical studies are welcome and necessary. It is important to examine how different institutions, including international courts, are organized and function from a constitutional perspective. Such studies should form the basis for any concrete normative proposals.

Dunoff and Trachman would also prefer a bottom-up rather than the top-down approach, which the book is claimed to apply. The intention of the book is certainly not to impose specific constitutional solutions. I agree that such choices should be up to

---

[10] And just for the record (and again not without irony), I am sometimes deemed overly critical of constitutionalization, as reflected in earlier writings. See, e.g., Jan Klabbers (2004) 'Constitutionalism Lite', 1 *International Organizations Law Review* 31–58.

policy-makers. But it is the role of academics to develop the choices available if certain constitutional values are to be respected. This may actually empower the policy-makers in choosing the option that best responds to their objectives. Finally, a constitutional approach does not mean a farewell to positive law. But it means to accept that international law is not limited to treaties and customary international law. International decisions (binding and non-binding) and judgments are of increasing importance. This growing public character of international law raises not only normative issues, but also questions of the legal significance of such decisions and judgments in positive law.

Daniel Bodansky is right in asking about the added value of a constitutional perspective, especially in relation to global administrative law. I would say that the two approaches have much in common. Global administrative law has set out accountability standards, such as transparency, participation, and reasoned decisions. But international constitutional law asks specifically how international institutions could learn from national constitutional law, and how they should interact with national constitutional organs. It should also ask how national constitutional organs should respond to the new international setting, as has been argued by Mattias Kumm. Bodansky also asks whether it might be better to study the different elements of constitutionalism, such as judicial review and democracy, rather than constitutionalism as such. But only a constitutional approach studies the inter-relationship between such elements, for example how to balance legal control represented by judicial review while ensuring ultimate political accountability.

So, a constitutional approach to international law brings a useful perspective. Traditional sources of international law in the form of treaties and customary international law continue to play important roles. But the constitutional approach is of increasing importance as the public character of international law is growing.

13. Constitutionalization Continued: A Rejoinder

Anne Peters

It is an honour to receive comments by distinguished experts on constitutionalism and international law. And it is fun to engage in a substantial discussion on difficult issues.

Method

All commentators raised important methodological issues.

Description and ('top down') prescription

Dunoff and Trachtman reproach us for a 'top down' approach to constitutionalism. In the introductory chapter, it was made clear that the book is, as such, a normative exercise, on a middle level of abstractness, and hooking onto existing legal rules, principles, and institutions. To the extent that this was meant to 'extrapolate' trends (of constitutionalization), the study included the claim that these trends actually exist (a claim which was openly formulated in the book).

Dunoff and Trachtman also reproach us for embracing an 'overly heroic vision of the law'. This critique manifests a disciplinary rift in the approaches of the two books, ours and the one edited by our critics. Dunoff and Trachtman espouse a more empirical method, more informed by social science. In contrast, we as a trio have not attempted to apply sociological methods, neither in quantitative nor in qualitative terms. Our arguments are, as declared in chapter 1, normative ones.

International constitutional law and politics

Steven Wheatley points out that the 'language and metaphors of constitutionalism suggests a realm of ('neutral' and 'objective') discourse that sits above ... politics', whereas in reality the 'global constitutional settlement ... is the product of political debate, discourse, and will'. Along that line, Dunoff and Trachtman suspect us of underestimating and downplaying the role of international politics.

Dunoff and Trachtman are right in saying that the enactment of positive law is only a 'starting point, rather than a culmination'. Nevertheless, any (political) action does need a starting point. Under the rule of law, positive law is indeed a *conditio sine qua non* of governmental action. I postulate that there is an international rule of law which requires international governance to be based on legal rules (i.e. on formal and general prescriptions) as opposed to governance by ad hoc decisions.

Moreover, law and politics should not be viewed as distinct realms, but rather, as described in chapter 7, as deeply intertwined. Still, the 'legalization' of political problems (conceiving of constitutionalization as a special type of legalization) modifies the debate surrounding those problems by introducing a different, juridical logic. Against Dunoff, Trachtman, and Wheatley, it might be argued that such a (relative) de-politization of international relations is not a disadvantage, but a plus, because international relations are as a general matter rather too politicized. The introduction of legal and even constitutional principles contributes to the stability of expectations, legal certainty, and equal treatment of the relevant actors. This remains true although international legal rules, and especially those which might be called constitutional ones, are linguistically open, and allow room for value judgements. Powerful political players might deploy constitutionalism in order to realize individual interests under the cover of legal argument.

For this reason, there is dialectic at work. While the evolutionary dynamics of constitutionalism leads to a legalization of politics (as argued above), it also leads to a stronger politization of law. As pointed out in chapter 7, the call for constitutionalism precisely *triggers* political contestation, and does not deny or pre-empt it.

International constitutional scholarship and politics

In parallel, international constitutional scholarship does comprise a moral and political commitment, as critical legal scholars have unmasked it—but this is not a death blow to scholarship as scholarship. The saturation of international constitutional scholarship with values is no methodological flaw per se. The 1920s' debate on preconceptions (*Vorverständnis*) in sociology and the 1970s' positivism debate have yielded the insight that international legal scholarship can (in a limited sense) be separated from political engagement. Historical experience shows, moreover, that scholarship and politics *should* be separated. This does not mean that political problems should be excluded from the academic discourse, but merely that value judgements should not be packaged as scholarly findings.

Hence, international constitutional scholarship may be called 'value-neutral'(only) to the extent that it does not generate norms, but merely theories about norms. An international (constitutional) scholar can only argue *ex suppositione* in favour of norms: if norm A and B are valid, then norm C must also be valid. For example, if there is an international legal principle requiring new states and territories under international administration to be organized in a democratic fashion, and if a purely transitive justification of international institutions via democratic governments does not work, then international institutions themselves have to be democratized through mechanisms of participation of natural persons. In that way, international constitutionalist scholarship may offer suggestions which may be picked up by political actors vested with formal law-making power—or not. Seen in this way, there is nothing to prevent scholars from advising the law-making bodies, so long as the researchers make clear to themselves and the reader, 'exactly at which point the scientific investigator becomes silent and the evaluating and acting person begins to speak', as Max Weber famously put it.[11]

But this separation of international constitutional scholarship from international constitutional politics is far from watertight. By highlighting the trends of constitutionalization, legal scholars in fact contribute to strengthening them. The reason is twofold: first, and generally speaking, the gain of new scholarly insights is not separable from the question of what these mean for our picture of the world. It is therefore inescapable and desirable that scholars reflect about the meaning of their findings for society at large and for the view of humans of the world. This is a political, but most of all an intellectual obligation.[12] The second reason is more specific to legal scholarship. Description and creation of the law may (despite being theoretically distinct) in some instances as a practical matter coincide. The object of both the legal process and of legal scholarship is the law, and the observer standpoint ('scholarly' description) and the participant standpoint ('political' creation) are easily confounded. The not uncommon changes of professional roles (from law professor to a judge, a diplomat, or a government official and vice versa) facilitate this. In international law, this confluence is acknowledged as legitimate by Article 38 (1) lit. d) ICJ-Statute which admits 'the teachings of the most highly qualified publicists' as a 'subsidiary means for the determination of the rules of law'.

But despite the overlap and interaction of law creation (i.e. legal politics) and legal analysis, the main objective and potential of legal scholarship is not to shape the political landscape and to take decisions, but to generate knowledge and to contribute to a better understanding of the law, including a better understanding of the law's (and a

---

[11] Max Weber, 'Objectivity in Social Sciences', in *The Methodology of the Social Sciences* 49–112 (Edward A Shils & Henry A. Finch trans. and eds, New York Free Press 1949, orig. 1904), at 60.

[12] Emil Angehrn, 'Die Wissenschaften und die Frage nach dem Menschen', Basler Universitätsreden 108. Heft, Rede gehalten am Dies academicus der Universität Basel am 26. November 2010 (Basel Schwabe Verlag), at 13.

constitution's) functions in politics. I personally aspired to do this, but there is probably always room for improvement.

Ideal and non-ideal theorizing

Jean Cohen finds that no energy should be spent on 'endless normative arguments and ideal theorizing'. I think that it is the legal scholar's role to come forward with ideal and non-ideal theories. Theories are conceived here as models or structures rather than as systems of statements. Theories should express the patterns or structures of data or of phenomena in the field under observation, as parsimoniously and concisely as possible. They should condense or compress the data and reduce complexity. Theories in that sense do not comprise the declaratory versus the constitutive 'theory' of recognition of statehood, nor the constitutional against the internationalist 'theory' with regard to Art. 46 Vienna Convention on the Law of Treaties, nor the absolute against the relative 'theory' of reservations to multilateral treaties. These are not theories, but merely singular recommendations for solutions to individual legal questions.

By contrast, there are theories in law that do reduce complexity, and in our book, we drew on the reservoir of constitutional theory. An example of such a 'data-condensing' theory is that of subsidiarity. The idea of subsidiarity forms the common basis of different rules (e.g. the local remedies rule, the priority of regional organizations over UN peacekeeping operations, and the complementarity of the International Criminal Court to domestic courts in the prosecution of international crimes under Art. 17 ICC Statute). On the basis of this reduction of complexity, scholars can show that the subsidiary responsibility of the international community for guaranteeing human security when the territorial state fails in its duty to protect 'fits' into the international legal system. Demonstrating such a doctrinal, systemic, and ideational fit means to demonstrate constitutionalization.

Idealism and pragmatism

Constitutionalism 'might produce a euphoria that distorts vision and obscures the need for the pragmatic, ongoing efforts', write Dunoff and Trachtman. There is a danger in that sense, but the opposite danger of exaggerated pragmatism exists as well. Resorting to the vocabulary of constitutionalism might not only 'narcotize', but also increase awareness of the difficulties in implementing constitutionalist ideas.

International legal scholars should and can steer a middle course between idealism and pragmatism or rather combine both attitudes, because both perform different functions on different intellectual levels. Idealism in the sense of the adage *'soyons réalistes, demandons l'impossible'* functions not as a recipe for solving practical questions but as a reflective tool, as a consciousness-sharpener. On the one hand, a scholar suggesting a particular legal institution *de lege ferenda* should think beforehand about the political chances of success. On the other hand, overly 'pragmatic' and 'realist' legal solutions which anticipate the expected political and practical difficulties of implementation would hardly be innovative. Moreover, the expert proposal will anyway be modified in the political debate leading to its adoption. The scholar should not practice anticipatory obedience to reality, because then she gives up a distinct quality of law, namely its counter-factualness. It is along this line that a constitutional role for business actors and NGOs in law-making and law-enforcement was suggested.

Holism and particularism

Daniel Bodansky points out that constitutionalism is a 'too protean concept ... that it does not provide clear answers to many questions'. Because the meaning of 'constitutionalism' is so unclear, it may not really be a helpful shorthand, but on the contrary confusing.

Indeed, as admitted in chapter 7, there is the danger that reliance on constitutionalism is actually counterproductive because it may postpone rather than encourage concrete debates on concrete problems. However, the added value of the constitutionalist paradigm might lie in its comprehensive nature. The normative claim is that the different features of constitutionalism are not merely additive, but that the whole is more than the sum of its parts. The various constitutionalist features, such as more inclusive and transparent decision-making and judicial review, should go together, and that in combination they take on a special normative significance. If this is true, the constitutionalist reconstruction does possess an additional explicative and prescriptive value. It reminds us, to repeat this point once again, that the various features of constitutionalism are linked, and calls for complementing the existing constitutional features of international law with missing ones, such as democracy and judicial review of acts of international organizations. To some extent, as argued in chapter 7, there is indeed constitutionalist bootstrapping.

The global constitutional community

In his comment on chapter 5, Steven Wheatley asks two questions: first, is it analytically meaningful to speak of a global constitutional community? And, second, is the 'constitutionalist concern to establish political legitimacy' not normatively flawed?

Wheatley's answer to the first question is that, with a view to the 'fragmented systems, it is difficult to conclude that the plurality of regulatory regimes construct (even hypothetically) a Global Constitutional Community'.

My response to the first, analytical, question is that the idea of an international community is entrenched in positive law, and often referred to, e.g. in Security Council resolutions. It is mentioned in Art. 53 VCLT and in Art. 42 lit. b) and 48 sec. 1 lit.b) of the ILC-Articles on the Responsibility of States for International Wrongful Acts of 2001. As argued in chapter 1 and elsewhere in the book, constitutionalism indeed responds to the fragmentation of international law by offering some overarching (constitutional) principles.

Two aspects must be kept in mind in this context. First, fragmentation as such is not obnoxious for a legal order. It may result in differenciation and pluralism, which is positive. Detrimental consequences are possibly resulting legal inconsistencies, legal lacunae, conflicts of jurisdiction, and so forth. Until today, such legal consequences have materialized to a lesser extent than predicted by pessimists. On the contrary, monitoring bodies and courts in different regimes have frequently relied on general principles or have transferred specific institutions from one field to the other. For example, the precautionary principle, as elaborated in environmental law has been applied in the law of humanitarian assistance. One possible explanation of such transfers is that the transferred principle is indeed a constitutional one.

The second aspect is that constitutionalization might also be conceived as a sectoral phenomenon, with different regimes having their own constitution. Gunter Teubner's constitutionalization approach based on general systems offers a theoretical basis for this view. The result would indeed be not one constitutional community, but various ones.

Steven Wheatley does not clearly answer his second, normative, question but seems to tend to the view that the idea of a constitutional community is an 'elite project imposing a liberal paradigm on all communities in world society'. This reminds me of Prosper Weil's famous critique that the concept of an international community conceals a *de facto* oligarchy. Weil pointed out that there 'is a danger of the implantation in international society of a legislative power enabling certain states—the most powerful or numerous ones—to promulgate norms that will be imposed on the others'. Thus, concepts such as that of the '"international community" may become code words, lending themselves to all kinds of manipulation, under whose cloak certain states may strive to implant an ideological system of law'.

In response to Wheatley's—and Weil's—normative critique, I submit, as in chapter 5, that the constitutionalist paradigm is both a useful extension of the concept of the international community and apt to counter the critique of concealed oligarchy. Stating that the international community is a *constitutional* community evokes the constitutionalist principle of democracy and thus offers leverage for making visible and arguing against the privileges of some states, such as the permanent members of the Security Council. Moreover, constitutionalism provides both a parsimonious explanation for the existing community-like features of the international legal order, and allows extrapolating these features in an adequate way.

For example, the constitutionalist paradigm explains the existence of *erga omnes* norms. Why should certain obligations create rights or at least interests for non-affected actors, and possibly even allow those to apply countermeasures or to raise claims? One answer could be that those actors are members of the constitutional community. A body of (international) constitutional law, even if not codified in one single document, provides some glue to hold actors together, because it sets out common objectives or aspirations, and defines the rules of interaction. This type of integration makes the legal possibility of claims by not directly affected actors much more plausible. On the other hand, the establishment of hierarchical centralized enforcement mechanisms, which would be an important component of an international constitutional order, could also render the concept of *erga omnes* norms superfluous. *Erga omnes* norms seem to be a device to facilitate the protection of community interests in a 'horizontal' manner in the absence of hierarchical enforcement.

Moreover, a constitutionalist reading allows overcoming the dichotomy between original, full international legal subjects on the one hand and derivative and partial legal subjects on the other. This dichotomy was in reality only a reification of the distinction between states as the makers of international law and all other, newer, subjects, such as international organizations or individuals. In opposition to this view, the constitutionalist approach decentres the state. If the international system is conceived as possessing constitutional law, the following argument can be raised: once a constitutional order has been set in place by the global multiple *pouvoirs constituants*, it no longer makes sense to speak of 'original' legal subjects, because all subjects have been transformed into *pouvoirs constitués*. Therefore, the distinction between 'original' and 'derivative' subjects breaks down. The various types of members of a constitutional community have different rights and obligations, as defined by constitutional law, but there is no categorical distinction between states and all others.

I do not deem it fair to qualify constitutionalism, or—more specifically—the idea of a constitutional community—as an 'elite project', apart from pointing to the obvious fact that scholarly writing is done only by a very small number of people. Constitutionalist thought has in historic terms been developed in Europe. But even in 18th- and 19th-century Europe, constitutionalism was asserted *against* the establishment, such as the nobility and the clergy, and *against* a culture of hierarchy, intransparency, and pre-determination of social options. Constitutionalism is the opposite of power politics, as such directed against the domination of many powerless by a few powerful actors, and thus the opposite of elitism. It is a reaction to the universal experience of subjugation, marginalization, and discrimination. In that sense, constitutionalism is universalizable.

Constitutionalism and democracy

Jean Cohen and Steven Wheatly have commented on chapter 6 'Dual Democracy'. Chapter 6 does *not* equate constitutionalism and democracy. Quite to the contrary, as a scholar raised in the German constitutional tradition, I am aware of the (somewhat simplified) distinction between two historical constitutionalisms: the German one which espoused constitutionalism (in form of a written constitutional document) *without* democracy (in the form of law-making by the people) as opposed to the Anglo-American tradition of viewing the rule of law and popular (or parliamentary) sovereignty as going hand in hand.

Our book devotes one chapter to the constitutional principle of democracy, not because it is more important than other constitutional principles but because democracy is more conspicuously absent in global governance, and because it seems particularly difficult to build in democratic elements in the design and operation of global governance.

Steven Wheatley asks why I posit that all rule over persons should be democratic. The answer is that I consider democracy to reconcile best individual freedom and equality with life in society. Moreover, democracy specifically accommodates the basic facts of diversity, disagreement, and cognitive bias, and is therefore particularly relevant for the global scale. Political institutions should be designed so as to equally advance the interests of persons who are substantially affected by (or as Steven Wheatley calls it 'subjected' to) those institutions. Because the diverse interests and backgrounds make people cognitively biased towards their own interests, the objective of equally advancing affected persons' interests can only be realized through an equal say. This reasoning is especially pertinent for global decision-making, because on a global level there is particularly strong disagreement about how the world should be shaped. This calls for a global collective decision-making process which grants each human an equal say in decisions affecting him or her.

However, as Jean Cohen agrees, affectedness as such is no operational criterion for determining who has a relevant interest in a certain development policy measure. In times of globalization, almost everybody in the world is affected by some decisions taken at any other place on the globe, especially in the field of finance, economy, and environment. Not every remote affectedness should be allowed to trigger a person's right to democratic participation in that decision. A threshold would have to be defined. This is difficult but unavoidable.

In chapter 6, it is argued that the promotion of democracy within nation states is a central principle of global constitutionalism because domestic democracy is the foundation of a transitive global democracy, and because domestic democracy promotes global goods such as peace. But, as Jean Cohen rightly points out, it would neither be feasible nor desirable to exclude China, as an undemocratic state, from the UN. The international (constitutional) principle which requires states to strive towards democracy indeed operates differently on 'old' and 'new' states. The successor states of the Soviet Union and Yugoslavia, East Timor and Eritrea, all of them created after 1989, were from the outset established as democratic states. While this may have initially been done as a matter of political expediency, this practice gave rise to the international constitutional principle that new states must be democratic. It would have been inconceivable, for example, to create an undemocratic state of Kosovo. The international constitutional precept has not prevented some states from sliding into totalitarianism. International sanctions against those states, such as Belarus, have been weak, but still manifest a political, and I would argue, also a legal commitment (enshrined in numerous UN documents), to democracy. In contrast, 'old' states such as China are treated differently under international law. They are not divested of their legal status as a state because they lack democratic government. The difference in treatment is justified because it is in practical terms more difficult to reorganize a state than to create new democratic structures in a situation where there is anyway an institutional vacuum. The different evaluation of new and old states does not amount to double standards as long as the normative direction imposed on them, towards more democracy, is the same.

Another difficult question, asked by Steven Wheatley, is 'how democratic systems of state law should react to the jurisdictional assertions of systems of global regulation'. In the absence of a normative hierarchy which ascribes priority to global rules, other techniques of coordination must be found. One technique might be a qualified rule of recognition as long as (*solange*) minimum equivalent (but not necessarily identical) constitutional standards are respected by the conflicting or competing regime.

A final issue raised in the comment on chapter 6 is that of 'political form' (Jean Cohen). Also, Jean Cohen misses a more explicit discussion of the federal analogy of a political entity composed of individuals and states. To the extent that 'political form' is meant to pay more attention to political feasibility and political will, I have discussed this above. But the quest for giving a political form to the combined setting of global and national governance should not mean a debate on the 'constitutional form' in the style of the ancient writers and their commentators. Samuel Pufendorf had called the German Empire '*monstro simile*' because it did not correspond to one of the established forms: monarchy, oligarchy or democracy, and this has been recalled in many debates on the EU. Instead of giving labels, concrete institutions such as parliamentary assemblies or consultative referendums should be described. Surely, this can, in future work, be made more specific.

Bibliography

Abbott, Kenneth W, Robert O Keohane, Andrew Moravcsik, Anne-Marie Slaughter, and Duncan Snidal 'The Concept of Legalization' (2000) 54 *International Organization* 401–419

Ackerman, Bruce 'The Rise of World Constitutionalism' (1997) 83 *Virginia Law Review* 771–797

Agamben, Giorgio *Homo Sacer: Sovereign Power and Bare Life* (Stanford UP Palo Alto1998 [orig. 1995] Heller-Roazen trans)

Albrow, Martin *Abschied vom Nationalstaat* (Suhrkamp Frankfurt am Main 1998/1996)

Alexander, Larry (ed) *Constitutionalism: Philosophical Foundations* (CUP Cambridge 1998)

Alkema, Evert Albert 'The European Convention as a Constitution and its Court as a Constitutional Court' in Paul Mahoney, Franz Matscher, Herbet Petzold, and Luzius Wildhaber (eds) *Protecting Human Rights: The European Perspective: Mélanges à la mémoire de Rolv Ryssdal* (Carl Heymans Köln 2000) 41–63

—— 'The Third-Party Applicability or "Drittwirkung" of the European Convention on Human Rights' in Franz Matscher and Heinrich Petzold (eds) *Protecting Human Rights: The European Dimension (Studies in Honour of Gérard J Wierarda)* (Carl Heymanns Verlag Köln 1988) 33–45

Allan, T R S *Constitutional Justice: A Liberal Theory of the Rule of Law* (OUP Oxford 2001)

Allott, Philip *Eunomia: New Order for a New World* (OUP Oxford 1990)

Alston, Philip '"Core Labour Standards" and the Transformation of the International Labour Rights Regime' (2004) 15 *EJIL* 457–521

—— 'Conjuring up New Human Rights: A Proposal for Quality Control' (1984) 78 *AJIL* 607–621

Alvarez, José E *International Organizations as Law-makers* (OUP Oxford 2005)

—— 'Do Liberal States Behave Better? A Critique of Slaughter's Liberal Theory' (2001) 12 *EJIL* 183–244

—— 'Judging the Security Council' (1996) 90 *AJIL* 1–39

Ambos, Kai *Völkerstrafrecht* (Beck München 2006)

Amerasinghe, Chittharanjan Felix *Principles of the Institutional Law of International Organizations* (2nd edn CUP Cambridge 2005)

—— *Jurisdiction of International Tribunals* (Kluwer Law International The Hague 2003)

Anderson, Benedict *Imagined Communities* (Verso London 1983)

Anderson, Gavin W *Constitutional Rights after Globalization* (Hart Oxford and Portland 2005)

Anderson, Kenneth 'Book Review: Squaring the Circle? Reconciling Sovereignty and Global Governance through Global Government Networks' (2005) 118 *Harvard Law Review* 1255–1312

Angehrn, Emil, Die Wissenschaften und die Frage nach dem Menschen, Basler Universitätsreden 108. Heft, Rede gehalten am Dies academicus der Universität Basel am 26. November 2010 (Schwabe Verlag Basel 2010).

Andrews, William (ed) *Constitutions and Constitutionalism* (2nd edn Princeton UP 1963)

Appadurai, Arjun *Modernity at Large: Cultural Dimensions of Globalization* (University of Minnesota Press Minneapolis 1998)

Appiah, Kwame Anthony *Cosmopolitanism: Ethics in a World of Strangers* (Norton New York 2006)

Archibugi, Daniele 'From the United Nations to Cosmopolitan Democracy' in Daniele Archibugi and David Held (eds) *Cosmopolitan Democracy: An Agenda for a New World Order* (Polity Press Cambridge 1995) 121–162

—— and David Held 'Editors' Introduction' in Daniele Archibugi and David Held (eds) *Cosmopolitan Democracy: An Agenda for a New World Order* (Polity Press Cambridge 1995) 1–16

Arendt, Hannah 'Karl Jaspers: Citizen of the World?' in *idem Men in Dark Times* (Harcourt Brace and Company San Diego 1968) 81–94

—— *The Origins of Totalitarianism* (Harcourt, Brace and Company New York 1951)

Armingeon, Klaus and Karolina Milewicz 'Compensatory Constitutionalism: A Comparative Perspective' (2008) 22 *Global Society* 179–196

d'Asprémont, Jean 'La création internationale d'Etats démocratiques' (2005) 109 *Revue Générale de Droit International Public* 889–908

—— 'Softness in International Law: A Self-serving Quest for New Legal Materials' (2008) 19 *EJIL* 1075–1093

—— *L'Etat non démocratique en droit international* (Pedone Paris 2008)

Aust, Anthony 'Peaceful Settlement of Disputes: A Proliferation Problem?' in Tafsir Malick Ndiaye, Rüdiger Wolfrum, Thomas A Mensah, and Chie Kojima (eds) *Law of the Sea, Environmental Law and Settlement of Disputes* (Brill Leiden 2007) 131–141

—— *Modern Treaty Law and Practice* (CUP Cambridge 2000, 2nd edn 2007)

Austin, John Langshaw *How To Do Things With Words* (2nd edn Clarendon Press Oxford 1975)

—— *Lectures on Jurisprudence* vol I (John Murray London 1911)

Ayling, Julie 'Serving Many Voices: Progressing Calls for an International Environmental Organisation' (1997) 9 *Journal of Environmental Law* 243–270

Ayala, Baltasar de *De jure et officiis bellicis et disciplina militari libri tres* (Carnegie Institution Washington 1912 (orig. 1581) Westlake ed)

Aznar Gòmez, Mariano J *La Administración internacionalizada del territorio* (Atelier Barcelona 2008)

Azoulay, Loïc 'La constitution et l'integration: Les deux sources de l'Union Européenne en formation' (2003) 19 *Revue Française de Droit Administratif* 859–875

Bankowski, Zenon and Andrew Scott (eds) *The European Union and its Order: The Legal Theory of European Integration* (Blackwell Oxford 2000)

Barkawi, Tarak and Mark Laffey 'Introduction: The International Relations of Democracy, Liberalism, and War' in Tarak Barkawi and Mark Laffey (eds) *Democracy, Liberalism, and War: Rethinking the Democratic Peace Debate* (Lynne Rienner Boulder 2001) 1–19

Barnett, Michael and Martha Finnemore *Rules for the World: International Organizations in Global Politics* (Cornell UP Ithaca NY 2004)

Basdevant, Jules 'La conclusion et la redaction des traités et des instruments autres que les traités' (1926/V) 15 *Recueil des Cours* 539–643

Baxter, Richard R 'International Law in "Her Infinite Variety"' (1980) 29 *ICLQ* 549–566

Bayart, Jean-François, Stephen Ellis, and Béatrice Hibou (eds) *The Criminalization of the State in Africa* (James Currey Oxford 1999)

Beatty, David *The Ultimate Rule of Law* (OUP Oxford 2004)

Beaulac, Stéphane 'An Inquiry into the International Rule of Law' (2007) 14 *European University Institute Workings Papers MWP*

Beck, Ulrich *Was ist Globalisierung?* (Suhrkamp Frankfurt am Main 1997)

Bederman, David 'Diversity and Permeability in Transnational Governance' (2007) 57 *Emory Law Journal* 201–231

Bedjaoui, Mohammed *The New World Order and the Security Council: Testing the Legality of its Acts* (Martinus Nijhoff Leiden 1995)

Beetham, David *The Legitimation of Power* (MacMillan Basingstoke 1991)

Beitz, Charles *Political Theory and International Relations* (Princeton UP 1979)

Bellamy, Richard *Political Constitutionalism. A Republican Defence of the Constitutionality of Democracy* (CUP Cambridge 2007)

Benhabib, Seyla, Jeremy Waldron, Bonnie Honig, Will Kymlicka, Robert Post *Another Cosmopolitanism* (OUP Oxford 2006)

Benhabib, Seyla 'Hospitality, Sovereignty, and Democratic Iterations' in Seyla Benhabib, Jeremy Waldron, Bonnie Honig, Will Kymlicka, and Robert Post *Another Cosmopolitanism* (OUP Oxford 2006) 147–186

Benvenisti, Eyal 'Exit and Voice in the Age of Globalization' (1999) 98 *Michigan Law Review* 167–213

Benz, Arthur *Der moderne Staat: Grundlagen einer politologischen Analyse* (2nd edn Oldenbourg München 2008)

—— Carol Harlow, and Yannis Papandopoulos 'Introduction' (2007) 13 *European Law Journal* 441–446

Berman, Paul Schiff 'Global Legal Pluralism' (2007) 80 *Southern California Law Review* 1155–1238

Berridge, Geoff R *Diplomacy: Theory and Practice* (Prentice Hall Hemel Hempstead 1995)

Bienen, Derk, Volker Rittberger, and Wolfgang Wagner 'Democracy in the UN System, Cosmopolitan and Communitarian Principles' in Daniele Archibugi, David Held, and Martin Köhler (eds) *Re-Imagining Political Community: Studies in Cosmopolitan Democracy* (Polity Press Cambridge 1998) 287–308

Biermann, Frank and Steffen Bauer (eds) *A World Environment Organization: Solution or Threat for Effective International Environmental Governance* (Ashgate Aldershot 2005)

Binder, Guyora *Treaty Conflict and Political Contradiction: The Dialectic of Duplicity* (Praeger New York 1988)

Bittner, Ludwig *Die Lehre von den völkerrechtlichen Vertragsurkunden* (Deutsche Verlags-Anstalt Stuttgart 1924)

Bloom, Evan T 'Establishment of the Arctic Council' (1999) 93 *AJIL* 712–722

Bluntschli, Johann Caspar *Das moderne Völkerrecht der civilisirten Staaten als Rechtsbuch dargestellt* (3rd edn Beck Nördlingen 1878)

Bodansky, Daniel 'Is there an International Environmental Constitution?' (2009) 16 *Indiana Journal of Global Legal Studies* 565–584

—— 'The Legitimacy of International Governance: A Coming Challenge for International Environmental Law?' (1999) 93 *AJIL* 596–624

Bodin, Jean *Les six livres de la République,* livre I, chapter 8, reprint of the edition of Paris 1583, first edition of 1576 (Scientia Aalen 1977)

Bogdandy, Armin von 'General Principles of International Public Authority: Sketching a Research Field' (2008) 9 *German Law Journal* 1909–1939

—— 'Law and Politics in the WTO—Strategies to Cope with a Deficient Relationship' (2001) 5 *Max Planck Yearbook of United Nations Law* 609–675

—— and Matthias Goldmann 'The Exercise of Public Authority Through National Policy Assessment' (2008) 5 *International Organizations Law Review* 241–298

—— Philip Dann, and Matthias Goldmann 'Developing the Publicness of Public International Law: Towards a Legal Framework for Global Governance Activities' (2008) 9 *German Law Journal* 1375–1400

—— *et al* (eds) *The Exercise of Public Authority by International Institutions: Advancing International Institutional Law* (Springer Berlin 2009) forthcoming

Bohman, James *Democracy across Borders: From Demos to Demoi* (MIT Press Cambridge MA 2007)

Bolton, John R 'Is There Really "Law" in International Affairs?' (2000) 10 *Transnational Law and Contemporary Problems* 1–48

Börzel, Tanja and Thomas Risse 'Public-Private Partnerships: Effective and Legitimate Tools of International Governance?' in Edgar Grande and Louis W Pauly (eds) *Complex Sovereignty: Reconstituting Political Authority in the 21st Century* (University of Toronto Press 2005) 195–216

Bothe, Michael 'Security Council's Targeted Sanctions against Presumed Terrorists' (2008) 6 *Journal of International Criminal Justice* 541–555

—— 'The Role of National Law in the Implementation of International Humanitarian Law' in Christophe Swinarski (ed) *Studies and Essays on International Humanitarian Law and Red Cross Principles in Honour of Jean Pictet* (Martinus Nijhoff Dordrecht 1984) 301–312

Bourquin, Maurice 'Règles Générales du Droit de la Paix' (1931/I) 35 *Recueil des Cours* 5–229

Boutros-Ghali, Boutros 'Democracy: A Newly Recognized Imperative' (1995) 1 *Global Governance* 3–11

Bowman, Michael 'Towards a Unified Treaty Body for Monitoring Compliance with UN Human Rights Conventions? Legal Mechanisms for Treaty Reform' (2007) 7 *Human Rights Law Review* 225–251

Boyle, Alan 'Relationship between International Environmental Law and other Branches of International Law' in Daniel Bodansky, Jutta Brunnée, and Ellen Hey (eds) *The Oxford Handbook of International Environmental Law* (OUP Oxford 2007) 125–147

—— and Christine Chinkin *The Making of International Law* (OUP Oxford 2007)

Brander, Sonia and María Martin Estebanez 'The OSCE Matures: Time for Legal Status' (2007) 2–5 *Helsinki Monitor*

Brierly, James Leslie 'The Basis of Obligation in International Law' in James Leslie Brierly *The Basis of Obligation in International Law and Other Papers* (Scientia Aalen 1977 (orig. 1928))

—— 'Règles Générales du Droit de la Paix' (1936/IV) 58 *Recueil des Cours* 5–237

Broms, Bengt 'The Definition of Aggression' (1977) 154 *Recueil des Cours* 297–400

Brunnée, Jutta and Stephen J Toope 'International Law and Constructivism: Elements of an Interactional Theory of International Law' (2000–2001) 39 *Columbia Journal of Transnational Law* 19–74

—— 'Persuasion and Enforcement: Explaining Compliance with International Law' (2002) 13 *Finnish Yearbook of International Law* 273–295

Buchanan, Allen *Justice, Legitimacy, and Self-determination: Moral Foundations for International Law* (OUP Oxford 2004)

—— and Robert O Keohane 'The Legitimacy of Global Governance' (2006) 20 *Ethics and International Affairs* 405–437

—— and Russell Powell 'Constitutional Democracy and the Rule of International Law: Are they Compatible?' (2008) 16 *Journal of Political Philosophy* 326–349

Buchanan, James MacGill and Gordon Tullock *The Calculus of Consent* (University of Michigan Press Ann Arbor 1962

Bueno Mesquita, Bruce and George W Downs 'Development and Democracy' (2005) 84 *Foreign Affairs* 77–86

Buergenthal, Thomas 'Proliferation of International Courts and Tribunals: Is It Good or Bad?' (2001) 14 *Leiden Journal of International Law* 267–275

Bull, Hedley *The Anarchical Society: A Study of Order in World Politics* (MacMillan Houndmills 1977)

Bùrca, Gráinne de, 'The European Court of Justice and the International Legal Order after *Kadi*' *Jean Monnet Working Paper* 01/09, NYU School of Law

Caflisch, Lucius 'Independence and Impartiality of Judges: The European Court of Human Rights' (2003) 2 *The Law and Practice of International Courts and Tribunals* 169–173

Campbell, Tom D, Keith D Ewing, and Adam Tomkins *Sceptical Essays on Human Rights* (OUP Oxford 2001)

Cane, Peter and Mark Tushnet (eds) *The Oxford Handbook of Legal Studies* (OUP Oxford 2005)

Caney, Simon *Justice Beyond Borders: A Global Political Theory* (OUP Oxford 2005)

Cannizzaro, Enzo *Il principo della propozionalitá nell'ordinamento internazionale* (Giuffrè Milan 2000)

Canovan, Margaret *The People* (Cambridge Polity 2005)

Carozza, Paolo G 'Subsidiarity as a Structural Principle of Human Rights Law' (2003) 97 *AJIL* 38–79

Carter, April 'Transnational Citizenship and Direct Action' in Wayne Hudson and Steven Slaughter (eds) *Globalisation and Citizenship: the Transnational Challenge* (Routledge Abingdon 2007) 127–136

—— *The Political Theory of Global Citizenship* (Routledge London 2001)

Cass, Deborah Z *Constitutionalization of the World Trade Oragnization* (OUP Oxford 2005)

—— 'The Constitutionalization of International Trade Law: Judicial Norm-Generation as the Engine of Constitutionalization' (2001) 13 *EJIL* 39–77

Cassese, Antonio *International Law* (2nd edn OUP Oxford 2005)

Cassese, Sabino 'Les transformations du droit administratif du XIXe au XXIe siècle' (2002) 41 *Droit Administratif* 6–9

Charney, Jonathan I 'Is International Law Threatened by Multiple International Tribunals?' (1998) 271 *Recueil des Cours* 101

—— 'Universal International Law' (1993) 87 *AJIL* 529–551

—— 'The Impact on the International Legal System of the Growth of International Courts and Tribunals' (1999) 31 *New York University Journal of International Law & Politics* 697–708

Charnovitz, Steve 'Nongovernmental Organizations and International Law' (2006) 100 *AJIL* 348–372

—— 'A World Environment Organization' (2002) 27 *Columbia Journal of Environmental Law* 323–362

—— 'WTO Cosmopolitics' (2002) 34 *New York University Journal of International Law and Politics* 299–354

Cheng, Tai-Heng 'Power, Authority, and International Investment Law' (2005) 20 *American University International Law Review* 465–520

Chesterman, Simon '"I'll Take Manhattan": The International Rule of Law and the United Nations Security Council' (2009) 1 *Hague Journal on the Rule of Law* 1–7.

—— 'The UN Security Council and the Rule of Law' (2008) New York University School of Law, Public Law and Legal Theory Research Paper Series, Working Paper No 08–57

Childers, Erskine and Brian Urquhart *Renewing the United Nations System* (Dag Hammarskjöld Foundation Uppsala 1994)

Chinkin, Christine *Third Parties in International Law* (OUP Oxford 1993)

—— 'The Challenge of Soft Law: Development and Change in International Law' (1989) 38 *ICLQ* 850–866

Christiano, Thomas 'Democratic Legitimacy and International Institutions' in Samantha Besson and John Tasioulas *Philosophy of International Law* (Oxford OUP 2010) 119–137

—— *The Constitution of Equality* (OUP Oxford 2008)

Churchill, Robin and Geir Ulfstein 'Autonomous Institutional Arrangements in Multilateral Environmental Agreements: A Little-Noticed Phenomenon in International Law' (2000) 94 *AJIL* 623–660

Churchill, Winston *His Complete Speeches 1897–1963* (Chelsea House Publishers New York 1974)

Cohen, Jean 'A Global State of Emergency or the Further Constitutionalization of International Law: A Pluralist Approach' (2008) 15 *Constellations* 456–484

Cohen, Joshua and Charles Sabel 'Global Democracy?' (2005) 37 *New York University Journal of International Law & Politics* 763–797

Coicaud, Jean-Marc 'Conclusion: International Organizations, the Evolution of International Politics, and Legitimacy' in Jean Marc Coicaud and Veijo Heiskanen (eds) *The Legitimacy of International Organizations* (United Nations UP Tokyo, New York, Paris 2001) 519–552

Commission on Global Governance *The Report of the Commission on Global Governance, Our Global Neighbourhood* (OUP Oxford 1995)

Corell, Hans 'Reforming the United Nations' (2005) 2 *International Organizations Law Review* 373–391

Corten, Olivier 'Convention de Vienne de 1969, Article 52' in *idem* and Pierre Klein (eds) *Les Conventions de Vienne sur le droit des traités: Commentaire article par article* (Bruylant Bruxelles 2006)

Cosnard, Michel 'Rapport introductif' in Société française pour le droit international (ed) *Colloque de Mans: Le sujet en droit international* (Paris 2005) 13–53

Cottier, Thomas 'Limits to International Trade: The Constitutional Challenge' (2000) 94 *Proceedings of the American Society of International Law* 220–222

Craig, Paul 'Constitutions, Constitutionalism, and the European Union' (2001) 7 *European Law Journal* 125–150

Craven, Matthew *The Decolonization of International Law: State Succession and the Law of Treaties* (OUP Oxford 2007)

Crawford, James *The Creation of States* (2nd edn CUP Cambridge 2006)

—— 'Multilateral Rights and Obligations in International Law' (2006) 319 *Recueil des Cours* 325–482

—— '"Marbury v. Madison" at the International Level' (2004) 36 *George Washington International Law Review* 505–514

—— 'International Law and the Rule of Law' (2003) 24 *Adelaide Law Review* 3–12

—— 'The UN Human Rights Treaty System: A System in Crisis?' in Philip Alston and James Crawford (eds) *The Future of UN Human Rights Treaty Monitoring* (CUP Cambridge 2000) 1–15

—— *Democracy in International Law* (CUP Cambridge 1994)

van Creveld, Martin *Aufstieg und Untergang des Staates* (Gerling-Akademie-Verlag München 1999 Klaus Fritz und Norbert Juraschitz trans)

Crouch, Colin *Post-Democracy* (Polity Cambridge 2004)

Dahl, Robert A 'Can International Organizations be Democratic?' in Ian Shapiro and Casiano Hacker-Cordón (eds) *Democracy's Edges* (CUP Cambridge 1999) 19–34

—— *Democracy and its Critics* (Yale UP New Haven 1989)

—— and Edward Tufte *Size and Democracy* (Stanford UP Palo Alto 1973)

Dahm, Georg, Jost Delbrück, and Rüdiger Wolfrum *Völkerrecht* (2nd edn de Gruyter Berlin 2002) vol I/3

Danilenko, Gennadij Michajlovič *Law-making in the International Community* (Martinus Nijhoff Dordrecht 1993)

Davies, Gareth 'Subsidiarity: The Wrong Idea, in the Wrong Place, at the Wrong Time' (2006) 43 *Common Market Law Review* 63–84

Davies, Howard and David Green *Global Financial Regulation: The Essential Guide* (Polity Cambridge 2008)

—— 'Developing Democracy Beyond the State' (2008) 46 *Columbia Journal of Transnational Law* 102–158

Delanty, Gerard 'Theorising Citizenhip in a Global Age' in Wayne Hudson and Steven Slaughter (eds) *Globalisation and Citizenship: The Transnational Challenge* (Routledge Abingdon 2007) 15–29

Delbrück, Jost 'Prospects for a "World (Internal) Law"? Legal Developments in a Changing International System' (2002) 9 *Indiana Journal of Global Legal Studies* 401–431

Delmas-Marty, Mireille *Le pluralisme ordonné* (Seuil Paris 2006)

—— *Vers un droit commun de l'humanité* (2nd edn Textuel Paris 2005)

Dembour, Marie-Bénédicte *Who Believes in Human Rights? Reflections on the European Convention* (CUP Cambridge 2006)

Deutch, Sinai 'Are Consumer Rights Human Rights?' (1994) 32 *Osgoode Hall Law Journal* 537–578

Dewey, John *The Public and its Problems* (Swallow Press Athens OH 1927)

Diggelmann, Oliver *Der liberale Verfassungsstaat und die Internationalisierung der Politik: Veränderungen von Staat und Demokratie in der Schweiz* (Stämpfli Bern 2005)

Dingwerth, Klaus 'The Democratic Legitimacy of Public-Private Rule Making: What can we Learn from the World Commission on Dams' (2005) 11 *Global Governance* 65–83

Disraeli, Benjamin *Sybil, or the Two Nations* (Thomas Nelson London 1845)

Doehring, Karl *Völkerrecht* (2nd edn CF Müller Heidelberg 2004)

Dörr, Oliver 'Privatisierung des Völkerrechts' (2005) 60 *Juristen-Zeitung* 905–916

Dorsen, Norman, Michel Rosenfeld, András Sajó, and Susanne Baer *Comparative Constitutionalism, Cases and Materials (American Casebook)* (West Publishing Co. St. Paul Minn. 2003)

Dougan, Michael 'Direct Democracy and the European Union ... is that a Threat or a Promise?' (2008) 45 *Common Market Law Review* 929–940

Douglas, Zachary 'The Hybrid Foundations of Investment Treaty Arbitration' (2004) 74 *BYIL* 151–290

Doyle, Michael W 'Kant, Liberal Legacies, and Foreign Affairs' (parts 1 and 2) (1983) 12 *Philosophy and Public Affairs* 205–235 and 323–353

Drechsler, Wolfgang 'On the Viability of the Concept of Staatswissenschaften' (2001) 12 *European Journal of Law and Economics* 105–111

Dryzek, John S *Deliberative Global Politics* (Polity Cambridge 2006)

—— *Deliberative Democracy and Beyond: Liberals, Critics, and Contestations* (OUP Oxford 2000)

Dunoff, Jeffrey L 'Constitutional Conceits: The WTO's "Constitution" and the Discipline of International Law' (2006) 17 *EJIL* 647–675

Dupuy, Pierre-Marie *Droit international public* (7th edn Dalloz Paris 2004)

—— 'L'unité de l'ordre juridique international' (2002) 297 *Recueil des Cours* 9–490

—— 'The Constitutional Character of the Charter of the United Nations Revisited' (1997) 1 *Max Planck Yearbook of United Nations Law* 1–33

Dupuy, René-Jean *La Communauté internationale entre le mythe et l'histoire* (Economica Paris 1986)

Dworkin, Ronald *Freedom's Law: The Moral Reading of the American Constitution* (Harvard UP Cambridge MA 1996)

—— *Taking Rights Seriously* (Duckworth London 1977)

Economidès, Constantin P and Alexandros G Kolliopoulou 'La clause de déconnexion en faveur du droit communautaire: Une pratique critiquable' (2006) 110 *Revue Générale de Droit International Public* 273–302

Eisemann, Pierre-Michel 'Le gentlemen's agreement comme source de droit international' (1979) 106 *Journal du Droit International* 326–348

Emiliou, Nicholas 'Subsidiarity: Panacea or Fig Leaf?' in David O'Keeffe and Patrick M Twomey (eds) *Legal Issues of the Maastricht Treaty* (Chancery Law Chichester 1994) 65–83

Emmerich-Fritsche, Angelika *Vom Völkerrecht zum Weltrecht* (Duncker & Humblot Berlin 2007)

Enders, Christoph *Die Menschenwürde in der Verfassungsordnung: zur Dogmatik des Art. 1 GG* (Mohr Siebeck Tübingen 1997)

Engström, Viljam *Realizing the Global Compact* (Erik Castrén Institute Helsinki 2002)

Erdmann, Gero and Ulf Engel 'Neopatrimonialism Revisited: Beyond a Catch-all Concept' (2006) 16 *German Institute of Global and Area Studies Working Papers*

Eriksen, Thomas Hylland *Globalization: The Key Concepts* (Berg New York 2007)

Esty, Daniel 'Good Governance at the Supranational Scale: Globalizing Administrative Law' (2006) 115 *Yale Law Journal* 1490–1562

Evans, Gareth 'The Responsibility to Protect: Rethinking Humanitarian Intervention' (2004) 98 *Proceedings of the American Society of International Law* 78–89

Falk, Richard and Andrew Strauss 'Toward Global Parliament' (2001) 80 *Foreign Affairs* 212–220

—— 'On the Creation of a Global Peoples Assembly: Legitimacy and the Power of Popular Sovereignty' (2000) 36 *Stanford Journal of International Law* 191–220

Farrall, Jeremy Matam *United Nations Sanctions and the Rule of Law* (CUP Cambridge 2007)

Fassbender, Bardo ' "We the Peoples of the United Nations": Constituent Power and Constitutional Form in International Law' in Martin Loughlin and Neil Walker (eds) *The Paradox of Constitutionalism: Constituent Power and Constitutional Form* (OUP Oxford 2007) 269–290

—— 'Targeted Sanctions Imposed by the UN Security Council and Due Process Rights: A Study Commissioned by the UN Office of Legal Affairs and Follow-Up Action by the United Nations', (2006) 3 *International Organizations Law Review* 437–485

—— 'Sovereignty and Constitutionalism in International Law' in Neil Walker (ed) *Sovereignty in Transition* (Hart Oxford 2003) 115–143

—— 'Review Essay: *Quis judicabit?* The Security Council, its Powers and its Legal Control' (2000) 11 *EJIL* 219–232

—— 'The United Nations Charter as the Constitution of the International Community' (1998) 36 *Columbia Journal of Transnational Law* 529–619

Fawcett, James E S 'The Legal Character of International Agreements' (1953) 30 *BYIL* 381–400

Feichtner, Isabel 'Subsidiarity' *Max Planck Encyclopedia of Public International Law* (OUP Oxford 2009)

Feinstein, Lee and Anne-Marie Slaughter 'A Duty to Prevent' (2004) 83 No 1 *Foreign Affairs* 136–150

Finke, Jasper 'Competing Jurisdiction of International Courts and Tribunals in the Light of the *MOX Plant* Dispute' (2006) 49 *German Yearbook of International Law* 307–326

Fischer, Frank *Technocracy and the Politics of Expertise* (Sage Publications Newbury Park Cal. 1990)

Fischer-Lescano, Andreas and Gunther Teubner, *Regime-Kollisionen: Zur Fragmentierung des Globalen Rechts* (Suhrkamp Frankfurt am Main 2006)

—— 'Regime-Collisions: The Vain Search for Legal Unity in the Fragmentation of Global Law' (2004) 25 *Michigan Journal of International Law* 999–1046

Fish, Stanley *Doing What Comes Naturally: Change, Rhetoric, and the Practice of Theory in Literary Studies* (Clarendon Press Oxford 1989)

Fitzmaurice, Sir Gerald 'Some Problems Regarding the Formal Sources of International Law' in F M van Asbeck, J Donner, PN Drost, JLF van Essen, WJM van Eysinga, JPA Francois, CL Patijn (eds) *Symbolae Verzijl* (Martinus Nijhoff The Hague 1958) 153–176

Flauss, François 'Vers un aggiornamento des conditions d'exercice de la protection diplomatique?' in *idem* (ed) *La protection diplomatique: Mutations contemporaines et pratiques nationales* (Bruylant Bruxelles 2003) 29–61

Florini, Ann *The Coming Democracy: New Rules for Running the World* (Island Press Washington DC 2003)

Flynn, E J 'The Security Council's Counter-terrorism Committee and Human Rights' (2007) 7 *Human Rights Law Review* 371–384

Føllesdal, Andreas 'Survey Article: Subsidiarity' (1998) 6 *The Journal of Political Philosophy* 90–218

—— Ramses Wessel, and Jan Wouters (eds) *Multilevel Regulation and the EU: The Interplay between Global, European and National Normative Processes* (Martinus Nijhoff Leiden 2008)

Foster, Robert J *Coca-Globalization: Following Soft Drinks from New York to New Guinea* (Palgrave MacMillan New York 2008)

Fox, Gregory H 'The Right to Political Participation in International Law' in Gregory H Fox and Brad R Roth (eds) *Democratic Governance and International Law* (CUP Cambridge 2000) 48–90

—— 'Democracy, Right to, International Protection' *Max Planck Encyclopedia of Public International Law* (OUP Oxford 2009)

—— 'The Right to Political Participation in International Law' (1992) 17 *Yale Journal of International Law* 539–607

Franck, Thomas 'Legitimacy and the Democratic Entitlement' in Gregory H Fox and Brad R Roth (eds) *Democratic Governance and International Law* (CUP Cambridge 2000) 25–47

—— 'The Emerging Right to Democratic Governance' (1992) 86 *AJIL* 46–91

—— *The Power of Legitimacy Among Nations* (OUP Oxford 1990)

Fraser, Nancy 'From Redistribution to Recognition?' in Stephen Seidman and Jeffrey C Alexander *The New Social Theory Reader* (Routledge London and New York 2001) 285–293

Friedman, Jonathan 'Diasporization, Globalization, and Cosmopolitan Discourse' in André Levy and Alex Weingrod (eds) *Homelands and Diasporas: Holy Lands and Other Places* (Stanford UP Palo Alto 2005) 140–165

—— 'Globalization' in David Nugent and Joan Vincent (eds) *A Companion to the Anthropology of Politics* (Blackwell London 2004) 179–197

Friedman, Milton *Capitalism and Freedom* (Chicago UP 1962)

Frouville, Olivier de 'Domesticating Civil Society at the UN' in Pierre-Marie Dupuy and Luisa Vierucci (eds) *NGOs in International Law: Efficiency and Flexibility* (Edward Elgar Northampton 2008) 71–115

Frowein, Jochen A 'Konstitutionalisierung des Völkerrechts' (2000) 39 *Berichte der Deutschen Gesellschaft für Völkerrecht* 427–447

Fuller, Lon L *The Morality of Law* (rev edn Yale UP New Haven CT 1969)

Gardam, Judith 'Proportionality and Force in International Law' (1993) 87 *AJIL* 391–413

Gardbaum, Stephen 'Human Rights as International Constitutional Rights' (2008) 19 *EJIL* 749–768

Geis, Anna, Harald Müller, and Wolfgang Wagner (eds) *Schattenseiten des demokratischen Friedens* (Campus Frankfurt and New York 2007)

—— Lothar Brock, and Harald Müller 'Demokratische Kriege als Antinomien des Demokratischen Friedens: Eine komplementäre Forschungsagenda' in Anna Geis, Harald Müller, and Wolfgang Wagner (eds) *Schattenseiten des demokratischen Friedens* (Campus Frankfurt and New York 2007) 69–91

Gellner, Ernest *Nations and Nationalism* (Basil Blackwell Oxford 1983)

Gerson, Allan 'Peace Building: The Private Sector's Role' (2001) 95 *AJIL* 102–119

Gill, Stephen 'Globalisation, Market Civilisation, and Disciplinary Neoliberalism' (1995) 24 *Millennium: Journal of International Studies* 399–423

Glendon, Mary Ann *Rights Talk: The Impoverishment of the Political Discourse* (The Free Press New York 1991)

Glennon, Michael J *Constitutional Diplomacy* (Princeton UP 1990)

Goldmann, Matthias 'Inside Relative Normativity: From Sources to Standard Instruments for the Exercise of International Public Authority' (2008) 9 *German Law Journal* 1865–1908

Goldsmith, Jack L and Eric A Posner *The Limits of International Law* (OUP Oxford 2005)

Goldstein, Judith, Miles Kahler, Robert O Keohane, and Anne-Marie Slaughter (eds) *Legalization and World Politics* (2000) 54 *International Organization* (special issue)

Gray, John *Two Faces of Liberalism* (New Press New York 2000)

—— *False Dawn: The Delusions of Global Capitalism* (Granta London 1998)

Grewe, Wilhem G (ed) *Fontes Historiae Iuris Gentium: Sources Relating to the History of the Law of Nations* vol 2 (de Gruyter Berlin 1988)

Grimm, Dieter 'Does Europe Need a Constitution?' (1995) 1 *European Law Journal* 282–307

Gruchalla-Wesierski, Tadeusz 'A Framework for Understanding "Soft Law"' (1984) *McGill Law Journal* 37–88

Guéneau, Stéphane 'Certification as a New Private Global Forest Governance System: The Regulatory Potential of the Forest Stewardship Council' in Anne Peters, Lucy Koechlin, Till Förster, Gretta Fenner Zinkernagel (eds) *Non-State Actors as Standard Setters* (CUP Cambridge 2009) 379–408

Guillaume, Gilbert 'The Future of International Judicial Institutions' (1995) 44 *ICLQ* 848–862

Haas, Peter 'Introduction: Epistemic Communities and International Policy Coordination' (1992) 46 *International Organization* 1–35

Habermas, Jürgen *The Divided West* (Polity Cambridge 2006 Cronin trans)

—— 'Does the Constitutionalization of International Law still have a Chance?' in *idem The Divided West* (Polity Cambridge 2006 Cronin ed and trans) 115–210

Haegel, Peter 'Standard Setting for Capital Movements: Reasserting Sovereignty over Transnational Actors?' in Anne Peters, Lucy Köchlin, Till Förster, and Gretta Fenner Zinkernagel (eds) *Non-state Actors as Standard Setters* (CUP Cambridge 2009) 351–378

Haltern, Ulrich 'Internationales Verfassungsrecht' (2003) 128 *Archiv des öffentlichen Rechts* 511–556

Harlow, Carol 'Global Administrative Law: The Quest for Principles and Values' (2006) 17 *EJIL* 187–214

Harmon, Michael *Responsibility as Paradox: A Critique of Rational Discourse on Government* (Sage Thousand Oaks CA 1995)

Hart, H L A *The Concept of Law* (Clarendon Press Oxford 1961)

Harten, Gus van *Investment Treaty Arbitration and Public Law* (OUP Oxford 2007)

Hartley, Trevor C *The Foundations of European Community Law* (6th edn OUP Oxford 2007)

Haufler, Virginia *A Public Role for the Private Sector: Industry Self-regulation in a Global Economy* (Carnegie Endowment for International Peace Washington DC 2001)

Hayek, Friedrich August von *The Road to Serfdom* (Routledge London 2001 [1944])

Hegel, Georg W F *The Philosophy of Right* (Encyclopedia Britannica Chicago etc. 1952 Benton publ, Knox trans) (*Grundlinien der Philosophie des Rechts* 1821)

—— *Vorlesungen über die Philosophie der Geschichte, I. Band: Einleitung—Die Vernunft in der Geschichte* (Meiner Leipzig 1920 Lasson ed)

Heilborn, Paul *Grundbegriffe des Völkerrechts. Handbuch des Völkerrechts* vol 1 (Kohlhammer Stuttgart 1912)

Held, David *Democracy and the Global Order: From the Modern State to Cosmopolitan Governance* (CUP Cambridge 1995)

—— 'Democracy, the Nation-state and the Global System' in David Held (ed) *Political Theory Today* (Polity Press Cambridge 1991) 197–235

Helfer, Laurence R 'Redesigning the European Court of Human Rights: Embeddedness as a Deep Structural Principle of the European Human Rights Regime' (2008) 19 *EJIL* 125–159

—— 'Overlegalizing Human Rights: International Relations Theory and the Commonwealth Caribbean Backlash against Human Rights Regimes' (2002) 102 *Columbia Law Review* 1832–1911

—— and Anne-Marie Slaughter 'Why States Create International Tribunals: A Response to Professors Posner and Yoo' (2005) 93 *California Law Review* 901- 56

Henckaerts, Jean-Marie and Louise Doswald-Beck *Customary International Humanitarian Law* vol I, Rules (CUP Cambridge 2005)

Henderson, Errol A *Democracy and War: The End of an Illusion?* (Lynne Riener Boulder 2002)

Henkin, Louis 'International Law: Politics, Values and Functions' (1989/V) 216 *Recueil des Cours* 9–416

Herdegen, Matthias *Internationales Wirtschaftsrecht* (3rd edn Beck München 2002)

Higgins, Rosalyn 'Conceptual Thinking about the Individual in International Law' (1978) 4 *British Journal of International Studies* 1–19

—— 'A Babel of Judicial Voices' (2006) 55 *ICLQ* 791–805

Hirschl, Ran *Towards Juristocracy: The Orgins and Consequences of the New Constitutionalism* (Harvard UP Cambridge MA 2004)

Hobbes, Thomas *Leviathan* (CUP Cambridge 1991 [orig. 1651] Tuck ed)

Hobsbawm, Eric J *Nations and Nationalism Since 1780: Progamme, Myth, Reality* (2nd edn Canto Cambridge 1992)

Hoekman, Bernard, and Michel Kostecki *The Political Economy of the World Trade Organization: From GATT to WTO* (OUP Oxford 1995)

Höffe, Otfried *Demokratie im Zeitalter der Globalisierung* (2nd edn Beck München 2002)

—— 'Vision Weltrepublik: Eine philosophische Antwort auf die Globalisierung' in Winfried Brugger, Ulfrid Neumann, and Stephan Kirste (eds) *Rechtsphilosophie im 21. Jahrhundert* (Suhrkamp Frankfurt am Main 2008) 380–396

Honig, Bonnie *Democracy and the Foreigner* (Princeton UP 2001)

Howse, Robert and Kalypso Nicolaidis 'Enhancing WTO Legitimacy: Constitutionalization or Global Subsidiarity' (2003) 16 *Governance* 73–94

Hurd, Ian *After Anarchy: Legitimacy and Power at the United Nations Security Council* (Princeton UP 2007)

Hurrell, Andrew *On Global Order: Power, Values, and the Constitution of International Society* (OUP Oxford 2007)

Hurrelmann, Achim, Stephan Leibfried, Kerstin Martens, and Peter Mayer 'The Transformation of the Golden-Age Nation State: Findings and Perspectives' in *idem* (eds) *Transforming the Golden-Age Nation State* (Palgrave Macmillan Hampshire 2007) 193–205

Hursthouse, Rosalind *On Virtue Ethics* (OUP Oxford 1999)

Ignatieff, Michael 'The Attack on Human Rights' (2001) vol 80 No 6 *Foreign Affairs* 102–116

Ihering, Rudolf von *Geist des römischen Rechts auf den verschiedenen Stufen seiner Entwicklung* part II (5th edn von Breitkopf und Härtel Leipzig 1898)

Independent International Commission on Kosovo *The Kosovo Report: Conflict, International Response, Lessons Learned* (OUP New York 2000)

Jackson, John H *Sovereignty, the WTO and Changing Fundamentals of International Law* (CUP Cambridge 2006)

—— 'Sovereignty-Modern. A New Approach to an Outdated Concept' (2003) 97 *AJIL* 782–802

—— *World Trade Law and the Law of GATT* (Bobbs Merrill Indianapolis 1969)

Jackson, Vicki C and Mark Tushnet (eds) *Defining the Field of Comparative Constitutional Law* (Praeger Westport CN 2002)

Jahn, Beate 'Kant, Mill, and Illiberal Legacies in International Affairs' (2005) 59 *International Organization* 177–207

Jennings, Robert 'What is International Law and how do we tell it when we see it?' (1981) 37 *Schweizerisches Jahrbuch für Internationales Recht* 59–88

—— 'The Judiciary, International and National and the Development of International Law' (1996) 45 *ICLQ* 1–12

Joerges, Christian and Florian Rödl 'Informal Politics, Formalised Law and the "Social Deficit" of European Integration: Reflections after the Judgments of the ECJ in *Viking* and *Laval* ' (2009) 15 *European Law Journal* 1–19

Johnston, Douglas M 'World Constitutionalism in the Theory of International Law' in Ronald MacDonald and Douglas M Johnston (eds) *Towards World Constitutionalism: Issues in the Legal Ordering of the World Commmunity* (Martinus Nijhoff Leiden 2005) 3–29

Johnstone, Ian 'Legislation and Adjudication in the UN Security Council: Bringing down the Deliberative Deficit' (2008) 102 *AJIL* 275–308

Johnstone, Rachael Lorna 'Cynical Savings or Reasonable Reform? Reflections on a Single Unified UN Human Rights Treaty Body' (2007) 7 *Human Rights Law Review* 173–201.

Kadelbach, Stefan 'Ethik des Völkerrechts unter Bedingungen der Globalisierung' (2004) 64 *Zeitschrift für ausländisches öffentliches Recht und Völkerrecht* 1–20

Kahler, Miles 'Defining Accountability up: The Global Economic Multilaterals' (2004) 39 *Government and Opposition* 132–158

Kaiser, Karl 'Transnational Relations as a Threat to the Democratic Process' (1971) 25 *International Organization* 706–720

Kaldor, Mary *Global Civil Society: An Answer to War* (Polity Press Cambridge 2003)

Kälin, Walter 'Der Menschenrechtsschutz der UNO: Ein Beispiel für die Konstitutionalisierung des Völkerrechts?' in Walter Kälin and Thomas Cottier (eds) *Die Öffnung des Verfassungsrechts: Symposium zum 65. Geburtstag von Prof. Jörg Paul Müller* (Stämpfli Verlag AG Bern 2005) 42–49

Kant, Immanuel 'Perpetual Peace' in *idem Perpetual Peace, and Other Essays on Politics, History, and Morals* (Hackett Publ Indianapolis 1983 (German orig. 1795 Humphrey trans)

—— *Die Metaphysik der Sitten, erster Theil, metaphysische Anfänge der Rechtslehre* (orig. Königsberg 1798) in *idem Die Metaphysik der Sitten*, works (Werkausgabe) vol VIII (3rd edn Suhrkamp Frankfurt am Main 1978 Weischedel ed)

Keller, Helen and Alec Stone Sweet *A Europe of Rights* (OUP Oxford 2008)

Kelsen, Hans *General Theory of Norms* (Clarendon Press Oxford 1991 Hartney trans)

—— *Principles of International Law* (2nd edn Holt Rinehart and Winston New York 1967)

—— 'Les Rapports de Système entre le Droit Interne et le Droit International Public' (1926/IV) 14 *Recueil des Cours* 231–329

Kennedy, Duncan *A Critique of Adjudication {Fin de Siècle}* (Harvard UP Cambridge MA 1997)

Kingreen, Thorsten *Die Struktur der Grundfreiheiten des Europäischen Gemeinschaftsrechts* (Duncker & Humblot Berlin 1999)

Kingsbury, Benedict 'Foreword: Is the Proliferation of International Courts and Tribunals a Systemic Problem?' (1999) 31 *New York University Journal of International Law & Politics* 679–696

—— Nico Krisch, and Richard B Stewart 'The Emergence of Global Administrative Law' (2005) 68 *Law and Contemporary Problems* 15–62

—— Nico Krisch, Richard B Stewart, and Jonathan B Wiener 'Foreword: Global Governance as Administration—National and Transnational Approaches to Global Administrative Law' (2005) 68 *Law and Contemporary Problems* 1–14

Klabbers, Jan 'Contending Approaches to International Organizations: Between Functionalism and Constitutionalism' in Jan Klabbers and Åsa Wallendahl (eds) *Research Handbook on International Organizations Law: Between Functionalism and Constitutionalism* (Edward Elgar Cheltenham 2011)

—— 'Goldmann Variations' in Armin von Bogdandy, Philipp Dann and Matthias Goldmann (eds) *The Exercise of Public Authority by International Institutions: Advancing International Institutional Law* (Springer Berlin 2010) 713–725

—— *Treaty Conflict and the European Union* (CUP Cambridge 2009)

—— 'Constitutionalism and the Making of International Law. Fuller's Procedural Natural Law' (2008) 5 *No Foundations: Journal of Extreme Legal Positivism* 84–112

—— 'Possible Islands of Predictability: The Legal Thought of Hannah Arendt' (2007) 20 *Leiden Journal of International Law* 1–23

—— 'Reluctant *Grundnormen*: Articles 31(3)(c) and 42 of the Vienna Convention on the Law of Treaties and the Fragmentation of International Law' in Matthew Craven, Malgosia Fitzmaurice, and Maria Vogiatzi (eds) *Time, History and International Law* (Martinus Nijhoff Leiden 2007) 141–161

—— 'The Commodification of International Law' (2006) 1 *Select Proceedings of the European Society of International Law* 341–358

—— 'International Organizations in the Formation of Customary International Law' in Enzo Cannizzaro and Paolo Palchetti (eds) *Customary International Law on the Use of Force* (Martinus Nijhoff Leiden 2005) 179–195

—— 'Reflections on Soft International Law in a Privatized World' (2005) 16 *Finnish Yearbook of International Law* 313–328

—— 'Straddling Law and Politics: Judicial Review in International Law' in Ronald St J MacDonald and Douglas M Johnston (eds) *Towards World Constitutionalism: Issues in the Legal Ordering of the World Community* (Martinus Nijhoff Leiden 2005) 809–835

—— 'The Concept of Legal Personality' (2005) 11 *Ius Gentium* 35–66

—— 'Two Concepts of International Organization' (2005) 2 *International Organizations Law Review* 277–293

—— 'Constitutionalism Lite' (2004) 1 *International Organizations Law Review* 31–58

—— '(I Can't Get No) Recognition: Subjects Doctrine and the Emergence of Non-state Actors' in Jarna Petman and Jan Klabbers (eds) *Nordic Cosmopolitanism: Essays in International Law for Martti Koskenniemi* (Martinus Nijhoff Leiden 2003) 351–369

—— 'Restraints on the Treaty-making Powers of Member States Deriving from EU Law' in Enzo Cannizzaro (ed) *The EU as an Actor in International Relations* (Kluwer The Hague 2002) 151–175

—— *An Introduction to International Institutional Law* (CUP Cambridge 2002)

—— 'Institutional Ambivalence by Design: Soft Organizations in International Law' (2001) 70 *Nordic Journal of International Law* 403–421

—— 'Clinching the Concept of Sovereignty: Wimbledon *Redux*' (1998) 3 *Austrian Review of International and European Law* 345–367

—— 'The Redundancy of Soft Law' (1996) 65 *Nordic Journal of International Law* 167–182

—— *The Concept of Treaty in International Law* (Kluwer The Hague 1996)

Klein, Naomi *The Shock Doctrine* (Penguin London 2007)

Knox, John H 'Horizontal Human Rights Law' (2008) 102 *AJIL* 1–47

Kolb, Robert *Ius contra bellum: le droit international relatif au maintien de la paix* (2nd edn Helbing Lichtenhahn Basel 2009)

—— 'Nouvelle observation sur la détermination de la personalité juridique internationale' (2002) 57 *Zeitschrift für öffentliches Recht* 229–241

Kooijmans, Pieter 'The ICJ in the 21st Century: Judicial Restraint, Judicial Activism, or Proactive Judicial Policy' (2007) 56 *ICLQ* 741–755

—— 'Article 31' in Andreas Zimmermann, Karin Oellers-Frahm, and Christian Tomuschat (eds) *The Statute of the International Court of Justice. A Commentary* (OUP Oxford 2006) 495–506

Kooijmans, Pieter Hendrik *The Doctrine of the Legal Equality of States: An Inquiry into the Foundations of International Law* (AW Sijthoff Leiden 1964)

Koopmans, Tijmen *Courts and Political Institutions: A Comparative View* (CUP Cambridge 2003)

Koskenniemi, Martti 'Constitutionalism as Mindset: Reflections on Kantian Themes about International Law and Globalization' (2007) 8 *Theoretical Inquiries in Law* 9–36

—— 'Formalism, Fragmentation, Freedom: Kantian Themes in Today's International Law' (2007) 4 *No Foundations: Journal of Extreme Legal Positivism* 7–28

—— 'On the Idea and Practice for Universal History with a Cosmopolitan Purpose' in Bindu Puri and Heiko Sievers (eds) *Terror, Peace, and Universalism: Essays on the Philosophy of Immanuel Kant* (OUP Oxford 2007) 122–148

—— *Fragmentation of International Law: Difficulties Arising from the Diversification and Expansion of International Law. Report of the Study Group of the International Law Commission* (Erik Castrén Institute Research Reports 21/2007 Helsinki 2007)

—— 'The Fate of Public International Law: Between Technique and Politics' (2007) 70 *Modern Law Review* 1–30

—— 'International Legislation Today: Limits and Possibilities' (2005) 23 *Wisconsin International Law Journal* 61–92

—— 'Legitimacy, Rights, and Ideology: Notes Towards a Critique of the New Moral Internationalism' (2003) 7 *Associations* 349–373

—— *The Gentle Civilizer of Nations: The Rise and Fall of International Law 1870–1960* (CUP Cambridge 2001)

—— 'Intolerant Democracies: A Reaction' (1996) 37 *Harvard International Law Journal* 231–235

—— and Päivi Leino 'Fragmentation of International Law? Postmodern Anxieties' (2002) 15 *Leiden Journal of International Law* 553–579

Kovach Hetty, Caroline Nelligan, and Simon Burall *The Global Accountability Report: Power without Accountability?* (One World Trust London 2003)

Krasner, Stephen D *Sovereignty: Organized Hypocrisy* (Princeton UP 1999)

Kratochwil, Friedrich V 'Of False Promises and Good Bets: A Plea for a Pragmatic Approach to Theory-building (the Tartu Lecture)' (2007) 10 *Journal of International Relations and Development* 1–15

—— *Rules, Norms, and Decisions: On the Conditions of Practical and Legal Reasoning in International Relations and Domestic Affairs* (CUP Cambridge 1989)

Kretzmer, David 'Political Agreements—A Critical Introduction' (1992) 26 *Israel Law Review* 407–437

Krisch, Nico 'The Pluralism of Global Administrative Law'' (2006) 17 *EJIL* 247–278

—— 'More Equal than the Rest? Hierarchy, Equality and US Predominance in International Law' in Michael Byers and Georg Nolte (eds) *United States Hegemony and the Foundations of International Law* (CUP Cambridge 2003) 135–175

—— and Benedict Kingsbury 'Introduction: Global Governance and Global Administrative Law in the International Legal Order' (2006) 17 *EJIL* 1–13

Krut, Riva *Globalization and Civil Society: NGO Influence in International Decision-Making* (United Nations Research Institute for Social Development Geneva 1997)

Ku, Charlotte 'Forging a Multilayered System of Global Governance' in Ronald St J MacDonald and Douglas M Johnston (eds) *Towards World Constitutionalism: Issues in the Legal Ordering of the World Community* (Martinus Nijhoff Leiden 2005) 631–651

Kull, Andrew 'Reconsidering Gratuitous Promises' (1992) 21 *Journal of Legal Studies* 39–65

Kumm, Mattias 'Democratic Constitutionalism Encounters International Law: Terms of Engagement' in Sujit Choudhry (ed) *The Migration of Constitutional Ideas* (CUP Cambridge 2006) 256–293

—— 'The Legitimacy of International Law: A Constitutionalist Framework for Analysis' (2004) 15 *EJIL* 907–931

Kuper, Andrew *Democracy Beyond Borders: Justice and Representation in Global Institutions* (OUP Oxford 2004)

Lacey, Nicola *A Life of H.L.A. Hart: The Nightmare and the Noble Dream* (OUP Oxford 2004)

Lachmayer, Konrad 'The International Constitutional Approach: An Introduction to a New Perspective on Constitutional Challenges in a Globalising World' (2007) 1 *Vienna Journal on International Constitutional Law* 91–99

Lagrange, Evelyne 'L'application de la Convention de Rome à des actes accomplis par les états parties en dehors du territoire nationale' (2008) 112 *Revue Générale de Droit International Public* 521–565

Lamy, Pascal 'Emergence des preferences collectives dans le champ de l'échange international: Quelles implications pour la regulation de la mondialisation?' Speech of 15 September 2004

—— *La démocratie-monde. Pour une autre gouvernance globale* (Seuil Paris 2004)

Lane Jan-Erik *Constitutions and Political Theory* (Manchester UP 1996)

Lasson, Adolf *System der Rechtsphilosophie* (Guttentag Berlin and Leipzig 1882)

—— *Princip und Zukunft des Völkerrechts* (Wilhelm Hertz Berlin 1871)

Lauterpacht, Hersch 'The Subjects of the Law of Nations (Part I)' (1947) 63 *The Law Quarterly Review* 428–460

—— 'The Grotian Tradition of International Law' (1946) 23 *BYIL* 1–53

Leibfried, Stephan and Michael Zürn (eds) *Transformations of the State?* European Review 13 Suppl. No 1 (CUP Cambridge 2005).

Lenaerts, Koen 'Constitutionalism and the Many Faces of Federalism' (1990) 38 *American Journal of Comparative Law* 205–263

Letsas, George *A Theory of Interpretation of the European Convention on Human Rights* (OUP Oxford 2007)

Liivoja, Rain 'The Scope of the Supremacy Clause of the United Nations Charter' (2008) 57 *ICLQ* 583–612

Limbach, Jutta, Pedro Cruz Villalón, Roger Errera, Anthony Lester, Tamara Morshchakova, Stephen Sedley, and Andrzej Zoll *Judicial Independence: Law and Practice of Appointments to the European Court of Human Rights* (Interrights London 2003)

Lincoln, Abraham *His Speeches and Writings* (World Publishing Cleveland 1946 Basler ed)

Lindblom Anna-Karin *Non-Governmental Organisations in International Law* (CUP Cambridge 2005)

Linklater, Andrew *The Transformation of Political Community: Ethical Foundations of the Post-Westphalian Era* (Polity Cambridge 1998)

Lipschutz, Ronnie 'Reconstructing World Politics: The Emergence of Global Civil Society' (1992) 21 *Millennium: Journal of International Studies* 389–420

Locke, John *Two Treatises of Government* (CUP Cambridge 1960 (orig. 1690) Laslett ed)

Lord, Christopher and Erika Harris *Democracy in the New Europe* (Palgrave Houndmills Basingstoke Hampshire 2006)

Lorimer, James *The Institutes of the Law of Nations* vol 1 (William Blackwood Edinburgh and London 1883)

Loughlin, Martin 'The Functionalist Style in Public Law' (2005) 55 *University of Toronto Law Journal* 361–403

—— *Swords and Scales: An Examination of the Relationship Between Law & Politics* (Hart Oxford 2000)

—— and Neil Walker (eds) *The Paradox of Constitutionalism: Constituent Power and Constitutional Form* (OUP Oxford 2007)

Lowe, Vaughan 'Corporations as International Actors and International Lawmakers' (2004) 14 *Italian Yearbook of International Law* 23–38.

—— 'Overlapping Jurisdiction in International Tribunals' (1999) 20 *Australian Yearbook of International Law* 191–204

Lowenfeld, Andreas F *International Economic Law* (2nd edn OUP Oxford 2008)

Lukes, Steven *Power: A Radical View* (MacMillan London 1974)

MacCormick, Neil *Questioning Sovereignty? Law, State, and Practical Reason* (OUP Oxford 1999)

—— *Legal Reasoning and Legal Theory* (Clarendon Press Oxford 1978)

MacDonald, Ronald and Douglas M Johnston 'Introduction' in *idem* (eds) *Towards World Constitutionalism: Issues in the Legal Ordering of the World Commmunity* (Martinus Nijhoff Leiden 2005) xiii–xviii

MacGillivray, Alex *A Brief History of Globalization* (Robinson London 2006)

Mackenzie, Ruth 'The *Amicus Curiae* in International Courts: Towards Common Procedural Approaches?' in Tullio Treves, Marco Frigessi di Rattalma, Attila Tanzi, Alessandro Fodella, Cesare Pitea, and Chiara Rani (eds) *Civil Society, International Courts and Compliance Bodies* (TMC Asser The Hague 2005) 295–311

—— and Philippe Sands 'International Courts and Tribunals and the Independence of the International Judge' (2003) 44 *Harvard International Law Journal* 271–285

MacLachlan, Campbell 'The Principle of Systemic Integration and Article 31(3)(c) of the Vienna Convention' (2005) 54 *ICLQ* 279–320

Madison, James 'Federalist No. 10' in Alexander Hamilton, James Madison, and John Jay *The Federalist Papers* (New York 1961, orig. 1788, Rossiter ed)

Magnette, Paul *Citizenship: The History of an Idea* (European Consortium for Political Research (ecpr) Colchester 2005)

Mahoney, Paul 'The International Judiciary—Independence and Accountability' (2008) 7 *The Law and Practice of International Courts and Tribunals* 313–349

Majone, Giandomenico 'Independence versus Accountability? Non-Majoritarian Institutions and Democratic Government in Europe' (1994) 1 *The European Yearbook of Comparative Government and Public Administration* 117–140

Mancewicz, Andrzej 'What's Behind the Window Dressing? Legal Ways of Enforcing Multinational Corporations' Human Rights Codes of Conduct' (unpublished master's dissertation, Helsinki/Venice 2007, on file with the authors)

Mann, Erika 'Parliamentary Dimensions in the WTO—More than Just a Vision?' (2004) 7 *Journal of International Economic Law* 659–665

Mann, Frederick Alexander 'Reflections on a Commercial Law of Nations' (1957) 33 *BYIL* 20–51

Mansfield, Edward D and Jon C Pevehouse 'Democratization and International Organizations' (2006) 60 *International Organization* 137–167

Manusama, Kenneth *The United Nations Security Council in the Post-Cold War Era: Applying the Principle of Legality* (Martinus Nijhoff Leiden 2006)

Marks, Susan *The Riddle of All Constitutions: International Law, Democracy, and the Critique of Ideology* (OUP Oxford 2000)

Marmor, Andrei 'Are Constitutions Legitimate?' (2007) *Canadian Journal of Law and Jurisprudence* 69–94

Marschall, Stefan *Transnationale Repräsentation in Parlamentarischen Versammlungen* (Nomos Baden-Baden 2005)

Martenczuk, Bernd 'The Security Council, the International Court and Judicial Review: What Lessons from Lockerbie?' (1999) 10 *EJIL* 517–547

Martini, Chiara 'States' Control over New International Organization' (2006) 6 *The Global Jurist Advances* 1–25

Maupain, Francis 'L'OIT, la justice sociale et la mondialisation', (1999) 278 *Recueil des Cours* 201–396

McDorman, Ted L 'Iceland, Whaling and the U.S. Pelly Amendment: The International Trade Law Context' (1997) 66 *Nordic Journal of International Law* 453–474

McDougal, Myres 'International Law, Power, and Policy: A Contemporary Conception' (1953/I) *Recueil des Cours* 137–259

McGinnis, John O and Ilya Somin 'Should International Law be Part of our Law?' (2007) 59 *Stanford Law Review* 1175–1248

—— and Mark L Movsesian 'The World Trade Constitution' (2000) 114 *Harvard Law Review* 511–605

Mead, George Herbert *Mind, Self and Society* (The University of Chicago Press 1934)

Mégret, Frédéric 'International Prosecutors: Accountability and Ethics' (2008) 18 *Working Paper: Leuven Centre for Global Governance Studies*

—— and Florian Hoffmann 'The UN as a Human Rights Violator? Some Reflections on the United Nations Changing Human Rights Responsibilities' (2003) 25 *Human Rights Quarterly* 314–342

Menon, P K 'The Legal Personality of Individuals' (1994) 6 *Sri Lanka Journal of International Law* 127–156

Meron, Theodor *The Humanization of International Law* (Martinus Nijhoff Leiden 2006)

—— 'Judicial Independence and Impartiality in International Criminal Tribunals' (2005) 99 *AJIL* 359–369

Merrills, John G *International Dispute Settlement* (4th edn CUP Cambridge 2005)

Michelman, Frank I *Brennan and Democracy* (Princeton UP 1999)

Mill, John Stewart 'A Few Words on Non-Intervention (1859)' in *The Collected Works of John Stewart Mill vol 21 (1984), Essays on Equality, Law and Education* (University of Toronto Press Toronto and Routledge and Kegan Paul London 1963–1991) 111–124

—— *Considerations on Representative Government* (Indianapolis 1958, orig. 1861 Shields ed)

Milward, Alan Steele *The European Rescue of the Nation-State* (Routledge London 1994)

Monaco, Riccardo 'Le caractère constitutionnel des actes institutifs d'organisations internationales' in *Mélanges offerts à Charles Rousseau, La communauté internationale* (Pédone Paris 1974)

Moore, Sally Falk 'Law and Social Change: The Semi-autonomous Social Field as an Appropriate Subject of Study' (1973) *Law and Society Review* 719–746

Moravcsik, Andrew 'Is there a "Democratic Deficit" in World Politics? A Framework for Analysis' (2004) 39 *Government and Opposition* 336–363

Morgenthau, Hans Joachim *Politics among Nations: The Struggle for Power and Peace* (7th edn McGraw-Hill Higher Education Boston 2005 [orig. 1948] Thompson and Clinton eds)

Mosler, Hermann *The International Society as a Legal Community* (Sijthoff & Noordhoff The Netherlands 1980)

—— 'Die Erweiterung des Kreises der Völkerrechtssubjekte' (1962) 22 *Zeitschrift für ausländisches öffentliches Recht und Völkerrecht* 1–48

Movsesian, Mark L 'Judging International Judgments' (2007) 48 *Virginia Journal of International Law* 65–118

Muchlinski, Peter *Multinational Enterprises and the Law* (2nd edn OUP Oxford 2007)

Müller, Adam Heinrich 'Von der Idee des Staates' in *idem Ausgewählte Abhandlungen* (Gustav Fischer Jena 1921 [orig. 1809]) 3–16

Münkler, Herfried 'Enzyklopädie der Ideen der Zukunft: Solidarität' in Jens Beckert, Julia Eckert, Martin Kohli, and Wolfgang Streeck (eds) *Transnationale Solidarität: Chancen und Grenzen* (Campus Frankfurt am Main 2004) 15–28

Nagel, Thomas *Equality and Partiality* (Oxford UP New York 1991)

Neuhold Hans-Peter, Waldemar Hummer, and Christoph Schreuer (eds) *Österreichisches Handbuch des Völkerrechts* (4th edn Manz Wien 2004) vol 1

Neves, Marco, *Symbolische Konstitutionalisierung* (Duncker & Humblot Berlin 1998)

Nguyen Quoc, Dinh, Patrick Daillier, and Alain Pellet *Droit international public* (LGDJ Paris 2002)

Nijman, Janne Elisabeth *The Concept of International Legal Personality: An Inquiry into the History and Theory of International Law* (TMC Asser Press Den Haag 2004)

—— and André Nollkaemper (eds) *New Perspectives on the Divide between National and International Law* (OUP Oxford 2007)

Nollkaemper, André 'Rethinking the Supremacy of International Law' (2010) 65 *Zeitschrift für öffentliches Recht* 65–85

—— 'The Internationalized Rule of Law' (2009) 1 *Hague Journal on the Rule of Law* 74–78

Noortmann, Math 'Who Really Needs Art. 71?' in Wybo P Heere (ed) *From Government to Governance: The Growing Impact of Non-state Actors on the International and European Legal System* (TMC Asser Press The Hague 2004) 113–120

Nordstrom, Carolyn *Global Outlaws: Crime, Money, and Power in the Contemporary World* (University of California Press Berkeley CA 2007)

Nowak, Manfred *U.N. Covenant on Civil and Political Rights: CCPR Commentary* (2nd rev. edn N.P. Engel Kehl 2005)

Nowrot, Karsten *Normative Ordnungsstruktur und private Wirkungsmacht: Konsequenzen der Beteiligung transnationaler Unternehmen an den Rechtssetzungsprozessen im internationalen Wirtschaftssystem* (Berliner Wissenschaftsverlag 2006)

—— 'Nun sag, wie hast du's mit den Global Players? Fragen an die Völkerrechtsgemeinschaft zur internationalen Rechtsstellung transnationaler Unternehmen' (2004) 79 *Die Friedens-Warte* 119–150

—— The New Governance Structure of the Global Compact: Transforming a 'Learning Network' into a Federalized and Parliamentarized Transnational Regulatory Regime (Beiträge zum Transnationalen Wirtschaftsrecht 47 Universität Halle 2000)

Nussbaum, Martha C 'Patriotism and Cosmopolitanism' in *idem* (ed) *For Love of a Country: Debating the Limits of Patriotism* (Beacon Press Boston 1996) 3–17

O'Flaherty, Michael and Claire O'Brien 'Reform of UN Human Rights Treaty Monitoring Bodies: A Critique of the Concept Paper on the High Commissioner's Proposal for a Unified Standing Treaty Body' (2007) 7 *Human Rights Law Review* 141–173

Oakeshott, Michael 'The Rule of Law' in Michael Oakeshott *On History and Other Essays* (Liberty Fund Indianapolis 1999 [1983]) 129–178

Oberthür, Sebastian *Participation of Non-governmental Organisations in International Environmental Co-operation: Legal Basis and Practical Experience* (Schmidt Berlin 2002)

—— and Thomas Gehring 'Reforming International Environmental Governance: An Institutionalist Critique of the Proposal for a World Environment Organisation' (2004) 4 *International Environmental Agreements: Politics, Law and Economics* 359–381

Odello, Marco 'Thirty Years After Helsinki: Proporals for OSCE's Reform' (2005) 10 *Journal of Conflict and Security Law* 435–449

Oellers-Frahm, Karin 'Multiplication of International Courts and Tribunals and Confliction Jurisdiction—Problems and Possible Solutions' (2001) 5 *Max Planck Yearbook of United Nations Law* 67–105

Offe, Claus '"Homogeneity" and Constitutional Democracy: Coping with Identity Conflicts through Group Rights' (1999) 6 *The Journal of Political Philosophy* 113–141

Ohmae, Kenichi *The End of the Nation State* (Harper Collins London 1995)

Ommeren, F J van and H J de Ru (eds) *Convenanten tussen overheid en maatschappelijke organisaties* (Staatsdrukkerij en –uitgeverij The Hague 1993)

Onuf, Nicholas 'The Constitution of International Society' (1994) 5 *EJIL* 1–19

Oppenheim, Lassa *International Law*, vol I (6th edn Longmans, Green and Co New York 1912)

Orakhelashvili, Alexander 'R (on the application of Al-Jedda) (FC) v Secretary of State for Defence' (2008) 102 *AJIL* 337–345

—— *Peremptory Norms in International Law* (OUP Oxford 2006)

Orford, Anne *Reading Humanitarian Intervention* (CUP Cambridge 2003)

Ost, François and Michel van der Kerchove *De la pyramide au réseau: pour une théorie dialectique du droit* (Facultés universitaires Saint-Louis Bruxelles 2002)

Ovey, Clare and Robin C A White *Jacobs and White European Convention on Human Rights* (3rd edn OUP Oxford 2002)

Parekh, Bhikhu C 'Cosmopolitanism and Global Citizenship' (2003) 29 *Review of International Studies* 3–17

Pateman, Carol *Participation and Democratic Theory* (CUP Cambridge 1970)

Patomäki, Heikki 'Rethinking Global Parliament: Beyond the Indeterminacy of International Law' (2007) 13 *Widener Law Review* 369–387

Paulus, Andreas *Die internationale Gemeinschaft im Völkerrecht* (Beck München 2001)

Pauwelijn, Joost *Conflict of Norms in Public International Law: How WTO Law Relates to other Rules of International Law* (CUP Cambridge 2003)

Pellet, Alain 'Article 38' in Andreas Zimmermann, Karin Oellers-Frahm, Christian Tomuschat (eds), Christian Tams (assistant ed) *The Statute of the International Court of Justice: A Commentary* (OUP Oxford 2006) 677–792

Pergantis, Vasileios 'Towards a "Humanization" of Diplomatic Protection?' (2006) 66 *Zeitschrift für ausländisches öffentliches Recht und Völkerrecht* 351–397

Perkins, John *Confessions of an Economic Hitman* (Ebury Press London 2005)

Pernice, Ingolf 'Multilevel Constitutionalism in the European Union' (2002) 27 *European Law Review* 511–529

Peters, Anne 'Humanity as the A and Ω of Sovereignty' (2009) 20 *EJIL* 513–544

—— 'Unequal Treaties' *Max Planck Encyclopedia of International Law* (OUP Oxford 2008)

—— 'The Globalization of State Constitutions' in Janne Elisabeth Nijman and André Nollkaemper (eds) *New Perspectives on the Divide between National and International Law* (OUP Oxford 2007) 251–308

—— 'Compensatory Constitutionalism: The Function and Potential of Fundamental International Norms and Structures' (2006) 19 *Leiden Journal of International Law* 579–610

—— 'Privatisierung, Globalisierung und die Resistenz des Verfassungsstaates' in Philippe Mastronardi and Denis Taubert (eds) *Staats- und Verfassungstheorie im Spannungsfeld der Disziplinen* Beiheft Archiv für Rechts- und Sozialphilosophie 105 (Franz Steiner Stuttgart 2006) 100–159

—— 'The Constitutionalization of the European Union—Without the Constitutional Treaty' in Sonja Puntscher Riekmann and Wolfgang Wessels (eds) *The Making of a European Constitution* (VS Verlag für Sozialwissenschaften Wiesbaden 2006) 35–67

—— 'The Growth of International Law between Globalization and the Great Power' (2003) 8 *Austrian Review of International and European Law* 109–139

—— *Elemente einer Theorie der Verfassung Europas* (Duncker & Humblot Berlin 2001)

—— *Das Gebietsreferendum im Völkerrecht: Seine Bedeutung im Licht der Staatenpraxis nach 1989* (Nomos Baden-Baden 1995)

—— and Simone Peter 'Lehren vom "gerechten Krieg" aus völkerrechtlicher Sicht' in Georg Kreis (ed) *Der 'gerechte Krieg'* (Schwabe Basel 2006) 43–96

Petersmann, Ernst-Ulrich 'Multilevel Judicial Governance of International Trade Requires a Common Conception of Rule of Law and Justice' (2007) 10 *Journal of International Economic Law* 529–552

—— 'Time for a United Nations "Global Compact" for Integrating Human Rights into the Law of Worldwide Organizations' (2002) 13 *EJIL* 621–650

Pettit, Philip *Republicanism: A Theory of Freedom and Government* (Clarendon Oxford 1997)

Picciotto, Sol 'Constitutionalizing Multilevel Governance?' (2008) 6 *I Con* 457–479

Pitea, Cesare 'The Legal Status of NGOs in Environmental Non-compliance Procedures: An Assessment of Law and Practice' in Pierre-Marie Dupuy and Luisa Vierucci (eds) *NGOs in International Law* (Edward Elgar Northampton 2008) 181–203

Poferl, Angelika 'Solidarität ohne Grenzen? Probleme sozialer Ungleichheit und Teilhabe in europäischer Perspektive' in Martin Heidenreich (ed) *Die*

Europäisierung sozialer Ungleichheit (Campus Frankfurt and New York 2006) 231–252

Poiares Maduro, Miguel 'Interpreting European Law: Judicial Adjudication in a Context of Constitutional Pluralism' (2007) 1 *European Journal of Legal Studies* 1–21

—— 'Contrapunctual Law: Europe's Constitutional Pluralism in Action' in Neil Walker (ed) *Sovereignty in Transition* (Hart Oxford 2003) 501–537

Posner, Eric A 'Human Welfare, not Human Rights' (2008) 108 *Columbia Law Review* 1758–1801

—— 'Reply to Helfer and Slaughter' (2005) 93 *California Law Review* 957–973

—— and John C Yoo 'Judicial Independence in International Tribunals' (2005) 93 *California Law Review* 3–74

Powell, Haywood Jefferson *Constitutional Conscience: The Moral Dimension of Judicial Decision* (University of Chicago Press 2008)

Power, Jonathan *Like Water on Stone: The Story of Amnesty International* (Penguin London 2002)

Preuss, Ulrich K 'Equality of States—Its Meaning in a Constitutionalized Global Order' (2008) 9 *Chicago Journal of International Law* 17–49

Prost, Mario 'All Shouting the Same Slogans: International Law's Unities and the Politics of Fragmentation' (2006) 17 *Finnish Yearbook of International Law* 131–159

Puurunen, Tapio *Dispute Resolution in International Electronic Commerce* (doctoral dissertation University of Helsinki 2005)

Quill, Lawrence *Liberty after Liberalism: Civic Republicanism in a Global Age* (Palgrave Macmillan Basingstoke and New York 2006)

Raab, Dominic and Hans Bevers 'The International Criminal Court and the Separation of Powers' (2006) 3 *International Organizations Law Review* 93–135.

Ratner, Steven 'Business' in Daniel Bodansky, Jutta Brunnée, and Ellen Hey (eds) *The Oxford Handbook of International Environmental Law* (OUP Oxford 2007) 807–828

Rawls, John *Political Liberalism* (expanded edn Columbia UP New York 2005)

—— *The Law of Peoples* (Harvard UP Cambridge MA 1999)

Raz, Joseph 'The Problem of the Nature of Law' in Joseph Raz *Ethics in the Public Domain: Essays in the Morality of Law and Politics* (rev. edn Clarendon Press Oxford 1994) 195–209

—— 'Legal Validity' in Joseph Raz *The Authority of Law: Essays on Law and Morality* (Clarendon Press Oxford 1979) 146–159

Rebasti, Emanuele 'Beyond Consultative Status: Which Legal Framework for an Enhanced Interaction between NGOs and Intergovernmental Organizations?' in Pierre-Marie Dupuy and Luisa Vierucci (eds) *NGOs in International Law: Efficiency and Flexibility* (Edward Elgar Northampton 2008) 21–70

Reinisch, August 'The Use and Limits of *Res Judicata* and *Lis Pendens* as Procedural Tools to Avoid Conflicting Dispute Settlement Outcomes' (2004) 3 *The Law and Practice of International Courts and Tribunals* 37–77

—— 'Developing Human Rights and Humanitarian Law Accountability of the Security Council for the Implementation of Economic Sanctions' (2001) 95 *AJIL* 851–871

Renan, Ernest 'Qu'est-ce qu'une nation? in idem *Oeuvres complètes* I (Calmann-Lévy Paris 1947, orig. 1882) 887–906

Rickert, Gottfried *Technokratie und Demokratie* (Peter Lang Frankfurt am Main 1991)

Rivers, Julian 'Proportionality and Discretion in International and European Law' in Nicholas Tsagourias (ed) *Transnational Constitutionalism: International and European Perspectives* (CUP Cambridge 2007) 107–131

Roberts, Simon 'After Government? On Representing Law Without the State' (2005) 68 *Modern Law Review* 1–24

Rosato, Sebastian 'Explaining the Democratic Peace' (2005) 99 *American Political Science Review* 467–472

—— 'The Flawed Logic of Democratic Peace Theory' (2003) 97 *American Political Science Review* 585–602

Rosenau, James R and Ernst-Otto Czempiel (eds) *Governance without Government: Order and Change in World Politics* (CUP Cambridge 1992)

Roth, Brad R *Governmental Illegitimacy in International Law* (Clarendon Press Oxford 1999)

Rousseau, Jean Jacques 'Du contrat social' in *idem Du contrat social et autres oeuvres politiques* (éditions Garnier Frères Paris 1954 [orig. 1762]) 235–336

Rubenfeld, Jed 'Unilateralism and Constitutionalism' (2004) 79 *New York University Law Review* 1971–2028

Russell, Harold 'The Helsinki Declaration: Brobdingnag or Lilliput?' (1976) 70 *AJIL* 242–272

Russett, Bruce and John R Oneal *Triangulating Peace: Democracy, Interdependence and International Organisations* (Norton & Company New York 2001)

Sabel, Robbie *Procedure at International Conferences* (2nd edn CUP Cambridge 2006)

Saladin, Peter *Wozu noch Staaten?* (Stämpfli Bern 1995)

Sand, Peter H 'To Treaty or Not To Treaty: A Survey of Practical Experience' (1993) 87 *Proceedings of the American Society of International Law* 378–383

Santos, Boaventura de Sousa *Towards a New Legal Common Sense* (2nd edn Butterworths London 2002)

Sapiro, Miriam 'Changing the CSCE into the OSCE: Legal Aspects of a Political Transformation' (1995) 89 *AJIL* 631–637

Sarooshi, Dan *International Organizations and their Exercise of Sovereign Powers* (OUP Oxford 2005)

Sassen, Saskia *A Sociology of Globalization* (Norton New York 2007)

Sassòli, Marco and Antoine A Bouvier *How does Law Protect in War* (ICRC Geneva 1999)

Sato, Tetsuo *Evolving Constitutions of International Organizations: A Critical Analysis of the Interpretative Framework of the Constituent Instruments of International Organizations* (Kluwer The Hague 1996)

Scalia, Antonin 'A Conversation between US Supreme Court Justices' (2005) 3 *Journal of International Constitutional Law* 519–541

Scelle, Georges *Précis de Droit des Gens, Principes et Systématique* vol I, Introduction, le milieu intersocial (Sirey Paris 1932)

—— *Une crise de la société des nations* (Presses universitaires de France Paris 1927)

Schachter, Oscar 'The Decline of the National State and its Implications for International Law' (1997) 36 *Columbia Journal of Transnational Law* 7–23

—— 'The Invisible College of International Lawyers' (1977) 72 *Northwestern University Law Review* 217–226

—— *International Law in Theory and Practice* (Martinus Nijhoff The Hague 1991)

Scharpf, Fritz W *Governing in Europe: Effective and Democratic?* (OUP Oxford 1999)

Schauer, Frederick *Playing by the Rules: A Philosophical Examination of Rule-based Decision-making in Law and in Life* (Clarendon Press Oxford 1991)

Schelling, Friedrich Wilhelm *Vorlesungen über die Methode (Lehrart) des akademischen Studiums* (2nd edn Felix Meiner Hamburg 1990 [orig. 1803])

Scheuner, Ulrich 'Die grossen Friedensschlüsse als Grundlage der europäischen Staatenordnung zwischen 1648 und 1815' in *idem Schriften zum Völkerrecht* (Duncker & Humblot Berlin 1984 Tomuschat ed) 352–354

Schmidt, Manfred G *Demokratietheorien* (4th edn VS Verlag Opladen 2006)

Schmitt, Carl 'Der Gegensatz von Parlamentarismus und moderner Massendemokratie' in *idem Positionen und Begriffe im Kampf mit Weimar—Genf—Versailles 1923–1939* (Duncker & Humblot Berlin 1988, orig. 1926)

—— *Der Begriff des Politischen* (Duncker & Humblot München 1932)

—— *Politische Theologie: vier Kapitel zur Lehre von der Souveränität* (Duncker & Humblot München 1922)

Scholing, Eberhard and Vincenz Timmermann 'Der Zusammenhang zwischen politischer und ökonomischer Freiheit: Eine empirische Untersuchung' (2000) 136 *Schweizerische Zeitschrift für Volkswirtschaft und Statistik* 1–23

Scholte, Jan Aart 'Civil Society and Democratically Accountable Global Governance' (2004) 39 *Government and Opposition* 211–233

Schücking, Walther 'Le développement du Pacte de la Société des Nations' (1927/V) 20 *Recueil des Cours* 349–458

Schultz, Alexander *Das Verhältnis von Gemeinschaftsgrundrechten und Grundfreiheiten des EGV* (Duncker & Humblot Berlin 2005)

Scott, Craig (ed) *Torture as Tort: Comparative Perspectives on the Development of Transnational Human Rights Litigation* (Hart Oxford 2001)

Searle, John R *The Construction of Social Reality* (Penguin London 1995)

—— *Speech Acts: An Essay in the Philosophy of Language* (CUP Cambridge 1969)

Seidl-Hohenveldern Ignaz 'International Economic "Soft Law"' (1979/II) 163 *Recueil des Cours* 165–246

Selle, Per and Øyvind Østerud 'The Eroding of Representative Democracy in Norway' (2006) 13 *Journal of European Public Policy* 551–568

Sellers, Mortimer *Republican Principles in International Law: The Fundamental Requirements of a Just World Order* (Palgrave MacMillan New York 2006)

—— 'Republican Principles in International Law' (1996) 11 *Connecticut Journal of International Law* 403–432

Sen, Amartya *Development as Freedom* (Knopf New York 1999)

—— 'Property and Hunger' (1988) 4 *Economics and Philosophy* 57–68

Seyersted, Finn *Common Law of International Organizations* (Martinus Nijhoff Leiden 2008)

Shahabuddeen, Mohamed 'Consistency in Holdings by International Tribunals' in Nisuke Ando, Edward McWhinney, and Rüdiger Wolfrum (eds) *Liber Amicorum Judge Shigeru Oda* (Kluwer Law International Leiden 2002) 633–650

—— *Precedent in the World Court* (CUP Cambridge 1996)

Shaffer, Gregory 'Parliamentary Oversight of WTO-Rulemaking? The Political, Normative, and Practical Contexts' (2004) 7 *Journal of International Economic* 629–654

—— *Defending Interests: Public-Private Partnerships in WTO-Litigation* (Brooking Institution Press Washington DC 2003)

Shanks, Cheryl, Harold K Jacobson, and Jeffrey H Kaplan 'Inertia and Change in the Constellation of International Governmental Organizations, 1981–1992' (1996) 50 *International Organization* 593–627

Shany, Yuval *Regulating Jurisdictional Relations between National and International Courts* (OUP Oxford 2007)

—— 'Toward a General Margin of Appreciation Doctrine in International Law?' (2005) 16 *EJIL* 907–940

—— *The Competing Jurisdictions of International Courts and Tribunals* (OUP Oxford 2003).

Shaw, Jo *The Transformation of Citizenship in the European Union: Electoral Rights and the Restructuring of Political Space* (CUP Cambridge 2007)

Shelton, Dinah 'Editor's Concluding Note: The Role of Non-binding Norms in the International Legal System' in Dinah Shelton (ed) *Commitment and Compliance: The Role of Non-binding Norms in the International Legal System* (OUP Oxford 2000) 544–546

—— 'The Participation of Nongovernmental Organizations in International Judicial Proceedings' (1994) 88 *AJIL* 611–642

Shikaki, Khalil, Mudar Kassis, and Jihad Harb (eds) *The State of Reform in the Arab World 2008* (The Arab Reform Initiative and the Palestine Center for Policy and Survey Research April 2008)

Sicilianos Linos-Alexandre *L'ONU et la démocratisation de l'Etat* (Pedone Paris 2000)

Simma, Bruno 'From Bilateralism to Community Interests in International Law' (1994/VI) 250 *Recueil des Cours* 217–384

—— 'Self-contained Regimes' (1985) 16 *Netherlands Yearbook of International Law* 112–136

—— and Dirk Pulkowski 'Of Planets and the Universe: Self-contained Regimes in International Law' (2006) 17 *EJIL* 483–529

—— and Philip Alston 'The Sources of Human Rights Law: Custom, Jus Cogens, and General Principles' (1991) 12 *Australian Yearbook of International Law* 82–108

Simpson, Gerry *Great Powers and Outlaw States* (CUP Cambridge 2004)

Singer, Peter W *Corporate Warriors: The Rise of the Privatized Military Industry* (Cornell UP Ithaca NY 2003)

Slaughter Anne-Marie *A New World Order* (Princeton UP 2004)

—— 'International Law in a World of Liberal States' (1995) 6 *EJIL* 503–538

Slaughter, Steven 'Cosmopolitan Citizenship and Republican Citizenship' in Wayne Hudson and Steven Slaughter (eds) *Globalisation and Citizenship: The Transnational Challenge* (Routledge Abingdon 2007) 85–99

Slim, Hugo 'By what Authority? The Legitimacy and Accountability of Non-governmental Organisations' (2002) *The Journal of Humanitarian Assistance* <http://www.jha.ac/articles/a082.htm> (last visited 9 July 2009)

Sloan, Blaine 'The United Nations Charter as a Constitution' (1989) 1 *Pace Yearbook of International Law* 61–126

Steffek, Jens 'The Legitimation of International Governance: A Discourse Approach' (2003) 9 *European Journal of International Relations* 249–275

Stein, Eric 'International Integration and Democracy: No Love at First Sight' (2001) 95 *AJIL* (2001) 489–534

—— 'Lawyers, Judges, and the Making of a Transnational Constitution' (1981) 75 *AJIL* 1–27

Steinberg, Richard H 'Judicial Lawmaking at the WTO: Discursive, Constitutional, and Political Constraints' (2004) 99 *AJIL* 247–275

Steiner, Henry 'Individual Claims in a World of Massive Violations: What Role for the Human Rights Committee?' in Philip Alston and James Crawford (eds) *The Future of UN Human Rights Treaty Monitoring* (CUP Cambridge 2000) 1–15

—— 'Political Participation as a Human Right' (1988) 1 *Harvard Human Rights Yearbook* 77–134

Steiner, Henry J, Philip Alston, and Ryan Goodman *International Human Rights in Context. Law, Politics, Morals* (3rd edn OUP Oxford 2006)

Sternberger, Dolf 'Verfassungspatriotismus' (1982) in *idem Schriften*, vol X (Insel Verlag Frankfurt am Main 1990 Haungs, Landfried, Orth and Vogel eds) 17–31

Stone Sweet, Alec and Jud Mathews 'Proportionality Balancing and Global Constitutionalism' (2008) 47 *Columbia Journal of Transnational Law* 72–164

Strange, Susan *The Retreat of the State: The Diffusion of Power in the World Economy* (CUP Cambridge 1996)

Suy, Eric *Les actes juridiques unilatéraux en droit international public* (Pédone Paris 1962)

Swaan, Abram de 'Verdriet en lied van de kosmopoliet' in Abram de Swaan *De draagbare De Swaan* (2nd edn Bert Bakker Amsterdam 2008) 230–242

Szasz, Paul 'The Security Council Starts Legislating' (2002) 96 *AJIL* 901–904

Szurek, Sandra 'La responsabilité de protéger, nature de l'obligation et responsabilité internationale' in Société française pour le droit international (ed) *Colloque de Nanterre, La responsabilité de protéger* (Pedone Paris 2008) 91–134

—— 'La Charte des Nations Unies Constitution Mondiale?' in Jean-Pierre Cot, Alain Pellet, and Mathias Forteau (eds) *La Charte des Nations Unies: commentaire article par article* vol. 1 (Economica Paris 2005) 29–68

Talmon, Stefan 'The Security Council as World Legislator' (2005) 99 *AJIL* 175–194

Tamanaha, Brian Z *On the Rule of Law. History, Politics, Theory* (CUP Cambridge 2004)

—— *A General Jurisprudence of Law and Society* (OUP Oxford 2001)

Tams, Christian *Enforcing Obligations Erga Omnes in International Law* (CUP Cambridge 2005)

Tarasofsky, Richard G 'The WTO Committee on Trade and Environment: Is it Making a Difference?' (1999) 3 *Max Planck Yearbook of United Nations Law* 471–488

Teivainen, Teivo 'The World Social Forum and Global Democratisation: Learning from Porto Alegre' (2002) 23 *Third World Quarterly* 621–632

Terris, Daniel, Cesare P R Romano, and Leigh Swigart *The International Judge: an Introduction to the Men and Women who Decide the World's Cases* (OUP Oxford 2007)

Terry, Larry D *Leadership of Public Bureaucracies: The Administrator as Conservator* (2nd edn Sharpe Armonk NY 2003)

Tesón, Fernando *A Philosophy of International Law* (Westlake Boulder 1998)

—— *Humanitarian Intervention: An Inquiry into Law and Morality* (2nd edn Transnational Publishers New York 1997)

Teubner, Gunther 'Societal Constitutionalism: Alternatives to State-Centred Constitutional Theory?' in Christian Joerges, Inger-Johanne Sand, and Gunther Teubner (eds) *Transnational Governance and Constitutionalism* (Hart Oxford and Portland 2004) 3–28

—— ' "Global Bukowina": Legal Pluralism in the World Society' in Gunther Teubner (ed) *Global Law Without a State* (Ashgate Aldershot 1997) 3–28

—— *Law as an Autopoietic System* (Blackwell Oxford 1993 Bankowska and Adler trans)

Thirlway, Hugh 'Judicial Activism and the International Court of Justice' in Nisuke Ando, Edward McWhinney, and Rüdiger Wolfrum (eds) *Liber Amicorum Judge Shigeru Oda* (Kluwer Law International Leiden) 75–105

Tocqueville, Alexis de *Democracy in America* (The Library of Amercia New York 2004 [orig. 1835–1840] Goldhammer trans)

Tomkins, Adam *Public Law* (Clarendon Press Oxford 2003)

Tomuschat, Christian 'Annotation' (*Kadi* and *Yusuf* cases) (2006) 43 *Common Market Law Review* 537–551

—— 'International Law: Ensuring the Survival of Mankind on the Eve of a New Century' (1999) 297 *Recueil des Cours* 9–438

—— 'Die internationale Gemeinschaft' (1995) 33 *Archiv des Völkerrechts* 1–20

Toth, Akos G 'A Legal Analysis of Subsidiarity' in David O'Keeffe and Patrick M Twomey (eds) *Legal Issues of the Maastricht Treaty* (Chancery Law Chichester 1994) 37–48

Trachtman, Joel P 'Constitutional Economics of the WTO', in Jeffrey L Dunoff and Joel P Trachtman (eds) *Ruling the World: Constitutionalism, International Law and Global Governance* (CUP Cambridge 2009)

—— 'The Constitutions of the WTO' (2006) 17 *EJIL* (2006) 623–646

Treves, Tullio, Marco Frigessi di Rattalma, Attila Tanzi, Alessandro Fodella, Cesare Pitea, and Chiara Rani (eds) *Civil Society, International Courts and Compliance Bodies* (TMC Asser The Hague 2005)

Tribe, Laurence H *The Invisible Constitution* (OUP Oxford 2008)

Triepel, Heinrich 'Les Rapports entre le Droit Interne et le Droit International' (1923) 1 *Recueil des Cours* 77–121

Tsagourias, Nicholas 'The Constitutional Role of General Principles of Law in International and European Jurisprudence' in *ibid* (ed) *Transnational Constitutionalism: International and European Perspectives* (CUP Cambridge 2007) 71–106

Tully, James 'The Imperialism of Modern Constitutional Democracy' in Martin Loughlin and Neil Walker (eds) *The Paradox of Constitutionalism: Constituent Power and Constitutional Form* (OUP Oxford 2007) 315–338

—— *Strange Multiplicity: Constitutionalism in an Age of Diversity* (CUP Cambridge 1995)

Tully, Stephen *Corporations and International Lawmaking* (Martinus Nijhoff Boston and Leiden 2007)

Twining, William 'Implications of "Globalisation" for Law as a Discipline' (unpublished paper on file with the authors)

—— *Globalisation and Legal Theory* (Butterworths London 2000)

Ulfstein, Geir 'Do We Need a World Court of Human Rights? in Ola Engdahl and Pål Wrange (eds) *Law at War—The Law as it was and the Law as it should be* (Brill Leiden 2008)

—— 'Treaty Bodies' in Daniel Bodansky, Jutta Brunnée, and Ellen Hey (eds) *The Oxford Handbook of International Environmental Law* (OUP Oxford 2007) 877–889

—— Thilo Marauhn, and Andreas Zimmermann (eds) *Making Treaties Work: Human Rights, Environment and Arms Control* (CUP Cambridge 2007)

Unger, Roberto M *Law in Modern Society: Towards a Criticism of Social Theory* (Free Press New York 1976)

Vajic, Nina 'Some Concluding Remarks on NGOs and the European Court of Human Rights' in Tullio Treves, Marco Frigessi di Rattalma, Attila Tanzi, Alessandro Fodella, Cesare Pitea, and Chiara Rani (eds) *Civil Society, International Courts and Compliance Bodies* (TMC Asser The Hague 2005) 93–104

Van den Bossche, Pieter 'NGO Involvement in the WTO: A Comparative Perspective' (2008) 11 *Journal of International Economic Law* 717–749

Van Harten, Gus *Investment Treaty Arbitration and Public Law* (OUP Oxford 2007)

Vasquez, John 'Ethics, Foreign Policy and Liberal Wars' (2005) 6 *International Studies Perspectives* 307–315

Vattel, Emer de *Le droit des gens ou principes de la loi naturelle, appliqués à la conduite et aux affaires de Nations et des Souverains*, vol I (London 1758), in James Brown Scott (ed) *The Classics of International Law* (Carnegie Institution Washington 1916 Fenwick trans)

Vedder, Anton (ed) *NGO Involvement in International Governance and Policy: Sources of Legitimacy* (Martinus Nijhoff Leiden 2007)

Verdross, Alfred *Die Quellen des universellenen Völkerrechts: Eine Einführung* (Rombach Freiburg 1973)

—— 'Forbidden Treaties in International Law' (1937) 31 *AJIL* 571–577

—— *Völkerrecht* (Springer Berlin 1937)

—— 'Le fondement du droit international' (1927/I) 16 *Receuil de Cours* 247–323

—— *Die Verfassung der Völkerrechtsgemeinschaft* (Springer Wien 1926)

Verhoeven, Joe 'La notion d'"applicabilité directe" du droit international' (1980) 15 *Revue Belge de droit international* 243–264

Vesting, Thomas 'Constitutionalism or Legal Theory: Comments on Gunther Teubner' in Christian Joerges, Inger-Johann Sand, and Gunther Teubner (eds) *Transnational Governance and Constitutionalism* (Oxford and Portland Oregon Hart 2004) 29–39

Vierucci, Luisa 'NGOs before International Courts and Tribunals' in Pierre-Marie Dupuy and Luisa Vierucci (eds) *NGOs in International Law* (Edward Elgar Northampton 2008) 155–180

Vitoria, Francisco de 'On Civil Power' in *idem Political Writings* (CUP Cambridge 1991 [orig. 1528] Pagden and Lawrance eds) 1–44

van Vollenhoven, Cornelis *De drie treden van het volkenrecht* (Martinus Nijhoff The Hague 1918)

Waldron, Jeremy *Law and Disagreement* (OUP Oxford 1999)

—— 'Cosmopolitan Norms' in Seyla Benhabib, Jeremy Waldron, Bounie Honig, Will Kymlicka, and Robert Post *Another Cosmopolitanism* (OUP Oxford 2006)

—— 'The Core of the Case Against Judicial Review' (2006) 115 *Yale Law Journal* 1346–1406

—— 'The Rule of International Law' (2006) 30 *Harvard Journal of Law and Public Policy* 15–30

Walker, Neil 'Beyond Boundary Disputes and Basic Grids: Mapping the Global Disorder of Normative Orders' (2008) 6 *Journal of International Constitutional Law* 373–396

—— 'The Idea of Constitutional Pluralism' (2002) 65 *Modern Law Review* 317–359

—— 'The EU and the WTO: Constitutionalism in a New Key' in Gráinne de Bùrca and Joanne Scott (eds) *The EU and the WTO: Legal and Constitutional Issues* (OUP Oxford 2001) 31–59

—— 'Flexibility within a Metaconstitutional Frame: Reflections on the Future of Legal Authority in Europe' in Gráinne de Bùrca and Joanne Scott (eds) *Constitutional Change in the EU: Between Uniformity and Flexibility?* (Hart Oxford 2000) 9–30

Walzer, Michael 'The Moral Standing of States: A Response to Four Critics' (1980) 9 *Philosophy and Public Affairs* 209–229

—— *On Toleration* (Yale UP New Haven CT 1997)

Wang, Jiangyu 'The Rule of Law in China: A Realistic View of the Jurisprudence, the Impact of the WTO, and the Prospects for Future Development' (2004) *Singapore Journal of Legal Studies* 347–389

Wates, Jeremy 'NGOs and the Aarhus Convention' in Tullio Treves, Marco Frigessi di Rattalma, Attila Tanzi, Alessandro Fodella, Cesare Pitea, and Chiara Rani (eds) *Civil Society, International Courts and Compliance Bodies* (TMC Asser The Hague 2005) 167–185

Watts, Arthur 'Enhancing the Effectiveness of Procedures of International Dispute Settlement' (2001) 5 *Max Planck Yearbook of United Nations Law* 21–39

—— 'The International Rule of Law' (1993) 36 *German Yearbook of International Law* 15–45

—— *International Law and the Antarctic Treaty System* (Grotius Cambridge 1992)

Weber, Max *Economy and Society: An Outline of Interpretive Sociology* (University of California Press Berkeley CA 1978 Roth and Wittich eds)

Weber, Max, 'Objectivity' in Social Sciences, in The Methodology of the Social Sciences 49–112 (Edward A. Shils & Henry A. Finch trans. and eds, Free Press New York 1949, orig. 1904

Weil, Prosper 'Le droit international en quête de son identité: Cours générale de droit international public' (19924/VI) 237 *Recueil des Cours* 9–370

—— 'Towards Relative Normativity in International Law?' (1983) 77 *AJIL* 413–442

Weiler, Joseph H H 'The Geology of International Law—Governance, Democracy and Legitimacy' (2004) 64 *Zeitschrift für ausländisches öffentliches Recht und Völkerrecht* 547–562

—— and Marlene Wind (eds) *European Constitutionalism Beyond the State* (CUP Cambridge 2003)

—— 'In Defence of the Status Quo: Europe's Constitutional *Sonderweg*' in Joseph H H Weiler and Marlene Wind (eds) *European Constitutionalism Beyond the State* (CUP Cambridge 2003) 7–23

—— 'A Constitution for Europe: Some Hard Choices' (2002) 40 *Journal of Common Market Studies* 563–580

Weinrib, Lorraine E 'Constitutional Conceptions and Constitutional Comparativism' in Vicki C Jackson and Mark Tushnet (eds) *Defining the Field of Comparative Constitutional Law* (Praeger Westport CN 2002) 3–34

Weiss, Linda 'Introduction: Bringing Domestic Institutions Back in' in *idem* (ed) *States in the Global Economy. Bringing Domestic Institutions Back in* (CUP Cambridge 2003) 1–36

Wellens, Karel 'Solidarity as a Constitutional Principle: Its Expanding Role and Inherent Limitations' in Ronald St MacDonald and Douglas M Johnston (eds) *Towards World Constitutionalism: Issues in the Legal Ordering of the World Commmunity* (Martinus Nijhoff Leiden 2005) 775–807

—— *Remedies against International Organizations* (CUP Cambridge 2004)

Wendehorst, Christiane C 'The State as a Foundation of Private Law Reasoning' (2008) 56 *American Journal of Comparative Law* 567–604

Wenger, Andreas and Daniel Möckli *Conflict Prevention. The Untapped Potential of the Business Sector* (Lynne Rienner Boulder 2003)

Werle, Gerhard *Völkerstrafrecht* (2nd edn Mohr Siebeck Tübingen 2007)

Werner, Wouter 'The Never-ending Closure: Constitutionalism and International Law' in Nicholas Tsagourias (ed) *Transnational Constitutionalism: International and European Perspectives* (CUP Cambridge 2007) 329–67

Wet, Erika de 'The Emergence of International and Regional Value Systems as a Manifestation of the Emerging International Constitutional Order' (2006) 19 *Leiden Journal of International Law* 611–632

—— 'The International Constitutional Order' (2006) 55 *ICLQ* 51–76

—— *The Chapter VII Powers of the United Nations Security Council* (Hart Oxford 2004)

—— and André Nollkaemper (eds) *Review of the Security Council by Member States* (Intersentia Antwerp 2003)

Wheare, Kenneth C *Federal Government* (OUP Oxford 1947)

Wheatley, Steven *The Democratic Legitimacy of International Law* (Hart Oxford 2010)

—— 'Democratic Governance beyond the State: The Legitimacy of Non-state Actors as Standard Setters' in Anne Peters, Lucy Köchlin, Till Förster, and Gretta Fenner Zinkernagel (eds) *Non-state Actors as Standard Setters* (CUP Cambridge 2009) 215–240

—— 'Democracy in International Law: A European Perspective' (2002) 51 *ICLQ* 225–247

White, Nigel D and Dirk Klaasen 'An Emerging Legal Regime?' in *idem* (eds) *The UN, Human Rights and Post-Conflict Situations* (Manchester UP 2005) 1–16

Wilder, Martijn 'Can Companies or Entities from a Non-Party to the Kyoto-Protocol participate in a Flexible Mechanism?' in David Freestone and Charlotte Streck (eds) *Legal Aspects of Implementing the Kyoto Protocol Mechanisms: Making Kyoto Work* (OUP Oxford 2005) 249–262

Wilke, Marie 'Emerging Informal Network Structures in Global Governance: Inside the Anti-Money Laundering Regime' (2008) 77 *Nordic Journal of International Law* 509–531

Williams, Oliver F (ed) *Peace through Commerce—Responsible Corporate Citizenship and the Ideals of the United Nations Global Compact* (University of Notre Dame Press 2008)

Witteveen, Willem J and Wibren van der Burg (eds) *Rediscovering Fuller* (Amsterdam UP 1999)

Wolff, Christian *Ius Gentium Methodo Scientifica pertractorum* vol II (Frankfurt 1764 Drake trans) in James Brown Scott (ed) *The Classics of International Law* (Clarendon Press Oxford 1934)

Wolfrum, Rüdiger 'Legitimacy of International Law from a Legal Perspective: Some Introductory Considerations' in *idem* and Volker Röben (eds) *Legitimacy in International Law* (Springer Berlin 2008) 1–24

Wood, Michael 'The Selection of Candidates for International Judicial Office: Recent Practice' in Tafsir Malick Ndiaye, Rüdiger Wolfrum, Thomas A Mensah, and Chie Kojima (eds) *Law of the Sea, Environmental Law and Settlement of Disputes* (Brill Leiden 2007) 357–368

Woods, Ngaire *The Globalizers: The IMF, the World Bank, and Their Borrowers* (Cornell UP Ithaca NY 2006)

World Trade Organization *A Handbook on the WTO Dispute Settlement System* (CUP Cambridge 2004)

Young, Ernest A 'The Trouble with Global Constitutionalism' (2003) 38 *Texas International Law Journal* 527–554

Zorn, Albert *Grundzüge des Völkerrechts* (2nd edn Verlagsbuchhandlung von J.J. Weber 1903)

Zumbansen, Peer 'Law after the Welfare State: Formalism, Functionalism, and the Ironic Turn of Reflexive Law' (2008) 56 *American Journal of Comparative Law* 769–808

Zürn, Michael 'Institutionalisierte Ungleichheit in der Weltpolitik. Jenseits der Alternativen "Global Governance" versus "American Empire" ' (2007) 48 *Politische Vierteljahresschrift* 680–704

Index